THE AMERICAN MUSICAL FILM SONG ENCYCLOPEDIA

Thomas S. Hischak

GREENWOOD PRESS
Westport, Connecticut • London

Library of Congress Cataloging-in-Publication Data

Hischak, Thomas S.
    The American musical film song encyclopedia / Thomas S. Hischak.
        p.   cm.
    Includes bibliographic references (p.   ) and index.
    ISBN 0–313–30737–7 (alk. paper)
    1. Motion picture music—United States—Encyclopedias.   2. Songs,
English—United States—Encyclopedias.   I. Title.
ML102.M68H57   1999
782.1′4′097303—dc21   98–34723

British Library Cataloguing in Publication Data is available.

Library of Congress Catalog Card Number: 98–34723
ISBN: 0–313–30737–7

First published in 1999

Greenwood Press, 88 Post Road West, Westport, CT 06881
An imprint of Greenwood Publishing Group, Inc.

Printed in the United States of America

The paper used in this book complies with the
Permanent Paper Standard issued by the National
Information Standards Organization (Z39.48–1984).

10 9 8 7 6 5 4 3 2 1

*For Ron, Chris, Greg, and Angela . . . who grew up
watching the movies with me.*

Contents

Preface

While this book is intended to be a companion to *The American Musical Theatre Song Encyclopedia* and uses the same format and philosophy of that earlier volume, writing about film songs has been quite a different experience. Film is not theatre, even when they both sing and dance, and film songs, while they share most of the same songwriters with the stage, are written, produced, and remembered in quite a different way. Audiences, critics, and Hollywood itself have been trying to define exactly what a film musical is since those early years when the Warner brothers made "talkies" sing. Ironically, Hollywood had little interest in actors talking on film. In fact, there seemed to be little enthusiasm on the audience's part for talking movie stars. But singing was a different matter. Most of *The Jazz Singer* is silent, but when Al Jolson sings we know we are going places we've never gone on film before.

As movies learned how to incorporate singing and dancing on celluloid, the differences from Broadway started to surface. Film musicals, for instance, required fewer songs than stage musicals. The typical Broadway show had a dozen musical numbers whereas the true movie musical—that is, one conceived and written as a movie rather than as a film adaptation of a musical play—usually had half as many. In fact, using dance sequences and some reprises, there are many classic film musicals that have only three or four songs. There is more reason for this beyond the fact that films are shorter than musical plays. At first, songs in movie musicals tended to exist as entertainment pieces added to nonmusical plots, and so character songs were rarely needed. Hollywood seemed very nervous about film actors just breaking out into song in the way performers so naturally did on stage. The character had to have an *excuse* for singing (a nightclub act, the big Broadway show, a radio broadcast, even a strolling musician to provide a logical reason for music), and there had to be an onscreen audience for him or her to sing to. Songs dealing with plot were just as rare. A story told through song seemed too artificial for the new medium. Even ensemble numbers were suspect unless sung by a chorus of a Broadway show in the film. With songs being used in such an isolated way, no wonder many of the Hollywood songwriters were able to turn out whole scores while knowing little or nothing of the film's plot or characters.

Film songs tend to be shorter than Broadway numbers. Verses, the standard introductory section used by all songwriters until the 1950s, were often written for film songs but just as often were cut from the final print by the studios. Reprises were also avoided (outside of a quick repeat for the finale or the end credits), and encores were just about unheard of. Some numbers emphasized dance and reduced the song to one brief refrain to set up the subject or theme. Hollywood loved song, but it was always cautious of a film getting *too* musical. Studios were less wary of dance, since choreographed bodies were visual in a way singing actors could never be.

Of the many differences between film songs and movie songs, the one that is hardest to pinpoint is the way a performer is linked to a song on celluloid. A Broadway show, though it be reviewed, photographed, recorded, and sometimes even videotaped, exists in a moment of time and is gone. The nature of theatre means the event occurs before a live audience and then disappears, leaving only memories and some evidence of its existence. Film, in contrast, is forever. It does not change even though time, audiences, and attitudes do. Alfred Drake as Curly was the first to sing "Oh, What a Beautiful Mornin'" on stage in the original 1943 Broadway production of *Oklahoma!* But there have been countless other Curlys since then, and each performance and each production is different. But Fred Astaire singing "The Way You Look Tonight" in the 1936 film *Swing Time* will never change. The song has often been recorded by others, but the celluloid version is permanent and indelible. One might say that the character Curly sings "Oh, What a Beautiful Mornin'" but the performer Fred Astaire sings "The Way You Look Tonight."

Although much has been written about film musicals, the songs themselves have only rarely been thoroughly identified and cataloged. David Ewen, Stanley Green, Robert Lissauer, and a few others have done admirable work in this area. But *The American Musical Film Song Encyclopedia* hopes to go beyond this. In addition to identifying the song's source, authors, and original performers, the *Encyclopedia* tries to *explain* the songs heard in movie musicals: what kind of song it is, what it is about and what purpose it had in the film, what aspects of it musically or lyrically are memorable, what is the song's history, and what may be unique about this particular number. One could say this book is about songs as little moments of screenwriting.

As in *The American Musical Theatre Song Encyclopedia*, the task of selecting which songs to include has been a frustrating one. In an effort to keep the encyclopedia to a manageable, one-volume size, I have chosen only songs written for and originally heard in movie musicals. Songs from Broadway that were performed on screen and songs from Tin Pan Alley that were interpolated into films are not included. For example, of such songs, only the three numbers John Kander and Fred Ebb wrote for the film version of *Cabaret* are discussed here. (Much of the rest of the Broadway score is covered in the *Theatre Song Encyclopedia*.) Musical sequences from films, such as ballets or lyricless dance numbers, are not included because they are not *songs* as such. The *Encyclopedia* is limited to American movies, though some British films with substantial Hollywood backing or talent are included. Animated films are covered but shorts, whether live action or animated, are not. Finally, only film *musicals* are considered. For the purposes of this book, I define a musical as having at least three songs that are sung by the characters in the story. It is not a thorough definition, I admit, but it does provide guidelines for discussing songs as part of a larger musical experience. *Saturday Night Fever*, for example, has an extensive musical score but that score consists of songs heard only on the soundtrack and not sung on screen. Comedies or dramas that boasted a single hit song, such as "Moon River" or "High Hopes," are not included because such films as *Breakfast at Tiffany's* and *A Hole in the Head* can hardly be described as musicals.

Even with these limitations it was difficult to narrow the field to the 1,760 songs from the 500 film musicals that are covered. I have tried to represent all the majors musicals, songwriters, performers, genres, and eras, selecting songs for their popularity, high quality, individual uniqueness, historical importance, or association with a particular performer. The song entries are presented alphabetically, but the "Film Musicals" list at the end of the book includes all the songs discussed from a particular movie. Song titles are often a matter of confusion. I have chosen what is generally considered the most common title for a song, but the "Alternate Song Titles" section identifies some of the many variations. Also, in order to provide a consistency of terminology, a "Glossary of Film Song Terms" is included at the start. And, lastly, some appendices regarding Academy Awards for film musicals and songs, as well as a list of memorable songs from Broadway and Tin Pan Alley heard in film musicals, are attached.

I wish to acknowledge the continued assistance from the staff at the Cortland Free Library and the Memorial Library at the State University of New York College at Cortland. William Whiting was very helpful in checking the text, the staff at Greenwood Press performed their usual superb and exacting talents on the manuscript, and my wife, Cathy, as ever, was always there, always supporting, and often watching film after film with me.

Glossary of Film Song Terms

ballad   A term with too many meanings in music and literature. In modern popular music it is any sentimental or romantic song, usually with the same melody for each stanza. Ballads were often the big sellers in a film musical, the songs that could move listeners without benefit of the movie's plot or characters. Most ballads written since World War Two have a foxtrot (4/4) base. A *narrative ballad* is more like poetry's definition of the term (a song that tells a story), but narrative ballads are rare in film musicals because there are usually more cinematic ways to tell a story within a story, as, for example, with a flashback.

character song   Any musical number that is concerned with revealing a character's personality or reaction to the events of the plot. A person's first character song is often his or her "I am" song. Character songs usually do not travel outside the context of the film as easily as ballads often do.

charm song   A musical number that is less about character development than it is about utilizing the characters' warmth and/or comic entertainment value. Although charm songs are often expendable to the plot, they have been audience favorites on occasion.

chorus   A group of characters that sing or dance together; hence, a vocal chorus made up of singers or a dancing chorus made up of dancers. Because of the ability of *dubbing*, film choruses usually did both singing and dancing, whereas in the theatre the groups were distinct until the 1960s. The chorus is sometimes called the *ensemble* in a film. A *chorus number* is a song sung primarily by a group. Chorus is also another term for the *refrain* of a song, although that definition is not used in this book.

dubbing Adding or replacing an actor's singing and/or speaking voice on the film's soundtrack. Songs were sometimes dubbed during the initial recording session, or sometimes were added after the production was filmed. When the information is available, both the singer appearing on the screen and the singer who dubbed the song are identified in this book.

"I am" song Often a solo, but any song that introduces a character or group of characters in a film musical by revealing their wishes, dreams, confusions, and so on. "I am" songs usually occur early in the movie. Sometimes called an "I wish" song as well, they became requisite in the musical theatre with the advent of the integrated musical play. In films they are less common but have been used effectively since the first talkies.

interpolation A song added to a movie musical that has not been written by the same songwriters who wrote the rest of the score. Interpolations were much more common in films than they were in the theatre, but the reasons were often the same: to improve a weak score or take advantage of a hit Tin Pan Alley song. A common practice in film musicals was to interpolate old standards in a new movie musical.

list song Any song, serious or comic, that is structured as a list of examples or a series of items. They are sometimes called "laundry list" songs, although the result is intended to be much more interesting than that.

lyric A line from a song or the entire set of lines written for a song. A lyric is written by a lyricist, as opposed to a screenwriter (librettist in the theatre) who writes the dialogue. The plural form *lyrics* refers to the words to all the songs a lyricist has written for a score; one writes a *lyric* for a song and the *lyrics* for the score. In this book, when a songwriter is not referred to specifically as a lyricist or a composer, it can be assumed that he or she wrote both music and lyric for the song.

montage A film term that means different things in different parts of the world. In Europe, for example, it refers to the editing process. In this book montage is a series of scenes edited together to create a flashback or to quickly show how a series of events occurred over a period of time.

pastiche song Any musical number that echoes the style, either musically or lyrically, of an earlier era. Such songs are written to spoof the past or to recapture the period for the setting of the new work.

refrain The main body of a song, that is, the section that follows the *verse* and repeats itself with the same melody and/or lyric. The most familiar part of a popular song is usually the refrain section. The refrain is sometimes called the *chorus*, but the latter term is too often confused with a group of singers, so it is not used in this book.

release A section of the refrain that departs from the repeated melody and explores a new musical line that may or may not have been suggested in the main melody. The release (also sometimes called the *bridge*) helps keep a song from being too predictable or monotonous.

reprise The repeating of all or part of a song later in a film musical, either by the same or different characters. Reprises differ from *encores* in that the latter are repeats that are sung immediately after a song is first sung. Reprises were common in movie musicals, but encores (once popular in the theatre) are rare on the screen.

soliloquy A solo in which the character is alone and reveals his or her thoughts, confusions, concerns, and so on. The most effective soliloquies are songs that show a character debating two sides of an issue or trying to come to a decision. A later development of the soliloquy on film is having the character's thoughts sung only on the soundtrack. Thus, it was possible to have a soliloquy when the character was with other people.

specialty number A song that highlights a performer's unique talents rather than the character or the plot. Audiences expected certain stars to perform certain characteristic songs in each film musical, and the studios often obliged them.

torch song In popular music a torch song is usually a sentimental song involving unrequited love, but in film musicals torch songs may be comic or sarcastic as well. In the rapid character development in a movie, any disagreement or misunderstanding between lovers is excuse enough to sing a torch song.

verse The introductory section of a song. The melody is usually distinct from that of the refrain that follows, and verses tend to be shorter. Most songs written in this century are more known for their refrains than for their verses. While verses were considered requisite for theatre and Tin Pan Alley songs, film scores often neglected verses in an effort to keep movies short and streamlined. Too often songwriters (who usually came from Broadway) wrote verses for all their songs and saw them recorded and filmed, only to be cut by the studio during the editing process. But a superior verse to a song sets up the number's important images or ideas and gives the song its full potency.

A

"About a Quarter to Nine" is Al Jolson's bouncy song of anticipation that he sang in *Go Into Your Dance* (1935) as he looked forward to his date with Ruby Keeler. The Harry Warren (music) and Al Dubin (lyric) song was used as a nightclub number with Jolson backed by a top-hatted male chorus. The song was then turned into the obligatory Jolson minstrel number with the star and chorus in blackface. Jolson recorded the song and sang it in two other films, though only his voice was heard. He provided the singing for Larry Parks in *The Jolson Story* (1946), where he sang it in a duet with Evelyn Keyes, and in *Jolson Sings Again* (1949). A popular recording of "About a Quarter to Nine" by Ozzie Nelson and his Orchestra was used decades later in the background of the Depression-era comedy *Paper Moon* (1973). On Broadway, Tammy Grimes and Wanda Richert sang the number in *42nd Street* (1980) as they anticipated the show's curtain rising at 8:45 P.M. The song was recorded by jazz singer Sarah Partridge in 1998.

"Abraham" was one of the handful of holiday songs Irving Berlin wrote for *Holiday Inn* (1942), this one celebrating Lincoln's Birthday at the inn, which opened only for holidays. Bing Crosby and Marjorie Reynolds (dubbed by Martha Mears) sang the number in blackface (Bing wishes to keep the identity of Reynolds from Fred Astaire) for the holiday patrons while the African-American housekeeper Louise Beavers sang some of it to her children in the kitchen. Although Crosby and Reynolds' stereotypic costumes and makeup render the scene somewhat offensive today, Berlin's jubilant song is a sincere Negro folklore tribute to Abe Lincoln. In *White Christmas* (1954), the music was used for a tap dance sequence by Vera-Ellen and George Chakiris (who was going by the name George Kerris at the time).

"Absolutely Green" is the ecological ballad that Cynthia Weil (lyric) and Barry Mann (music) wrote for the animated fantasy *A Troll in Central Park* (1994). Stanley the Troll (voice of Dom DeLuise with the St. Patrick's Cathedral Choir) sang the fervent number to a little girl as flowers magically grew from wherever he touched his green thumb. At the end of the film the song was reprised by the chorus as the island of Manhattan was turned into a giant garden.

"Ac-cent-tchuate the Positive" is the Johnny Mercer (lyric) and Harold Arlen (music) hit song from *Here Come the Waves* (1944), which was featured on *Your Hit Parade* for thirteen weeks and was nominated for an Oscar. One story has it that Mercer recalled the title phrase from his school days in the South. Another version says the title came from a sermon by Harlem revivalist preacher Father Divine; the phrase was printed in a newspaper article which was sent to Mercer by a friend and the lyricist kept the clipping for years before using it for a lyric. In either case, Mercer suggested the phrase to Arlen as they drove together to the Paramount studio one day and they completed the song by the time they arrived at work. The revival-like number has a playful lyric with Jonah and Noah warning not to bother with "Mr. In-Between" while Arlen's music bounces from measures of steady accents to those with syncopated patterns. Mailman Bing Crosby and doorman Sonny Tufts, both in blackface, introduced the song in a U.S. Navy show in the film, but the song is better remembered for popular recordings by the Andrews Sisters, Artie Shaw (vocal by Imogene Lynn), Crosby's solo recording, and a record with the Andrews Sisters. Other notable recordings were made by Mercer, Kay Kyser (vocal by Dorothy Mitchell), Julie Wilson, and Barbara Cook. Gospel-singer-turned-pop-vocalist Aretha Franklin recorded the song in 1962, and according to James R. Morris, she "catches the mock-spiritual quality of the music and animates the song, in an arresting forecast of the coming rage for soul music." The song was used effectively on the soundtrack for *The Blue Dahlia* (1946) and was sung by Brooks Ashmanskas, Angelo Fraboni, Kevyn Morrow, Timothy Edward Smith, and Nancy Lemenager in the Broadway Mercer revue *Dream* (1997).

"Accidents Will Happen" is a pleasing ballad by Johnny Burke (lyric) and James Van Heusen (music) about a stubborn lover who is nonetheless willing to hope that he will change his tune someday. Bing Crosby, as a reluctant songwriter, sang the song with Dorothy Kirsten in *Mr. Music* (1950) and later recorded it.

"According to the Moonlight" was a hit single record for Alice Faye after she sang it in the Broadway backstager *George White's Scandals* (1935). Faye performed the Jack Yellen, Herb Magidson (lyric), and Joseph Meyer (music) ballad as a small town girl who makes it big on Broadway. Harry

Richman had a successful recording of the song, as did the Victor Young Orchestra (vocal by Jimmy Ray).

"Across the Breakfast Table (Looking at You)" is a lovely, too-little-known ballad by Irving Berlin about married love. Al Jolson, as the faded star of a minstrel company in *Mammy* (1930), sang the song as a gushing proposal of marriage, but Berlin's simple, heartfelt lyric and enticing melody is much more sincere than that. Fred Waring and the Pennsylvanians (vocal by Gene Austin) were among the first to record the number, and Michael Feinstein is probably the most recent. The song is often listed as "Looking at You."

"Adam and Evil" is the light rock-and-roll number that Elvis Presley, as the leader of a musical combo out on the road, sang in a small California club in *Spinout* (1966). Fred Wise and Randy Starr wrote the song about the dangerous lure that women have, going all the way back to Eve, but one is willing to risk it all the same.

"Adelaide" is one of three songs Frank Loesser wrote for the 1955 film versioi of his Broadway hit *Guys and Dolls*, this one to give Frank Sinatra as Nathan Detroit (basically a nonsinging role) a chance to deliver a ballad. After being tricked into marrying his long-time fiancée Adelaide (Vivian Blaine), Sinatra and his fellow gamblers sang this spirited paean to the long-suffering gal who "is taking a chance on me."

"Adorable" is the title number from the 1933 costume musical scored by George Marion, Jr., (lyric) and Richard Whiting (music). Janet Gaynor, as a Ruritanian princess, and French actor Henri Garat, as the naval officer who loves her, sang the florid duet. *Adorable* was Garat's Hollywood debut and Gaynor's last film musical. Recordings of the song have been made over the years by Wayne King and his Orchestra, pianist Lee Sims, Little Jack Little, and Freddie Martin and the Hotel Bossert Orchestra.

"Afraid to Dream" is a charming ballad by Mack Gordon (lyric) and Harry Revel (music) about a lover's insecurity regarding romance. It was introduced by Don Ameche in the backstage musical *You Can't Have Everything* (1937) and reprised later in the film by Alice Faye and Tony Martin. Benny Goodman's recording was fairly popular.

"Afraid to Fall in Love" was the romantic duet that teenage lovers Mickey Rooney and Gloria De Haven sang in a pristine garden in *Summer Holiday* (1948), the film musicalization of Eugene O'Neill's domestic Broadway comedy *Ah, Wilderness!* Ralph Blane (lyric) and Harry Warren (music) wrote the youthful ballad that listed several the famous lovers of the past who were not fearful of romance.

"After Sundown" is the song that many feel made Bing Crosby a singing star on film. He sang the Latin-flavored ballad on the soundtrack of *Going Hollywood* (1933) during a montage of romantic scenes between Marion Davies and himself. Crosby's subsequent recording of the song was a hit single and helped make the movie successful. Nacio Herb Brown wrote the flowing music and Arthur Freed provided the ardent lyric.

"Age of Not Believing" is a tender ballad about the loss of a child's innocence that Richard M. and Robert B. Sherman wrote for the musical fantasy *Bedknobs and Broomsticks* (1971). The friendly witch Angela Lansbury and her three youthful evacuees prepared a magic flying bed for travel but the eldest, eleven years old going on twelve, doubted her powers of sorcery. So Lansbury sang of the age when a child starts to question everything and "when all the make believe is through."

"Ah, But Is It Love?" was a clever musical sequence from the Depression backstager *Moonlight and Pretzels* (1933). Song plugger Roger Pryor played his schmaltzy, would-be classical composition on the piano for sassy Lillian Miles, but she preferred jive. So he played it again as an arresting mixture of schmaltz and jive that led into a production number in a theatre. Jay Gorney composed the intriguing music and E. Y. Harburg provided the lively lyric.

"Ah Still Suits Me" was one of the three new songs Oscar Hammerstein (lyric) and Jerome Kern (music) wrote for the 1936 film version of their Broadway classic *Show Boat*, this one a charming character number for Paul Robeson and Hattie McDaniel. While dockhand Robeson shelled peas in the show boat's kitchen and sang of his laid-back contentment in life, his sharp-tongued wife McDaniel made cutting comments on his eternal laziness. Hammerstein's penchant and honest lyric keeps the scene from descending into the racial stereotypic, and both performers are at their understated best. The song, sometimes listed as "I Still Suits Me," was sung by Scott Holmes and Elisabeth Welch in the 1986 Broadway revue *Jerome Kern in Hollywood*.

"Ain't Got a Dime to My Name" is the easygoing ballad of idle happiness by Johnny Burke (lyric) and James Van Heusen (music) that Bing Crosby sang as he wandered the streets of Morocco looking for partner Bob Hope in *Road to Morocco* (1942). The song, which dismisses wealth with a musical "ho hum," was sung by Lewis Cleale and Michael McGrath in the Broadway revue *Swinging on a Star* (1995).

"Ain't It a Shame About Mame?" is a delightful narrative ballad that Johnny Burke (lyric) and James Monaco (music) wrote for Mary Martin to sing as she auditioned a song she had supposedly co-written with Bing Crosby in *Rhythm on the River* (1940). The number tells the frolicsome tale of everyday Mame, who encountered all sorts of trouble when she moved up in the world and married "Sir Reginald What's-His-Name."

"Ain't Nature Grand" is the bouncy musical observation made by farmgirl-swimmer Esther Williams and salesman Fernando Lamas in the aquatic musical *Dangerous When Wet* (1953).Williams' Ma (Charlotte Greenwood), her Pa (William Demarest), her sisters (Barbara Whiting and Denise Darcel), and Jack Carson reprised the number by Johnny Mercer (lyric) and Arthur Schwartz (music) that celebrated all the things nature provides, including the lover of one's dreams.

"Ain't No Road Too Long" is the keep-on-goin' country-western number from the children's film *Follow That Bird* (1985). The snappy number was sung by truck driver Waylon Jennings and Big Bird (voice of Carroll Spinney) as they rode along in a pickup full of turkeys. Throughout the song were shots of Big Bird's various friends combing the countryside looking for him and singing the same tune. Jeff Penning, Jeff Harington, and Steve Pippin wrote the optimistic number.

"Ain't There Anyone Here for Love?" is the sexy, athletic number that gold digger Jane Russell sang in the film version of *Gentlemen Prefer Blondes* (1953). The Harold Adamson (lyric) and Hoagy Carmichael (music) song was staged by choreographer Jack Cole in the gymnasium of an ocean liner where Russell worked out with a troop of male body builders as she presented her musical question.

"Alice in Wonderland" is the dreamy title number that was sung by a chorus on the soundtrack at the beginning and end of the 1951 animated fantasy. Bob Hilliard wrote the chorale-like lyric and Sammy Fain composed the warm music.

"All at Once" is the love ballad from the odd but likable musical fantasy *Where Do We Go From Here?* (1945). Contemporary writer Fred MacMurray sang the song of romantic discovery to June Haver and then reprised it later to Joan Leslie when a genie sends him back in time to seventeenth-century New Amsterdam. Kurt Weill, in one of his rare film assignments, composed the music and Ira Gershwin wrote the colloquial lyric. Kay Armen and the Guy Lombardo Orchestra, Don Cornell, and Cab Calloway and his Orchestra all had popular recordings of the song.

"All God's Chillun Got Rhythm" is the memorable revival number written by Gus Kahn (lyric), Walter Jurmann, and Bronislau Kaper (music) for the Marx Brothers vehicle *A Day at the Races* (1937). Harpo, as a flute-playing Pied Piper, led Ivy Anderson and the Crinoline Choir, as a troop of Negro children, through the town as they proclaimed him Gabriel and celebrated the God-given gift of rhythm. The jubilant song was often recorded, including noteworthy disks by Anderson, Bunny Berigan, Duke Ellington, Maynard Furguson, Sonny Stitt, Artie Shaw, and Judy Garland in her record debut.

"All I Do Is Dream of You" is the wistful and perennial favorite by Arthur Freed (lyric) and Nacio Herb Brown (music) in which the lover revels in the idle pursuit of daydreaming about his true love. Gene Raymond introduced the ballad in *Sadie McKee* (1934), and that same year Chico played it on the piano in *A Night at the Opera*. An unidentified French singer crooned the song standard in *Broadway Melody of 1936* (1935), and Debbie Reynolds sang it in both *Singin' in the Rain* (1952) and *The Affairs of Dobie Gillis* (1953), where she was joined by Bobby Van. Twiggy gave the song an understated interpretation in *The Boy Friend* (1971), and Vangle Charmichael sang it for *Lucky Lady* (1975). The oft-recorded ballad was a popular selection by Benny Goodman and Judy Garland, and there were recordings of interest by the orchestras of Jan Garber, Henry Busse, and Freddie Martin. A 1953 disk by Johnnie Ray revived interest in the old favorite.

"All I Owe Ioway" is the rousing tribute to the Midwest state sung by William Marshall, Vivian Blaine, Charles Winninger, Fay Bainter, Donald Meek, and other Iowans in the rural musical *State Fair* (1945). Oscar Hammerstein (lyric) and Richard Rodgers (music) wrote the number, which bears some resemblance to the title song of their recent Broadway hit *Oklahoma!* (1943). The 1962 remake of *State Fair* was reset in Texas and so the number was not used, but John Davidson and company sang it in the 1996 Broadway version of the musical.

"All I Want Is Just One Girl" is the sprightly love song that Maurice Chevalier sang in the early film revue *Paramount on Parade* (1930). Leo Robin (lyric) and Richard Whiting (music) wrote the number which Chevalier sang as a gendarme strolling through a French park where, noticing all the pairs of lovers there, he yearned for a sweetheart of his own. The song was reprised later in the film by Chevalier and the young Mitzi Green, who playfully imitated his famous accent. Early records by Chevalier, the Gus Arnheim Orchestra, and others helped make the song popular.

"All in a Golden Afternoon" is the operetta-like choral number that various flowers sing in the animated fantasy *Alice in Wonderland* (1951). Bob

Hilliard (lyric) and Sammy Fain (music) wrote the lyrical number in which the various flora celebrated their beauty in front of Alice, who they think is also a flower until she sings off key.

"All My Life" is an intoxicating, dreamy ballad by Sidney Mitchell (lyric) and Sam H. Stept (music) about a long-awaited love coming true. Phil Regan introduced the song in *Laughing Irish Eyes* (1936), and the ballad has resurfaced on occasion over the years. Ella Fitzgerald (with Teddy Wilson's band), Thomas "Fats" Waller, Ted Fio Rito, and the Benny Goodman Trio (vocal by Helen Ward) each made popular recordings of the ballad. It was featured in the backstager *Johnny Doughboy* (1943), and Julia Roberts sang it in the film musical *Everyone Says I Love You* (1997).

"All That I Am" is the appealing romantic ballad that Sid Tepper and Roy Bennett wrote for the Elvis Presley vehicle *Spinout* (1966). On a camping trip in the California mountains, band singer Presley sang the profession of love to authoress Diane McBain while other members of the group sang backup from inside their tents. The Presley disk of the number was moderately popular.

"All the Time" is a serviceable ballad from the serviceman musical *No Leave, No Love* (1946). British musical comedy star Pat Kirkwood (in her only Hollywood film) sang the Ralph Freed (lyric) and Sammy Fain (music) number as part of a USO show with Guy Lombardo's Orchestra, and the song enjoyed some popularity through recordings by Lombardo and his Royal Canadians (vocal by Kirkwood), Mike Douglas with Kay Kyser's band, and others.

"All the Way" is the Oscar-winning song by Sammy Cahn (lyric) and James Van Heusen (music) that Frank Sinatra introduced in *The Joker Is Wild* (1957) and was long associated with him on record and in concert. Sinatra sang the standard as lounge singer Joe E. Lewis on opening night of a ritzy Chicago nightclub, later reprising the song on a record that was playing. The lyric denotes a character of deep and unending devotion even though the film character was far from that. But the song became very popular, and when the dark film failed at the box office it was reissued as *All the Way*. A distinctive recording of the ballad was made by Lena Horne, and the Sinatra disk was used on the soundtrack for *Once Is Not Enough* (1974).

"All Through the Day" is arguably Jerome Kern's last superior ballad. It was written for the nostalgic musical *Centennial Summer* (1946), which Kern completed only a few months before his death. Oscar Hammerstein's warm lyric concerns the way one daydreams throughout the sunlight hours, looking forward to the night when one will be with one's beloved. The ballad was sung by Larry Stevens, Cornel Wilde, and Jeanne Carson (dubbed by Louanne Hogan) during a demonstration of a magic lantern showing slides of the Philadelphia Centennial Exposition of 1876. The Oscar-nominated song received several recordings, most memorably by Frank Sinatra with Alex Stordahl's Orchestra, Perry Como with Andre Kostalanetz's Orchestra, and Margaret Whiting with Carl Kress's Orchestra.

"All Together Now" is the lighthearted sing-along song that the Beatles (in live action) sang at the end of the animated fantasy *Yellow Submarine* (1968). Paul McCartney wrote the nursery song–like number for the film, and it enjoyed some popularity, especially at soccer matches and other large crowd gatherings.

"All You Want to Do Is Dance" is a song of romantic frustration crooned by Bing Crosby in *Double or Nothing* (1937) because his sweetheart prefers footwork over embracing. Johnny Burke (lyric) and Arthur Johnston (music) wrote the song, and Crosby's recording was a moneymaker.

"Allegheny Al" is a breezy song of low–down fun, a type not often associated with Oscar Hammerstein (lyric) and Jerome Kern (music). Dorothy Lamour (breaking away from her current sarong persona) and Irene Dunne, as traveling showgirls in nineteenth-century rural Pennsylvania, let down their hair and gave the number their cornball best in *High, Wide and Handsome* (1937).

"All's Fair in Love and War" is a sardonic look at the battle of the sexes by Al Dubin (lyric) and Harry Warren (music) that Dick Powell, Lee Dixon, Joan Blondell, Rosalind Marquis, and the chorus sang in *Gold Diggers of 1937* (1936). It was Dubin, whose own marriage was a battleground, who came up with the idea for the song, which compares romantic skirmishes to military maneuvers. Busby Berkeley's staging of the number, complete with seventy white-helmeted chorus girls goosestepping and being reflected on the polished floor, took the lyric literally.

"Alma Mammy" is the spirited school song by George Marion, Jr., (lyric) and Richard Whiting (music) that was heard throughout the early college musical *Sweetie* (1929). At one point in the film Jack Oakie, as a vaudeville hoofer, and the students at Pelham College all donned blackface and sang the song in the football stadium cheering section. The number was written because Oakie, envious of Jolson's blackface film performances, wanted a similar number in his career. The song was among the first recorded by Fred Waring and the Pennsylvanians.

"Alone" is a melancholy love song sung by sweethearts Kitty Carlisle and Allan Jones on board an ocean liner in the Marx Brothers' *A Night at the Opera*

(1935). The Arthur Freed (lyric) and Nacio Herb Brown (music) duet was a mating call of sorts from one lonely heart to another. Later in the film Harpo reprised the melody on his harp, and Judy Garland sang the ballad as a solo in *Andy Hardy Meets Debutante* (1940). Recordings were made by the orchestras of Tommy Dorsey, Hal Kemp, and Al Donahue.

"Always in All Ways" is the uptempo ballad in which impoverished countess Jeanette MacDonald and royalty-disguised-as-hairdresser Jack Buchanan sang together in *Monte Carlo*. (1930). Leo Robin's melting lyric about loyalty and unspoken love may be a bit thick, but Richard Whiting's music soars above the deliberately cute title. Despite Buchanan's charming screen presence, he would not appear in a Hollywood musical again for twenty-three years.

"Am I Blue?" is the renowned torch standard that was the highlight of the early backstage musical *On With the Show* (1929) and the first hit song introduced by an African-American on a film soundtrack. Ethel Waters, dressed as a plantation worker in a Broadway show, and the Harmony Emperors Quartet sang the intoxicating lament by Grant Clarke (lyric) and Harry Akst (music) of a woman whose lover has gone and left her "the sad and lonely one." The bluesy number has been heard in many subsequent films, including renditions by Charlotte Greenwood in *So Long, Letty* (1930), Joan Leslie in *The Hard Way* (1942), Nan Wynn in *Is Everybody Happy?* (1943), Hoagy Carmichael and Lauren Bacall (dubbed by a young Andy Williams) in *To Have and Have Not* (1944), and Barbra Streisand in *Funny Lady* (1975). A distinguished recording by Billie Holiday is arguably the finest disk, but standout records were made by Libby Holman, Ben Selvin's Orchestra, saxophonist Carmen Leggio, Dinah Washington, and Waters herself, whose recording was used on the soundtrack of *The Cotton Club* (1984). More recent recordings include those by Linda Ronstadt, Rita Coolidge, and George Strait, whose 1987 version was a Number One hit on the country music chart. "Am I Blue?" has been a stable in Broadway revues as well: Leslie Uggams, Debbie Shapiro, and Jean Du Shon sang it in *Blues in the Night* (1982), the whole cast performed it in the 1988 revue *Blues in the Night*, and Carrie Smith featured it in *Black and Blue* (1989).

"Am I in Love?" is a waggish list song by Al Dubin (lyric) and Harry Warren (music) in which a lover catalogues all the symptoms and comes to the conclusion that this is true love. Kenny Baker, as a small-town crooner, sang the number in *Mr. Dodd Takes the Air* (1937), and Gene Nelson revived it years later in *She's Working Her Way Through College* (1952), where he sang it and then performed an athletic dance in a gymnasium. Recordings by Hal Kemp, George Hall, and Jolly Coburn helped keep the song alive in the interim.

"Am I in Love?" is the Oscar-nominated duet sung by timid Harvard grad

Bob Hope and lady bandit Jane Russell as she shaves his face in a barber chair in the musical sequel *Son of Paleface* (1952). Jack Brooks wrote the bright and sportive number in which the two characters seek an answer to their amorous query, only to conclude that "all I know is I want to sing."

"Amapola (Pretty Little Poppy)" is the captivating Spanish song by Joseph M. Lacalle that had been heard in the United States since 1924 but became a hit when Albert Gamse added a new English lyric and Deanna Durbin, as a teenage orphan living with obnoxious relatives, trilled it in *First Love* (1939). The ballad was featured on *Your Hit Parade* for nineteen weeks and remained popular throughout the 1940s. Jimmy Dorsey's Orchestra (vocal by Bob Eberle and Helen O'Connell) had its first major hit with the song, selling over a million records; his band also played it in *The Fleet's In* (1942). Xavier Cugat (vocal by Carmen Castillo) also had success with the ballad, and it was featured in the Gene Autry film *Saddle Pals* (1947).

"America" is the driving rock song by Neil Diamond that celebrated those immigrants still coming to America in the 1980s looking to fulfill their dreams. The number was written for the third film version of *The Jazz Singer* (1980), where Diamond sang it on the soundtrack over the opening credits and in a concert at the end of the film. Diamond's recording was in the Top Ten on the charts.

"Amor" was a hit song in Mexico and became popular in the United States when radio singer Ginny Simms sang an English version of it in the backstager *Broadway Rhythm* (1944). Gabriel Ruiz wrote the enticing melody, Lopez Mendez penned the Spanish lyric, and Sunny Skylar provided the English one. Recordings by Bing Crosby, Andy Russell, Xavier Cugat, and others kept the song popular, and it was also featured in *Swing in the Saddle* (1946). The love song was revived in the next decade by a successful 1954 disk by the Four Aces with Jack Pleis and his Orchestra.

"And I Love Her" is the gentle love song sung by the Beatles in their first film *A Hard Day's Night* (1964). John Lennon and Paul McCartney wrote the number, their first traditional ballad, for the film (McCartney came up with the idea of having the title start in midsentence), and it was sung by the group as they recorded a television show. The song immediately became a hit single with over 300 different recordings over the years. Esther Phillips' 1965 recording as "And I Love Him" was also a hit, and there was a successful version by Smokey Robinson and the Miracles as well.

"And Then You Kissed Me" is the crooning ballad that Sammy Cahn (lyric) and Jule Styne (music) wrote for *Step Lively* (1944), the musicalization of the farce *Room Service*. Singing playwright Frank Sinatra sang the number about how his life changed after a kiss from a certain someone.

"And You'll Be Home" is an easygoing ballad that Johnny Burke (lyric) and James Van Heusen (music) fashioned for Bing Crosby's inimitable style. The lyric advises one to pursue one's own dream: Follow your heart, and happiness is yours. Crosby introduced the song as a lazy, carefree songwriter in *Mr. Music* (1950).

"Angel" is the lush ballad that heiress Lucille Bremer (dubbed by Trudi Erwin) sang in the exotic fairy tale musical *Yolanda and the Thief* (1945). Arthur Freed (lyric) and Harry Warren (music) wrote the song about a naive girl's guardian angel who has come to life (she believes) in the form of Fred Astaire. Kay Kyser (vocal by Mike Douglas) had a popular recording of the number.

"Animal Crackers in My Soup" is the gleeful kind of children's song only Shirley Temple could deliver without a trace of camp: A list song of different edible animals and the funny people she has met who remind her of them. It was written by Irving Caesar, Ted Koehler (lyric), and Ray Henderson (music) for *Curly Top* (1935), where Temple sang it at the Lakeside Orphanage to entertain other children, who beat out the song's rhythm with spoons on the tables. Temple reprised the song in *Rebecca of Sunnybrook Farm* (1938), where, at the ripe old age of ten, she performed a medley of her past hits. Don Bestor and his Orchestra had a popular disk, and in the 1960s Barbra Streisand and Tiny Tim made fun recordings of the ditty.

"Anniversary Song" was the only new song in the bio–musical *The Jolson Story* (1946), but it was the sleeper number of the film and swept the country, remaining on *Your Hit Parade* for seventeen weeks. Al Jolson and Saul Chaplin co-wrote the sentimental favorite, basing the melody on an 1880 waltz "Donauwellen" by J. Ivanovici, and Jolson dubbed for Larry Parks, who serenaded his parents on a California veranda as the family celebrated their fiftieth wedding anniversary. The Jolson recording sold over a million disks, and he repeated it on the soundtrack of *Jolson Sings Again* (1949). Other hit recordings of the song were made by Dinah Shore with Morris Stoloff's Orchestra, Tex Beneke (vocal by Garry Stevens), Guy Lombardo (vocal by Kenny Gardner), organist Ken Griffin, and Andy Russell with Paul Weston's Orchestra.

"Another Night Like This" is an atmospheric Latin number that Dick Haymes, as a Costa Rican singer who returns to his homeland, crooned in *Carnival in Costa Rica* (1947). The song was an adaptation of a Cuban ballad by Ernesto Lecuona with a new lyric by Harry Ruby; Haymes' recording of it, with Desi Arnez and his Orchestra, was very popular.

"Any Gal From Texas" is the Broadway-style cowboy song that Ralph Blane, Robert Wells (lyric), and Josef Myrow (music) wrote for the Jane Russell vehicle *The French Line* (1954). Texas millionairess Russell and her Lone Star pal Marty McCarty, dressed in skimpy cowgirl outfits, sang the sassy number performing in a benefit show on an ocean liner, stating how a true Texan gal is always looking for a straight-shooting kind of love.

"Any Moment Now" is a rapturous ballad about the anticipation of everlasting love that Deanna Durbin sang as she surveyed a beautiful western vista in *Can't Help Singing* (1944). E. Y. Harburg wrote the lighthearted lyric and Jerome Kern composed the music that, according to Gerald Bordman, starts "with sweet, simple phrases of the sort Kern had employed often in earlier days but quickly resorts to the darker, more advanced harmonies he preferred at the close of his career."

"Any Time's the Time to Fall in Love" is the upbeat love duet that Elsie Janis (lyric) and Jack King (music) wrote for the early Hollywood revue *Paramount on Parade* (1930). Lillian Roth, Charles "Buddy" Rogers, and the chorus performed the number, Rogers also making a record of it and singing the tune again in *Along Came Love* (1931). Phil Spitalny's Orchestra made an early recording of interest.

"Anything Can Happen in New York" is a sly paean to Manhattan that Mickey Rooney, Ray MacDonald, and Richard Quine delivered with straw hats and canes in a spaghetti restaurant floor show in the backstager *Babes on Broadway* (1941). Burton Lane composed the honky–tonk melody, and E. Y. Harburg provided the tongue-in-cheek lyric about how anyone one can climb to the top in New York, filled with references to John D. Rockefeller, Eddie Cantor, Walter Winchell, Thomas Dewey, Irving Berlin, and Joe DiMaggio. The song has enjoyed some interest recently through a recording by Michael Feinstein.

"Anything to Please the Queen" is a delightful musical conversation between the diplomat Maurice Chevalier and Queen of Sylvania Jeanette MacDonald in the early film operetta *The Love Parade* (1929). Victor Schertzinger composed the merry music and Clifford Grey wrote the comic lyric, a series of questions by the queen regarding her happiness that he answers with "anything!"

"Anywhere" is the Oscar-nominated song that Janet Blair, as a London showgirl during the Blitz, sang in *Tonight and Every Night* (1945), a film tribute to the enduring quality of the theatre. Sammy Cahn penned the dreamy lyric and Jule Styne composed the gentle music. The song was also featured in the film musical *Glamour Girl* (1948).

"Anywhere I Wander" is Frank Loesser's tender song about the loneliness of a wanderer that Danny Kaye sang in *Hans Christian Andersen* (1952) as he repaired the ballet slippers of the ballerina he is quietly in love with. Loesser's music is quiet and very evocative with an unusually short refrain of only twelve bars. Mel Tormé's recording of the ballad was a bestseller, and a disk by Julius LaRosa with Archie Bleyer's Orchestra was also popular.

"Applause, Applause" is a rousing tribute to show business that avoids clichés and doesn't take itself too seriously. The Ira Gershwin (lyric) and Burton Lane (music) ditty was performed by Debbie Reynolds and Gower Champion as the finale of a Broadway revue in *Give a Girl a Break* (1953). Lane's music is vigorous yet silly, and Gershwin's lyric, praising the power that audience appreciation has on all performers from actors to animal trainers, is nimble and filled with fun rhymes such as "Rockaway" and "a block away." Although the song was too sly to became an industry anthem, it has received some interesting recordings over the years, including a 1975 disk by Gershwin and Lane and a 1991 cut by Lane and Michael Feinstein.

"An Apple for the Teacher" is one of those coy love songs that Bing Crosby could sing and still come across as sincere: The lover asks his sweetheart to be kept after school so that he can learn about romance from the teacher. The Johnny Burke (lyric) and James Monaco (music) ballad was sung by Crosby to Linda Ware in *The Star Maker* (1939), a bio-musical about kiddie act impresario Gus Edwards. Crosby and Connie Boswell each recorded the song, and Gene Autry sang it in *The Last Roundup* (1947).

"April Love" is the ballad of young love that Pat Boone put at the top of the charts after singing it in the 1957 musical of the same title. Paul Francis Webster (lyric) and Sammy Fain (music) wrote the Oscar-nominated song, which Boone, as a troubled teen sent to a farm in Kentucky, sang to entertain guests at a dance. Later in the film the number was reprised by Boone and Shirley Jones, the neighboring farmgirl he falls in love with. Johnny Mathis' recording was also popular.

"April Played the Fiddle" is a pleasant ballad that Bing Crosby sang in *If I Had My Way* (1940), a sentimental tale about vaudevillians in New York. James Monaco wrote the delicate melody and Johnny Burke provided the warm lyric about spring and the blossoming of romance that it brings. Crosby recorded the number as well.

"Arabian Nights" is the psuedo-exotic opening number for the animated adventure *Aladdin* (1992) by Alan Menken (music) and Howard Ashman (lyric). A Middle Eastern merchant, voiced by Robin Williams, introduces the film, but Bruce Adler provided his singing voice as the sly salesman croons about the enchanted land of many stories. Because some found Ashman's lyric about the inhabitants' barbaric tendency "to cut off your ear if they don't like your face" offensive, the lyric was changed to complaints about the flat terrain and the intense heat for the video version.

"Are You Makin' Any Money, Baby?" is the standout rhythm number that Herman Hupfeld wrote for the oddly named backstager *Moonlight and Pretzels* (1933). Lillian Miles sang the rousing song as part of a Broadway show in which she was backed by a gambler. Paul Whiteman's Orchestra (vocal by Ramona) recorded it.

"Aren't You Glad You're You?" is a mellow but bright song of self-esteem that Bing Crosby (reprising his *Going My Way* role of Father O'Malley) played on the piano and sang to the dejected youth Joan Carroll to cheer her up in *The Bells of St. Mary's* (1945). Johnny Burke (lyric) and James Van Heusen (music) wrote the song which was nominated for an Oscar and was a hit record for Crosby and, to a lesser extent, for the Pied Pipers, Les Brown, Tommy Dorsey, and Johnny Long (vocal by Helen Young).

"Aren't You Kind of Glad We Did?" is a charming duet that was delivered by Dick Haymes and Betty Grable as they rode through the streets of 1874 Boston in an open carriage in *The Shocking Miss Pilgrim* (1947). Ira Gershwin penned the cunning lyric in which the two Bostonians realize that they've been sightseeing together without a chaperone but neither regrets the fact. Because the lyric's double entendres, such as "whatever made us do it?" and "wasn't it fun?" made the song a bit too risqué outside the context of the plot, radio play of recordings, such as that by Vaughan Monroe and Betty Norton, was limited. The number's music was an old trunk tune by George Gershwin, who had died ten years earlier, and Ira worked it into, as he named it, a "mid-Victorian colloquy." Sarah Vaughan made a distinctive recording years later.

"The Aristocats" is the title song by Richard M. and Robert B. Sherman for the 1970 animated film, the last time Maurice Chevalier was heard in a movie musical. Chevalier came out of retirement to sing (in English and French) over the opening credits the French cafe–style number about upper–class felines.

"Arthur Murray Taught Me Dancing in a Hurry" is the comic ditty that Betty Hutton (in her film debut) delivered with Jimmy Dorsey's Orchestra in her brash and energetic style at San Francisco's Swingland Dance Hall in *The Fleet's In* (1942) and it made her a star. The silly number by Johnny

Mercer (lyric) and Victor Schertzinger (music) told the animated tale of a gal who took a crash course in ballroom dancing at the famous franchise. At first Arthur Murray objected to the song because of the way it trivialized his teaching methods; but as the song became popular across the country, his business boomed and all objections ended. Among the handful of recordings of the number were bestsellers by Jimmy Dorsey (vocals by Bob Eberle and Helen O'Connell) and the King Sisters.

"Artists and Models" is the tuneful title song by Jack Brooks (lyric) and Harry Warren (music) for the 1955 musical vehicle for Dean Martin and Jerry Lewis. Martin sang the number, about how beautiful subjects inspire great art, over the opening credits; he and Lewis then sang it as part of a production number later in the film, the stage filled with lovely models in various colors on a giant palette.

"As Long as I'm Dreaming" is a soothing Johnny Burke (lyric) and James Van Heusen (music) ballad that Bing Crosby, as a young doctor new in town, sang in *Welcome Stranger* (1947). Crosby's recording was moderately popular, as were disks by Tex Beneke and Glenn Miller (vocal by Garry Stevens).

"As Long as There's Music" is a dreamy ballad that young playwright Frank Sinatra crooned in *Step Lively* (1944), the musical remake of the Broadway farce *Room Service*. Jule Styne composed the pleasing music, and Sammy Cahn penned the enticing lyric that promised that music and his true love, as long as she is near, will be the song.

"At Last" is an uptempo ballad about a long-awaited love coming true that Glenn Miller performed in two different films. Mack Gordon (lyric) and Harry Warren (music) wrote the number for *Sun Valley Serenade* (1941), but only the music was used in a sequence with Miller's orchestra. The song was heard in full form in *Orchestra Wives* (1942), where Ray Eberle and Lynn Bari (dubbed by Pat Friday) sang it with the famous band at a concert in Iowa City. A Miller-Eberle recording of the number became a hit, and a decade later Ray Anthony (vocal by Tommy Mercer) had a Top Ten record with it. The song enjoyed a revival in 1961 as a result of an Etta James recording.

"At the Balalaika" is a languid tango number used throughout the Nelson Eddy vehicle *Balalaika* (1939), an operetta about Russian exiles in Paris. Though originally a London stage piece with music by George Posford, the title tune was adapted for the film by Herbert Stothart, and George Forrest and Robert Wright provided the new lyric. Ilona Massey and the Russian Art Choir first sang the number at the Cafe Balalaika, then it was reprised by Walter Woolf

King and the soldiers in the trenches, and finally it was heard again when Eddy sang the number at the cafe. The number was recorded by the orchestras of Orrin Tucker and Abe Lyman.

"At the Cafe Rendezvous" is the silly character song that Sammy Cahn (lyric) and Jule Styne (music) wrote for the Hollywood spoof *It's a Great Feeling* (1949). Waitress and singer wanna-be Doris Day sang the zesty number in a thick and playful French accent.

"At the Codfish Ball" is a perky soft-shoe number that Shirley Temple and Buddy Ebsen sang and danced as they entertained the residents of a fishing village in *Captain January* (1936). Lew Pollack provided the catchy music, and Sidney D. Mitchell devised the gamesome lyric about an underwater dance hall.

"Aurora" is the musical paean to an entrancing lady of Brazil that Harold Adamson (lyric), Mario Lago, and Roberto Roberti (music) wrote for the Abbott and Costello farce *Hold That Ghost* (1941). The Andrews Sisters sang the rhythmic number wth Ted Lewis' Orchestra at an outdoor nightclub and their recording proved popular.

B

"Babes on Broadway" is the rollicking title number from the 1941 backstager about a bunch of teens who put on a show on the Great White Way. Burton Lane provided the catchy music, and Ralph Freed wrote the enthusiastic but sly lyric that spoke of rural teens milking applause rather than cows. But the clever number was reduced to barely a refrain in the final cut: An offscreen chorus sang a few lines over the opening credits, and in the finale Mickey Rooney, Judy Garland, Virginia Weidler, Ray McDonald, Richard Quine, and a chorus of youths sang the last refrain of the celebratory number about performing on Broadway. Michael Feinstein's 1990 recording of the full lyric (with Lane at the piano) revived interest in the song.

"Baby, Baby, Baby" is the pop hit sung by Teresa Brewer in the period musical *Those Redheads From Seattle* (1953) and on records. Mack David (lyric) and Jerry Livingston (music) wrote the repetitive declaration of love Brewer sang as a city girl who finds herself in love in the middle of the Yukon gold rush. Tommy Edwards also had a hit recording of the number.

"Baby Doll" is a light and breezy song of affection that Johnny Mercer (lyric) and Harry Warren (music) wrote for Gene Kelly to sing in *Take Me Out to the Ball Game* (1949), but the ballad was never used. The number was interpolated into the later *The Belle of New York* (1952), where wealthy playboy Fred Astaire woos Salvation Army gal Vera-Ellen with the song and they end up dancing all over the mission. Mercer's lyric describes the lady as a doll that Santa left under the Christmas tree, a girl one longs to take for a walk and show off. Later in the musical the number was reprised by Astaire and a male quartet. Kelly's cut soundtrack recording of the number was later released.

"Baby, I Don't Care" is the rock-and-roll ballad by Jerry Leiber and Mike Stoller that proclaims true love for a girl who doesn't "know the latest dance steps" but it doesn't matter. Elvis Presley, as an ex-con who has become a singing superstar, sang the number to entertain guests at a Hollywood pool party in *Jailhouse Rock* (1957). Years later Joni Mitchell revived the song with success. The number is sometimes listed as "You're So Square, Baby, But I Don't Care."

"Baby, It's Cold Outside" was written by Frank Loesser as a novelty duet for him and his wife to sing at Hollywood parties. Guests enjoyed the snappy number so much that it was interpolated into *Neptune's Daughter* (1949), where it was sung by Esther Williams and Ricardo Montalban. Later in the movie Red Skelton and Betty Garrett comically reprise the number. The song hardly blends into the plot — moments before he sings it, Montalban entreats Williams to stay with him on "this warm summer evening" — yet it became the musical highlight of the film and won the Oscar for Best Song. The contrapuntal duet is actually a musical conversation between a man-on-the-make (Loesser called him "the Wolf" in the sheet music) and his reluctant escort ("the Mouse") as he tries to convince her to stay indoors with him rather than face the weather outside. The song works so effectively as a duet that rarely has the oft-recorded number been sung as a solo. Memorable records include duets by Johnny Mercer and Margaret Whiting, Dinah Shore and Buddy Clark, Ella Fitzgerald and Louis Jordan, and Pearl Bailey and Hot Lips Page. A 1962 recording by Ray Charles and Betty Carter revived interest in the old favorite, and it was later sung by Bette Midler and James Caan in the film musical *For the Boys* (1991).

"Baby Mine" is the heartbreaking lullaby ballad that Ned Washington (lyric) and Frank Churchill (music) wrote for the animated circus tale *Dumbo* (1941). The singing voice of an uncredited female was heard on the soundtrack as young Dumbo is comforted by his mother, who is locked up as dangerous and can touch him only with her outstretched trunk. Les Brown (vocal by Betty Bonney) and Jane Froman both had popular records of the Oscar-nominated song.

"Baby, Take a Bow" is the Lew Brown (lyric) and Jay Gorney (music) song that introduced moppet Shirley Temple to American film audiences. Legend has it that while they were recording the score for *Stand Up and Cheer* (1934), six-year-old Temple was brought to the recording studio and started to improvise dance steps to the music, catching the attention of studio bosses, who signed her up on the spot. In the film Temple, in a polka dot ballet dress, and her father James Dunn performed the number, with Temple crawling out between his legs, curtsying, and then singing and dancing her way to stardom. The simple little ditty inspired Temple's next feature, *Baby, Take a Bow* (1934), and the song clip from the original was added to her later vehicle *Young People* (1940).

"Baby, Won't You Say You Love Me?" is the suggestive musical question that saloon shimmy dancer Betty Grable asked in the period musical *Wabash Avenue* (1950). Grable first sang the number in a fast and coquettish manner at rehearsal but during the performance at a World's Fair casino, Victor Mature made the orchestra slow down the tempo and Grable was forced to sing the ballad with a smooth and sincere delivery. Mack Gordon (lyric) and Josef Myrow (music) wrote the romantic number which was successfully recorded by Ella Fitzgerald, Herb Jeffries, and Ray Robbins.

"Baby, You Knock Me Out" is a driving rhythm song with a Big Band sound that Betty Comden, Adolph Green (lyric), and André Previn (music) wrote for *It's Always Fair Weather* (1955). In Stillman's gym, boxing enthusiast Cyd Charisse talk-sang the number with a bunch of pugilists, each proclaiming the powerful effect that they have on each other.

"The Back Bay Polka" is the satiric number by the Gershwins that was the comic highlight of *The Shocking Miss Pilgrim* (1947). Ira Gershwin took a trunk melody by his brother, George (who had died in 1937), and wrote the acerbic lyric about the narrow-mindedness of conservative Boston, where no one speaks the naked truth and "even a salad must have dressing." It was sung in an 1874 Boston boarding house by a quartet of "outcasts" — painter Arthur Shields, lexicographer Lillian Bronson, poet Allyn Joslyn, composer Charles Kemper — with radical landlady Elizabeth Patterson and feminist Betty Grable in order to prepare Grable to meet some of Boston's bluebloods. The song, sometimes listed as "Boston" and "But Not in Boston," was recorded by the quartet of Barbara Cook, Anthony Perkins, Bobby Short, and Elaine Stritch years later.

"Back in Business" is a bouncy pastiche number that Stephen Sondheim wrote in the Depression-be-damned style for *Dick Tracy* (1990), where it was sung by a line of nightclub chorines during a montage showing Big Boy Caprice's illegal enterprises booming. Sondheim's energetic melody and dancing lyrics were somewhat lost in the busy editing, but the song has resurfaced on several occasions. Julie Andrews, Stephen Collins, Christopher Durang, Michael Rupert, and Rachel York sang it in the Off-Broadway revue *Putting It Together* (1993); Liza Minnelli and Elaine Stritch sang and recorded the song in the 1992 *Sondheim: A Celebration at Carnegie Hall*; and Alet Oury made a complete recording of the number with Julie Alderfer, Farah Alvin, Heidi Godt, Kelli Shrewsbury, and Gretchen Weiss in 1997.

"Back to Back" is Irving Berlin's tongue-in-cheek answer to his own ballad "Cheek to Cheek," promoting a dance where the couples dance holding hands but facing away from each other. It was sung by Mary Healy on a nightclub dance floor in the Sonja Henie vehicle *Second Fiddle* (1939), in which all the patrons at the club tried out the awkward but fun dance. This uptempo number slyly makes fun of swing, calling it merely a "fad," but some bandleaders were not amused and refused to play it. Jimmy Dorsey (vocal by Helen O'Connell) and Glenn Miller each had a best-selling recording of the song, and Carroll Gibson's Orchestra had a record on the charts in England. Dorothy Loudon and Bobby Short made a larkish duet recording of the number in 1966.

"Back to School Again" is the lively 1960s pastiche number that opens *Grease 2* (1982) with an extended musical sequence that includes the credits and director-choreographer Patricia Birch's clever staging of the students descending on Rydell High School for the start of the 1961–62 school year. Howard Greenfield (lyric) and Louis St. Louis (music) wrote the vibrant song which was sung on the soundtrack by the Four Tops.

"The Bad Humor Man" is a fun novelty number by Johnny Mercer (lyric) and Jimmy McHugh (music) from the offbeat musical thriller *You'll Find Out* (1940). Ish Kabibble, as a grouchy ice cream vendor, sang the song (with Kay Kyser and his Kollege of Musical Knowledge) that spoofed the power the Good Humor Man had to drive the neighborhood kids to hysteria simply by ringing his bell. Jimmy Dorsey (vocal by Helen O'Connell) had a successful recording, and the silly song was rather popular in its day.

"Balboa" is one of the three songs Judy Garland belted out in her feature film debut in *Pigskin Parade* (1936). Sidney Mitchell (lyric) and Lew Pollack (music) wrote the zesty number which Garland sang as a pig-tailed hillbilly in the collegiate musical with Dixie Dunbar, Betty Grable, Jack Haley, Johnny Downs, Patsy Kelly, and the Yacht Club Boys.

"Bali Boogie" is the slaphappy specialty number Sylvia Fine wrote for the Danny Kaye fantasy vehicle *Wonder Man* (1945). Kaye, Jack Norton, Vera-Ellen (in her film debut, dubbed by June Hutton), and the Goldwyn Girls sang and cut capers with the nonsense song that spoofed swing and Polynesian tunes.

"The Bare Necessities" is the Oscar-nominated song of low-down, low-key philosophy by Terry Gilkyson that was featured in the animated film *The Jungle Book* (1967). Baloo the Bear (voice of Phil Harris) sang to the Man-cub Mowgli (voice of Bruce Reitherman) about taking the easy road in life and looking for the creature comforts as the two cavorted through the Indian jungle. Harris' recording enjoyed some popularity, and later there were distinctive records by Harry Conick, Jr., in 1995 and the Jazz Networks in 1996.

"Be a Clown" is the raucous Cole Porter song that celebrates the joy of bringing foolish fun to the world, as presented in *The Pirate* (1948). The film starred Gene Kelly, who suggested the idea to Porter, saying that the costume musical needed a knockout comic number. The music was first used for a vigorous dance sequence by Kelly and the Nicholas Brothers. Near the end of the film, when pirate Kelly was about to be hanged and given one last chance to perform, he and Judy Garland, in baggy clown costumes, performed the vivacious number for the crowd. Kelly and Garland also recorded the song as a duet. "Be a Clown" was closely copied for the "Make 'Em Laugh" number in *Singin' in the Rain* (1952).

"Be Careful, It's My Heart" is the tender Irving Berlin ballad that was used effectively to advance plot and character in the film classic *Holiday Inn* (1942). Bing Crosby sang the gentle plea for attention to Marjorie Reynolds during a rehearsal for the inn's Valentine's Day show. But Fred Astaire entered during the song, saw Reynolds, and was entranced by her, the two of them moving into a romantic dance while Crosby sang on unaware that he has lost her. Berlin's repetitive use of the same half and quarter notes and the unexpected jump from the key of F to A flat make the song difficult to sing but all the more alluring. In addition to Crosby's recording, Tommy Dorsey (vocal by Frank Sinatra), Joe Bushkin and his Orchestra, George Shearing, and Vera Lynn all had popular disks of the ballad.

"Be Honest With Me" is a soul-searching ballad that Gene Autry wrote (with Fred Rose) and sang in the cowboy musical *Ridin' on a Rainbow* (1941) and that was nominated for an Oscar. Jimmy Wakely sang it in *Strictly in the Groove* (1942), and records by Autry, Bing Crosby, and Freddy Martin (vocal by Clyde Rodgers and Eddie Stone) were all popular.

"Be My Love" is the bombastic aria hit that Mario Lanza sang in *The Toast of New Orleans* (1950) and became forever identified with him. The Sammy Cahn (lyric) and Nicholas Brodszky (music) ballad, in which the world "eternally" becomes an amorous call to arms, was performed in the film as a duet by Lanza, as a singing Louisiana fisherman, and Kathryn Grayson, as an opera singer. Lanza's recording, with Ray Sinatra's Orchestra and the Jeff Alexander Choir, sold over two million copies. The Oscar-nominated number later became the theme song for Lanza's television show *The Coca-Cola Hour*. Years later opera star Placido Domingo had modest success with his recording of the aria. In the Lanza vehicle *Because You're Mine* (1952), Doretta Morrow sang the ballad over the phone as part of an audition, and Connie Francis tearfully crooned it in *Looking for Love* (1964).

"Be Our Guest" was the Busby Berkeley–like production number in the animated musical *Beauty and the Beast* (1991) that affectionately spoofed the Hollywood musicals of the past. The enchanted candelabra Lumiere (voice of

Jerry Orbach) led the silverware, plates, and other kitchen paraphernalia in this psuedo–French music hall number about the joy of dining. Howard Ashman penned the slapstick lyric, Alan Menken composed the catchy melody, and the song was nominated for an Oscar.

"Be Prepared" is a sinister call to arms written by Tim Rice (lyric) and Elton John (music) for the animated *The Lion King* (1994) in which the scheming lion Scar (voice of Jeremy Irons) urged the hyenas to aid him in overthrowing the lion king and to put himself on the throne. While the three main hyenas (voices of Whoopi Goldberg, Cheech Marin, and Jim Cummings) provide the comic element, the song is a Fascistic promise of a new age that is uncomfortably chilling. In the 1997 Broadway version of *The Lion King,* the number was sung by John Vickery as Scar and Tracy Nicole Chapman, Stanley Wayne Mathis, and Kevin Cahoon as the three hyenas.

"The Beautiful Briny" is the carefree song about traveling underwater that was used in a mixed animation and live-action sequence in the musical fantasy *Bedknobs and Broomsticks* (1971). Angela Lansbury and David Tomilson sang the song as they traveled below the surface on a magic bed with three children (Roy Snart, Ian Weighill, and Cindy O'Callaghan) and observed the animated flowers and sea life. The scene climaxed with an acrobatic dance at the Beautiful Briny Ballroom where Lansbury and Tomilson won a trophy for their fancy footwork. The sequence was similar to a superior one in the previous *Mary Poppins* (1964), where Julie Andrews entered an animated world and won a trophy for a horse race. But "The Beautiful Briny" has a charm all its own. Richard M. and Robert B. Sherman wrote the jovial song, having fun with 'b' alliteration in the lyric.

"Beautiful City" is the only new song Stephen Schwartz wrote for the 1973 film version of his Off-Broadway hit musical *Godspell*. Jesus (Victor Garber) and his disciples sang the bright optimistic song about an ideal community built not of alabaster but of dreams. The number has an early 1960s pop sound to it, in contrast to the more driving 1970s temperament of the rest of the score. Laurie Beechman made a notable recording of the song.

"Beautiful Coney Island" is the sly pastiche salute to the "paradise far away from it all" that Leo Robin (lyric) and Ralph Rainger (music) wrote for the period musical *Coney Island* (1943). The waiters and patrons of a Coney Island saloon sang the number at the top of the film then it was later reprised by saloon singer Betty Grable and saloon owner George Montgomery on a pier as a gang of harmonica–playing beachcombers accompanied them. While Robin's lyric is very tongue-in-cheek, Rainger's music is a warm version of a ballad at the turn of the century, the film's setting.

"Beautiful Girl" is the musical proposal of marriage to a ravishing female that Bing Crosby sang in *Going Hollywood* (1933) as he cut a new record in the studio. The Arthur Freed (lyric) and Nacio Herb Brown (music) ballad was recorded by Crosby with Jimmie Grier's Orchestra, as well as by Bernie Cummins and Freddy Martin (vocal by Terry Shand). Jimmy Thompson sang it in *Singin' in the Rain* (1952), and in the 1985 Broadway version of that film classic it was sung by Don Corria and the ensemble.

"Beauty and the Beast" is the entrancing title ballad from the 1991 animated musical: The teapot Mrs. Potts (voice of Angela Lansbury) sang the number while the Beast and Belle danced in the castle ballroom. Howard Ashman wrote the simple but affecting lyrics and Alan Menken composed the entrancing music. A record three songs from the film were nominated for the Oscar and this one won. Recordings were made by Peabo Bryson and Celine Dion, flutist James Galway, harpist Carmen Dragon, Barbara Cook, the Jazz Networks, Debbie Shapiro Gravitte, and others.

"Because You're Mine," the title ballad for the 1952 Mario Lanza vehicle, was an attempt by Sammy Cahn (lyric) and Nicholas Brodszky (music) to provide Lanza with an ardent aria like "Be My Love," which they wrote for him two years before. The attempt was not a futile one: Lanza's recording of "Because You're Mine" sold over a million disks. Nat "King" Cole also had a hit record of the Oscar-nominated song.

"Beginner's Luck" is the intoxicating song by Ira Gershwin (lyric) and George Gershwin (music) that Fred Astaire sang to Ginger Rogers on an ocean liner in *Shall We Dance* (1937), declaring that he was lucky because his first time in love is with her. Astaire recorded the number with Johnny Green's Orchestra and Tommy Dorsey (vocal by Edythe Wright) had a hit record of the song, which is sometimes listed as "I've Got Beginner's Luck." In 1990 Bobby Short made a standout recording of the jaunty number.

"Being in Love" is the only new song that Meredith Willson wrote for the 1962 film version of his Broadway hit *The Music Man*, though sections of the ballad used parts of the stage song "My White Knight." Shirley Jones, as a strong-willed librarian in a small Iowa town, sang of her dream of marrying a quiet, intelligent man "more interested in me" than in himself.

"Bella Notte" is the warm Italian serenade written by Sonny Burke and Peggy Lee for the animated canine tale *Lady and the Tramp* (1955). A chorus sang the romantic number on the soundtrack during the film's most affecting scene, the spaghetti dinner shared by the street-wise dog Tramp and the refined cocker spaniel Lady as they dined in the alley behind Tony's Restaurant.

"Belle" is the extended musical sequence by Howard Ashman (lyric) and Alan Menken (music) that opened the story proper in the animated fairy tale *Beauty and the Beast* (1991). As the French country girl Belle (voice of Paige O'Hara) sang about the predictable ways of the townsfolk and dreamt of something better for herself, the villagers commented on the beautiful but odd girl who didn't seem to fit in. In a masterful interplay of song and dialogue reminiscent of the best musical plays, characters were introduced and attitudes were established. Belle reprised the song later in the film after turning down a marriage proposal from the brutish Gaston and wondered if she will ever find happiness in such a place. The Oscar-nominated song was sung by Susan Egan and the ensemble in the 1994 Broadway version of the film.

"The Bells of Notre Dame" is the prologue number for *The Hunchback of Notre Dame* (1996), one of the most complex musical sequences ever devised for an animated film. The narrator Clopin (voice of Paul Kandel) related in song and storytelling the history of the hunchback: how he was born and nearly killed, how he was hidden away, and how Paris had become subject to the powerful judge Frollo. Alan Menken composed the vivid music and Stephen Schwartz penned the lyric that utilizes sections of Latin religious texts.

"Beloved" is one of the three new songs Paul Francis Webster (lyric) and Nicholas Brodszky (music) were commissioned to write to augment the famous Sigmund Romberg score for the operetta favorite *The Student Prince* (1954). It was hoped that Mario Lanza would play the royal Heidelberg student, but he had grown too stout for the role and so it was given to Edmund Purdom. Lanza, however, provided the voice for this lush serenade sung to pretty barmaid Ann Blyth.

"A Bench in the Park" was the silly romantic production number in the early musical revue *King of Jazz* (1930) by Jack Yellen (lyric) and Milton Ager (music) in which dozens of couples dallied and smooched in a public park. The song was sung by the Brox Sisters and George Chiles with Paul Whiteman's Orchestra and featured the Rhythm Boys: Harris Barris, Al Rinker, and Bing Crosby (his film debut). Russell Markert devised the clever choreography that effectively used the large chorus (he would go on to create the Rockettes a few years later), and the number compares favorably to Busby Berkeley's "Pettin' in the Park" sequence three years later in *Gold Diggers of 1933*. Whiteman recorded the song with the Rhythm Boys.

"Bend Down, Sister" is a delightful comic number by Ballard MacDonald, David Silverstein (lyric), and Con Conrad (music) from the Eddie Cantor vehicle *Palmy Days* (1931) about fake spiritualists. Long-legged comedian Charlotte Greenwood, as a health nut in a bakery, and the female bakers sang the jocular number that taught one to keep pastries and such "on the outside looking in" if one wants to remain slim. The song was followed by an athletic dance sequence choreographed by Busby Berkeley that featured an early use of his kaleidoscope pattern technique.

"The Best Things Happen When You're Dancing" is the smooth Irving Berlin dance song that Danny Kaye sang to Vera-Ellen in *White Christmas* (1954) as they glided across a Miami nightclub dance floor and out onto a deserted veranda. The number was an unusually straight and sophisticated one for comic Kaye, but the role (and the song) was intended for Fred Astaire, who had to drop out of the movie because of illness. Kaye recorded the ballad with the Skylarks.

"Better Luck Next Time" is the plaintive but sincere lament that Irving Berlin wrote for *Easter Parade* (1948). The number was sung by Judy Garland to an understanding bartender when she realizes that her dancing partner Fred Astaire is still in love with his old flame Ann Miller. Berlin's lyric is a quiet masterwork, avoiding the maudlin and allowing the singer to refute the title phrase and pledge that there would be no "next time" for her. Jo Stafford made an effective recording of the ballad which was revived in 1987 by Michael Feinstein.

"Between You and Me" is Cole Porter's lyrical song of romantic camaraderie that he wrote for *Broadway Melody of 1940* (1940). Broadway-hopeful George Murphy sang it as he auditioned as Eleanor Powell's new leading man; then the two of them performed a sleek dance together.

"Beware My Heart" is a torchy ballad by Sam Coslow that was one of the few contemporary songs in *Carnegie Hall* (1947), a film that featured many classical pieces performed by world-famous concert artists. Vaughn Monroe crooned the number accompanied by his own orchestra, and Margaret Whiting and June Christie each had successful recordings of the song.

"Beyond the Blue Horizon" is the hit song by Leo Robin (lyric), Richard Whiting, and W. Franke Harling (music) from *Monte Carlo* (1930) that provided the text for one of the most memorable sequences in early film musicals. Princess Jeanette MacDonald ran away from her fiancé and boarded a train to Monte Carlo. From her compartment she gazed out the window, singing and waving to the peasants working in the fields, who sang back in harmony. The orchestration effectively included the sounds of clicking train rails, and the number built in intensity as the song soared to a climax. Gerald Mast calls the Ernst Lubitsch–directed scene "the first sensational Big Number in an American film musical, the first extended musical sequence in which song, story, style and meaning combine with a pyrotechnical display of cinema's visual devices." At the end of the film the song was reprised by MacDonald and Jack Buchanan. MacDonald also sang "Beyond the Blue Horizon" in *Follow the Boys* (1944), but the line referring to "rising sun" was changed to "shining sun" because of the former expression's association with Japan. MacDonald and others made early recordings of the song, many retaining the locomotive accompaniment, and it has remained a standard over the years, heard as recently as 1988 when it was sung on the soundtrack by Lou Christie in the film *Rain Man*. On Broadway the number was sung by the cast of the revue *A Day in Hollywood—A Night in the Ukraine* (1980).

"Bibbidi, Bobbidi, Boo" is the gleeful nonsense song that the Fairy Godmother (voice of Verna Felton) sang in the animated fairy tale *Cinderella* (1950) to cheer up the young orphan while performing her magical powers. Mack David (lyric), Al Hoffman, and Jerry Livingston (music) wrote the bouncy number and Perry Como had a hit recording of it. Dinah Shore, Ilene Woods, and, in a duet version, Gordon MacRae and Jo Stafford also recorded the Oscar-nominated song, and Bobby McFerrin sang it in a 1995 version of the complete score.

"Big Bottom" is the mock heavy-metal song performed in concert by a fictitious British group touring America in the parody rockumentary *This Is Spinal Tap* (1984). Christopher Guest, Rob Reiner, Harry Shearer, and Michael McKean wrote the pulsating number about a girl with large buttocks who is too good "to leave behind." Guest, McKean, Shearer, R. J. Parnell, and David Kaff performed the outrageously prankish number as the members of the group Spinal Tap. A decade later the actors regrouped and played this song and others in actual concerts and on a television special.

"Big City Blues" is a psuedo-blues number in a psuedo-Broadway show that Sidney D. Mitchell (lyric), Archie Gottler, and Con Conrad (music) provided for the early backstager *Fox Movietone Follies of 1929* (1929). Lola Lane, as a chorus girl in the show who takes over the lead spot when the temperamental star refuses to go on, sang the number. (The contrived plot device, predating *Forty-Second Street* by four years, was actually somewhat original for its time.) The song provided successful recordings by Annette Hanshaw and by the orchestras of Bert Lown, George Olsen, Lou Gold (vocal by Irving Kaufman), and Arnold Johnson (vocal by Scrappy Lambert).

"Birmingham Bertha" is a determined song of amorous revenge that Ethel Waters sang in the early backstager *On With the Show* (1929). Harry Akst composed the bluesy music and Grant Clarke penned the lyric, which told of a gal who traveled to Chicago to get even with the man who jilted her back in

Birmingham. Waters recorded the number, as did Jimmy Noone, B. A. Rolfe, Don Voorhees, Miff Mole, and Walter Barnes.

"Birmin'ham" is a lively duet that Rosalind Russell and Eddie Albert sang in *The Girl Rush* (1955), the musical about Las Vegas gambling casinos. Hugh Martin and Ralph Blane wrote the carefree tribute to the Southern city.

"The Black Hills of Dakota" is a soothing ballad about the beauty of the land that Paul Francis Webster (lyric) and Sammy Fain (music) wrote for the frontier musical *Calamity Jane* (1953). Doris Day, Howard Keel, and other guests riding in the moonlight in carriages to a ball at the fort sang the song about "the beautiful Indian country that I love." The number is sometimes listed as "Take Me Back to the Black Hills of Dakota."

"Black Moonlight" is a suicidal dirge that Sam Coslow (lyric) and Arthur Johnston (music) wrote for the Bing Crosby vehicle *Too Much Harmony* (1933). Because of Crosby's hit recording (with Jimmie Grier's Orchestra), the torch song was long associated with him, but it was sung in the film by Kitty Kelly as a Harlem resident in a Broadway-bound show. A popular Perry Como recording in the 1950s revived interest in the song.

"Blah, Blah, Blah" is a wry love song by Ira Gershwin (lyric) and George Gershwin (music) that makes fun of love songs. In *Delicious* (1931), Swedish-accented comedian Ed Brendel and his cohort Manya Roberti sang the number to illustrate to some Russian immigrants how easy it is to write love songs in America. Ira Gershwin's lyric playfully includes all the predictable clichés ("moon . . . croon . . . month of May . . . clouds of gray") and then uses the title phrase to fill in all the blanks. Shot for the film but edited out in the final print was a "Russian" refrain that spoofed actual Russian celebrities and terms; Gershwin would file away the idea and use it in 1941 for the Broadway song "Tschaikowsky" in *Lady in the Dark*. "Blah, Blah, Blah" has resurfaced on occasion over the years: Barbara Lea had success with it in her cabaret act, Diahann Carroll recorded it, and Tommy Tune sang it in the Broadway musical *My One and Only* (1983).

"Blame It on the Samba" is the Latin number that organist Ethel Smith and the Dinning Sisters performed on the soundtrack of the animated anthology film *Melody Time* (1948) when Donald Duck and Joe Carioca, reunited from *The Three Caballeros* (1945), danced and frolicked. Ernesto Nazareth composed the exotic music for the original Brazilian song and Ray Gilbert provided the nimble English lyric for the film.

"Blame My Absent-Minded Heart" is the regretful ballad that waitress Doris Day sang in *It's a Great Feeling* (1949), the musical farce about Hollywood. Sammy Cahn (lyric) and Jule Styne (music) wrote the lament which was recorded by Mindy Carson with Henri René's Orchestra.

"Bless Your Beautiful Hide" is the crude but heartfelt song of affection that mountain man Howard Keel sang in *Seven Brides for Seven Brothers* (1954) as he wandered the streets of the frontier town looking for a wife, knowing he has found her when he saw Jane Powell. Johnny Mercer wrote the crusty lyric and Gene De Paul composed the melodic country-flavored music, which was also used, in a faster tempo, behind the famous competitive dance at the barn raising later in the film. David-James Carroll performed the song in the 1982 Broadway version of *Seven Brides for Seven Brothers*, and Edmund Hockridge sang it in the 1994 British recording of the complete film score.

"Blossoms on Broadway" is the appealing title ballad by Leo Robin (lyric) and Ralph Rainger (music) for the unusual pop-opera film of 1937. Shirley Ross, as a con lady posing as a gold-mine owner, sang the graceful number about how bustling Broadway turns into a quiet and romantic country lane when one is in love.

"Blue Bayou" is the atmospheric number by Ray Gilbert (lyric) and Bobby Worth (music) that provided the background for a lyrical sequence in the animated musical anthology *Make Mine Music* (1946). The Ken Darby Chorus sang the song on the soundtrack during a "Tone Poem" in which an egret stops at a bayou to rest, finds a companion, and the two fly off toward the moon reflected in the water.

"Blue Hawaii" is the hit tropical ballad that pineapple businessman Bing Crosby sang to a reluctant Shirley Ross in *Waikiki Wedding* (1937) to convince her of the magical qualities of the islands, the moonlight, and himself. Leo Robin (lyric) and Ralph Rainger (music) wrote the Oscar-winning song that was a popular record for Crosby and for many instrumental groups, from an early recording by Billy Vaughn and his Orchestra to pan flutist Kim Kahuna and the Royal Palms Orchestra. Elvis Presley sang the ballad over the credits of the film *Blue Hawaii* (1962), and his recording was also a hit.

"Blue Lovebird" is a gay nineties pastiche number that Gus Kahn (lyric) and Bronislau Kaper (music) wrote for the period biographical musical *Lillian Russell* (1940). Alice Faye, as the hour-glass-figured Russell, sang this plaintive ballad that aped the kind of music hall numbers that the great lady had excelled at. Although the lyrics were purposely dated, band leaders liked the melody, which was recorded by Larry Clinton, Mitchell Ayres, Frankie Masters, and Kay Kyser (vocal by Ginny Simms).

"Blue Monday" is the blues standard that Antoine "Fats" Domino wrote (with Dave Bartholomew) and sang in a guest spot in *The Girl Can't Help It* (1957), the rock-and-roll spoof starring Jane Mansfield. Domino's recording of the cool blues number was a bestseller.

"Blue Shadows on the Trail" is the pleasing cowboy ballad that Bob Nolan and the Sons of the Pioneers sang on the soundtrack for the "Pecos Bill" segment of the animated anthology film *Melody Time* (1948). Johnny Lange (lyric) and Elliot Daniel (music) wrote the bucolic song, and Roy Rogers, Bing Crosby, and Vaughn Monroe and his Orchestra all had successful recordings of it.

"Blueberry Hill" is the perennial blues-country favorite by Al Lewis, Larry Stock, and Vincent Rose that has remained popular since it was first sung by Gene Autry in *The Singing Hills* (1941). Glenn Miller's Orchestra (vocal by Ray Eberle) and Kay Kyser made recordings that kept the song alive throughout the 1940s, and Antoine "Fats" Domino's 1957 recording sold a million copies and kept the number popular into the 1960s. The song was also a specialty for Louis Armstrong in concert and on records. Domino reprised his legendary rendition of "Blueberry Hill" in the film rockumentary *Let the Good Times Roll* (1973).

"Bluebirds in My Belfry" is the frenetic specialty number written by Johnny Burke (lyric) and James Van Heusen (music) for comedienne Betty Hutton. She sang the animated lament as part of a sister act called the "Angels" in the wartime musical *And the Angels Sing* (1944).

"Bluebirds in the Moonlight" is the swinging Big Band number that the mythical Lilliputians sang and danced to in the animated adventure *Gulliver's Travels* (1940). At a dinner honoring giant Gulliver for his help in battle, the miniature citizens of Lilliput sang the bouncy song of thanks and the king did a jitterbugging dance with Gulliver's huge fingers. Ralph Rainger composed the very contemporary music, and Leo Robin provided the jubilant lyric in which the Lilliputians proclaimed their appreciation was enough to make bluebirds sing at night. Popular recordings of the song were made by Dick Jurgens (vocal by Eddie Stone), Glenn Miller (vocal by Marion Hutton), and Benny Goodman (vocal by Mildred Bailey).

"Blues in the Night" is arguably the most potent blues number to come out of Hollywood. The Johnny Mercer (lyric) and Harold Arlen (music) standard was heard in the 1941 film of the same title, a dark musical melodrama about the lives of itinerant jazz musicians. (The film was to be called *Hot Nocturne*, but the studio heads changed the title once they heard the Mercer-Arlen song.)

William Gillespie, as a black inmate in a St. Louis jail cell, sang the number about a two-timing woman while Jimmy Lunceford's Orchestra accompanied him. A Lunceford recording (vocal by Willie Smith), in which the song was delivered in two contrasting styles, was released just before the film was, and the song hit the charts right away. Mercer's lyric uses Southern vernacular in a potent manner, avoiding cliché and finding words of brute strength that have a rhythm of their own. Arlen's music (written in an unusually long fifty-eight measures) uses a traditional three-stanza, twelve-bar pattern typical of authentic blues folk songs and even uses classic blues phrases, yet the song is uniquely its own, "certainly a landmark," according to Alec Wilder, "in the evolution of American popular music, lyrically as well as musically." The song was nominated for an Oscar, and Jerome Kern, whose own "The Last Time I Saw Paris" was nominated (and won), actively campaigned for "Blues in the Night" to win. Of the many recordings over the years, most noteworthy were those by Dinah Shore in 1941 (her first million-selling record), Judy Garland, the Benny Goodman Sextet, Jimmy Lunceford, Artie Shaw, Cab Calloway, Woody Herman, Frank Sinatra, Rosemary Clooney, Ella Fitzgerald, and Julie Wilson. John Garfield, as a comic gangster, sang it in the 1943 film musical *Thank Your Lucky Stars*. The song also provided the title for two Broadway revues, sung by Leslie Uggams and Debbie Shapiro in a 1982 show and by the company in a 1988 version. Lesley Ann Warren sang "Blues in the Night" in the Broadway revue of Mercer songs entitled *Dream* (1997).

"Boa Noite" is the romantic goodnight song that Mack Gordon (lyric) and Harry Warren (music) wrote for the Latin musical *That Night in Rio* (1941). Don Ameche sang the tender lullaby to a bevy of beauties in evening gowns as part of a Rio de Janeiro nightclub floor show. Later in the film Alice Faye reprised the number in her bedroom, singing to Ameche in his bedroom next door.

"Bojangles of Harlem" is the swinging tribute to dancer Bill Robinson that was long associated with Fred Astaire, who danced to it in *Swing Time* (1936) but never actually sang it. The Dorothy Fields (lyric) and Jerome Kern (music) number was presented as a nightclub act at the Silver Sandal in New York with Astaire (in blackface) dancing in Robinson's inimitable style while a chorus of girls sang of Bojangles' dancing genius. The number climaxed with Astaire dancing with three huge silhouettes of himself. The music, a rhythm number with a distinct march tempo, is unusual for Kern, who disliked swing. Legend has it that Astaire had to tap out the rhythm for Kern as he wrote in his hotel room. Although the song is primarily a dance piece, it was successfully recorded by Astaire, Bob Howard, the Tempo Kings Combo, Bobby Short, and most recently Barbara Cook. The song was also performed by the cast of the 1986 Broadway revue *Jerome Kern Goes to Hollywood*.

"Bonjour, Paris!" is the enthusiastic song of greeting that Leonard Gershe (lyric) and Roger Edens (music) added to the Gershwin musical romance *Funny Face* (1957). Photographer Fred Astaire and fashion magazine editor Kay Thompson brought young model Audrey Hepburn to Paris, where the trio sang their salute to the City of Light in a montage that took them all over town, ending up on the Eiffel Tower.

"Bonne Nuit — Goodnight" is the lullaby that reporter Bing Crosby sang to the two French orphans he hopes to adopt in *Here Comes the Groom* (1951). Jay Livingston and Ray Evans wrote the warm bilingual ballad.

"The Boogie Man" is an odd but interesting rhythm number by Sam Coslow (lyric) and Arthur Johnston (music) from the musical farce *Many Happy Returns* (1934). Guy Lombardo's Orchestra (vocal by Lebert Lombardo) performed the song in the sleeping car of a train, the musicians clad in their pajamas and perched on upper and lower berths.

"Boogie Woogie Bugle Boy (of Company B)" is the 1940s standard that the Andrews Sisters sang in the wartime musical *Buck Privates* (1941) and were forever after associated with. Hugh Prince composed the contagiously bouncy music, and Don Raye provided the frantic lyric that saluted the company's bugler. The Andrew Sisters reprised the Oscar-nominated song in *Swingtime Johnny* (1943), and the number became popular all over again when Bette Midler revived it in 1973 on record, in concerts, and later in the film *Divine Madness* (1980). In 1995 the Osborne Sisters recorded the electric number with the Cincinnati Pops Orchestra.

"Born in a Trunk" is the show biz song that opens and closes the intricate fifteen-minute section of *A Star Is Born* (1954), showing the rise of an ambitious singer (Judy Garland) from vaudeville to the big time. The Leonard Gershe (lyric) and Roger Edens (music) song sequence was filmed after the principal photography for the movie was complete; in fact, Ira Gershwin and Harold Arlen, who wrote the rest of the film's score, were not available, and the scenes were staged not by director George Cukor but by Richard Barston and Edens. During the exhilarating sequence, sections of "Black Bottom," "My Melancholy Baby," "Swanee," and other standards were sung by Garland. The film-within-a-film is one of the highlights of *A Star Is Born*, and Garland's throbbing rendition of "Born in a Trunk" and how she was bred with show business in her blood was a standout in her career. Years later her daughter Liza Minnelli made a similar kind of musical montage called "Happy Endings" in *New York, New York* (1977).

"The Boulevard of Broken Dreams" is the mellow torch song by

Al Dubin (lyric) and Harry Warren (music) that inspired a lavish production number in *Moulin Rouge* (1934). Constance Bennett sang the psuedo-French lament with Tullio Carminati, Russ Columbo, and the Boswell Sisters as part of a show in a Paris theatre. Warren's music is in a moody minor key, and Dubin's lyric about the unhappy affair between a gigolo and a loose woman was purposely morose. Yet the song became somewhat popular through recordings by Hal Kemp, Frances Langford with Harry Sosnik's Orchestra, Jan Garber (vocal by Lee Bennett), Ted Weems (vocal by Elmo Tanner), and others. Tony Bennett revived the song in 1950 (it was his first hit record), and the number was most recently recorded by Diana Krall.

"A Boulevardier From the Bronx" is a daffy duet sung by Jack Oakie and Joan Blondell in the forgotten Ruby Keeler–Dick Powell musical *Colleen* (1936). Harry Warren composed the lighthearted music, and Al Dubin wrote the silly lyric that spoofed ballroom dancers.

"Bounce Me Brother With a Solid Four" is one of those fast and robust wartime novelty songs filled with jive slang that the Andrews Sisters excelled at. They introduced this Don Raye and Hugh Prince number in *Buck Privates* (1941) as a trio of Pied Pipers singing their heart out for the war effort. Their recording was very popular.

"The Boy Next Door" is the unforgettable ballad of wistful yearning that Judy Garland sang in *Meet Me in St. Louis* (1944) as she quietly soliloquized her love for neighbor Tom Drake. Ralph Blane and Hugh Martin wrote the song, which is distinctive both musically and lyrically. The number employs a waltz tempo yet has none of the predictability of waltz ballads. The verse is unusually long, using twenty-four repeated notes to gracefully compliment the lyric that cites the lengthy house address numbers of the two young folk. The refrain is a series of suspended chords that provides the number with simplicity and yet creates an effective tension. Garland's performance of the song is one of her finest, adding unique moments of hesitation in the refrain to convey the youthful anxiety of the character. Vic Damone sang the song as "The Girl Next Door" in *Athena* (1954), and Donna Kane sang it in the 1989 Broadway version of *Meet Me in St. Louis*.

"Brave Man" is the coy tribute to courage that saloon singer Rosemary Clooney and the chorus sang in the western musical spoof *Red Garters* (1954). Jay Livingston and Ray Evans wrote the agreeable number which was popular for a time.

"Brazil" is the durable samba number that has remained a Latin standard over the decades. Ary Barroso wrote the music and the original Portuguese lyric (the title then was "Aquarela do Brazil"), but Bob Russell provided an English lyric when the song was interpolated into the animated musical *Saludos Amigos* (1942), where it was performed on the soundtrack by Eddy Duchin and his Orchestra. The number was also featured in *The Gang's All Here* (1943), where it was sung by Carmen Miranda, Aloysio de Oliveira, and the chorus; in *Jam Session* (1944), where it was sung by Nan Wynn; and by Big Bands in *Road to Rio* (1948) and *The Eddy Duchin Story* (1956). Both Xavier Cugat (vocal by the band members themselves) and Jimmy Dorsey (vocal by Bob Eberle and Helen O'Connell) had best-selling records of the serenade, and Les Paul recorded a unique version using multitrack guitars. The song was a hit once again in 1975 as a top-selling disco version by the group Richie Family. "Brazil" inspired three film titles, where it was played on the soundtrack: the 1943 Roy Rogers western, the 1944 Tito Guizar–Virginia Bruce musical, and the 1985 sci-fi satire.

"Bring on the Beautiful Girls" is the requisite paean to gorgeous show girls that Earl Brent (lyric) and Roger Edens (music) wrote for the film revue *Ziegfeld Follies* (1946). Fred Astaire sang the opening number to a bevy of chorines dressed in pink and riding a carousel with real horses on it. Cyd Charisse then did a specialty ballet sequence, model Lucille Ball "tamed" some catlike females with her whip, and finally Virginia O'Brien reprised the number as "Bring on Those Wonderful Men" while she rode horseback and lamented the scarcity of males in the production number.

"Broadway Melody" is the upbeat anthem to the street that "always wears a smile" and the title song for the historic 1929 musical that boasted, among other things, the first complete score written for a film. Arthur Freed (lyric) and Nacio Herb Brown (music) wrote the brash song, which Charles King sang in the film three times: first as he auditioned the new song for the producer, then as he taught it to vaudeville sisters Bessie Love and Anita Page in their hotel room, and finally in top hat and tails as he strutted across the stage in a large production number. King recorded the number, and the orchestras of Ben Selvin and Nat Shilkret made early disks as well. The song was heard in the background of a handful of films over the years, and its title inspired a series of MGM musicals in the 1930s. Harry Stockwell sang it in *Broadway Melody of 1936* (1935), the King recording was used in *This Happy Breed* (1944), and Gene Kelly used the song for the renowned "Broadway Ballet" sequence in *Singin' in the Rain* (1952).

"Broadway Rhythm" is the Arthur Freed (lyric) and Nacio Herb Brown (music) rhythm song that Frances Langford sang in a lavish nightclub in *Broadway Melody of 1936* (1935) while Eleanor Powell danced with Vilma and Buddy Ebsen, June Knight, and Nick Long, Jr. The swinging number was reprised by Powell in *Broadway Melody of 1938*, Judy Garland performed it in both *Babes in Arms* (1939) with Betty Jaynes and *Presenting Lily Mars* (1943) with Tommy Dorsey's Orchestra, and Gene Kelly sang it in *Singin' in the Rain* (1952) while Cyd Charisse danced to it. Guy Lombardo and his Royal Canadians had the most successful of the many recordings of the song.

"Broadway's Gone Hillbilly" is the slaphappy discovery that country music is here to stay, sung by Sylvia Froos in one of several specialty numbers in *Stand Up and Cheer* (1934). Jay Gorney composed the Broadwayized country ditty, and Lew Brown wrote the raffish lyric about the way all the shows on the Great White Way seem to want to go back to the farm.

"Brooklyn Bridge" is the crooning tribute to the local landmark from *It Happened in Brooklyn* (1947). Sammy Cahn (lyric) and Jule Styne (music) wrote the song, and ex-GI Frank Sinatra returning home to Brooklyn sang it.

"Buds Won't Bud" is a sly torch song that was cut from two shows before Ethel Waters introduced it in the musical spy thriller *Cairo* (1942). E. Y. Harburg (lyric) and Harold Arlen (music) wrote the number for the Broadway musical *Hooray for What!* (1937), but it was dropped before opening. Judy Garland recorded it for the film *Andy Hardy Meets Debutante* (1940), but again it was cut. When Waters was cast as Jeanette MacDonald's maid in *Cairo*, the song was interpolated to fill out her part. Waters delivered the number in a light and witty manner that illustrated what a fine comedienne she was but too rarely given the opportunity to be so. Arlen's music is carefree for a torch song, and Harburg's lyric, about how nature is neglecting itself since her lover left her, is filled with crafty wit and fun hyperbole. Distinctive recordings over the years include those by Tommy Dorsey (vocal by Connie Haines), Benny Goodman (vocal by Helen Forrest), Phil Harris, and Julie Wilson.

"Bugsy Malone" is the lazy bluesy title song by Paul Williams for the 1976 gangster musical cast completely with children. Williams sang the number, about a good-hearted racketeer ("he's a sinner, candy-coated"), over the opening credits and later during a montage when Bugsy (Scott Baio) takes chorus girl Blousie (Florrie Dugger) for an outing in the country.

"Build a Better Mousetrap" is the brash novelty number that Johnny Mercer (lyric) and Victor Schertzinger (music) wrote for the screen debut of equally-brash comedienne Betty Hutton. She sang it as Dorothy Lamour's sidekick and roommate in the wartime musical *The Fleet's In* (1942), and it was an auspicious debut.

"Build a Little Home" is a bright-eyed ditty suited to the talents of Eddie Cantor, who sang it to a group of Oklahoma townspeople being evicted for failure to meet their mortgages in *Roman Scandals* (1933). Al Dubin (lyric) and Harry Warren (lyric) wrote the optimistic song, which enjoyed recordings by Eddy Duchin, Ruth Etting, Barney Rapp, and Joe Venuti's Orchestra (vocal by Howard Phillips).

"A Bundle of Old Love Letters" is a tender ballad by Arthur Freed (lyric) and Nacio Herb Brown (music) from the early musical *Lord Byron of Broadway* (1930). Charles Kaley, as a scriptwriter who gets his writing ideas from his friends' hard luck stories, was shown by Gwen Lee a stack of letters her old flame once wrote her, and so he wrote this ballad about it. Paul Whiteman and his Orchestra had a successful recording of the number.

"Busy Doing Nothing" is a merry trio number from the costume fantasy *A Connecticut Yankee in King Arthur's Court* (1949). Johnny Burke (lyric) and James Van Heusen (music) wrote the song of contented idleness sung by New England blacksmith Bing Crosby, Cedric Hardwicke as Arthur, and William Bendix as Round Table knight Sir Sagrimore as they wander the countryside disguised as medieval hoboes. Jack Smith had a popular record of the song.

"But Beautiful" is the philosophical ballad by Johnny Burke (lyric) and James Van Heusen (music) that sees life as a series of contrasts (sad/funny, joyous/heartbreaking, quiet/maddening, etc.), but beautiful all the same. Musician-on-the-lam Bing Crosby sang the charming ballad to South American heiress Dorothy Lamour on board a ship heading to Rio de Janeiro in *Road to Rio* (1947). Crosby recorded the romantic number, as did Frank Sinatra, Margaret Whiting, Art Lund, the Norman Luboff Choir, Englebert Humperdinck, Johnny Mathis, Ann Hampton Callaway, vocalist-pianist Shirley Horn, and others. Terry Burrell performed the song in the Broadway revue *Swinging on a Star* (1995).

"But Definitely" is the spunky song of affection by Mack Gordon (lyric) and Harry Revel (music) that Shirley Temple sang in *Poor Little Rich Girl* (1936). Temple demonstrated that her talents went far beyond just cuteness in this effective rhythm number, as she professionally used a chuckle or an ad lib between the lyrics, asking questions such as "do I adore you?" and answering them all with the title phrase (which she pronounced as "but definally"). Adults also had success with the song: Bunny Berigan and his Orchestra, Ray Noble (vocal Al Bowlly), and Joe Reichman (vocal by Buddy Clark) had popular records of the number.

"But the World Goes 'Round" is the bluesy song about time's indifference to personal problems that Fred Ebb (lyric) and John Kander (music) wrote for the 1940s pastiche musical *New York, New York* (1977). Nightclub singer Liza Minnelli sang the hard-as-nails lament in a dark recording studio, both the atmosphere and the song reminding film audiences of her mother Judy Garland's rendition of "The Man That Got Away" in *A Star Is Born* (1954). Later in the film Minnelli, now a Hollywood star, reprised the song in a ritzy Manhattan nightclub. Brenda Pressley and the cast sang the song in the 1991 Off-Broadway revue *And the World Goes 'Round*. The number is sometimes listed as "And World Goes 'Round" and "The World Goes 'Round."

"But Where Are You?" is a wistful torch song by Irving Berlin that Harriet Hilliard sang in *Follow the Fleet* (1936) at a garden party after thinking she has lost Randolph Scott forever. It was recorded by Hilliard with future husband Ozzie Nelson and his Orchestra and by Jane Froman.

"Buttons and Bows" is the tuneful Oscar-winning song by Ray Evans and Jay Livingston about longing for the creature comforts of back East when one is out West. Bob Hope, as a timid dentist-turned-cowboy, sang the song to Jane Russell in a covered wagon as they traveled along and he played the concertina in *The Paleface* (1948). Russell reprised the number in *Son of Paleface* (1952) with Roy Rogers while Hope made sarcastic doggerel commentary. A chorus was also heard singing the catchy ditty in *Sunset Boulevard* (1950). Dinah Shore's recording with the Happy Valley Boys sold over a million disks, and Hope's recording was a bestseller as well. Evelyn Knight also recorded it, and the Dinning Sisters and Betty Garrett each made notable records later on.

"By a Waterfall" is the echoing song of aquatic romance in *Footlight Parade* (1933) that led into one of Busby Berkeley's most fanciful production numbers. When producer Jimmy Cagney saw some black children playing in the water from an open fire hydrant, he got an idea for his next show. The scene shifted to Dick Powell and Ruby Keeler lounging near a pristine waterfall and singing how they love to meet near the splashing water. The number then opened up to show dozens of chorus girls swimming, diving, sliding, and making kaleidoscopic patterns in a huge pool. The entire sequence (supposedly taking place in a theatre) lasted fifteen minutes, and Berkeley never ran out of aquatic ideas. Irving Kahal (lyric) and Sammy Fain (music) wrote the song, which Powell recorded, as did Rudy Vallee, Guy Lombardo (vocal by Carmen Lombardo), Leo Reisman, Ozzie Nelson's Orchestra, and Adrian Rollini.

"Bye Bye Birdie" is the sassy pop song that Lee Adams (lyric) and Charles Strouse (music) wrote for the 1963 film version of their Broadway hit of the same name. After major production was completed, the studio insisted that a movie musical needed to have a title song, so Ann-Margaret sang this gleeful farewell ditty to the camera at the beginning of the film.

"Bye Low" is the entrancing ballad that Eliot Daniel wrote for the Damon Runyon–based musical fable *Bloodhounds of Broadway* (1952). Georgia hillbilly Mitzi Gaynor, who dreamed of going to Broadway to perform, sang the tenderhearted number.

C

"Ça, C'est L'Amour" is one of a handful of Cole Porter's love songs in which the lover breaks into a French phrase when trying to describe the emotions stirring inside. This one was sung by Taina Elg in a breathy voice to Gene Kelly in *Les Girls* (1957) as they rode along in a rowboat on a lake in France. The ballad is melodically similar to Porter's earlier "C'est Magnifique" but was distinct enough to become popular, thanks to a best-selling record by Tony Bennett.

"Cae Cae" was a Portuguese song by Pedro Barrios (lyric) and Roberto Martina (music) that was given an English lyric by John Latouche and was featured in the Latin musical *That Night in Rio* (1941). Carmen Miranda and the Banda Da Lua performed the number at an outdoor party at a ritzy Rio de Janeiro estate, and audiences enjoyed it enough that the song was reprised by Grace McDonald in *She's for Me* (1943).

"Caldonia (What Makes Your Heart So Hard?)" is the jaunty swing number by Fleecie Moore that Louis Jordan and his Tympany Five performed in a nightclub in *Swing Parade of 1946* (1945). Jordan recorded the song as "Caldonia Boogie," and his recording sold a million disks. Woody Herman and Erskine Hawkins (vocal by Ace Harris) also had hit recordings of the jumpin' number.

"California Rose" is the gentle cowboy ballad that Ray Evans (lyric) and Jay Livingston (music) wrote for the musical sequel *Son of Paleface* (1952). Roy Rogers, as a government agent disguised as a singing cowboy, serenaded lady bandit Jane Russell outside her window with his guitar, ironically claiming that the gal of his heart was soft and pleasant.

"Californ-i-ay" is the robust ode to the territory where "the hills have more splendor and the girls have more gender," as sung by Deanna Dubin, Robert Paige, and the other wagon train arrivals in the frontier operetta *Can't Help Singing* (1944). The waltzing E. Y. Harburg (lyric) and Jerome Kern (music) number was obviously inspired by the popular title song in *Oklahoma!* the year before, yet Harburg's lyrics are more tongue-in-cheek, filled with such hyperbolic claims as the ocean there is wetter than elsewhere and it rains champagne. Kern's music is also distinctive, effectively employing sections of the verse in the refrain. In the Broadway revue *Jerome Kern Goes to Hollywood* (1986), the rollicking number was sung by the ensemble.

"Can I Forget You?" is the hit ballad by Oscar Hammerstein (lyric) and Jerome Kern (music) from the pioneer musical *High, Wide and Handsome* (1937), where Irene Dunne sang the lovely farewell song to Randolph Scott. The lyric is lush and romantic without being cloying, and the music, according to Gerald Bordman, "is sweet without becoming saccharine, memorably melodic and, reflecting Kern's acute ear, captures a period flavor while remaining contemporary." The ballad was sung by the ensemble in the Broadway revue *Jerome Kern Goes to Hollywood* (1986), and Andrea Marcovicci made a distinctive recording of it in 1997.

"Can You Feel the Love Tonight?" is the Oscar-winning love song by Tim Rice (lyric) and Elton John (music) from the animated film *The Lion King* (1994). On the soundtrack Joseph Williams and Sally Dworsky sang the thoughts of lions-in-love Simba and Nala while meercat Timon (voice of Nathan Lane) and warthog Pumba (voice of Ernie Sabella) made comments on the side about how love will destroy their threesome. Although the song was a traditional pop ballad in music and lyric, the African tribal accompaniment gave the number a distinctive and haunting tone. John's recording was a bestseller, and in the 1997 Broadway version of the tale the number was sung by Jason Raize and Heather Headley with commentary by Max Casella and Tom Alan Robbins.

"Candle on the Water" is the heart-tugging ballad that Al Kasha and Joel Hirschhorn wrote for the part–animated, part–live–action fantasy *Pete's Dragon* (1977). Helen Reddy, as a lighthouse keeper's daughter, sang the number as she looked out to the ocean from the lighthouse tower and prayed that her sailor-boyfriend, who has been lost at sea, will return. Reddy's recording of the Oscar-nominated song enjoyed some popularity.

"The Candy Man" is the sprightly ode to the provider of sweets sung by candy vendor Aubrey Wood as he distributed samples to the children in his shop in *Willy Wonka and the Chocolate Factory* (1971). Leslie Bricusse and Anthony

Newley wrote the flavorful song, and Sammy Davis, Jr.'s 1972 record was a Number One hit. Newley, Floyd Cramer, and Roy Orbison each made a noteworthy recording as well.

"Can't Buy Me Love" is the driving pop song that was added to the Beatles' musical film *A Hard Day's Night* (1964) when the director was dissatisfied with how "I'll Cry Instead" fit into the loose plot. John Lennon and Paul McCartney wrote the bouncing testament to the power of love over money, which was sung by the group on the soundtrack while the foursome ran down the fire escape of a theatre and out onto an open field where they played an imaginary game of soccer. McCartney has denied the suggestion that the song was about prostitution.

"Can't Get Out of This Mood" is the contemplative torch song ("heartbreak, here I come") by Frank Loesser (lyric) and Jimmy McHugh (music) that was featured in the wartime musical *Seven Days Leave* (1942). Ginny Simms, backed by Freddie Martin's Orchestra, sang the lament in a silky and sophisticated manner, accentuating, according to Roy Hemming, McHugh's "directly appealing and simple melodic line." Both Kay Kyser (vocal by Harry Babbitt) and Johnny Long (vocal by the Four Teens) had top records of the song, which was most recently recorded by Tommy Tune.

"Can't Help Falling in Love (With You)" is that rare thing: an Elvis Presley waltz. Hugo Peretti, George David Weiss, and Luigi Creatore wrote the number for the Presley vehicle *Blue Hawaii* (1961), and Presley's recording of the tender song sold over a million copies. At a barbecue in Hawaii Elvis presented an Austrian music box as a birthday present to his girlfriend's mother. He then sang along with the sentimental waltz, the sound soon augmenting into a full orchestra with a large choral number following. At the end of the number all reverted to the simple tune coming from the music box. The song received new popularity in 1970 through hit recordings by Al Martino and Andy Williams, and Corey Hart's 1987 record was also popular. The ballad is sometimes listed as "I Can't Help Falling in Love With You."

"Can't Help Singing" is the lilting title number from the 1944 pioneer musical, as sung by senator's daughter Deanna Durbin as she drove a carriage through the countryside near Washington, D.C. The number was reprised later in the film by Durbin and Robert Paige out West as each sat in wooden outdoor bathtubs separated by a wall, their voices joining in a silly, sensual manner. Jerome Kern composed the no-holds-barred waltz music, E. Y. Harburg penned the expansive lyric, and musicologist Alec Wilder accurately described the song as "cheery, direct, uncomplex and spring-like."

"The Carioca" is a landmark musical number because it introduced the team of Fred Astaire and Ginger Rogers, as well as a new Latin sound, to the nation. The Edward Eliscu, Gus Kahn (lyric), and Vincent Youmans (music) standard was danced by the Brazilian Turunas in an outdoor nightclub in *Flying Down to Rio* (1933); it was then sung by Etta Moten, encouraging the couples to join in the Brazilian dance that asked the couples to press their heads together while they danced across the floor. Astaire and Rogers, in supporting roles in the plot, stepped onto the dance floor and magic occurred, the two ending up dancing on seven white grand pianos that came together to form a circular stage. The whole sequence lasted thirteen minutes, and by the end America's most beloved dance team was born. "The Carioca" (the title is a Brazilian nickname for a native of Rio de Janeiro) is also distinctive as a song. The lyric describes the dance, admits to "the meter that is tricky," and promises to finish off all other dance forms. (The song became very popular, but the actual dance never caught on in ballrooms because it was far too difficult for the average person to execute.) Youmans' music uses the kind of "maxie" meter similar to the tangos that Vernon and Irene Castle popularized twenty years before, yet the song has its own character, utilizing three distinct melodies in its structure. Latin studies expert John Storm Roberts cites "The Carioca" as "the earliest samba-based number to have substantial success in the United States." The Oscar-nominated song has been recorded hundreds of times, most memorably by Enric Madriguera, Harry Sosnik, Artie Shaw, Xavier Cugat, Jack Jones, Art Lund, Oscar Peterson, Mel Tormé, Les Paul, Andre Kostalanetz, Bobby Short, and the Boston Pops Orchestra.

"Carry Me Back to the Lone Prairie" is the popular cowboy folk song by Carson Robison that was introduced, ironically, by an operatic tenor. Hotel-porter-turned-radio-star James Melton (in his film debut) delivered the wistful ballad in *Stars Over Broadway* (1935). Melton's recording of the song was a big hit, and the number soon became a staple of singing cowboys. The ballad has been recorded and listed under several different titles, such as "Bury Me Not on the Lone Prairie," "The Dying Cowboy," and "The Ocean Burial."

"'Cause My Baby Says It's So" is a lighthearted song of undying trust and naivete that Al Dubin (lyric) and Harry Warren (music) wrote for *The Singing Marine* (1937). U. S. Marine Dick Powell entered a radio contest, sang the breezy number, and soon he was a big radio star. Powell's recording was a modest success on the real airwaves, as were versions by Mal Hallett and Kay Kyser.

"Champagne" is the orgasmic number that Pete Townsend wrote for the 1975 film version of his rock opera *Tommy* and one of the most bizarre sequences in a film filled with them. Distraught Ann-Margaret got drunk on champagne while watching her son Roger Daltry on television as he rose to fame. She sang about her elation and her misery as she rolled across the floor in sexual frustration. The number climaxed with various liquids spewing forth from the television set and Ann-Margaret wallowing in the muck.

"Change of Heart" is the Oscar-nominated ballad by Harold Adamson (lyric) and Jule Styne (music) that was featured in *Hit Parade of 1943* (1943), a musical about the pop song market. John Carroll, as a played-out songwriter, introduced the song, which became popular enough that the studio changed the film's title to *Change of Heart* when the movie was reissued for television.

"Change Partners (and Dance With Me)" is the intoxicating ballad by Irving Berlin that integrates into the plot of *Carefree* (1938) in a way rarely seen in movie musicals of the time. Therapist Fred Astaire wooed his patient Ginger Rogers at a country club dance by sending her fiancé Ralph Bellamy to answer a bogus phone call so that he can stop the two of them from dancing together and keep Ginger to himself. The same situation is reflected in the lyric, one of Berlin's finest, with the interesting twist at the end: If you change partners with him, she'll never want to change partners again. Astaire recorded the Oscar-nominated song, and popular records were also made by Jimmy Dorsey (vocal Bob Eberle), Larry Clinton (vocal by Dick Todd), and Lawrence Welk and his Orchestra. Michael Feinstein made a superb recording of the ballad in 1987, and Barbara Cook and Andrea Marcovicci are among the female singers to record the number.

"Changing My Tune" is the knowing "I am" song by the Gershwin brothers that was used effectively in the period musical *The Shocking Miss Pilgrim* (1947). Ira Gershwin wrote the lyric about taking a new lease on life and seeking a bright future, and he set it to a trunk tune by his deceased brother, George. Betty Grable, as a newly graduated "typewriter," sang the number as she anticipates her new job in Boston and later her new lodgings. After she fell in love with her boss Dick Haymes, she reprised the song as she saw a different future for herself. Judy Garland made a zesty recording of the number, as did Mel Tormé and the Mel-Tones with Artie Shaw's Orchestra and, years later, Anthony Perkins and Barbara Cook as a duet.

"Charlotte's Web" is the haunting title song by Richard M. and Robert B. Sherman from the 1973 animated musical version of the E. B. White children's classic. A male chorus sang the lyrical ballad on the soundtrack about the spider Charlotte, who mysteriously and diligently spent the whole night spinning a special web that would save her friend Wilbur the pig from the slaughterhouse.

"The Charm of You" is the pleasing ballad that sailor-on-leave Frank Sinatra sang in *Anchors Aweigh* (1945) and later recorded with success. Jule Styne composed the romantic music, and Sammy Cahn provided the list song lyric that catalogued the various pleasures in life that compared to the charms of one's beloved.

"Charming" is an ingratiating ballad from the early operetta *Devil May Care* (1929) that used the film medium is an original and inventive way. French officer Ramon Novarro was disguised as a footman and sat in the courtyard cleaning Dorothy Jordan's shoes. As he sang, his tenor voice (and the camera) rose up to Jordan's room in the mansion, where she was charmed by his sentiments. Later in the film Novarro and Jordan reprised the ballad as a duet. The Clifford Grey (lyric) and Herbert Stothart (music) number was recorded by Smith Ballew, Frank Munn, and Leo Reisman and his Orchestra.

"Chattanooga Choo-Choo" is the sensational Big Band number that was a highlight of *Sun Valley Serenade* (1941) and one of the shining moments for the Big Band era. Harry Warren composed the swinging, contagious music, and Mack Gordon wrote the bouncy lyric that told of a passenger who leaves Penn Station in New York, travels through Baltimore, wakes up to breakfast in the diner in the Carolinas, and arrives in the Tennessee city of Chattanooga. The number was seen in the film as a rehearsal, Glenn Miller and his Orchestra playing it while Tex Beneke, Paula Kelly, and the Modernaires sang it. Then a teenage Dorothy Dandridge sang it with the Nicholas Brothers before their breaking into a furiously delightful dance in front of a painted drop of the famous train. The Oscar-nominated song showed up in several nonmusicals and such subsequent musicals as *Springtime in the Rockies* (1942), where Carmen Miranda sang it in Portuguese; *You're My Everything* (1949) with Dan Dailey performing it; and *The Glenn Miller Story* (1954), where Frances Langford and the Modernaires sang it with Miller's orchestra. The popular song was on *Your Hit Parade* for thirteen weeks and received many orchestral recordings, none more popular than Miller's, which sold a million copies and remained one of his biggest hits on disk and on the radio. Years after the Big Band era there were three best-selling recordings: a piano version by Floyd Cramer in 1962, a Number One recording by Harper's Bizarre in 1967, and a disco rendition by the group Tuxedo Junction in 1978.

"Cheek to Cheek" is the enchanting, romantic Irving Berlin ballad for Fred Astaire and Ginger Rogers that led to one of filmdom's smoothest and most intoxicating musical numbers. At a ritzy Lido resort in Venice in *Top Hat* (1935), Astaire sang to Rogers and then they danced, her long feathered gown creating magical patterns as they moved. As effortless as the number seemed, it took days to film because the loose feathers kept getting into Astaire's eyes and mouth. Dance critic Arlene Croce cites "Cheek to Cheek" as the "high point" of all the Astaire-Rogers numbers. The song's music is unusual, being uncommonly long (seventy-two measures) and having no verse and two distinct releases. The lyric, as Philip Furia and others have pointed out, is disappointing, containing a few too many clichés. But the graceful music carries the song, and in the indelible opening phrase about being in heaven, the words, music, and romance were never better suited to each other. Although the Oscar-nominated song was written with Astaire in mind (he also recorded it), many singers and orchestras have had success with the number, ranging from Eddy Duchin and his Orchestra to Ella Fitzgerald to Joe Bushkin's Orchestra to Andrea Marcovicci. In a 1995 recording, opera singers Frederica von Stade and Jerry Hadley sang it as a duet. "Cheek to Cheek" shows up in the background of many films, most memorably in 1938's *Alexander's Ragtime Band*. The Ritz Brothers performed it with altered lyrics in *On the Avenue* (1937), and the original *Top Hat* footage was used for the bittersweet ending of the nonmusical *The Purple Rose of Cairo* (1985).

"Chica Chica Boom Chic" is the eruptive samba nonsense song that Carmen Miranda introduced in *That Night in Rio* (1941). In a lavish Rio de Janeiro nightclub, Miranda sang the silly number and was then joined by U. S. Navy officer Don Ameche and a large dancing chorus. Later in the film Ameche and Alice Faye reprised the song. Harry Warren composed the rapid Latin music, and Mack Gordon wrote the antic lyric that could be interpreted as sexy or just nonsensical. Miranda's recording was a wartime hit, and a Xavier Cugat disk was also popular.

"Chicago, Illinois" is the jazzy, sexy tribute to the Second City sung by gangster's moll Lesley Ann Warren in a nightclub act in *Victor/Victoria* (1982). Henry Mancini composed the bump-and-grind music, and Leslie Bricusse wrote the deadpan lyrics that claimed that the city's name starts out with "chic" and that someday the city may even get its own airport. In the 1995 Broadway version of the story, Rachel York and the chorus girls sang the facetious number.

"Chicago Style" is the merry narrative ballad by Johnny Burke (lyric) and James Van Heusen (music) that tells of a Chicago trombone player with plenty of style. The number was performed as a vaudeville song-and-dance routine by Bing Crosby and Bob Hope on stage in a Melbourne, Australia, music hall in *Road to Bali* (1953), where they sang the song, played (and destroyed) two trombones, and did a silly dance step up and down a miniature staircase.

"Chim Chim Cheree" is the Oscar-winning ditty by Richard M. and Robert B. Sherman that was used effectively in *Mary Poppins* (1964). The melody was first heard as sidewalk artist Dick Van Dyke, as a one-man band, performed it for a small crowd gathered in a London park. Later he sang the number to cheer up glum children Karen Dotrice and Matthew Garber, Julie Andrews joining him in the song. Although the lyric is in the vein of a nonsense song, the music has a haunting quality and the number has an almost reverent mood at times. The New Christy Minstrels and Burl Ives each had successful records of the song, which in the original script was titled "Pavement Artist." Louis Prima and Gia Maione recorded it as a duet, and in 1996 the number got a new interpretation by the Jazz Networks.

"Chin Up, Cheerio, Carry On!" is an unusual patriotic song that was used in an odd but powerful manner in *Babes on Broadway* (1941). Judy Garland and a chorus of youths sang the supportive song on a broadcast at a block party for British war orphans. As the cheery number progressed, a montage of wartime London was superimposed on the faces of the weeping orphans. Rarely had a wartime film (especially a musical) shown the agony and aftermath of the current war. Burton Lane wrote the uptempo music, and E. Y. Harburg penned the optimistic lyric that urged the British troops to struggle on, free the homeland, and "turn the Blitz on the Fritz."

"Chitty Chitty Bang Bang" is the rhythmic title song for the 1968 musical that Richard M. and Robert B. Sherman scored, hoping to capture the success of their earlier hit "Chim Chim Cheree." The effort was less accomplished, but the song was nominated for an Oscar and was entertainingly used in the film. Crackpot inventor Dick Van Dyke constructed a flying–floating car, and the odd noise pattern of the motor inspired him to sing the number with his children Adrian Hill and Heather Ripley. Later Sally Ann Howes joined the trio and they all sang the pulsating song as they flew across the countryside, praising the powers of their "four-fendered friend." Paul Mauriat and his Orchestra had a hit recording of the catchy song.

"Cinderella Sue" is a forgotten gem from *Centennial Summer* (1946) that compares favorably with Jerome Kern's finest character songs. Avon Long and a group of children sang the pseudo-Negro folk song for passersby and then went into a bouncy dance on the sidewalk. E. Y. Harburg's narrative lyric, about a shantytown Cinderella with a "Dixie nose" and "patches on her gown," is wily and yet involving. Kern's toe-tapping music and harmonica accompaniment recalls the ethnic songs he wrote for *Show Boat*. George Reinholt made a recording of the number in the early 1970s.

"Cinderella's Fella" is the sassy number Fifi D'Orsay sang about her beau Bing Crosby in *Going Hollywood* (1933). Later in the film the Arthur Freed (lyric) and Nacio Herb Brown (music) number was reprised by Crosby's new love, French teacher Marion Davies. Ferde Grofe's Orchestra made a successful recording of the song.

"The Circle of Life" is the stirring song about the mysterious and primitive ways of nature that opened the animated film *The Lion King* (1994). As the various animals on the savanna gathered to pay tribute to the birth of Simba, the future Lion King, Carmen Twillie sang the moving number on the soundtrack with assist by Lebo M, whose African chanting made the Tim Rice (lyric) and Elton John (music) song soar to an almost spiritual level. John's recording, less inspiring but more pop in flavor, was a success. In the 1997 Broadway version of the tale, the narrator Rafiki, played by Tsidii Le Loka, led the ensemble in the stunning opening number.

"The Closer You Are" is a pleasing ballad by Leo Robin (lyric) and Jule Styne (music) from the musical *Two Tickets to Broadway* (1951) that was, despite the title, about entertainers hoping to break into television. Tony Martin, as an unemployed singing songwriter, crooned his latest creation to his girlfriend Janet Leigh in an open-air eatery in New York City.

"Cocktails for Two" was one of the best-selling love songs of the 1930s, but because of outside circumstances the number today is known mostly as a comic novelty. Sam Coslow and Arthur Johnston wrote the highly romantic ballad for Carl Brisson to sing in the musical thriller *Murder at the Vanities* (1934). Prohibition had just been repealed, and the studio wanted a song that showed drinking as respectable and romantic. Ironically, Johnston was on one of his famous alcoholic binges, so Coslow wrote most of the number himself, about a five o'clock rendezvous when two lovers hold hands, look out over the avenue, and enjoy cocktails. The song was a major success with hit recordings by Brisson, Kitty Carlisle (who was also in the film), Tommy Dorsey, Duke Ellington, Billy May, Carmen Cavallaro, and others. Then in 1944 Spike Jones and his City Slickers made an outrageously antic recording of the ballad, speeding up the tempo and adding hiccups and the sounds of shattering glass. Coslow was furious but he was helpless to stop the record — Jones did not change one note or word of the original — and his only consolation was his royalties from the two million copies the Jones disk sold. The song was heard in a handful of films: Miriam Hopkins sang it in *She Loves Me Not* (1934), the City Slickers performed their famous comic version in *Ladies' Man* (1947), and Danny Kaye delivered the number in a groaning Marlene Dietrich manner in *On the Double* (1961). The ballad was heard on Broadway when the ensemble sang it in the revue section of *A Day in Hollywood — A Night in the Ukraine* (1980).

"Coffee in the Morning (and Kisses at Night)" is the love song from *Moulin Rouge* (1934) that the Hays office found too suggestive: The lyric had to be changed from an illicit offer of a one-night stand to a proposal of marriage. Al Dubin (lyric) and Harry Warren (music) wrote the infatuated ballad, which Constance Bennett sang as part of a rehearsal. Later in the film the actual performance was shown with the Boswell Sisters singing the song with Bennett and Russ Columbo in a large production number. Eddy Duchin, Columbo, the Andrew Sisters, and Gus Arnheim each had popular recordings of the song.

"Coffee Time" is the vivacious finale number by Arthur Freed (lyric) and Harry Warren (music) for the experimental musical fantasy *Yolanda and the Thief* (1945). Set during a festive Latin American carnival, Fred Astaire, Lucille Bremer, and the ensemble sang and danced about the leading export of the community. Kay Kyser (vocal by Mike Douglas) had a successful recording of the number, and the catchy song was published and recorded as a lively instrumental piece under the title "Java Junction."

"College Rhythm" is the bouncy title song for the 1934 musical about rival department stores and rival colleges. Mark Gordon (lyric) and Harry Revel (music) wrote the catchy number about a new campus dance, and ex–football star Jack Oakie sang it with Lyda Roberti. Oakie and Roberti recorded the number as a duet and separately, and there were also band recordings by Johnny "Scat" Davis, Jolly Coburn, and Jimmie Grier.

"College Swing" is the Big Band title number that Frank Loesser (lyric) and Hoagy Carmichael (music) wrote for the 1938 musical that was a revue disguised behind a thin plot about a college filled with vaudevillians. Betty Grable, Martha Ray, and Skinnay Ennis performed the song in the swing style that was growing more and more popular.

"Colors of the Wind" is the Oscar-winning song of inspiration about nature and racial tolerance that Stephen Schwartz (lyric) and Alan Menken (music) wrote for the animated romance *Pocahontas* (1995). (It was Menken's fourth Best Song Oscar in six years.) Pocahontas (sung by Judy Kuhn) showed Captain John Smith the wonders of nature in the New World, arguing that it must be preserved to be understood, as he must walk in the footsteps of the Native American in order to understand her people. Menken's expansive music and Schwartz's vivid imagery kept the song potent without being preachy. Vanessa Williams' recording was a pop favorite.

"Come Get Your Happiness" is the optimistic call for everyday contentment that Shirley Temple and a female chorus sang on a radio broadcast from a farmhouse in *Rebecca of Sunnybrook Farm* (1938). Samuel Pokrass composed the uptempo music and Jack Yellen provided the lyric that listed all the riches in the world, from sunbeams and moonbeams to Mother Nature, that are free and not taxable.

"Come Out, Come Out, Wherever You Are" is the swinging song of longing that Sammy Cahn (lyric) and Jule Styne (music) wrote for *Step Lively* (1944), the musical version of the farce *Room Service*. In a scene from the musical play being produced, Gloria De Haven first sang parts of the song, calling to that special someone who might be hiding, and then a chorus of men on stage and scattered throughout the auditorium answered her call. Finally, Frank Sinatra, at the zenith of his popularity with the women of America, appeared and sang the full number, verse and refrain. Charlie Barnet's Orchestra (vocal by Kay Starr) had a successful record, and Michael Feinstein revived the number as a romantic ballad in a 1991 recording.

"Come Up and See Me Sometime" is the vampy number from *Take a Chance* (1933) that was inspired by the famous invitation by Mae West, then at the peak of her popularity. Arthur Swanstrom (lyric) and Louis Alter (music) wrote the song, which was sung by Lillian Roth in the film about carnival hucksters.

"Conchita, Marquita, Lolita, Pepita, Rosita, Juanita Lopez" is the satirical love song by Herb Magidson (lyric) and Jule Styne (music) that had fun with the wave of South American beauties that seemed to be everywhere during the war years. Johnnie Johnston sang the number in *Priorities on Parade* (1942), a patriotic musical about swing musicians and comely gals working in an airplane factory to aid the war effort.

"Confidentially" is the love ballad that bandleader John Payne sang to Margaret Lindsay in the intimate musical romance *Garden of the Moon* (1938). Harry Warren composed the tender music, and Johnny Mercer and Al Dubin collaborated on the heartfelt lyric.

"Constantly" is the romantic pledge not just for tonight but forever, written by Johnny Burke (lyric) and James Van Heusen (music) for *Road to Morocco* (1942). Princess Dorothy Lamour sang the number to Bob Hope in her boudoir as he was attended to by her servants and a hidden Bing Crosby looked on in disbelief. Crosby got to sing the ballad on record, and his recording was somewhat popular.

"The Continental," the first song to win the Oscar, was a seventeen-minute dance sequence that climaxed *The Gay Divorcee* (1934). Fred Astaire and Ginger Rogers heard the song in a hotel room as the music came from a dance floor. They sang together about the new dance craze that involved kissing as well as footwork, and then they snuck out of the room to join the dancers. The song was then picked up by Erik Rhodes and Lillian Miles, who sang a lyric that listed all the places in Europe where the dance had caught on. Finally, Astaire and Rogers took to the floor and performed a tango that then moved into an athletic Russian dance. Herb Magidson penned the lyric, and Con Conrad composed the snappy music that is very adventurous in the way the long song (seventy-two bars) moves in a new direction for each section, repeating phrases often enough to give the number unity. Leo Reisman and his Orchestra made an early and distinctive recording of the song, and the Three Suns had a success with it years later.

"Cooking Breakfast for the One I Love" is a cynical yet touching lament by Billy Rose (lyric) and Henry Tobias (music) that Fanny Brice sang in *Be Yourself* (1930). Brice delivered the self-parodying tribute to married life as she fried bacon and set the table for the sleeping Robert Armstrong. The number is unique in early film musicals for the way it was staged: all movement yet it was not a dance number. Brice's recording was popular, as were records by Annette Hanshaw and Libby Holman (with Roger Wolfe Kahn's Orchestra).

"Corns for My Country" is one of those comic patriotic numbers that flourished during the World War Two. The Andrews Sisters sang the song by Jean Barry, Dick Charles, and Leah Worth in *Hollywood Canteen* (1944) and on record, complaining about the condition of their feet after jitterbugging with soldiers at the canteen all night long.

"Cosi Cosa" is the merry sing-along number (patterned after the popular "Funiculi — Funicula") that Allan Jones sang while entertaining the steerage passengers on an ocean liner in the Marx Brothers classic *A Night at the Opera* (1935). Jones recorded the Ned Washington (lyric), Bronislau Kaper, and Wallace Jurmann (music) ditty and performed it again in *Everybody Sing* (1938).

"Could I Fall in Love?" is the soft romantic ballad by Randy Starr from *Double Trouble* (1967) that asks the rhetorical question of two people only "a kiss apart." Elvis Presley, as an American singer on a European tour, sang the number to English "bird" Annette Day over tea in her apartment, singing along with a record by himself and the Jordanaires that was playing on the phonograph.

"Couldn't We Ride?" is the engaging travel song that Joe Raposo wrote for the musical farce *The Great Muppet Caper* (1981). Kermit the Frog (voice of Jim Henson), Miss Piggy (voice of Frank Oz), and various other puppet characters sang the dreamy number as they rode bicycles through London's Hyde Park.

"Count on Me" is the exuberant proclamation of support that was added to the Leonard Bernstein score when the Broadway musical *On the Town* was brought to the screen in 1949. Betty Comden and Adolph Green wrote the lyric (as they had on Broadway), Roger Edens composed the music, and the cheery number was sung by sailors-on-leave Gene Kelly, Jules Munchin, and Frank Sinatra in a bar with New Yorkers Ann Miller, Betty Garrett, and Alice Pearce.

"Count Your Blessings (Instead of Sheep)" is the Oscar-nominated ballad-lullaby that Bing Crosby and Rosemary Clooney sang in a Vermont ski lodge in *White Christmas* (1954). Irving Berlin wrote the delicate song that suggested a reevaluation of life's little gifts as a cure for insomnia. The ballad remained on *Your Hit Parade* for thirteen weeks and led to popular records for Crosby, Clooney and, later, Eddie Fisher. Most recently the ballad received a superb recording by Patti LuPone.

"The Country's Going to War" is the daffy patriotic number that Groucho Marx and the citizens of Freedonia sang once they heard that they were at war in *Duck Soup* (1933). The Bert Kalmar (lyric) and Harry Ruby (music) song has been accurately described by Ethan Mordden as "a lampoon of production numbers made up of noncontiguous elements — black, spiritual, hillbilly, swing — each with its own performers, costumes and choreography."

"County Fair" is the happy song about an Indiana rural fair in 1903 where the young Bobby Driscoll brought his pet ram hoping to win a prize in *So Dear to My Heart* (1948). Mel Tormé and Robert Wells wrote the number, and Tormé sang it on the soundtrack during an animated sequence showing scenes from the fair.

"A Couple of Song and Dance Men" is the intentionally hokey vaudeville number that entertainers Fred Astaire and Bing Crosby sang (with Cliff Nazarro at the piano) and danced in an impromptu performance at a rehearsal in *Blue Skies* (1946). Irving Berlin wrote the jovial number (one of four original ones added to a score of old favorites), which allowed for plenty of clowning around for Astaire and Crosby, who later recorded it as a duet.

"A Couple of Swells" is the dandy psuedo-sophisticated song that Fred Astaire and Judy Garland, in hobo costumes and missing teeth, sang as they strolled up a fashionable avenue in a Broadway revue in *Easter Parade* (1948). The number was a last-minute addition that Irving Berlin wrote at producer Arthur Freed's request for a silly song to enliven the period musical, and it is one of the songwriter's finest lightweight efforts. Berlin's music is delicate and highbrow with lots of flutes in the accompaniment yet the song has a low-down rhythmic quality as well. His lyric, with its name-dropping and overly genteel language, is sly and droll: The two bums decide that they would much rather walk to their destination than ride there.

"Cover Girl" is the lush paean to magazine model Rita Hayworth and the title song of the 1944 musical scored by Ira Gershwin (lyric) and Jerome Kern (music). The production number, with a male chorus singing and dancing with Hayworth as she ran down a long winding ramp on stage in a Broadway show, is the stuff of parody, but the song itself is rather intriguing with Kern's music smoothly rising and falling in an effective manner. The number is sometimes listed as "The Girl on the Cover."

"Cowboy From Brooklyn" is the psuedo-rustic title song by Johnny Mercer (lyric) and Harry Warren (music) from the 1938 Dick Powell vehicle. Powell, as a singing city slicker who gets a job on a ranch and becomes a radio star, sang the tongue-in-cheek number, which was later recorded by Mercer, Tommy Dorsey, Jimmy Dorsey, and others.

"Cow-Cow Boogie" is the swinging nonsense song by Don Raye, Gene De Paul, and Benny Carter from the wartime bobbysoxer musical *Reveille With Beverly* (1943). Ella Mae Morse sang the swinging cowboy song, and popular recordings were made by Freddy Martin and his Orchestra (vocal by Morse) and Ella Fitzgerald with the Ink Spots, the last used on the soundtrack for the boxing film *Raging Bull* (1980).

"Crawfish" is the plaintive but haunting song selling seafood that Fred Wise (lyric) and Ben Wiseman (music) wrote for the dark Elvis Presley vehicle *King Creole* (1958). Near the opening of the film, pushcart peddler Kitty White sang out about her wares on a New Orleans street while restless teenager Presley echoed her bluesy call from the terrace of his French Quarter apartment. As directed by Michael Curtiz, the scene has an eerie and forebodding quality rarely encountered in Presley's films.

"Crazy Feet" is the rhythm song that made for one of the most unusual production numbers in early pre–Busby Berkeley musicals. In *Happy Days* (1930), Dixie Lee and a flock of chorines sang the Sidney D. Mitchell, Con Conrad, and Archie Gottler song as they emerged out of a pair of gigantic pants legs and, masquerading as shoelaces, danced down an endless staircase.

"Crazy People" is the rhythmic number the Boswell Sisters sang in the trend-setting musical about radio *The Big Broadcast* (1932). Edgar Leslie (lyric) and James Monaco (music) wrote the song, which was recorded with success by the Boswells, Cliff "Ukelele Ike" Edwards, Gene Kardos, and Benny Kruger.

"Crazy World" is the flowing ballad that Leslie Bricusse (lyric) and Henry Mancini (music) wrote for Julie Andrews to sing in the gender-bending musical *Victor/Victoria* (1982). "Vicki" sings the song about the confusions and contradictions in life and in love, something she knows about, since she is impersonating a man who is a female impersonator. Johnny Mathis recorded it, and Andrews sang the number in the 1995 Broadway version of the story.

"Cryin' for the Carolinas" is the jazzy homesick lament of former Carolinians that Sam Lewis, Joe Young (lyric), and Harry Warren (music) wrote for *Spring Is Here* (1930). The Brox Sisters sang the number as lively entertainers at a party, but the song caught on later after it had been recorded by others as a tender ballad. Ruth Etting, Belle Barker, Guy Lombardo, Arthur Schutt, Sid Garry, Fred Waring and his Pennsylvanians, and Ben Bernie's Orchestra all had successful records. "Cryin' for the Carolinas" was the first film song by prolific Hollywood composer Warren.

"Cuanto Le Gusta (La Parranda)" was one of Carmen Miranda's greatest movie song successes and the musical highlight of *A Date With Judy* (1948). The catchy Latin number by Ray Gilbert (lyric) and Gabriel Ruiz (music) urged one, in English and in Spanish, to go where the music was hot and vowed that romance was in the air. The sassy number was a winner on *Your Hit Parade*, and recordings by Miranda with the Andrews Sisters, Xavier Cugat (who was in the film) and his Orchestra, and Jack Smith were all popular.

"Cuban Love Song" is the ardent title song from the 1931 musical romance sung by U.S. Marine Lawrence Tibbett and Havana peanut seller Lupe Velez. The Dorothy Fields (lyric), Herbert Stothart, and Jimmy McHugh (music) ballad, a passionate pledge of undying devotion, was reprised by Tibbett later in the film in a unique duet with himself. The renowned opera singer recorded the song first as a baritone and then again in a tenor voice, and the two tracks were mixed (arguably the first such multiple recording in film history) so that Tibbet the Marine sang it on screen while Tibbet the ghost was seen standing beside him and harmonizing along. Recordings by Tibbett, Ruth Etting, Guy Lombardo, Paul Whiteman (vocal by Jack Fulton), and Art Jarrett made the ballad popular. It was revived years later by a successful record by Gordon MacRae. In the Broadway revue *Sugar Babies* (1979), the song was sung by Scot Stewart and Michele Rogers.

"Curly Top" is the title song of affection for a "little bundle of joy" that Ted Koehler, Irving Caesar (lyric), and Ray Henderson (music) wrote for the 1935 Shirley Temple vehicle. Millionaire John Boles sang the tribute to the blonde moppet as he played at a white piano, and then orphan Temple danced a tap routine on top of it.

D

"Daddy-O (I'm Gonna Teach You Some Blues)" is the swinging song about the latest music trends that Don Raye and Gene De Paul wrote for the Danny Kaye vehicle *A Song Is Born* (1948). Nightclub singer Virginia Mayo (dubbed by Jerri Sullivan) and the Page Cavanaugh Trio sang the kiss-off number to an unfaithful lover, promising "to teach you some blues." Dinah Shore's recording (coupled with "Buttons and Bows") sold a million copies.

"Dames" is the snappy title song for the 1934 backstager and the inspiration for one of Busby Berkeley's most dazzling production numbers. Al Dubin (lyric) and Harry Warren (music) wrote the song that argued the only thing a hit show needs is a bevy of beautiful chorus girls. Dick Powell sang the persuasive serenade to a group of theatre backers to raise money for a Broadway show; the scene next shifted to the performance as the girls were introduced in a series of closeups. The chorines were then celebrated by a male chorus as the girls were seen waking up, bathing, getting dressed, and rushing to the theatre where they performed the requisite geometric patterns. The nine-and-a-half-minute sequence climaxed with each girl flying up to the camera for a final closeup and smile. (The effect was achieved by lowering each girl on a wire from a high camera down to the floor and then showing the film in reverse and speeded up.) Eddy Duchin and his Orchestra had a hit recording of the song, and in the Broadway musical *42nd Street* (1980) it was sung by Lee Roy Reams and the ensemble.

"Dancing on a Dime" is the mostly forgotten title song from the 1941 backstage musical where Robert Paige and Grace McDonald sang the amorous number while fox trotting on a crowded dance floor. Frank Loesser wrote the heartfelt lyric about finding romantic seclusion even in a small space, and Burton

Lane composed the evocative music that effortlessly climbs the scale in a appealing way. Michael Feinstein recorded the lovely ballad in 1990.

"Danger — Love at Work" is the uptempo cautionary song that Mack Gordon (lyric) and Harry Revel (music) wrote for the show biz musical *You Can't Have Everything* (1937). Alice Faye, as the granddaughter of Edgar Allan Poe with playwriting ambitions, sang the number with Louis Prima and his Band. The song inspired the title for a 1937 film comedy, where it was sung by Jack Haley and Ann Sothern.

"Dark Is the Night" is the melancholy torch song from *Rich, Young and Pretty* (1951) about the end of a romance and the darkening days and nights to come. Jane Powell, as a rich Texas girl visiting Paris, sang the Sammy Cahn (lyric) and Nicholas Brodszky (music) number after a falling out with sweetheart Vic Damone.

"Datin' " is the bouncy duet that pilot Elvis Presley and pre–teen Donna Butterworth sang together while flying across the islands in his helicopter in *Paradise, Hawaiian Style* (1966). Fred Wise and Randy Starr wrote the sprightly number about how adults start to act as silly as kids when they go dating. Presley recorded the song as a solo and included it on two of his albums.

"The Day After Forever" is the ballad of everlasting love by Johnny Burke (lyric) and James Van Heusen (music) that was used creatively in *Going My Way* (1944). At St. Dominic's church rectory, wayward singer Jean Heather sang the number in a sexy manner with odd hand gestures to show priest Bing Crosby that she has talent. Crosby gave her some suggestions on how to better perform the song, sitting at the piano and giving the number a quiet and sincere interpretation. They ended singing it as a duet, though the effect was necessarily more of teacher-pupil than two lovers. Crosby and Andy Russell each had successful recordings of the ballad.

"Day Dreaming (All Night Long)" is the wistful song of longing that radio crooner Rudy Vallee and Rosemary Lane sang in *Gold Diggers in Paris* (1938). Harry Warren wrote the gentle music, and Johnny Mercer provided the lyric that dreamt of an ideal romance that will someday become a reality.

"The Day You Came Along" is the hyperbolic song that Judith Allen sang in a nightclub about how her whole world changed when she met Broadway singer Bing Crosby in *Too Much Harmony* (1933). Crosby reprised the number later in the film and had a best-selling record of it as well. Arthur Johnston and Sam Coslow wrote the song (which includes the title phrase no less than nine times in the lyric); it was also recorded by Meyer Davis, Will Osborne, Victor

Young (vocal by Scrappy Lambert), and Conrad Thibault.

"The Deadwood Stage" is the tuneful western song sequence by Paul Francis Webster (lyric) and Sammy Fain (music) that opened the frontier musical *Calamity Jane* (1953). Sharpshooter Doris Day sang the number about how she loves the sound of the whip cracking as she rode atop a stagecoach and shot at Indians that are chasing them. When the stage arrived in Deadwood, the number moved into a list song with Day showing the townspeople some of the exciting things the coach has brought them. The number concluded in the Golden Garter Saloon, where the other major characters were introduced, some kidding Calamity about her tomboy ways, and ended with drinks for all at the bar, Day insisting only on a "sasparilla."

"Dearest, Darest I?" is the comic love song that Eddie "Rochester" Anderson sang illustrating his tentative way of seduction in *Love Thy Neighbor* (1940), the musical about the Jack Benny–Fred Allen radio feud. James Van Huesen provided the jazzy music, and Johnny Burke penned the sly lyric inspired by Anderson's unique comedy talents. Ray McKinley, with Will Bradley's Orchestra, made a recording of the number.

"Dearly Beloved" is the alluring song about a marriage ceremony by Johnny Mercer (lyric) and Jerome Kern (music) that Rita Hayworth (dubbed by Nan Wynn) and Fred Astaire sang and danced to Xavier Cugat's Orchestra at a wedding reception in *You Were Never Lovelier* (1942). Kern's music, which some have pointed out bears a resemblance to the duet "Or son contenta" in Puccini's *Madama Butterfly*, is a favorite for study by musicologists because of its ingenious chromatics; the song is written in the key of C, but the main theme is in alternating G and F chords. The Oscar-nominated song remained on *Your Hit Parade* for seventeen weeks, and among those who have recorded it are Dinah Shore, George Shearing, Glenn Miller (vocal by Skip Nelson), Alvino Rey (vocal by Bill Schallen), Ted Fio Rito (vocal by Jimmy Baxter), Dorothy Kirsten, and, most recently, Andrea Marcovicci. The number was also featured in the Broadway revues *Jerome Kern Goes to Hollywood* (1986), where it was sung by Liz Robertson, and in *Dream* (1997), where it was performed by Jonathan Dokuchitz and Darcie Roberts.

"Delishious" was the first hit the Gershwin brothers had with a song written directly for the screen, a playful number used in a dream sequence called "Welcome to the Melting Pot" in *Delicious* (1931). The number was sung by Russian songwriter Raul Roulien when he hears immigrant Janet Gaynor mispronounce the movie's title. George Gershwin composed the engaging music, and Ira Gershwin invented words like "caprishee-us" and "ambishee-us" to fill out the lighthearted number. Nat Shilkret and his Orchestra made a successful recording of the song, and in the Gershwin bio-musical *Rhapsody in Blue* (1945) the number was sung by Joan Leslie (dubbed by Sally Sweetland). Cabaret singer Bobby Short made a noteworthy recording of the song in 1990.

"Derry Down Dilly" is the flavorful nonsense song Marge Champion, as the distaff half of a song-and-dance couple, sang and danced to in *Everything I Have Is Yours* (1952). Johnny Green composed the music, and Johnny Mercer wrote the meaningless words that seemed to mean so much.

"The Dickey Bird Song" is the musical announcement that spring has arrived, sung by divorced mom Jeanette MacDonald and her offspring Jane Powell, Mary Eleanor Donahue (dubbed by Beverly Jean Garbo), and Ann E. Todd (dubbed by Pat Hyatt) in *Three Darling Daughters* (1948). MacDonald's new love José Iturbi later reprised the song at the piano. The chipper number by Howard Dietz (lyric) and Sammy Fain (music) became rather popular, thanks to records by Freddy Martin and his Orchestra (vocal by Glen Hughes) and Larry Clinton (vocal by Helen Lee and the Dipsy Doodles).

"Did You Ever See a Dream Walking?" is the enduring song favorite by Mack Gordon (lyric) and Harry Revel (music) about a romantic vision that becomes a reality. The standard was introduced by Ginger Rogers and Art Jarrett in the show biz musical *Sitting Pretty* (1933), and it was heard in the background in several films thereafter. Two recent and unusual uses of the ballad on film: a Bing Crosby recording heard on the soundtrack but with new footage in *Pennies from Heaven* (1981) and a chilling use of the song as a sinister leit motif in *Lady in White* (1988). In addition to Crosby, Eddy Duchin (vocal by Lew Sherwood) had a hit record of the song and there were successful recordings by Guy Lombardo, Meyer Davis, the Pickens Sisters, Eddie Cantor, Gene Austin, Vaughn Monroe, and others.

"Ding Dong! The Witch Is Dead" is the unifying song in the beloved Munchkinland sequence in the fantasy classic *The Wizard of Oz* (1939). E. Y. Harburg (lyric) and Harold Arlen (music) wrote the comic operetta-like scene that was sung or delivered in rhymed verse throughout. The first section, "Come Out, Come Out, Wherever You Are," was sung by Glinda the Good Witch (enacted by Billie Burke but dubbed by Lorraine Bridges) as she encouraged the hiding Munchkins to present themselves to Dorothy (Judy Garland). Then Garland sang "It Really Was No Miracle," explaining how the tornado lifted up her Kansas house and dropped it on the Wicked Witch. The 150 citizens of Munchkinland then celebrated with "Ding Dong! The Witch Is Dead" and selected Munchkins and dignitaries honored Garland and sang various versions of "We Welcome You to Munchkinland." The whole ensemble broke into a jubilant reprise of "Ding Dong! The Witch Is Dead," which was cut off at the climax by the appearance of the surviving Wicked Witch (Margaret Hamilton). The entire sequence is one of the most imaginatively written and staged in musical film. Arlen's music is melodic and frolicsome, Harburg's lyrics are filled with playful rhymes, Bobby Connolly choreographed the marches and dance specialties with finesse, and Victor Fleming directed the sequence with just the right touch of fantasy and farce. The group the Fifth Estate had a hit record of the "Ding Dong! The Witch Is Dead" section in 1967.

"Do You Know What It Means to Miss New Orleans?" is the jazzy tribute to the jazz center of the world, written by Eddie De Lange (lyric) and Louis Alter (music) for *New Orleans* (1947), a musical in which Dorothy Patrick is torn between the study of classical music and the study of jazz. The number was performed by Patrick, Louis Armstrong and his All Stars, Billie Holiday, and Woody Herman. The song is a favorite in New Orleans, where several jazz clubs have adopted it as their theme song. Armstrong's recording is definitive but memorable versions have also been made by Bob Scobey and his Band and by clarinetist Pete Fountain who made it his theme song.

"Do You Know Why?" is the questioning love ballad by Johnny Burke (lyric) and James Van Heusen (music) that Mary Martin and the Merry Macs sang in *Love Thy Neighbor* (1940), the musical about radio stars. Tommy Dorsey (vocal by Frank Sinatra), Glenn Miller, Bob Crosby, and Dick Todd all made recordings of the number.

"Do You Play, Madame?" is a sly duet in which millionaire Charles "Buddy" Rogers and *Follies* gal Kathryn Crawford sang of their love match using golf metaphors throughout the number. It was written by George Marion, Jr., (lyric) and Richard Whiting (music) and was featured in the early musical *Safety in Numbers* (1930).

"Doctor, Lawyer, Indian Chief" is the energetic comic number by Paul Francis Webster (lyric) and Hoagy Carmichael (music) that hat-check girl Betty Hutton sang with wild abandon in *Stork Club* (1945). Hutton's recording was a bestseller, and disks by Carmichael and Les Brown (vocal by Butch Stone) were also successful.

"Doin' It the Hard Way" is one of the many high-powered, farcical novelty numbers written for Betty Hutton's maniacal comic talents. Johnny Burke (lyric) and James Van Heusen (music) wrote this one for Hutton in *Duffy's Tavern* (1945), a musical loosely based on the popular radio program.

"Doin' the Uptown Lowdown" is the swinging dance song Frances Williams sang in a nightclub in *Broadway Thru a Keyhole* (1933). Harry Revel wrote the music, and Mack Gordon penned the lyric about a new Harlem dance that was attracting all the tourists to uptown Manhattan. The number enjoyed several recordings, including ones by Mildred Bailey, Richard Himbler (vocal by Johnny Mercer), Ted Weems (vocal by Parker Gibbs), Isham Jones, Abe Lyman (vocal by Ella Logan), and Joe Venuti.

"Dolores" is the ballad that introduced Frank Sinatra to film audiences. Frank Loesser (lyric) and Louis Alter (music) wrote the song praising a girl who is "not Marie or Emily or Doris," and Sinatra (in his screen debut) sang it in *Las Vegas Nights* (1941) with Tommy Dorsey's Orchestra and some assist by Bert Wheeler. Bing Crosby's record of the Oscar-nominated ballad was a hit, but it was Sinatra's recording that made the song and helped launch his film career.

"The Donkey Serenade" is the hit song interpolated into the film score of Rudolf Friml's stage operetta *The Firefly* (1937) and became Allan Jones' signature song throughout his career. Jones sang it, with Robert Spindola and guitarist Manuel Alvarez Maciste, to Jeanette MacDonald as they rode through the Spanish mountains on a donkey-drawn coach, the tempo of the song set by the hoof beats of the domestic animals. The number was based on a 1920 piano piece by Friml that was turned into a song with lyrics by Sigmund Spaeth. For the film, Herbert Stothart adapted the music and Robert Wright and George Forrest wrote a new lyric. Jones' recording was a bestseller and the song was forever associated with him, but it was also recorded by Frank Perry, Lanny Ross, organist Eddie Dunstedter, Artie Shaw, Horace Heidt, Tony Martin, and Jerry Hadley. "The Donkey Serenade" also showed up in a number of films: Jones reprised it in a cameo role in *Crazy House* (1943), José Iturbi played it on the piano in *Anchors Aweigh* (1945), Dean Martin and Jerry Lewis sang it in *My Friend Irma* (1949), and Jones' famous recording was heard on the radio in *Radio Days* (1987).

"Don't Ask Me Why" is the quiet rock ballad by Fred Wise (lyric) and Ben Wiseman (music) that pleads for a lover not to forsake one. Bourbon Street singer Elvis Presley sang the torchy number as he accompanied himself on the guitar at a New Orleans nightclub in the gritty musical melodrama *King Creole* (1958). Presley's recording was very popular.

"Don't Be a Do-Badder" is the nimble song of advice by Sammy Cahn (lyric) and James Van Heusen (music) that teaches one how to avoid bad behavior and "climb the stepladder" to heaven. Bing Crosby and the young boys in an orphanage dormitory sang and danced to the merry lesson in the gangster musical spoof *Robin and the Seven Hoods* (1964). At the end of the film the song was reprised by reformed hoods Frank Sinatra, Sammy Davis, Jr., and Dean Martin dressed in Santa Claus suits and collecting money for the poor.

"Don't Carry Tales Out of School" is a tongue-in-cheek love song from *Pin-Up Girl* (1944) that uses wartime jargon to make its point. Betty Grable and a male quartet performed the supposedly impromptu number in New York's Club Chartreuse to convince war hero John Harvey that she is a Broadway star. James Monaco composed the gently swinging music, and Mack Gordon wrote the clever lyric that warned her beau to keep mum regarding her love, referring also to military secrets because "loose lips sink ships."

"Don't Fence Me In" is the atypical Cole Porter hit about the wide open prairie that took quite a while before it was heard. Porter based his lyric on a poem by Montana miner Robert Fletcher and wrote the woeful lament of a jailed cowboy who longs for the open spaces of the land. The number was written in the 1930s for a film that was never released, but it was eventually interpolated into *Hollywood Canteen* (1944), where it was sung by Roy Rogers and the Sons of the Pioneers and later reprised by the Andrews Sisters. The song was on *Your Hit Parade* for sixteen weeks, aided by a recording by Kate Smith with Four Chicks and a Chuck, and a version by Bing Crosby and the Andrews Sisters sold over a million copies. Other memorable recordings were made by Sammy Kaye and his Orchestra, Gene Autry, the Sons of the Pioneers, and Nero Young. Rogers reprised the ballad in *Don't Fence Me In* (1945), and it was featured in the Porter bio-musical *Night and Day* (1946).

"Don't Give Up the Ship" is the patriotic rouser that Dick Powell and the naval cadets sang in *Shipmates Forever* (1935); it later became the official song of the U.S. Naval Academy. Al Dubin (lyric) and Harry Warren (music) wrote the stirring tribute to the U.S. Navy, and it was recorded by Powell and by Tommy Dorsey.

"Don't Let It Bother You" is the toe-tapping opening number by Mack Gordon (lyric) and Harry Revel (music) in *The Gay Divorcee* (1934). A chorus of girls in a Paris nightclub sang and danced to the cheery forget-your-troubles number, and then Fred Astaire, in order to prove that he is a famous tap-dancing star from America, took to the stage and danced to the jaunty music. Thomas "Fats" Waller made a notable recording of the song.

"Don't Let That Moon Get Away" is the hit ballad about seizing the romantic moment that Bing Crosby introduced in *Sing You Sinners* (1938) when called upon to entertain at a roadside nightclub. Crosby's recording of the Johnny Burke (lyric) and James Monaco (music) song was a bestseller that was also recorded by Hal Kemp and by Shep Fields. Eugene Fleming sang the ballad in the Broadway revue *Swinging on a Star* (1995).

"Don't Mention Love to Me" is the languid ballad by Dorothy Fields (lyric) and Oscar Levant (music) that Hollywood-star-in-disguise Ginger Rogers sang in *In Person* (1935), warning prospective beaus that her heart was not a "play thing" and that casual romances are not for her. Recordings were made by Rogers, Isham Jones' Orchestra, and Kay Thompson.

"Don't Rock the Boat, Dear" is the cautionary duet that married TV stars Betty Grable and Dan Dailey sang in *My Blue Heaven* (1950). Harold Arlen composed the music and collaborated with Ralph Blane on the lyric.

"Don't Say Goodnight" is the waltzing production number by Al Dubin (lyric) and Harry Warren (music) in *Wonder Bar* (1934) that gave Busby Berkeley the opportunity to use mirrors to create his magical illusions. After Dick Powell sang the song and Delores Del Rio and Ricardo Cortez danced to it, a chorus in white took to a stage full of large mirrors that moved in such a way that the eight chorines became a thousand dancing images. Gus Arnheim and Tal Henry each made orchestral recordings of the song.

"Dormi Dormi Dormi" is the tender Italian lullaby that Sammy Cahn (lyric) and Harry Warren (music) wrote for the Jerry Lewis vehicle *Rock-a-Bye Baby* (1958). Salvatore Baccaloni and Lewis sang the number to a set of infant triplets, trying to get them to sleep.

"Double Trouble" is the spunky song by Leo Robin (lyric), Ralph Rainger, and Richard Whiting (music) about a gal with two beaus and the problems of "trying to be true to two." Countess Lyda Roberti sang the number with boyfriend Henry Wadsworth and radio star Jack Oakie in *The Big Broadcast of 1936* (1935), and it was recorded by Ray Noble, Red McKenzie, Frank Dailey, and Babs and her Brothers. The ensemble sang the zippy number in the Broadway revue *A Day in Hollywood—A Night in the Ukraine* (1980).

"Down Argentina Way" is the Latin-flavored invitation to travel south of the border that Mack Gordon (lyric) and Harry Warren (music) wrote for *Down Argentine Way* (1940). Don Ameche (dubbed by Carlos Albert) sang in Spanish about his homeland to Betty Grable in a New York nightclub, and a little later in the film she sang it in English with the chorus and danced to it. The role was meant for Alice Faye, but she became ill as filming began. Grable, in her first major film role, so impressed audiences in this song and others in the movie that her stardom was launched. Dinah Shore had a hit recording of the Oscar-nominated song.

"Down at Baba's Alley" is one of those delicious novelty numbers written for Donald O'Connor to chew the scenery with. This comic number by Sidney Miller and Inez James, which satirically played off the *Arabian Nights*, was enacted by mathematician-turned-performer O'Connor in *Are You With It?* (1948).

"Down By the River" is a charming Rodgers and Hart ballad that riverboat singer Bing Crosby sang in the period musical *Mississippi* (1935) and on record, both with great success. Lorenz Hart's lyric, a pledge of love as deep and everflowing as the great river, is straightforward and unfussy. Richard Rodgers' music is spare, using few notes to wondrous effect, and the song, according to Alec Wilder, "has the hymn-like strength of Kern's songs."

"Down Old Ox Road" is a sentimental ballad with a rather squalid subtext that Sam Coslow (lyric) and Arthur Johnston (music) wrote for *College Humor* (1933). College professor Bing Crosby and some smooching students sang about taking a girl down a certain lovers' lane and how it implied much more than just a stroll. In fact, the title expression was a contemporary college euphemism for sexual seduction. Surprisingly, the censors did not see anything objectionable in the lyric that claimed Old Ox Road was not a place on any map but a "proposition." Crosby's recording of the ballad was very popular, and the song was also successfully recorded by Maxine Sullivan, Paul Whiteman (vocal by Peggy Healy and Al Dary), and Elliott Lawrence.

"Down on Ami-Oni-Oni Isle" is a flavorful Polynesian number from *Song of the Islands* (1942) that had a bit of wit in its writing and performing. At a luau on a small Pacific island, grass-skirted Betty Grable sang of the glories of her island. The song was taken up by native Hilo Hattie, and then everyone sang it as Grable and the girls did a hula production number choreographed by Hermes Pan. Harry Warren composed the Broadway–style Hawaiian music, and Mack Gordon wrote the wry lyric that listed all the things, from Jell-o to Alka Seltzer to Ginger Rogers films, that one didn't have to put up with on the secluded isle.

"Down Where the Trade Winds Blow" is the pseudo-Hawaiian ballad that Harry Owens wrote for the Bobby Breen vehicle *Hawaii Calls* (1938). Ten-year-old Breen, the male Shirley Temple of his day, belted out the atmospheric number as a stowaway who ends up on the Hawaiian Islands.

"Dream Dancing" is a neglected ballad with a lot of kick, another song about dreaming but this one rather upbeat and lighthearted. Cole Porter wrote the number for Fred Astaire to sing in *You'll Never Get Rich* (1941) and then to dance to with new co-star Rita Hayworth. But the song was left on the cutting room floor and only the dance remained. Astaire also recorded the song, but it was released during an ASCAP strike and received no radio play and so quickly disappeared. "Dream Dancing" was used in a nightclub scene in *This Could Be the Night* (1957) and has gathered a group of admirers over the years.

"A Dream Is a Wish Your Heart Makes" is the flowing ballad near the beginning of the animated fairy tale *Cinderella* (1949) that the title character (voice of Ilene Woods) sang as she awoke from dreaming of a better life. Mack Gordon, Jay Livingston, and Al Hoffman collaborated on the ballad, and Perry Como's recording was very popular. Michael Bolton's record in 1995 was a success, and the next year Linda Ronstadt recorded the song (and much of the rest of the score) in both Spanish and English. Stacy Sullivan made a noteworthy recording in 1998.

"Dream Lover" is the trilling song that introduced Jeanette MacDonald to film audiences. Clifford Grey (lyric) and Victor Schertzinger (music) wrote the ballad as the first number MacDonald would sing in her debut film *The Love Parade* (1929). As the queen of a fictional European country, MacDonald awoke in her royal bedchamber and sang the operetta aria to her nonplused handmaidens about the imaginary sweetheart she has been dreaming about. Later in the film she reprised it at the piano as the camera followed various couples in love. There were early recordings by Tom Gerun and Nat Shilkert, and Claudette Colbert sang the number in *Arise My Love* (1940).

"Dream Stuff" is the gentle song about the fleeting nature of dreams and how they must be protected or they will get stolen away. The lullabylike number's tender lyric was by Dr. Seuss (AKA Theodore Geisel), and Frederick Hollander composed the flowing music, written for the nightmarish fantasy *The 5,000 Fingers of Dr. T* (1953), where it was sung by plumber Peter Lind Hayes and the imaginative youth Tommy Rettig.

"The Dreamer" was one of those ardent wait-till-the-boys-return love songs so prevalent during World War Two. Frank Loesser (lyric) and Arthur Schwartz (music) wrote this one for the all-star musical *Thank Your Lucky Stars* (1943), where Dinah Shore, as a farmgirl in a charity show, sang lethargically about how long she has waited for her serviceman boyfriend and how she will continue to dream until he comes back home. The number was reprised by nonsinging stars Ida Lupino, Olivia De Havilland, and George Tobias as they jitterbugged to a scat version of the song. Shore and Kay Armen each had a popular record of the heavy-hearted ballad.

"The Dressing Song (My Do-Me-Do-Duds)" is the silly and word-crazy song that Hans Conried, as the diabolical piano teacher Dr. Terwilliger, sang with his attendants as he dressed in outlandish concert dress in a nightmare sequence in the fantasy musical *The 5,000 Fingers of Dr. T* (1953). Frederick Hollander wrote the jocular music, and Dr. Seuss (AKA Theodore Geisel) penned the intricate lyric that employed the kind of tongue twisters and alliteration that he was famous for in his popular children's books.

"Dues" is the heartbreaking lament written and sung by Ronee Blakely in the ambitious musical drama *Nashville* (1975) about the music industry. As a fragile country–music star performing at the Opryland theme park, Blakely sang of a marriage that has become a "battleground" and how weary she is of paying emotional dues for her mistakes. While most of the songs were parodies of country and pop songs, this ballad was painfully sincere, leading the star into a nervous breakdown on the stage.

"The Dwarf's Yodel Song" is the rompish but charming nonsense number that Larry Morey (lyric) and Frank Churchill (music) wrote for the landmark animated film *Snow White and the Seven Dwarfs* (1937). The seven little men sang, danced, and accompanied themselves on makeshift instruments as they entertained Snow White after dinner. The song consists of jokes with no meaning, sing-along sections, and high-flying yodeling. The number is also listed as "The Silly Song" and sometimes as "Isn't This a Silly Song?"

E

"An Earful of Music" is the exuberant opening number by Gus Kahn (lyric) and Walter Donaldson (music) for the Eddie Cantor vehicle *Kid Millions* (1934). Ethel Merman, as a salesgirl in a music store, belted out the zesty song about how listening to music and dancing with one's beloved is the way to total happiness. Merman recorded the song with Johnny Green's Orchestra, and there were also records by Cantor, George Hall (vocal by Loretta Lee), Emil Coleman, Mal Hallett, and Anson Weeks (vocal by Kay St. Germaine).

"Early Bird" is an optimistic little ditty that shipwrecked Shirley Temple sang in *CaptainJanuary* (1936) as she whistled and did a soft-shoe routine. Lew Pollack devised the happy music, and Sidney Mitchell wrote the lyric, which suggests that one should wake up and greet every new day as the early bird does.

"East Side of Heaven" is the title ballad from the 1939 Bing Crosby vehicle scored by Johnny Burke (lyric) and James Monaco (music). Singing cab driver Crosby sang the optimistic number anticipating a tenement rooftop rendezvous with an angel who can't afford the better locales and philosophizing that life was never perfection but it wasn't "always wrong" either. Crosby's recording enjoyed some popularity, and Bobby Short made a standout recording 1995.

"Easy to Love" is the indelible Cole Porter love song that was used throughout *Born to Dance* (1936). Jimmy Stewart sang it (barely) to Frances Langford as they strolled through Central Park at night. Then Eleanor Powell danced to the number, Langford reprised it, Reginald Gardiner mimed it, and Buddy Ebsen tapped to it. Legend has it that the studio planned on dubbing Stewart's singing but the song was so effective even in his uneven delivery that they left it as it was. Porter wrote the song for the Broadway musical *Anything Goes* (1934), but leading man William Gaxton objected to the high notes and the ballad was replaced by "All Through the Night." Among the many who have recorded the ballad are Langford, Hal Kemp (vocal by Bob Allen), Shep Fields (vocal by Dick Robertson), Dick Jurgen (vocal by Eddy Howard), Maxine Sullivan, Dinah Shore and Buddy Clark as a duet, Errol Garner, Judy Garland, and Billie Holiday. The song was heard in a handful of films over the years: on the soundtrack in the Porter bio-musical *Night and Day* (1946), by operatic tenor Lauritz Melchior in *This Time for Keeps* (1947), and by Tony Martin in *Easy to Love* (1953). On Broadway "Easy to Love" was eventually heard in the revue *A Day in Hollywood—A Night in the Ukraine* (1980), and Howard McGillin sang it in its originally intended spot in the 1988 revival of *Anything Goes*.

"Ebony Rhapsody" is a clever variation on the old rhapsody form that Sam Coslow (lyric) and Arthur Johnston (music) wrote for the musical mystery *Murder at the Vanities* (1934). The production number on a stage opened with an old-fashioned rhapsody sung by Carl Brisson and Kitty Carisle, but soon the tempo changed and Gertrude Michael and Duke Ellington's Orchestra moved into a syncopated variation of Liszt's "Second Hungarian Rhapsody." Ellington's recording was moderately popular.

"Eeny, Meeny, Miney, Mo" is that rare case when a songwriter sang one of his own songs in a feature film musical. Matt Malneck composed the music and Johnny Mercer penned the lyric for the rhythm number that used the expression to grab your "troubles by the toe" and let them go. Mercer, in a cameo role, sang it with the California Collegians in *To Beat the Band* (1935). His record with Ginger Rogers popularized the song and there were also successful recordings by Bing Crosby (who is mentioned in the comic lyric), Benny Goodman, and Billie Holiday.

"Empty Saddles" is the popular cowboy song that Bing Crosby sang in *Rhythm on the Range* (1936), his only musical western. The lyric was taken from a poem by J. Keirn Brennan, and Billy Hill wrote the easygoing music. Crosby sang it with the Sons of the Pioneers, one of them named Dick Weston at the time later changed his name to Roy Rogers. Crosby's recording was a hit, and later Rogers recorded it with the other Pioneers.

"Endlessly" is the devoted ballad that Kim Gannon (lyric) and Walter Kent (music) wrote for the backstager *Earl Carroll Vanities* (1945). Constance Moore, as the Princess Drinia from Turania who appears in a Broadway revue while on a trip to New York, sang the Oscar-nominated song.

"Evergreen" is the Oscar-winning song by Paul Williams (lyric) and Barbra

Streisand (music) that was featured in the 1976 remake of *A Star Is Born*. The highly emotional ballad about an undying love was heard at a recording session where up-and-coming singer Streisand sang it to self-destructive rock star Kris Kristofferson. Williams' lyric is rather spare and straightforward (love is "soft as an easy chair"), but Streisand's music climbs the scale perilously in a manner ideal for showing off her unique vocal talents. The Streisand recording was the Number One pop love song of the day, but the number has been effectively recorded as an instrumental piece as well, most memorably by clarinetist Acker Bilk and pianists Ferrante and Teicher. The song is sometime listed as "Love Theme from *A Star Is Born*."

"Every Day's a Holiday" is the swinging title number by Sam Coslow (lyric) and Barry Trivers (music) from the 1938 Mae West vehicle set at the turn of the century. West, as con woman Peaches O'Day, sang the celebratory song with Louis Armstrong's Orchestra, and there were successful recordings by Cab Calloway, Bob Crosby's Orchestra, Glenn Miller (vocal by Kathleen Lane), and Thomas "Fats" Waller. According to Coslow, West (who wrote the screenplay) was having trouble finding a title until she saw the lyric to the song.

"Every Little While" is a neglected Jerome Kern ballad that was the victim of film audience's loss of interest in musicals in the very early 1930s. Otto Harbach (lyric) and Kern (music) wrote the poignant love duet for *Men of the Sky* (1931), a musical melodrama about flying aces, where it was sung by American pilot Jack Whiting and French lass Irene Delroy. But musicals had become box office poison by 1931, so the studio cut all the songs and released the film as a drama. The number was recorded by George Dvorsky and Jeanne Lehman in 1993.

"Every Night at Seven" is the sparkling opening number in *Royal Wedding* (1951) in which the brother-sister act of Fred Astaire and Jane Powell (based on the actual team of Fred and Adele Astaire) performed a sexy romp with king Astaire chasing chambermaid Powell around the palace. Burton Lane composed the jazzy music and Alan Jay Lerner wrote the wry lyric in which the king, weary of long working days and budget problems, anxiously awaits the maid's arrival nightly at seven because he's "always in full bloom" when she is near. Roddy McDowell made an antic recording of the number.

"Everybody Has a Laughing Place" is the jumping comic number that Ray Gilbert (lyric) and Allie Wrubel (music) wrote for the innovative musical *Song of the South* (1946) that successfully mixed animation and live action for the first time. During one of the animated Uncle Remus tales, Brer Rabbit (voice of Johnny Lee), captured by Brer Fox and Brer Bear and about to be cooked, happily sang about his secret laughing place. The ploy worked, and Rabbit's captors let him free to see the special place, only to discover a bee hive that attacked the two and indeed provided Brer Rabbit with plenty to laugh about. Burl Ives' recording of the song was a popular children's record.

"Everybody Sing" is the effervescent call to vocalize that teenager Judy Garland and a group of performers sang in a Broadway producer's office in *Broadway Melody of 1938* (1937). Arthur Freed (lyric) and Nacio Herb Brown (music) wrote the buoyant number, which was on the first record Garland ever recorded.

"Everyone Says I Love You" is the bouncy list song by Bert Kalmar (lyric) and Harry Ruby (music) about all the amorous people throughout the world that was used throughout the Marx Brothers vehicle *Horse Feathers* (1932). Zeppo serenaded the college widow Thelma Todd with the song while she breakfasted in bed, and then Chico played it on the piano while he interjected insults at the same widow. Later Harpo played it on his harp, and finally Groucho accompanied himself on a ukelele as Todd paddled them across a lake in a canoe. Isham Jones (vocal by Eddie Stone) and Anson Weeks both had popular orchestral records, and the song inspired the title for the 1997 contemporary musical film where the Helen Miles Singers sang it on the soundtrack.

"Everything I Have Is Yours" is the hit love song from the backstager *Dancing Lady* (1933) written by Harold Adamson (lyric) and Burton Lane (music). Bandleader Art Jarrett sang the driving rhythm ballad about how love rids one of one's possessions while Joan Crawford danced with Franchot Tone. Early recordings by Ruth Etting, George Olson and his Orchestra, Rudy Vallee, and others helped popularize the song, but it became an even bigger hit in the late 1940s and early 1950s with recordings by Billy Eckstine and Eddie Fisher. Opera star Ezio Pinza sang the number in *Strictly Dishonorable* (1951), Monica Lewis performed it in *Everything I Have Is Yours* (1952), and Michael Feinstein revived it on record in 1991.

"Everything Is on the Up and Up" is the comic gem from the musical melodrama *Roadhouse Nights* (1930) that serves as a record of what the brilliant stage team of Durante, Jackson, and Clayton must have been like in vaudeville. As three comics performing at the River Inn, Eddie Jackson and Lou Clayton were the straightmen while Jimmy Durante (in his screen debut) got all the punch lines in the daffy song written by the trio.

"Everything's Been Done Before" is the light-footed ballad by Harold Adamson (lyric), Jack King, and Edwin H. Knopf (music) that argues falling in love is such an old and steadfast pastime, so why resist the tried and true? Allan Jones (in his screen debut) sang the song as part of a Broadway show in *Reckless* (1935), and Art Jarrett's recording of the number was so popular he made it his theme song.

"Ev'ry Day" is the dedicated ballad Rudy Vallee crooned in *Sweet Music* (1935) and later recorded and featured in his radio show. Sammy Fain composed the music and Irving Kahal penned the lyric, which advocated renewing one's love on a daily basis.

"Ev'ry Day I Love You (Just a Little Bit More)" is the pseudo-cowboy love song by Sammy Cahn (lyric) and Jule Styne (music) from the satiric western musical *Two Guys from Texas* (1948). Dennis Morgan, as a song-and-dance man who ends up on a dude ranch, sang the ballad, which was recorded by Vaughn Monroe, Dick Haymes, and Jo Stafford.

"Ev'rybody Wants to Be a Cat" is the contagious jazz number by Floyd Huddleston and Al Rinker about how all wish they had the new hot jazz sound written for the animated musical *The Aristocats* (1970). Alley cat Thomas O'Malley (voice of Phil Foster) and Scat Cat (voice of Scatman Crothers) and his band performed the swinging number while the sophisticated lady cat Duchess (voice of Eva Gabor) did a slower and cooler section of the song. The jumping sequence climaxed as their Paris townhouse collapsed from all the jubilant music.

F

"Face to Face" is the languishing ballad by Sammy Cahn (lyric) and Sammy Fain (music) about the remarkable things that happen when a boy and girl are close together. Jane Powell sang the song in a taxicab as she auditioned for a Broadway show in *Three Sailors and a Girl* (1953), and Gordon MacRae (who was one of the sailors in the film) made a record of it.

"Fair and Warmer" is the upbeat hang-the-Depression song that singing waiter Dick Powell sang with Ted Fio Rito's Orchestra in *Twenty Million Sweethearts* (1934), a backstage musical about radio. Harry Warren composed the jazzy music, and Al Dubin wrote the optimistic lyric that promised ideal weather when one was in love. Powell's recording was a modest hit, and the number became a favorite of dance bands at the time. The song is sometimes listed as "It's Getting Fair and Warmer."

"Faithful Forever" is actually two songs that Leo Robin (lyric) and Ralph Rainger (music) wrote for the animated adventure *Gulliver's Travels* (1939). Princess Glory (voice of Jessica Dragonette) sang the operetta-like "Faithful," the official song of Lilliput, while Prince David (voice of Lanny Ross) sang the equally lush ballad "Forever," the state song of the Kingdom of Lupescu. When the two lovers became engaged, a war broke out over which song would be played at the wedding. Gulliver solves the problem by combining the two songs, which blended together beautifully as David and Glory reprised them at the end of the film. The double ballad was on *Your Hit Parade* for nine weeks, and the Oscar-nominated song was recorded by Ross, Kenny Baker, Glenn Miller, Phil Harris, and Ginny Simms.

"Fame" is the pulsating Oscar-winning title number from the 1980 docu-musical about students and staff at Manhattan's High School for the Performing Arts. Student composer Lee Carreri had written a song about celebrity, so his cab driver father broadcast the music from loudspeakers on his cab and Irene Cara and the other students sang and danced the number on the sidewalk in front of the school, in the street, and on the rooftops of cars stalled in the traffic jam. Dean Pitchford wrote the driven lyrics, Michael Gore composed the catchy and repetitive music, and Cara's recording was a major hit.

"Family" is the easygoing soft-shoe number about mutual appreciation and camaraderie that Randy Newman wrote for *James and the Giant Peach* (1996), the fantasy that mixed live action and stop-action animation. The Grasshopper (voice of Simon Callow) played on his violin and sang the number to the orphaned James (voice of Paul Terry) as they floated through the sky on the giant peach, and they were joined in song by his friends the Earthworm (voice of David Thewlis), Spider (voice of Susan Sarandon), Glow Worm (voice of Miriam Margoyles), Lady Bug (voice of Jane Leeves), and Centipede (voice of Richard Dreyfuss).

"Fancy Meeting You" is a rather unusual love song, using reincarnation and evolution to explain the couple as "lovesick fish in the sea" who crawled out of the water millions of years ago. Dick Powell sang the ballad to Jeanne Madden in a museum in the backstager *Stage Struck* (1936), and he later recorded the number with Eddy Duchin's Orchestra. Harold Arlen composed the uptempo music, which Harold Meyerson has described as "a deadpan lilting fox trot," and E. Y. Harburg penned the lyric that poked fun at Darwin, the Shavian life force, romance magazine clichés, and reincarnation (Powell claimed that even as a prehistoric man he had loved her).

"Far Longer Than Forever" is the gushing love duet written by David Zippel (lyric) and Lex de Azevedo (music) for the animated fairy tale *The Swan Princess* (1994). Prince Derek (voice of Howard McGillin) and Princess Odette (voice of Liz Callaway) each sang the rhapsodic number in their separate kingdoms, but on the soundtrack their voices combined in loving harmony.

"Faraway Part of Town" is an entrancing ballad that Dory Langdon (lyric) and André Previn (music) wrote for the star-studded disappointment *Pepe* (1960). Judy Garland sang the Oscar-nominated song, but she was not seen; her voice came from a record player as Dan Dailey and Shirley Jones danced about the garden of a Hollywood producer's mansion.

"Fare Thee Well Annabelle" is the crooning ballad that bandleader Rudy Vallee sang in the early swing musical *Sweet Music* (1935). Mort Dixon (lyric) and Allie Wrubel (music) wrote the innocent number, and there were successful recordings by Glen Gray and the Casa Loma Orchestra and Guy Lombardo and his Royal Canadians.

"Fated to Be Mated" was one of two new songs Cole Porter wrote for the 1957 film version of his Broadway musical *Silk Stockings*. On a deserted film soundstage producer Fred Astaire and Russian official Cyd Charisse (dubbed by Carole Richards) sang the joyous marriage proposal and then went into one of the best dance sequences of the era, a diverse number that had the couple waltzing on a fake Paris street, tangoing in an artificial Spanish garden, and chasing each other through a fisherman's wharf.

"Feed the Birds" is the haunting lullaby-ballad by Richard M. and Robert B. Sherman that Julie Andrews sang in Disney classic *Mary Poppins* (1964). As the nanny Andrews put her two charges to bed and sang to them of the old bird woman who sits in front of St. Paul's Cathedral and sells bird seed at "tuppence a bag." As she sang, the scene dissolved to a dreamy view of St. Paul's and the old woman (veteran actress Jane Darwell in her last screen appearance) surrounded by loving pigeons. Louis Prima and Gia Maione recorded the ballad together.

"Feelin' High" is the high-flying number that Shirley Ross and Harry Barris sang in the star-packed *Hollywood Party* (1934). Howard Dietz wrote the breezy lyric about the buoyant feeling of love, and Walter Donaldson composed the music, one of only two songs the prolific songwriters ever collaborated on.

"A Fella With an Umbrella" is the nimble number Peter Lawford sang to Judy Garland as they got acquainted in *Easter Parade* (1948). During a surprise shower on a New York City street, Lawford grabbed a sidewalk vendor's oversized umbrella and protected Garland from the rain as he crooned the Irving Berlin song. Lawford could barely get the simple ditty out, but Bing Crosby's recording gave the number its full flavor.

"Fiddle Dee Dee" is the bouncy song by Sammy Cahn (lyric) and Jule Styne (music) that waitress Doris Day sang in the Hollywood spoof *It's a Great Feeling* (1949). Johnny Desmond recorded it, as did the bands of Lionel Hampton, Guy Lombardo, and Jimmy Dorsey.

"Fidgety One" is the effervescent song-and-dance number that Frank Loesser (lyric) and Matt Malneck (music) wrote for the Jack Benny vehicle *Man About Town* (1939). Eddie "Rochester" Anderson and Betty Grable (in a cameo role) performed the celebratory song about the need to dance, displaying some fancy footwork that was the highlight of the film.

"Fifi" is the sly Parisian pastiche song that Sam Coslow wrote for Mae West in *Every Day's a Holiday* (1937). The song tells of a Brooklyn gal who dons a black wig and tries to pass herself off as a French music hall star. According to Coslow, West was having so much trouble with the script that when she saw the song, she threw out most of the old screenplay and fashioned a new one based on the number.

"Fifi From the Folies Bergère" was a silly can-can number performed by Dorothy Lamour shaking off her sarong image in *Slightly French* (1949). Lester Lee and Allan Roberts wrote the song, which Irish cooch dancer Lamour sang after being coached in the Gallic nuances by Don Ameche.

"Fill the World With Love" is the inspiring school song that Leslie Bricusse wrote for the musical version of the beloved classic novella *Goodbye, Mr. Chips* (1969). It was sung by the students at the all-boy "public" school a handful of times throughout the film, and like any good school song, it is optimistic in its lyric and rather stirring in its music.

"A Fine Romance" is the marvelous duet from *Swing Time* (1936) that lyricist Dorothy Fields subtitled "a sarcastic love song" and is one of the best singing moments in any Fred Astaire and Ginger Rogers film. The song was actually cut up with bits of dialogue, making it a true musical scene, as Astaire and Rogers walked through a snowy woodland setting and sang about the strange (or lack of) romance they were experiencing. Jerome Kern composed the delectable music that abandons his usual operetta melody line and opts instead for brief groupings of notes with longer intervals. According to Alec Wilder, the music "keeps piling up, tossing in pleasantries and surprises, and has a wonderful quality of uninterrupted movement." Fields' lyric (which was, atypical for Kern, written before the music) is among her finest as she explores funny but apt metaphors (as chilly as leftover mashed potatoes or as difficult to steer as the *Ile de France*) and even subtly shifts the pronunciation of the word "romance" to create different meanings. Even the title is ambiguous; Philip Furia suggests it is taken from the expression "a fine kettle of fish" and thereby is meant to be sarcastic from the start. Astaire's recording was Number One on the charts, Bing Crosby and Dixie Lee made a popular duet recording of the song, and there have been memorable versions by Guy Lombardo and his Royal Canadians, Ella Fitzgerald and Louis Armstrong, Johnny Mercer and Martha Stilton, Billie Holiday, Lena Horne, Frederica von Stade, Ann Hampton Callaway, and Michael Feinstein (whose 1988 recording restored a lost verse for Astaire that was never used in the film). Virginia O'Brien sang "A Fine Romance" in the Kern film bio-musical *Till the Clouds Roll By* (1946), and in the Broadway revue *Jerome Kern Goes to Hollywood* (1986) the duet was performed by Elaine Delmar and Scott Holmes.

"The First Thing You Know" is one of the handful of new songs Alan Jay Lerner (lyric) and André Previn (music) wrote for the 1969 film version of Lerner and Frederick Loewe's Broadway gold rush musical *Paint Your Wagon*. Lone prospector Lee Marvin growled the song about how civilization was ruining everything in life.

"First You Have Me High, Then You Have Me Low" is the gutsy ballad by Lew Brown (lyric) and Harold Arlen (music) that laments the roller coaster of emotions during a love affair. Ethel Merman belted the number in the Eddie Cantor vehicle *Strike Me Pink* (1936) about the amusement park business.

"Five Minutes More" is the hit ballad from the musical remake *Sweetheart of Sigma Chi* (1946) that was on *Your Hit Parade* for sixteen weeks. Phil Brito sang the song by Sammy Cahn (lyric) and Jule Styne (music) that pleaded for more time with one's sweetheart. A recording by Frank Sinatra was a bestseller and other popular recordings were made by Tex Beneke and his Orchestra, Johnnie Johnston, the Three Suns, and Skitch Henderson (vocal by Ray Kellogg).

"The Five Pennies" is the Oscar-nominated title song from the 1959 bio-musical of jazz cornet player Red Nichols as played by Danny Kaye. Sylvia Fine wrote the childlike number that counted out five special pennies, each one a gift guaranteed to bring happiness. Kaye and Louis Armstrong sang it and played it together in a nightclub as a red hot jazz number, the original Nichols providing the cornet playing on the soundtrack and Armstrong holding his own. Later in the film Nichols' young daughter Susan Gordon sang the song contrapuntally with Kaye singing "Lullaby in Ragtime" and Armstrong singing "Good Night, Sleep Tight." At the end of the movie, Barbara Bel Geddes (dubbed by Eileen Wilson) reprised it tearfully as Kaye danced with his grownup daughter Tuesday Weld.

"Flirtation Walk" is the sugary title song by Mort Dixon (lyric) and Allie Wrubel (music) from the 1934 patriotic musical set at West Point Academy. Cadet Dick Powell and his girlfriend Ruby Keeler sang the number as they strolled across the famous campus. Popular recordings were made during the 1930s by Powell, Irving Aaronson (vocal by Lew Sherwood), Hal Kemp (vocal by Skinnay Ennis), George Hall (vocal by Sonny Schuyler), and Victor Young's Orchestra, and the serenade was revived in the 1950s by Elliott Lawrence and his Orchestra and, later, by Gordon MacRae. Powell's recording was used effectively on the soundtrack for the Depression comedy *Paper Moon* (1973).

"Flying Down to Rio" is the Latin-flavored title song from the 1933 landmark musical and the inspiration for one of Hollywood's silliest yet most memorable production numbers. Because the hotel in Rio de Janeiro could not get an entertainment permit, Fred Astaire sang the song and the chorus girls joined in on airplanes as they flew over the audience below. The sequence (staged by Dave Gould), with the girls strapped to the wings of the biplanes as they did barnstorming stunts, is one of the most ridiculous and sublime of all musical scenes, often parodied, as in the film *The Boy Friend* (1971) and the Broadway musical *Steel Pier* (1997). Gus Kahn and Edward Eliscu wrote the sprightly lyric, and Vincent Youmans (in his first screen assignment) composed the pioneering samba music that had the forceful propulsion of an airplane engine. Astaire and Rudy Vallee each made estimable recordings of the song.

"A Foggy Day (in London Town)" is the enthralling song by the Gershwin brothers that Fred Astaire sang and seemed to float on air with in *Damsel in Distress* (1937). Ironically, the song was featured in a scene far away from London. American entertainer Astaire wandered the foggy grounds of Totleigh Castle and recalled how his loneliness lifted up like the fog when that special someone first appeared to him. Legend has it that the effortlessly graceful ballad was written in less than an hour. George Gershwin's music is light as a feather, even with its Irish flavor in the verse, and Ira Gershwin's lyric is a classic example of words sitting so comfortably on the notes that music and lyric seem inseparable. Astaire recorded the song, as did Hal Kemp (vocal by Skinnay Ennis) and Bob Crosby (vocal by Kay Weber). Les Brown and his Orchestra revived interest in the ballad in the 1950s, Sarah Vaughan recorded it in the 1960s, and Frank Sinatra sang it with great success on records and in nightclubs. Bobby Short made a noteworthy recording in 1990.

"The Folks Who Live on the Hill" is the devoted domestic ballad, perhaps the finest of its kind in all filmdom, that Oscar Hammerstein (lyric) and Jerome Kern (music) wrote for the pioneer musical *High, Wide and Handsome* (1937). Irene Dunne, as a nineteenth-century Pennsylvania woman, sang the tender number about growing old together to her new husband Randolph Scott as they sat on their hill and dreamed of the future. Kern's music is appropriately simple and wistful, and Hammerstein's lyric is filled with the kind of rural charm that he would develop further six years later in the Broadway musical *Oklahoma!* Although written for the mid-1800s setting of the film, the ballad echoed the sentiments of many Americans just coming out of the Depression and the song was very popular. Bing Crosby, Maxine Sullivan, Guy Lombardo and his Royal Canadians, Stan Getz, and Ozzie Nelson (vocal by Harriet Hilliard) were among the best of the many early records, and recent recordings by Judy Kaye with David Green and by Andrea Marcovicci have shown that the song has lost none of its power. Scott Holmes sang the ballad in the Broadway revue *Jerome Kern Goes to Hollywood* (1986).

"Follow the Boys" is the throbbing Connie Francis hit song by Benny Davis and Ted Murray that served as the title number for the 1962 sequel to *Where the Boys Are* (1960). Francis, as one of a group of "seagulls" who follow sailors from port to port, sang the pop ballad, and her recording was a bestseller.

"Follow the Yellow Brick Road" is the brief but unforgettable musical number in *The Wizard of Oz* (1939) that leads into "We're Off to See the Wizard." The citizens of Munchkinland sang the musical advice (taken from the good witch Glinda) to Dorothy (Judy Garland), who joined them in singing it as she set off for the Emerald City. Harold Arlen composed the simple ascending-descending scales and E. Y. Harburg penned the lyric that suggested one pursue the man who "follows the dream," a phrase he would later develop into the beguiling ballad "Look to the Rainbow" eight years later on Broadway.

"Follow Your Heart" is the Parisian ditty by Jack Feldman, Bruce Sussman (lyric), and Barry Manilow (music) that was used throughout the animated fantasy *Thumbelina* (1994). At the beginning of the film, the sparrow Jacquesmo (voice of Gino Conforti) sang the catchy song about the magical things that will happen if you trust your heart. Later in the story he and a chorus of singing bugs reprised it to Thumbelina to encourage her to seek out her prince. The French-flavored number is also repeated by the chorus at the film's happy ending.

"For Every Man There's a Woman" is the Oscar-nominated hit ballad by Leo Robin (lyric) and Harold Arlen (music) that Tony Martin sang at various points in the exotic romance *Casbah* (1948). Algiers thief Martin first delivered the ballad of fated love as he stood on a balcony overlooking the Casbah section in Algiers. Later he crooned it to Marta Toren as they danced at a nightclub. Finally, Yvonne De Carlo sang it to Martin in her tobacco shop as she mocked his love for the unsuspecting Toren. Alec Wilder has accurately described Arlen's alluring music in the song as "a moaner, in minor, with a slow beat and many harmonic changes." Martin's recording of the number was very popular, as was Peggy Lee's with Benny Goodman's Orchestra.

"For You, for Me, for Evermore" is probably the last new love song by the Gershwin brothers to be heard in public. George Gershwin composed the melody around 1936 but filed it away unused. For the period musical *The Shocking Miss Pilgrim* (1947), composer Kay Swift helped Ira Gershwin adapt the deceased Gershwin's music, and with a new lyric it was sung by Boston businessman Dick Haymes and his "typewriter" Betty Grable as they sat on the staircase of the boarding house where she lived. Ira Gershwin's lyric, about the discovery of mutual love and the promise of eternally sustaining it, is one of his least slangy but most heartfelt. Haymes recorded the ballad as a duet with Judy Garland, and there were also successful records by Benny Goodman (vocal by Eve Young), Jane Froman, and Mel Tormé with Artie Shaw's Orchestra.

"Fortuosity" is the silly song of philosophy by Richard M. and Robert B. Sherman that optimistically believes that good luck will always turn up. Newly arrived Irish butler Tommy Steele sang the antic number in *The Happiest Millionaire* (1967) as he walked the streets of Philadelphia on his way to a job interview. Later in the period musical Steele reprised it as he chased down the pet alligators of his eccentric employer.

"Forty-Second Street" is the compelling title song by Al Dubin (lyric) and Harry Warren (music) from the landmark 1933 backstage musical. The song itself is dark and rather sinister as it hypnotically invites one to come to that "naughty, bawdy, gaudy, sporty" Manhattan thoroughfare. Busby Berkeley's brilliant staging of the number brought out all the song's tawdry elements. The song was first sung by cab driver Ruby Keeler as she tapped out the number on the roof of her cab. Then a montage of violent and seductive scenes of life on the street was seen, climaxing in a jealous lover stabbing his girl. Finally, Dick Powell and a chorus of girls standing on a staircase sang the song as they formed the skyline of Manhattan by holding up flat cutouts of various buildings. The orchestras of Don Bestor and Hal Kemp each had popular recordings of the song. In the 1980 Broadway version (spelled *42nd Street*), Wanda Richert, Lee Roy Reams, and the ensemble performed it as the musical's climax. In a 1994 recording of the complete *Forty-Second Street* score, Debbie Shapiro Gravitte sang the title number.

"Freebootin' " is the musical salute to laziness that Tom Sawyer (Johnny Whitaker) and Huck Finn (Jeff East) sang together in the period musical *Tom Sawyer* (1973). Richard M. and Robert B. Sherman wrote the breezy number about the art of wasting time.

"Freedonia Hymn" is the mock patriotic national anthem sung several times by the citizens of Freedonia in the Marx Brothers vehicle *Duck Soup* (1933). Bert Kalmar wrote the appropriately insipid lyric ("hail, hail, Freedonia, land of the free"), and Harry Ruby composed the music that, like many anthems, climbs the scale until no one can comfortably sing it.

"The French Lesson" is one of two new numbers written for the 1947 film version of the 1927 Broadway hit *Good News*. In a clever musical scene, librarian June Allyson tried to teach football star Peter Lawford the basics of the French language so he can pass an important test and be allowed to play in the big game. Roger Edens composed the sprightly music, and Betty Comden and

Adolph Green wrote the ingenious conversational lyric. Allyson and Lawford recorded the number as duet.

"Friend Like Me" is the show–stopping character song from the animated comic fantasy *Aladdin* (1992) in which the exuberant Genie (voice of Robin Williams), just released from the lamp after hundreds of years, sang to Aladdin about the magical powers he possessed and how his friendship will take the youth to the top. While the Oscar-nominated song has its charm, it was overshadowed by Williams' vocal pyrotechnics and the Disney animators' Hirschfeld–like artwork in bringing the Genie to life. The song was one of the few that Alan Menken (music) and Howard Ashman (lyric) completed years earlier, before they dropped the project. The delightful number was later interpolated into the Menken–Tim Rice score.

"Friendly Star" is the bittersweet song of longing that New England farm girl Judy Garland sang in the backstager *Summer Stock* (1950). Mack Gordon (lyric) and Harry Warren (music) wrote the touching plea for a kindred spirit, and Garland's recording was somewhat popular. A distinctive record of the ballad was also made by Margaret Whiting.

"From the Top of Your Head (to the Tip of Your Toe)" is the hyperbolic tribute to a sweetheart's physical perfection, as sung by songwriter Bing Crosby to his beloved Joan Bennett in *Two for Tonight* (1935). Mack Gordon (lyric) and Harry Revel (music) wrote the buoyantly affectionate number, and Crosby recorded it with success.

"From This Moment On" is the zesty Cole Porter hit that was Broadway's loss and Hollywood's gain. The eager ballad that looked forward to love and better times was written for the stage musical *Out of This World* (1950) but was cut from the show out of town. Porter interpolated it into the score for the 1953 film version of his Broadway smash *Kiss Me, Kate* where it was sung in the *Taming of the Shrew* show by Ann Miller and her three beaus (Tommy Rall, Bobby Van, and Bob Fosse), and then danced by all, with Carol Haney and Jeannie Coyne joining in to even out the couples. Parenthetically, the vibrant dance section was devised by Haney and Fosse, the first such staging attempt by future director-choreographer Fosse. Frank Sinatra's recording made the song popular.

"The Fuddy Duddy Watchmaker" is the novelty number that Frank Loesser (lyric) and Jimmy McHugh (music) wrote for dynamo Betty Hutton in the Caribbean-set musical *Happy Go Lucky* (1943). At a charity show at a ritzy hotel, Hutton and the Sportsmen sang the slaphappy number about a 103-year-old watchmaker whose talent for creating timepieces with a perfect beat is a mystery and sets everyone to swinging. Kay Kyser (vocal by Julie Conway) made a recording of the boogie–woogie number.

"Funny Girl" is the somber title song for the 1968 film version of the Broadway hit and one of three numbers added for the movie score. Bob Merrill (lyric) and Jule Styne (music) wrote the melancholy ballad, about the heartbreak of not being taken seriously, for the stage version, but it was cut before opening. In the film Fanny Brice (Barbra Streisand) sang the Oscar-nominated song quietly to herself after her husband Omar Sharif left her.

"The Funny Old Hills" is a playful comedy number that Leo Robin (lyric) and Ralph Rainger (music) wrote for the Bing Crosby vehicle *Paris Honeymoon* (1938). Texas millionaire Crosby and Edward Everett Horton sang the rhythmic number, comically echoing each other in both words and music. Crosby made a solo recording of the song, but it was not nearly as much fun.

G

"A Gal in Calico" is the pseudo–western favorite about a cowboy who longs to marry his pretty calico-clad sweetheart and make a home with her in Santa Fe. Arthur Schwartz wrote the melody in 1934 as the theme song for a radio show then, when a country tune was needed for *The Time, the Place and the Girl* (1946), Leo Robin wrote the narrative lyric, which was sung in the film by Dennis Morgan and Jack Carson as part of a Broadway-bound show. LeRoy Prinz staged the fun number with Martha Vickers (dressed in calico) as the sweetheart of the song and a chorus of cowgirls dancing and twirling ropes in a corral. The Oscar-nominated number is a superior rhythm song, Alec Wilder describing it as "cheery, strong, swinging and professional." Popular recordings of the country ditty were made by Bing Crosby, Johnny Mercer, Tex Beneke and his Orchestra, and Benny Goodman (vocal by Eve Young).

"Gaston" is the vigorous character song by Howard Ashman (lyric) and Alan Menken (music) about the broad-shouldered, thick-headed villain in the animated fairy tale *Beauty and the Beast* (1991). Gaston (voice of Richard White) had been turned down by Belle, so his sidekick Lefou (voice of Jesse Corti) and the patrons at Gaston's tavern cheered him up with this boneheaded tribute to the man of brawn. The number was reprised later by Gaston and Lefou with different lyrics as they planned to use Belle's father's insanity as a way to win Belle's hand in marriage. The fast-paced waltz number was sung by Burke Moses, Kenny Raskin, and the ensemble in the 1994 Broadway version of the tale.

"Get Thee Behind Me, Satan" is the hesitant Irving Berlin ballad that was written for Ginger Rogers to sing in *Top Hat* (1935) but was cut, so the song was interpolated into his score for *Follow the Fleet* (1936). Harriet Hilliard, having just met Randolph Scott and afraid that she'll fall in love with him, sang the quiet number in which Berlin cleverly used a biblical reference to convey a modern sentiment. Hilliard recorded the number with Ozzie Nelson's Orchestra.

"Getting Nowhere" is the philosophical ballad by Irving Berlin commenting on how much of life is taken up with endlessly meaningless activity, from a dog chasing its tail to a carousel revolving and going nowhere. The song was one of the four new numbers that Irving Berlin wrote for the hit-packed *Blue Skies* (1946), where Bing Crosby sang the lullabylike number to his daughter Karolyn Grimes as he played the toy piano in her bedroom. The song is sometimes listed as "Running Around in Circles Getting Nowhere."

"Gigi" is the scintillating title song from the 1958 period musical where Paris playboy Louis Jourdan realized that he has fallen in love with the tomboyish heroine. The song is a masterwork of dramatic and musical craftsmanship, Frederick Loewe's music gushing forth with discovery and Alan Jay Lerner's lyric finding refreshing ways to express newfound love. The number serves the same purpose as did the songwriting team's "I've Grown Accustomed to Her Face" in the play and film *My Fair Lady*, in both cases the stuffy bachelor being the last to realize he has fallen in love. Yet "Gigi" has a less-reserved sense of expression and imagery, citing that "warmth becomes desire" and describing the young girl as on the edge of new life. The number is unusual for a film song in that it has a very long verse that teases the audience before gliding into the sparkling refrain. "Gigi" won the Best Song Oscar, remained one of Lerner's favorites all his life, and received many recordings, the most popular being one by Vic Damone. In the 1973 Broadway version of the film, Daniel Massey sang the ballad.

"The Girl at the Ironing Board" is the Al Dubin (lyric) and Harry Warren (music) number that served as a springboard for one of choreographer Busby Berkeley's most ingenious routines. In the backstager *Dames* (1934), laundress Joan Blondell sang wistfully about a perfect mate to a stack of men's pajamas and underwear when suddenly the laundry came to life and washwoman and clothes did a dance routine together. The illusion was created by having fifty men in the rafters working the clothes like marionettes. Also, Blondell's movements are cleverly hidden throughout the number (the star was very much pregnant at the time of the shooting).

"The Girl Can't Help It" is the popular rhythm-and-blues title song from the 1957 Jane Mansfield vehicle that spoofed the rock-and-roll business. John Marascalco and Robert A. Blackwell wrote the robust song, and Little Richard sang it in the film and on a Top Ten record.

"Girl for All Seasons" is the daffy pastiche number from the musical sequel *Grease 2* (1982) that spoofed those catchy girl-group songs from the 1960s. Dominic Bugetti and Frank Musker wrote the ditty, heard in part at various rehearsals for the high school talent show. For the actual performance, it was sung by Lorna Luft, Michelle Pfeiffer, Maureen Teefy, and Alison Price, each ludicrously dressed as a different season of the year.

"The Girl Friend of the Whirling Dervish" is the hilarious novelty number written by Al Dubin, Johnny Mercer (lyric), and Harry Warren (music) for *Garden of the Moon* (1938). Nightclub bandleader John Payne, Johnny "Scat" Davis, Ray Meyer, Joe Venuti, and Jerry Colonna (in drag as the "girl friend") performed the narrative number, which told of a Hindu monk who fell for a two-timing gal and how he was left with the same old runaround. Van Alexander (vocal by Butch Stone), Skinnay Ennis, and Guy Lombardo each made recordings close to the time the film was released. Cabaret singer Spider Saloff made a distinctive recording in 1989, and the song was used as background in the film musical *For the Boys* (1991).

"The Girl I Love to Leave Behind" is a little-known Richard Rodgers and Lorenz Hart comedy song that Ray Bolger sang and danced to in the wartime musical *Stage Door Canteen* (1943). The songwriting team had originally written a number called "The Boy I Left Behind" for their 1942 Broadway musical *By Jupiter,* which starred Bolger. Hart reworked the lyric into a funny piece about the dreadful girls ("known to daddy as 'mother's mistake'") that forced men to enlist just so they could go overseas to escape their clutches.

"The Girl I Never Loved" is the torchy ballad by Randy Starr that admits an inability to tell a beloved one about his love for her. Millionaire-in-disguise Elvis Presley sang the number on a lonely beach in *Clambake* (1967) as he pined for gold digger Shelly Fabares.

"Girl in the Wood" is the crooning ballad Frankie Laine sang in the Hollywood satire *Rainbow Round My Shoulder* (1952). Brothers Terry, Neal, and Stuart Gilkyson wrote the throbbing number about a true love in the wild, and Laine's recording with Paul Weston's Orchestra was fairly popular.

"The Girl on the Police Gazette" is the Irving Berlin number in *On the Avenue* (1937) that pastiches the old-time songs saluting pretty women, the kind of song Berlin himself often wrote a few decades earlier. Dick Powell, Alice Faye, and the chorus performed the number, about one man's love for the girl in tights on the cover of the once-notorious tabloid, as part of a Broadway revue. Powell recorded the song, as did Russ Morgan, Shep Fields, Wayne King, and Abe Lyman (vocal by Sonny Schuyler).

"A Girl Worth Fighting For" is a delightfully ironic comic number that David Zippel (lyric) and Matthew Wilder (music) wrote for the animated adventure musical *Mulan* (1998). As they march through the mountains of China, a band of new recruits (voices by Harvey Fierstein, James Hong, Jerry Tondo, Wilder and the chorus) sang of the type of girl they desire, from a ravishing beauty to a good cook. When the girl-in-disguise Mulan (singing voice of Lea Salonga) suggests a bright woman who thinks for herself, the others dismiss the idea as unattractive.

"Girls Were Made to Take Care of Boys" is the pseudo-old-fashioned song with an old-fashioned sentiment that Ralph Blane wrote for the period musical *One Sunday Afternoon* (1948). Dorothy Malone sang the musical lesson, which encouraged girls to help boys by offering comfort, understanding, and affection, while the boys provided the worldly necessities. Rose Murphy and Herb Jeffries each recorded the song, and there were later notable disks by Gordon MacRae and Jo Stafford.

"Give a Little Whistle" is the tuneful song of warning to "always let your conscience be your guide" from the animated fairy tale classic *Pinocchio* (1940). Ned Washington (lyric) and Leigh Harline (music) wrote the snappy number, sung by Pinocchio (voice of Dickie Jones) and Jiminy Cricket (voice of Cliff Edwards) as they danced about Gepetto's toy shop and celebrated Jiminy being made Pinocchio's conscience by the Blue Fairy. Edwards recorded the song, which, as the title suggests, involved a certain amount of whistling.

"Give Her a Kiss" was perhaps the finest ballad Lorenz Hart (lyric) and Richard Rodgers (music) wrote for the political musical *The Phantom President* (1932), but it was practically hidden in the film. As George M. Cohan and Claudette Colbert drove out to the country, two unidentified vocalists were heard on the car's radio singing the gentle ballad that encouraged the shy suitor to take advantage of the pristine setting and kiss the girl.

"Give Me a Band and My Baby" is the vivacious call for music and love that Leo Robin (lyric) and Jule Styne (music) wrote for the musical version of *My Sister Eileen* (1955). The lively number was sung and danced to by sisters Betty Garrett and Janet Leigh with Tommy Rall and Bob Fosse (who also choreographed the piece).

"Give Me a Heart to Sing To" is the heartrending plea sung by casino singer Helen Morgan in *Frankie and Johnny* (1936), the musical based on the famous song. Ned Washington (lyric) and Victor Young (music) wrote the passionate number in 1934, but it and the whole film sat on the shelf for two years because of censorship problems. The ballad eventually found some favor through a recording by Guy Lombardo (vocal by Carmen Lombardo).

"Give Me a Moment, Please" is an operetta love duet that was sung, somewhat incongruously, over the telephone by countess-on-the-run Jeanette MacDonald and count-in-disguise Jack Buchanan in *Monte Carlo* (1930). Richard Whiting and W. Franke Harling collaborated on the Friml–like music, and Leo Robin provided the stylish lyric. The song became violinist Dave Rubinoff's theme song on his radio show.

"Give Me Liberty or Give Me Love" is the march-tempo torch song sung by fallen woman-turned-singing-star Claudette Colbert in the musical melodrama *Torch Singer* (1933). Leo Robin penned the urgent lyric, and Ralph Rainger composed the limited-range music for Colbert, who did her own singing and effectively pulled off a Marlene Dietrich kind of groaning lament. Recordings of the song were made by Mildred Bailey, Irene Taylor, and Annette Hanshaw.

"Give Me the Simple Life" is the upbeat ballad that yearns for a life free from complications and entanglements, as expressed by June Haver and John Payne in *Wake Up and Dream* (1946). Harry Ruby (lyric) and Rube Bloom (music) wrote the song, which became popular through a recording by Sammy Kaye and his Orchestra. Recordings were also made by Bing Crosby with Jimmy Dorsey's Orchestra and Benny Goodman (vocal by Liz Morrow). The song was featured in the film musical *Let's Make Love* (1960).

"Give Your Baby Lots of Lovin'" is the pathetically cheery song of advice that was used to great dramatic effect throughout the early musical drama *Applause* (1929). Over-the-hill burlesque queen Helen Morgan sang the number by Dolly Morse (lyric) and Joe Burke (music) to her daughter Joan Peers, and the song was used as a leit motif throughout the film to illustrate the affection between mother and daughter. Later, when the desperate Morgan sings the song onstage as part of a vulgar dance, Peers looks on in disgust. The same song was sung even later by Peers herself on stage, and the performance supposedly made her a star.

"Go Fly a Kite" is one of the ballads Bing Crosby sang as showman Gus Edwards in the bio-musical *The Star Maker* (1939). This childlike ditty was written by Johnny Burke (lyric) and James Monaco (music), and there were successful recordings of it by Crosby, Artie Shaw, and Tommy Dorsey.

"Go Home and Tell Your Mother (That She Certainly Did a Wonderful Job on You)" is the charming duet that Dorothy Fields (lyric) and Jimmy McHugh (music) wrote for the golf musical *Love in the Rough* (1930), their first Hollywood score. Store clerk Robert Montgomery and heiress Dorothy Jordan sang the number on the golf course with a caddie conveniently at hand to provide harmonica accompaniment. The number was reprised later in the film by the Biltmore Trio during a party scene. The song became quite popular thanks to recordings by Gus Arnheim, Johnny Marvin, Guy Lombardo and the Royal Canadians, and Don Voorhees's Orchestra.

"Go Into Your Dance" is the vivacious song of advice for chasing off the blues by Al Dubin (lyric) and Harry Warren (music) and the title number from the 1935 backstager starring Al Jolson, who performed the catchy song in a nightclub setting. In the Broadway musical *42nd Street* (1980), the number was performed by Wanda Richert, Lee Roy Reams, Karen Prunczik, Ginny King, Carole Cook, Jeri Kansas, and the chorus.

"Go the Distance" is the stirring "I am" song of the teenage Hercules (voice of Roger Bart) as he lamented his awkward super strength and set off to find his true identity in the animated adventure *Hercules* (1997). Alan Menken composed the penetrating music, David Zippell provided the eager lyrics, and Michael Bolton's recording of the Oscar-nominated song was very popular.

"Go to Sleep" is one of two new numbers that Alan Jay Lerner (lyric) and Burton Lane (music) wrote for the 1970 film version of their Broadway ESP musical *On a Clear Day You Can See Forever*. Naive but psychic Barbra Streisand was starting to fall for the dashing psychology professor Yves Montand even though she was engaged to a dull businessman. As she tried to go to sleep, she and her alter ego argued in duet format about her predicament. Lerner's lyric is an ingenious conversation in song, and Burton's music is light and frothy. Streisand performed the two contrasting characters and attitudes with effortless skill.

"Go West, Young Man" is the daffy comic song that Bert Kalmar (lyric) and Harry Ruby (music) wrote for Groucho Marx to sing in a nightclub sequence in *Copacabana* (1947), the comic's first movie without his famous brothers. Dressed in his traditional tails, glasses, and painted mustache, Marx sang the silly song in a Wild West setting filled with cacti and sexy cowgirls, encouraging one to take Horace Greeley's advice and go farther west than Buffalo. During the number Marx did shrewd impersonations of Al Jolson and Jeanette MacDonald.

"God Help the Outcasts" is the simple hymn that the gypsy girl Esmerelda (singing voice of Heidi Mollenbauer) and others in the cathedral sang in the animated romance *The Hunchback of Notre Dame* (1996). Alan Menken composed the unadorned music, and Stephen Schwartz wrote the fervent lyric that asks for a blessing on all of life's rejected ones. Bette Midler made a noteworthy recording of the song.

"Goin' to Heaven on a Mule" was the pseudo-Negro spiritual that served as the finale for *Wonder Bar* (1934), and it has not dated well, John Kobel aptly calling it "one of Busby Berkeley's most tasteless numbers." Al Jolson, in blackface, arrived at the gate of St. Peter's and viewed a minstrel show–like heaven with 200 Negro angel-residents eating watermelon and pork chops. The song by Al Dubin (lyric) and Harry Warren (music) is actually quite accomplished and sincere, but the number is usually cut for television showings of the film.

"Going Hollywood" is the jaunty title song of the 1933 musical, one of the first about Tinsel Town itself. Bing Crosby sang the jolly song by Arthur Freed (lyric) and Nacio Herb Brown (music) as he set out from Grand Central Station for the golden West.

"Going My Way" is the gentle title ballad by Johnny Burke (lyric) and James Van Heusen (music) from the popular 1944 musical about a struggling Catholic parish in Manhattan. Newly arrived priest Bing Crosby first sang the song about following one's own dream to a young couple as a song he had just written. Opera star Risë Stevens later saw the sheet music, and soon she and the Robert Mitchell Boys Choir were singing it on the stage of the Met as an audition for a music publisher. (The publisher turned it down as not commercial enough; he was probably right, as "Going My Way" was never as popular as the other songs in the film.) Burke's lyric carefully avoids any overtly romantic phrases, since the song had to be sung by a priest, only going so far as to "hope you're going my way too." Mary Clare Haran made a distinctive recording of the ballad in 1994, and Lewis Cleale sang it in the Broadway revue *Swinging on a Star* (1995).

"Good Mornin' " is the raucous greeting to the new day sung by mountain gal Martha Raye in the hillbilly musical *Mountain Music* (1937). Sam Coslow wrote the bombastic number, and Raye's recording was a hit, as was, to a lesser extent, one by Tommy Dorsey (vocal by Edythe Wright). The familiar ditty was also known as the musical jingle for twenty years of Kellogg's Corn Flakes commercials.

"Good Morning" is the chipper duet that Mickey Rooney and Judy Garland sang in a music publisher's office in the backstager *Babes in Arms* (1939). Arthur Freed (lyric) and Nacio Herb Brown (music) wrote the number that was added to the Rodgers and Hart stage score and seemed to fit right in. Abe Lyman and his Orchestra made a moderately popular recording at the time. The upbeat song was revived years later when Debbie Reynolds, Gene Kelly, and

Donald O'Connor sang it in *Singin' in the Rain* (1952) and recorded it as a trio. In the 1985 Broadway version of *Singin' in the Rain*, the number was sung by Mary D'Arcy, Don Correia, and Peter Slutsker.

"Good Morning Glory" is the appealing ballad by Mack Gordon (lyric) and Harry Revel (music) about waking up to thoughts of one's beloved. Songwriters Jack Haley and Jack Oakie, with Ginger Rogers and the chorus, sang the bright number in *Sitting Pretty* (1933), and it became a popular Depression-chaser. The Pickens Sisters and George Hall (vocal by Loretta Lee) each had successful records, and the Hall recording was used effectively as background in the Depression-era film comedy *Brighton Beach Memoirs* (1986).

"Goodnight, Lovely Little Lady" is one of several warm lullaby ballads sung by Bing Crosby in films, this one distinguished by the fact that he sang it to a bear. Mack Gordon (lyric) and Harry Revel (music) wrote the pleasant number for *We're Not Dressing* (1934), in which shipwrecked sailor Crosby crooned it to his oversized pet to put her to sleep.

"Goodnight, My Love" is a lullaby from a Shirley Temple movie but became popular because of a recording by Alice Faye. Mack Gordon (lyric) and Harry Revel (music) wrote the tender song for *Stowaway* (1936), where orphan Temple sang it to put herself to sleep. The number was reprised later by Faye as she danced with millionaire husband Robert Young on the moonlit deck of their luxury yacht. Faye's recording was one of the biggest hits of her career, and a disk by Benny Goodman (vocal by Ella Fitzgerald) went to the top of the charts as well. Records by Shep Fields and his Orchestra and Hildegarde were also popular.

"Good-Time Charley" is the lively song-and-dance number that conmen Bing Crosby and Bob Hope performed in a small theatre in *Road to Utopia* (1945). James Van Heusen composed the vaudeville pastiche music, and Johnny Burke wrote the lyric about a fun-loving guy who happened to be "the loneliest man in town."

"The Gospel Truth" is the spirited opening song by David Zippel (lyric) and Alan Menken (music) from the animated musical *Hercules* (1997). The mock-gospel number was sung by the Muses (voices of Lilias White, La Chanze, Tawatha Agee, Roz Ryan, Cheryl Freeman, and Vanessa Thomas) as they began the adventure story, giving expositional information about the baby Hercules and generally setting the comic tone for the film.

"Got My Mind on Music" is the winning swing number that Mack Gordon (lyric) and Harry Revel (music) wrote for the backstager *Sally, Irene and*

Mary (1938). Singing manicurists Alice Faye, Joan Davis, and Marjorie Weaver (with the Raymond Scott Quintet) sang the song about how thinking of music makes one think about love, which makes one think about that special someone.

"Gotta Feelin' for You" is the snappy number by Jo Trent (lyric) and Louis Alter (music) that was part of the stellar lineup for *The Hollywood Revue of 1929* (1929), the first all-star movie musical revue. Paul Gibbons and the Biltmore Trio sang the Charleston number while Joan Crawford energetically danced a flapper routine. A 1929 recording by Frank Luther and the High Hatters was popular, and the song was featured in the film musical *Chasing Rainbows* (1930).

"Gotta Have Me Go With You" is the swinging song of inseparable devotion that Ira Gershwin (lyric) and Harold Arlen (music) wrote for the first musical version of *A Star Is Born* (1954). Unknown band vocalist Judy Garland sang the number with Don McKay and Jack Harmon in a benefit performance at the L.A. Shrine Auditorium, where they were joined by drunken movie star James Mason, who did a sloppy impromptu dance with Garland. Arlen's music uses a very unusual structure of a verse of twenty-four bars, eight of which are used twice in the forty-eight-bar refrain.

"Grease" is the rhythmic title song written by Barry Gibb for the 1978 film version of the long-running Broadway musical about the 1950s. The jaunty number was sung by Frankie Valli (accompanied by Peter Frampton on the guitar) during the cleverly animated opening credits, proudly proclaiming that "grease is the word." The Valli recording was a Number One hit, and there were successful British records by Carl Wayne and John Barrowman.

"Grouch Anthem" is the amusingly satiric opening song by Jeff Penning, Steve Pippin, and Jeff Harrington for the *Sesame Street* feature film musical *Follow That Bird* (1985). In a delicious spoof of the opening of the film biography *Patton* (1970), Oscar the Grouch (voice of Carroll Spinney) appeared before a huge American flag and urged all the grouches in the audience to "just stand up and complain."

"A Guy Like You" is the comic vaudeville-style number by Stephen Schwartz (lyric) and Alan Menken (music) that seemed out of place in the dark animated romance *The Hunchback of Notre Dame* (1996) but was delightful in its own way. Three cathedral gargoyles (singing voices of Jason Alexander, Mary Stout, and Charles Kimbrough) tried to cheer up hunchback Quasimodo (voice of Tom Hulce) by pointing out his unique features and the unusual appeal he must have for the ladies.

"A Guy What Takes His Time" is the suggestive number Mae West sang in her first starring feature, *She Done Him Wrong* (1933), a movie that did more to establish the Hay's Office Production Code than any other. Ralph Rainger composed the music, and he and West collaborated on the song's slangy lyric, which was not as naughty as her moaning delivery of it implied.

"G'wan, Your Mudder's Callin' " is the merry specialty number that Ralph Freed (lyric) and Sammy Fain (music) wrote for Jimmy Durante, utilizing his colorful New Yorkese. Manhattan piano-playing saloon owner Durante sang the ditty in the period musical *Two Sisters From Boston* (1946).

H

"Hakuna Matata" is the dandy Oscar-nominated song of "problem-free philosophy" that Tim Rice (lyric) and Elton John (music) wrote for the animated musical *The Lion King* (1994). Meercat Timon (voice of Nathan Lane) and warthog Pumba (voice of Ernie Sabella) tried to cheer up the guilt-ridden lion cub Simba (singing voice of Jason Weaver) with this snappy number, the title being an African expression for "no worries for the rest of your days." Young Simba joined in, and in a montage showing the passage of time, grown-up Simba (voice of Matthew Broderick) joined them as well. In the 1997 Broadway version of *The Lion King*, the waggish number was sung by Max Casella, Tom Alan Robbins, Scott Irby-Ranniar, and Jason Raize.

"Half Moon on the Hudson" is the romantic duet that Alice Faye and Tony Martin sang in the moonlight in *Sally, Irene and Mary* (1938), proclaiming to be "more than half in love with you." Harold Spina composed the flowing music, and Walter Bullock penned the lyric that referred to Henry Hudson's famous ship and to the half moon in the sky for the lovers.

"Hallelujah, I'm a Bum" is the philosophical title song about being free and easy that Lorenz Hart (lyric) and Richard Rodgers (music) wrote for the experimental 1933 musical film. Al Jolson, in what is arguably his finest screen performance, played a Central Park bum and sang this exceptional number in the Depression musical. Both song and film title had to be changed to "Hallelujah, I'm a Tramp" in Great Britain (where "bum" means "buttocks"), and Jolson recorded the song with each title. Mary Cleere Haran made a distinctive recording of the number in 1998.

"Hallowe'en" is the lighthearted tribute to that musically neglected holiday on October 31. The verse of the song by Ralph Blane (lyric) and Harold Arlen (music) points out that Irving Berlin penned songs for just about all the holidays but he forgot Halloween. Betty Grable, Jane Wyatt, Dan Dailey, and David Wayne sang the happy paean as an impromptu entertainment piece in the show biz musical *My Blue Heaven* (1950).

"Hang on to Your Lids, Kids (Here We Go Again)" is the sparkling riff song by Johnny Mercer (lyric) and Harold Arlen (music) from *Blues in the Night* (1941), the musical melodrama about itinerant jazz musicians. Band singer Priscilla Lane and fellow band musicians sang the jumping number as stowaways being tossed about in a railroad boxcar. Arlen effectively repeats riffs in the perky music, and Mercer's lyric is full of colorful jive, such as hold on to "your hopes, dopes."

"Hang Your Heart on a Hickory Limb" is the upbeat precautionary song that warns one of the heartache of love, so it is best to avoid love at all costs. Johnny Burke (lyric) and James Monaco (music) wrote the tangy number for *East Side of Heaven* (1939), where it was sung in a cafe by singing cab driver Bing Crosby, owner Jane Jones, two chefs, and a host of waitresses called The Music Maids. Crosby recorded the number, which was the hit of the film.

"Happiness Ahead" is the optimistic title song by Mort Dixon (lyric) and Allie Wrubel (music) for the 1934 musical about the business world. Dick Powell, as the owner of a window–washing company, sang the number and also recorded it, as did the Pickens Sisters and Ted Lewis and his Orchestra. The song is sometimes listed as "There Must Be Happiness Ahead."

"Happiness Is (Just) a Thing Called Joe" is the beloved ballad of contentment that E. Y. Harburg (lyric) and Harold Arlen (music) wrote for the 1943 film version of the Broadway Negro folk musical *Cabin in the Sky*. Long-suffering wife Ethel Waters sang the optimistic blues number about her newly reformed gambling husband Eddie "Rochester" Anderson, and the Oscar-nominated song became popular partly as a result of a recording by Woody Herman (vocal by Frances Wayne). Judy Garland's record of the song was superlative, and years later Della Reese made a noteworthy recording as well. Arlen's music is smooth and seemingly effortless, and Harburg's straightforward and atypical unclever lyric is filled with homespun imagery ("he's got a smile that makes the lilac wanna grow") and hidden internal rhymes that gently fall into place without notice. Susan Hayward sang the ballad in the Lillian Roth bio-film *I'll Cry Tomorrow* (1955).

"Happy Days Are Here Again" is arguably the best of the

Depression-chasing songs and one that has remained popular over the decades. Jack Yellen (lyric) and Milton Ager (music) wrote the optimistic number for the backstager *Chasing Rainbows* (1930), but it was cut from the final script. George Olsen and his Band played the song in a hotel ballroom soon after the Crash for a crowd of downhearted patrons, and the room exploded with enthusiasm. In Hollywood the band at the Roosevelt Hotel played it one night, and when producer Irving Thalberg wanted to know why MGM never came up with such songs, he was informed that it was written for their own *Chasing Rainbows*. The number was recorded and written back into the film, where it was sung by Charles King and Bessie Love as they celebrate the end of World War One. The movie was not popular, but the whole country was soon singing the number, especially after it was adopted as Roosevelt's campaign song in 1932. (It would later serve the same purpose for the presidential campaigns of Harry Truman and John F. Kennedy.) The number became the theme song for Lucky Strike's radio show *Your Hit Parade*, so audiences heard it weekly for many years. Early recordings of "Happy Days Are Here Again" include popular disks by Ben Selvin and Leo Reisman, followed by dozens of others over the years. Barbra Streisand revived interest in the song in 1963 with her slow-tempo ballad approach to the rouser. The song has also been heard in several musical and nonmusical films, including *Thanks a Million* (1935), where it was sung by Fred Allen, Raymond Walburn, and Andrew Tombes; *Beau James* (1957); *This Earth Is Mine* (1959); and *Night of the Iguana* (1964) where it was sung by a bus load of American tourists. In the Broadway musical *Big Deal* (1986), the song was sung by Larry Marshall, Mel Johnson, Jr., Desiree Coleman, and the ensemble. A 1963 ASCAP poll cited "Happy Days Are Here Again" as one of the sixteen all-time *Hit Parade* songs.

"Happy Endings" is an expert song by Fred Ebb (lyric) and John Kander (music) about Hollywood's knack for finishing every story with a neat and satisfying conclusion. The number was used in an elaborate and lengthy production number in *New York, New York* (1977) that recalled the tongue-in-cheek "Born in a Trunk" sequence in *A Star Is Born* (1954). Usherette Liza Minnelli sang the song as she gazed at the movie screen and imagined that a Hollywood producer (Larry Kert) discovers her, makes her a Broadway star, and all ends happily. But the song and the stylized sequence was cut from the final print when *New York, New York* ran too long. It was restored in the 1981 reissue of the film, and Andrea Marcovicci made a wistful recording of the number in 1987.

"Happy Feet" is the toe-tapping number by Jack Yellen (lyric) and Milton Ager (music) from *King of Jazz* (1930) that inspired one of the most inventive sequences in early musical film. The song was performed by the Sisters G, Paul Whiteman's Orchestra, and the Rhythm Boys (Harry Barris, Al Rinker, and Bing

Crosby in their film debut); it was then danced to by Al Norman, the Markert Girls, and Paul Small. Director John Murray Anderson and choreographer Russell Markert came up with a dazzling production number using stop-action photography, double exposures, and special effects. A pair of disembodied shoes leapt out of a gift box and did a tap routine with Whiteman's Orchestra superimposed behind them. Then the Sisters G were seen in closeup, their faces seemingly floating in space and singing. Leo Reisman, Cab Calloway, and the Revelers each had successful early recordings of the song.

"Happy Go Lucky" is the title number about the anticipation of good fortune from the 1943 musical where gold digger Mary Martin and beachcomber Dick Powell sang the freewheeling song as a duet as they sailed along in his leaky boat. Jimmy McHugh composed the gently swinging music, and Frank Loesser supplied the carefree lyric.

"Happy Holiday" is the perennial ditty by Irving Berlin still heard around Christmastime, but the song makes no mention of that particular holiday. It was written as a sort of lietmotif for *Holiday Inn* (1942), where is was sung or played throughout the film to convey the passage of time and set up the various holiday shows. Inn owner Bing Crosby and entertainer Marjorie Reynolds (dubbed by Martha Mears) first sang the catchy number to the guests at the inn as part of the New Year's Eve show and soon all joined in. The release of the song is actually a different number, "Holiday Inn," in which Crosby and Reynolds/Mears urged folks to get away from the hustle and bustle of the city and come to the country retreat. Crosby's recording with John Scott Trotter's Orchestra was popular, and the song remains one of Berlin's most recognized compositions.

"A Hard Day's Night" is the hit title song by John Lennon from the Beatles' first film, the freewheeling 1964 musical film that took the form of a pseudo-documentary about a typical day for the popular foursome. The surging number was sung on the soundtrack by the Beatles (Paul McCartney was featured because he was the only one who could hit the high notes) during the opening credits of the film as they were seen running from a gang of overly eager female fans and again over the closing credits. The title came from an impromptu comment Ringo Starr had made after a tiring all-night recording session. Lennon took the phrase and in twenty-four hours the song was written, arranged, and recorded. The song's title was then made the title for the film. "A Hard Day's Night" was a Gold Record for the group, and an instrumental version by the Ramsey Lewis Trio in 1966 was also a hit. Diana Ross and the Supremes made a record of it, and British comic Peter Sellers made a novelty recording of the song, speaking the lyric as if he were Laurence Olivier reciting Shakespeare, and it made the Top Twenty in Britain.

"Hard Headed Woman" is the fast and furious rock-and-roll lament by Claude De Metrius that Elvis Presley sang in *King Creole* (1958). Presley's recording was a Number One hit. Ironically, only the last lines of the song were used in the film, and Presley's singing in a New Orleans club was heard offcamera while crowds gathered outside the Bourbon Street watering hole.

"Have You Got Any Castles, Baby?" is a swaggering song of confidence by Johnny Mercer (lyric) and Richard Whiting (music) offering to build castles and slay dragons, yet it was sung by a group of women. Priscilla Lane (in her screen debut) sang the number with the chorus girls of a college revue in a New York theatre in *Varsity Show* (1937). Dick Powell, who was also in the film, made a recording of the number popular enough to remain on *Your Hit Parade* for eleven weeks, helped by hit recordings by Tommy Dorsey and Dolly Dawn. In the Broadway revue of Mercer songs called *Dream* (1997), the song was sung by Lesley Ann Warren, Jonathan Dokuchitz, and the company.

"Have Yourself a Merry Little Christmas" is, after "White Christmas," the most popular and beloved Yuletime song to come from the movies. The tender Ralph Blane (lyric) and Hugh Martin (music) ballad from *Meet Me in St. Louis* (1944) was sung by Judy Garland to little sister Margaret O'Brien as they looked out the window at the snowmen they had built and the sisters contemplated moving from St. Louis to New York. The original lyric was rather despondent, citing this as the "last Christmas ever." But Garland requested a more optimistic tone, and Blane wrote the wistful lyric about troubles being far away and all being together in the future. Garland and Frank Sinatra each had early major hit recordings of the ballad, and there have been hundreds of others over the years. In the 1989 Broadway version of *Meet Me in St. Louis*, Donna Kane sang the song to Courtney Peldon.

"Havin' Myself a Time" is the high-flying number Martha Raye performed in *Tropic Holiday* (1938), the musical about Americans vacationing in Mexico. Leo Robin (lyric) and Ralph Rainger (music) wrote the song, and Billie Holiday made a distinctive recording of it.

"He Ain't Got Rhythm" is the playful Irving Berlin song about a brilliant scientist who discovers the fourth dimension but cannot find the beat in music. The number was sung by Alice Faye, the Ritz Brothers, and the chorus at the beginning of the backstage musical *On the Avenue* (1937). Popular recordings of the rhythm song were made by Ted Wilson (vocal by Billie Holiday), Benny Goodman (vocal by Jimmy Rushing), and Jimmy Lunceford and his Orchestra.

"He Loved Me Till the All-Clear Came" is the wartime lament of a gal who lost her man when the danger had passed, as sung by Cass Daley in the star-studded *Star-Spangled Rhythm* (1942). Johnny Mercer (lyric) and Harold Arlen (music) wrote the comic torch song, and Daley also sang it a year later in the film musical *Ridin' High* (1943).

"He Needs Me" is the melancholy ballad by Arthur Hamilton from the dark musical melodrama *Pete Kelly's Blues* (1955). Peggy Lee, as a down-on-her-luck nightclub singer who has taken to drink, sang the bluesy number in her inimitable cool style.

"He Needs Me" is the sweet and awkward ballad that Harry Nilsson wrote for the surreal musical *Popeye* (1980). Shelly Duvall, as the gangly Olive Oyl, sang the pathetically charming song on the streets of Sweethaven about her realization that Popeye loves her. As her gawking voice happily climbed the musical scale, all the neighbors slammed their windows shut, and she went into an odd disarming dance solo that is like a cartoon come alive.

"Heaven's Light/Hellfire" is the contrasting song combination by Stephen Schwartz (lyric) and Alan Menken (music) from the animated romance *The Hunchback of Notre Dame* (1996). When the lonely hunchback Quasimodo (voice of Tom Hulce) received a friendly smile from the gypsy girl Esmeralda, his heart filled with the kind of glow he has seen in others in love. This airy ballad is then overtaken by the prayer of the sinister judge Frollo (voice of Tony Jay), who lusted after Esmeralda and wanted her destroyed if he could not have her. "Hellfire," with its Latin chanting by priests in the background, the lyric's many references to Frollo's burning desire, and the sensual graphics as he saw the voluptuous Esmerelda in the fire of his imagination, is the most erotic scene to be found in any Disney animated film.

"Heigh-Ho" is the catchy marching song that the seven little miners sing and whistle going to and coming home from work in the animated classic *Snow White and the Seven Dwarfs* (1937). Larry Morey (lyric) and Frank Churchill (music) wrote the familiar ditty, which has been used as a work song in many situations over the years, such as in the comedy *Having Wonderful Time* (1938). Horace Heidt and his Musical Knights recorded the song. The number is very short and uses simple repetition, and it remains one of the most recognized of all Disney film songs.

"Heigh-Ho, Everybody, Heigh-Ho" is the welcome song Harry Woods wrote for Rudy Vallee for his film debut in *The Vagabond Lover* (1929). Vallee and his band had played at the Heigh-Ho Club in New York, where he opened his act with the title phrase. Woods took the phrase and fashioned it into a crooning number that Valle, as a saxophone-playing impostor at a Long Island mansion, sang in the film and recorded with great success.

"Heigh-Ho, the Gang's All Here" is the happy song-and-dance number that introduced Fred Astaire to movie audiences. Harold Adamson (lyric) and Burton Lane (music) wrote the anti-Depression number for *Dancing Lady* (1933), where Astaire, playing himself and wearing white tie and tails, sang the song and danced with Joan Crawford. The merry number ("we all have beer!") hardly showed off Astaire's talents (he appeared in only two numbers in the film), but he did make an impression on audiences so the studio decided to feature him in future films.

"Hell Hole" is the rock song parody by Christopher Guest, Rob Reiner, Harry Shearer, and Michael McKean that was featured in the mock documentary *This Is Spinal Tap* (1984) about a fictitious British rock group on tour in America. The angst-ridden number about the misery one is feeling when one's lover is gone was performed by Guest, Shearer, McKean, R. J. Parnell, and David Kaff in concert in the film, and the performers even made a mock video of the song.

"Help!" is the best-selling title song by John Lennon and Paul McCartney for the Beatles' 1965 musical farce. The lyric is a surging plea for help in escaping the blues, but according to Lennon, the title and the sentiment came from his desperation to come up with a title song for their second film. Originally written as a slower, more sincere ballad, the number was speeded up to make it more commercial (something Lennon always regretted). "Help" was sung by the foursome over the opening credits as they appeared on television screens set up inside the temple of a religious cult. Their recording of the song (with a slightly different lyric than on the soundtrack) was the Number One song for several weeks. Henry Gross sang "Help!" in the musical documentary *All This and World War Two* (1976). A pseudo-Beatles group of vocalists recorded the song for the Ford Motor Company, which used the version in television ads for Lincoln-Mercury in the 1980s.

"Here Comes Cookie" is the farcical but affectionate song of anticipation by Mack Gordon for Cookie who "takes the cake." Gracie Allen sang the baby-talk number in *Love in Bloom* (1935), and Glen Gray and the Casa Loma Orchestra (vocal by Pee Wee Hunt) had a best-selling recording of it. Ted Fio Rito (vocal by Muzzy Marcelino), Jan Garber, and Teddy Hill also made records of the song, which is sometimes listed as "Lookie, Lookie, Here Comes Cookie."

"Here Comes Heaven Again" is a romantic ballad that Harold

Adamson (lyric) and Jimmy McHugh (music) wrote for *Doll Face* (1945), a backstage musical loosely based on the career of Gypsy Rose Lee (some fifteen years before the Broadway musical and film *Gypsy*). Perry Como sang the pervasive song in the film, and his recording was popular.

"Here Lies Love" is the despondent torch song that Leo Robin (lyric) and Ralph Rainger (music) wrote for the star-filled *The Big Broadcast* (1932). Arthur Tracy sang the song in a speakeasy about the end of a love affair while radio crooner Bing Crosby read in a newspaper that he has been dumped by the girl he hoped to marry the next day. Later in the film Vincent Lopez and his Orchestra played the number in a club and, hearing it in his apartment in the same building, Crosby reprised the lament as he burned all the photographs he had of his ex-beloved. The song remained on *Your Hit Parade* for thirteen weeks thanks to recordings by Crosby, Ray Noble (vocal by Al Bowlly), Sam Coslow, and Jimmie Grier and his Orchestra. Most recently, cabaret singer Andrea Marcovicci recorded the mournful ballad.

"Here You Are" is a pastiche ballad in the style of early songwriter Paul Dresser that Leo Robin (lyric) and Ralph Rainger (music) wrote for Alice Faye to sing in the Dresser bio-musical *My Gal Sal* (1942). Faye never made the picture, but Rita Hayworth performed it beautifully, even though the dubbing by Nan Wynn was not in Faye's lower and sultry register. The lovely song was popular with big bands of the period and was recorded by Les Brown (vocal by Ralph Young), Glen Gray and the Casa Loma Orchestra (vocal by Kenny Sargent), Sammy Kaye (vocal by Elaine Beatty), Freddy Martin (vocal by Stuart Wade), and Chico Marx and his Orchestra.

"Here's Love in Your Eye" is the swinging number by Leo Robin (lyric) and Ralph Rainger (music) that Benny Fields and Larry Adler sang with Benny Goodman's Orchestra in the behind-the-scenes-in-radio musical *The Big Broadcast of 1937* (1936). Goodman's recording with a vocal by Helen Ward enjoyed some popularity.

"Here's the Key to My Heart" is the suggestive invitation that Alice Faye, being tested by the studio to see if she was star material, sang in *She Learned About Sailors* (1934). Sidney Clare (lyric) and Richard Whiting (music) wrote the eager number and Faye, as a Shanghai saloon singer, sang it as she threw prop keys to the sailors in the sleazy cafe. The film was not a hit, but Faye's rendition of the song — somewhat innocent, yet very knowing — demonstrated that the deep-voiced, sultry singer was a welcome relief from the trilling sopranos that filled the movie houses.

"Here's What I'm Here For" is a ballad of firm romantic resolution that Ira Gershwin (lyric) and Harold Arlen (music) wrote for Judy Garland to sing in *A Star Is Born* (1954). In a recording studio, up-and-coming singer Garland cut her first record as her boyfriend and mentor James Mason looked on. When the chorus took over, Garland quietly spoke with Mason and (we find out later) he has proposed to her. The whole scene and the song were cut by the studio before releasing the film, but in the 1980s it was found and restored to the musical classic. Garland's recording of the ballad was released even though the number was cut, and it was moderately popular.

"He's a Good Man to Have Around" is the vampy song by Jack Yellen (lyric) and Milton Ager (music) that Sophie Tucker, as a "red hot mama" nightclub singer, performed in the early show biz musical *Honky Tonk* (1929). Tucker recorded the number, as did Billy Murray with the Yuban Radio Orchestra, Libby Holman with the Cotton Pickers, and much later Kay Starr.

"He's a Tramp" is the cool and sexy tribute to an unfaithful lover that Peggy Lee and Sonny Burke wrote for the animated animal romance *Lady and the Tramp* (1955). When the well-bred cocker spaniel Lady was put in the dog pound, the worldy-wise feline Peg (voice of Lee) sang to her about the freewheeling mutt Tramp, who is "a bounder but I love him." The group the Jazz Networks made a notable recording of the song in 1996.

"He's So Unusual" is the comic lament of a girl whose football player boyfriend is more interested in playing ball rather than playing around with her. Al Lewis, Al Sherman (lyric), and Abner Silver (music) wrote the number for the early collegiate musical *Sweetie* (1929), and it was sung by baby-voiced Helen Kane, whose performance in the number made her a major film name for a while. Recordings were made by Kane, Annette Hanshaw, Meyer Davis, and Vaughan DeLeath.

"Hey, Babe, Hey! (I'm Nuts About You!)" is the vigorous cry of affection that James Stewart sang to Eleanor Powell on the patio of a New York nightclub in *Born to Dance* (1936). Cole Porter wrote the catchy oom-pah-pah melody and zesty lyric, and the number was reprised by Sid Silvers to Una Merkel, Buddy Ebsen, and Frances Langford, everyone then breaking into a cheery tap number.

"Hi-Diddle-Dee-Dee (an Actor's Life for Me)" is the tuneful ode to the lure of show business that Ned Washington (lyric) and Leigh Harline (music) wrote for the animated classic *Pinocchio* (1940). The sly fox J. Worthington Foulfellow (voice of Walter Catlett) sang of the glory of the stage to wooden puppet Pinocchio (voice of Dickie Jones) as he led him to enslavement with Stromboli's marionette troupe.

"High, Wide and Handsome" is the rollicking anthem to the rugged Pennsylvania wilderness and the title song by Oscar Hammerstein (lyric) and Jerome Kern (music) for the 1937 pioneer musical. Irene Dunne sang the rousing number as part of a medicine show run by her father. The song has been recorded on several occasions and in several different styles, from a dance arrangement by Gus Arnheim's Orchestra to swing versions by Egdar Hayes (vocal by Bill Darnell) and the Tempo King's Swing Combo, to a western approach by Tex Ritter.

"The Hills of Old Wyomin'" is the warm tribute to the countryside that aristocrat Frances Langford sang in *Palm Springs* (1936) after she fell in love with a cowboy. The absorbing song by Leo Robin (lyric) and Ralph Rainger (music) was recorded by Langford, Jan Garber (vocal by Lee Bennett), Russ Morgan (vocal by Dick Robertson), Tex Ritter, and the Sons of the Pioneers (which included the unknown Roy Rogers).

"His Rocking Horse Ran Away" is the swinging comic number that Betty Hutton sang in *And the Angels Sing* (1944) and on record. Johnny Burke (lyric) and James Van Heusen (music) wrote the silly ditty for her. It was also sung by Kathy Fitzgerald in the Broadway revue of Burke–Van Heusen songs called *Swinging on a Star* (1995).

"Hit the Road to Dreamland" is an offbeat but enticing lullaby by Johnny Mercer (lyric) and Harold Arlen (music) in which a couple in love are out all night and, feeling the dawn coming on, decide it is time to part and get some sleep. Mary Martin and Dick Powell performed it in *Star-Spangled Rhythm* (1942) as the last two customers in a railway dining car, and a counterpoint section was sung by the Golden Gate Quartet as the waiters who gently but firmly try to get the lovers to leave. The rhythmic number was successfully recorded by Bing Crosby, Freddie Slack (vocal by the Mellowaires), Dean Martin, and Diahann Carroll.

"Hold Me in Your Arms" is the no-holds-barred ballad that Ray Heindorf, Don Pippin, and Charles Henderson wrote for the musical tearjerker *Young at Heart* (1955). New Englander Doris Day sang the song in the film and recorded it with success.

"Hold My Hand" is a crooning invitation sung by Rudy Vallee in the backstager *George White's Scandals* (1934). Irving Caesar and Jack Yellen collaborated on the direct-delivery lyric, Ray Henderson provided the Vallesque music, and it was recorded by Vallee, Frances Langford, and the bands of Ray Noble, Ted Black, and Vincent Rose.

"Honeymoon Hotel" is the prankish but sublime song by Al Dubin (lyric) and Harry Warren (music) about the glories of a hostelry for newlyweds and the inspiration for one of Busby Berkeley's most coy musical sequences. In a narrative musical number on stage in *Footlight Parade* (1933), Dick Powell proposed to Ruby Keeler, they wed, and soon they were seen with other just-married couples as they checked into a Jersey City hotel. They were greeted in song by the bellboys, desk clerk, and other attendants; then they arrived in their room, where they were surprised by a half-dozen waiting relatives. Once the family was gone, the men all paraded down the hall to a washroom to change while the wives demurely slipped into sleepwear. The couples were finally reunited and snuggled in bed, and the scene faded to a closeup of a magazine with a baby on the cover. The jaunty song was recorded by Powell, Rudy Vallee's Orchestra (vocal by Alice Faye), Leo Reisman, Freddy Martin (vocal by Terry Shand), and Ozzie Nelson's Orchestra.

"Honolulu" is the pseudo-exotic title number from the 1939 musical farce set partially on the Hawaiian Islands. Gus Kahn (lyric) and Harry Warren (music) wrote the song about hoping to find romance on the Islands and Gracie Allen sang it on board an ocean liner as she plucked along on her ukele and an instrumental combo joined her on deck. This was followed by a tap routine by Allen and Eleanor Powell then an enthusiastic solo by Powell that had her skipping rope as she tapped all over the boat. The song became quite popular and was recorded by Tommy Dorsey (vocal by Edythe Wright), Glen Gray and the Casa Loma Orchestra, Van Alexander's Orchestra, and others.

"Honor to Us All" is the tuneful character song that David Zippel (lyric) and Matthew Wilder (music) wrote for the animated adventure *Mulan* (1998). Two Chinese women (voices of Beth Fowler and Marnie Nixon) sang the Oriental-flavored number as they prepared the maiden Mulan (singing voice of Lea Salonga) for presentation at the matchmaker's, hoping to get her a good husband and maintain the family heritage, while Mulan prays to her ancestors that she won't disappoint them.

"Hooray for Hollywood" is the satiric tribute to movieland by Johnny Mercer (lyric) and Richard Whiting (music) that later became the unofficial theme song for the film business with no satire intended. The lively tongue-in-cheek song was the opening number in the Tinsel Town musical *Hollywood Hotel* (1937) and was sung by Frances Langford, Johnny "Scat" Davis, Benny Goodman's Orchestra, and several others as they are seen riding in cars to the St. Louis airport to bid goodbye to Dick Powell, who is flying off to "screwy bally hooey Hollywood." The song was reprised by Davis with Powell and Rosemary Lane at the end of the film. The entertaining number was heard as background in many films and newsreels, and Sammy Davis, Jr., sang it in *Pepe* (1960).

"Hooray for Hollywood" was featured in two Broadway revues: The company sang it in *A Day in Hollywood — A Night in the Ukraine* (1980), and it was performed by Brooks Ashmanskas, Angelo Fraboni, Kevyn Morrow, and Timothy Edward Smith in *Dream* (1997).

"Hooray for Love" is the pleasing title song by Dorothy Fields (lyric) and Jerome Kern (music) for the 1935 musical about getting an intimate revue produced. Gene Raymond sang the number, which became a hit in the mid-1930s.

"Hooray for Love" is the bluesy duet from *Casbah* (1948) that was sung by French thief Tony Martin and Yvonne De Carlo as they danced in an Algiers tobacco shop. Leo Robin wrote the restrained lyric, and Harold Arlen composed the cool, almost detached music. Recordings of the number were made by Martin, Johnny Mercer, Julie Wilson, and others.

"Hopelessly Devoted to You" is one of the handful of songs interpolated into the 1978 film version of the runaway Broadway hit *Grease*. John Farrar wrote this pastiche number that parodied the heartbreak songs of the late 1950s and was sung by high school exchange student Olivia Newton-John about her crush on greaser John Travolta as she wandered in a suburban backyard in her nightgown and even saw his face appear in the kids' wading pool. Audiences took the Oscar-nominated ballad at face value, and Newton-John's solo record was a major hit. In England, Michaela Strachan and Shona Lindsay also had popular recordings of the song.

"Hot Lunch Jam" is the driving rock number from *Fame* (1980) that took the form of a spontaneous and improvised musical scene. In the cafeteria of Manhattan's High School for the Performing Arts, student musicians (led by pianist Lee Curreri) started to improvise an idle riff. Then music student Irene Cara started to sing, and soon the whole room exploded in a pulsating song and dance. The sequence was written by Robert F. Colesberry and Michael and Lesley Gore.

"How About You?" is the captivating and memorable ballad by Ralph Freed (lyric) and Burton Lane (music) that teenagers Mickey Rooney and Judy Garland sang and danced to in a Manhattan apartment in the backstager *Babes on Broadway* (1941). The Oscar-nominated number (known by many as "I Like New York in June" from the first line of the refrain) is a delectable list song in which the boy and girl each chronicles the simple everyday things that they like (a Gershwin tune, auto rides, banana splits, FDR's looks, and so on) then asks the other the title question. Lane's music is unusual for a list song in that it doesn't repeat itself but instead goes into various new directions with each new section.

Tommy Dorsey's recording with Frank Sinatra was a bestseller, and later Dick Jurgens and his Orchestra, Jane Froman, and Tony Bennett each made a noteworthy record of the song. Michael Feinstein's 1990 recording was the most complete, including the rarely–heard verse and a second lyric given to him by Lane.

"How Blue the Night" is the gushing ballad by Harold Adamson (lyric) and Jimmy McHugh (music) about lonely nights and long days when one is separated from one's sweetheart. Dick Haymes, as a soldier on a USO tour in *Four Jills in Jeep* (1044), sang the number to Mitzi Mayfair, who then launched into a tap routine while the chorus encored the song. Haymes' recording was very popular.

"How Could You Believe Me When I Said I Loved You When You Know I've Been a Liar All My Life?" is arguably the movie song with the longest title, yet the Alan Jay Lerner lyric sits so comfortably on Burton Lane's music that it is easier to remember than many songs. The vaudeville number was sung by Fred Astaire and Jane Powell in *Royal Wedding* (1951) as a couple of squabbling street toughs who added physical punches and kicks to their roughhouse choreography. Their performance was self-mocking and very funny, Powell using a low chest voice instead of her usual soprano trilling. Legend has it that Lerner and Lane were riding to the studio one day and discussed the possibility of a corny revue number to spice up their overly romantic tale. By the time they arrived at the studio the title, melody for the refrain, and much of the rest of the song were finished. Lerner's lyric is a masterwork of long phrases that trip off the tongue, and Lane's release section is a flamboyant mock blues for which Lerner wrote silly torch song lyrics. Astaire recorded the number, which is sometimes listed as "The Liar Song."

"How Do I Rate With You?" is an upbeat romantic duet by Sam Coslow (lyric) and Richard Whiting (music) that was featured in *Coronado* (1935). Millionaire Johnny Downs and struggling singer Betty Burgess sang the chipper ballad at the famous California resort, and it was successfully recorded by Tommy Dorsey and his Orchestra.

"How Do You Do?" is the merry musical greeting that Robert MacGimsey wrote for the groundbreaking folklore film *Song of the South* (1946). Brer Rabbit (voice of Johnny Lee) sang the lively number to the lifeless tar baby in one of the animated Uncle Remus tales told in the musical.

"How Do You Like Your Eggs in the Morning?" is the jitterbugging song of affection that Sammy Cahn (lyric) and Nicholas Brodszky (music) wrote for the Paris musical romance *Rich, Young and Pretty* (1951).

Texas tourist Jane Powell and Vic Damone (in his film debut) sang the bouncy number with the Four Freshmen, asking details about one's breakfast wishes and answering with no preference, as long as one got a kiss from the other.

"How Long Did I Dream?" is a winsome Big Band ballad sung by Ginny Simms with Kay Kyser's Band in *Playmates* (1942). The number was written by Johnny Burke (lyric) and James Van Heusen (music), and there were recordings by Simms, Frankie Masters (vocal by Lou Hurst), Lou Breese, and Art Jarrett and his Orchestra.

"How Lucky Can You Get?" is the breezy song of satisfaction that Fred Ebb (lyric) and John Kander (music) wrote for the bio-musical sequel *Funny Lady* (1975). The song was first heard coming from a record that Barbra Streisand, as entertainer Fanny Brice, played in her dressing room after she and her ex-husband Omar Sharif have parted for good. Then Streisand sang the optimistic number with a bittersweet subtext on a bare stage, turning it into a willing song of survival. Karen Mason performed the Oscar-nominated song in the Off-Broadway revue *And the World Goes 'Round* (1991).

"How Many Times Do I Have to Tell You?" is the fervent ballad by Harold Adamson (lyric) and Jimmy McHugh (music) that asks a familiar rhetorical question. Dick Haymes sang it in *Four Jills in a Jeep* (1944), a musical about a USO tour to England and North Africa. Haymes' recording with Emil Newman's Orchestra was popular for a while.

"How Sweet You Are" is a pastiche of a nineteenth-century ballad written by Frank Loesser (lyric) and Arthur Schwartz (music) for the star-studded *Thank Your Lucky Stars* (1943). Dinah Shore and a chorus sang the song as part of a revue for enlisted men, but to make the scene different for audiences during World War Two, it was set in 1861 and was performed for Union officers during the Civil War. Shore, Kay Armen, and Jo Stafford each made recordings of the simple song of affection.

"How'dja Like to Love Me?" is a jocular romantic proposal by Frank Loesser (lyric) and Burton Lane (music) that Bob Hope and Martha Raye performed in the academic frolic *College Swing* (1938). The music is so swinging and peppy that it hardly feels like a love song, and Loesser's casual lyric (filled with such domestic images as hanging toothbrushes side by side, going to meet mother, picking out his neckties, and so on) is more gamesome than romantic. The song was recorded by Larry Clinton (vocal by Bea Wain), Dolly Dawn, and the orchestras of Horace Heidt, Jimmy Dorsey, and Abe Lyman. Michael Feinstein's 1991 recording revived interest in the jolly number.

"A Hubba Hubba Hubba (or, Dig You Later)" is a silly but contagious rhythm number by Harold Adamson (lyric) and Jimmy McHugh (music) that uses jazz slang and clichés both musically and lyrically. Perry Como sang the lively song in the backstager *Doll Face* (1945), and his recording with the Satisfiers sold over a million disks.

"Humpty Dumpty Heart" is a pure-1940s ballad, full of heartbreak yet still very resilient. It was written by Johnny Burke (lyric) and James Van Heusen (music) for *Playmates* (1942), where it was sung by Harry Babbitt with Kay Kyser's band. Recordings were made by Glenn Miller (vocal by Ray Eberle), and the bands of Frankie Masters, Lou Breese, and Art Jarrett.

"Hushabye Mountain" is an infectious lullaby written by Richard M. and Robert B. Sherman for the musical fantasy *Chitty Chitty Bang Bang* (1968). Crackpot inventor Dick Van Dyke sang the enchanting song to his children Adrian Hill and Heather Ripley as he put them to bed, describing a magical place that you can sail to in a boat in your dreams.

I

"I Am the Words (You Are the Melody)" is the tender ballad by Buddy De Sylva, Lew Brown (lyric), and Ray Henderson (music) for the first (and practically only) sci–fi musical, *Just Imagine* (1930). The song, sometimes listed as "You Are the Melody," was sung by scientist John Garrick as he peered through a Martian telescope at Maureen O'Sullivan, her image superimposed on a distant view of planet earth. O'Sullivan talk-sang a weepy reprise of the ballad, which was also reprised later in the film by Garrick, Sullivan, and the chorus.

"I Begged Her" is the bragging song of amorous conquests sung by sailors Gene Kelly and Frank Sinatra to their buddies in *Anchors Aweigh* (1945) that led into a tap routine that had the boastful narrators jumping over beds in a servicemen's dormitory. Sammy Cahn wrote the hyperbolic lyric, Jule Styne composed the vigorous music, and Sinatra had a popular recording of the song.

"I Believe" is the upbeat optimistic number by Sammy Cahn (lyric) and Jule Styne (music) that returning soldier Frank Sinatra, janitor Jimmy Durante, and the tap-dancing Billy Roy performed in *It Happened in Brooklyn* (1947). Sinatra recorded the song, as did Jane Froman, who made it part of her repertoire in clubs for many years.

"I Believe in Love" is the driving ballad that rising star Barbra Streisand and her backup singers sang as part of a concert in the 1976 remake of *A Star Is Born*. Alan and Marilyn Bergman (lyric) and Kenny Loggins (music) wrote the disco-style number about being ready and accepting of love, and both Streisand's and Loggins' recordings were bestsellers.

"I Can Do Without Broadway (But Can Broadway Do Without Me?)" is the delightful specialty number that Jimmy Durante performed in the Hawaiian-located musical romance *On an Island With You* (1948). Durante wrote the comic ditty himself and delivered it with his distinctive sense of honky–tonk and Broadway pizzazz.

"I Can't Be Bothered Now" is the footloose plea, written by the Gershwin brothers for *Damsel in Distress* (1937), to be left alone because when one is dancing no one cares if "this old world stops turning." Fred Astaire, as an American hoofer in England, was prodded into performing by a handful of street buskers, so he sang and danced the carefree number amidst the busy London traffic. George Gershwin's music is made up of short, staccato musical phrases that Ira Gershwin matches with terse, dancing, lyric phrases. Tommy Tune and the male chorus performed the song at the top of the Broadway musical *My One and Only* (1983), and it was sung and danced by Harry Groener and the female chorus near the beginning of the "new" Gershwin stage musical *Crazy for You* (1992).

"I Can't Begin to Tell You" is the Oscar-nominated ballad by Mack Gordon (lyric) and James Monaco (music) that was interpolated into a score of old favorites for the period bio-musical *The Dolly Sisters* (1945). Composer John Payne first sang the soothing number about the inability to express the words that "refuse to leave my heart" as a song he'd just written, then he reprised it with Betty Grable as a romantic duet. The ballad became the hit of the film and was popular across the country thanks to recordings by Grable (with Harry James' Band), Bing Crosby (with Carmen Cavallaro's Orchestra), Sammy Kaye and, as late as 1983, by Willie Nelson. The song was featured in the movie musical *You're My Everything* (1949), and Ginger Rogers sang it in *Dreamboat* (1952).

"I Can't Escape From You" is the lazy ballad that singing hired hand Bing Crosby sang in the western musical *Rhythm on the Range* (1936). Richard Whiting composed the easygoing music, which has a nice steady rhythmic quality, and Leo Robin penned the lyric of a free and wandering lover who travels the globe but cannot get away from the memory of his beloved. Crosby recorded the ballad, and Jimmie Lunceford's instrumental disk was very popular.

"I Concentrate on You" is the alluring ballad Cole Porter wrote for Fred Astaire to sing in *The Broadway Melody of 1940* (1940), but it was actually sung by Douglas MacPhail as part of a Broadway revue number while Astaire and Eleanor Powell, dressed as Harlequin and Columbine, danced to it. The melody is upbeat and throbbing, and Porter's lyric is one of his most captivating, about how the thoughts of one's lover keeps away the gloom, and is filled with 'on' and 'en' diphthongs throughout that make the lyric lines smooth and echoing. The ballad was particularly popular with dance bands, and there were memorable recordings by Tommy Dorsey (vocal by Anita Boyer), Eddy Duchin (vocal by Stanley Worth), Glen Gray and the Casa Loma Orchestra (vocal by Kenny Sargent) and later by Percy Faith, Carmen MacRae, Diahann Carroll, and Nero Young.

"I Could Go on Singing" is the expansive title number by E. Y. Harburg (lyric) and Harold Arlen (music) from the 1963 musical tearjerker that starred Judy Garland and was, at times, uncomfortably close to her own troubled life. Garland, as a famous singer visiting England, belted the emotionally charged tribute to showmanship over the opening credits and then again at the film's finale. "I Could Go on Singing" was the last song Arlen composed for the movies, and the musical melodrama was also Garland's last film.

"I Could Use a Dream" is a romantic duet about selecting one's lover as dream material that Tony Martin and Alice Faye performed in the backstager *Sally, Irene and Mary* (1938). Harold Spina composed the smooth music, and Walter Bullock provided the gushing ("my lips upon your fingertips") lyric. Martin and Faye recorded the number together.

"I Couldn't Sleep a Wink Last Night" is the Oscar-nominated ballad that Frank Sinatra (in his screen debut) sang as a reconciliatory gift to Michele Morgan after a lovers' quarrel in *Higher and Higher* (1943). Harold Adamson (lyric) and Jimmy McHugh (music) wrote the gentle and apologetic love song, and Sinatra's recording was a Top Ten hit. Legend has it that McHugh had trouble sleeping one night and wrote the basic melody out on his bedsheet. The next day at the studio he couldn't recall the theme and so he called his housekeeper, but she had sent the linen to the laundry, which sent McHugh rushing to the cleaners to retrieve his song. Martha O'Driscoll sang the ballad in *Criminal Court* (1946), and Joan Blondell gave it her personal rendition in *The Blue Veil* (1951).

"I Don't Care Who Knows It" is the sultry ballad that Harold Adamson (lyric) and Jimmy McHugh (music) wrote for the period musical *Nob Hill* (1945). Vivian Blaine, as a cafe singer in San Francisco, sang the bold proclamation of love, and a Harry James recording (vocal by Kitty Kallen) was moderately popular.

"I Don't Know What I Want" was the lament sung by hare-brained Jane Powell, who was engaged to three different men in *The Girl Most Likely* (1958) and could not decide which one to marry. Ralph Blane and Hugh Martin wrote the pleasant number for the film, which was made in 1956 but not released for two years.

"I Don't Want to Cry Anymore" is a tearful torch song by Victor Schertzinger that was interpolated into the Johnny Burke–James Monaco score for *Rhythm on the River* (1940). Mary Martin, as a lyricist who ghostwrites songs for others, sang the delicate lament of a finished love affair in a nightclub setting.

"I Don't Want to Make History (I Just Want to Make Love)" is the droll number that heiress-on-the-outs Frances Langford sang in *Palm Springs* (1936). Ralph Rainger wrote the music, and Leo Robin penned the clever lyric that sees the accomplishments of Joan of Arc, Christopher Columbus, and Napoleon as small potatoes because love is the only conquest worth pursuing. Langford recorded the song, as did Bob Crosby's band, Hal Kemp, Snuff Smith's Combo (featuring Jonah Jones), and Vincent Lopez and his Orchestra.

"I Don't Want to Walk Without You" is the first of many top-drawer songs Frank Loesser (lyric) and Jule Styne (music) collaborated on, this one written for Judy Canova to sing in the B movie musical *Sis Hopkins* (1941). But the new team was so pleased with their first effort they saved it for a better project, and when contracted to score the college musical *Sweater Girl* (1942), the lovely plea for a sweetheart to return was given to Johnny Johnston to sing and was reprised by Betty Jane Rhodes. Johnston reprised the number in *You Can't Ration Love* (1944), and Lizbeth Scott sang it in *Dark City* (1950). The song launched the careers of Loesser and Styne when it became a wartime favorite with a Number One recording by Harry James (vocal by Helen Forrest) and popular disks by Bing Crosby and Dinah Shore. The ballad has remained an oft-recorded standard over the decades. Phyllis McGuire's 1964 record was a bestseller, Englebert Humperdinck made a pop recording soon after, Barry Manilow had a hit with it in 1980, and most recently the number has been revived again with records by Michael Feinstein, Andrea Marcovicci, and Judy Kuhn.

"I Don't Want Your Kisses (If I Can't Have Your Love)" is the bubble-headed love song by Fred Fisher (lyric) and Martin Broones (music) from the early campus musical *So This Is College* (1929). Football player Robert Montgomery introduced the number, later reprised by teammate Elliot Nugent at the piano to coed Sally Starr. All three stars were recruited from Broadway, but only Montgomery caught on with audiences, this film launching his career (which rarely included musicals).

"I Dream Too Much" is the entrancing title song by Dorothy Fields (lyric) and Jerome Kern (music) that was featured in the 1935 vehicle for Met opera star Lily Pons. The confessional song about dreaming "too much alone" was sung by Pons and the chorus as part of a musical written by her husband Henry Fonda and was reprised at the end of the film. When producer Pandro Berman heard the song, he changed the film's title from *Love Song* to that of the waltzing ballad. Designed to show off Pons' coloratura opera talents, Kern composed expansive and demanding music that David Ewen notes "is of special interest for its chromatic harmonies and for the leap of a minor ninth in the melody." Pons and Leo Reisman and his Orchestra each recorded the sweeping number, also sung by the ensemble in the Broadway revue *Jerome Kern Goes to Hollywood* (1986).

"I Dug a Ditch (in Wichita)" is the wartime novelty number about the life of an enlisted man by Ralph Freed, Lew Brown (lyric), and Burton Lane (music) that was heard in the star-filled revue *Thousands Cheer* (1943). Kathryn Grayson sang it with Kay Kyser's Orchestra, and then later Gene Kelly did an ingenious dance to it as the lone GI forced to clean the PX. Willie Kelly and his Orchestra made a best-selling record of the fun song.

"I Fall in Love Too Easily" is the bewitching ballad by Sammy Cahn (lyric) and Jule Styne (music) admitting that one's heart should be "well schooled" in matters of love. Sailor Frank Sinatra mournfully sang it as he played the piano on the large stage of the deserted Hollywood Bowl in *Anchors Aweigh* (1945). The Oscar-nominated song was recorded by Sinatra and Mel Tormé and has recently enjoyed new popularity thanks to disks by Karen Akers, Michael Feinstein, and Judy Kuhn. A distinctive recording was also made by saxophonist Carmen Leggio.

"I Fall in Love With You Every Day" is the upbeat ballad by Frank Loesser (lyric), Arthur Altman, and Manning Sherwin (music) about a romance that is renewed daily and was sung by campus sweethearts John Payne and Florence George in *College Swing* (1938). The flavorful love song was recorded by Larry Clinton (vocal by Bea Wain), Jimmy Dorsey (vocal by Bob Eberle), Dolly Dawn with George Hall's Orchestra, Abe Lyman, Horace Heidt, and most recently Karen Akers.

"I Feel a Song Comin' On" is the rhythmic anticipation of music by Dorothy Fields (lyric), Jimmy McHugh (music), and George Oppenheimer (who came up with the catchy title) that was featured in the backstager *Every Night at Eight* (1935). Struggling singers Alice Faye, Patsy Kelly, and Frances Langford harmonized together as an ambitious trio hoping to leave the factory for Broadway. Later in the film Faye reprised the number as a vampy torch song with a Mae West–like rendition. McHugh's music is a rhythmic marvel with, as

James R. Morris calls, "an extroverted character . . . [that] begins aggressively, with the first four measures dominated by long whole notes, setting up a syncopated release in the following four bars." Fields' lyric is equally exhilarating with wondrous word play and flowing rhymes such as "ringin' through ya" and "Hallelujah." The song was successfully recorded by Langford, Paul Whiteman (vocal by Ramona), Johnny "Scat" Davis, and Frank Dailey's Orchestra, and for many years it was a favorite opening number for nightclub singers. "I Feel a Song Coming On" was featured in the all-star film revue *Follow the Boys* (1944) and was sung by Ann Miller and the chorus in the Broadway revue *Sugar Babies* (1980).

"I Feel Like a Feather in a Breeze" is the slaphappy ditty sung by a group of campus coeds in *Collegiate* (1936). Harry Revel composed the airy music, and Mack Gordon wrote the whimsical lyric about feeling weightless when in love. Recordings were made by Richard Himber (vocal by Stuart Allen), Jan Garber (vocal by Lee Bennett), Johnny Johnston, and Art Karle.

"I Found a New Way to Go to Town" is the sly proclamation that vamp Mae West sang in *I'm No Angel* (1933), bragging that she has found a man who loves her constantly and "no man can shake me until I let him go." Gladys DuBois, Ben Ellison, and Harvey Brooks wrote the playful number and West recorded it.

"I Get the Neck of the Chicken" is the hit comic song by Frank Loesser (lyric) and Jimmy McHugh (music) about a girl with no luck and plenty of shortcomings. Marcy McGuire introduced it in the wartime musical *Seven Days Leave* (1942), and a recording by Freddy Martin (vocal by Eddie Stone) was a bestseller.

"I Go for That" is the appealing romantic ballad that Broadway star Dorothy Lamour sang on a show boat in Missouri in *St. Louis Blues* (1938). Matty Malneck composed the music, and Frank Loesser penned the lyric that approved of her guy because he played the ukelele. Lamour recorded the song as well.

"I Got a New Lease on Life" is the jaunty song by Dorothy Fields (lyric) and Oscar Levant (music) that finds the singer getting over the blues when she "bumped into love again." Ginger Rogers, as a famous Hollywood celebrity, sang and tap danced to the slangy number in *In Person* (1935), proclaiming she felt like "Popeye the sailor girl."

"I Got Love" is opera star Lily Pons' attempt to sing a swing number in *I Dream Too Much* (1935), and though some found her singing the jazzy song with Andre Kostalanetz's Orchestra in a Parisian cafe successful, others used this song as a reason for calling the film *I Scream Too Much*. Jerome Kern composed the low-down music (he himself had difficulty accepting swing as a legitimate form of music), and Dorothy Fields wrote the grasping lyric.

"I Got Out of Bed on the Right Side" is the delightful number that Johnny Mercer (lyric) and Arthur Schwartz (music) wrote for the Esther Williams vehicle *Dangerous When Wet* (1953). The diverting song about being lucky was sung by Williams, Fernando Lamas, Charlotte Greenwood, William Demarest, Barbara Whiting, and Donna Corcoran.

"I Gotta Gal I Love (in North and South Dakota)" is the gleeful song that naive country lad Eddie Bracken sang in New York City in *Ladies' Man* (1947). Sammy Cahn penned the wry lyric and Jule Styne contributed the cheery music.

"I Had the Craziest Dream" is the serene and entrancing ballad by Mack Gordon (lyric) and Harry Warren (music) that tries to turn a dream of love into a reality. The romantic number was sung by Helen Forrest with Harry James and his Orchestra as they entertained the patrons at a Lake Louise resort in *Springtime in the Rockies* (1942). Later in the film the music was reprised for a daffy dance solo by the long-legged, high-kicking Charlotte Greenwood. Gordon's lyric for the ballad is one of his most alluring, as he describes a kiss in his dream. Philip Furia notes how an "insistent progression of colloquial phrases is subtly sensuous and builds to a prosaically surreal climax." The recording by Forrest and James sold over a million copies; Nat "King" Cole, the Skylarks, and Johnny Mathis each made memorable records of the ballad; and in 1998 Judy Kaye recorded the number.

"I Have a Dream" is the wistful ballad that Harold Adamson (lyric) and Burton Lane (music) wrote for the silly historical musical *Jupiter's Darling* (1955). Esther Williams, engaged to the Roman dictator George Sanders but in love with the conqueror Hannibal (Howard Keel), sang the enraptured number.

"I Have Confidence in Me" is one of two songs Richard Rodgers wrote by himself after Oscar Hammerstein's death when preparing the film version of *The Sound of Music* (1965). The less-than-confident governess-to-be Julie Andrews sang the bright song as she traveled from the abbey where she has lived through beautiful Salzburg to the Von Trapp villa in the Austrian countryside. Ethan Mordden has noted that Rodgers' lyric is very much in the Hammerstein style and that his happy march music "sounds like a charge up a hill."

"I Have Eyes" is the alluring ballad by Leo Robin (lyric) and Ralph Rainger (music) about having vision only for one because the singer only has the eye for you. It was introduced by the chorus in the backstager *Artists and Models* (1937) and then was featured the next year in *Paris Honeymoon* (1938), where it was sung by Bing Crosby, Shirley Ross, and Franciska Gaal. Successful recordings were made by Crosby and the bands of Benny Goodman, Les Brown, Red Norvo, and Artie Shaw (vocal by Helen Forrest).

"I Have the Room Above Her" is the lilting romantic ballad that Oscar Hammerstein (lyric) and Jerome Kern (music) wrote for the 1936 film version of their Broadway classic *Show Boat*. Gambler-turned-actor Allan Jones sang the song from his room in the show boat *Cotton Blossom* to Irene Dunne, who is at the window of her room below his, and then the two joined in a lovely duet. Kern's music beautifully climbs the scale in fits and starts while Hammerstein's lyric is simple, succinct, and endearing. The song has often been interpolated into stage revivals of the musical and was featured in the Broadway revue *Jerome Kern Goes to Hollywood* (1986), where it was sung by Scott Holmes. Cy Young recorded the ballad in the early 1970s, and Mandy Patinkin gave it a moving rendition in a 1997 recording.

"I Haven't Time to Be a Millionaire" is the carefree ballad by Johnny Burke (lyric) and James Monaco (music) that takes life as it comes. Singing construction worker Bing Crosby sang the number in the musical tearjerker *If I Had My Way* (1940), and he recorded it as well.

"I Hear Music" is the rhythmic swing number by Frank Loesser (lyric) and Burton Lane (music) that young and eager performers Peter Lind Hayes, Eddie Quillan, Frank Jenks, and Robert Paige sang in the backstage musical *Dancing on a Dime* (1941). Lane's music, which Alec Wilder described as "witty, carefree, direct," is a favorite with jazz groups because of its unique construction: A musical phrase will begin, then is replaced by another, then a previous one returns and ties in cleverly with the whole. Loesser's lyric is a list song that playfully recalls all the everyday sounds (milk bottles clanking, coffee percolating, and so on) that become music with the right frame of mind. Among the recordings made of the song are those by Billie Holiday, Gene Krupa (vocal by Irene Day), Larry Clinton (vocal by Peggy Mann), Russ Morgan, George Shearing, and recently Michael Feinstein.

"I Heard the Birdies Sing" is the jolly production number that Betty Grable and a chorus of female boxers sang at a dress rehearsal in the Broadway backstage musical *Footlight Serenade* (1942). Ralph Rainger wrote the tuneful music, Leo Robin penned the animated lyric about love hitting you like a knockout, and Hermes Pan choreographed the number in which Grable did a pas de deux with her own sparring partner shadow, who punched her out at the end.

"I Just Can't Do Enough for You" is the smooth love song sung by Dan Dailey and Betty Grable that led to a sultry pas de deux as part of a rehearsal for a soldier show in *Call Me Mister* (1951). Sammy Fain composed the sensuous music, and Mack Gordon provided the adoring lyric.

"I Just Can't Wait to Be King" is the ambitious "I am" song for the young cub Simba (singing voice of Jason Weaver) in the animated musical *The Lion King* (1994). The future king sang enthusiastically of his plans while he frolicked across the savanna with young Nala (voice of Laura Williams) and tried to lose the hornbill Zazu (voice of Rowan Atkinson), who punctuated the song with wry comments about the young prince's faults. Soon various birds and other creatures joined in, and the scene turned into a mock Las Vegas revue number. Elton John wrote the rhythmic music, Tim Rice penned the busy lyric, and Mark Mancina provided the African arrangement that made the number bounce with joy. John recorded the song, which in the 1997 Broadway version of the tale was performed by Scott Irby-Ranniar, Kajuana Shuford, and Geoff Hoyle.

"I Know Now" is a forgotten romantic ballad by Al Dubin (lyric) and Harry Warren (music) that Marine-turned-radio-singer Dick Powell sang with his sweetheart Doris Weston in *The Singing Marine* (1937). The bittersweet number was not shown to its advantage in the film and Powell's recording was not a hit, but the song remained one of Warren's favorites all his life. Guy Lombardo and his Royal Canadians had modest success with their recording. Warren asked that it be included in the score for the 1980 Broadway musical *42nd Street*, and producer David Merrick begrudgingly obliged. Tammy Grimes sang the ballad, but it was not recorded with the rest of the score. When Warren died in 1981, Merrick cut the number from the show.

"I Know Why (and So Do You)" is a bright-eyed love ballad by Mack Gordon (lyric) and Harry Warren (music) that became a hit after Glenn Miller and his Orchestra played it in *Sun Valley Serenade* (1941). Gordon's lyric is an endearing list song that observes a series of unusual phenomena in nature (bluebirds singing in winter, violets growing in the snow, and so on) and explains that the reason is love. Lynn Bari (dubbed by Pat Friday), John Payne, and the Modernaires joined Miller as they auditioned for the Sun Valley Lodge; then later in the film the number was reprised on a phonograph record as Payne and Sonja Henie sang and danced to it in a ski hut. Miller's recording (vocal by Paula Kelly) was a bestseller, and the orchestra played it in *The Glenn Miller Story* (1954) with Jimmy Stewart (as Miller) conducting. Richard Himbler and his Orchestra also had a profitable recording of the number.

"I Like Him" is the genial realization that Barbra Streisand, as entertainer Fanny Brice, sang on the soundtrack as she watched the brash producer Billy Rose (played by James Caan) at rehearsal in the bio-musical *Funny Lady* (1975). As she sang her thoughts, the song blended contrapuntally with the standard "It's Only a Paper Moon" (which Rose co-authored) that the chorus girls were singing. A little later in the scene Caan reprised the song as "I Like Her" while Streisand talk-sang the standard for the girls. Fred Ebb (lyric) and John Kander (music) wrote the succinct, unsentimental number.

"I Like Myself" is the self-proclamation of self-contentment by Betty Comden, Adolph Green (lyric), and André Previn (music) that Gene Kelly sang and danced to in *It's Always Fair Weather* (1955). Discontented fight manager Kelly saw himself in a new light, breezily sang and whistled the number, and then did an athletic dance down Broadway on roller skates as the music turned into a vigorous march. The sequence, which took twelve days to rehearse and four to film, was the highlight of the movie.

"I Like to Do Things for You" is a sweet love serenade by Jack Yellen (lyric) and Milton Ager (music) that was featured in the early revue classic *King of Jazz* (1930). Paul Whiteman's Orchestra played the ballad while the Rhythm Boys (a trio that included the unknown Bing Crosby) sang it. Whiteman and the Rhythm Boys each recorded the song, as did Pletcher's Eli Prom Trotters, Leo Reisman's Orchestra, and Grace Hayes.

"I Lost My Sugar in Salt Lake City" is the bluesy lament by Leon René and Johnny Lange that was introduced by Mae E. Johnson singing backstage at a rehearsal in the landmark all-black musical *Stormy Weather* (1942). Johnny Mercer's recording with Freddie Slack's Band was a bestseller, and the number was performed in *Jam Session* (1944) by Jan Garber and his Orchestra.

"I Love a New Yorker" is the high-flying song-and-dance number from *My Blue Heaven* (1950), where Dan Dailey and Betty Grable sang their salute to those "bold, breezy and bright" citizens of New York City. Harold Arlen composed the snappy music and co-wrote the sassy lyric with Ralph Blane.

"I Love an Esquire Girl" is a tribute to the sexy ladies who graced the covers of the once-risqué magazine for men. Ralph Freed, Roger Edens, and Lew Brown collaborated on the number, which was seen in *DuBarry Was a Lady* (1943) in two parts: Red Skelton performed a comic version that listed the many fine qualities of the pin-up girls, and then Dick Haymes sang a serious paean to the twelve gals who graced the calendar months of 1943.

"I Love the Way You Say Goodnight" is the jaunty duet by Edward Pola and George Wyle that was interpolated into a score of old standards for the backstager *Lullaby of Broadway* (1951). As part of a benefit show, Gene Nelson and Doris Day sang the number about long goodnights filled with long kisses; they then danced to it with a dozen other couples, climaxing in a pas de deux filmed in slow motion.

"I Love to Laugh" is the buoyant song about the power of laughter that Richard M. and Robert B. Sherman wrote for *Mary Poppins* (1964). Governess Julie Andrews and chimney sweep Dick Van Dyke came to the aid of daffy Ed Wynn, who occasionally went into laughing fits that made him weightless. The three sang the song and, together with two children, had a tea party while floating in the air.

"I Love to Rhyme" is the clever Gershwin song from the Hollywood backstager *The Goldwyn Follies* (1938) that expresses lyricist Ira Gershwin's love of words and word play. Frustrated screen actor Phil Baker sang the number with Edgar Bergen and his puppet Charlie McCarthy (in their screen debut) at a Hollywood party, but the song was pretty much lost amid all the insults and jokes tossed back and forth. George Gershwin wrote the sprightly music, but the song's charm lies in its nimble lyric filled with rhymes and hoping that "*you* will rhyme with *me*." Bobby Short made a noteworthy recording in 1990.

"I Love to Sing-A" is the hearty proclamation song sung by Al Jolson and Cab Calloway in the show biz saga *The Singing Kid* (1936). Harold Arlen wrote the music and E. Y. Harburg contributed the playful lyric, an early example of his talent for suffix songs (which would culminate in "Something Sort of Grandish" a decade later), where he rhymes such invented words as "June-a" with "moon-a" and "south-a" with "mouth-a." Calloway made a successful recording of the number.

"I Love to Walk in the Rain" is the tuneful ditty by Walter Bullock (lyric) and Harold Spina (music) that Shirley Temple sang with the chorus in *Just Around the Corner* (1938). The ever-optimistic Temple thanked nature for the downpour ("I don't complain") because it gave her an opportunity to partake of her favorite pastime.

"I Love to Whistle" is a high-spirited "whistle" song by Harold Adamson (lyric) and Jimmy McHugh (music) that failed to catch on because of unfortunate timing. Swiss boarding school teen Deanna Durbin sang the cheerful number with her friends (accompanied on the soundtrack by Cappy Barra's Harmonica Band) as they bicycled through the hills of Switzerland in *Mad About Music* (1938). As appealing as the song was, audiences had been subjected to too many whistle songs in 1938 ("Whistle While You Work" was the most prevalent) and didn't want another one. Thomas "Fats" Waller made a notable recording of the song. A footnote: "I Love to Whistle" is not dissimilar in rhythm to Rodgers and Hammerstein's "I Whistle a Happy Tune," written a dozen years later.

"I Love You, Samantha" is a straightforward love song by Cole Porter that expresses itself simply ("my love will never die") and effectively ("I'm a one-gal guy"). Millionaire Bing Crosby sang the number about his ex-wife Grace Kelly (whose nickname was Samantha) in *High Society* (1956) as he dressed for a formal Newport party. Crosby is accompanied by Louis Armstrong's trumpet solo coming from another room in the mansion. The upbeat ballad was sung by Dennis Lotis in the 1994 British recording of the complete *High Society* score. In the 1998 Broadway version the ballad was sung by Daniel McDonald to Melissa Errico.

"I Love You So Much" is the eager song of unsubtle affection by Bert Kalmar (lyric) and Harry Ruby (music) that made for a clever musical scene in *The Cuckoos* (1930). Fortuneteller Bert Wheeler wanted to kiss Dorothy Lee in an apple orchard, but she insisted that he give her a bite of his apple for each kiss. So Wheeler fetched a bushel of apples, and by the end of the song the camera revealed the empty basket and the two sweethearts passed out from too many apples and kisses. Arlene Dahl and a male chorus sang the number in the Kalmar-Ruby bio-musical *Three Little Words* (1950), and the song was recorded by many, including Aileen Stanley, the California Ramblers, Smith Ballew, the Arden-Ohman Orchestra, Bob Haring, and Eddie Walters. The number was revived in 1953 by a popular record by Vicki Young.

"I Never Felt Better" is the paean to good health and a sunny disposition that Hugh Martin and Ralph Blane wrote for *Athena* (1954), the musical about a family of physical fitness advocates. Healthy sisters Jane Powell and Debbie Reynolds sang the jaunty number.

"I Never Knew Heaven Could Speak" is the hyperbolic revelatory ballad by Mack Gordon (lyric) and Harry Revel (music) about heaven personified by a true love's voice. Alice Faye, as a Fanny Brice–like performer, sang the rhapsodic love song at a backstage party in *Rose of Washington Square* (1939), and there were recordings by Bob Crosby (vocal by Marion Mann), Hal Kemp (vocal by Bob Allen), and Red Nichols (vocal by Bill Darnell).

"I Never Met a Rose" is a beguiling song from the musical allegory *The Little Prince* (1974), where stranded aviator Richard Kiley sang about the various flowers and women he has seen as he traveled the world, claiming he has never found fulfillment with any of them. Frederick Loewe composed the jazzy music that pastiched a 1920s lament (Kiley even sang parts of the song using a rolled-up paper as a megaphone), and Alan Jay Lerner wrote the ambiguously enchanting lyric.

"I Only Have Eyes for You" is the romantic standard by Al Dubin (lyric) and Harry Warren (music) from the backstager *Dames* (1934) and one of the team's loveliest ballads. The song was used throughout the film, often as background music, and in two celebrated scenes. Dick Powell sang the lyrical paean to Ruby Keeler on the Staten Island ferry at night, praising her beauty and preferring her eyes to the stars shining in the heavens. Then in a famous ten-minute sequence devised by Busby Berkeley, Powell rode a subway and imagined he sees Keeler's face in all the ads on the wall. The scene dissolved into a dream number where dozens of girls wearing Keeler masks appeared and eventually formed a giant jigsaw puzzle of Keeler's face. The song was heard throughout the sequence and eleven other times in the film, and even Warren commented that he was sick of the melody by the final reel. But audiences were not, and the ballad was often recorded and used in many other films. James R. Morris has written that the music's appeal is attributable to "the weightless melody and its adroitly linked phrases that flow gracefully into one another." The song was featured in *The Girl From Jones Beach* (1949); *My Dream Is Yours* (1949); *Tea for Two* (1950), where it was sung by Gordon MacRae and Virginia Gibson; and *Jolson Sings Again* (1959), where Al Jolson dubbed the singing for Larry Parks. Memorable recordings include those by Eddy Duchin, Jane Froman, Billie Holiday, Frank Sinatra (one of his first solo records), Helen Forrest, Eddy Duchin (vocal by Lew Sherwood), the Lettermen, Jackie Gleason's and Percy Faith's Orchestras, the Flamingos in 1959 (that was used in the 1973 film *American Graffiti*), Jerry Butler in 1972, and Art Garfunkle in 1975.

"I Poured My Heart Into a Song" is a delectable Irving Berlin ballad that never caught on quite as his other hits had, but it is a wondrous little gem all the same. Stanley Green notes that it is "possibly the one piece that best reveals Berlin's songwriting credo: Sincerity, not smartness or cleverness or *Hit Parade* standing, is the most important element." Berlin wrote the number for *Second Fiddle* (1939), where press agent Tyrone Power wrote the ballad for client Rudy Vallee to use to win Sonja Henie; later Vallee reprised it himself at a posh nightclub. Although "I Poured My Heart Into a Song" was nominated for an Oscar and was recorded by Vallee and such bands as those of Jimmy Dorsey, Artie Shaw, and Jan Garber, the ballad is mostly forgotten today.

"I Promise You" is the heartfelt pledge for mutual love that Johnny Mercer (lyric) and Harold Arlen (music) wrote for the wartime romance *Here Come the Waves* (1944). Celebrity-crooner-turned-sailor Bing Crosby and

WAVE member Betty Hutton sang the number as part of a benefit show for the U.S. Navy.

"I Remember It Well" is the charmingly satiric duet by Alan Jay Lerner (lyric) and Frederick Loewe (music) that Maurice Chevalier and Hermione Gingold sang in *Gigi* (1958) and one of Hollywood's finest character numbers. Two former lovers accidentally meet after many years at a seaside resort and fondly recall their past affair, though his memory of events is much less accurate than hers. Loewe's music is elegant but with a twinkle of humor in it, and Lerner's lyric, filled with contradictory details (a lost glove, a carriage ride, the music they heard, and so on) and warm affection, is a gentle showstopper. The number was shot in a studio months after the principal filming on location in Paris was complete. Lerner felt a duet for the two comic leads was necessary and recalled a song "I Remember It Well" that he had written for a disagreeing husband and wife to sing in the Broadway show *Love Life*. The scene (staged by Charles Walters since director Vincente Minnelli's work was done) was rather crudely shot and not nearly as lush as the rest of the musical, but the song was a highlight in the film. Steve Lawrence and Eydie Gorme recorded the duet, and in the 1973 Broadway version of *Gigi* the number was sung by Alfred Drake and Maria Karnilova.

"I Remember You" is the perennial favorite from the war years that Johnny Mercer (lyric) and Victor Schertzinger (music) wrote for *The Fleet's In* (1942). Dorothy Lamour sang the languid ballad about the "one who made my dreams come true" on a beach at night; then the number was reprised by Bob Eberle, Helen O'Connell, and some sailors with Jimmy Dorsey's Orchestra. The ballad has been recorded often over the decades, most memorably by Lamour, Eberle, Harry James (vocal by Helen Forrest) in the 1940s, the George Shearing Trio in the 1950s, and Ella Fitzgerald, the Four Freshmen, and Frank Ifield (a bestseller in Britain) in the 1960s. Bette Midler and James Caan revived the number in the musical film *For the Boys* (1991), Mary Clare Haran made a notable recording in 1994, and Jessica Molaskey sang it in the Broadway revue *Dream* (1997).

"I Said No" is a clever novelty song by Frank Loesser (lyric) and Jule Styne (music) in which a girl keeps refusing a man's continual offers until her resistance is shattered and she agrees, in the last line, to subscribe to *Liberty* magazine. Betty Jane Rhodes sang the double entendre number in *Sweater Girl* (1942) and recorded it, as did Alvino Rey (vocal by Yvonne King), Jimmy Dorsey (vocal by Helen O'Connell), and recently Andrea Marcovicci.

"I Saw You First" is a robust duet written by Harold Adamson (lyric) and Jimmy McHugh (music) for *Higher and Higher* (1943), where it was sung by

Frank Sinatra and Marcy McGuire as they teased each other over who can lay the first claim of affection on the other. Later in the film various women fought over Sinatra and sang the number as "I Saw Him First."

"I See Two Lovers" is the throbbing ballad by Mort Dixon (lyric) and Allie Wrubel (music) about picturing future happiness together and was sung by West Point cadet Dick Powell in *Flirtation Walk* (1934). Helen Morgan sang the lyrical song in *Sweet Music* (1935) and recorded it, as did Eddy Duchin and Russ Columbo.

"I Should Care" is a charming ballad by Sammy Cahn (lyric), Alex Stordahl, and Paul Weston (music) in which the lover claims to be indifferent to the romance at hand but obviously is not. Newlywed Esther Williams sang the number in *Thrill of a Romance* (1945) after meeting Van Johnson while on her honeymoon, and it was later reprised by Robert Allen. The oft-recorded song provided Frank Sinatra with a best-selling disk, and there were also recordings by Tommy Dorsey (vocal by Bonnie Lou Williams and the Sentimentalists), Jimmy Dorsey (vocal by Teddy Walters), and Martha Tilton. The ballad was revived in the 1950s with hit records by Harry Prime and Jeff Chandler.

"I Should Have Known Better (With a Girl Like You)" is the not-so-torchy torch song that John Lennon wrote for the Beatles' first film *A Hard Day's Night* (1964). The number was heard on the soundtrack (Lennon sang and the foursome played) as the fab group and "grandfather" Wilfred Brambell bounced along inside the mail car of a train. The group recorded the song for an album as well and sang it in many concerts in the mid-1960s.

"I Sing the Body Electric" is the stirring graduation song sung by the music, dance, and acting students of the High School for the Performing Arts in *Fame* (1980). Michael Gore composed the fervent music and Dean Pitchford wrote the lyric based on Walt Whitman's celebrated poem.

"I Speak to the Stars" is a wistful ballad about a secret love proclaimed to the heavens that Paul Francis Webster (lyric) and Sammy Fain (music) wrote for the backstager *Lucky Me* (1954). Doris Day, as an entertainer stranded in Miami, sang the pleasing number in the film and recorded it with success.

"I Used to Be Color Blind" is the intoxicating ballad by Irving Berlin that Fred Astaire sang to Ginger Rogers in *Carefree* (1938) as part of a dream sequence. The scene was originally intended to be in color, so Berlin used the idea of discovering color as a sign of true love. But the studio kept the whole film in black and white, and the song had to stand on its own. Psychiatrist Astaire suggests that patient Rogers eat lobster with mayonnaise before going to sleep so that her dreams will be vivid and he can then interpret them. The sequence was indeed vivid, with Astaire singing to her at first and then the couple easing into a graceful slow-motion dance that brought them across oversized lily pads and ended with one of the longest kisses in screen history. Astaire and Rogers each recorded the captivating song.

"I Wanna Be a Dancing Man" is the loving and personal tribute to dance that Johnny Mercer (lyric) and Harry Warren (music) wrote for Fred Astaire to perform in the period musical *The Belle of New York* (1952). Turn-of-the-century playboy Astaire, disguised as a singing waiter to win the heart of Salvation Army gal Vera-Ellen, did the song and dance number on the stage of a New York beer hall, vowing to leave "my footsteps" on the "sands of time." The scene is one of Astaire's most personal moments on screen, for as Jane Feuer explains, he "breaks out of the character to play his first and best screen role — himself dancing. There is no better example of the legendizing of Astaire within his films than this 1952 number which breaks out of the narrative in order to allow Astaire to pay tribute to his own art." Astaire recorded the song, and it was later performed by the company of the Broadway revue *Dancin'* (1978).

"I Wan'na Be Like You" is one of the most swinging and contagious of all Disney songs, a jazzy number by Richard M. and Robert B. Sherman that was a highlight of the animated Kipling tale *The Jungle Book* (1967). The orangutan King Louis of the Apes (voice of Louis Prima) sang the enthusiastic number to the kidnapped "man-cub" Mowgli about how he wishes he were human too, and then he and the other chimps broke into a wild and farcical dance.

"I Wanna Go Back to Bali" is a novelty number by Al Dubin (lyric) and Harry Warren (music) that dance troupe manager Rudy Vallee crooned in *Gold Diggers in Paris* (1938). Freddie "Schnicklefritz" Fisher's band, which was featured in the film, recorded the number, as did Jimmie Grier's Orchestra.

"I Wanna Go to the Zoo" is the snappy number of anticipation of seeing animals that orphaned Shirley Temple sang on a yacht in *Stowaway* (1936). Mack Gordon wrote the animated lyric, and Harry Revel provided the perky music. Songstress Hildegarde recorded the number and often sang it in her nightclub act.

"I Wanna Wander" is the exuberant number that Mack Gordon (lyric) and Josef Myrow (music) wrote as a specialty number for Donald O'Connor in *I Love Melvin* (1953). Photographer's assistant O'Connor sang the song about seeing the wide world. Later in the film he performed a knockabout dance, filled with his characteristic pratfalls and rubber-faced expressions, that took him all over the globe.

"I Want to Be a Minstrel Man" is the boisterous song-and-dance number by Harold Adamson (lyric) and Burton Lane (music) that was featured in the Eddie Cantor vehicle *Kid Millions* (1934). A very young Fayard Nicholas sang the tribute to minstrelry with the Goldwyn Girls as the opening portion of an entertainment on a boat heading to Egypt. Lane retrieved his melody years later and used it for "You're All the World to Me" (with a new lyric by Alan Jay Lerner) in *Royal Wedding* (1951).

"I Want to Go Places and Do Things" is the simple vaudeville ditty that Nancy Carroll (in her musical film debut) sang in the early musical melodrama *Close Harmony* (1929). Leo Robin (lyric) and Richard Whiting (music) wrote the eager little ballad, and Carroll sang it with a chorus on the stage of the Babylon Theatre. The scene, directed by John Cromwell and Edward Sutherland, was curiously staged, with a closeup on Carroll for most of the number and the chorines (which included an unknown Jean Harlow) barely visible behind her.

"I Was Alone" is a melancholy ballad that Otto Harbach, Oscar Hammerstein (lyric), and Jerome Kern (music) interpolated into their Broadway score for the 1930 film version of *Sunny*. Marilyn Miller, re-creating her stage role as a circus performer who stowed away on a ship heading to New York, sang the lonely number twice in the film.

"I Was Doing All Right" is the cheerful lament of a gal who was happy before she met her true love and now is miserable when he's away, but that she is "doing better than ever now." George Gershwin composed the music (one of his last songs before his early death), Ira Gershwin penned the gamesome lyric, and it was sung by Ella Logan in the Hollywood backstager *The Goldwyn Follies* (1938). Like other numbers in the film, the song was only briefly heard in the background, Logan's voice coming from a radio program. The ballad was recorded by Logan, Red Norvo's Orchestra (vocal by Mildred Bailey), Larry Clinton, and Jimmy Dorsey (vocal by Bob Eberle).

"I Was Lucky" is the exuberant proclamation sung by music hall comedian Maurice Chevalier in *Folies Bergère* (1935) when he realized he has found the girl of his dreams. Jack Meskill (lyric) and Jack Stern (music) wrote the zesty number, which was recorded by Benny Goodman and his Orchestra.

"I Was Saying to the Moon" is a casual ballad delivered casually by Mae West in *Go West Young Man* (1937). Johnny Burke (lyric) and Arthur Johnston (music) wrote the number, and West sang it as a movie star stuck in the countryside. The song was recorded by several bands, including those of Reggie Childs, George Hamilton, Dick Stabile, and Rudy Vallee.

"I Wish I Could Tell You" is the tentative song of affection written by Harry Ruby (lyric) and Rube Bloom (music) for the postwar musical melodrama *Wake Up and Dream* (1946). June Haver, as a waitress looking for her lost GI boyfriend, sang the ballad, and there were popular recordings by Dick Haymes, Benny Goodman's Orchestra, and Phil Brito.

"I Wish I Didn't Love You So" is the Frank Loesser torch song that Betty Hutton, as silent movie queen Pauline White, sang in the bio-musical *The Perils of Pauline* (1947). Hutton recorded the Oscar-nominated ballad, as did Dinah Shore, Dick Haymes, and Vaughn Monroe and his Orchestra.

"I Wish I Knew" is a luscious duet written by Mack Gordon (lyric) and Harry Warren (music) about the uncertainty of knowing whether one's loved one loves one back. Show girl Betty Grable and stage-struck doctor Dick Haymes sang the number (accompanied by Carmen Cavallero) in *Diamond Horseshoe* (1945), and Haymes recorded it as well. Years later the song was revived by a recording by Englebert Humperdinck.

"I Wish We Didn't Have to Say Goodbye" is an absorbing ballad of parting that for some reason or other never caught on and has pretty much disappeared. Perry Como (in his screen debut) and Vivian Blaine sang the number by Harold Adamson (lyric) and Jimmy McHugh (music) in the wartime musical *Something for the Boys* (1944).

"I Wished on the Moon" is the hit ballad, about finding the right mate after consulting the heavens, that Bing Crosby introduced in the star-packed *Big Broadcast of 1936* (1935), where he sang it on an early form of television called the Seeing Eye. Ralph Rainger composed the enticing music (his first *Your Hit Parade* success) and poet-wit Dorothy Parker wrote the romantic lyric. The popular song was recorded by Crosby, Billie Holiday (with Teddy Wilson's Orchestra), Ray Noble (vocal by Al Bowlly), Lanny Ross, Little Jack Little, and much later Teddi King. Nick Lucas was heard singing the ballad in the Hollywood drama *The Day of the Locust* (1975).

"I Wonder Where My Easy Rider's Gone" is the narrative lament that Bowery gal Mae West sang in her first starring vehicle, *She Done Him Wrong* (1933), telling of the plight of a woman who lost her jockey lover. Shelton Brooks wrote the honky–tonk number and West recorded it.

"I Won't Dance" is the scintillating rhythm song by Dorothy Fields (lyric) and Jerome Kern (music) that was written for the 1935 film version of Kern's Broadway hit *Roberta*. Fred Astaire sang the tangy refusal to Ginger Rogers as they danced in a Paris nightclub, and then Astaire broke into a fiery tap solo. It was Astaire who requested a faster and more jumping number for the near-operatic score, and Kern obliged with one of his few rhythm songs. The result was music that is, as Gerald Mast put it, "bizarrely meandering," with a simple and catchy main theme but a very tricky release, "perhaps the most difficult release Kern ever wrote," according to Alec Wilder, because it jumps from the key of C to A flat then to D flat to B. The melody was not entirely original. Kern and Oscar Hammerstein had written a similar number for the short-lived London musical *Three Sisters*, but Fields' lyric sent the song in a whole new direction. It is one of her finest lyrics: snappy, sensual, and slightly ambiguous. She even makes a reference to the "Continental," the song and dance made popular the year before by Astaire and Rogers. "I Won't Dance" became a big hit, somewhat as a result of Eddy Duchin's best-selling recording, and it was reprised by Van Johnson and Lucille Bremer in the Kern bio-musical *Till the Clouds Roll By* (1946), and by Marge and Gower Champion in the remake of *Roberta* called *Lovely to Look At* (1952). Kaye Ballard and Jack Cassidy made a lively recording of the song, and in the Broadway revue *Jerome Kern Goes to Hollywood* (1986) it was sung by Liz Robertson.

"I Won't Say (I'm in Love)" is the contradictory love song that the calculating Meg (voice of Susan Egan) sang, with the gospel-singing Muses backing her up, in the animated adventure *Hercules* (1997). Alan Menken composed the impelling music and David Zippel wrote the lyric denying her true feelings ("no way!") yet admitting that she is quite taken with the brawny but naive hero.

"I Won't Take a Million" is the optimistic ditty by Mack Gordon (lyric) and Harry Warren (music) that refuses to put a price tag on love and denies wealth and fame because his career is "here in your caress." Down-and-out vaudevillian Jack Oakie sang the number with his adopted ten-year-old daughter Shirley Temple in *Young People* (1940).

"I, Yi, Yi, Yi, Yi (I Like You Very Much)" is the sprightly samba number by Mack Gordon (lyric) and Harry Warren (music) that was one of Carmen Miranda's greatest hits. She sang the approving ditty (sprinkled with a few Portuguese words) at a lavish outdoor party in *That Night in Rio* (1941), backed by the male guitar group Banda da Lua. Miranda's recording was a top seller, and she sang it again in *Four Jills in a Jeep* (1944). Almost as popular was a recording of the samba by the Andrews Sisters, and most recently the zesty number was recorded by Judy Kaye.

"Ice Cold Katie" is a vibrant black mini-musical that was presented as part of a charity benefit in *Thank Your Lucky Stars* (1943) and an important sequence in the development of African-American roles in cinema. Frank Loesser (lyric) and Arthur Schwartz (music) wrote the musical scene that featured Hattie McDaniel, Willie Best, Rita Christina, Jesse Lee Brooks, and a black chorus. Newly enlisted soldier Best was off to war, but his girl Katie (McDaniel) refused to do her "patriotic duty" and marry him first. Best, their friends, and the chorus pleaded until Katie relented, a wedding was held, and Best was shipped off. The scene is devoid of stereotypes, and Allen Woll comments that the "number is quite an advance. McDaniel and Best are no longer maid and butler, but woman and soldier, separated by the coming of war, a dilemma common to both whites and blacks."

"I'd Know You Anywhere" is the Oscar-nominated ballad by Johnny Mercer (lyric) and Jimmy McHugh (music) from *You'll Find Out* (1940), an example of that rarest of genres, the musical whodunit. At a party in a haunted mansion, Ginny Simms and Harry Babbitt (with Kay Kyser's Kollege of Musical Knowledge) sang the song about recognizing one's true love by having seen him or her previously in one's dreams. Simms, Babbitt, and Kyser recorded the infatuated number.

"I'd Love to Take Orders from You" is a chirpy love duet that Al Dubin (lyric) and Harry Warren (music) wrote for *Shipmates Forever* (1935). Reluctant sailor Dick Powell and his sweetheart Ruby Keeler sang the romantic-military number, and there were popular recordings of the song by Mildred Bailey, Phil Harris, and Enric Madriguera.

"I'd Rather Be Blue Over You (Than Be Happy With Somebody Else)" is the bittersweet blues lament that struggling star Fanny Brice sang in the early talkie *My Man* (1928). Fred Fisher wrote the sassy music, and Billy Rose penned the Jewish-flavored lyric ("oucha-m'goucha!") specifically tailored to Brice's unique talents. Brice recorded the number with success. Barbra Streisand, as a young struggling Fanny Brice, sang the number on roller skates as part of a vaudeville act in *Funny Girl* (1968) and rescued the little gem from obscurity.

"I'd Rather Be Me" is the hit ballad that telegram boy Eddie Bracken sang in *Out of This World* (1945) but out of his mouth came Bing Crosby's voice. The gimmick (part of the plot of the film) didn't keep the Crosby recording from selling well. Sam Coslow, Ed Cherkose (lyric), and Felix Bernard (music) wrote the ballad about self-contentment in love, and it was interpolated into the Mercer-Arlen score.

"I'd Rather Lead a Band" is the toe-tapping opening number by Irving Berlin for the nautical romance *Follow the Fleet* (1936). Sailor Fred Astaire and a small jazz band performed the number on the deck of a U.S. Navy vessel when asked by an admiral and his visiting party for some entertainment. After Astaire sang the vivacious song, he did a solo tap routine and the sailors performed drills to the insistent tapping of his feet. Astaire recorded the number, as did Bunny Berigan, Glen Gray and the Casa Loma Orchestra (vocal by Pee Wee Hunt), and Nat Brandwynne's Orchestra. In 1966 Bobby Short, Dorothy Loudon, and Blossom Dearie recorded the rhythm song as a trio.

"I'd Rather Listen to Your Eyes" is the oxymoric ballad by Al Dubin (lyric) and Harry Warren (music) that sailor Dick Powell sang to dancing teacher Ruby Keeler in *Shipmates Forever* (1935). Mildred Bailey had a popular recording of the song, which was also recorded by the bands of Phil Harris, Enric Madriguera, Chick Bullock, and Jacques Renard.

"If He Cared" is the heart-throbbing torch lament that Clifford Grey (lyric) and Herbert Stothart (music) wrote for the early film operetta *Devil May Care* (1929). Marion Harris, a popular singer from Broadway, sang the aria–like number in the period musical, her only film.

"If I Didn't Have You" is the comic duet that the two-headed dragon (voices of Eric Idle and Don Rickles) sang, each half claiming to have been able to accomplish great things if he hadn't been stuck with the other, in the animated adventure *Quest for Camelot* (1998). Carole Bayer Sager (lyric) and David Foster (music) wrote the farcical number that moved from vaudeville to rock and roll.

"If I Had a Dozen Hearts" is a fun character duet by Paul Francis Webster (lyric) and Harry Revel (music) from the nightclub backstager *Stork Club* (1945). Betty Hutton, as a hat-check girl at the famed Manhattan nightspot who comes into a fortune, sang the number about the enormity of her passion with a tentative Andy Russell.

"If I Had a Million Dollars" is a song of affection hyperbolized into a monetary amount by Johnny Mercer (lyric) and Matt Malneck (music) and sung by the Boswell Sisters as shipboard entertainment on deck an ocean liner in *Transatlantic Merry-Go-Round* (1934). The number was popular throughout the Depression years thanks to records by the Boswells, Eddie Stone, and Jack Fulton and band recordings by Emil Coleman, Richard Himber, and Joe Haymes. The upbeat ballad was revived in the 1940s because of a best-selling recording by Betty and Rosemary Clooney with Tony Pastor's Band.

"If I Had a Talking Picture of You" is the hit ballad by Buddy De Sylva, Lew Brown (lyric), and Ray Henderson (music) from the early and influential musical *Sunny Side Up* (1929). At a wealthy Long Island estate, poor Manhattan girl Janet Gaynor and millionaire Charles Farrell sang the sweet but sly number as part of a charity show, and then the song was reprised by a gang of kindergarten children. Later in the film Farrell sang the song to a photograph of Gaynor, and the mocking lyric, imagining one's lost lover as a film with repeated showings in one's heart, made much more sense. Paul Whiteman and his Orchestra made a noteworthy recording of the popular song, and there was a memorable duet version by Johnny Mercer and Martha Stilton. "If I Had a Talking Picture of You" was performed by Byron Palmer in the DeSylva-Brown-Henderson bio-musical *The Best Things in Life Are Free* (1956) and by Vangle Charmichael in *Lucky Lady* (1975).

"If I Only Had a Brain" is the astute "I am" song for the scarecrow Ray Bolger in *The Wizard of Oz* (1939) and, with different lyrics, for the tin man Jack Haley's wish for a heart and for the cowardly lion Bert Lahr's hope for "da nerve." The song triplet was written by E. Y. Harburg (lyric) and Harold Arlen (music) for the fantasy classic, though the basic melody had been used for "I'm Hanging on to You," a song by the team cut from the Broadway musical *Hooray for Love* (1937). Although each section of the number vividly introduces the three *The Wizard of Oz* characters, the songs were originally much longer with a full verse for each character. All three verses were cut (despite some wonderfully witty lyrics by Harburg), and the lion's number was shortened to only ten lines in the final cut. Regardless, "If I Only Had a Brain/Heart/the Nerve" remains one of Hollywood songdom's finest (and most familiar) comic character number.

"If I Should Lose You" is the hit ballad that government agent John Boles and vigilante-in-disguise Gladys Swarthout sang together in the operetta *Rose of the Rancho* (1936). Leo Robin wrote the heartwrenching lyric, and Ralph Rainger composed the passionate music that adventurously keeps changing keys and, according to Alec Wilder, is "bordering at times on the pretentious but escapes miraculously." Among the many recordings were those by Isham Jones (vocal by Woody Herman), Harry Richman, Richard Himber's Orchestra, June Christy, and Milt Hinton.

"If I Steal a Kiss" is the moody ballad that reluctant desperado Frank Sinatra sang in the musical romance *The Kissing Bandit* (1948). Nacio Herb Brown composed the languid music, and Edward Heyman penned the lyric claiming a stolen kiss can be returned but a stolen heart is lost forever. Sinatra's recording enjoyed some popularity.

"If I Were in Love" is the sole original song added to the opera-highlights score for the Luciano Pavarotti vehicle *Yes, Giorgio* (1982). The famous tenor sang the expansive ballad by Alan and Marilyn Bergman (lyric) and John Williams (music) as a famous tenor on a concert tour of the United States.

"If I Were King" is the passionate song of political and romantic dreaming that outlaw-poet Dennis King sang to the aristocratic Jeanette MacDonald in the 1930 film version of the Broadway operetta *The Vagabond King*. Leo Robin (lyric), Newell Chase, and Sam Coslow (music) wrote three new songs to be added to the famous Rudolf Friml score, and the film version was slated to be called *If I Were King*, the title of the original play on which the operetta was based. The studio insisted on a title song so the lyrical duet was written, recorded, and filmed. When Friml found out about the interpolations into his score he sued because a clause in his contract forbade any non-Friml songs. The studio changed the film title back to that of the operetta and paid Friml $50,000 to use the songs he did not write. King, who had played the same role on stage, recorded the new song.

"If I Were King of the Forest" is the delicious mock aria that cowardly lion Bert Lahr sang in *The Wizard of Oz* (1939) as he anticipated being king of the jungle with his newfound courage. E. Y. Harburg, who had written specialty material for Lahr on Broadway, wrote the comic lyric and Harold Arlen composed the regal march music, much of which Lahr spoke rather than sang. The hilarious ditty, as written, was much longer but was cut by the studio for reasons of length and for the lyric phrase naming him the "king of kings" which was considered irreverent.

"If I'm Dreaming, Don't Wake Me Too Soon" is a song of an awakening love as sung by struggling dancer Marilyn Miller and millionaire Alexander Gray in the 1929 film version of the Broadway hit *Sally*. Al Dubin (lyric) and Joe Burke (music) wrote the duet, which was interpolated into the Jerome Kern score and was recorded by Wayne King and his Orchestra and by Elmo Tanner.

"If This Be Slav'ry" is the dancing song of affection that ancient Roman Gower Champion sang to Marge Champion in the Esther Williams vehicle *Jupiter's Darling* (1955); then the two of them did an energetic dance together. The coy number was written by Harold Adamson (lyric) and Burton Lane (music).

"If You Feel Like Singing, Sing" is the carefree chase-the-blues-away song that Mack Gordon (lyric) and Harry Warren (music) wrote for the backstager *Summer Stock* (1950). Farmgirl Judy Garland sang the cheerful number while taking a shower.

"If You Stub Your Toe on the Moon" is the bright-eyed ballad by Johnny Burke (lyric) and James Van Heusen (music) that warns one that having big dreams may cause you momentary distress but one should pursue them anyway. New England blacksmith Bing Crosby sang the delightful number with the local kids of the village in *A Connecticut Yankee in King Arthur's Court* (1949) as he tried to repair an automobile, tapping the engine with his hammer in time with the music. Crosby and Tony Martin each had popular recordings of the dreamy song.

"If You Want the Rainbow (You Must Have the Rain)" is the musical bit of philosophy that struggling performer Fanny Brice sang in the early show biz melodrama *My Man* (1928). Mort Dixon, Billy Rose (lyric), and Oscar Levant (music) wrote the number for Brice's film debut. Brice recorded the song, as did Eva Taylor, and it was sung by the chorus in the Brice bio-musical *Funny Lady* (1975).

"If You Were Mine" is an agreeable ballad by Johnny Mercer (lyric) and Matt Malneck (music) that Roger Pryor sang in the Hugh Herbert vehicle *To Beat the Band* (1935). Billie Holiday made a distinctive recording of the love song with Teddy Wilson's Band, and there were also disks by Lanny Ross, Jan Garber, and Jerry Cooper.

"If You Were the Only Girl in the World" is the crooning ballad that sax player Rudy Vallee sang with the Connecticut Yankees in the early musical comedy of manners *The Vagabond Lover* (1929). Clifford Grey (lyric) and Nat D. Ayer (music) wrote the hyperbolic number, which was revived in 1946 by a popular recording by Perry Como. The ballad was also sung by Ann Blyth (dubbed by Gogie Grant) in the bio-musical *The Helen Morgan Story* (1957).

"If You Were There" is the breezy song of affection by Pony Sherrell and Phil Moody that discounts the allure of Paris in the spring or a Manhattan autumn, arguing that any place at any time is special when that certain someone is near. Sailor Gene Nelson and American singer Gloria De Haven sang the light-footed number in a Parisian nightclub after hours in *So This Is Paris* (1955), dancing on the stage and empty tables in an effortless manner.

"I'll Always Be in Love With You" is the sprightly ballad that Morton Downey introduced in the early backstager *Syncopation* (1929). Bud Green, Herman Ruby (lyric), and Sam Stept (music) originally wrote the catchy number for the film *Stepping High* the previous year, but only the melody was used as background music. The ballad was recorded by Downey, Frank Milne, and (most successfully) Fred Waring and his Pennsylvanians. In 1957 Jack Pleis and his Orchestra revived the number with a popular recording.

"I'll Be Loving You" is the swinging love song that Sammy Cahn (lyric) and Vernon Duke (music) wrote for *She's Working Her Way Through College* (1952), the musical version of the campus comedy *The Male Animal*. Students Virginia Mayo and Gene Nelson sang the number from their upcoming student show in Ronald Reagan's classroom and then launched into a vigorous dance together that had them jumping atop the desks and chairs.

"I'll Buy That Dream" is the Oscar-nominated ballad by Herb Magidson (lyric) and Allie Wrubel (music) that Anne Jeffreys sang in *Sing Your Way Home* (1945), the postwar musical about Americans returning from Europe. The simple but effective love song became a standard thanks to best-selling records by Helen Forrest and Dick Haymes with Victor Young's Orchestra and by Harry James (vocal by Kitty Kallen).

"I'll Capture Your Heart Singing" is the playful Irving Berlin number that opens the musical classic *Holiday Inn* (1942). In a New York City nightclub show, song-and-dance team Bing Crosby and Fred Astaire tried to win Virginia Dale, Crosby using his singing voice and Astaire using his fancy footwork. At one point each spoofed the other, Fred singing a few "boo boo boo boo's" and Crosby furiously dancing. The silly routine parallels the plot in which Astaire has won Dale away from Crosby by offering her a dancing partnership. At the end of the film, the swinging song is reprised as a quartet with Marjorie Reynolds joining the threesome in a happy ending.

"I'll Dream Tonight" is the pleasing ballad about mutual fantasies that singing ranch hand Dick Powell and his sweetheart Priscilla Lane sang in *Cowboy from Brooklyn* (1938). The lyrical number by Johnny Mercer (lyric) and Richard Whiting (music) was recorded by the bands of Tommy Dorsey, Eddy Duchin, Orrin Tucker, and Teddy Wilson (vocal by Nan Wynn).

"I'll Give You Three Guesses" is the coy pastiche number by Johnny Mercer (lyric) and Henry Mancini (music) from the World War One–era musical *Darling Lili* (1970). Mata Hari–like entertainer-spy Julie Andrews (accompanied by a male quartet strumming banjos) sang the coquettish song in a Paris music hall offering three chances to guess who she's in love with. Later in the film Andrews reprised the song as a striptease number using the same sweet, old-fashioned lyric.

"I'll Never Let a Day Pass By" is the fervent love ballad that Frank Loesser (lyric) and Victor Schertzinger (music) wrote for the Hollywood satire *Kiss the Boys Goodbye* (1941), where it was sung by Southern starlet Mary

Martin and film director Don Ameche. The number was originally titled "I'll Never Let a Day Go By," but Ameche asked that it be changed because the original title could sound like an ethnic insult. The ballad was recorded by Charlie Barnet, Harry James (vocal by Dick Haymes), and Charlie Spivak.

"I'll Never Stop Loving You" is the Oscar-nominated ballad of unending love that Sammy Cahn (lyric) and Nicholas Brodszky (music) put into a score of old standards for the Ruth Etting bio-musical *Love Me or Leave Me* (1955). Doris Day, as Etting, sang the torchy number in a recording studio sequence and Day's record was a bestseller.

"I'll Remember April" is the hit ballad that Don Raye, Patricia Johnston (lyric), and Gene De Paul (music) wrote for the Abbott and Costello vehicle *Ride 'Em Cowboy* (1942) that became a standard. Singer Dick Foran, masquerading as a cowboy on a dude ranch, sang the wistful song about the memory of a past love affair and the number was soon heard everywhere, no recording more popular than one by Woody Herman and his Orchestra. Kirby Grant and Gloria Jean sang "I'll Remember April" in the 1945 film named after the song.

"I'll Si-Si Ya in Bahia" is the catchy Leo Robin (lyric) and Harry Warren (music) ditty that producer Bing Crosby sang at a rehearsal to demonstrate how the samba number ought to be done in *Just for You* (1952). The lyric tells of a young man at a crowded airport who hopes to fly down to the Brazilian resort city and bring his beloved back to the United States.

"I'll Sing You a Thousand Songs" is the ambitious boast of gondolier David Carlyle (who later became Robert Paige) as he and the chorus serenaded Marion Davies in a mammoth Venice production number in *Cain and Mabel* (1936). Al Dubin (lyric) and Harry Warren (music) wrote the gushing ballad, the middle section allowing for some snatches of other standards, including a few by Dubin-Warren, to be heard to support the title's musical claim. Years later Warren revealed that the other tunes were inserted because the two songwriters were not pleased with the main song and the studio wanted the sequence to be lavish and long. (The number runs eight minutes in the final cut.) The song enjoyed some popularity, no doubt helped by the strong promotion it received by William Randolph Hearst, Davies' lover and patron. Eddy Duchin and his Orchestra had a Number One chart recording of the song.

"I'll String Along With You" is the breezy love song by Al Dubin (lyric) and Harry Warren (music) in which an over-romantic lover gives up his idealized fantasy of an angelic beauty and happily settles for his flesh-and-blood sweetheart. Singing-waiter-turned-radio star Dick Powell sang the upbeat ballad in *Twenty Million Sweethearts* (1934), where he was joined on the air by Ginger Rogers (in her first important screen role). The popular number was sung in a handful of subsequent films, most memorably by Jack Carson and Joan Leslie in *The Hard Way* (1942), Doris Day in *My Dream Is Yours* (1949), and Danny Thomas in *The Jazz Singer* (1953). Among the many recordings was a best-selling one by Ted Fio Rito and a distinctive disk by Buddy Clark.

"I'll Take Romance" is the waltzing title song by Oscar Hammerstein (lyric) and Ben Oakland (music) from the 1937 musical about the world of grand opera. Grace Moore sang the gentle song, a yearning for love while one is young enough to give one's heart away, as she played the piano for opera manager Melvyn Douglas. Rudy Vallee and Tony Martin each had popular recordings of the ballad, which was heard in such subsequent films as *Good Girls Go to Paris* (1939), *Manhattan Angel* (1948), *Holiday in Havana* (1949), *Jolson Sings Again* (1949), and *The Eddy Duchin Story* (1956).

"I'll Take Sweden" is the pop title song for the 1965 musical about the generation gap. Diane Lampert and Ken Lauber wrote the genial ditty, and impoverished singer Frankie Avalon sang it as part of a lakeside production number.

"I'll Take Tallulah" is the lively number by E. Y. Harburg (lyric) and Burton Lane (music) that Bert Lahr and Red Skelton clowned with in *Ship Ahoy* (1942) and then Eleanor Powell danced to the music of Tommy Dorsey's Orchestra. A Dorsey recording with Frank Sinatra and the Pied Pipers was recorded.

"I'll Take You Dreaming" is the touching lullaby that Sylvia Fine and Sammy Cahn wrote for the Danny Kaye vehicle *The Court Jester* (1956). Kaye, as a medieval carnival clown disguised as a jester to get into the royal court, sang the gentle ballad to an infant prince while hiding the babe from a royal usurper.

"I'll Walk Alone" is the oft-recorded wartime ballad by Sammy Cahn (lyric) and Jule Styne (music) about being more than happy to be alone while waiting for one's beloved to return home. The song sold over one million copies of sheet music, the biggest hit in Cahn's career. Doris Day sang the Oscar-nominated song in the star-studded *Follow the Boys* (1944) and her record was a bestseller. Other popular recordings soon followed, including those by Frank Sinatra, Mary Martin, Martha Tilden, and Jane Froman. Froman sang it again for the dubbed Susan Hayward in the bio-musical *With a Song in My Heart* (1952) and interest in the song was revived, also through the 1952 recordings by Margaret Whiting, Richard Hayes and, in particular, through a hit record by Don

Cornell. Englebert Humperdinck recorded it in the 1970s, and most recently Michael Feinstein and Andrea Marcovicci have made distinctive disks of it.

"I'll Walk With God" is the simple and inspirational hymn that Paul Francis Webster (lyric) and Nicholas Brodszky (music) interpolated into the Sigmund Romberg score for the 1954 film version of *The Student Prince*. Operatic favorite Mario Lanza was originally slated to play the royal student Prince Karl, but his weight problem soon made the project impractical. So Lanza recorded the score and Edmund Purdom played the role on screen using the opera singer's familiar singing voice. Lanza's recording of the hymn was a bestseller, and the song became a standard in churches and for choral groups.

"Illusions" is the heavy–handed torch song by Frederick Hollander about the loss of one's illusions in life and love. Berlin cabaret singer Marlene Dietrich sang the dirge in the spy melodrama with songs *A Foreign Affair* (1948).

"I'm a Dreamer (Aren't We All?)" is the wistful song of longing by Buddy De Sylva, Lew Brown (lyric), and Ray Henderson (music) from the early musical romance *Sunny Side Up* (1929). Working girl Janet Gaynor sang the tender ballad in her Yorkville tenement apartment as she accompanied herself on the zither. (The scene was originally filmed with a full orchestra, but because Gaynor's weak singing voice was lost in the orchestrations, it was replaced by the zither.) Later in the film Gaynor reprised the number at a charity show at a Long Island mansion. The ballad became popular on records and on radio, and Paul Whiteman recorded it and featured the song for years in his orchestral concerts. The song was heard in *Holy Terror* (1931) and in *Everyone Says I Love You* (1997), where it was sung Olivia Hayman dubbing for Drew Barrymore.

"I'm a Gypsy" is a delightful comic wooing song that fortune hunter Bert Woolsey sang to rich matron Jobyna Howland while strumming a guitar caballero-style in the early musical farce *The Cuckoos* (1930). Harry Ruby composed the flighty music and Bert Kalmar provided the funny lyric that professed to love devotedly as long as his beloved's money holds out.

"I'm a Happy-Go-Lucky Fellow" is a chirping number by Ned Washington (lyric) and Leigh Harline (music) that Jiminy Cricket (voice of Cliff Edwards) sang on a floating leaf in a lily pond to introduce the first part of the animated anthology *Fun and Fancy Free* (1947). The song had originally been written and recorded by Edwards for the animated *Pinocchio* but was cut from the final print.

"I'm a Ruler of a South Sea Island" is a slaphappy comic number by Ralph Blane (lyric) and Harold Arlen (music) from *Down Among the*

Sheltering Palms (1953), a musical about GIs stationed in a Pacific Island after World War Two. Officer and war hero William Lundigan and his sidekick David Wayne sang the daffy number about being Pacific royalty.

"I'm a Square in a Social Circle" is the playful lament written by Ray Evans and Jay Livingston for the nightclub backstager *Stork Club* (1945). Hat-check girl Betty Hutton, who suddenly found herself favored by a millionaire, sang the comic specialty number.

"I'm Against It" is the zany song of philosophy that Bert Kalmar (lyric) and Harry Ruby (music) wrote for the Marx Brothers vehicle *Horse Feathers* (1932). Groucho Marx, as the incoming president of Huxley College, sang the number in front of a line of bearded deans who eventually joined in with shimmies and kicks. The song, in which Marx nonsensically lists all the things he is against, has been aptly described by Ethan Mordden as "a mixture of Gilbertian patter and rhythmic quickstep." The number is sometimes listed as "Whatever It Is, I'm Against It."

"I'm an Old Cowhand (From the Rio Grande)" is the popular cowboy song by Johnny Mercer (his first Hollywood hit song) that gently spoofs the "home on the range" kind of western ballad, the singer confiding that he cannot be much of a cowboy because he has never even seen a cow. Mercer even adds a "Yippy-I-O-Ki-ay" at the end of each refrain to give the song a satirical flavor. Singing cowboy Bing Crosby introduced the ballad in *Rhythm on the Range* (1936) and had a major hit record of the number with Jimmy Dorsey's Orchestra. The song was revived when Roy Rogers sang it in *King of the Cowboys* (1943); his record with the Sons of the Pioneers was also a bestseller.

"I'm Bubbling Over" is the spirited song of romantic enthusiasm by Mack Gordon (lyric) and Harry Revel (music) from *Wake Up and Live* (1937), a backstager about radio. Grace Bradley and the Brewster Twins sang the number as a specialty act during a radio broadcast; later in the film it was reprised by the Condos Brothers with Ben Bernie's Orchestra at another broadcast from the High Hat Club.

"I'm Cookin' With Gas" is the sassy rhumba number by Stella Unger (lyric) and Alec Templeton (music) that Carmen Miranda sang with Xavier Cugat and his Orchestra at a rehearsal in *A Date With Judy* (1948). The lyric consisted of several everyday expressions that were hilarious when mispronounced by Miranda (the title phrase came out "cookin' with glass") as she tried to explain how she "digs the music."

"I'm Doing It for Defense" is the sly comic number by Johnny Mercer (lyric) and Harold Arlen (music) about excusing one's overly romantic behavior as all part of the war effort. Betty Hutton sang the jaunty song as she and some sailors rode along in a jeep in *Star-Spangled Rhythm* (1942). Andrea Marcovicci made a shrewd recording of the number in 1990, and it was sung by Darcie Roberts in the Broadway Mercer revue *Dream* (1997).

"I'm Easy" is the carefree folk song with a sensual subtext that Keith Carradine wrote and sang in the satirical *Nashville* (1975) about the music business. The lyric is disarming, offering casual sex from a man who "plays the game" and yearns for something more from an unattainable woman. Folksinger Carradine sang sections of the song at various points in the film (once it was heard on a tape player while he bedded a fellow singer), but its most memorable use in the film was at a small Nashville nightclub where Carradine sang it to Lily Tomlin in the audience while three of his other sexual conquests looked on uncomfortably. Carradine's solo record was a bestseller and the song won the Oscar.

"I'm Feelin' Like a Million" is the breezy duet that Eleanor Powell and George Murphy performed in the opulent *Broadway Melody of 1938* (1937). Arthur Freed wrote the high-flying optimistic lyric and Herb Nacio Brown composed the bouncy music.

"I'm Glad I Waited for You" is the embullient song by Sammy Cahn (lyric) and Jule Styne (music) that Coast Guard member Alfred Drake sang to Janet Blair in the wartime musical *Tars and Spars* (1946). Popular recordings of the ballad were made by Peggy Lee, Helen Forrest, Frankie Carle and his Orchestra, and Freddy Martin (vocal by Clyde Rogers).

"I'm Glad I'm Not Young Anymore" is the delicious character song that Maurice Chevalier, as an aging boulevadier seated in a Paris sidewalk cafe, sang to the camera in *Gigi* (1958), explaining how comfortable life can be when one is past all the troubles of youth. Frederick Loewe composed the soft-shoe music hall melody and Alan Jay Lerner provided the superb lyric that called the fountain of youth "dull as paint." The idea for the song came from Chevalier himself when he remarked to Lerner one day that he was too old for passion, physical sport, and heavy drinking, that his audience was the only vice still available to him. Lerner then wrote the jaunty lyric, including a third refrain that was considered too risque and was cut by the studio. During the recording of the song, Chevalier asked Lerner if his accent was okay. When Lerner assured him he could understand every word, Chevalier inquired "but was there enough?" The song became Chevalier's signature tune for his nightclub act during the last decade of his life. In the 1973 Broadway version of *Gigi*, Alfred Drake sang the number (including the racy third refrain).

"I'm Going Shoppin' With You" is a bright song by Al Dubin (lyric) and Harry Warren (music) that medical student Dick Powell (working as a hotel clerk) sang to wealthy Gloria Stuart as they went on a shopping spree in *Gold Diggers of 1935* (1935). Winifred Shaw, who was also in the film, recorded the song with Dick Jurgens' Orchestra, as did Russ Morgan and Little Jack Little.

"I'm Going to Go Back There Some Day" is the wistful ballad by Kenny Asher and Paul Williams about missed opportunity and the desire to try something again. The hoarse-voiced muppet Gonzo (voice of Dave Goelz) sang the quiet song to his traveling companions in *The Muppet Movie* (1979) as they camped out in the desert and sat around a campfire in the moonlight.

"I'm Gonna Ring the Bell Tonight" is the merry declaration that Doris Day sang in *April in Paris* (1952) in the galley of a French ocean liner as she announced to the chefs and waiters that she was tired of behaving and planned to "rock the boat tonight." Sammy Cahn (lyric) and Vernon Duke (music) wrote the lively number that combined Parisian can-can with Broadway belting, and diplomat Ray Bolger did a drunken dance to the music with Day.

"I'm Gonna Swing My Way to Heaven" is the zesty proclamation that Frances Langford sang in the radio backstager *Swing It, Soldier* (1941). Eddie Cherkose and Jacques Press wrote the jubilant number that claims swing music is heaven's music.

"I'm Hans Christian Andersen" is the title storyteller's signature song by Frank Loesser that was used throughout the romanticized bio-musical *Hans Christian Andersen* (1952). Danny Kaye first sang the engaging "I am" song as he walked to Copenhagen and rehearsed what he would say to the people there about his unconventional characters and ability to tell stories. He reprised the number as he set himself up in a shoe shop in town and later reprised it again, with a different lyric, when his first story was published.

"I'm in Love" is the no-holds-barred romantic ballad that Sammy Cahn (lyric) and Jule Styne (music) wrote for the shipboard musical *Romance on the High Seas* (1948). Doris Day (in her film debut) sang the number as a singer disguised as a socialite, and her recording was a bestseller.

"I'm in the Market for You" is the naive but endearing love song by Joseph McCarthy (lyric) and James Hanley (music) that society gent Charles Farrell and shop girl Janet Gaynor sang in the musical melodrama *High Society*

Blues (1930). Johnny Marvin had an early recording with Bob Haring's Orchestra, and a disk by George Olson's Orchestra was a hit. Subsequent recordings were made by Louis Armstrong, Sammy Fain, the Keynotes, and Harry James.

"I'm in the Mood for Love" is one of the most popular standards to come out of Hollywood, a soulful ballad by Dorothy Fields (lyric) and Jimmy McHugh (music) that factory girl and would-be singer Frances Langford (in her film debut) sang in *Every Night at Eight* (1935). McHugh's music is sad yet romantic, and Fields' lyric brilliantly inserts casual expressions like "funny" and "simply" before lush praises that makes the song so confidential and even conversational. Langford recorded the ballad, sang it over the credits for *Palm Springs* (1938), and reprised it again in *People Are Funny* (1946). It is estimated that over 500 different records of the song have been made, selling well over three million disks. Among the many memorable recordings over the decades have been those by Little Jack Little (a Number One seller), Louis Prima and Keely Smith, the McGuire Sisters, Louis Armstrong, Billy Eckstine, and more recently Barbara Cook. The song has also been very popular in films, being sung by Gloria De Haven in *Between Two Women* (1944), Lizbeth Scott in *Dark City* (1950), Dean Martin in *That's My Boy* (1951), Shirley Booth in *About Mrs. Leslie* (1954), a chorus on the soundtrack of *Ask Any Girl* (1959), and others.

"I'm Late" is the furious ditty by Bob Hilliard (lyric) and Sammy Fain (music) that is heard in quick snatches throughout the animated fantasy *Alice in Wonderland* (1951). The White Rabbit (voice of Bill Thompson) sang the number as he rushed down the rabbit hole near the beginning of the film, and he repeated it as he reappeared in various places in Wonderland.

"I'm Learning a Lot From You" is an amiable song of affection by Dorothy Fields (lyric) and Jimmy McHugh (music) from the lighthearted musical romance *Love in the Rough* (1930). Golf champ Robert Montgomery and his sweetheart Dorothy Jordan sang the number on a golf course and were joined by comic sidekicks Benny Rubin and Dorothy McNulty. The scene is unique in that it is one of the very few musical numbers in early talkies that is not presented as part of a show or performance of some kind. But the studio worried about the logic of music coming out of nowhere on a golf course, so a harmonica-playing caddy was added to the scene.

"I'm Like a Fish Out of Water" is a frolicsome number about being caught in awkward situations that saxophonist Dick Powell and movie-star-stand-in Rosemary Lane sang in *Hollywood Hotel* (1947) as they waded barefoot in a fancy hotel fountain. Richard Whiting composed the sprightly music, and

Johnny Mercer wrote the jocuse lyric that included such examples of awkwardness as Ginger Roger managing the Brooklyn Dodgers and J. P. Morgan trying to play a pipe organ.

"I'm Making Believe" is a starry-eyed ballad that Mack Gordon (lyric) and James Monaco (music) wrote for Benny Goodman and his Orchestra to feature in *Sweet and Low Down* (1944), a backstager about the Big Band business. Ella Fitzgerald's recording of the Oscar-nominated song with the Ink Spots was a bestseller.

"I'm No Angel" is the sultry title song sung by sideshow hussy Mae West in the 1933 musical filled with suggestive sex and overt comedy. Gladys DuBois, Ben Ellison, and Harvey Brooks wrote the number urging one to "love me until I just don't care" and West recorded it.

"I'm Old Fashioned" is the bewitching ballad by Johnny Mercer (lyric) and Jerome Kern (music) that was introduced in *You Were Never Lovelier* (1942) when Rita Hayworth (dubbed by Nan Wynn) sang it to Fred Astaire, and then they both danced to Xavier Cugat's Orchestra in a Buenos Aires garden. Mercer's lyric lists old-fashioned favorites such as moonlight and the sound of raindrops, yet it rises far above mawkishness. (Mercer once stated that this lyric came closest to his personal philosophy of life.) Kern's music, a carefully disguised waltz, has been described by Gerald Bordman as "an imaginative series of theme and variations, all played out in a range of just over an octave." In fact, the refrain has unusually few notes, none shorter than a quarter note. The music is also a masterpiece of building up melody and harmony in an effortless but captivating way. The oft-recorded song received memorable recordings by Cugat, Ella Fitzgerald, Glen Gray and the Casa Loma Orchestra (vocal by Kenny Sargent), Astaire (whose recording was heard in the 1971 film *A Safe Place*), Dorothy Kirsten, Barbara Carroll, and recently Mandy Patinkin. Elaine Delmar sang the ballad in the Broadway revue *Jerome Kern Goes to Hollywood* (1986), and Darcie Roberts and Jonathan Dokuchitz performed it in the Broadway Mercer revue *Dream* (1997).

"I'm Olga from the Volga" is a comic ditty that comedienne Joan Davis performed in the Sonja Henie vehicle *Thin Ice* (1937). Mack Gordon wrote the wacky lyric, and Harry Revel provided the mock-Russian music.

"I'm Putting All My Eggs in One Basket" is the delightful Irving Berlin love song that playfully admits that all of one's romantic hopes are being put on one sweetheart. Sailor Fred Astaire sang the song at the piano in *Follow the Fleet* (1936) as part of a rehearsal for a benefit show on a yacht. Then he and his former vaudeville partner Ginger Rogers broke into a competitive dance routine that took them all over the ship. Astaire's recording was a bestseller, and the number was also recorded by Jan Garber, Guy Lombardo and his Orchestra, the Boswell Sisters, Louis Armstrong, Joe Bushkin and his Orchestra, Carmen McRae, the Snuff Smith Combo, and more recently Michael Feinstein.

"I'm Ridin' for a Fall" is the jaunty admission of romance by Frank Loesser (lyric) and Arthur Schwartz (music) from the star-studded wartime musical *Thank Your Lucky Stars* (1943). Songwriter Joan Leslie and singer Dennis Morgan sang the jovial but fatalistic duet.

"I'm Shooting High" is the optimistic love song that Alice Faye sang with Jack Oakie, Warner Baxter, and the team of Shaw and Lee, then danced with Nick Long, Jr., in the backstager *King of Burlesque* (1935). Jimmy McHugh composed the energetic music, and Ted Koehler wrote the spunky lyric about aiming high, even climbing up a rainbow if necessary, to get one's love. The bright number was popular with audiences beginning to recover from the worst of the Depression, and there were successful recordings made by Faye, Louis Armstrong, Jan Garber (vocal by Lee Bennett), Lud Gluskin (vocal by Buddy Clark), and Little Jack Little. In the Broadway revue *Sugar Babies* (1980), Mickey Rooney and Ann Miller performed the high-flying number.

"I'm Sitting High on a Hilltop" is the song of self-satisfaction that governor-elect Dick Powell sang in the political musical comedy *Thanks a Million* (1935). Gus Kahn (lyric) and Arthur Johnston (music) wrote the number, recorded by Paul Whiteman, the Mound City Blue Blowers, the Original Dixieland Jazz Band, Guy Lombardo and his Royal Canadians, Dolly Dawn, Paul Pendarvis, and Johnny Hamp.

"I'm Sorry for Myself" is the nimble torch song by Irving Berlin whose lively rhythm keeps the sad lyric from being too earnest. Mary Healy and the chorus sang the ballad at a studio wrap party in the Hollywood backstager *Second Fiddle* (1939). The orchestras of Glenn Miller, Ben Bernie, and Hal Kemp (vocal Nan Wynn) made recordings of the rhythmic number.

"I'm Sorry, I Want a Ferrari" is the sly duet sung by longshoreman union mobster James Cagney (in his last singing role) and his worldy-wise "girl Friday" Cara Williams in the gangster musical comedy *Never Steal Anything Small* (1959). In a Manhattan car showroom, Williams insisted Cagney buy her a $14,000 Ferrari to convince her to carry out his latest scheme, then the two danced a clever pas de deux (choreographed by Hermes Pan) on a treadmill moving between the various cars on display. Maxwell Anderson (lyric) and Allie Wrubel (music) had originally written the cynical number for a Broadway show that never materialized.

"I'm Still Crazy for You" is the slaphappy love duet that chorine Betty Grable and her fiancé John Payne sang on a Manhattan rooftop in the Broadway backstager *Footlight Serenade* (1942). Ralph Rainger composed the winning melody, and Leo Robin wrote the frolicsome lyric in which the lovers confess to having seen each other at their worst (e.g. unshaven, hair in a mess, even drunk) but claim they are still in love.

"I'm Talking Through My Heart" is the musical pledge of sincerity by Leo Robin (lyric) and Ralph Rainger (music) from the radio backstager *The Big Broadcast of 1937* (1936). Small-town radio announcer Shirley Ross (in her first leading role) sang the heartfelt ballad.

"I'm the Last of the Red Hot Mammas" is the caustic number nightclub singer Sophie Tucker (in her film debut) performed, as described by Ethan Mordden, as "a combination of speech, recitative, and all-out singing" in *Honky Tonk* (1929). Milton Ager composed the jazzy music and Jack Yellen wrote the lyric, whose title came from Tucker's catch-phrase in her act. Tucker also recorded the number, which became one of her signature songs for the rest of her career.

"I'm True to the Navy Now" is the self-mocking song of fidelity that Elsie King (lyric) and Jack King (music) wrote for the early film revue *Paramount on Parade* (1930). Clara Bow, in a sexy sailor outfit, sang and danced the slick number with Jack Oakie and dozens of mariners aboard a ship. The song (and Bow) were so popular that the studio quickly made a vehicle for her using the song and released it later that year as *True to the Navy* (1930).

"I'm Wishing" is the echoing song of yearning that Larry Morey (lyric) and Frank Churchill (music) wrote for the animated classic *Snow White and the Seven Dwarfs* (1937). Snow White (voice of Adriana Caselotti) sang the winsome number into a wishing well about her hopes of a true love, and her own voice echoed back to her. At the end of the song the Prince (voice of Harry Stockwell) appeared behind her and, his face reflected in the water, sang the last notes of the song for her.

"Imagine" is the sprightly romantic duet that Hugh Martin and Ralph Blane wrote for the physical fitness musical *Athena* (1954). Health-nut Debbie Reynolds and crooner Vic Damone sang the merry list song that let them imagine themselves as everything from a shipwrecked couple to a moth attracted to a flame. Reynolds and Damone recorded the number together and it enjoyed some popularity.

"In Acapulco" is the vivacious tribute to the resort city that Mack Gordon (lyric) and Harry Warren (music) wrote for Carmen Miranda to sing in *Diamond Horseshoe* (1945), but she wasn't available for the film and so it was sung instead by Betty Grable and the chorus at a nightclub with Carmen Cavallaro at the piano. Cavallaro and Georgia Gibbs each had successful recordings of the lively number.

"In-Between" is the touching lament written by Roger Edens about being at that awkward age when a girl is caught between "toys" and "boys." Overlooked teenager Judy Garland sang the entrancing ballad in *Love Finds Andy Hardy* (1938).

"In Love in Vain" is the lyrical ballad of unrequited love that Leo Robin (lyric) and Jerome Kern (music) wrote for the nostalgic period musical *Centennial Summer* (1946). Philadelphian Jeanne Crain (dubbed by Louanne Hogan) sang the not-so-torchy torch song and was joined by William Eythe and the chorus. It was recorded by Mildred Bailey, Sarah Vaughn, Barbara Carroll, and recently Andrea Marcovicci.

"In Old Chicago" is the vivacious title number by Mack Gordon (lyric) and Harry Revel (music) that praised the Second City in the 1938 musical that climaxed with the famous fire of 1871. Music hall singer Alice Faye and the chorus sang the boisterous number in a rowdy beer hall, and Dick Stabile made a popular recording of the zesty anthem.

"In Our United State" is the patriotic song of connubial love by Ira Gershwin (lyric) and Burton Lane (music) from *Give a Girl a Break* (1953) that looks forward to "star-spangled happiness." Bob Fosse sang the sly list song that used government metaphors to express long-term romance; then he and Debbie Reynolds danced in a Brooklyn Heights park along the East River, Fosse falling into the water at the end of the number. Michael Feinstein made a sportive recording of the song in 1990.

"In the Cool, Cool, Cool of the Evening" is the Oscar-winning standard by Johnny Mercer (lyric) and Hoagy Carmichael (music) that looked forward to romance once the hot sun went down. Laid-back journalist Bing Crosby and perspective sweetheart Jane Wyman sang the number as they prepared for a party in *Here Comes the Groom* (1951). The Crosby-Wyman recording was a bestseller, and a duet version by Frankie Laine and Jo Stafford was also popular. Margaret Whiting and the John Pizzarelli Trio sang the ballad in the Broadway Mercer revue *Dream* (1997).

"In the Cool of the Evening" is the romantic ballad that Walter

Bullock (lyric) and Jule Styne (music) wrote for the radio backstager *Hit Parade of 1941* (1940). Small-time radio singer Frances Langford sang the number and later recorded it. The song was also heard in *Is Everybody Happy?* (1943).

"In the Dark of the Night" is the driving Russian number that Rasputin (singing voice of Jim Cummings) sang in the animated *Anastasia* (1997). As he vowed to revenge himself on the Romanoff family (the surviving Anya in particular), Rasputin conjured up his minions from hell and sent them on their deadly mission. Lynn Ahrens wrote the demonic lyric and Stephen Flaherty composed the surging music.

"In the Middle of Nowhere" is the dreamy ballad that Harold Adamson (lyric) and Jimmy McHugh (music) wrote for the wartime musical farce *Something for the Boys* (1944), the Cole Porter Broadway hit that was brought to the screen with only one of Porter's songs surviving. Perry Como (in his film debut) introduced the poignant song of loneliness.

"In the Park in Paree" is a charming Gallic number by Leo Robin (lyric) and Ralph Rainger (music) that ex–big game hunter Maurice Chevalier sang in *A Bedtime Story* (1933). He reprised the song three decades later in *A New Kind of Love* (1963), and there were instrumental recordings by Paul Whiteman, Ted Fio Rito, Roy Smeck, Paul Tremaine, and Freddy Martin.

"In the Spirit of the Moment" is an expansive ballad that Bernie Grossman (lyric) and Walter Jurman (music) wrote for *His Butler's Sister* (1943), a musical about the world of classical music in New York. Singing hopeful Deanna Durbin sang the impetuous number about getting carried away with song.

"In the Still of the Night" is the intoxicatingly lyrical Cole Porter ballad in which a lover stares at the moon in a hushed reverie and contemplates whether or not his love is returned. College football player Nelson Eddy sang the number to princess Eleanor Powell in a romantic garden in the fictional kingdom of Romanza in *Rosalie* (1937). The ballad is not only one of Porter's finest, but among his most unusual structurally. The long (seventy-two measures) refrain has a sixteen-measure stretch labeled "appassionato" that is tricky and exhilarating. The lyric is also atypical of Porter, being a sincere, aching lyric devoid of any sophistication and climaxing with a series of short descriptive phrases that gently peak with the title phrase. Eddy was not comfortable with the song and wanted it cut from the score, but Porter played the ballad for producer Louis B. Mayer, who (legend has it) wept upon hearing it and kept the song in the film. Eddy himself must have had a change of heart because he later sang it on radio and included the number in his concerts for several years. The oft-recorded ballad has remained a staple over the decades with distinctive records by Tommy Dorsey (vocal by Jack Leonard), Leo Reisman's Orchestra, Vaughn Monroe, Helen O'Connell, Ella Fitzgerald, Della Reese (her first hit record), Nero Young, and Englebert Humperdinck. "In the Still of the Night" was sung by Dorothy Malone, Cary Grant, and the chorus in the Porter bio-musical *Night and Day* (1946).

"In the Valley (Where the Evening Sun Goes Down)" is Judy Garland's "I am" song at the beginning of the prairie musical *The Harvey Girls* (1946), a wistful ballad that she sang on the back platform of a train taking her westward for a new life. Harry Warren composed the haunting music, and Johnny Mercer penned the pastoral lyric about the magical valley where she hopes to go after she weds and make a home with her true love.

"In Your Own Quiet Way" is a ballad about finding love in an nonaggressive manner, as sung by Broadway director Dick Powell in the backstager *Stage Struck* (1936). Harold Arlen wrote the flowing music and E. Y. Harburg penned the disarming lyric.

"The Inch Worm" is a simple yet indelible children's song that Frank Loesser wrote for the bio-musical *Hans Christian Andersen* (1952) and one of his own favorites of all his works. The short (only sixteen bars) and gentle song is based on an Andersen tale about an inch worm slowly "measuring the marigold" who best appreciates the beauty of nature. Loesser's number was a contrapuntal duet with storyteller Danny Kaye singing about the inch worm as he and his apprentice Joey Walsh watched one in the garden while the voices of children in the schoolhouse sang addition equations. The resulting scene was thematically and lyrically magical.

"Innamorata" is the tearful Italian ballad by Jack Brooks (lyric) and Harry Warren (music) that invites one to romance using the odd Italian phrase here and there for effect. The lyrical song was used cleverly in the Dean Martin–Jerry Lewis vehicle *Artists and Models* (1955), where struggling artist Martin sang it to illustrator Dorothy Malone but she thought the voice was coming from the radio. Then Shirley MacLaine reprised the number as a silly seductive song and dance for Lewis, turning the Italian ballad into a screeching mating call. Martin's flowing recording of the song enjoyed some popularity.

"Irresistible You" is the swinging song of affection by Don Raye and Gene De Paul that Ginny Simms and George Murphy sang with Tommy Dorsey's Orchestra in the backstager *Broadway Rhythm* (1944). Simms recorded the number, as did Woody Herman and his Orchestra and Johnny Johnston.

"Is That Good?" is the delightful comic number by Leo Robin (lyric) and Ralph Rainger (music) that asks if lack of sleep, a fluttering of the heart, and absent-mindedness are signs of true love. Texas short-order cook Charlotte Greenwood and Florida hotel waiter Jack Haley sang the dandy character number in *Moon Over Miami* (1941) and then they launched into a high-kicking antic pas de deux.

"Is You Is or Is You Ain't My Baby?" is the ungrammatical plea for affection that Billy Austin and Louis Jordan wrote for the all-star wartime musical *Follow the Boys* (1944). Jordan sang the number in the film and his record with his Tympani Five was a bestseller. Popular recordings were also made by Bing Crosby, Glenn Miller, and the Delta Rhythm Boys, who also sang it in the film *Easy to Look At* (1945). The Andrews Sisters sang the fun number the same year in *Her Lucky Night* (1945). Buster Brown's 1960 disk revived the song, which was later performed by the company of the Broadway revue *Five Guys Named Moe* (1992).

"Isn't It Kinda Fun?" is a casual but endearing love song that farmboy Dick Haymes and entertainer Vivian Blaine sang in the rural musical *State Fair* (1945). Richard Rodgers composed the catchy music that comfortably uses repeated notes, and Oscar Hammerstein penned the easygoing lyric that considers this romance may be just a momentary fling but also perhaps the real McCoy. In the 1962 remake of the musical the number was jazzed up and sung by Ann-Margaret and David Street as a bump-and-grind act on stage. Andrea McArdle and Scott Wise performed the song in the 1996 Broadway version of *State Fair*.

"Isn't It Romantic?" is the brilliant opening number in the early classic musical *Love Me Tonight* (1932) and one of filmdom's most effective uses of a song as a way to introduce a movie's story. Tailor Maurice Chevalier sang the enthralling song of wishful romance in his Paris shop; it was then picked up by various Parisians and carried across town. Soon a regiment of soldiers marching into the countryside were continuing the number, which ended up being sung by aristocrat Jeanette MacDonald in her rural chateau. Lorenz Hart (lyric) and Richard Rodgers (music) wrote the infectious number and director Rouben Mamoulian staged the sequence, which has rarely been equaled though much copied by others over the years. Rodgers' music uses a snappy four-note musical phrase repeatedly (eight times in the refrain alone), and Hart's lyric is sly and knowing even as it embraces romance. (A stanza about an ideal wife who is equally adept at scrubbing the floors and one's back was deleted in the final print.) The popular song was featured in several films, including *Isn't It Romantic?* (1948), *Sabrina* (1954), *It's Only Money* (1962), and *The Day of the Locust* (1975), and was recorded by such artists as Harold Stern and his Orchestra, Carmen McRae, Joe Bushkin, and Ella Fitzgerald and more recently by Joan Morris and William Bolcom as a duet and by Michael Feinstein (who included the politically incorrect stanza).

"Isn't That Just Like Love?" is the spirited, matter-of-fact song about romance by Johnny Burke (lyric) and James Van Heusen (music) that Mary Martin sang with a knowing look with the Merry Macs in the radio backstager *Love Thy Neighbor* (1940). The number was recorded by the bands of Glenn Miller, Tommy Dorsey, and Bob Crosby.

"Isn't This a Lovely Day (to Be Caught in the Rain)?" is the delectable song about using a sudden rain shower as a way to romance that Irving Berlin wrote for *Top Hat* (1935), his first full score for Hollywood. Fred Astaire and Ginger Rogers were caught in the London rain and dashed into a park bandstand where Astaire sang the jaunty number to Rogers and then slipped into a challenge dance, with her imitating his fancy footwork all over the empty pavilion. Berlin's music has plenty of rests in the melodic line to accommodate dancing, and musicologists have pointed out the Gershwin–like musical phrases in the song. Alec Wilder found the last section the most ambitious, "not only unexpected but difficult to sing" as the music does an unexpected turn. Astaire's recording of the gently rhythmic song remains the definitive one.

"Isn't This Better?" is a beguiling ballad by Fred Ebb (lyric) and John Kander (music) from the bio-musical *Funny Lady* (1975) about contentment being better than passionate love. Barbra Streisand, as entertainer Fanny Brice, sang the song to her sleeping husband James Caan in a train compartment on their honeymoon, happy to know her second marriage was based on friendship rather than the complicated love of her first.

"It Can't Go on Like This" is the impressionable torch song by E. Y. Harburg (lyric) and Jay Gorney (music) from *Roadhouse Nights* (1930), the musical melodrama about rum-running. Helen Morgan, as a chanteuse in a seedy nightclub outside of Chicago, sang the tormented song of unrequited love.

"It Could Happen to You" is the wry song of caution sung by band singer Dorothy Lamour and bandleader Fred MacMurray in *And the Angels Sing* (1944). James Van Heusen wrote the flowing music and Johnny Burke penned the lyric that warned of romantic temptation but admitted that no one has ever heeded the advice. Jo Stafford and Bing Crosby each had a best-selling recording of the ballad, and years later Johnny Mathis, Shirley Horn, and Ann Hampton Callaway each recorded the number, which was also sung by Alvaleta Guess in the Broadway revue *Swinging on a Star* (1995).

"It Doesn't Cost a Dime to Dream" is a breezy lullaby by Ray

Evans and Jay Livingston about the low cost of big dreams of travel, wealth, and happiness. Con-man Bob Hope and nightclub singer Marilyn Maxwell introduced the light-hearted song of optimism to a group of homeless old ladies as they sang them to sleep in a makeshift dormitory in *The Lemon Drop Kid* (1951).

"It Don't Worry Me" is a lazy song of freedom from the world's crises that was used effectively in the country–music backstager *Nashville* (1975). Keith Carradine wrote the lackadaisical number, which he was heard singing on a tape recorder in a hotel room. At the end of the film, struggling singer Barbara Harris took to the stage of a political rally after a country star is murdered and sang the number to and with the crowd.

"It Happened in Monterey" is the hit ballad by Billy Rose (lyric) and Mabel Wayne (music) about the fond memory of a romance that took place in Mexico. The song was introduced in a lavish production number in the early revue *King of Jazz* (1930), where John Boles and Jeanette Loff, set amid giant palms and cacti and surrounded by smiling señoritas, sang the song with Paul Whiteman's Orchestra and were then joined by the Sisters G, George Chiles, and the Markert Girls. Whiteman recorded the ballad, as did Ruth Etting, George Olson's Orchestra, organist Jesse Crawford, and the Regents Club Orchestra.

"It Happened in Sun Valley" is the happy narrative ballad by Mack Gordon (lyric) and Harry Warren (music) about a skiing accident where the girl fell in the snow and the guy fell in love. Lynn Bari (dubbed by Pat Friday) sang the song in *Sun Valley Serenade* (1941) as she auditioned for a job at the Sun Valley Lodge, and later it was heard as members of Glenn Miller's band sang it as they rode in sleighs to the lodge. Miller's recording, with vocals by Tex Beneke, Bob Eberle, and the Modernaires, was popular.

"It Happens Every Time" is the charming admission by Ira Gershwin (lyric) and Burton Lane (music) that every time one is with one's beloved one falls in love all over again. Gower Champion sang it to Marge Champion in the backstage musical *Give a Girl a Break* (1952) and then they danced to the upbeat number. Michael Feinstein made a distinctive recording of the merry ballad in 1991.

"It Might As Well Be Spring" is the Oscar-winning ballad by Oscar Hammerstein (lyric) and Richard Rodgers (music) about the restless feeling of spring fever hitting one out of season. The song served as farmgirl Jeanne Crain's (dubbed by Louanne Hogan) "I am" song in *State Fair* (1945) as she sang it in her bedroom and wondered why she seems so discontent. In one rarely recorded section of the song she fantasized about her ideal lover, a combination of Ronald Coleman, Charles Boyer, and Bing Crosby, and an image of each appeared to her and sang to her in her imagination. Later in the film she reprised the song with different lyrics (also rarely recorded) about the squeaky-clean and loveless life she anticipated with her dull husband-to-be. The ballad is a masterwork of music and lyric writing. Rodgers uses the odd shift from the key of C to F sharp in the release to give the song a strange off-balance feel to mirror the character's confusion, and his melody bounces up and down the scale when she sings of being "jumpy as a puppet" on strings, purposely using a "wrong note" (F natural) on the word "string" to send it askew. Hammerstein originally wrote the song as a straightforward bout of spring fever until he recalled that all state fairs are held at the end of the summer. So he rewrote the lyric about it *feeling* like spring fever when it cannot be and the change is what makes the song so fascinating. "It Might As Well Be Spring" has been recorded often, most memorably by Margaret Whiting with Paul Weston's Orchestra, Dick Haymes, a jazz version by Stan Getz, and Barbara Cook. It was sung by Pamela Tiffin (dubbed by Anita Gordon) in the 1962 remake of *State Fair*, Lynne Wintersteller performed it in the Broadway revue *A Grand Night for Singing* (1993), and Andrea McArdle sang it in the 1996 Broadway version of the homespun tale.

"It Must Be You" is a larkish duet by Edward Eliscu and Manning Sherwin about the inevitability of romance with each other. It was sung in the golf musical *Follow Through* (1930) by shy millionaire Jack Haley (in his film debut) and perky Zelma O'Neal, who wooed him with her mysterious "love perfume."

"It Only Happens When I Dance With You" is the flowing Irving Berlin dance song that was heard three times in the period musical *Easter Parade* (1948). Entertainer Fred Astaire sang it to dance partner Ann Miller in an Edwardian apartment; then the two ingeniously danced in the small space, seductively moving about the furniture and out onto a balcony. Later in the film Astaire's new dancing partner Judy Garland sang it to him and, even later, the music was used for a pas de deux by Astaire and Miller as they performed at the New Amsterdam rooftop theatre. The song is one of Berlin's smoothest with an effortless fluttering of notes to propel the music forward. Frank Sinatra made a best-selling disk of the song, and recently it has been recorded by Andrea Marcovicci, Mandy Patinkin, and Tommy Tune.

"It Was So Beautiful" is the popular ballad by Arthur Freed (lyric) and Harry Barris (music) that was featured in two different movies made by two different studios in 1932. Kate Smith sang it in the radio backstager *The Big Broadcast* while Marion Davies sang it in the Broadway backstager *Blondie of the Follies*. Among the recordings of the romantic number were those by Ruth

Etting, Harry Richman, Enric Madriguera and his Orchestra, and Ozzie Nelson and his Orchestra.

"It Was Written in the Stars" is the romantic song about the power of fate that Leo Robin (lyric) and Harold Arlen (music) wrote for the exotic musical romance *Casbah* (1948). Dashing thief Tony Martin and his beloved Marta Toren strolled through a street festival in Algiers and listened to the natives sing. Martin then translated and sang to Toren in a stiff and sophisticated way, followed by Katherine Dunham and her dancers interpreting the song in a passionate manner. Ella Fitzgerald's recording of the number was a bestseller.

"It's a Blue World" is the lush ballad by Robert Wright and George Forrest that was featured in the Big Band musical *Music in My Heart* (1940). Tony Martin, as a foreigner looking for a singing job so that he can stay in America, sang the ballad and his recording was a top-selling record. The Oscar-nominated song was also recorded by Glenn Miller (vocal by Ray Eberle).

"It's a Bore" is the acidic "I am" song for the restless French aristocrat Louis Jourdan in the period musical classic *Gigi* (1958). As Jourdan rode through Paris in an open carriage with his uncle Maurice Chevalier, he complained how spring, the Eiffel Tower, the River Seine, horse racing, and all his former joys now bored him and he bluntly refuted each of Chevalier's arguments to the contrary. Frederick Loewe composed the busy and restless music, and Alan Jay Lerner penned the expert lyric that describes Venice as "a town without a sewer" and discounts the Tower of Pisa as a "bore." The musical number was performed by Daniel Massey and Alfred Drake in the 1973 Broadway version of *Gigi*.

"It's a Grand Night for Singing" is one of Richard Rodgers' most intoxicating waltz songs, described by Alec Wilder as "a charmingly direct, four-square, old-fashioned back-porch waltz." He wrote it with Oscar Hammerstein (lyric) for the rural musical *State Fair* (1945), where it was sung by William Marshall, Vivian Blaine, Dick Haymes, Jeanne Crain (dubbed by Louanne Hogan), Dana Andrews, and other fairgoers as they danced at an outdoor pavilion of the Iowa State Fair. In the 1962 remake of the film, the waltz was sung by Pat Boone, Pamela Tiffin (dubbed by Anita Gordon), Bob Smart, Ann-Margaret, Bobby Darrin, and Alice Faye. The celebratory number is one of Rodgers and Hammerstein's most recognized songs and has been popular with choral groups for decades. The waltz was sung by the casts of the Broadway revue *A Grand Night for Singing* (1993) and the 1993 Broadway version of *State Fair*.

"It's a Great Big World" is a somber character song that Johnny Mercer (lyric) and Harry Warren (music) wrote for the out-West musical *The*

Harvey Girls (1946). Three waitresses at the Harvey House restaurant — Judy Garland, Virginia O'Brien, and Cyd Charisse (dubbed by Marion Doenges) — sang the number on the balcony of their room above the restaurant at night, wistfully making plans for the future and yet afraid of the uncertainty of what awaits them if they must leave town. The trio recorded the waltzing number.

"It's a Great Day for the Irish" is the joyous tribute to St. Patrick's Day in Manhattan that Roger Edens wrote for the sentimental ethnic musical *Little Nelly Kelly* (1940). Judy Garland and Douglas MacPhail led the crowd in the spirited number. Freddy Martin and his Orchestra had a popular recording of the rousing anthem.

"It's a Great Feeling" is the bubbly title song by Sammy Cahn (lyric) and Jule Styne (music) for the 1949 musical spoof about moviemaking in Hollywood. The Oscar-nominated song was sung by Doris Day as a waitress in Tinsel Town waiting for her one big break, and Day later recorded it with success.

"It's a Hap-Hap-Happy Day" is the chipper song of celebration that Sammy Timberg, Winston Sharples, and Al J. Neiburg wrote for the animated adventure *Gulliver's Travels* (1939). When the giant Gulliver helped defeat the enemy in battle, the Lilliputians sang this merry ditty as they sewed new clothes and groomed their newfound hero. The bright number was recorded by Ginny Simms, Eddy Duchin (vocal by the Earbenders), and Guy Lombardo (vocal by the Lombardo Trio).

"It's a Long, Dark Night" is the flexible song by Leo Robin (lyric) and Ralph Rainger (music) that was used creatively throughout the musical melodrama *Torch Singer* (1933) in different contexts, much like "Let Me Entertain You" was used in the play and film *Gypsy* years later. Fallen woman Claudette Colbert took up singing in clubs and used the torchy number throughout her career, first as an awkward beginner and finally as a high-style chanteuse. Robin's lyrics are suggestive enough to be used in various ways, being both coy and sultry. Rainger himself played Colbert's pianist in one scene.

"It's a Lovers' Knot" is a diverting character song by Mack Gordon (lyric) and Harry Warren (music) from the Sonja Henie vehicle *Iceland* (1942). Icelandic skating champ Henie sang the merry number about the entanglements of love with Jack Oakie and John Payne.

"It's a Most Unusual Day" is the popular rhythm song by Harold Adamson (lyric) and Jimmy McHugh (music) that celebrates a spring day of clear skies, high spirits, and romance in the air. Teenager Jane Powell introduced the lilting number in *A Date With Judy* (1948) while rehearsing for a high school dance, and it was reprised twice: by rival teen Elizabeth Taylor (dubbed by an uncredited singer), who gave it a sultry interpretation, and by Powell and the crowd at formal anniversay party at the end of the film. The song is one of McHugh's few waltzes and one of his most exhilarating efforts: a long (seventy-two measures) and soaring melody that is done "in one" (three beats of the measure are conducted with one sweep of the baton). The most popular of the many recordings was that by Ray Noble (vocal by Anita Gordon).

"It's a New World" is the optimistic ballad by Ira Gershwin (lyric) and Harold Arlen (music) that foresees no more pain or unhappiness now that true love has come into one's life. The eager number was used effectively throughout the legendary musical *A Star Is Born* (1954): Up-and-coming singer Judy Garland was heard singing it on the radio, then she later sang it to husband James Mason in their home, and finally she was heard singing it in the background when Mason went out onto the beach to commit suicide. Gershwin rewrote some the lyrics in 1963 when Lena Horne performed the inspiring song at Carnegie Hall in a benefit for the March on Washington for Jobs and Freedom.

"It's All in a Lifetime" is the bright-eyed song of optimism that Alice Faye and the male chorus sang in *The Great American Broadcast* (1941), the musical about the early days of radio. Harry Warren wrote the banjo-strumming music and Mack Gordon penned the happy lyric that promises that lady luck will get around to you eventually.

"It's Always You" is the tender ballad by Johnny Burke (lyric) and James Van Heusen (music) that finds one's true love in the stars, the roses, the breeze, and in melody itself. Conman Bing Crosby sang it to conlady Dorothy Lamour in *Road to Zanzibar* (1941) as they paddled along in a canoe in Africa, Crosby even getting a harp glissendo when he runs his hand through the water. Crosby recorded the ballad, and a disk by Tommy Dorsey (vocal by Frank Sinatra), made at the time of the film but not released until two years later, became a bestseller.

"It's Anybody's Spring" is the jaunty song of optimism that prospector Bing Crosby sang in a talent contest aboard a ship heading for Alaska in *Road to Utopia* (1945) while fellow prospector Bob Hope accompanied him on the accordion. James Van Heusen composed the warm but gleeful music, and Johnny Burke wrote the philosophical lyric that dismisses fame and fortune for the hopeful possibilities of new beginnings.

"It's Bigger Than You and Me" is the eager ballad of affection by Leo Robin (lyric) and Jule Styne (music) from the 1955 musical film version of the popular comedy *My Sister Eileen*. New York magazine publisher Jack Lemmon sang the number to aspiring writer Betty Garrett from Ohio, arguing that their mutual attraction could not be overlooked.

"It's Dynamite" is the zesty number that cowgirl-entertainer Ann Miller sang and exuberantly danced with male dancers (who incongruously wore cowboy outfits with Indian feathers and tom-toms) at a party for wealthy Texans in the midway musical *Texas Carnival* (1951). Dorothy Fields wrote the powerhouse lyric, and Harry Warren provided the spirited music.

"It's Easy to Remember (and So Hard to Forget)" is the infectious ballad that remembers a lost love that riverboat singer Bing Crosby (in one of his few costume roles) performed with a chorus of Southern belles in the period musical *Mississippi* (1935). The score for the film, written by Lorenz Hart (lyric) and Richard Rodgers (music), was completed and the two songwriters were back in New York when original star Lanny Ross was replaced by Crosby, who asked for a ballad written in his crooning style. The team quickly responded and sent a demo record of the new song to Hollywood. Rodger's music is unusually sparse, utilizing a narrow range and repeated notes but feeling expansive all the same. Alec Wilder calls it "an instance of conveying the most within the confines of required simplicity." Crosby's recording of the ballad, sometimes listed as "Easy to Remember," was on the top of the charts.

"It's Fate, Baby, It's Fate" is the comic number that Betty Garrett sang to timid baseballer Frank Sinatra in the period musical *Take Me Out to the Ball Game* (1949) as he protested mildly in song. Roger Edens composed the snappy music, and Betty Comden and Adolph Green provided the sly lyric in which Garrett made clear that time was running out and Sinatra had better "play ball with me."

"It's Love I'm After" is the forthright song of romantic hunting that Sidney Mitchell (lyric) and Lew Pollock (music) wrote for the youth musical *Pigskin Parade* (1936). Freckled hillbilly gal Judy Garland (in her first feature film) belted out the exuberant number during halftime of a football game between a small Texas college and Yale. Mildred Bailey, Tony Martin, and the bands of Charlie Barnet and Al Donahue made recordings of the vigorous ballad.

"It's Magic" is the Oscar-nominated song that made Doris Day a marketable movie star. She sang the enticing ballad by Sammy Cahn (lyric) and Jule Styne (music) in a Latin nightclub in *Romance on the High Seas* (1948), and her recording of the song sold over a million copies. The slow tango melody had been written two years earlier but not used in the project because it was too Spanish sounding. Cahn remembered the tune when the new film required a

Latin number, and he wrote the expansive lyric of realization that love is found in a sweetheart's voice, even a sigh. Styne's music is a series of descending scales that end with the title phrase in a bewitching manner. Gene Nelson and Janice Rule sang the number in *Starlift* (1951), and among the many recordings of the ballad were memorable ones by Dick Haymes, Gordon MacRae, Bobby Hackett, Sarah Vaughn, Tony Martin, and Vic Damone. The Platters revived the song with their 1962 record, and most recently Michael Feinstein recorded it.

"It's On, It's Off" is a delicious comic number by Sam Coslow and Al Siegel about the genteel art of the striptease and Martha Raye performed it with aplomb in *Double or Nothing* (1937). The satiric song is a sort of forerunner for Rodgers and Hart's more famous number "Zip," written for the Broadway musical *Pal Joey* a few years later.

"It's Swell of You" is a song of appreciation by Mack Gordon (lyric) and Harry Revel (music) for the one who showed "the way to love" from the radio backstager *Wake Up and Live* (1937). Ben Bernie's Orchestra played the song during a radio broadcast while the Condos Brothers tap danced to the music. Later in the film microphone-shy Jack Haley (dubbed by Buddy Clark) sang it with the same orchestra into what he thought was a dead microphone. Alice Faye, who was in the film, and Ruth Etting each recorded the song, as did the bands of Ozzie Nelson, Chick Webb, Duke Ellington, Little Jack Little, Teddy Wilson, and Emery Deutsch.

"It's the Animal in Me" is the vivacious song about a woman's sensual powers that Mack Gordon (lyric) and Harry Revel (music) wrote for Ethel Merman to sing in *We're Not Dressing* (1934) as she swung from tree to tree in a Tarzan outfit, ending up on the back of an elephant. The sequence was recorded and filmed before it was cut from the final print, but the bizarre scene was interpolated into *The Big Broadcast of 1936* (1935), where it was shown as part of an early form of television called the "Seeing Eye." Merman recorded the feisty song.

"It's the Natural Thing to Do" is the romantic list song by Johnny Burke (lyric) and Arthur Johnston (music) arguing that all sorts of animals fall in love so it must be all right for us. (The song might be described as a less risqué version of Cole Porter's risqué list song "Let's Do It.") Bing Crosby sang the number in *Double or Nothing* (1937), and his recording and one by Mildred Bailey were both bestsellers.

"It's the Same Old Dream" is the slow tempo ballad by Sammy Cahn (lyric) and Jule Styne (music) about the ageless power of love from *It Happened in Brooklyn* (1947). Returning GI Frank Sinatra worked as a salesman in a record store, but the teenage customers urged him to sing and so he did in a quiet and rather bland manner. But the teens were bored and reprised the number in a jazzed-up swinging version that prompted Sinatra to sing the ballad again, this time with depth and feeling. In addition to Sinatra's recording were standout ones by Tommy Dorsey (vocal by Stuart Foster) and the Pied Pipers with June Hutton.

"I've a Strange New Rhythm in My Heart" is the robust number by Cole Porter that princess Eleanor Powell sang and tapped out in a college dorm in the romantic fairy tale *Rosalie* (1937). The rhythm is indeed strange in the song, which is, according to Ethan Mordden, "cross-metered from fox trot to waltz and back again." (One section of the number breaks into Porter's "Night and Day.") Artie Shaw (vocal by Leo Watson) made a memorable recording of the catchy number.

"I've Got a Date With a Dream" is the hit ballad that Mack Gordon (lyric) and Harry Revel (music) wrote for the Sonja Henie vehicle *My Lucky Star* (1938). Art Jarrett, Buddy Ebsen, Joan Davis, and the chorus girls introduced the song in the film, and there were best-selling recordings by the orchestras of Benny Goodman and George Hall.

"I've Got a Feeling I'm Falling" is the bittersweet song of realization by Billy Rose (lyric), Harry Link, and Thomas "Fats" Waller (music) that looks at the prospect of new love with mixed emotions. Aging burlesque singer Helen Morgan sang the ballad in the groundbreaking musical melodrama *Applause* (1929), and Waller's recording of it was popular. Nell Carter performed the number in the Broadway Waller revue *Ain't Misbehavin'* (1978).

"I've Got a Feeling You're Fooling" is the lighthearted song by Arthur Freed (lyric) and Herb Nacio Brown (music) that suspects romantic insincerity but accepts it all the same. Robert Taylor and June Knight sang it in a ritzy penthouse apartment in *Broadway Melody of 1936* (1935), where furniture kept popping up from the floor; then Knight danced to the song with Nick Long, Jr. Later in the film Frances Langford reprised the number. The delectable song was revived decades later when Susan Hayward (dubbed by Jane Froman) sang it in the Froman bio-musical *With a Song in My Heart* (1952), and that same year it was sung by the chorus during a montage sequence in *Singin' in the Rain*. On Broadway it was sung by Mary D'Arcy and the girls in the 1985 version of *Singin' in the Rain* and by Gary Chapman, Cleavant Derricks, Bernard J. Marsh, and the ensemble of the musical *Big Deal* (1986).

"I've Got a Gal in Kalamazoo" is the swinging song by Mack Gordon (lyric) and Harry Warren (music) that eagerly looks forward to seeing an old flame from Michigan because she was a "real pipperoo." Glenn Miller and his Orchestra introduced the peppy number at a casino in *Orchestra Wives* (1942) with vocals by Tex Beneke, Marion Hutton, the Modernaires, and the Nicholas Brothers, who also performed a vigorous dance to it. The Miller recording was at the top of the charts, and the song was even popular in England, where no one was familiar with the oddly named town. It was performed by James Alexander and the company of the Off-Broadway revue *A Brief History of White Music* (1996).

"I've Got a Pocketful of Dreams" is the laid-back ballad that brothers Bing Crosby (on guitar), Fred MacMurray (on clarinet), and Donald O'Connor (on accordion) performed in *Sing, You Sinners* (1938). James Monaco composed the smooth music and Johnny Burke wrote the carefree lyric that admitted to material poverty but lots of imagination. Crosby's recording was a bestseller, and one by Russ Morgan and his Orchestra was also popular.

"I've Got My Eyes on You" is a breezy Cole Porter love song that promises to keep close to one's true love and hopes "you'll keep your eyes on me." Fred Astaire introduced the song in *Broadway Melody of 1940* (1940) in an empty theatre after a rehearsal when he saw a picture of Eleanor Powell on some sheet music and then sang to and danced with the photo. Powell entered and watched, and soon they were performing a tap routine together. Both Tommy Dorsey (vocal by Alan DeWitt) and Bob Crosby (vocal by Marion Mann) made profitable recordings of the ballad, and Kathryn Grayson sang it in *Andy Hardy's Private Secretary* (1941).

"I've Got My Fingers Crossed" is the rhythmic song hoping for true love that Dixie Dunbar and Thomas "Fats" Waller sang in the backstager *King of Burlesque* (1935). Ted Koehler (lyric) and Jimmy McHugh (music) wrote the number, and there were successful recordings by Alice Faye, Louis Armstrong, Lud Gluskin (vocal by Buddy Clark), Wingy Manone, and the Mound City Blue Blowers. In the Broadway Waller revue *Ain't Misbehavin'* (1978) the number was sung by Armelia McQueen, Ken Page, and Charlaine Woodard.

"I've Got My Love to Keep Me Warm" is "one of the most smiling of all (Irving) Berlin's songs," according to Alec Wilder, "breezy, healthy and forthright with no aspect of contrivance about it." Dick Powell, Alice Faye, and E. E. Clive sang the rhythm number as part of a Broadway revue in the backstager *On the Avenue* (1937), claiming that gloves and overcoats were not necessary to keep away the cold when one is in love. Les Brown and his Orchestra revived the song in 1949 with a record that went to the top of the charts. The merry love song was also recorded by Faye, Powell, Billie Holiday,

Art Lund, the Mills Brothers, and Della Reese as well as the orchestras of Skitch Henderson, Ray Noble, Joe Bushkin, and a 1949 bestseller by Les Brown.

"I've Got News for You" is a satiric song by Bill Giant, Bernie Baum, and Florence Kaye that was used for comic effect in the Elvis Presley vehicle *Girl Happy* (1965). Fort Lauderdale stripper Nita Talbot sang the mock-striptease number while she removed fabric newspaper that she was wearing. Later in the film millionaire's daughter Shelly Fabares reprised the song on stage in a drunken stupor and a brawl broke out. The number has also been listed as "Good News" and "Read All About It."

"I've Got No Strings" is the carefree song of freedom by Ned Washington (lyric) and Leigh Harline (music) that the puppet Pinocchio (voice of Dickie Jones) sang and danced to as he performed at Stromboli's marionette theatre in the animated classic *Pinocchio* (1940). The simple ditty had an amusing section in which puppets from different nations sang and danced with Pinocchio in a mock Folies Bergère routine. Barbra Streisand made a spirited recording of the song in the 1960s, and the Gipsy Kings recorded it in 1995.

"I've Got to Hear That Beat" is the rhythmic number by Leo Robin (lyric) and Nicholas Brodszky (music) that inspired a memorable Busby Berkeley sequence in *Small Town Girl* (1953). Ann Miller sang the pounding song on a stage set with holes cut in the floor through which dozens of musicians' hands and arms protruded playing their instruments, creating a surreal effect worthy of Salvador Dali.

"I've Got to Sing a Torch Song" is the upbeat lament by Al Dubin (lyric) and Harry Warren (music) that is far from torchy. Songwriter-singer Dick Powell sang the number for a Broadway producer in *Gold Diggers of 1933* (1933), and the producer was so impressed that when Powell finished the producer shouted "Fire Dubin and Warren!" Ginger Rogers then sang the number, but it was cut from the final print; her recording of the song was uncovered and released in 1995. Powell also recorded the song, as did Bing Crosby, Ramona with Roy Bargy, Hal Kemp, and Freddie Martin. A recording by Fletcher Henderson in 1942 revived interest in the number.

"I've Got You Under My Skin" is one of the finest ballads Cole Porter ever wrote for the movies, an intoxicating song in which there is a subtle but unmistakable subtext that suggests the love affair is fated not to last. The song was first heard in *Born to Dance* (1936) as the music for a dance routine by the team of Georges and Jalna. Later in the film temperamental Broadway star Virginia Bruce sang the ballad to James Stewart on the terrace of an elegant penthouse apartment. The Oscar-nominated number is one of Porter's most unusual songs. It has no verse yet is rather long (fifty-six measures) and filled with unexpected key changes. Porter departs from the traditional AABA structure for an intriguing AABCD one with more than one musical climax. And although it has the familiar beguine tempo that Porter favors, the song is more haunting than rhythmic. "I've Got You Under My Skin" has been a favorite in films and records over the decades. It was sung by Ginny Simms in the Porter bio-musical *Night and Day* (1946), Marina Koshetz in *Luxury Liner* (1948), and Debbie Reynolds and Tony Randall in *The Mating Game* (1959). Early records were made by Hal Kemp (vocal by Skinnay Ennis), Ray Noble (vocal by Al Bowlly), Dick Jurgens (vocal by Eddy Howard), and Frances Langford. Frank Sinatra's 1956 best-selling recording was superb, and there were also later records by Peggy Lee, Louis Prima and Keely Smith, Stan Getz, Nero Young, Julie Wilson, and even a novelty version by Stan Freberg. A 1966 recording by the Four Seasons put the beloved ballad back on the charts again, and in 1995 opera singer Frederica von Stade recorded it with the Cincinnati Pops Orchestra.

"I've Heard That Song Before" was the first song written by the prolific team of Sammy Cahn (lyric) and Jule Styne (music). They wrote the Oscar-nominated number about the familiarity of music for the campus musical *Youth on Parade* (1942), where it was sung by Martha Driscoll (dubbed by Margaret Whiting) with Bob Crosby and his Orchestra. The uptempo number remained on *Your Hit Parade* for fifteen weeks, and a record by Harry James (vocal by Helen Forrest) sold over a million copies. Edra Gale sang the song in *Farewell, My Lovely* (1975), and it has remained a favorite concert opening number. More recently Michael Feinstein recorded it with Styne providing the musical accompaniment. The song is sometimes listed as "It Seems I Heard That Song Before."

"I've Hitched My Wagon to a Star" is the dreamy ballad that Johnny Mercer (lyric) and Richard Whiting (music) wrote for *Hollywood Hotel* (1938), the musical backstager about Tinsel Town. Dick Powell, as a saxophonist who wins a trip to Hollywood, sang the starry-eyed song with Raymond Paige's Orchestra.

"I've Taken a Fancy to You" is a pastiche number by Sidney Clare (lyric) and Lew Pollock (music) from the period musical *In Old Chicago* (1938). Music hall singer Alice Faye sang the old-time song of affection in 1871 Chicago, complete with sentimental lyrics and a waltzing melody typical of the nineteenth century.

J

"Jack's Lament" is the eerie but romantic "I am" song by Danny Elfman for Jack Skellington the Pumpkin King in the stop-motion animation fantasy *The Nightmare Before Christmas* (1993). Jack (singing voice by Elfman) strolled through a cemetery and admitted to himself that he found the thrill of Halloween was gone and he hoped for more out of life than the annual sound of screams.

"Jailhouse Rock" is the propulsive title song by Jerry Leiber and Mike Stoller about a jam session in a cell block from the 1957 Elvis Presley vehicle. Ex-con Presley made it to the big time and on a television special performed the rock-and-roll number with male dancers on a stylized prison set. Presley's recording of the song was at the top of the charts. Dan Aykroyd and James Belushi sang the number in *The Blues Brothers* (1980), and it was performed by Michael Park in the Broadway revue *Smokey Joe's Cafe* (1995) and by the company of the Off-Broadway revue *A Brief History of White Music* (1996).

"Jammin' " is the eruptive musical excuse for making merry all night, as proposed by Phil Harris and his Orchestra in *Turn Off the Moon* (1937), a satirical musical about astrology. Sam Coslow wrote the exhilarating song, which was recorded by Harris and by Tommy Dorsey (vocal by Edythe Wright). The Andrews Sisters made their first record singing the song with Leon Belasco's Orchestra and it was a hit.

"Jeepers Creepers" is the sassy song of affection by Johnny Mercer (lyric) and Harry Warren (music) that praises a true love's eyes with delicious 1930s slang. The raffish ditty was introduced by Louis Armstrong and his Band (vocal help by Maxine Sullivan) as they rode along side a race course in an open truck in *Going Places* (1938) because the race horse Jeepers Creepers would run only when he heard his favorite song. The number caught on quickly and was in the first spot on *Your Hit Parade* for five weeks. Armstrong's recording was a bestseller and remains the definitive version of the popular standard. There were also standout recordings by Al Donohue and his Orchestra, Gene Krupa, Larry Clinton (vocal by Ford Leary), Ethel Waters, Paul Whiteman (vocal by the Modernaires), Lester Young, Stan Kenton (vocal by Chris Connors), and Don Elliott. The Oscar-nominated song was also featured in several films, including *Yankee Doodle Dandy* (1942), *My Dream Is Yours* (1949), *The Day of the Locust* (1975), and *The Cheap Detective* (1978) and was performed by the John Pizzarelli Trio in the Broadway revue *Dream* (1997). "Jeepers Creepers" was Mercer's first song hit, and the title expression immediately entered the slang vernacular.

"Jericho" is the swinging pseudo-gospel number by Leo Robin (lyric) and Richard Myers (music) that Fred Waring and his Pennsylvanians introduced in the vaudeville backstager *Syncopation* (1929). It was revived years later when Lena Horne (with Hazel Scott at the piano) sang it in *I Dood It* (1943).

"The Jockey on the Carousel" is a sentimental lullaby by Dorothy Fields (lyric) and Jerome Kern (music) that Lily Pons sang in *I Dream Too Much* (1935) to cheer up a lonely child at a fairground as they rode a merry-go-round. Fields' lyric tells the tale of a carousel horse jockey who is always chasing after his sweetheart on the horse ahead of him but never seems to get any closer. Kern's music is adventurous, according to Gerald Bordman, as it "jumped through several moods and key changes, including a five-sharped key of B, a key which Kern knew discouraged sheet music sales." Opera singer Pons recorded the bittersweet ballad.

"Johnny Fedora and Alice Blue Bonnet" is the delightful narrative song by Ray Gilbert (lyric) and Allie Wrubel (music) that told one of the stories in the animated anthology *Make Mine Music* (1946). The harmonizing Andrews Sisters sang the smooth ballad on the soundtrack as the tale was told from a hat's point of view. Johnny and Alice sat side by side in a hat shop window and were in love but were separated when bought by two different patrons. As Johnny was worn all over town, he struggled and strained to find Alice; but eventually Johnny was discarded. At the last minute he was rescued by an iceman who put the hat on one of his horses and, lo and behold, Alice was sitting on the head of the companion horse.

"The Joint Is Really Jumpin' in Carnegie Hall" is a boogie-woogie number by Roger Edens, Ralph Blane, and Hugh Martin that Judy Garland sang in an all-star variety show in *Thousands Cheer* (1943) while José Iturbi attempted to perform the classics. The slangy lyric tells of the day the famous concert hall was invaded by swing, commenting that Bach, Beethoven, and Brahms were passé and that it was time to "get in the groove."

"Jolly Holiday" is the flavorful song by Richard M. and Robert B. Sherman from *Mary Poppins* (1964) that provided one of filmdom's finest sequences of live action mixed with animation. Julie Andrews, as governess Mary Poppins, her two charges Karen Dotrice and Matthew Garber, and sidewalk artist Dick Van Dyke magically entered one of his chalk drawings. At an outdoor cafe staffed with penguin waiters, Van Dyke sang that a day outing with Mary was like a holiday, and she returned the compliment. After doing an ingenious dance with the penguins, Van Dyke joined Andrews and the two children on a merry-go-round where the horses took off and ran a country race, Mary coming in first place. The Sherman brothers' song is happy and carefree with the flavor of an old vaudeville soft-shoe routine. Louis Prima and Gia Maione recorded the number together.

"The Jolly Tar and the Milkmaid" is a satiric number pastiching old English madrigals that was written by the Gershwins for *Damsel in Distress* (1937). In Totleigh Castle, Fred Astaire, Jan Duggan, Mary Dean, Pearl Amatore, Betty Rone, and some madrigal singers performed the narrative ballad about a sailor who proposes marriage to a maid but she declines, being already married and the mother of three; so the sailor admits that he has three wives already. George Gershwin composed the mock-eighteenth-century tune and Ira Gershwin provided the insidious lyric. The song is sometimes listed as "The Mother of Three."

"Joobalai" is a gypsy song by Leo Robin (lyric) and Ralph Rainger (music) that Texas millionaire Bing Crosby sang with peasant girl Franciska Gaal in *Paris Honeymoon* (1939). Rainger's music is appropriately Bohemian, and Robin's lyric admits that the whole song comes "straight from Romany," a reference to the gypsy standard "Romany Life."

"A Journey to a Star" is the warm ballad by Leo Robin (lyric) and Harry Warren (music) that was used throughout the wartime musical favorite *The Gang's All Here* (1943). Show girl Alice Faye sang the enchanting love song to soldier James Ellison in the moonlight on the deck of the Staten Island Ferry. Later, at a benefit show on a Long Island estate, Faye reprised the song with Benny Goodman's Orchestra and then it was danced by Sheila Ryan and Tony DeMarco. The number was heard again in the elaborate Busby Berkeley–directed finale with the central characters each singing a line of the song as they poked through colorful moving panels.

"Journey to the Past" is the stirring "I am" song for the lost princess

Anya in the animated romance *Anastasia* (1997). The orphan Anya (singing voice of Liz Callaway) sang the ballad full of fear and excitement as she set off in the snow from the orphanage where she has lived to search for her family and her past. Stephen Flaherty composed the driving music, and Lynn Ahrens wrote the knowing lyric in which Anya searches for the strength to go through with her task. The singer Aaliyah recorded the Oscar-nominated ballad, and there was a Spanish-language version called "Viaje Tiempo Atrás" (lyric by Patricia Azar and Juan Carlos Garcia) that singer Thalia released at the time the film opened.

"Jubilee" is the rousing number that Stanley Adams (lyric) and Hoagy Carmichael (music) wrote for the Mae West period vehicle *Every Day's a Holiday* (1937). Louis Armstrong and his Orchestra introduced the swinging song, and there were records by Armstrong, Cab Calloway, Harry James (vocal by Helen Humes), and Kay Thompson with the Williams Brothers.

"Judaline" is the old-fashioned serenade that Don Raye and Gene De Paul wrote for the teenage romance *A Date With Judy* (1948). Jane Powell sang the crooning ballad with Scotty Beckett and a male quartet in a radio studio, the boys singing the praises of the gal called Judaline, and Powell worrying about how she will ever be able to live up to their expectations. Beckett and the foursome reprised the slightly swinging number later in the film when they serenaded Powell outside her bedroom window one night.

"June Comes Around Every Year" is the flowing ballad by Johnny Mercer (lyric) and Harold Arlen (music) about the perennial arrival of new love each summer. Singing telegram boy Eddie Bracken sang the song in *Out of This World* (1945), but whenever he opened his mouth Bing Crosby's singing voice was heard. Crosby recorded the number, as did Tommy Dorsey (vocal by Stuart Foster) and Woody Herman and his Orchestra.

"June in January" is the best-selling ballad by Leo Robin (lyric) and Ralph Rainger (music) that millionaire Bing Crosby and European princess Kitty Carlisle sang in *Here Is My Heart* (1934). When Robin suggested the title, Rainger thought it an impossible idea for a song, but the enticing lyric explained how snow can be like summer blossoms when spring (and love) is in your heart. The title expression quickly entered the vernacular, the song remained on *Your Hit Parade* for ten weeks, and Crosby's solo recording went to the top of the charts. There were also notable records by Harry Richman and the bands of Ted Fio Rito, Art Kassel, Guy Lombardo, Al Kavelin, Richard Himber, and Little Jack Little. Frank Sinatra sang the ballad in *The Joker Is Wild* (1957) and revived interest in it once again, a Dean Martin recording finding favor in the 1960s.

"Just a Kiss at Twilight" is a sentimental ballad that was twisted about by comedienne Martha Raye in the musical farce *Give Me a Sailor* (1938). Raye first sang the wistful number as she fried an egg in a skillet into the shape of a heart. In the film's finale, she did a wide-mouthed mocking rendition of the song, some of it swing style, some of it in scat singing. Ralph Rainer composed the flexible music, and Leo Robin wrote the languishing lyric.

"Just Around the Riverbend" is the exhilarating "I am" song for the Native American heroine in the animated romance *Pocahontas* (1995). The Indian princess Pocahontas (singing voice of Judy Kuhn) contemplated the future, wondering if she should marry the noble but cold tribesman Kokomo. Alan Menken composed the stirring music, and Stephen Schwartz penned the expert lyric filled with nature imagery and a rich imagination.

"Just Blew in From the Windy City" is the vigorous list song by Paul Francis Webster (lyric) and Sammy Fain (music) that sharpshooter Doris Day sang in the frontier musical *Calamity Jane* (1953). Having just returned from "Chicagee" to her hometown of Deadwood, Day told the patrons at the Golden Garter Saloon all about the wonders of the big city but concluded "they ain't got what we got." The zestful number is similar to the "Kansas City" tribute from *Oklahoma!* a decade before, with Day even going into a dance to demonstrate the soft-shoe she saw performed there.

"Just Leave Everything to Me" is the rapid patter number that served as matchmaker Barbra Streisand's "I am" song in the 1969 film version of the Broadway blockbuster *Hello, Dolly!* As the indeflatible Dolly Levi, Streisand marched through the streets of old New York handing out business cards and listing her many talents, especially for arranging other people's lives. Jerry Herman wrote the bright number, which replaced "I Put My Hand In" from his Broadway score.

"Just Let Me Look at You" is the languid ballad by Dorothy Fields (lyric) and Jerome Kern (music) that was used throughout the backstager *Joy of Living* (1938). Broadway star Irene Dunne (in her last musical film) rehearsed the new song at home before it was to be added to her hit show. She reprised it later in her limo, where Douglas Fairbanks, Jr., who was hitching a ride on the vehicle's luggage rack, listened to her dreamily. Finally, Dunne sang it seductively to the judge in a courtroom scene. Fields' sunny lyric claims that one speechlessly in love can only look with adoration at one's beloved. Kern's music has been described by Alec Wilder as "a beautiful, uncluttered song which proceeds from melodic point to point in one long flowing line." (Stanley Green has pointed out that the song's melody recalls Tchaikowsky's "None But the Lonely Heart.") George Reinholt made a distinctive recording of the ballad in the

1970s, and Liz Robertson sang it in the Broadway revue *Jerome Kern Goes to Hollywood* (1986).

"Just Shows to Go Ya" is the prankish but endearing pastiche song by Larry Gelbart (lyric) and Ralph Burns (music) from the double-feature spoof *Movie Movie* (1978). Struggling songwriter Barry Bostwick got an idea for a song from chorine Rachel York when she stumbled over the title expression when they first met on the roof of a Manhattan tenement. Pushing aside the laundry hanging out to dry to reveal a piano, he immediately composed and sang the romantic duet to York, and she joined him in the psuedo-1930s ditty.

"Just You, Just Me" is the exquisite love song by Jesse Greer (lyric) and Raymond Klages (music) that calls for only a twosome to find perfect happiness. The number was sung as a duet by World War One private Lawrence Gray and French lass Marion Davies in the early musical *Marianne* (1929). The most memorable of the many recordings of the winsome ballad were those by Cliff "Ukelele Ike" Edwards (atypically straightforward and tender), by Benny Goodman, and by Betty Carter and Ray Charles in a duet version. The song was featured in *This Could Be the Night* (1957) and was sung by Liza Minnelli in *New York, New York* (1977) and by Edward Norton and various New Yorkers in *Everybody Says I Love You* (1997).

K

"Keep on Doin' What You're Doin'" is the sultry number by Bert Kalmar (lyric) and Harry Ruby (music) that Ruth Etting sang in the Wheeler and Woolsey musical farce *Hips Hips Hooray* (1934). Successful recordings of the come-hither ballad were made by Benny Goodman and Adrian Rollini's Ramblers.

"Keep Young and Beautiful" is the perky song of instruction that Eddie Cantor, as a delivery boy who dreams he's a food-taster in ancient Rome, sang to the ladies of the emperor's court in *Roman Scandals* (1933). Busby Berkeley staged the number with dozens of scantly clad girls doing exercises, applying cosmetics, and lounging about a Roman bath. Al Dubin (lyric) and Harry Warren (music) wrote the diverting number, which is similar in nature to (though not as pleasing as) their "Young and Healthy" in the previous year's *Forty-Second Street*.

"Keep Your Fingers Crossed" is the clever love song by Sam Coslow (lyric) and Richard Whiting (music) that uses a series of superstitions to convey one's affections. Millionaire Johnny Downs and hotel singer Betty Burgess sang the duet with Eddy Duchin's Orchestra in *Coronado* (1935), a musical romance set in the famous California resort. Freddie Martin's Orchestra recorded the number with success.

"Keepin' Myself for You" is the devoted ballad by Sidney Clare (lyric) and Vincent Youmans (music), about the frustrations of saving oneself for true love, that was interpolated into Youmans' score for the 1930 film version of his Broadway success *Hit the Deck*. Cafe owner Polly Walker and sailor Jack Oakie sang the number in the film's finale, which used the new Technicolor process. When the story was remade in 1955, Tony Martin and Ann Miller sang it with the chorus girls. Notable recordings of the uptempo ballad were made by the orchestras of Bert Lown, Paul Specht, and Artie Shaw (in a hit record with the Gramercy Five in 1940), and the song was later revived by Mel Tormé on record.

"The Kid's Song" is the heartfelt character solo that young Tommy Rettig sang in the musical fantasy *The 5,000 Fingers of Dr. T* (1953), arguing that just because kids are "closer to the ground" is no reason to always keep them down. Frederick Hollander composed the simple music, and Dr. Seuss (AKA Theodore Geisel) wrote the straightforward lyric that contained little of his characteristic wordplay but captured the philosophy of the famous children's writer-artist.

"Kinda Lonesome" is the bluesy number by Sam Coslow, Leo Robin (lyric), and Hoagy Carmichael (music) that Maxine Sullivan sang with the Hall Johnson Choir in the show biz musical *St. Louis Blues* (1938). Sullivan and Dorothy Lamour (who was the star of the film) each recorded it, but Jimmy Dorsey's disk (vocal by Lee Leighton) was the biggest seller. There were also recordings by Benny Goodman (vocal by Martha Tilton), Eddy Duchin (vocal by Stanley Worth), and Shep Fields and his Rippling Rhythm.

"The Kindergarten Conga" is the playful narrative number by Leo Robin (lyric) and Ralph Rainger (music) about a kindergarten teacher who went to Havana and taught the locals to dance a conga to the words various nursery rhymes. Gold digger Betty Grable sang the number on a hotel dance floor in *Moon Over Miami* (1941), and Hermes Pan staged the colorful dance she performed with the chorus, utilizing Latin, ballroom, and tap in one pleasing sequence. Robin managed to include several nursery rhymes, from "Little Tommy Tucker" to "Ring Around the Rosie," in his wry lyric.

"King of the Whole Wide World" is the swinging rock-and-roll number by Ruth Batchelor and Bob Roberts that Elvis Presley sang over the opening credits of the boxing musical *Kid Galahad* (1962), claiming that "the man who can sing" is royalty. Presley's recording was a bestseller.

"The Kiss in Your Eyes" is the flowing ballad that American phonograph salesman Bing Crosby sang to Austrian countess Joan Fontaine on an island in a Tyrolean lake in the costume musical *The Emperor Waltz* (1948). The romantic music came from Richard Heuberger's *Der Opernball* and Johnny Burke provided the English lyric that blamed the come-hither look in her eyes for his amorous attention.

"The Kiss Polka" is the festive love song in polka time that Mack Gordon (lyric) and Harry Warren (music) wrote for the Big Band musical *Sun Valley Serenade* (1941). Glenn Miller's Orchestra played the number, a trio of waitresses sang it, and couples inside a ski hut danced to it, including Norwegian refugee Sonja Henie and band member John Payne. (It was one of the rare occasions where Henie danced without wearing skates.) Gordon's lyric cleverly leaves space in the lyric for a kiss to replace the word "kiss." Miller's recording with the Modernaires was very popular.

"Kiss the Boys Goodbye" is the coyly satirical title song by Frank Loesser (lyric) and Victor Schertzinger (music) that Southern belle Mary Martin sang in the 1941 musical about the search for someone to play Scarlett O'Hara in *Gone With the Wind*. The lyric suggests one last fling with old boyfriends before marriage to "daddy," a follow-up of sorts to the Cole Porter song "My Heart Belongs to Daddy," which Martin performed on stage and screen. Martin recorded "Kiss the Boys Goodbye," as did Bea Wain, but the biggest selling version was by Tommy Dorsey (vocal by Connie Haines). Shirley Booth sang the insidious song in *About Mrs. Leslie* (1954).

"Kiss the Girl" is the calypso-flavored love song that Sebastian the Crab (voice of Samuel E. Wright) sang with other marine animals in the animated fairy tale *The Little Mermaid* (1989) as they urged Prince Eric to kiss Ariel and make her human forever. The Oscar-nominated song was written by Howard Ashman (lyric) and Alan Menken (music). The group Soul II Soul recorded the song with Kolfi in 1995, and The Jazz Network did a notable version in 1996.

"A Kiss to Build a Dream On" is the hit ballad by Bert Kalmar, Oscar Hammerstein (lyric), and Harry Ruby (music) that Kay Brown and Louis Armstrong sang in the musical melodrama *The Strip* (1951). Kalmar and Ruby had written the song for *A Night at the Opera* (1935), but it was never used. Hammerstein reworked the lyric, about a farewell kiss that will launch a thousand dreams, and the number became very popular due to Armstrong's recording. The Oscar-nominated song also received a distinctive recording by Hugo Winterhalter and his Orchestra.

"Kissin' Cousins" is the crooning title song by Fred Wise and Randy Starr that Elvis Presley sang over the opening credits of the 1964 hillbilly musical. At the end of the film, U.S. Army officer Presley and his backwoods cousin (also played by Presley) reprised the rock-folk number with the crowd of Tennessee locals, praising their romantic kinfolk, including a comely female cousin who is a distant relative, which makes it "all right." Presley's recording became a Gold Record.

"Kokomo, Indiana" is the charming pastiche number by Mack Gordon (lyric) and Josef Myrow (music) that sings praises for the simple life in small-town America. Vaudevillians Betty Grable and Dan Dailey, in top hat and tails, sang the cheery number in the show biz musical *Mother Wore Tights* (1947), and there were successful recordings of the song by Vaughn Monroe and his Orchestra and Doris Day with Sonny Burke's Orchestra.

L

"Ladies-in-Waiting" is the sly Cole Porter ditty that Mitzi Gaynor, Taina Elg, and Kay Kendall, performing in Louis IV court gowns, sang in *Les Girls* (1957) as part of their nightclub act. Porter's crafty lyric lists all the joys of being the king's servants and then ends each stanza with a sour punchline.

"The Lady Dances" is the energetic production number that Lew Brown (lyric) and Harold Arlen (music) wrote for the Eddie Cantor vehicle *Strike Me Pink* (1936). The dancing song was performed by amusement park entrepreneur Cantor with Rita Rio (later Donna Drake) and the Goldwyn Girls.

"The Lady in Red" is the rhythmic number by Mort Dixon (lyric) and Allie Wrubel (music) about the naughty but nice gal who is the toast (and the talk) of the town. Wini Shaw and a seductive chorus of toreador-hatted girls sang the number in *In Caliente* (1935) in a dark cafe in the Mexican resort town of Caliente. The song was danced by the DeMarcos, and then Judy Canova did a hillybilly rendition as she tried to seduce Edward Everett Horton. The catchy song was recorded by Ethel Merman with Johnny Green's Orchestra, Xavier Cugat (vocal by Don Reid), Louis Prima, Henry Busse, and Stan Getz. Both song and Busby Berkeley's staging of it were lampooned in *Here Comes Cookie* (1935), where Gracie Allen sang a spoof called "Vamp of the Pampas."

"The Lady in the Tutti-Frutti Hat" is one of director-choreographer Busby Berkeley's most famous production numbers, a silly and extravagant cavalcade from *The Gang's All Here* (1943), his first film in color. Leo Robin (lyric) and Harry Warren (music) wrote the song about a gal with a colorful headdress that, despite the tropical plantation setting, is more Broadway than Latin in flavor. Carmen Miranda sang the ditty and played the lady in question.

The fruit of choice was the banana, and Miranda was surrounded by a chorus waving huge bananas in kaleidoscope patterns; the number ended with the illusion that hundreds of bananas were protruding from Miranda's fruity headgear.

"A Lady Loves" is the dapper song Debbie Reynolds sang in the show biz musical *I Love Melvin* (1953) itemizing all the things a star admires, from penthouses to Riviera holidays, but mostly she "loves to love." Mack Gordon (lyric) and Josef Myrow (music) wrote the number in which the star-struck chorus girl Reynolds imagines herself a famous film star beseiged by photographers and reporters.

"The Lady Loves Me" is a lighthearted duet written by Sid Tepper and Roy C. Bennett for the Elvis Presley vehicle *Viva Las Vegas* (1964). Race car driver Presley strummed his guitar and sang to swimming instructor Ann-Margaret (who was in the ladies' room changing) that she loves him but she "doesn't know it yet." Ann-Margaret came out and joined him, sarcastically sings "The Lady Loves Him," and the duet ended with her pushing him into the hotel pool.

"The Lady's in Love With You" is a charming list song by Frank Loesser (lyric) and Burton Lane (music) that explains the clues (she keeps you waiting, a gleam in her eye, a preference for sitting in the balcony at the movies, and so on) that will tell if she loves you. Sideshow barker Bob Hope and his sweetheart Shirley Ross performed the number with Gene Krupa's Band in the carnival-set musical *Some Like It Hot* (1939). Krupa (vocal by Irene Daye) recorded the catchy number, as did Hope and Ross together. Other notable recordings were made by the orchestras of Glenn Miller (vocal by Tex Beneke), Benny Goodman, and Bob Crosby. A Nellie Lutcher disk revived the song in 1947, and Michael Feinstein recorded it in 1991.

"Lafayette" is a spirited march that Dorothy Fields (lyrics) and Jerome Kern (music) wrote for the remake of *Roberta* called *Lovely to Look At* (1952). American tourists Red Skelton, Howard Keel, and Gower Champion arrived in Paris and announced to the dead French general that they, as in the famous quote, "are here." As they toured the town the threesome tried out some French phrases and habits but with little success.

"Last Call for Love" is the chipper announcement of romance that E. Y. Harburg, Burton Lane, and Margery Cummings collaborated on for *Ship Ahoy* (1942), a Big Band musical set aboard a cruise ship in the Caribbean. Tommy Dorsey's Orchestra performed the gently swinging number, and the vocalists were Frank Sinatra, Connie Haines, and the Pied Pipers. They all recorded the number together, and it was moderately popular.

"The Lately Song" is the vivacious song by Sammy Cahn (lyric) and Sammy Fain (music) that provided for an outstanding dance sequence (choreographed by Gene Nelson and LeRoy Prinz) in the nautical show biz musical *Three Sailors and a Girl* (1954). Nelson, Gordon MacRae, and Jack E. Leonard were the title tars who performed the number with title gal Jane Powell.

"The Latin Quarter" is the bubbly tribute to the famous Parisian neighborhood that Al Dubin (lyric) and Harry Warren (music) wrote for *Gold Diggers in Paris* (1938). Americans Rudy Vallee, Rosemary Lane, Allen Jenkins, and Mabel Todd performed the production number as they toured the Left Bank.

"Laugh, You Son-of-a-Gun" is the no-nonsense order from Shirley Temple to stop whining about the Depression and start smiling . . . or else. The cheering song by Leo Robin (lyric) and Ralph Rainger (music) was sung by orphan Temple and Dorothy Dell in *Little Miss Marker* (1934).

"Lavender Blue (Dilly Dilly)" is the simple but unforgettable ditty that Larry Morey and Eliot Daniel fashioned from a seventeenth-century English folk song to be used in the nostalgic musical *So Dear to My Heart* (1949). Blacksmith Burl Ives (in his film debut) played the guitar and sang the childlike song of affection for Beulah Bondi, Bobby Driscoll, and Luana Patten in the farmhouse one evening after supper. The Oscar-nominated song was recorded by Ives (with "Captain Stubby and the Buccaneers") and by Dinah Shore, and each had a hit with it. Records were also made by Sammy Kaye (vocal by the Three Kaydets) and Jack Smith, and it was revived by a Sammy Turner recording in 1959. Vera Lynn sang the number in *A Safe Place* (1971).

"Le Jazz Hot" is the steamy nightclub number by Leslie Bricusse (lyric) and Henry Mancini (music) that introduced the female impersonator Count Victor Grazinsky, played by Julie Andrews in drag, to Paris cafe society in the cross-dressing musical *Victor/Victoria* (1982). Andrews and the chorus sang the 1920s pastiche song entreating the band to play nothing but American-style jazz. Andrews reprised the gender-bending role and the song in the 1995 Broadway version of *Victor/Victoria*.

"The Leader Doesn't Like Music" is the jumping nonsense song by Gus Kahn (lyric) and Harry Warren (music) that provided the comic (if incongruous) highlight of the musical farce *Honolulu* (1939). At a costume party on board an ocean liner heading for Hawaii, Gracie Allen (dressed as Mae West) sang the ditty about a conductor who hated every kind of music from classical to swing, and she was joined by the King's Men (led by Ken Darby) dressed as the Marx Brothers, the foursome consisting of a Chico, Harpo and two identical Grouchos.

"Learn to Croon" is the ballad in which Bing Crosby first delivered his trademark "boo boo boo boo," which would be associated with (and haunt) him for the next fifty years. College professor Crosby sang the song, written by Sam Coslow (lyric) and Arthur Johnston (music), in the campus musical *College Humor* (1933), where he taught one that the murmur of "boo boo boo boo" to your sweetheart will win her heart. While the silly expression was part of the original lyric, it would be squeezed into many Crosby ballads in the future, often between lines of the lyric or during musical transitions. Crosby recorded "Learn to Croon," and the disk was heard in the background in *Jolson Sings Again* (1949). Fran Frey and Al Bowlly each recorded it as well, as did the bands of Billy Cotton, Jack Hylton, Don Bestor, Jimmie Grier, and Jack Payne.

"Les Girls" is the tangy title number by Cole Porter (his last film score) for the *Roshomon*-like 1957 musical. As part of their nightclub act, hoofer Gene Kelly introduced the three lovely mademoiselles of the show (Taina Elg, Mitzi Gaynor, and Kay Kendall) and sang of their alluring qualities.

"Let Me Dance for You" is one of the two songs that Edward Kleban (lyric) and Marvin Hamlisch (music) interpolated into their Broadway score for the 1984 film version of *A Chorus Line*. Former chorus girl Alyson Reed had failed as a featured actress and wanted to return to the "line," so she sang this fervent ballad to the director (her former lover) asking to dance again and, by implication, seeking acceptance and love.

"Let Me Sing and I'm Happy" might be described as the theme song for Irving Berlin's career (though there are several songs that could be said for), a cheery salute to the joy of entertaining with music. Al Jolson, as the star of a traveling minstrel show, introduced the number in *Mammy* (1930) and sang it on the soundtrack for Larry Parks in the bio-musical *The Jolson Story* (1946). The same clip was used in the sequel *Jolson Sings Again* (1949). The exuberant song, a favorite opener for nightclub singers, was recorded by Jolson, Ruth Etting, Gene Austin (with Fred Waring's Pennsylvanians), Ben Selvin's Orchestra (vocal by Smith Ballew), and Sid Gary. Bing Crosby and Danny Kaye sang it in *White Christmas* (1954), and there have been recent recordings by Michael Feinstein, Barbara Cook, and Patti LuPone.

"Let That Be a Lesson to You" is the comic song of warning by Johnny Mercer (lyric) and Richard Whiting (music) from *Hollywood Hotel* (1938). Dick Powell, Rosemary Lane, and most of the cast performed the number at a drive-in diner with Benny Goodman and his Orchestra on hand. Director Busby Berkeley staged the humorous sequence making clever use of the cars and carhops at the diner. Louis Armstrong and his Orchestra recorded the sportive number.

"Let the Worry Bird Worry for You" is a vivacious antidepressant number that Leo Robin (lyric) and Jule Styne (music) wrote for the early backstager about television *Two Tickets to Broadway* (1951). Dancing hopeful Ann Miller performed the number, which is sometimes listed as "The Worry Bird."

"Let Yourself Go" is one of Irving Berlin's best rhythm songs, a contagious invitation to let loose on the dance floor. Dance hall hostess Ginger Rogers sang the number at a dime-a-dance ballroom in *Follow the Fleet* (1936), and she was soon accompanied by fellow workers Betty Grable, Joy Hodges, and Jennie Gray. Customer Fred Astaire then joined Rogers, and their fancy footwork won them the dance contest trophy. Astaire recorded the jubilant song, as did the Boswell Sisters and the orchestras of Ray Noble and Bunny Berigan. More recently it has been recorded by Mandy Patinkin, Patti LuPone, and Andrea Marcovicci.

"The Letter Song" is a reworked version of "The Glamorous Life," Stephen Sondheim's astute song about the theatre profession that was heard in the 1973 Broadway musical *A Little Night Music*. For the 1978 film version Chloe Franks, as the young daughter of a famous actress, sang about how "unordinary" her mother was and about the series of letters she gets from her touring parent. While the song was heard, her famous mother (Elizabeth Taylor) was seen traveling, performing, and wearily charming the crowds wherever she went. Betsy Joslyn recorded the knowing number in 1985, and Cassidy Ladden recorded it in 1997.

"Let's Be Common" is a delectable comic duet written by Clifford Grey (lyric) and Victor Schertzinger (music) for the comic operetta *The Love Parade* (1929). The lusty maid Lillian Roth and the count's butler Lupino Lane sang the merry song about ignoring the ways of the upper classes because the lower have more fun. The rubber-faced London comic Lane then performed an acrobatic dance routine and displayed his unique sense of physical comedy that made him a West End favorite.

"Let's Be Domestic" is a sly and sexy duet performed by fun-loving Lillian Roth and Skeets Gallagher (as a millionaire masquerading as a butler) in the musical farce *Honey* (1930). W. Franke Harling composed the bouncy music, and Sam Coslow penned the clever lyric that begins by describing everyday chores, such as window washing and grass cutting, but soon suggests more amorous activities.

"Let's Call a Heart a Heart" is a sentimental ballad from the sentimental Bing Crosby vehicle *Pennies From Heaven* (1936) that he expertly performed just short of mawkishness. Crosby recorded the number by Johnny Burke (lyric) and Arthur Johnston (music) and there were popular disks also by Billie Holiday and Artie Shaw (vocal by Peg La Centra).

"Let's Call the Whole Thing Off" is the scintillating Gershwin song that gleefully suggests ending a relationship because of verbal incompatibility. Phony Russian Fred Astaire and stage star Ginger Rogers sang the zesty number in *Shall We Dance* (1937) and then performed a marvelous dance on roller skates in Central Park. The sequence, which took thirty "takes" over four days to shoot, was so enjoyable that too few appreciated the song itself and recognition would come only after recordings were made. George Gershwin's music uses repeated notes and phrases beautifully as the song moves comically along. Ira Gershwin's lyric is one of his most accomplished, using alternating pronunciations of the words "potato," "tomato," "either," and "neither" to illustrate the trivial nature of the bickering. The lighthearted quarrel ends with the sly and romantic idea of calling off the calling off. The song was the first Gershwin number to make *Your Hit Parade*. Astaire recorded the number with Johnny Green's Orchestra, and there were notable disks by Billie Holiday, the Ink Spots, and the bands of Eddy Duchin (vocal by Jerry Cooper), Jimmy Dorsey, and years later Sarah Vaughan.

"Let's Do the Copacabana" is the flowing Latin number by Sam Coslow that turns into the swing finale for the musical farce *Copacabana* (1947). Carmen Miranda sang the number that invited one to do a new dance that's unknown now but is sure to catch on; then a chorus of high-hatted dancers sang it with Gloria Jean, who then danced some of it with Groucho Marx.

"Let's Face the Music and Dance" is arguably Irving Berlin's most haunting movie ballad, a song so alluring and mysterious that it is too often mistakenly attributed to the Gershwins. (Alec Wilder notes that there is an awful lot of Cole Porter in certain strains as well.) But the ballad is pure Berlin in its simplicity, flowing melody, and uncluttered lyric. The number was introduced as part of a fundraising revue aboard a yacht in *Follow the Fleet* (1936), and the sequence was set on a sleek art deco rooftop where Fred Astaire and Ginger Rogers each considered suicide, then found each other, and ignoring the "trouble ahead" decided to tackle love and life head on. Astaire sang the song to Rogers; they then performed an elegant but passionate dance, her heavy beaded dress doing a show of its own. (The gown weighed so much that it knocked Astaire all over the stage in rehearsals.) Notable recordings of the ballad were made by Astaire, Mel Tormé, and the orchestras of Ted Fio Rita and Ray Noble. In the film *Pennies From Heaven* (1981), Steve Martin and Bernadette Peters watched the "Let's Face the Music and Dance" scene in a dirty movie theatre and then replaced Astaire and Rogers on the screen for the dance section.

"Let's Fall in Love" is the hit title song by Ted Koehler (lyric) and Harold Arlen (music) for the 1934 musical that spoofed Hollywood's fascination for European actresses. Art Jarrett introduced the fervent proposal, reprised a few times by fake Swedish movie star Ann Sothern. Arlen's music (this was his first screen assignment) is ardent, and Koehler's lyric, according to Philip Furia, has a "brassy pugnacity" that turns "clichés of romantic proposal into an aggressive sales pitch with rhetorical questions." Eddy Duchin and his Orchestra recorded the ballad, which went to the top of the charts. The song was revived by Peaches and Herb in 1967, and it too was a bestseller. "Let's Fall in Love" was sung in numerous films by various performers, including Don Ameche and Dorothy Lamour in *Slightly French* (1949), Robert Cummings in *Tell It to the Judge* (1949), Jack Lemmon and Judy Holliday in *It Should Happen to You* (1954), pianist Carmen Cavallaro playing for Tyrone Power in the bio-musical *The Eddy Duchin Story* (1956), Jack Jones in *Juke Box Rhythm* (1959), and Bing Crosby in *Pepe* (1960).

"Let's Get Lost" is the dreamy and seductive ballad about getting away from it all that Frank Loesser (lyric) and Jimmy McHugh (music) wrote for the Caribbean-set musical *Happy Go Lucky* (1943). Vacationing gold digger Mary Martin sang the song (orchestra accompaniment coming from the radio) to nonplussed millionaire Rudy Vallee during a tropical picnic. The ballad was twelve weeks on *Your Hit Parade* thanks to a Number One record by Vaughn Monroe with the Four Lee Sisters. Other recording were made by Kay Kyser (vocal by Julie Conway), Harry Babbitt, Max Williams, Jack Martin, and Jimmy Dorsey (vocal by Bob Eberle).

"Let's Give Three Cheers for Love" is the romantic call to arms by Mack Gordon (lyric) and Harry Revel (music) that student tenor Lanny Ross sang in the campus frolic *College Rhythm* (1934). Ross recorded the upbeat number, as did the bands of Little Jack Little, Tom Croakley, and Jimmie Grier.

"Let's Go Bavarian" is the tongue-in-cheek duet written by Harold Adamson (lyric) and Burton Lane (music) for *Dancing Lady* (1933) that is mostly remembered for introducing Fred Astaire to movie audiences. He sang and danced the number with Joan Crawford, both of them dressed in ridiculous "German" outfits, but the Astaire sparkle was evident all the same. George Olson recorded the song with Ethel Shutta and Fran Frey doing the vocals and it was popular.

"Let's Go Fly a Kite" is the uplifting finale song from *Mary Poppins*

(1964) by Richard M. and Robert B. Sherman. Edwardian father David Tomilson realized it was time to enjoy life and his own family and sang the joyous number with wife Glynis Johns as they joined the other Londoners in the park singing and flying kites. Burl Ives made a memorable recording of the song, as did Louis Prima with Gia Maione.

"Let's Go to the Movies" is a happy production number that Martin Charnin (lyric) and Charles Strouse (music) added to their score of the Broadway hit *Annie* when it was brought to the screen in 1982. Orphan Aileen Quinn and secretary Ann Reinking started the song as they dressed to go out to the movies with millionaire Albert Finney. As they arrived at the Radio Music Hall, all the ushers and usherettes joined in the singing and then went into a high-kicking dance in the huge lobby. Finally the live show before the film repeated the song as a Busby Berkeley–like extravaganza filled the mammoth stage.

"Let's Hear It for Me" is the propulsive number by Fred Ebb (lyric) and John Kander (music) that celebrates one's ability to survive and thrive. Barbra Streisand, as entertainer Fanny Brice, sang the eager song in the musical sequel *Funny Lady* (1975) after a scene with her ex-husband Omar Sharif in which she called the shots. Because the song was delivered while she drove in her car to the airport and ended with her flying off in a private biplane, the sequence was reminiscent of a *Funny Girl* scene where Streisand sang the similarly themed song "Don't Rain on My Parade" as she rode on a tugboat out of the New York harbor.

"Let's K-nock K-nees" is the silly but adorable ditty by Mack Gordon (lyric) and Harry Revel (music) about a dancing twosome who keep getting injured while bumping their knees on the dance floor. Betty Grable (accompanying herself on a ukelele) and Edward Everett Horton sang the prankish number in *The Gay Divorcee* (1934).

"Let's Not Be Sensible" is the call for irrational love that conman Bing Crosby and spy Joan Collins sang in *The Road to Hong Kong* (1962), the last of the Hope-Crosby "Road" comedies. Sammy Cahn (lyric) and James Van Heusen (music) wrote the romantic duet.

"Let's Put It Over With Grover" is the tuneful campaign song for candidate Grover Cleveland at the 1888 Democratic Convention in the political period musical *The One and Only, Genuine, Original Family Band* (1968). Richard M. and Robert B. Sherman wrote the brash number, sung by avid Democrat Walter Brennan, his Nebraska family members Buddy Ebsen, Lesley Ann Warren, Janet Blair and the children as they auditioned for a representative from the convention.

"Let's Put Our Heads Together" is an archly romantic song by E. Y. Harburg (lyric) and Harold Arlen (music) that provided director Busby Berkeley with a standout scene in *Gold Diggers of 1937* (1936). Dick Powell sang the number to Joan Blondell as they sat in oversized rocking chairs, and soon they were joined by Lee Dixon, Rosalind Marshall, Jack Norton, Glenda Farrell, and Victor Moore, all rocking away in time to the music. Roy Hemming has described the genial number as having "an easy-going, ingratiating melody and tongue-in-cheek June-moon lyrics." Dick Powell recorded the ballad with success.

"Let's Sing Again" is the optimistic title song for the 1936 musical melodrama that introduced child-star Bobby Breen to audiences. Eight-year-old Breen, as an orphan on the run from a small-time circus, sang the outgoing ballad by Gus Kahn (lyric) and Jimmy McHugh (music) and recorded it as well, his first of many recordings. Thomas "Fats" Waller, Ted Weems (vocal by Elmo Tanner), and Mal Hallett also recorded it.

"Let's Start the New Year Right" is one of the two holiday songs Irving Berlin wrote for New Year's Day in *Holiday Inn* (1942). This jaunty number claims that kissing the old year out and the new year in is the correct way to celebrate the holiday. Inn owner Bing Crosby and his star attraction Marjorie Reynolds (dubbed by Martha Mears) sang it in the kitchen as they prepared salads for the guests, and Crosby later recorded the song.

"Let's Take the Long Way Home" is the romantic suggestion written by Johnny Mercer (lyric) and Harold Arlen (music) that the roundabout path will prolong an evening of joy. Singing idol Bing Crosby and struggling singer Betty Hutton sang the duet in *Here Come the Waves* (1944). The number is a sequel of sorts to a song Arlen had written with lyricist E. Y. Harburg for Broadway called "Let's Take a Walk Around the Block." Both Jo Stafford and Cab Calloway had hit recordings of the Mercer–Arlen song, and years later Diahann Carroll made a distinctive record of it.

"Life Begins When You're in Love" is an agreeable song of romantic contentment that Lew Brown, Harry Richman (lyric), and Victor Schertzinger (music) wrote for the show biz musical *The Music Goes 'Round* (1936). Richman sang the number in the film and recorded it, as did Isham Jones (vocal by Woody Herman), Teddy Wilson, and Richard Himber (vocal by Allen Stuart).

"Life Is So Peculiar" is the simple song of philosophy by Johnny Burke (lyric) and James Van Heusen (music) that was used throughout *Mr. Music* (1950). Songwriter Bing Crosby sang it with guest stars Peggy Lee and the Merry Macs, then Marge and Gower Champion danced to the number. Later it was reprised by Crosby and Groucho Marx in a comedy sketch. Notable recordings of the song were made by Crosby with the Andrew Sisters and by Louis Armstrong with Louis Jordan. The number was sung by the company in the Broadway revue *Five Guys Named Moe* (1992).

"Life's Full of Consequence" is a delectable comic duet that E. Y. Harburg (lyric) and Harold Arlen (music) interpolated into the score for the 1943 film version of the Broadway Negro folk musical *Cabin in the Sky*. Eddie "Rochester" Anderson sang the number with the seductress Lena Horne, arguing that all of life's sins have their penalties but he cannot decide whether or not to succumb to them. Anderson's wide-eyed rendition of the song, making the word "consequence" both funny and suggestive, is a comic classic. The song originally contained a verse that stated "De Lord" made sin and the five senses to enjoy it, but he also "provided the consequences." When the studio insisted on a less irreverent lyric, Harburg revised it, but the whole verse was cut out of the final print.

"Like Someone in Love" is the starry-eyed ballad by Johnny Burke (lyric) and James Van Heusen (music) that listed the symptoms of love: star gazing, hearing guitar music, walking on air, and so on. Saloon singer Doris Day sang the number in *Belle of the Yukon* (1944); her recording, as well as one by Bing Crosby, was a bestseller. Denise Faye sang the ballad in the Broadway revue *Swinging on a Star* (1995).

"Listen My Children and You Will Hear" is the raucous number that Depression lass Martha Raye, in a singing style most resembling an air raid siren, delivered in *Double or Nothing* (1937) when she and her friends came into a fortune. Ralph Freed (lyric) and Burton Lane (music) wrote the comic rouser, and Count Basie and his Orchestra recorded it.

"Little Drops of Rain" is a winsome ballad about the dripping of water and the dropping grains of sands and how all signal the passing of time, so it is best to enjoy all the little things in life. E. Y. Harburg (lyric) and Harold Arlen (music) wrote the song for the animated romance *GayPurr-ee* (1962), where it was sung by the country cat Mewsette (voice of Judy Garland) and reprised by the town cat Jaune-Tom (voice of Robert Goulet).

"A Little Kiss Each Morning (a Little Kiss Each Night)" is the theme song offering a prescription for romantic happiness that was used throughout *The Vagabond Lover* (1929), Rudy Vallee's first starring film. Vallee, as a small-town bandleader, sang the Harry Woods number to Sally Blane, and then it was heard in the background several times after. Vallee's recording with the Connecticut Yankees and Guy Lombardo's disk with his Royal Canadians were both popular, and the orchestras of Seger Ellis and Hal Kemp also recorded the ballad. Twenty-five years after the film the song was revived in a best-selling recording by Bing Crosby.

"Little Pal" was an unsubtle attempt by Lew Brown, Buddy De Sylva (lyric), and Ray Henderson (music) to create another paean to a young boy along the lines of their phenomenally successful "Sonny Boy." Radio star Al Jolson sang the number in *Say It With Songs* (1929) about his son Davey Lee (whom Jolson had sung "Sonny Boy" about in *The Singing Fool*), and Jolson's record hit the top of the charts. There were also recordings by Gene Austin and Gene Waldron, but "Little Pal" soon faded from memory while "Sonny Boy" went on and on.

"The Little Prince (From Who Knows Where)" is the fragile title song by Alan Jay Lerner (lyric) and Frederick Loewe (music) for the 1975 allegorical fantasy based on the famous Antoine de Saint-Exupéry novella. Pilot Richard Kiley sang the heartfelt song of affection to the dying child-prince Steven Warner, who has changed his life. The score for *The Little Prince* proved to be Loewe's last, and Lerner later argued that the music was "filled with melody and bubbling with the innocence of youth" but that director Stanley Donen "took it upon himself to change every tempo, delete musical phrases at will and distort the intention of every song until the entire score was unrecognizable." Regardless, the ballad was nominated for an Oscar.

"The Little Things You Used to Do" is the morbid torch song that gangster mistress Helen Morgan sang in a nightclub in the dark show biz saga *Go Into Your Dance* (1935). Harry Warren wrote the somber music, and Al Dubin penned the lyric that recalls the unglamorous details (cigarette ashes on the floor, a stain on his shirt, the way he lied to her) that remind her of him. Morgan, whose alcoholism destroyed her film career, appeared in the cameo role because of the insistence of Al Jolson, the musical's star. Morgan recorded the lament, as did the orchestras of Johnny Green, Enric Madriguera, and Jack Shilkret.

"A Little White Gardenia" is the musical offering of a flower to a lover, telling her she can wear it if she loves him or toss it away. Sam Coslow wrote the ballad for the British singer Carl Brisson to perform in *All the King's Horses* (1935), and it became the crooner's signature song. Coslow got the idea for the number from Brisson, who told him that an unknown woman had sent him a white gardenia every week when he was performing in *The Merry Widow* on the London stage. In addition to Brisson's popular recording, there were disks by Al Bowlly, Morton Downey, and the orchestras of Hal Kemp, Emil

Coleman, and Art Kassel.

"Live and Love Tonight" is the melting ballad by Arthur Johnston (lyric) and Sam Coslow (music) that Carl Brisson and Kitty Carlisle, as the leading actors in a Broadway show, sang in the musical whodunit *Murder at the Vanities* (1934). Recordings were made by Brisson and the orchestras of Duke Ellington, Johnny Green, and Will Osborne.

"Live Hard, Work Hard, Love Hard" is the song that introduced Mitzi Gaynor to movie audiences, a life-affirming number that she sang in the sentimental musical *My Blue Heaven* (1950). The optimistic ballad was written by Ralph Blane (lyric) and Harold Arlen (music).

"Living in the Sunlight — Loving in the Moonlight" is the musical prescription for a happy life that Al Lewis (lyric) and Al Sherman (music) wrote for the Maurice Chevalier vehicle *The Big Pond* (1930). Chevalier sang the upbeat number to a group of businessmen in the film and later recorded it. There were instrumental records made by Ben Bernie, Paul Whiteman, and Bernie Cummins' New Yorker Orchestra.

"Lonesome Polecat" is the rhythmic song of romantic frustration that Johnny Mercer (lyric) and Gene De Paul (music) wrote for the frontier musical *Seven Brides for Seven Brothers* (1954). Backwoodsman Bill Lee and five of his brothers sang the bluesy lament in the snow as they chopped down trees and sawed logs to the insistent beat of the music. The number was originally set in the brothers' bunkhouse, but choreographer Michael Kidd suggested the scene be moved outside, where the brothers' yearning for feminine companionship could be illustrated with an activity. The McGuire Sisters and Freddy Martin and his Orchestra each made notable recordings of the song.

"Long Ago (and Far Away)" is arguably the last great song composer Jerome Kern wrote, and although lyricist Ira Gershwin never liked it all that much, it was the biggest seller of his career. The enchanting ballad was introduced by heartsick entertainer Gene Kelly in an empty nightclub in *Cover Girl* (1944) while Phil Silvers quietly played the piano and the unseen Rita Hayworth looked on. Near the end of the film Kelly and Hayworth (dubbed by Martha Mears) briefly reprised the number. Told by the producer to "keep it simple," Gershwin labored through several drafts before he wearily submitted the lyric about a long past dream that finally comes true. It is an atypically simple lyric for a Gershwin song but perfectly phrased all the same. Another strength of the song is Kern's music, which keeps returning to the same musical theme, something rarely done in popular music. As Alec Wilder notes, "Kern daringly restates his principal idea a minor third higher after only eight measures . . . I was convinced that this device would be too much for the public ear, but not so." In fact, the song sold over 600,000 copies of sheet music the first year. Among the many recordings of the ballad are those by Bing Crosby, Helen Forrest and Dick Haymes, Perry Como, Guy Lombardo (vocal by Tony Craig), Glenn Miller, Jo Stafford, Carmen Dragon, Dorothy Kirsten, Englebert Humperdinck, and more recently Andrea Marcovicci. Kathryn Grayson sang the number in the Kern bio-musical *Till the Clouds Roll By* (1946).

"Look at You, Look at Me" is a forgotten gem by Frank Loesser (lyric) and Jule Styne (music) from the campus musical *Sis Hopkins* (1941). The torchy ballad concerns two parted lovers: He's smoking too much and she's drinking too much; both are miserable and wonder if they weren't better off together. Katharine Alexander sang the number with Bob Crosby and his Band in the film, and fifty years later it was revived by a Michael Feinstein recording.

"Look Out Broadway" is the comic music hall number that Fred Wise and Randy Starr wrote for the Elvis Presley period vehicle *Frankie and Johnny* (1966). Having been offered a shot at the big time, riverboat entertainers Presley, Harry Morgan, Donna Douglas (dubbed by Eileen Wilson), and Audrey Christie celebrated in their cabin with this joyous warning to the Great White Way. Presley recorded the number as a solo.

"Look What I've Got" is a vibrant song of optimism that Leo Robin (lyric) and Ralph Rainger wrote for the Maurice Chevalier vehicle *A Bedtime Story* (1933). Leah Ray, as one of big-game-hunter Chevalier's old sweethearts, sang the happy-go-lucky number, which became moderately popular through recordings by Paul Whiteman, Freddy Martin, and Ted Fio Rito.

"Look What You've Done" is a slaphappy love duet for phony matador Eddie Cantor and platinum blonde sidekick Lyda Roberti in the musical farce *The Kid From Spain* (1932). Bert Kalmar (lyric), Harry Ruby, and Harry Akst (music) wrote the snappy song, which was recorded by Cantor as well as by Ozzie Nelson and his Orchestra.

"Lookin' for Trouble" is the striptease number that Texas millionairess Jane Russell sang as she seductively posed during a Paris fashion show in *The French Line* (1954), claiming she was on the lookout for a man who didn't care about propriety. Ralph Blane, Robert Wells (lyric), and Josef Myrow (music) wrote the suggestive number, but Russell's sheer black outfit was even more suggestive, causing the director to film the scene at such a distance that she was almost lost in the long shot. It didn't make any difference to religious groups, though, who condemned the film primarily because of the scene.

"Looking for Love" is the howling title song by Hank Hunter and Stan Vincent for the 1964 youth musical starring Connie Francis. The song of romantic yearning was tearfully sung by Francis, as a switchboard operator looking for a singing job as well as romance, and her recording was a big seller.

"Looking for Someone to Love" is the lightfooted torch song by Pony Sherrell and Phil Moody that served as a specialty number for Gene Nelson in *So This Is Paris* (1955). American sailor Nelson, on leave in Paris, sang of his searching for a romantic partner as he tripped along the streets of the city late at night. The tempo then speeded up and Nelson performed an athletic dance (choreographed by Nelson and Scott Lee) utilizing buildings, cars, and various Parisians that he encountered.

"Looking Through Your Eyes" is the pop ballad that Carole Bayer Sager (lyric) and David Foster (music) wrote for the animated adventure *Quest for Camelot* (1998). The ambitious maiden Kayley (singing voice of LeeAnn Rimes) and the blind hermit Garrett (singing voice of Bryan White) sang the fervent duet, promising to love and guide each other.

"Lose That Long Face" is a painfully ironic production number from the 1954 version of *A Star Is Born* that was among the twenty-seven minutes cut by the studio before the film was released. Movie star Judy Garland was worried about her alcoholic husband James Mason but must go on the sound stage and shoot a big optimistic number. Dressed as a freckle-faced newsboy, she belted the optimistic song and danced with a variety of New Yorkers on the street, but her determined but pathetic performance is overshadowed by the song's subtext. Harold Arlen composed the upbeat music, and Ira Gershwin provided the lyric that rhymed "critical" with "Pollyannalytical." The sequence was rediscovered and restored to the film when it was reissued in the early 1980s.

"Lost Horizon" is the lyrical title song for the 1973 musical version of the famous James Hilton tale. Hal David (lyric) and Burt Bacharach (music) wrote the number that urged one to flee one's troubles and come to the mythical land of Shangri La and it was sung over the opening credits by Shawn Phillips.

"A Lot in Common (With You)" is a sprightly duet that lists everything the couple shares, from being left-handed to being "lonesome and stranded." It was sung by war hero Fred Astaire and sweetheart Joan Leslie (dubbed by Sally Sweetland) at a servicemen's club in *The Sky's the Limit* (1943), then the two did a lively tap dance together. Harold Arlen composed the bouncy music, and Johnny Mercer wrote the sly lyric that had Astaire referring to his ex-co-star Ginger Rogers and Leslie referring to her ex-co-star James Cagney. The song is also called "I've Got a Lot in Common With You."

"Louise" is perhaps the quintessential Maurice Chevalier song, a romantic but dapper number by Leo Robin (lyric) and Richard Whiting (music) that Chevalier introduced in his first American feature film, *Innocents of Paris* (1929), and one he was always associated with. As he sat on a garden fence in the moonlight, Paris junk dealer Chevalier serenaded Sylvia Beecher and a new movie star was born. Chevalier reprised the song in *A New Kind of Love* (1963), but it had been sung in earlier films by Johnny Johnston and Betty Jane Rhodes in *You Can't Ration Love* (1944), Jerry Lewis and Dean Martin in *The Stooge* (1952), and Neil Diamond in *The Jazz Singer* (1980). Even the Marx Brother lip-synced to the famous Chevalier recording in *A Night at the Opera* (1935). Recordings were made by Chevalier (his first American disk), Paul Whiteman and the Rhythm Boys, Dick Robertson, Bobby Dukoff, and organist Ken Griffin. The familiar song was sung by the cast of the Broadway revue *A Day in Hollywood—A Night in the Ukraine* (1980).

"Love" is the sultry list song about the various faces of romance that Lena Horne performed in a tropical cafe setting in the star-packed revue *Ziegfeld Follies* (1946). Ralph Blane and Hugh Martin wrote the pulsating number and Horne recorded it, but Judy Garland's recording was the bigger seller.

"Love" is the romantic ballad by Floyd Huddleston (lyric) and George Bruns (music) from the animated adventure *Robin Hood* (1973). The Oscar-nominated song was sung on the soundtrack by Nancy Adams during a montage showing the fox Robin Hood falling in love with the vixen Maid Marian. While the lyric is in the courtly love vein, the music has a driving pop flavor.

"Love and Learn" is the trilling ballad about romantic experience that the trilling Lily Pons sang in *That Girl from Paris* (1937). Edward Heyman (lyric) and Arthur Schwartz (music) wrote the song, which was popular with orchestras, being recorded by Artie Shaw (vocal by Peg La Centra), Eddy Duchin, Shep Fields, Abe Lyman, and Miff Mole.

"Love Him" is the bombastic announcement that love has arrived, delivered by Betty Hutton, as vaudeville singer Blossom Seeley, and Ralph Meeker, as her husband Benny Fields, at a benefit show in the period bio-musical *Somebody Loves Me* (1952). Jay Livingston and Ray Evans wrote the World War One–era number.

"Love in Bloom" is the Oscar-nominated ballad by Leo Robin (lyric) and Ralph Rainger (music) that is one of the most recognized melodies in pop culture because it served as Jack Benny's theme song for decades on radio and television. The song, about spring being not a natural phenomenon but a romantic one, was introduced by Bing Crosby and Kitty Carlisle in *She Loves*

Me Not (1934) and the effect (if you can ignore the comic connection) is hauntingly romantic. The studio and various music publishers thought the song too rangy and lyrically too highbrow for audiences, but Crosby's recording was a bestseller and a half million copies of sheet music were sold in 1934 alone. Other recordings were made by Paul Whiteman, Hal Kemp, George Price, and Claude Hopkins, and even Spike Jones did a spoof of the popular ballad. Benny sang the number in *College Holiday* (1937) and played it on the violin in *Man About Town* (1939). "Love in Bloom" was featured in two other films: Lynn Overman sang it in *New York Town* (1941), and Judy Canova did her own unique version of it in *True to the Army* (1942).

"Love Is Back in Business" is the celebratory song by Mack Gordon (lyric) and Sammy Fain (music) that eagerly looks forward to normalcy after World War Two. Betty Grable, Dan Daily, Danny Thomas, Benay Venuta, and the cast of a soldier show sang the jubilant number at the end of *Call Me Mister* (1951).

"Love Is Greater Than I Thought" is the revelatory ballad that Jay Livingston and and Ray Evans wrote for the western musical spoof *Red Garters* (1954). Joanne Gilbert of the prairie town of Paradise Lost sang the number, which is sometimes listed as "This Is Greater Than I Thought."

"Love Is Here to Stay" is the beloved Gershwin standard that took years to become popular but survives as one of the most expert of all movie ballads. It is the song George Gershwin was working on for *The Goldwyn Follies* (1938) when he died prematurely in 1937. Vernon Duke completed the music using Gershwin's notes and Oscar Levant's remembering the melody from hearing it played by the late composer. The music is flowing but restrained and uses no rhythmic tricks, "a model love song" as James Morris describes it. Ira Gershwin wrote the entrancing lyric that looks at the world's "passing fancies" but sees a long life for a romance that is going "a long, long way." Kenny Baker sang the ballad on a radio program while his girlfriend Andrea Leeds and studio boss Adolphe Menjou listened to him on the radio, talking over parts of the number. Needless to say, the song attracted little attention, and despite recordings by Red Norvo (vocal Mildred Bailey), Larry Clinton, and Jimmy Dorsey (vocal by Bob Eberle), the lovely ballad pretty much disappeared until Gene Kelly sang it to Leslie Caron in *An American in Paris* (1951) and it was rediscovered by audiences. Kelly recorded the number, as did Nat King Cole, Jackie Gleason's Orchestra with trumpeter Bobby Hackett, Tony Bennett, and many others. Known also as "Our Love Is Here to Stay," the song is one of the most performed and recorded in the Gershwin repertoire. Diana Ross sang it in the Billie Holiday bio-musical *Lady Sings the Blues* (1972), and there have been distinctive recent recordings by Natalie Cole, Michael Feinstein, and Ann

Hampton Callaway.

"Love Is Just Around the Corner" is the Depression-era love song that shrewdly uses Herbert Hoover's promise "Prosperity is just around the corner." Millionaire crooner Bing Crosby sang the breezy invitation to romance in *Here Is My Heart* (1934) and his recording was very popular. Leo Robin wrote the clever lyric that included the memorable compliment of being cuter than Venus and, even better, "you've got arms," and Lewis Gensler composed the upbeat music. Philip Furia rightfully calls the song "one of the wittiest metaphors of the golden age." Henry Busse (vocal by Marion Holmes) made a notable record of the ballad, and Bob Cummings sang it in *Millions in the Air* (1935). The song was performed by Wayne Cilento and Bruce Anthony Davis in the Broadway musical *Big Deal* (1986).

"Love Is Never Out of Season" is the romantic ballad by Lew Brown (lyric) and Sammy Fain (music) that Harriet Hilliard and William Brady sang in the backstager *New Faces of 1937* (1937). Hilliard recorded the number with Ozzie Nelson's Orchestra, and there were also records by Tommy Dorsey (vocal by Jack Leonard), George Hall (vocal by Dolly Dawn), and the bands of Gene Kardos and Emery Deutsch.

"Love Is on the Air Tonight" is the rousing finale number by Johnny Mercer (lyric) and Richard Whiting (music) for a college musical revue on Broadway in *Varsity Show* (1937). Priscilla and Rosemary Lane led the crowd of students in military fashion down a huge staircase and sang about a heart-to-heart hookup over the radio that will unite the nation with love. The Busby Berkeley–staged number then featured a baton-twirling display, Fred Waring and his Pennsylvanians (in their film debut) sang and toss footballs about, and the sequence ended with an overhead shot that revealed the names of celebrated colleges spelled out by the students below. Dick Powell, who was in the film, made a noteworthy recording of the uptempo song.

"Love Is Only Love" is the reticent ballad by Jerry Herman from the 1969 film version of his Broadway blockbuster *Hello, Dolly!* As widowed matchmaker Barbra Streisand brushed her hair in her lonely apartment and prepared to go out to rejoin the human race by getting married again, she sang this ballad about accepting a quieter and more practical kind of love the second time around. Herman had originally written the song for the musical *Mame,* but it was cut before opening.

"Love Is Where You Find It" is the sentimental ballad by Al Dubin, Johnny Mercer (lyric), and Harry Warren (music) from the nightclub backstager *Garden of the Moon* (1938) that believes romance can be found in the most unlikeliest of places, be it in Kalua or Kokomo. Band leader John Payne sang the number with Johnny "Scat" Davis in the film, and there were memorable recordings by Jimmy Dorsey (vocal by Bob Eberle), the Andrews Sisters, and Kay Kyser (vocal by Harry Babbitt).

"Love Is Where You Find It" is the later and more popular song of the same name that advises one to grab romance where one can. Earl Brent (lyric) and Nacio Herb Brown (music) wrote the passionate song for the Frank Sinatra vehicle *The Kissing Bandit* (1948), where it was sung by Kathryn Grayson, who also recorded it. Later that same year Jane Powell sang the Spanish-flavored aria in *A Date With Judy* (1948).

"Love Isn't Born, It's Made" is the sly song of pragmatic advice that Ann Sheridan and Joyce Reynolds sang to a dorm full of coeds as part of a big charity revue in *Thank Your Lucky Stars* (1943). Arthur Schwartz composed the swinging music, and Frank Loesser wrote the lyric that argued that certain shy men will not find love on their own, so women must go out to create a little romance for them. Fay DeWitt and Stephen Berger sang the number in the Off-Broadway revue *Nightclub Confidential* (1984).

"Love Me Forever" is the ardent title song by Gus Kahn (lyric) and Victor Schertzinger (music) that was one of only two contemporary numbers in the 1935 musical about grand opera. Grace Moore, as a Metropolitan soprano, sang the love song in the film and recorded it as well.

"Love Me, Love My Pekinese" is a delightful comic number by Cole Porter that wryly put some conditions on love. Temperamental Broadway star Virginia Bruce performed the campy number to a flock of ogling sailors in the backstager *Born to Dance* (1936).

"Love Me Tender" is the popular title song that Elvis Presley sang in his first film, a 1956 period musical set right after the Civil War. Texas farmboy Presley sang the simple folk ballad about endless devotion as he strummed his guitar and entertained family members on the porch of their farmhouse. Presley and Vera Matson adapted George R. Poulton's 1861 song "Aura Lee," and Presley's record sold over a million copies. Richard Chamberlain's 1962 disk was nearly as popular, and the number was revived in 1967 by a pop version by Percy Sledge. The ballad was featured in *All Hands on Deck* (1962) and was sung by Linda Ronstadt in *FM* (1978).

"Love Me Tonight" is the title song by Lorenz Hart (lyric) and Richard Rodgers (music) for the 1932 landmark musical comedy. The tailor Maurice Chevalier dreamt that he was singing with the haughty but beautiful princess

Jeanette MacDonald, the two of them urging the other not to wait, but to seize romance now because no one knows what tomorrow may bring.

"The Love of My Life" is a swinging love song that Johnny Mercer (lyric) and Artie Shaw (music) wrote for the varsity–Big Band musical *Second Chorus* (1940). Trumpet-playing college student Fred Astaire (Bobby Hackett dubbed the horn playing) performed the Oscar-nominated number that was an invitation to romance, and he and Shaw's Orchestra (vocal by Anita Boyer) each made recordings of it. The song is sometimes listed as "How Would You Like to Be the Love of My Life?"

"Love of My Life" is the fervent Cole Porter ballad, written for the very stylized musical *The Pirate* (1948), that is straightforward in its romanticism. Just as Gene Kelly was about to be hanged as the Caribbean pirate Macoco, villager Judy Garland sang the heartfelt song to him saying that he was the love she had long dreamed about. The poignant number, the quietest in this hyperactive musical, provoked the real Macoco to come forward and save Kelly's life. Garland recorded the ballad, as did Harry James (vocal by Marion Morgan).

"Love on the Rocks" is the quiet rock ballad that pop singer Neil Diamond sang in a recording studio trying to forget an unhappy past in the 1980 version of *The Jazz Singer*. Diamond wrote the English lyric for Gilbert Becaud's French torch song, and the Diamond recording was popular.

"Love Thy Neighbor" is the love song by Mack Gordon (lyric) and Harry Revel (music) that uses the biblical commandment as a way to romance. Shipwrecked on a tropical island, Bing Crosby, Ethel Merman, and Leon Errol sang the merry song as they built a primitive hut in *We're Not Dressing* (1934). Crosby's recording was a bestseller; the number was also recorded by Raymond Paige and his Orchestra.

"Love Walked In" is the Gershwin brothers' "airily confident romantic ballad," as described by Roy Hemming, that was heard throughout the Hollywood backstager *The Goldwyn Follies* (1938). Short order cook Kenny Baker introduced the popular song of romantic revelation as he grilled hamburgers in a Hollywood diner. He later reprised the ballad with sweetheart Andrea Leeds (dubbed by Virginia Verrill) as they were sunbathing on a California beach; the song was also sung at a Hollywood party at the end of the film by Baker, Leeds/Verrill, and opera singer Helen Jepson. George Gershwin's music, written several years earlier, was self-described as "Brahmsian" (his brother Ira called it "churchy"), and Alec Wilder pronounced it "very restrained, lucid, direct, warm, and without pretense." Ira Gershwin's lyric beautifully personifies love as a welcome stranger entering a room and one's life forever after. The lyricist felt the melody deserved better words, but the song went on to be very popular, remaining on *Your Hit Parade* for thirteen weeks. Sammy Kaye's recording was Number One on the charts, and there were also hit records by Louis Armstrong and Chet Baker. The 1950s recordings by the Hilltoppers and the Flamingos were bestsellers, and Dinah Washington had success with the song in a 1960 disk. Stephen Richards (dubbed by Bill Days) sang "Love Walked In" in the Gershwin bio-musical *Rhapsody in Blue* (1945).

"Love With All the Trimmings" is the erotic recipe for love that Alan Jay Lerner (lyric) and Burton Lane (music) wrote for the 1970 film version of their Broadway ESP musical *On a Clear Day You Can See Forever*. Barbra Streisand, as an elegant lady of wealth in Regency England, was heard singing her thoughts on the soundtrack as she eyed a handsome man at a dinner party. Lerner's lyric is very suggestive in its many food metaphors ("piping hot with all the trimmings"), and Streisand's silky rendition and her tactile fingering of her wine glass make the scene very sensual.

"Love, You Didn't Do Right By Me" is the gentle torch song that Irving Berlin wrote for *White Christmas* (1954), an affecting number that stops short of mawkishness. Rosemary Clooney sang it in a nightclub while Bing Crosby was in the audience, each of them aware that the lyric applies to their recent quarrel. Clooney recorded the ballad, as did Peggy Lee.

"The Loveliest Night of the Year" is the popular waltz ballad introduced in the bio-musical *The Great Caruso* (1951). Although Mario Lanza played the renowned tenor in the film and his recording of the song sold over a million disks, the number was introduced by Ann Blyth as Mrs. Caruso as she waltzed with her husband during his birthday celebration in a New York restaurant. Irving Aaronson wrote the music, adapting the melody from Juventino Rosas' "Over the Waves," and Paul Francis Webster penned the lyric that rejoiced in the evening. Recordings by Helen O'Connell and organist Ethel Smith were notable yet, curiously, over the years the song is mostly known as the preferred musical background for performing seals.

"Lovely Lady" is the waltzing tribute to Alice Faye that Kenny Baker sang in a production number in *King of Burlesque* (1935). Ted Koehler (lyric) and Jimmy McHugh (music) wrote the ardent love song, and there were recordings made by Bing Crosby, Glen Gray and the Casa Loma Orchestra, Vincent Lopez, Tommy Dorsey, and Dick Robertson.

"Lovely to Look At" is the enchanting tribute to beauty that Dorothy Fields (lyric) and Jerome Kern (music) interpolated into Kern's score for the 1935 film version of the Broadway musical *Roberta*. It was their first collaboration, although Fields wrote the lyric to Kern's lead sheet before she even met the famous composer. The result was a haunting, intoxicating song and the birth of one of the finest songwriting teams in the history of Hollywood. Irene Dunne introduced the song in the film; later the ballad was reprised by Fred Astaire and danced by Astaire and Ginger Rogers. Told that the number must serve as a love song and also be used for the film's fashion show finale, Fields came up with an elegant lyric that sits on Kern's dreamy melody effortlessly. The song's refrain is unusually short (only sixteen measures), and when asked why, Kern replied, "That was all I had to say." But the last four measures are very complex and the studio feared the song was too difficult to become popular. To their surprise the cascading love song was at the top of *Your Hit Parade's* listing, Eddy Duchin's recording was Number One on the charts, and it was nominated for an Oscar. The 1952 remake of *Roberta* was called *Lovely to Look At* because of the song, which was sung by Howard Keel and Kathryn Grayson. Recordings of note include those by Leo Reisman and his Orchestra, Joan Roberts and Stephen Douglass, and recently Andrea Marcovicci. Elisabeth Welch sang the ballad in the Broadway revue *Jerome Kern Goes to Hollywood* (1986).

"A Lovely Way to Spend an Evening" is the crooning ballad by Harold Adamson (lyric) and Jimmy McHugh (music) that observes the enchanting night and yearns to spend them all with a certain person. Frank Sinatra (in his film debut) sang the love song to Michelle Morgan in *Higher and Higher* (1943) as they sat on a bench in Central Park and the music from an outdoor concert supplied the accompaniment. When Sinatra went to record the song, a musicians' strike forced him to use the Bobby Tucker Singers as his accompaniment. The record was a hit all the same, and there were noteworthy recordings by Louis Prima, Englebert Humperdinck, and others. The ballad, sometimes listed as "This Is a Lovely Way to Spend an Evening," was sung by Martha O'Driscoll in *Criminal Court* (1946) and by Lizbeth Scott in *The Racket* (1951).

"Lover" is the familiar operatic-like aria by Lorenz Hart (lyric) and Richard Rodgers (music) from *Love Me Tonight* (1932) that is both grandiose and silly. French aristocrat Jeanette MacDonald sang the high-trilling number to her horse as she happily galloped across the countryside in a buggy. Hart's lyric is filled with "whoa" and other comments to the horse, and Rodgers' music ascends and descends the scale in a furious manner that can only be described as mock opera. (When Rodgers played the song for studio head Darryl F. Zanuck, the mogul asked him if he could "make it better.") While there were recordings of "Lover" in the 1930s by Paul Whiteman and others, the song did not become popular until a decade later when it was used as the opening number at a military school dance in *The Major and the Minor* (1942). Gloria Jean sang it in *Moonlight in*

Vermont (1943), Deanna Dubin (with revised lyrics) in *Because of Him* (1946), Peggy Lee in *The Jazz Singer* (1953), Fred Astaire in *The Pleasure of His Company* (1961), and Jerry Lewis in *The Errand Boy* (1962). Other recordings were made by Les Paul (a 1948 release using multitrack recording techniques), Ella Fitzgerald, Greta Keller, and in 1995 opera diva Frederica von Stade.

"Loving You" is the sensitive title ballad that Jerry Leiber and Mike Stoller wrote for the 1957 Elvis Presley vehicle and the only gentle number in the rock-and-roll score. Rising singing star Presley, accompanying himself on guitar, sang of hoping to spend his whole life loving just one person as he entertained Dolores Hart and her family at a picnic on their farm. Later in the film Presley reprised the song on a television broadcast. In the Lieber and Stoller Broadway revue called *Smokey Joe's Cafe* (1995), the number was performed by Ken Ard and the cast.

"Lowdown Lullaby" is the heartfelt ballad that Leo Robin (lyric) and Ralph Rainger (music) wrote for *Little Miss Marker* (1934), but it was, as described by Roy Hemming, a "cynically wistful" number and was sung by Dorothy Dell rather than the film's chipper star Shirley Temple. Dell gave the melancholy song a sultry interpretation that is quite estimable. Paramount was grooming Dell as its next star, but she died in a car accident soon after the film was released.

"Lullaby in Ragtime" is the lightly swinging ballad by Sylvia Fine that was used effectively in the bio-musical of Red Nichols called *The Five Pennies* (1959). Danny Kaye (as Nichols) and his wife Barbara Bel Geddes (dubbed by Eileen Wilson) sang the number to their infant daughter as they rode on the touring band bus, members of the band quietly accompanying them vocally and on their instruments. Later in the film, in a nightclub six years later, Kaye reprised the lullaby contrapuntally with Louis Armstrong's singing of "Good Night, Sleep Tight" and daughter Susan Gordon's singing of "The Five Pennies."

"Lullaby of Broadway" is the Oscar-winning standard by Al Dubin (lyric) and Harry Warren (music) that is purportedly about the theatre district in New York but in many ways is the quintessential Hollywood song. It was introduced in an elaborate production number as part of a show at a resort hotel in *Gold Diggers of 1935* (1935) and inspired one of choreographer Busby Berkeley's finest narrative scenes. The sequence began with a closeup of Wini Shaw's face that enlarged to become the skyline of Manhattan. She sang of a hedonistic chorus girl on Broadway who slept all day, partied all night, and came to a tragic end. Scenes in the theatre district illustrated the tale as escort Dick Powell (who sang a section of the song) and his "Broadway baby" were seen partying at a nightspot where hundreds of couples engaged in decadent and jazzy dancing, culminating when the show girl was accidentally pushed out a window to her death. Her empty apartment was then seen, with no one to pour milk for the hungry cat, and the sequence ended with Manhattan reverting to Shaw's face, which receded into the distance. When the song was first played for studio head Jack Warner, he disliked the downbeat lyric and requested new words; but Warren refused to couple his music with any other lyric. The music is unusual in the way it does not establish its predominant key until late in the song. As Ethan Mordden comments, "While it opens with a jazzy, stepping strain, it does indeed work up to a lullaby." "Lullaby of Broadway" was Number One on *Your Hit Parade* with best-selling recordings by Shaw, the Dorsey brothers, Hal Kemp, and others. Bette Midler made a distinctive recording years later with a trio version, using a triple track and providing all three voices herself, and in 1998 Mary Cleere Haran made a notable recording. The popular number was used in *The Jolson Story* (1946) and *Young Man With a Horn* (1950) and became the title of a 1951 musical where it was sung by Doris Day and danced by Day and Gene Nelson. Jerry Orbach and the company sang the number in the Broadway musical *42nd Street* (1980).

"Lulu From Louisville" is the jazzy Southern-flavored number by Leo Robin (lyric) and Ralph Rainger (music) that was briefly featured in the turn-of-the-century musical *Coney Island* (1943). On a riverboat wharf setting on the stage of a Coney Island saloon, Betty Grable (made up as a light-skinned Negress) and a chorus of minstrel performers sang about the naughty and enticing gal from Kentucky, then did a rousing cakewalk together.

"Lulu's Back in Town" is the jaunty song by Al Dubin (lyric) and Harry Warren (music) that insists that with tuxedo pressed, shoes shined, "I look my best" because the idolized Lulu is due soon. Dick Powell introduced the jazzy number with the Mills Brothers in the radio backstager *Broadway Gondolier* (1935). Powell and the Mills Brothers each recorded it, as did Thomas "Fats" Waller, Ted Fio Rito, Mel Tormé, and Jerry Vale.

"Lydia, the Tattooed Lady" is arguably the finest song ever written for the Marx Brothers, if not one of the best comic songs in all movie musicals. E. Y. Harburg (lyric) and Harold Arlen (music) wrote the hilarious description of the tattoos that grace Lydia's body and it was sung by Groucho Marx (with Chico at the piano) to entertain passengers on a train in *At the Circus* (1939). The music is rather unadventurous for Arlen, but he had to tailor his tune to Marx's limited singing range. Knowing Groucho's love of Gilbert and Sullivan songs, Harburg tried for a similar kind of lyric, but the result was much racier than any Victorian operetta would allow. The rhymes throughout the lyric are classic, from "torso" and "adore so" to the arch rhyming of "encyclopedia" with the lady's name. The studio objected to the song because of the censorship code, but when Harburg added a last verse in which Lydia married the admirable, the number was approved. Virginia Weidler sang the ditty in *The Philadelphia Story* (1940), Frank Ferrante performed it in the Off-Broadway show *Groucho: A Life in Revue* (1986), Bobby Short recorded it, and Kermit the Frog (voice of Jim Henson) sang it on television and records, but the definitive version is still that by Groucho Marx, who sang it throughout his long career.

M

"Mack the Black" is the rousing production number by Cole Porter from the colorful stylized musical *The Pirate* (1948). Caribbean maiden Judy Garland and the inhabitants of the island of San Sebastian told about the legendary pirate Macoco in song and story. Porter's lyric is very raffish, pronouncing the word "Caribbean" different ways to suit his nimble wordplay.

"Madame, I Love Your Crepes Suzettes" is the comic love song by Ralph Freed, Lew Brown (lyric), and Burton Lane (music) that Red Skelton sang with Tommy Dorsey's Orchestra in the film version of *DuBarry Was a Lady* (1943), which dropped most of the Cole Porter Broadway score. The suggestive number, dismissing a gal's cooking abilities and favoring the lady herself because she is "my favorite dish," was not up to Porter's urbane level, but it was clever in its own right and was gleefully performed.

"Magic" is the top-selling disco ballad by John Farrar about a muse's power to inspire one's imagination. It was introduced in the flashy musical *Xanadu* (1980) by the muse Olivia Newton-John (with the Electric Light Orchestra), who was heard on the soundtrack singing "we are magic" as she roller-skated through an abandoned building and Michael Beck, looking on unseen, fell in love with her. Newton-John's recording was a Number One bestseller.

"Magic Dance" is a rompish rock number that David Bowie wrote for the musical fantasy *Labyrinth* (1986). The King of the Goblins (Bowie in a fright wig) sang the joyous song to the human infant that he has stolen, and all of his court of grotesque Muppet creatures joined him in the singing and dancing frolic.

"Main Street" is the exuberant song by Betty Comden, Adolph Green (lyric), and Roger Edens (music) that salutes "small town people, the backbone of American civilization." Sailor Gene Kelly sang and dancer Vera-Ellen joined him and danced the number in a rehearsal hall in *On the Town* (1949), dropping their phony sophistication and admitting to each other that they came from small towns; in fact, the same small town.

"Make a Wish" is the hopeful title song by Paul Francis Webster (lyric) and Oscar Straus (music) for the 1937 musical melodrama. The youth Bobby Breen sang the number with Basil Rathbone, the composer with writer's block who is inspired by the boy.

"Make 'Em Laugh" is the only new song written for the musical classic *Singin' in the Rain* (1952) and the last song ever penned by the illustrious team of Arthur Freed (lyric) and Nacio Herb Brown (music). A comic number was needed for Donald O'Connor to sing and dance to cheer up Gene Kelly in the film, but nothing in the Freed-Brown repertoire (the source of the rest of the score) seemed to fit and so the old collaborators were reunited one last time. The result is a merry number that is uncomfortably close to Cole Porter's previous "Be a Clown" in theme, melody, and rhythm, but it did provide for O'Connor's tour de force performance that is arguably the funniest musical number ever captured on film. On a sound stage filled with props, O'Connor performed "Make 'Em Laugh" with athletic comedy bits and outrageous facial expressions, raising low-down clowning to a high art. The number was performed by Peter Slutsker in the 1985 Broadway version of *Singin' in the Rain*.

"Make Way for Tomorrow" is the vibrant song about an optimistic future that Ira Gershwin, E. Y. Harburg (lyric), and Jerome Kern (music) wrote for the fashion magazine musical *Cover Girl* (1944). Struggling entertainers Gene Kelly, Rita Hayworth (dubbed by Nan Wynn), and Phil Silvers sang the uplifting number as they left their favorite late-night diner and pranced down a Brooklyn street, using Brownstone stoops, garbage can lids, and other found objects in their ingenious dancing. The three friends also reprised the song briefly at the end of the film. Kern's music is a merry march that continues to rise throughout the song and the Gershwin-Harburg lyric has fun with clichés about smiles, clouds, and sunshine. Barbara Cook, Cy Young, and Bobby Short recorded the trio in the 1970s, and the number was sung by the ensemble in the Broadway revue *Jerome Kern Goes to Hollywood* (1986).

"The Maladjusted Jester" is the comic character song for medieval performer Danny Kaye, who disguised himself as the royal "king of jesters and jester to kings" in the musical farce *The Court Jester* (1956). Sylvia Fine wrote the specialty number for Kaye, who turned it into an eruption of tongue twisters and other verbal clowning as he explained to the court how he "made a fool" of himself.

"Mama, That Moon Is Here Again" is the comic lament by Leo Robin (lyric) and Ralph Rainger (music) that Martha Raye belted in the shipboard musical *The Big Broadcast of 1938* (1938). Having scared off a man with her overeager ways, Raye sang out to her mother back home (the word "Mama" coming out of her mouth like something approaching an air raid siren) about how she has been left high and dry again. She then engaged in a very physical and silly dance with a bunch of sailors who tossed her about the deck like a wet mop. Shep Fields and his Rippling Rhythm (who appeared in the film) recorded the song, as did Glen Gray and his Casa Loma Orchestra (vocal by Pee Wee Hunt) and Isham Jones (vocal by Eddie Stone).

"Mammy's Gone" is the touching lullaby that the hard-working father Clarence Muse sang to his grandson and granddaughter as he rocked them to sleep in the trail-blazing early black musical *Hearts in Dixie* (1929). Buddy De Sylva, Lew Brown (lyric), and Ray Henderson (music) wrote the captivating number that was interpolated into a score comprised mostly of Negro spirituals.

"A Man and His Dream" is a ballad about fantasizing in the moonlight that Johnny Burke (lyric) and James Monaco (music) wrote for *The Star Maker* (1939), the bio-musical about talent search impresario Gus Edwards. Bing Crosby, as showman Edwards, sang the languishing number and recorded it as well.

"A Man Chases a Girl (Until She Catches Him)" is one of the few new songs Irving Berlin wrote for his hit-packed compilation musical *There's No Business Like Show Business* (1954). After he has been given the cold shoulder by singer Marilyn Monroe, vaudevillian Donald O'Connor sang the breezy song about the mysterious ways the female behaves as he danced about in a Florida park outside her bungalow. (Monroe joined in the number from inside her room.) When O'Connor was hit by a coconut falling from one of the park's palm trees, he dreamt that the statues in the fountain came to life and exuberantly danced with them. Eddie Fisher recorded the number with success.

"The Man That Got Away" is the driving lament by Ira Gershwin (lyric) and Harold Arlen (music) that became Judy Garland's signature song for the last years of her career, a compelling number that alternates between despair, off-hand dismissal, and vainglorious hope. Garland introduced the torch song as a struggling young singer in *A Star Is Born* (1954), where she sang it for some musician friends in a Sunset Strip nightclub after hours. Arlen's music is disturbing and very bluesy, though David Ewen points out it "is more a blues of

Tin Pan Alley variety than New Orleans or Chicago." The song's musical structure, which extends an unusual fifty-six measures, is more like that of an opera aria than a popular song. The opening musical phrase is repeated five times, giving the song a relentless drive right from the start, and the number climaxes with heartbreaking hope. Gershwin's lyric is terse and expert, the title avoiding the more grammatically correct "man who got away," so that it recalls the slangy boast of "the fish that got away." Garland's recording of the Oscar-nominated song remained popular for years, and few singers recorded the number because her rendition was so pervasive. (Julie Wilson made a distinctive recording in 1990 that made an effort to break away from the Garland approach.) Frank Sinatra recorded the song as "The Gal That Got Away," but the result was far less satisfying.

"March of the Grenadiers" is the operetta call to arms that Clifford Grey (lyric) and Victor Schertzinger (music) wrote for Jeanette MacDonald to trill in *The Love Parade* (1929). Dressed in uniform, European queen MacDonald sang the pounding march to and with her troops as they paraded past her. The song left plenty of opportunities for MacDonald to display her considerable soprano talents, sometimes holding notes endlessly while the men continued the melody without her.

"Marry the Mole" is a comic song of advice that Carol Channing sang on the soundtrack for the animated fantasy *Thumbelina* (1994). A matchmaking mouse (voice of Channing) told the miniature Thumbelina to forget about her lost fairy prince and wed the rich mole who has proposed to her. Jack Feldman and Bruce Sussman wrote the funny lyric, and Barry Manilow composed the soft-shoe music that turned into a bump-and-grind for Channing's raspy singing voice.

"May I?" is a narrative ballad by Mack Gordon (lyric) and Harry Revel (music) about a tongue-tied suitor who can barely speak when with his beloved, but when he gets the words out they request a passionate love affair and *then* a wedding. Sailor Bing Crosby sang the sly number to guests on a yacht in *We're Not Dressing* (1934) and recorded it as well.

"Maybe This Time" is one of the three new songs Fred Ebb (lyric) and John Kander (music) wrote for the 1972 film version of their Broadway hit *Cabaret*. American singer Liza Minnelli sang the hopeful ballad, about romantic success after a long line of failures, as she performed in the Berlin Kit Kat Klub; the song was intercut with scenes of her blossoming romance with British author Michael York. Director Bob Fosse shot the number simply, using the smoke in the club and a single follow spot in ingenious ways. If the song sounded more like contemporary Las Vegas than 1920s Berlin, it was because

Kander and Ebb had written it for Minnelli's nightclub act seven years earlier but it was never used. Brenda Pressley sang the pungent number in the Off-Broadway revue *And the World Goes 'Round* (1991) and Natasha Richardson sang it in the 1998 Broadway revival of *Cabaret*.

"Mean Green Mother from Outer Space" is the only new song added to the 1986 film of the Off-Broadway sci–fi musical *Little Shop of Horrors*. Howard Ashman (lyric) and Alan Menken (music) wrote the Oscar-nominated rock number that was sung by the flesh-eating plant Audrey II (singing voice of Levi Stubbs) as it tried to devour his human protégé Rick Moranis.

"Meet the Beat of My Heart" is the rhythmic call for affection that Mack Gordon (lyric) and Harry Revel (lyric) wrote for the Mickey Rooney vehicle *Love Finds Andy Hardy* (1938). Overlooked teenager Judy Garland sang the urgent number, which was recorded by Garland, Hal Kemp (vocal by Bob Allen), Charles "Buddy" Rogers (vocal by Bob Hannon), and Gene Krupa and his Orchestra.

"Meet the Sun Half Way" is a song of hope for tomorrow that singing construction worker Bing Crosby sang in the sentimental musical *If I Had My Way* (1940). Johnny Burke (lyric) and James Monaco (music) wrote the ballad, which was recorded by Crosby, Hal Kemp (vocal by Janet Blair), the Smoothies, and Barry Wood.

"Meetcha 'Round the Corner (at Half Past Eight)" is the humorous seduction number sung by saloon hostess Iris Adrian to dentist Bob Hope in *The Paleface* (1948) as she suggested that they get away from the crowd and be alone together. Jay Livingston and Ray Evans wrote the wry ditty based on the familiar phrase.

"Mein Herr" is the stylized homage to Marlene Dietrich that songwriters Fred Ebb (lyric) and John Kander (music) and director Bob Fosse devised for the dark musical *Cabaret* (1972). American singer Liza Minnelli and the Kit Kat Girls, dressed in black stockings and bowler hats, performed the farewell song to an ex-lover as they posed and gyrated on chairs in a Berlin nightclub. In the Broadway version, the Minnelli character was British and was introduced with the coy music hall number "Don't Tell Mama." For the film, the satiric "Mein Herr" served as her "I am" song and paid tongue-in-cheek tribute to Dietrich's famous "Falling in Love Again" number in the German melodrama *The Blue Angel* (1930). Natasha Richardson and the girls sang "Mein Herr" in the 1998 Broadway revival of *Cabaret*.

"The Merry-Go-Runaround" is a frolicsome trio written by Johnny Burke (lyric) and James Van Heusen (music) for the familiar love triangle of Bing Crosby, Bob Hope, and Dorothy Lamour in *Road to Bali* (1953). Stranded on a Pacific Island, vaudevillians Crosby and Hope each sang to Polynesian princess Lamour how he loved her but her indecision about which one to marry was wearing on them all. Lamour joined the duo in singing how she is giving them the runaround; then all three went into a silly dance that had them swinging from vines Tarzan-style.

"The Merry Old Land of Oz" is the catchy song of welcome that the citizens of the Emerald City sang as Dorothy (Judy Garland) and her three friends (Ray Bolger, Jack Haley, and Bert Lahr) entered the shining city. Then the four guests sang sections of the number as they were groomed to meet the Wizard. Harold Arlen wrote the caliope-like music, and E. Y. Harburg penned the jolly lyric that was filled with such onomatopoeic words as "buzz," "pat," "chirp," and plenty of "ho ho ho"s and "ha ha ha"s. An introductory verse explaining how anyone can fit in and be happy in Oz was written to make the transition into the song less abrupt, but it was cut from the film before opening.

"Midnight in Memphis" is the acid rock lament by Tony Johnson about the loneliness and restlessness of touring on the rock concert circuit. Drugged-out singer Bette Midler sang the number in concert in the thinly disguised Janis Joplin bio-musical *The Rose* (1979).

"Midnight in Paris" is the resounding aria that struggling opera singer Nino Martini sang in the grand opera backstager *Here's to Romance* (1935). Herb Magidson (lyric) and Con Conrad (music) wrote the surging number that invited one to experience the romantic joys of the City of Light.

"Military Man" is the big tap finale for *Poor Little Rich Girl* (1936) in which socialite tot Shirley Temple, vaudevillians Jack Haley and Alice Faye, and the chorus all donned military garb and sang the praises of the man in uniform. Mack Gordon (lyric) and Harry Revel (music) wrote the tuneful march, which is sometimes listed as "I Love a Military Man."

"Milkman, Keep Those Bottles Quiet" is the loud-mouthed musical complaint of defense plant workers who needed their sleep to do their best for the war effort, as delivered by Nancy Walker and Ben Blue as part of a summer stock musical revue in *Broadway Rhythm* (1944). Don Raye and Gene De Paul wrote the raucous comedy number, which was recorded by Ella Mae Morse, Woody Herman and his Orchestra, the King Sisters, and very recently Judy Kaye.

"A Million Miles Away Behind the Door" is one of the handful of songs Alan Jay Lerner (lyric) and André Previn (music) wrote for the 1969 film version of the Broadway musical *Paint Your Wagon* scored by Lerner and composer Frederick Loewe. Ex-Mormon wife Jean Seberg (dubbed by Anita Gordon) sang the mellow song yearning for domestic peace and contentment as she gazed out from her cabin in the wilds of 1840 California.

"Mimi" is the funny, naughty tribute to a lady whose best attributes can only be hinted at, as performed by Maurice Chevalier with lewd winks and mumbling words of appreciation in *Love Me Tonight* (1932). Richard Rodgers wrote the French can-can music, Lorenz Hart supplied the double entendre lyric, and Parisian tailor Chevalier sang it to French aristocrat Jeanette MacDonald after he has rescued her from a runaway horse and buggy. (The lady's name is not Mimi but it sounded sexier than Jeanette, the character's name in the script.) C. Aubrey Smith, Charlie Ruggles, and Charles Butterworth reprised the number later in the film with Elizabeth Patterson, Ethel Griffies, and Blanche Friderici. In the original release Myra Loy also sang a reprise of "Mimi," but in 1950 censors noticed that Loy's navel was visible through her nightgown when she sang it and so the reprise was cut from subsequent showings. Chevalier recorded the song, sang it again in *Pepe* (1960), and yet again in *A New Kind of Love* (1963).

"Mind If I Make Love to You?" is, despite its title, a rather casual and off-hand invitation, written by Cole Porter for *High Society* (1956), but charming all the same. Journalist Frank Sinatra sang the ballad to wealthy socialite Grace Kelly as they danced by the pool of her Newport mansion. Carl Wayne sang the number for a 1994 British recording of the *High Society* score.

"Minnie From Trinidad" is the rhythmic production number from the backstager *Ziegfeld Girl* (1940) in which *Follies* singer Judy Garland described herself as a very bad lady from the Caribbean but being very good at it. Roger Edens wrote the song that Busby Berkeley staged on a lush tropical setting with a fervent dance by Sergio Orta.

"Miss Brown to You" is the sly, affectionate ballad that Leo Robin (lyric), Richard Whiting, and Ralph Rainger (music) wrote for the radio backstager *The Big Broadcast of 1936* (1935). Bill Robinson and the Nicholas Brothers performed the number with Ray Noble's Band as a radio broadcast with a Harlem setting, celebrating the arrival of "huggable Emily Brown," who was leaving Tennessee to be with her man up north. Billie Holiday recorded the song with Teddy Wilson's Orchestra and it was long associated with her.

"A Mist Over the Moon" is the Oscar-nominated ballad that Oscar

Hammerstein (lyric) and Ben Oakland (music) wrote for the musical murder mystery *The Lady Objects* (1938). Football halfback Lanny Ross sang the dreamy number filled with atmospheric imagery.

"Mister Five By Five" is the bouncing blues number by Don Raye and Gene De Paul about a short, fat musician who is as wide as he is tall. The song was introduced by Grace McDonald with Sonny Dunham's Orchestra in the Ritz Brothers vehicle *Behind the Eight Ball* (1942). The lyric was said to have been inspired by the corpulent blues singer James Rushing, who could not have been too offended by the song because he later recorded it. The best-selling records of the popular ditty were by Freddie Slack (vocal by Ella Mae Morse) and Harry James and his Orchestra. Jane Frazee sang it in *Almost Married* (1942), and the Andrews Sisters performed it in *Always a Bridesmaid* (1943) and recorded it as well.

"Misto Cristofo Colombo" is the slangy tribute to Columbus by Jay Livingston and Ray Evans in which the famous navigator is merrily applauded because he was able to convince "all the squares" that Earth was indeed round. Bing Crosby, Dorothy Lamour, Phil Harris, Louis Armstrong, and Cass Daley sang it together in an airplane cabin in *Here Comes the Groom* (1951).

"Moments Like This" is the driving ballad that Florence George sang in *College Swing* (1938) as she admitted her cool and nonchalant exterior hides the glow inside because she is in love. Frank Loesser wrote the succinct lyric, and Burton Lane composed the compelling music that was still very romantic. The ballad was recorded by Maxine Sullivan, Dick Stabile and his Orchestra, and Teddy Wilson (vocal by Nan Wynn). A 1986 Tony Bennett recording revived interest in the song, and more recently Michael Feinstein recorded it.

"Money, Money (Makes the World Go Round)" is the rapid-fire, sexy paean to wealth that nightclub performers Liza Minnelli and Joel Grey sang at the Berlin Kit Kat Klub in *Cabaret* (1972). John Kander composed the vivacious honky–tonk music, and Fred Ebb penned the funny lyric that turned the possession of money into a sensual obsession. The comic ditty, which replaced a production number called "The Money Song" in the Broadway original, was sung by the company in the Off-Broadway revue *And the World Goes 'Round* (1991) and by Alan Cumming and the Kit Kat Girls in the 1998 Broadway revival of *Cabaret*.

"Money Burns a Hole in My Pocket" is the easygoing ballad by Bob Hilliard (lyric) and Jule Styne (music) that Dean Martin sang in *Living It Up* (1954), a film version of the Broadway musical *Hazel Flagg*. Hilliard and Styne interpolated the lovely song about impetuousness into their stage score, and the number was recorded by Martin with Dick Stabile's Orchestra.

"The Moon and the Willow Tree" is the enticing ballad by Johnny Burke (lyric) and Victor Schertzinger (music) about two conflicting views about romance, one joyous (the "smiling moon") and the other melancholic (the "weeping willow"). Polynesian gal-on-the-run Dorothy Lamour awoke in the middle of the night and sang the number to the moon in the first of the "Road" pictures, *Road to Singapore* (1940). Lamour recorded it, as did Jack Teagarden (vocal by Kitty Kallen).

"The Moon Got in My Eyes" is the dreamy ballad by Johnny Burke (lyric) and Arthur Johnston (music) that considers a trick of the moon may be responsible, but it seems like true love this time. Bing Crosby sang the song in *Double or Nothing* (1937) and recorded it, and later Mildred Bailey had a successful disk of the ballad.

"Moon Song (That Wasn't Meant for Me)" is the torchy ballad by Sam Coslow (lyric) and Arthur Johnston (music) that Kate Smith introduced in *Hello, Everybody!* (1933) and was long associated with her. Radio singer Smith sang the lyrical lament about a love affair that was never meant to be after Randolph Scott, whom she had fallen in love with, was attracted to her pretty sister. Smith recorded the number and sang it on the radio for years, and there were also recordings by Annette Hanshaw, Frances Langford, Irene Beasley, Jack Denny, Wayne King, and years later Frank Sinatra.

"Moonburn" is the lighthearted romantic ballad by Edward Heyman (lyric) and Hoagy Carmichael (music) that was interpolated into the 1935 film version of the Cole Porter– scored Broadway hit *Anything Goes*. Bing Crosby sang the song through a ship's porthole to Ida Lupino, claiming that his healthy appearance was not from a sun tan but from the glow caught from moonlight and romance. Crosby, who also recorded the ballad, had heard Carmichael sing the number at a Hollywood party and asked if it could be added to the film's score.

"Moonlight Becomes You," arguably the finest ballad to come from the "Road" pictures, is an entrancing love song by Johnny Burke (lyric) and James Van Heusen (music) that compliments a beloved's beauty in the perfect atmosphere, noting "you certainly know the right thing to wear." Shipwrecked entertainer Bing Crosby serenaded Moroccan princess Dorothy Lamour with the ballad in a garden beneath her window in *Road to Morocco* (1942). Later in the film Crosby reprised the song with Lamour and Bob Hope as part of a fantasy brought on by the desert heat, and the wrong voices came out of each of their mouths. Crosby's recording was popular, but it was a 1943 disk by Harry James (vocal by Johnny McAlfee) that sold over a million copies. Other distinctive recordings were made by Glenn Miller (vocal by Skip Nelson and the Modernaires), Jackie Gleason's Orchestra with cornet player Bobby Hackett, the Hi-Lo's, George Shearing, Englebert Humperdinck, Mary Clare Haran, and most recently Tommy Tune. Lewis Cleale sang the warm ballad in the Broadway revue *Swinging on a Star* (1995).

"Moonstruck" is the contemplative ballad by Sam Coslow (lyric) and Arthur Johnston (music) that wonders if this love is true love or just moonlight illusion. Drama professor Bing Crosby sang the song in the campus musical *College Humor* (1933), and he recorded it, as did Al Bowlly, with success.

"More" is a snazzy pastiche number, written by Stephen Sondheim for the cartoonish musical *Dick Tracy* (1990), in which the hedonistic lyric cries out for excess in love, money, and fame. The jazzlike song was first heard at a rehearsal where club owner–gangster Al Pacino was running his chorus girls through their paces, demonstrating how the number should be performed. Later in the film nightclub star Madonna and the girls sang the song onstage as part of a New Year's Eve celebration. The number, like most of those in the film, was intercut with scenes in other locales and was barely intact in the final cut. Jennifer Simard recorded the complete song in 1997.

"More and More" is the Oscar-nominated ballad by E. Y. Harburg (lyric) and Jerome Kern (music) about an ever-growing feeling of love that is overwhelming one. Pioneer gal Deanna Durbin sang the intoxicating song to cardsharp Robert Paige in a moonlit frontier setting in *Can't Help Singing* (1944); according to Roy Hemming, it was "the best song she ever got to introduce in any of her movies." Kern's music is unusually expansive and, as Gerald Bordman notes, "never repeats itself, moving along on an ABCD frame . . . yet the song is tied together by variations of the initial theme." Kern's last hit song in his lifetime, "More and More" was on *Your Hit Parade* for fifteen weeks. The ballad was recorded by Durbin and many others, the top sellers being records by Tommy Dorsey (vocal by Bonnie Lou Williams) and Perry Como.

"The More I See You" is the zesty romantic duet written by Mack Gordon (lyric) and Harry Warren (music) for the nightclub backstager *Diamond Horseshoe* (1945). Show girl Betty Grable and stage-struck doctor Dick Haymes sang the song about their love that increases with frequent viewing. Haymes recorded the number with Victor Young's Orchestra. Harry James (vocal by Buddy De Vito) also had a notable recording, and the song was revived twenty years later with a best-selling record by Chris Montez. Englebert Humperdinck subsequently recorded the ballad with success.

"More Than Just a Friend" is a comic song of affection from the 1962 remake of *State Fair* and probably the only love song in the movies ever sung to a hog. Farmer Tom Ewell groaned the number to the "sweet hog of mine" when the animal got sick at the Texas State Fair. Because lyricist Oscar Hammerstein had died since the original *State Fair*, Richard Rodgers wrote both music and lyric for the odd song.

"Mother Earth and Father Time" is the lyrical ballad by Richard M. and Robert B. Sherman about the passing of the seasons and the birth and rebirth that occurs in nature. The spider Charlotte (voice of Debbie Reynolds) sang the lovely number in the animated children's musical *Charlotte's Web* (1973).

"Mother of Mine, I Still Have You," being the only original number in the landmark film *The Jazz Singer* (1927), has the distinction of being the first song ever written expressly for a talkie. Grant Clarke (lyric), Louis Silvers, and Al Jolson (music) wrote the Southern-style ballad, and Jolson sang it in blackface at a dress rehearsal while his mother (Eugenie Besserer) watched tearfully from the wings. The lyric is a highly emotional cry of thanks to a mother who has stood by him through all his troubles and remained steadfast when all his fair-weather friends have left him. Jolson delivered the ballad chokingly, more talking than singing; and since the lyric followed the film's plot closely, "Mother of Mine, I Still Have You" can also be defined as the first integrated musical number in the history of movie musicals. Jolson recorded the sentimental number which was very popular on radio and in sheet music sales.

"The Mountie Who Never Got His Man" is the comic specialty number about a failed Canadian law enforcer that Herbert Baker (lyric) and George Stoll (music) wrote for the inspired clown Bert Lahr. Mountie and comic sidekick Bert Lahr sang the ditty in the third film version of the operetta *Rose-Marie* (1954). The number is sometimes listed as "I'm a Mountie Who Never Got His Man."

"Movin' Right Along" is a rhythmic traveling song that Kenny Ascher and Paul Williams wrote for *The Muppet Movie* (1979), the first film musical featuring the famous cast of cloth characters from television. Kermit the Frog (voice of Jim Henson) and Fozzie Bear (voice of Frank Oz) sang the peppy number as they drove along the highway on their way to Hollywood.

"Mr. and Mrs. Is the Name" is the happy announcement of long-lasting romance that Mort Dixon (lyric) and Allie Wrubel (music) wrote for the West Point Academy musical *Flirtation Walk* (1934). Cadet Dick Powell and sweetheart Ruby Keeler sang the joyous number, and recordings were made by

Powell, George Hall (vocal by Loretta Lee and Sonny Schuyler), and Victor Young's Orchestra.

"Mr. Booze" is the cautionary rhythm number by Sammy Cahn (lyric) and James Van Heusen (music) that spoke of the evils of the bottle but was so dandy a song it seemed a bit inebriated itself. Bing Crosby led Frank Sinatra, Dean Martin, Sammy Davis, Jr., and an ensemble of fake participants in a fake mission in singing the revival song in the musical parody *Robin and the Seven Hoods* (1964). The musical was Crosby's sixty-first and last film.

"Muchacha" is the vibrant Latin song of amorous conquest ("tonight I've got-cha where I want-cha") by Al Dubin (lyric) and Harry Warren (music) that Mexican dancer Dolores Del Rio, singing "bandido" Phil Regan, and a chorus of dancing couples performed in *In Caliente* (1935). Busby Berkeley staged the lavish number, which transformed a hotel patio into a bandits' hideaway where eight horses joined in the hot-blooded dancing.

"Murder, He Says" was one of Betty Hutton's signature songs, a frantic jive number written by Frank Loesser (lyric) and Jimmy McHugh (music) about a hepcat's slang that is not only unromantic but downright incomprehensible. Hutton introduced the novelty number at a floor show in *Happy Go Lucky* (1943), recorded it, and then sang it on radio and in clubs for years. Dinah Shore's recording was also a bestseller. Teddy Powell and his Orchestra performed the song in *Jam Session* (1944), and Kim Basinger sang it in *The Marrying Man* (1991).

"Music in My Heart" is the tuneful song of musical appreciation by Paul Francis Webster, Louis Alter (lyric), and Oscar Straus (music). Child-star Bobby Breen merrily belted out the ballad in the musical melodrama *Make a Wish* (1937).

"Music in the Night" is the operatic duet that Met tenor Jan Kiepura and co-star Gladys Swarthout sang in the grand opera backstager *Give Us This Night* (1936). Hollywood symphonic composer Erich Wolfgang Korngold wrote the passionate music and Oscar Hammerstein provided the romantic lyric.

"Music Is Better Than Words" is the breezy song by Roger Edens (lyric) and André Previn (music) that urged a fellow to forget about the words and "sing her a song." It was sung by mistress of ceremonies Dolores Gray (in her screen debut) on a television program in *It's Always Fair Weather* (1955). Because the song was a last–minute addition, Edens wrote the lyric after Betty Comden and Adolph Green, lyricists for the rest of the score, had returned to New York. Gray reprised the number in *Designing Woman* (1957).

"Music Makes Me" is the enthralling rhythm number by Gus Kahn, Edward Eliscu (lyric), and Vincent Youmans (music) that seeks to explain the effect the right kind of music has on romance. Ginger Rogers sang the ballad with Gene Raymond's Band in a floor show at a Miami hotel in *Flying Down to Rio* (1933). Youmans' music is exhilarating, with measures containing half notes contrasted those with quarter notes, concluding in two very rhythmic measures.

"The Music Stopped" is the gently swinging ballad by Harold Adamson (lyric) and Jimmy McHugh (music) that recollects an evening when a couple danced together in oblivious bliss even after the music ended and the orchestra had left. Frank Sinatra sang the number at a social event in *Higher and Higher* (1943), where he serenaded and danced with both Michelle Morgan and Barbara Hale. The song was used effectively at the end of the film when Jack Haley and Morgan literally danced on a cloud "way up in the blue" while Sinatra reprised the ballad. A recording by Woody Herman (vocal by Frances Wayne) was a bestseller, and the number has always been a favorite of jazz musicians.

"Mutiny in the Nursery" is the lively rhythm number that jockey Dick Powell and socialite Anita Louise sang with bandleader Louis Armstrong and vocalist Maxine Sullivan in *Going Places* (1938), the musical about horse racing. Johnny Mercer wrote both music and lyric for the electric number.

"My Baby Just Cares for Me" is the perennial favorite by Gus Kahn (lyric) and Walter Donaldson (music) that brags about how one's sweetheart prefers one to all worldly treasures. Hypochondriac Eddie Cantor disguised himself as a blackfaced singing waiter to escape from the deputies out West and sang the delightful testament to true love to prove he really is a singing waiter in *Whoopee* (1930). The songwriters, who had written the score for the stage musical on which the film was based, were requested by producer Samuel Goldwyn to come up with a new song for Cantor for the next day's filming, and Donaldson and Kahn obliged with the new hit. There were early recordings by Cantor, Isham Jones, Smith Ballew, and Ted Weems (vocal by Art Jarrett), while over the years there have been notable recordings by Joni James, Harry Cool, Mel Tormé, Maurice Chevalier, Count Basie (vocal by Joe Williams), and Nina Simone. "My Baby Just Cares for Me" was interpolated into the 1979 Broadway revival of *Whoopee*, where it was sung by Charles Repole and the ensemble, and the number was performed by Edward Norton, Natasha Lyonne, and some overzealous clerks in a jewelry shop in the contemporary film musical *Everyone Says I Love You* (1997).

"My Baby Said Yes" is a cheerful romantic duet that Sid Robin and Ted Walters wrote for the radio backstager *Blonde from Brooklyn* (1945). Ex-GI Bob

Haymes (AKA Bob Stanton) and jukebox singer Lynn Merrick introduced the number, which was later recorded by Bing Crosby and Louis Jordan with the Tympany Five, and Charlie Spivak (vocal by Irene Daye).

"My Bluebird's Singing the Blues" is the musical parody of saccharine kids' songs of optimism that were quite the rage in vaudeville and in Depression-era films. Eight-year-old Baby Rose Marie (later television comedienne Rose Marie) delivered the tongue-in-cheek number in *International House* (1933) with a sweetly innocent voice that quickly turned into a down-and-dirty growl filled with cynicism. Leo Robin wrote the cunning lyric and Ralph Rainger composed the uptempo music.

"My Campfire Dreams" is the catchy ballad of youthful imagination sung by child-star Bobby Breen in *Make a Wish* (1937). Paul Francis Webster, Louis Alter (lyric), and Oscar Straus (music) wrote the tuneful number, which was popular for a time.

"My Dancing Lady" is the rhythmic song of appreciation for a gal who is light of foot that Dorothy Fields (lyric) and Jimmy McHugh (music) wrote for *Dancing Lady* (1933). Crooner Art Jarrett sang the number while Broadway hoofer Joan Crawford danced around him.

"My Dream Is Yours" is the gushing title song by Ralph Blane (lyric) and Harry Warren (music) from the 1949 radio backstager. Struggling singer Doris Day and pompous radio singer Lee Bowman introduced the number in the film. Day's recording was quite popular.

"My Dreams Are Getting Better All the Time" is the uptempo love song by Mann Curtis (lyric) and Vic Mizzy (music) in which a growing love feeds one's dreams. Marion Hutton sang the ballad in the Abbott and Costello vehicle *In Society* (1944), and a recording by Les Brown (vocal by Doris Day) was a bestseller. There were also notable records by Johnny Long (vocal by Dick Robertson) and the Phil Moore Four with Billy Daniels.

"My Future Just Passed" is a delectable ballad by George Marion (lyric) and Richard Whiting (music) in which the singer knows with one look that his future will be with the person in question. Millionaire Charles "Buddy" Rogers sang the number to Follies gal Joan Crawford in *Safety in Numbers* (1930). Whiting's music, according to James R. Morris, contains a "graceful melody with an infectious bounce," the bounce coming from alternating measures that place the downbeat in different places to intriguing effect. The composer's daughter, Margaret Whiting, made a successful record of "My Future Just Passed" and Teddi King's 1957 recording of the ballad with George Siravo and his Orchestra is very distinctive.

"My Girl Back Home" is the character song that Oscar Hammerstein (lyric) and Richard Rodgers (music) wrote for their Broadway score for *South Pacific*, but it was cut before opening. The number was restored to the score for the 1958 film version, where John Kerr (dubbed by Bill Lee) sang about his sweetheart back in Philadelphia; Kerr was joined by Mitzi Gaynor, who sang of how she missed her home in Little Rock, Arkansas.

"My Heart and I" is an ardent love song by Leo Robin (lyric) and Frederick Hollander (music) that was interpolated into Cole Porter's score for the 1936 film version of the Broadway hit *Anything Goes*. Stowaway Bing Crosby sang the ballad to wealthy girlfriend Ida Lupino from inside a lifeboat on the ship's deck, swearing that both heart and self are in love with her. Crosby's recording of the song was a success.

"My Heart Is a Hobo" is a free-and-easy ballad about a life of no cares or worries that Johnny Burke (lyric) and James Van Heusen (music) wrote for the sentimental small town musical *Welcome Stranger* (1947). Young doctor Bing Crosby sang the happy song as he went fishing with the older town physician Barry Fitzgerald. Crosby recorded it, as did Tex Beneke with the Glenn Miller Orchestra (vocal by the Mello-Larks).

"My Heart Is an Open Book" is the enamored ballad by Mack Gordon (lyric) and Harry Revel (music) that vows romantic affection and trust with nothing concealed. Young songwriter Joe Morrison sang the number in the musical melodrama *Love in Bloom* (1935) then carnival gal Dixie Dunbar joined him for a duet version.

"My Heart Is Singing" is the hit ballad of musical joy that Gus Kahn (lyric), Walter Jurmann, and Bronislau Kaper (music) wrote for teenager Deanna Durbin's feature film debut. Durbin sang the expansive number in *Three Smart Girls* (1937) and it became very popular.

"My Heart Is Taking Lessons" is the heartfelt song in which veterinary surgeon Bing Crosby claimed he was learning how to sing and how to love from his sweetheart in *Doctor Rhythm* (1938). Johnny Burke (lyric) and James Monaco (music) wrote the ballad, which and Crosby recorded with John Scott Trotter's Orchestra.

"My Heart Sings" is the pop standard that started out as a French song, was Americanized for the film *Anchors Aweigh* (1945), and then became popular again in France when the English lyric was translated and sung there. Jean Marie

Blanvilliar (lyric) and Henri Herpin (music) wrote "Ma Mie," which was a big success in France. On a dare with his publisher, Harold Rome wrote a new lyric that had nothing to do with the original; his song was interpolated into the film where struggling singer Kathryn Grayson sang the explosive number about newfound love. Grayson, Guy Lombardo, Martha Stewart, Hildegarde, Johnny Johnston, and others recorded the song, which was revived in 1959 with a top seller by Paul Anka. Six years later Mel Carter also had a hit record with the ballad, which is sometimes listed as "All of a Sudden My Heart Sings."

"My Heart Tells Me" is the winning ballad by Mack Gordon (lyric) and Harry Warren (music) in which one's heart warns against a romantic entanglement because it is too weak to resist. Saloon singer Betty Grable sang the number while in a bathtub filled with bubbles as part of a naughty beer hall show in the period musical *Sweet Rosie O'Grady* (1943). The song remained on *Your Hit Parade* for nineteen weeks, and a recording by Glen Gray and the Casa Loma Orchestra (vocal by Eugenie Baird) was a Number One hit.

"My Idaho Home" is the country–music ballad by Ronee Blakeley that fondly recalls growing up on the farm and the struggles one encountered but also the love and strength she got from her family. Country music superstar Blakeley sang the lively but sincere number at a political concert in *Nashville* (1975), and the sentiments of the song disturbed a fanatic fan so much that he opened fire on the singer just after she finished singing it.

"My Ideal" is the enticing ballad by Leo Robin (lyric), Newell Chase, and Richard Whiting (music) that wonders if an ideal lover will ever be found. Maurice Chevalier, as a waiter who has inherited millions but is still romantically unsatisfied, introduced the number in *Playboy of Paris* (1930), but only the refrain was used and the drunken Chevalier's rendition was not likely to make the song popular. Chevalier and others recorded it, but the number only gained attention in France when a Gallic film version of the story was made. In America, it was Margaret Whiting's 1943 record that launched her singing career and made the ballad popular enough to remain on *Your Hit Parade* for seven weeks. Other recordings were made by Isham Jones, Helen Forrest, Jimmy Dorsey and his Orchestra, Eartha Kitt, and Maxine Sullivan. Charles "Buddy" Rogers sang the number in the film *Along Came Youth* (1931). "My Ideal" remained Richard Whiting's favorite of all his song, and he often commented that he would never be able to top it.

"My Kind of Town (Chicago Is)" is the Oscar-nominated ode to the Windy City that Sammy Cahn (lyric) and James Van Heusen (music) wrote for the musical spoof *Robin and the Seven Hoods* (1964). Gangster Frank Sinatra (in his last film musical) sang the breezy anthem on the steps of the courthouse after he had been acquitted of murder; the citizens of Chicago joined him in saluting their town. Sinatra's recording was very popular, and later that year Cahn rewrote the lyric as "My Kind of Guy" for Robert Kennedy's Senate race.

"My Love Parade" is the airy serenade by Clifford Grey (lyric) and Victor Schertzinger (music) from the comic operetta *The Love Parade* (1929) that catalogs a woman's charms, concluding that they all add up to a parade. Diplomat Maurice Chevalier sang it to queen Jeanette MacDonald (in her film debut), comparing her to the great women of Paris; he then talk-sang it so that audiences could catch all the inventive lyric. At the end of the film the couple reprised the song in her boudoir, and then MacDonald slyly closed the window curtain, cutting off the audience's view of the wedding night activities. Chevalier recorded the song, as did Tom Gerun.

"My Mother's Eyes" is the signature song for George Jessel, a heartrending tribute to motherhood that he introduced in the early talkie *Lucky Boy* (1929). L. Wolfe Gilbert (lyric) and Abel Baer (music) wrote the sentimental ballad that Jewish jeweler's son Jessel sang at an amateur show and at three subsequent times in the film. Jessel recorded the song and used it as his trademark number throughout his long career in vaudeville, radio, and television. Bette Midler revived the number fifty years later with a recording and by singing it in *Divine Madness* (1980).

"My! My!" is a romantic ditty that Frank Loesser (lyric) and Jimmy McHugh (music) wrote specially for Eddie "Rochester" Anderson to sing in the Jack Benny vehicle *Buck Benny Rides Again* (1940). The number made clever use of Anderson's stock expression "My! My!" in Benny's radio show. Anderson sang it with a raffish twinkle in his eye to maid Theresa Harris, arguing that he cannot find any other words to say to such a beautiful gal. Harris joined in singing it (even imitating his raspy "My! My!"s) and then the two performed a comic dance all over a Manhattan penthouse apartment. Anderson recorded the song, as did Glenn Miller (vocal by Marion Hutton), Tommy Dorsey (vocal by Jo Stafford and the Pied Pipers), and Horace Heidt.

"My Old Flame" is the smooth and sensuous ballad by Sam Coslow (lyric) and Arthur Johnston (music) that show girl Mae West moaned when requested to sing her favorite song in the period musical *Belle of the Nineties* (1934). The cool-headed torch song about a lost and forgotten love became an oft-recorded standard beginning with West's record with Duke Ellington's Orchestra (who accompanied her in the film). The music has a haunting and sultry quality, twice using the device of dropping down to a note not in the scale of the key in which the number is written. Coslow's lyric is ambivalent and very muted in its affection, making it all the more distinctive. Among the many notable recordings of "My Old Flame" are those by Ellington (vocal by Ivy Anderson), Ted Lewis, Billie Holiday, Stan Getz, Jo Stafford, Peggy Lee (both with Benny Goodman and years later as a solo), Dinah Washington, a spoof version by Spike Jones, Benny Morton, Oscar Peterson, the Platters, and Linda Ronstadt.

"My One and Only Highland Fling" is a delightful comic duet for Fred Astaire and Ginger Rogers as they performed in Scottish kilts and dour facial expressions as part of a Broadway revue in *The Barkleys of Broadway* (1949). Harry Warren wrote the pseudo-Gaelic music, and Ira Gershwin provided the farcical lyric that had a field day with Scottish names: Andy McPherson, an "impossible person," Maggie McDermott, "make me a hermit," Bobbie MacDougal, "he was too frugal," and so on. Astaire wrote in his autobiography that "My One and Only Highland Fling" was one of his favorite musical numbers. Jo Stafford and Gordon MacRae made a delicious duet recording of the song.

"My Own" is the Oscar-nominated ballad by Harold Adamson (lyric) and Jimmy McHugh (music) that teenager Deanna Durbin sang in a variety show in *That Certain Age* (1938). The lilting song about private and special dreams was ideally suited to Durbin's voice, and her recording of the ballad was a major hit. There were also records by Tommy Dorsey (vocal by Edythe Wright), Ozzie Nelson's Orchestra, Gene Krupa (vocal by Irene Daye), and Henry King and his Orchestra.

"My Personal Property" is the spunky "I am" song for taxi dancer Shirley MacLaine in the 1969 film version of the Broadway hit *Sweet Charity*. MacLaine sang the number as she frolicked through Central Park claiming that all New York was hers because she was in love. Dorothy Fields (lyric) and Cy Coleman (music) wrote the number that replaced their "You Should See Yourself" from the Broadway score. Bobby Short made a noteworth recording of "My Personal Property" in 1995.

"My Resistance Is Low" is a wry song about amorous vulnerability that casino nightclub performers Jane Russell and Hoagy Carmichael sang in *The Las Vegas Story* (1952). Carmichael composed the music and Harold Adamson provided the knowing lyric.

"My Shining Hour" is the entrancing standard by Johnny Mercer (lyric) and Harold Arlen (music) that tearfully bids farewell to a loved one, the moment of leave taking being the bright spot until they are reunited. The music is hymnlike with what James R. Morris describes as "even, measured phrases that have a classical dignity." The loving ballad was introduced in *The Sky's the Limit* (1943), where Joan Leslie (dubbed by Sally Sweetland) sang it with Freddie Slack's Orchestra. Later in the film war hero Fred Astaire reprised the number in a more lighthearted tempo and with a less fatalistic lyric. Then Astaire and Leslie danced to the music on a penthouse terrace. The Oscar-nominated ballad was recorded by Glen Gray and the Casa Loma Orchestra (vocal by Eugenie Baird) and became a bestseller. Mabel Mercer sang it on disk and in clubs for many years, and more recently Sammy Davis, Jr., Diahann Carroll, Julie Budd, Mary Clare Haran, Andrea Marcovicci, and Ann Hampton Callaway recorded it. "My Shining Hour" was sung by Margaret Whiting and the company of the Broadway revue of Mercer songs called *Dream* (1997).

"My Sweeter Than Sweet" is the infatuated ballad by George Marion, Jr., (lyric) and Richard Whiting (music) that was heard no less than six times in the early campus musical *Sweetie* (1929). Nancy Carroll, as a show girl who inherited a men's college, introduced the number, which was reprised by football hero Stanley Smith and the King's Men. Among the many recordings of the song were those by Rudy Vallee, the Ipana Troubadors, Sammy Fain, and the orchestras of Leo Reisman and Frankie Trumbauer.

"My Walking Stick" is the rhythmic Irving Berlin song that delighted in the masculine cane as a sign of panache, one of the few new songs in the Berlin-scored *Alexander's Ragtime Band* (1938). Ethel Merman, in top hat, cutaway, and cane, belted the merry number as a chorus of girls twirled canes and Tyrone Power conducted the orchestra. The song, sometimes listed as "Hand Me Down My Walking Stick," was recorded by Tony Martin with Ray Noble's Orchestra, Ruby Newman's Orchestra, and Roger Pryor and his Orchestra.

"My Wonderful One, Let's Dance" is a vivacious dance song by Nacio Herb Brown, Arthur Freed, and Roger Edens that Lana Turner and George Murphy sang and danced to in the backstager *Two Girls on Broadway* (1940). The number was recorded by the bands of Ben Bernie and Gene Krupa and was heard on the soundtrack of *Two Girls and a Sailor* (1944).

N

"The Nango" is a swing version of a tango that Mack Gordon (lyric) and Harry Warren (music) wrote for Carmen Miranda to sing in *Week-End in Havana* (1941). The song, about a new Latin dance, was presented as a nightclub act with Miranda and a chorus of girls all dressed like her performing Hermes Pan's odd choreography that switched from tango to jitterbug.

"The Nearness of You" is the romantic standard by Ned Washington (lyric) and Hoagy Carmichael (music) that celebrates the glow one gets from the presence of a sweetheart. Hungarian peasant Gladys Swarthout introduced the ballad in the operetta *Romance in the Dark* (1938) and it has remained popular ever since. Carmichael's music is beautifully structured, according to James R. Morris: "Its opening phrase traverses a downward path for six measures, then arches gracefully upward for two measures in a gesture that neatly rounds off the idea." The song remained a personal favorite of Carmicheal's and there were notable recordings over the years by Connie Boswell, Dinah Shore, Bob Manning, Dick Haymes, Jo Stafford, John Gary, Bobby Short, and the bands of Guy Lombardo, Glenn Miller, Larry Clinton, and Ray Herbeck.

"Never" is the Oscar-nominated ballad that Eliot Daniel (lyric) and Lionel Newman (music) wrote for the bio-musical *Golden Girl* (1951) about the famous nineteenth-century actress Lotta Crabtree. Dennis Day, as the timid admirer of the perennially youthful actress, sang the fervent number in the film and on record.

"Never Gonna Dance" is the dark and broodingly romantic song of denial by Dorothy Fields (lyric) and Jerome Kern (music) that provided for one of Fred Astaire and Ginger Rogers' most alluring musical numbers. Astaire sang the song to Rogers in *Swing Time* (1936), claiming to forgo dancing if he cannot dance with her. The two of them then glided into a dance in an empty nightclub in which they tried to part ways yet were pulled back together by the music. (The dance sequence reportedly took forty-eight takes to get right.) Gerald Bordman describes the music as "a smoky, sometimes wailing rhythm number that resorts to the tempo and key changes Kern so loved." Fields' lyric is also a marvel with phrases like "la belle, la perfectly swell romance" that Philip Furia comments "combined the colloquial with the romantic . . . (that) perfectly characterizes Astaire and Rogers." The lyric also refers to Rogers' character by name ("Penny"), and it remained that way for the published version of the song, something rarely done at the time. The creative team was so pleased with the scene that the movie was slated to be called *Never Gonna Dance*, but the studio feared that an Astaire and Rogers film that sounded like it had no dancing would keep audiences away. Two distinctive recordings of the song were made decades later by Bobby Short and Andrea Marcovicci.

"Never in a Million Years" is the hyperbolic ballad by Mack Gordon (lyric) and Harry Revel (music) that pledges long-lasting love and fidelity with never one moment of neglect. Alice Faye and Jack Haley (dubbed by Buddy Clark) introduced the number in the radio backstager *Wake Up and Live* (1937), and there were recordings by Faye, Bing Crosby with Jimmy Dorsey's Orchestra, Mildred Bailey, and Glen Gray and the Casa Loma Orchestra.

"Never Look Back" is the torchy number that Chilton Price wrote for the musical bio about Ruth Etting called *Love Me or Leave Me* (1955), one of the few new songs written for a score filled with old Etting standards. Doris Day, as the troubled stage and nightclub performer, sang the number in the film.

"Never Say No to a Man" is the kindly (and fearfully outdated) musical advice that mother Alice Faye sang to daughter Pamela Tiffin in the 1962 remake of *State Fair*. Richard Rodgers wrote both music and lyric (Oscar Hammerstein had died in 1960), and Faye came out of a seventeen-year retirement to play the character, her first maternal role. Tiffin took her advice and ended up with Bobby Darin.

"A New Moon Is Over My Shoulder" is the ardent ballad by Arthur Freed (lyric) and Nacio Herb Brown (music) that Phil Regan, as captain of the college rowing team, sang to Maxine Doyle in the campus musical *Student Tour* (1934). The romantic number became moderately popular through recordings by Regan, Jane Froman, and the orchestras of Isham Jones (vocal by Joe Martin), Johnny Green, Joe Reichman, and Anson Weeks.

"Nice Work If You Can Get It" is a brilliant and carefree ballad that became popular despite its rather unusual introduction in *Damsel in Distress* (1937), where it was sung by Fred Astaire and a trio of Madrigal Singers (Jan Duggan, Mary Dean, Pearl Amatore) as an entertainment at Totleigh Castle. The swift little number was over before you knew it, but subsequent records (often at a slower and more reflective pace) put the song on *Your Hit Parade* for ten weeks. George Gershwin composed the sprightly music (originally intended for the Broadway show *Girl Crazy* but never used), whose release, cited by Alec Wilder as "one of the best he ever wrote," has a musical allusion to his own "I Got Rhythm." Ira Gershwin penned the knowing lyric about how fortunate lovers are, another example of his taking a popular expression and turning it into a love song. Astaire's recording was a top seller, and there were successful disks by the Andrews Sister, Maxine Sullivan, and Mel Tormé as well. George Guetary and Oscar Levant performed "Nice Work If You Can Get It" in the Gershwin classic *An American in Paris* (1951), Twiggy sang it in the Broadway musical *My One and Only* (1983), and Harry Groener and the girls' chorus sang and danced it on Broadway in *Crazy for You* (1992).

"A Nickel's Worth of Jive" is the swinging song by Mack Gordon (lyric) and Harry Warren (music) about the music you can get from a jukebox for a small fee. Showgirl Betty Grable sang the slangy number in the nightclub backstager *Diamond Horseshoe* (1945).

"The Night Is Young" is the lush title number by Oscar Hammerstein (lyric) and Sigmund Romberg (music) for the 1935 sentimental operetta. Archduke Ramon Novarro and ballet dancer Evelyn Lane sang the passionate duet, and Paul Whiteman and his Orchestra recorded it.

"Night Over Shanghai" is a dark and exotic ballad by Johnny Mercer (lyric) and Harry Warren (music), an Oriental version of Warren and Al Dubin's "Lullaby of Broadway." (Dubin was slated to write the lyric, but a bout of alcohol and depression kept him away and so a new songwriting team was created.) The song was introduced in a production number in a nightclub in *The Singing Marine* (1937), and Busby Berkeley staged the haunting sequence: classical harmonicist Larry Adler was seen playing the Puccini-like melody on a mouth organ; then marine Dick Powell heard the song and was drawn hypnotically into a basement cabaret where crude men and tough women engaged in drinking and fighting, ending with a Chinese girl being killed in a brawl. Berkeley added some surreal touches such as using light on only parts of the patrons in the bar, giving the illusion of disembodied limbs. (Berkeley said he got the idea watching Jean Cocteau's antirealistic films.) Tony Thomas describes the number as "an excellent piece of material, a superior, almost operatic song full of minor modes and a sultry, quite Oriental feeling."

"The Night They Invented Champagne" is the contagious song of celebration by Alan Jay Lerner (lyric) and Frederick Loewe (music) that provided a turning point in *Gigi* (1958) in much the same way that "The Rain in Spain" did in the same team's *My Fair Lady*. Parisian bachelor Louis Jourdan had promised the young Gigi (Leslie Caron, dubbed by Betty Wand) and her aunt Hermione Gingold that he would take them both to the resort city of Trouville if they could beat him at cards. They did and the trio burst out into song, sipping champagne and dancing about the small Paris apartment. The scene was filmed in a Hollywood soundstage by Charles Walters weeks after director Vincente Minnelli and the Paris crew had finished the film because Lerner and Loewe were very unhappy with the original footage. The song was performed by Daniel Massey, Karin Wolfe, and Maria Karnilova in the 1973 Broadway version of *Gigi*.

"The Night They Raided Minsky's" is the pastiche title song for the 1968 period musical about the birth of the striptease. Lee Adams (lyric) and Charles Strouse (music) wrote the facetious number, which was sung by narrator Rudy Vallee on the soundtrack.

"Niña" is the enamored Cole Porter number from *The Pirate* (1948) that uses ridiculous rhyme in an affectionate way. Wandering actor Gene Kelly went through the streets of a Caribbean town greeting all the pretty girls with the song, calling each one Niña (a South American term of endearment). After rhyming the name with "I've seen ya," "neurathenia," "schizophrenia," and other phrases, Kelly launched into an athletic dance routine that took him all over the quaint street setting.

"The Nina, the Pinta and the Santa Maria" is a delightful operetta-within-a-musical that Ira Gershwin (lyric) and Kurt Weill (music) devised for the clever fantasy *Where Do We Go From Here?* (1945). Frustrated draft-rejectee Fred MacMurray was sent back in time by a genie and found himself a sailor on Columbus' expedition. Carlos Ramirez and the other sailors on the *Santa Maria* complained about the hardships of the voyage, missed home cooking, and considered the voyage ridiculous because they knew the world was flat. The sailors planned a mutiny, but MacMurray sang about the glories of the New World that they would soon discover and the uprising was calmed. The whole sequence was sung, Gershwin using his talent for multiple rhymes and Weill (in a rare movie assignment) providing the vigorous music.

"No Love, No Nothin' (Until My Baby Comes Home)" is the street-smart lament of a gal who has forsworn romance until her true love comes back from the war. Leo Robin (lyric) and Harry Warren (music) wrote the ballad for the wartime musical *The Gang's All Here* (1943), and Alice Faye sang it at a rehearsal of a nightclub show, lounging about an empty apartment and expressing sultry loneliness. Phil Silvers sang it in a less serious manner the next year in *Four Jills in a Jeep* (1944). Johnny Long (vocal by Patti Dugan) had a popular record of the song, also recorded by Ella Mae Morse, Judy Garland, and Jan Garber and his Orchestra. Jane Russell revived the number decades later when she sang it in *Fate Is the Hunter* (1964).

"No More Love" is the torch song by Al Dubin (lyric) and Harry Warren (music) that was used in an erotic (and notorious) scene of sexual submission that closed the era before the Production Code took over. Busby Berkeley staged the infamous sequence from *Roman Scandals* (1933) in which courtesan Ruth Etting sang the lament in a Roman slave market while seemingly naked slave girls (barely covered by their long hair) were chained to walls and a grotesque guard went about lashing his whip at the writhing creatures. Etting recorded the song, as did Irene Taylor, Barney Rapp, and Joe Venuti (vocal by Howard Phillips).

"No Strings (I'm Fancy Free)" is the scintillating Irving Berlin song that celebrates the freedom to dance and do just about anything else that strikes one's fancy. Broadway hoofer Fred Astaire sang the number to his producer Edward Everett Horton in *Top Hat* (1935), tap dancing all over Horton's hotel suite and waking up Ginger Rogers in the room below. Berlin's music is lighter than air and his lyric carelessly joyous, claiming to be "free for anything fancy." Patti LuPone made an estimable recording of the song.

"No Two People (Have Ever Been So in Love)" is the flavorful duet that Frank Loesser wrote for the bio-musical *Hans Christian Andersen* (1952). Storyteller Danny Kaye imagined himself with ballet star Zizi Jeanmarie (dubbed by Jane Wyman), and in his fantasy they were bride and groom singing and dancing the lighthearted ballad together. The number is a refreshing love song that sees the two lovers as friendly and familiar with each other rather than gushing over each other. Doris Day and Donald O'Connor made a popular recording of the duet, and Loesser himself recorded a solo version.

"No Wonder (He Loves Her)" is the entrancing ballad by Alan and Marilyn Bergman (lyric) and Michel Legrand (music) that was used so effectively in the Eastern European musical *Yentl* (1983). Barbra Streisand, as a country girl disguised as a male Yeshiva student, went with fellow student Mandy Patinkin to the home of the beautiful Jewess Amy Irving and, watching her perfect manners and alluring feminine ways, sang on the soundtrack her thoughts about the lady's charm and understood why Patinkin loved her. Streisand reprised the number with different lyrics later in the film when she herself must court Irving.

"Nobody" is a wistful torch song that Roger Edens wrote for Judy Garland to sing in the backstager *Strike Up the Band* (1940). As she went through a deserted library putting away books, Garland contemplated all the famous duos (Romeo and Juliet, Lunt and Fontanne, Minneapolis and St. Paul, Metro-Goldwyn and Mayer) and yearned to be part of a pair herself. The gentle number was made particularly moving by Busby Berkeley's staging (in rare subtle form) with Garland dwarfed by the tall stacks of books that surround her.

"Nobody But You" is the breezy love song by Joe Goodwin (lyric) and Gus Edwards (music) that Cliff "Ukelele Ike" Edwards introduced in *Hollywood Revue of 1929* (1929), the first plotless, all-star movie musical revue. The nimble number was recorded by Frankie Trumbauer's Orchestra, the Les Paul Trio (vocal by Clancy Hayes), and Margaret Whiting.

"Nobody Loves a Riveter" is the tuneful opening number by Lorenz Hart (lyric) and Richard Rodgers (music) for the romantic musical *The Hot Heiress* (1931). Riveter Ben Lyon was working on a skyscraper, and the residents of the neighboring building (including society dame Ona Munson) complained about the noise in song, Lyon noting that the only person who loves a riveter is his mother.

"Nobody's Using It Now" is a comic torch song by Clifford Grey (lyric) and Victor Schertzinger (music) that Maurice Chevalier delivered in *The Love Parade* (1929) directly to the screen as if in one of his music hall acts. (Clive Hirschhorn notes that it is "the first musical soliloquy in a talking picture.") Count Chevalier listed all of the things he had (loving arms, a bridal suite, a sofa with springs barely used) that were going to waste without the right girl. Chevalier recorded the number, keeping all the lusty implications in tact, and Marion Harris also made a disk of the song.

"Not Mine" is an agreeable ballad by Johnny Mercer (lyric) and Victor Schertzinger (music) that was sung and danced to by Dorothy Lamour, Eddie Bracken, Betty Hutton, and others at the Swingland Dancehall in *The Fleet's In* (1942). Jimmy Dorsey provided their accompaniment in the film, and his recording with Bob Eberle and Helen O'Connell was very popular.

"Nothing Can Compare With You" is the affectionate song that Bobby Beverly and By Dunham wrote for the generation gap musical *I'll Take Sweden* (1965). Widower Bob Hope sang the number to interior decorator Dina Merrill, whom he met when he was transferred to Sweden by his company.

"Nothing's Gonna Stop Us Now" is the lively gospel number by Randy Newman that served as the pastiche finale for the animated spoof of

Hollywood *Cats Don't Dance* (1996). Studio feline extras Sawyer (voice of Natalie Cole) and Danny (voice of Scott Bakula) led the other animals on the lot in a live stage show after a film premiere, singing and dancing on a Noah's Ark mockup and spoofing the grand finales of old Hollywood musicals.

"Now I Know" is the Oscar-nominated ballad by Ted Koehler (lyric) and Harold Arlen (music) that Dinah Shore (in her film debut) sang in *Up in Arms* (1944), making an amateur record so that departing soldier Danny Kaye (also in his film debut) had something to remember her by. Later in the film Kaye played the record and comically mimed the lyric. Shore's recording of the gentle song about newly realized love was very popular.

"Now I'm a Lady" is the slinky song of determination that Sam Coslow, Sammy Fain, and Irving Kahal collaborated on for the Mae West vehicle *Goin' to Town* (1935). Wealthy cattle queen West sang the number as she tried to break into high society with wisecracks and sexual allure. Ramona recorded the song with Paul Whiteman's Orchestra, and there was a disk by Joe Haymes' Orchestra as well.

"Now It Can Be Told" was the Oscar-nominated ballad by Irving Berlin and a new standard that was added to all the old standards heard in *Alexander's Ragtime Band* (1938). Pianist Don Ameche played the number in a deserted San Francisco ballroom, and when asked by band singer Alice Faye what he was playing, he sang the tender song to her. Later in the film Faye sang it with Tyrone Power's band and the two fell in love, much to the chagrin of Ameche, who was silently watching. Berlin's music has a beautiful intensity as it contrasts repeated eighth notes in one phrase with a series of long notes in another. The sentimental ballad was recorded by Bing Crosby, Hildegarde, and the orchestras of Tommy Dorsey, Ruby Newman, Roger Pryor, Ray Noble (vocal by Tony Martin), Red Norvo (vocal by Mildred Bailey), and Teddy Wilson (vocal by Nan Wynn).

"Now That I Need You (Where Are You?)" is a dire torch song by Frank Loesser that Betty Hutton delivered with uncharacteristic heartbreak in the musical whodunit *Red, Hot, and Blue* (1949). Doris Day and Frankie Laine also made records of the suicidally romantic number, which is sometimes listed "Where Are You Now That I Need You?"

"Now You Has Jazz" is the vibrant recipe song by Cole Porter for creating hot jazz music. Millionaire Bing Crosby and bandleader Louis Armstrong sang the sassy number in *High Society* (1956) and also recorded the song together. Kenny Ball and his Jazzmen sang it in the 1994 British recording of the full *High Society* score.

"Nowhere Guy" is the torchy lament written by Mack Gordon (lyric) and Joseph Myrow (music) for the backstager *The Girl Next Door* (1953). Musical comedy star June Haver introduced the number in the film, after which she retired from show business and entered a convent.

O

"O'Brien Has Gone Hawaiian" is the facetious song that Betty Grable sang as part of a Pacific island luau celebration of St. Patrick's Day in *Song of the Islands* (1942). Mack Gordon wrote the lyric, which mixed Irish and Hawaiian clichés (with a reference to a "uke-shelegh"), and Harry Owens composed the music, which alternated between exotic Polynesian strains and Hibernia folk song. Hermes Pan staged the number, which had Grable and the island girls (in green grass skirts) dancing the hula and an Irish jig interchangeably.

"An Occasional Man" is the sly narrative ballad by Ralph Blane and Hugh Martin that told the story of an idyllic Pacific island where a gal has everything from sunshine to sandy beaches, with an occasional man thrown in for fun. Gloria De Haven sang the undulating number in a production number in a Las Vegas hotel show in *The Girl Rush* (1955). Jeri Southern made a distinctive recording of the suggestive ditty.

"Occidental Woman (in an Oriental Mood for Love)" is the sexy come-hither song that Gene Austin wrote for Mae West to sing in *Klondike Annie* (1936). West, as a San Francisco broad disguised as a Salvation Army lass in the Klondike, sang the ingratiating number, giving a religious service a much-neededkick.

"Oh, But I Do" is the exclamatory song of amorous affirmation that Dennis Morgan sang to Martha Vickers as they danced in a nightclub in the backstager *The Time, the Place and the Girl* (1946). Leo Robin (lyric) and Arthur Schwartz (music) wrote the number, which was recorded by Margaret Whiting with Jerry Gray's Orchestra and by Tex Beneke (vocal by Artie Malvin).

"Oh Me, Oh Mi-ami" is the diverting ode to the Florida city that Leo Robin (lyric) and Ralph Rainger (music) wrote for the sunny musical *Moon Over Miami* (1941). The chorus sang of the colorful city "where a million dreams come true" as scenes of Miami were shown. Later in the film three Texas gold diggers Betty Grable, Carole Landis, and Charlotte Greenwood sang the number in their hotel room as they began their scheme to land a Florida millionaire.

"Oh Mother, What Do I Do Now?" is the archly coy song by Robert Wright and George Forrest that seeks an answer to a romantic predicament. Chorus-girl-turned-stripper Lucille Ball sang the number in the backstager *Dance, Girl, Dance* (1940) and, perhaps for the first time, revealed that her talents lay not in playing naughty women but in comedy.

"Oh, My Goodness" is a lengthy musical sequence in the Shirley Temple vehicle *Poor Little Rich Girl* (1936) that asked the child star to sustain a number beyond a short ditty followed by a dance. Neglected rich tot Temple sang the song to a collection of international dolls, each stanza of the song addressing one doll in the style of her native land. The number, written by Mack Gordon (lyric) and Harry Revel (music), climaxed with a "hi-de-ho" style for America.

"Oh, Oh, Oklahoma" is a rousing production number by Harold Adamson (lyric) and Jimmy McHugh (music) that is quite a curiosity piece looking back at it now. The chorus members of a Broadway show in *You're a Sweetheart* (1937) sang the tribute to Oklahoman Will Rogers (who had died in a plane crash the year before) by praising the "okay" state with a "Yip-yip-yipee-I-ay!" Though no threat to the famous Rodgers and Hammerstein song written six years later, the number is remarkably similar.

"Oh Sing, Sweet Nightingale" is a brief operatic aria written by Al Hoffman, Mack Davis, and Jerry Livingston that was used in contrasting ways in the animated fantasy *Cinderella* (1950). The ugly stepsisters (voices of Rhoda Williams and Lucille Bliss) practiced vocalizing and playing the flute in the music room, destroying music and shattering the ears, while downstairs Cinderella (voice of Ilene Woods) scrubbed the floor and sang the same aria, her lovely voice lifting up like the soap bubbles rising from her wash bucket. The number, which is sometimes listed as "Sing, Sweet Nightingale," was recorded as a duet by David Sanborn and David Benoit in 1995.

"Oh, That Mitzi!" proved once again that Maurice Chevalier could take a woman's name or a simple "oh" and turn it into a lusty exclamation. He did both in this song by Leo Robin (lyric) and Oscar Straus (music) from the comic operetta *One Hour With You* (1932). Although he was happily married to

Jeanette MacDonald, Chevalier kissed the provocative Mitzi (Genevieve Tobin) and later told the camera about her difficult-to-dismiss attraction.

"Oh, You Nasty Man" is the song that launched Alice Faye's movie career and quickly established her as the sultry but warm heroine that she would play over the next dozen years. Jack Yellen, Irving Caesar (lyric), and Ray Henderson (music) wrote the easygoing scolding to a philanderer, and Faye (in her film debut) sang it as part of a production number early in the backstager *George White's Scandals* (1934). One story has it that producer White saw the number on the dailies and decided to put Faye into the film's leading role. Other sources claim that Lillian Harvey was slated to play the heroine in the tale but quit and that Rudy Vallee recommended his band singer Faye for the role. Regardless, Faye made quite an impact on audiences and got star billing from then on. The song's title came from a popular expression at the time, originated by comic Joe Penner in his variety act. The number is sometimes listed as "Nasty Man."

"Okay Toots" is the merry song of affirmation that Gus Kahn (lyric) and Walter Donaldson (music) wrote for the Eddie Cantor vehicle *Kid Millions* (1934). Wealthy heir Cantor arrived in Egypt to claim his inheritance and sang this dandy song about his sweetheart back in Brooklyn to a sheik's many seductive wives (played by the Goldwyn Girls). Canter recorded the happy ditty, and there were also records by the orchestras of George Hall (vocal by Loretta Lee), Tom Coakley, and Mal Hallett.

"An Old-Fashioned Tune Is Always New" is another of of Irving Berlin's songs that expressed a quaint (and very personal) view toward popular music. This song's sentiment was demonstrated in a big production number in the Hollywood backstager *Second Fiddle* (1939), where Rudy Vallee and a chorus sang the song as they sat on a mountain of sheet music, the bars of music serving as perches and literally supporting the singers.

"The Old Music Master" is a swinging narrative ballad by Johnny Mercer (lyric) and Hoagy Carmichael (music) that tells the tale of a little "Memphis boy" who convinces a classical composer to get hep by switching to "swing, boogie-woogie and jive." Dick Powell delivered the fiery number in *True to Life* (1943), and Paul Whitman's recording with vocalists Mercer and Jack Teagarden was moderately popular.

"An Old Straw Hat" was the tuneful song by Mack Gordon (lyric) and Harry Revel (music) that promoted comfortable old farm clothes over fancy city duds and was used effectively throughout *Rebecca of Sunnybrook Farm* (1938). Shirley Temple sang the number to farmhand Bill Robinson as they set off from the farmhouse to collect berries. Then she reprised it at the living room piano, her voice recognized by a radio producer; she then encored the number over the phone long distance to New York. Finally she began the number as part of a big-time network broadcast but lost her voice before getting past the first few notes.

"Old Souls" is a rock-and-roll ballad that Paul Williams wrote for the cult favorite *Phantom of the Paradise* (1974), the disco version of the famous *Phantom of the Opera* story reset in the world of the record business. Disco club singer Jessica Harper sang the number about two old loves being reborn in a "new life baby."

"On a Little Two-Seat Tandem" is the merry vaudeville song that Mack Gordon (lyric) and Josef Myrow (music) wrote for the period musical *Mother Wore Tights* (1947). Barnstorming variety couple Betty Grable and Dan Dailey sang the song as part of their act, dressed in turn-of-the-century stripes and riding the bicycle-built-for-two about the little stage in front of a painted backdrop of Central Park.

"On a Sunday Afternoon" was a specialty number for the team of Buddy and Vilma Ebsen, who lit up many a 1930s film musical. This atmospheric number by Arthur Freed (lyric) and Nacio Herb Brown (music) was sung by the team as a pair of Broadway hopefuls in *Broadway Melody of 1936* (1935). The orchestras of Don Bestor, Archie Blyer, and Richard Himber each made a recording of the jaunty number.

"On the Atchison, Topeka and the Santa Fe" is the Oscar-winning standard by Johnny Mercer (lyric) and Harry Warren (music) that, if not the best movie song ever written about a train, is surely one of the finest train sequences in any film musical. The propulsive ballad was written for the western musical *The Harvey Girls* (1946), and while most remember Judy Garland singing it, the number was actually a complex musical scene involving several characters and locales that built up gradually to a powerhouse finale. The sequence began in a saloon in Sandrock, New Mexico, where the train whistle was first heard. Porter Ben Carter announced the arrival of the train coming from Philadelphia and heading to California, and a group of cowboys sang about the train on the station platform. Soon engineer Vernon Dent and fireman Jack Clifford were singing it with the passengers (including Ray Bolger and Virginia O'Brien). Then a middle section (written by Roger Edens and Kay Thompson) allowed each of the arriving Harvey girls (including Judy Garland) to sing about their origin and their hopes for a new life out West. The train arrived at the platform, all sang the catchy song as the passengers disembarked, and the scene climaxed with Garland and Bolger leading the ensemble in a high-kicking dance as the steam surrounded them and the train pulled out of the station. Later in the film Bolger did a tap dance specially to the song's melody. The main part of the number was written a year before but never used until Mercer and Warren were commissioned to score *The Harvey Girls* and found the perfect showcase for the song. Mercer's recording with the Pied Pipers was the biggest-selling of the many recordings, and there were notable records by Bing Crosby (with Six Hits and a Miss), Garland and the Merry Macs (with Lyn Murray's Orchestra), Tommy Dorsey (vocals by the Sentimentalists), and more recently Mandy Patinkin, and Leslie Uggams with the Singing Hoosiers. The standard was sung by the cast of the Broadway revue of Mercer songs called *Dream* (1997).

"On the Boards" is a snappy music hall ditty by Herbert Kretzmer (lyric) and Anthony Newley (music) that argued for a life on the stage, saying it was better to be a starving actor than a well-fed clerk. Old-time vaudevillian Bruce Forsythe sang and danced the soft-shoe number in the surreal adult musical *Can Heironymus Merkin Ever Forget Mercy Humppe and Find True Happiness?* (1969) before dropping dead on the stage.

"On the Boardwalk in Atlantic City" is a freewheeling song of anticipation that gold diggers Vera-Ellen (dubbed by Carol Stewart), Vivian Blaine, and June Haver sang as they traveled to the New Jersey resort to nab rich husbands in *Three Little Girls in Blue* (1946). Mack Gordon (lyric) and Josef Myrow (music) wrote the rollicking song, and Dick Haymes and the Charioteers each recorded it.

"On the Bumpy Road to Love" is the upbeat ballad by Al Hoffman, Al Lewis, and Murray Mencher that teenager Judy Garland sang in the domestic musical *Listen Darling* (1938). The number was recorded by the Merry Macs, Terry Shand, Teddy Wilson (vocal by Nan Wynn), and Ozzie Nelson and his Orchestra.

"On the Good Ship Lollipop," arguably the most popular kiddie song of the 1930s and 1940s, was introduced by Shirley Temple (in her first starring role) in *Bright Eyes* (1934) and became her signature. Sidney Clare (lyric) and Richard Whiting (music) wrote the happy number, about a child's fantasy of a ship that travels to an overabundant candy shop, and within months over 400,000 copies of sheet music were sold. Mae "Betty Boop" Questel's recording alone sold over a million disks. The simple ditty has appeared in other films as well: Temple reprised it in *Rebecca of Sunnybrook Farm* (1938) as part of a medley of her past hits, Shari Robinson and Dan Dailey performed it in *You're My Everything* (1949), and Helen Mirren sang it in *The Fiendish Plot of Dr. Fu Manchu* (1980). Though never completely forgotten, the song was revived by Tiny Tim's recording in the 1960s, and in 1998 Judy Kaye made a smooth and enticing version of the ditty. In the Broadway revue *A Day in Hollywood—A Night in the Ukraine* (1980), the cast sang it as part of a tribute to Whiting.

"On the Riviera" is the Gallic title number by Sylvia Fine for the 1951 Danny Kaye vehicle in which the comedian played two lookalikes. An off-camera chorus sang the sprightly number about the lure of the Riviera during the opening credits; then in a nightclub Kaye delivered the song with a broad Maurice Chevalier impersonation, which was an inside joke: Chevalier had played lookalikes in the much earlier (and very similar) musical *Folies Bergère* (1935).

"On the Road" is a silly samba number written by Jack Feldman, Bruce Sussman (lyric) and Barry Manilow for the animated fantasy *Thumbelina* (1994). When Mrs. Toad (voice of Charo) discovered the lovely singing voice of Thumbelina (voice of Jodi Benson), the crafty old woman and her fellow toads (voices of Domenick Allen, Larry Kenton, and Rick Riso) sang to the miniature girl about the success they will find when they go on tour. The fast and furious Latin number parodies the Carmen Miranda–type songs so popular in the 1940s and the lyric is often incomprehensible, but as Mrs. Toad explained, they cannot sing any slower and "we don't do ballads."

"On the Sentimental Side" is the gentle ballad by Johnny Burke (lyric) and James Monaco (music) that acknowledges a failed love affair but noted that the sentimental streak inside keeps hoping it can be revived. Young doctor Bing Crosby and orphaned Mary Carlisle sang the number in *Doctor Rhythm* (1938), and there were recordings by Crosby with Scott Trotter's Orchestra, Billie Holiday, and Abe Lyman and his Orchestra.

"On Top of the World, Alone" is the torchy theme song for *Innocents of Paris* (1929), Maurice Chevalier's first Hollywood film. Leo Robin (lyric) and Richard Whiting (music) wrote the number that Chevalier sang three times in the musical, showing his rise from a Paris junk dealer to a music hall star.

"Once and for Always" is the amiable ballad by Johnny Burke (lyric) and James Van Heusen (music) that pledges long-term affection. Bing Crosby, as a New England blacksmith magically transported to Camelot, and the medieval lady Rhonda Fleming sang the duet on a castle balcony in the musical fantasy *A Connecticut Yankee in King Arthur's Court* (1949). Later in the film Crosby reprised it as he and Fleming were prisoners in a medieval dungeon. Crosby and Jo Stafford each made a successful record of the ballad.

"Once in a Blue Moon" is the romantic ballad by Mack Gordon (lyric) and Harry Revel (music) that cites just how often that special someone comes along. Sailor Bing Crosby sang the fond number to socialite Carole Lombard in *We're Not Dressing* (1934) as they walked along the beach of the deserted island where they have been shipwrecked. Crosby's recording of the ballad was popular.

"Once Too Often" is the sultry narrative ballad by Mack Gordon (lyric) and James Monaco (music) about a New Orleans fancy woman who gives her lover the brush off because he's been unfaithful "once too often." Betty Grable sang the number in a nightclub act in *Pin-Up Girl* (1944) and then danced to Charlie Spivak's Orchestra with choreographer Hermes Pan (in one of his rare screen appearances). Ella Fitzgerald made a memorable recording of the dark ballad.

"Once Upon a December" is the enchanting memory song that Lynn Ahrens (lyric) and Stephen Flaherty (music) wrote for the animated romance *Anastasia* (1997). The fragile ballad, about a past filled with distinct images but no complete picture, was used three times in the film. Before the Russian Revolution, the Dowager Empress Marie (voice of Angela Lansbury) sang the the song as she gave her young granddaughter Anastasia a gift. Years later the grown-up Anya (singing voice of Liz Callaway) sang it when she entered the deserted Winter Palace ballroom and images and ghosts from the past overwhelmed her. The song was briefly reprised when Anastasia and her grandmother were reunited in Paris. Deana Carter recorded the haunting ballad at the time of the film's release.

"Once Upon a Dream" is the waltzing love ballad that the princess Aurora (voice of Mary Costa) sang to herself as she danced through the forest with her animal friends in the animated fairy tale *Sleeping Beauty* (1959). The princess was soon observed by Prince Philip (voice of Bill Shirley), who joined her in song, and the two danced beside a stream, their bodies reflected in the water. Jack Lawrence (lyric) and Sammy Fain (music) wrote the song, which was adapted from Tchaikowski's *Sleeping Beauty* ballet.

"Once Upon a Time in New York City" is the catchy opening song by Howard Ashman (lyric) and Barry Mann (music) from the animated contemporary version of *Oliver Twist* called *Oliver and Company* (1988). Over the opening credits, Huey Lewis sang the number about the tough city that was home to a thousand stories and dreams and how you should overcome your shyness and get out and experience the metropolis for yourself.

"The One and Only, Genuine, Original, Family Band" is the boastful title song by Richard M. and Robert B. Sherman for the 1968 political musical about the 1888 Democratic Convention. Nebraska family patriarch Walter Brennan sang the proud march number with family members Buddy Ebsen, Lesley Ann Warren, Janet Blair, and the seven children as they rehearsed at the beginning of the film.

"One Day When We Were Young" is the simple and unembellished memory of young love that Fernand Gravet, as composer Johann Strauss, and his beloved Miliza Korjus sang together in the musical bio-musical *The Great Waltz* (1938). Dimitri Tiomkin adapted a Strauss waltz for the song's music, and Oscar Hammerstein provided the straightforward lyric that is highly romantic without gushing.

"One for My Baby (and One More for the Road)" is the oft-recorded standard by Johnny Mercer (lyric) and Harold Arlen (music) that is so famous that its bluesy, drunken lyric has almost become a cliché. War hero Fred Astaire went into a New York City cocktail lounge to forget his troubles in *The Sky's the Limit* (1943) and sang the torch ballad to the bartender, getting drunker and more depressed until he was dancing with frustration on the bar. Arlen called it a "wandering song" because of its unusual length (forty-eight bars) and the way it shifts keys in a blues manner. There is also an old-time piano-player flavor to the music, which gives it just the right touch of honky–tonk. As for Mercer's lyric, few popular songs create as vivid a picture as that detailed in the words. Astaire regarded the song as "one of the best pieces of material that was ever especially written for me." Yet the song is mostly associated with Frank Sinatra, who recorded it after singing the ballad in *Young at Heart* (1955), and his disk remains the biggest seller of all. Other distinctive recordings were made by Lena Horne with Horace Henderson's Orchestra, Mel Tormé, Tony Bennett (his first major success), Fran Warren, Oscar Peterson, Julie Wilson, and Mercer himself. Ida Lupino sang "One for My Baby" in *Roadhouse* (1948), Jane Russell performed it in *Macao* (1955), and hundreds of saloon singers have used it in their acts over the years. Margaret Whiting sang the standard in the Broadway Mercer revue *Dream* (1997).

"One Hour With You" is the engaging title song, written by Leo Robin (lyric) and Richard Whiting (music) for the 1932 musical comedy of manners that happily pleads for a brief but amorous interlude. Jeanette MacDonald, Maurice Chevalier, Genevieve Tobin, Charles Ruggles, and Donald Novis each had an opportunity to sing it in the film as various intrigues were afoot. The melodic song was kept alive by Eddie Cantor's singing it (with altered lyrics) at the conclusion of his popular weekly radio show for many years. Cantor himself provided the singing voice when "One Hour With You" was sung by Keefe Brasselle in *The Eddie Cantor Story* (1954). Chevalier, MacDonald, and Novis each recorded the song, as did Morton Downey, Andy Sanella, and Jimmie Grier (vocal by Novis). This last recording was used effectively on the soundtrack for *Paper Moon* (1973).

"The One I Love" is an adoring ballad by Gus Kahn (lyric), Bronislau Kaper, and Walter Jurmann (music) filled with expectations of love returned. Allan Jones introduced the number in *Everybody Sing* (1938), though the song was originally written for Jeanette MacDonald to sing in *San Francisco* (1936) but was cut.

"One in a Million" is the laudatory title song by Sidney Mitchell (lyric) and Lew Pollack (music) for the 1936 musical that introduced skating champion Sonja Henie to the screen. The hyperbolic number was used throughout the film: Leah Ray, the featured vocalist in Adolphe Menjou's all-girl band, sang it during a rehearsal on a train heading to a hotel in the Swiss Alps. It was later reprised by Borrah Minevitch's Harmonica Rascals, then yet again by a chorus while Henie skated at Madison Square Garden. Recordings of the number were made by Thomas "Fats" Waller, Bunny Berigan, and Mal Hallett's Orchestra.

"One Jump Ahead" is the frantic "I am" song for the title "street rat" in the animated adventure *Aladdin* (1992). Howard Ashman (lyric) and Alan Menken (music) wrote the lightfooted song, which Aladdin (voice of Brad Kane) sang as he dodged angry merchants and ran from the sultan's guards through the streets of Agrabah. Later, in a quieter moment, he reprised the song, revealing his hopes of bettering his lot someday. Debbie Shapiro Gravitte made a recording of note in 1994.

"One Little Star" is a simple and unpretentious lullaby written by Jeff Moss for the *Sesame Street* feature film *Follow That Bird* (1985). The lost and lonely Big Bird (voice of Carroll Spinney) sang the song as he looked up at a star and asked it to shine on the friends he had to leave behind. Meanwhile the scattered friends sang the number as well as they searched for their oversized friend.

"One Never Knows, Does One?" is the questioning ballad by Mack Gordon (lyric) and Harry Revel (music) that Alice Faye introduced in the Shirley Temple vehicle *Stowaway* (1936). The song about the uncertainty of love became popular on the radio through a recording by Hal Kemp (vocal by Skinnay Ennis). There were also successful recordings by Billie Holiday and the bands of Shep Fields, Mal Hallett, and Ruby Newman.

"One Night of Love" is the melodic title number by Gus Kahn (lyric) and Victor Schertzinger (music) for the 1934 Grace Moore vehicle about the world of opera, her greatest film success. Struggling opera soprano Moore sang the song of yearning as she imagined a night of romantic perfection. Much of the rest of the score consisted of opera highlights, so the fact that Schertzinger's music was deliberately based on Puccini's *Madame Butterfly* duet was in keeping with the show. Moore recorded the ballad, as did Jack Fulton and the orchestras of Freddy Martin and Lud Gluskin.

"One Song" is the operatic "I am" song for the handsome Prince Charming in the landmark animated fairy tale *Snow White and the Seven Dwarfs* (1937). Larry Morey (lyric) and Frank Churchill (music) wrote the number, which the prince (voice of Harry Stockwell) sang, claiming he had only one song in his heart and he was saving it for that special someone. True to his word, the prince sang no other song in the film.

"One, Two, Button Your Shoe" is the pleasant ballad by Johnny Burke (lyric) and Arthur Johnston (music) that Bing Crosby sang in *Pennies from Heaven* (1936) while waiting for his sweetheart to get dressed, anticipating an evening of romance. The lyric is a gentle variation on the familiar nursery rhyme, and the song is as innocent as a child's prayer. Crosby recorded the ballad with George Stoll's Orchestra, and there were also records by Ray Noble, Shep Fields, Jimmy Dorsey (vocal by Bob Eberle), Billie Holiday, Joe Haymes, and Artie Shaw. Denise Faye and Michael McGrath sang the song as a duet in the Broadway revue *Swinging on a Star* (1995).

"Only Forever" is the Oscar-nominated ballad by Johnny Burke (lyric) and James Monaco (music) that poses several questions, all answered by the song title. Composer Bing Crosby sang the song to his lyricist-collaborator Mary Martin aboard his houseboat in *Rhythm on the River* (1940), and the two of them reprised the ballad on a radio broadcast from a Manhattan nightclub at the end of the film. Crosby's recording was a Number One bestseller, and there was also a noteworthy record by Tommy Dorsey and his Orchestra.

"Only When You're in My Arms" was the only new song in the bio-musical *The Story of Vernon and Irene Castle* (1939), which was filled with period standards from the early years of the century. Bert Kalmar, Con Conrad, and Harry Ruby collaborated on the romantic dance duet, which was performed by Fred Astaire and Ginger Rogers as the famous dance team of the film's title.

"Oo-De-Lally" is the enjoyable pseudo-medieval folk ballad that Roger Miller wrote for the animated adventure *Robin Hood* (1973), an easygoing number that provided exposition at the top of the film. The rooster Alan-a-Dale (voice of Miller) acted as the musical's narrator and lazily sang and whistled the folk song.

"Oops!" is a playful song by Johnny Mercer (lyric) and Harry Warren (music) that admits that the heart went "oops!" when it first met you and it still does every time we meet. Playboy Fred Astaire sang the song to Salvation Army lass Vera-Ellen in the period musical *The Belle of New York* (1952) as they rode in a horse-drawn trolley. The upbeat number was punctuated by the bounce of the trolley, and the clever dance that followed ended with Fred riding on the horse.

"Open Your Eyes" is an entrancing ballad by Alan Jay Lerner (lyric) and Burton Lane (music) that encourages one to see and experience the world around us. It was sung by American entertainer Jane Powell in *Royal Wedding* (1951) as she performed for fellow passengers on an ocean liner heading to England for the marriage ceremony of Elizabeth II. The song was followed by a dance routine with her brother Fred Astaire, but the rocking of the ship sent the couple tumbling down before the big finish. Lane's music is appropriately expansive, and Lerner's lyric is rich in imagery, describing the ocean as "a carpet of jade around us." Dorothy Loudon and Michael Feinstein have each recorded the number.

"Orange Blossom Time" is the seasonal ballad by Joe Goodwin (lyric) and Gus Edwards (music) that was sung by Charles King in *Hollywood Revue of 1929* (1929) then danced to by the Albertina Rasch Ballet and the Belcher Child Dancers. Recordings were made by Cliff "Ukelele Ike" Edwards, Tom Waring, and Earl Burtnett.

"Orchids in the Moonlight" is the intoxicating Latin number by Gus Kahn, Edward Eliscu (lyric), and Vincent Youmans (music) from *Flying Down to Rio* (1933), one of the few movie tangos to become a standard. Raul Roulien sang the atmospheric number and then Fred Astaire and Dolores Del Rio danced a tango to it. Early records by Rudy Vallee and the Connecticut Yankees and by Enric Madriguera and his Orchestra helped the romantic song become popular. Also notable of the many recordings that followed over the years were instrumental ones by Paul Weston and Andre Kostalanetz.

"Ordinary Fool" is the superb but overlooked torch song that Paul Williams wrote for the children's gangster musical spoof *Bugsy Malone* (1976). Nightclub singer Florrie Dugger (singing voice of Julie McWirder) was stood up by hood-with-a-heart Bugsy, so she sang this absorbing number, wondering what to do when her "ordinary dreams fall through."

"Our Big Love Scene" is a melting ballad by Arthur Freed (lyric) and Nacio Herb Brown (music) that uses the metaphor of acting to describe a love that moves from rehearsal to a performance of true love. In *Going Hollywood* (1933) Bing Crosby was heard singing the number on the radio while the lovesick schoolteacher Marion Davies listened intently. Crosby recorded the ballad, which enjoyed moderate popularity.

"Our Home Town" is the amiable opening number from the period musical *Summer Holiday* (1948) that was based on Eugene O'Neill's domestic comedy *Ah! Wilderness!* Beautifully staged by Rouben Mamoulian, the number began with newspaper editor Walter Huston singing the song in his office; it was then picked up and sung by various members of his family in different rooms in their house. (The sequence recalls Mamoulian's legendary opening for *Love Me Tonight* sixteen years earlier.) Ralph Blane (lyric) and Harry Warren (music) wrote the number, which effectively integrates song and dialogue. Mickey Rooney, Agnes Moorehead, Selena Royle, Shirley Johns, Frank Morgan, and Butch Jenkins made up the New England family that sang about their sleepy Connecticut town. The song is sometimes listed as "It's Our Home Town."

"Our Love Affair" is the Oscar-nominated ballad by Arthur Freed (lyric) and Roger Edens (music) promising that a teenage romance will still be true love when they are in old age. Stagestruck youths Mickey Rooney and Judy Garland sang the song as they rehearsed at her house in *Strike Up the Band* (1940), Rooney arranging fruit on the dining room table to illustrate the members of the orchestra he envisions. The pieces of fruit then magically turned into the heads of musicians and instruments of an orchestra, and they all played the song. Vincente Minnelli directed the clever sequence, based on an idea given to him by Busby Berkeley. The uptempo love song was recorded by the orchestras of Tommy Dorsey (vocal by Frank Sinatra), Glenn Miller (vocal by Ray Eberle), and Dick Jurgens (vocal by Harry Cool).

"Our Song" is the love ballad by Dorothy Fields (lyric) and Jerome Kern (music) that foresees a romance with the lovers as closely united as the words and music in a song. Australian opera singer Grace Moore sang the number to American Cary Grant as they strolled through a misty forest in *When You're in Love* (1937). Moore recorded the ballad, as did Eddy Duchin (vocal by Jerry Cooper).

"Our State Fair" is the musical boast sung by Iowans Percy Kilbride, Charles Winninger, Fay Bainter, and others at the top of the rural musical *State Fair* (1945). Richard Rodgers wrote the merry march melody, and Oscar Hammerstein provided the folksy lyric that made the indisputable claim that the Iowa State Fair was the "best state fair in our state." In the 1962 remake of the tale, it was sung by Tom Ewell, Alice Faye, Pamela Tiffin (dubbed by Marie Green), Pat Boone, and various Texans (the locale being changed to the Lone Star State). The number was sung by John Davidson, Kathryn Crosby, Andrea

McArdle, Ben Wright, and the ensemble in the 1996 Broadway version of *State Fair*.

"Out for No Good" is the risqué ditty that Al Dubin (lyric) and Harry Warren (music) wrote for the radio backstager *Twenty Million Sweethearts* (1934). Ginger Rogers, in her first major film role, sang the questioning number that asked "why do we park the car?" if lovemaking wasn't the reason. Rogers recorded the saucy song.

"Out Here on My Own" is the rebelliously ambitious song by Lesley Gore (lyric) and Michael Gore (music) of a youth demanding recognition and success in the entertainment business. Irene Cara, as a student at Manhattan's High School for the Performing Arts, sang the number in the contemporary musical *Fame* (1980). The song was nominated for an Oscar, and Cara's recording was very popular.

"Out of Sight, Out of Mind" is the gently swinging lament by Dorothy Fields (lyric) and Oscar Levant (music), declaring that because the singer has been burnt by love, she will stay out of the running until the perfect lover comes along. Movie star Ginger Rogers sang and danced to the uptempo ballad in the Hollywood backstager *In Person* (1935).

"Out of This World" is the title ballad by Johnny Mercer (lyric) and Harold Arlen (music) for the 1945 musical farce and a love song that uses sci fi imagery: He is lifted off the planet when he looks at her and hears strange extraterrestrial music. Telegram boy Eddie Bracken sang the ballad, but when he opened his mouth the singing voice of Bing Crosby came out. Crosby's recording was popular, and there were also disks by Jo Stafford, Tommy Dorsey (vocal by Stuart Foster), Diahann Carroll, and Julie Wilson. Darcie Roberts sang the song in the Broadway revue *Dream* (1997).

"Out There" is the stirring "I am" song for the deformed Quasimodo (voice of Tom Hulce) in the animated romance *The Hunchback of Notre Dame* (1996). Stephen Schwartz (lyric) and Alan Menken (music) wrote the expansive ballad that the lonely hunchback sang as he climbed about the towers of Notre Dame and looked down at the ordinary people on the street, wishing he could be like them and with them.

"Outside of You" is a ballad of exclusive admiration that Al Dubin (lyric) and Harry Warren (music) wrote for the radio backstager *BroadwayGondolier* (1935). Cab-driver-turned-radio-star Dick Powell sang the number in the film and recorded it with Victor Arden's Orchestra. Ted Fio Rito and his Band also made a recording of the ballad.

"Over and Over" is the pop love ballad that Don Crawford wrote for the campus musical *C'mon Let's Live a Little* (1967). Jackie De Shannon, as the dean's daughter, and Bobby Vee, as an Arkansas folk singer taking classes on campus, sang the romantic ditty that enjoyed some popularity at the time.

"Over the Rainbow," one of the most beloved and popular songs ever to come out of Hollywood, is the inspiring "I am" song for farmgirl Judy Garland in *The Wizard of Oz* (1939) and became her signature song throughout her career. As the troubled teenager Dorothy, Garland sang the number to her dog Toto on her Kansas farm as she dreamed of a better world on the other side of the rainbow. Harold Arlen wrote the music first, and lyricist E. Y. Harburg strongly objected to it when he first heard it, saying it was too operatic for a twelve-year-old girl on a farm to ever sing. Ira Gershwin suggested that the tempo be slowed down and the harmony given a simpler and thinner texture. Arlen did so, and Harburg then wrote the lyric, using a rainbow as the central image because he felt it was probably the only bit of vibrant color the girl had ever seen. Arlen's ambitious music (with its famous leap at the beginning of the refrain) and Harburg's dreamy lyric blended beautifully and the sequence was filmed simply and effectively. But the studio felt the song was slowing the film down and three times tried to cut it, each time producer Arthur Freed fighting to have it reinstated. (As it was, the song's verse, one of the finest Harburg ever wrote, was edited out of the final print.) The ballad immediately became popular, won the Oscar, and was recorded by Garland (several times throughout her career) and countless others. An ASCAP poll conducted in 1963 named "Somewhere Over the Rainbow" one of the sixteen best songs of the past fifty years. James Stewart warbled the ballad in *The Philadelphia Story* (1940) and conducted it in *The Glenn Miller Story* (1954). Eleanor Parker (dubbed by Eileen Farrell) sang it as opera star Marjorie Lawrence in *Interrupted Melody* (1955), and Elizabeth Hartman sang it in *A Patch of Blue* (1965).

P

"Painting the Clouds With Sunshine" is the torchy song by Al Dubin (lyric) and Joe Burke (music) about hiding one's misery behind a cheerful demeanor. The sunny lament was introduced in the first "Gold Diggers" musical called *Gold Diggers of Broadway* (1929), where Nick Lucas sang it in a colorful production number using an early form of Technicolor. Lucas, accompanying himself on guitar, delivered the song to Ann Pennington, who danced with two chorus boys in front of a giant artist's palette. Later that same year the song was interpolated into *Little Johnny Jones* (1929), and decades later the song title was used for a 1951 musical where the number was sung by Dennis Morgan and Lucille Norman. Lucas recorded the song, and there was a hit recording by Jean Goldkette's Orchestra (vocal by Frank Munn).

"Pan American Jubilee" is the star-studded finale for *Springtime in the Rockies* (1942), a Broadway production number utilizing all the principals in the film. Betty Grable and John Payne (with Harry James and his Orchestra) sang the swinging number about joining our neighbors to the south of us for the jubilee, followed by a chorus of gaily colored carnival couples who also sang it. Carmen Miranda and Cesar Romero joined the festivities, then Edward Everett Horton and Charlotte Greenwood as well. Mack Gordon wrote the salutatory lyric and Harry Warren composed the music, which switched back and forth between jitterbug and rumba. Grable recorded the number with James' Orchestra.

"Panamania" is the swinging Latin number by Sam Coslow (lyric) and Al Siegel (music) that described a new dance craze "named for the Canal Zone." Dorothy Lamour introduced the song in *Swing High, Swing Low* (1937) and recorded it as well.

"Papa, Can You Hear Me?" is the prayerlike song that the determined village girl Barbra Streisand sang to her father's grave in *Yentl* (1983) asking him to understand her decision to disguise herself as a boy and study at a Yeshiva. The Oscar-nominated song was written by Alan and Marilyn Bergman (lyric) and Michel Legrand (music), and Streisand's recording was moderately popular. Opera diva Jessye Norman recorded it, and Michael Crawford made a notable disk of the song with "A Piece of Sky" from the same film.

"Parade of the Wooden Soldiers" is the swinging march by Lew Pollack, Sidney Mitchell, and Raymond Scott that happily anticipates a military parade. Shirley Temple sang the short, tuneful number as part of a network broadcast in *Rebecca of Sunnybrook Farm* (1938); she was then joined by Bill Robinson and a chorus of uniformed soldiers for a spiffy tap routine.

"Paree" is the coloratura aria that aristocratic Jeanette MacDonald sang to the shipboard passengers on the way to the New World in *New Moon* (1940), the second film version of the 1928 Broadway operetta. Oscar Hammerstein (lyric) and Sigmund Romberg (music) wrote the song about the unique ways of the French for the original stage production, but it was dropped before opening. Bypassed for the 1930 film, it was pulled out of the trunk and introduced in the 1940 version. It is sometimes listed as "The Way They Do It in Paree." Stanley Green has pointed out that the number is more Spanish in its flavor than French, parts of the song similar to José Padilla's "El Relicario."

"Paris Holds the Key (to Your Heart)" is the French music hall number by Lynn Ahrens (lyric) and Stephen Flaherty (music) from the animated romance *Anastasia* (1997). Transplanted Russian Sophie (voice of Bernadette Peters) showed some new arrivals the nightlife of the City of Light, and, as they hopped from the Folies Bergère to a can-can show, there were cameo appearances by Maurice Chevalier, Sigmund Freud, Josephine Baker, and others residing in Paris in the 1920s.

"Paris in the Spring" is the title love song, written by Mack Gordon (lyric) and Harry Revel (music) for the 1935 musical, that suggests the perfect city at the perfect time of the year for the perfect romance. Mary Ellis and Tullio Carminati sang the number, which was interpolated into the following year's *The Princess Comes Across* (1936). Recordings were made by the orchestras of Freddie Martin, Ray Noble, and Frank Dailey.

"Paris Is a Lonely Town" is the torchy ballad that E. Y. Harburg (lyric) and Harold Arlen (music) wrote for the animated tale *Gay Purr-ee* (1962). The country cat Mewsette (voice of Judy Garland) was alone and frightened in the big city and she noted that even Paris is a dreary place when love is "a laugh and you're a clown."

"Paris, Stay the Same" is the wistful farewell song to the City of Light that Maurice Chevalier sang (in French and English) to balconies full of female admirers in *The Love Parade* (1929). The number, by Clifford Grey (lyric) and Victor Schertzinger (music), was reprised later in the film by Lupino Lane and a barking dog. Chevalier recorded the fervent and zesty number.

"The Parisians" is the fierce "I am" song for tomboy Leslie Caron (dubbed by Betty Ward) in *Gigi* (1958) that is more familiarly known as "I Don't Understand the Parisians." Alan Jay Lerner (lyric) and Frederick Loewe (music) wrote the delicious character song that found fault with the attitude of all the adults in Paris, finding love in everything they see and do.

"Part of Your World" is the lyrical "I am" song by Howard Ashman (lyric) and Alan Menken (music) for the title character in the animated fairy tale *The Little Mermaid* (1989). The mermaid princess Ariel (voice of Jodi Benson) looked through her collection of objects from humans and sang of her desire to join them on the land and live as they do. The song is somewhat similar in sentiment and melody to the same songwriters' "Somewhere That's Green" from the Off-Broadway musical *Little Shop of Horrors* (1982) in which a city girl yearned for a life in the suburbs. Debbie Shapiro Gravitte recorded "Part of Your World" in 1994.

"Pass That Peace Pipe" is a pulsating "Indian" number by Ralph Blane, Hugh Martin, and Roger Edens that was interpolated into the 1947 film version of the Broadway college musical *Good News*. Joan McCracken sang the vivacious song in a campus ice cream shop and then did a rousing dance with Ray MacDonald and other students. The Oscar-nominated song had actually been written for Fred Astaire and Gene Kelly to perform in *Ziegfeld Follies* (1946) but was never used. Bing Crosby and Margaret Whiting each had successful recordings of the number.

"The Peanut Vendor" is the unlikely hit song, about selling one's wares, that U.S. Marine Lawrence Tibbitt sang to the Havana peanut seller Lupe Velez in *The Cuban Love Song* (1931). The melody came from a Spanish tune by Moises Simons, and an English lyric was written by L. Wolfe Gilbert and Marion Sunshine for the *Madame Butterfly*–like tale. Tibbett sang the rumba number to Velez to teach her how better to sell her peanuts. Ten years later he heard a Cuban orchestra play the song in a Manhattan nightclub, and it triggered his memory of the love affair. Finally, it was sung by Tibbitt and Velez's ten-year-old son, the song helping the ex-Marine to identify him. Don Azpiazu and his Havana Casino Orchestra played the song at the Palace Theatre and helped launch its popularity. Orchestral recordings by Guy Lombardo, Paul Whiteman, Louis Armstrong, and Xavier Cugat also helped, and later there were distinctive records by Desi Arnez, Stan Kenton, and Morton Gould. Jane Powell sang the rumba number in *Luxury Liner* (1947), and Judy Garland performed it in *A Star Is Born* (1954).

"Pecos Bill" is the narrative ballad by Johnny Lange (lyric) and Eliot Daniel (music) that provided the tale for the final sequence in the animated anthology *Melody Time* (1948). In a live action introduction, Roy Rogers and the Sons of the Pioneers sang to Bobby Driscoll and Luana Patten about why coyotes howl, and then the animated tall tale of Pecos Bill was told: A boy was raised on the desert by coyotes; after he loses his sweetheart Slue Foot Sue, he returns to his animal friends and in his misery bays at the moon.

"Pennies From Heaven" is the Oscar-nominated song of optimism by Johnny Burke (lyric) and Arthur Johnston (music) that envisions it raining money if you are open to love in the world. The ballad was written for the sentimental 1936 film of the same name, where it was sung by good-hearted crooner Bing Crosby. The number was featured on *Your Hit Parade* for thirteen weeks thanks to Crosby's best-selling record, and over the years there have been notable recordings by Hildegarde, Arthur Tracy, the Norman Luboff Choir, Mary Cleere Haran, and Mandy Patinkin. Dick Haymes sang it in *Cruisin' Down the River* (1953), Crosby reprised it in *Pepe* (1960), and it was heard in the film dramas *From Here to Eternity* (1954) and *Picnic* (1956). In the dark 1981 spoof *Pennies From Heaven,* the Tracy recording was used on the soundtrack as a hobo danced in a shower of pennies. In the Broadway revue *Swinging on a Star* (1995), the song was performed by Lewis Cleale and reprised by the ensemble.

"Pennsylvania Polka" is the swing polka by Lester Lee and Zeke Manners that praised a new dance "mania" from the Keystone State. The Andrews Sisters, as a trio of elderly aunts, sang the number in *Give Out, Sisters* (1942), had a hit record with it, and then sang it again in *Follow the Boys* (1944).

"People Like You and Me" is the jumping love song by Mack Gordon (lyric) and Harry Warren (music) that ascribes to the philosophy that love and all of life's charms are free of charge and were created for lovers just like us. One section of the song turns very patriotic, proclaiming the men overseas are fighting for victory for folks "like you and me." The number was introduced in a recording studio in the swing musical *Orchestra Wives* (1942) by Benny Goodman and his Orchestra with vocals by Marion Hutton, Tex Beneke, and the Modernaires. Charlie Spivak and his Orchestra had a hit record of the song.

"Pepe" is the childlike title song that Shirley Jones sang to a group of Mexican children in an Acapulco square as she held up a puppet named Pepe in the 1960 musical. After she sang it, Jones was joined by Cantinflas and they happily danced on the streets of the resort town. The song had originated as a German ditty by Hans Wittstatt called "Andalusian Girl," but Dory Langdon Previn wrote a new English lyric for the film song. An instrumental record by Duanne Eddy was popular at the time.

"Perfect Gentlemen" is the satiric number by Lee Adams (lyric) and Charles Strouse (music) that boasts of highbrow quality in a lowbrow manner. Rival burlesque comics Jason Robards and Norman Wisdom sang the comic song in the period musical *The Night They Raided Minsky's* (1968).

"Perfect Isn't Easy" is the decadent "I am" song for the pampered French poodle Georgette (voice of Bette Midler) in the animated *Oliver Twist* musical called *Oliver and Company* (1988). Barry Manilow, Bruce Sussman, and Jack Feldman wrote the amusing character song in which the wealthy Manhattan pet lamented the trials of being perfect, her indifferent yawns turning into feline screeches of pleasure.

"Personality" is the zesty and suggestive hit song that show girl Dorothy Lamour sang in the Golden Rail Saloon in Skagway, Alaska, in *Road to Utopia* (1945). James Van Heusen wrote the catchy music, and Johnny Burke penned the sassy list song, which mentioned all the great ladies of history, from DuBarry to Salome to Juliet, who knew how to use their sexual appeal and physical assets, all euphemistically called "personality." Johnny Mercer's recording with the Pied Pipers was a major hit, a rare instance when a songwriter had a hit with another writer's material. Also popular were recordings by Pearl Bailey, Bing Crosby with Eddie Condon's Orchestra, and Dinah Shore. Kathy Fitzgerald, Denise Faye, and Terry Burrell sang the bawdy number in the Broadway revue *Swinging on a Star* (1995).

"Pet Me, Poppa" is the feline nightclub number that Frank Loesser wrote and interpolated into the 1955 film version of his Broadway smash *Guys and Dolls*. Vivian Blaine and the chorines, all dressed as sexy cats and prowling about an alley, used a variety of double entendres as they pleaded to be pampered by their master. The song replaced, for some inexplicable reason, the popular "Bushel and a Peck" number from the stage play and was never as successful as the original, though Rosemary Clooney made a notable recording of "Pet Me, Poppa."

"Pete Kelly's Blues" is the haunting title song that Sammy Cahn (lyric) and Ray Heindorf (music) wrote for the 1955 musical melodrama that used a variety of standards in its nightclub milieu. Ella Fitzgerald, as a saloon singer, introduced the mellow song of lament.

"Pettin' in the Park" is the cutsey ditty about public show of affection that choreographer Busby Berkeley turned into a humorously risqué production number. Al Dubin (lyric) and Harry Warren (music) wrote the tuneful song that Dick Powell and Ruby Keeler introduced in *Gold Diggers of 1933* (1933) in a scene from a Broadway revue. In a Central Park setting, Powell sang the song and Keeler tapped to it while couples embraced on park benches. As the seasons passed, everything from snowball fights to roller skating occupied the lovers until the women, after a fight with their sweethearts, all donned metallic bathing garb and the midget Billy Barty offered a can opener to Powell to pry open Keeler's protective gear. The song was a bit daring for its day because several cities across the nation were on a morals crusade and were passing legislation against public petting. The bizarre sequence ran a little over seven minutes as the incessant Dubin-Warren tune was reprised over and over again. Consequently, few who have ever seen the film can forget the catchy melody. Powell recorded the song for those who wanted to hear it yet again.

"Phantom's Theme" is a moody rock-and-roll soliloquy that record impressario Paul Williams sang in the cult musical *Phantom of the Paradise* (1974), a disco version of the classic *Phantom of the Opera* tale. Subtitled "Beauty and the Beast," the oddly alluring song explores all the "good guys and the bad guys" that are lurking inside the evil businessman. Williams also penned the number.

"Piccadilly Lily" is the soft-shoe number by Herbert Kretzmer (lyric) and Anthony Newley (music), about a gal from the famed London thoroughfare, that served as the theme song for the pseudo-erotic musical fantasy *Can Heironymus Merkin Ever Forget Mercy Humppe and Find True Happiness?* (1969). Lecherous performer Newley sang the number several times in the film, using it as everything from a vaudeville routine on a music hall stage to a slick crooner's signature song in a nightclub lounge.

"The Piccolino" is the festive dance number by Irving Berlin, the tunesmith who wrote more popular songs about dance than anyone else. This one was introduced at a Venice carnival in *Top Hat* (1935), where Ginger Rogers and the chorus sang it and then she and Fred Astaire danced to its exquisite melody. Berlin's lyric describes the new dance as the product of a Latin who found himself in Brooklyn and composed the sprightly melody that became the rage on the Lido.

"Pick Yourself Up" is a swinging polka that Dorothy Fields (lyric) and

Jerome Kern (music) wrote for Fred Astaire and Ginger Rogers to perform in *Swing Time* (1936) and it made for an unusual musical scene. Astaire told dancing instructor Rogers that he knew nothing about hoofing and required lessons, whereupon he performed an ingenious routine with her filled with elegant mistakes and rhythmic pratfalls. (The lyric suggests that one get up, dust oneself off, and "start all over again.") Fields wrote the lyric first (very unusual in collaborations with Kern), and the composer used an old Bohemian musical motif to match her rapid-fire words. The result is one of Kern's finest rhythm songs and one of Astaire and Rogers' most intricate pas de deux. Astaire recorded the number with Johnny Green's Orchestra, and there were also disks by Rosemary Clooney, Benny Goodman, Mel Tormé and, decades later, the George Shearing Trio, whose improvisational rendition made the song a favorite with jazz musicians. "Pick Yourself Up" was featured in two Broadway shows in 1986: Elaine Delmar and Liz Robertson sang it in the revue *Jerome Kern Goes to Hollywood,* and it was performed by Cleavant Derricks, Larry Marshall, Mel Johnson, Jr., Alan Weeks, and Alde Lewis, Jr., in *Big Deal.*

"Picture Me Without You" is the tearjerking ballad that Ted Koehler (lyric) and James Van Heusen (music) wrote for Shirley Temple to sing in *Dimples* (1936), guaranteeing there be no dry eye in the house. Temple sang the song to her pickpocket grandfather Frank Morgan, clutching herself to him and describing how hollow and lonely life would be without him, pleading to stay with him rather than be adopted by a wealthy New York couple. Recordings of the sob ballad were later made by Ted Weems (vocal by Perry Como) and Red Norvo (vocal by Mildred Bailey).

"A Piece of Sky" is the stirring finale number by Alan and Marilyn Bergman (lyric) and Michel Legrand (music) that brought *Yentl* (1983) to its hopeful conclusion. Eastern European student Barbra Streisand sang the emotional song looking forward to the future as she and other immigrants huddled on the deck of a ship taking them to America. The number effectively incorporated reprises of two songs heard earlier in the film, "Papa, Can You Hear Me?" and "Where Is It Written?" bringing together the character's ambition for knowledge and her ties to her ethnic heritage. The sequence was reminiscent of Streisand's other big number on a boat, "Don't Rain on My Parade" in *Funny Girl* (1968), though thematically the two songs are very different.

"Pig Foot Pete" is the Oscar-nominated character number that Martha Raye delivered in high comic style in the Abbott and Costello vehicle *Keep 'Em Flying* (1941). Don Raye (lyric) and Gene De Paul (music) wrote the rambunctious number that enjoyed a good deal of popularity at the time, helped by recordings by Dolly Dawn, Ella Mae Morse, and Freddie Slack's Orchestra.

"Pink Elephants on Parade" is the unusual march song by Oliver Wallace, Ned Washington, and Frank Churchill that was used in a famous dream sequence in the animated circus musical *Dumbo* (1941). When some alcohol was accidentally dumped into the water trough and the young elephant Dumbo drank it, he had surreal visions of elephants that are pink and other colors, the chorus singing the hypnotic march as the visuals went berserk and created one of the most surreal scenes in film animation.

"Play Me an Old-Fashioned Melody" is a pastiche number by Mack Gordon (lyric) and Harry Warren (music) that captures the feel of an 1890s ballad. William Gaxton and Beatrice Kay, as nightspot entertainers who specialized in old-time numbers, performed the nostalgic song in *Diamond Horseshoe* (1945). It was one of the rare film appearances by Broadway favorite Gaxton.

"Please" is the ardent plea for requited love that Leo Robin (lyric) and Ralph Rainger (music) wrote for Bing Crosby to sing in the radio backstager *The Big Broadcast* (1932). The lyric is unabashed and heartfelt and the music expansive, the song starting with its highest note. Radio singer Crosby sang it accompanied by jazz guitarist Eddie Lang as they practiced in a broadcast studio. At the film's finale the number was reprised by Crosby, Lang, and Stuart Erwin. Crosby's recording went to the top of the charts, and the song remained on *Your Hit Parade* for twenty-two weeks. There were also successful recordings by the bands of George Olson, Ray Noble, and Sam Coslow; and later, disks by Al Hibbler with Johnny Hodge's Orchestra, and by Giselle MacKenzie. Jack Oakie performed "Please" in *From Hell to Heaven* (1933), and the song was sung by an unidentified Chinese character in *Stowaway* (1936).

"Please Don't Monkey With Broadway" is the wry Cole Porter song that pleads with the city fathers to make what changes they must in New York but leave the old theatre district alone. The soft-shoe number was sung by the down-and-out vaudeville team of George Murphy and Fred Astaire in *Broadway Melody of 1940* (1940), and then the two top-hatted hoofers did a dance that ended with the two dueling with their canes.

"Please Don't Say No (Say Maybe)" is the hit love ballad by Ralph Freed (lyric) and Sammy Fain (music) from the operatic *Thrill of a Romance* (1945). The King Sisters sang the pleading number with Tommy Dorsey's Orchestra; it was then reprised later in the film by opera tenor Lauritz Melchior, who hid in the bushes, in a *Cyrano de Bergerac*-like scene, and did the singing for air force hero Van Johnson as he wooed Esther Williams with the musical deception.

"Please Don't Stop Loving Me" is the tearful ballad by Joy Byers that contrite riverboat singer Elvis Presley sang to angered sweetheart Donna Douglas in the period musical set on the Mississippi called *Frankie and Johnny* (1966). Presley recorded the lament with the Jordanaires.

"Please Pardon Us, We're in Love" is the apologetic love song by Mack Gordon (lyric) and Harry Revel (music) from the backstager *You Can't Have Everything* (1937). Alice Faye, as a struggling playwright who happened to be the granddaughter of Edgar Allen Poe, introduced the ballad.

"The Polka Dot Polka" is a routine dance song by Leo Robin (lyric) and Harry Warren (music) that was distinguished by the dazzling Busby Berkeley staging of the nightclub scene in *The Gang's All Here* (1943). Alice Faye sang the polka number with a group of children in costumes of different periods; then a brightly attired chorus entered and danced in front of two giant revolving mirrors that created endless kaleidoscopic images, the effect being a before-its-time psychedelic experience.

"Poor Boy" is the upbeat torch song that Texas farmboy Elvis Presley sang in his film debut in *Love Me Tender* (1956). At a country fair soon after the end of the Civil War, Presley entertained the locals by playing his guitar and gyrating on a makeshift stage as he happily proclaimed "I ain't lonesome" or "blue" because he still had a lot of memories of the girl he loves. Presley and Vera Matson were credited with writing the sprightly country-western number, but it was later revealed that Matson wrote it with her husband Ken Darby. Presley's recording was moderately popular.

"Poor Unfortunate Souls" is the dandy character song for the villainous squid Ursula (voice of Pat Carroll) that Howard Ashman (lyric) and Alan Menken (music) wrote for the animated fairy tale *The Little Mermaid* (1989). Ursula sang about those seeking her help and how she always managed to oblige them . . . for a price. She agreed to make princess Ariel (voice of Jodi Benson) human but wanted the young mermaid's voice. The song then turned into an enthralling chant, filled with mock-Latin evocations, as the sea witch transformed the mermaid into a girl. Debbie Shapiro Gravitte recorded the number in 1994.

"Poor You" is a lighthearted love song by E. Y. Harburg (lyric) and Burton Lane (music) that avoids the "I love you" approach by cleverly sympathizing with the lover because he or she will "never know what loving you can be." Passengers Red Skelton, Frank Sinatra, and Virginia O'Brien sang the number with Tommy Dorsey's Orchestra on board a ship to Puerto Rico in *Ship Ahoy* (1942). Sinatra and Dorsey recorded the ballad together, and decades later Michael

Feinstein made a beguiling recording of it.

"Pop! Goes Your Heart" is the robust ballad by Mort Dixon (lyric) and Allie Wrubel (music) that celebrates love at first sight and the luck that immediately comes to one. Dick Powell, as the manager of a window–cleaning company, sang the ballad in *Happiness Ahead* (1934) when he flipped over heiress Josephine Hutchinson. Powell recorded the number, as did the orchestras of Ted Lewis, Raymond Paige, and Vincent Rose (vocal by Chick Bullock).

"Popo the Puppet" is the bright childlike number that Danny Kaye, dressed as a marionette with strings attached, sang with three lady puppets in a televised nightclub show in *On the Riviera* (1951). Sylvia Fine wrote the specialty number, which listed all the remarkable things Popo could do as long as someone pulled the right strings.

"Poppa, Don't Preach to Me" is the raucous narrative song by Frank Loesser that provided Betty Hutton with one of her biggest hits, singing it in the period bio-musical *The Perils of Pauline* (1947) about silent film star Pauline White and recording it with best-selling success. The song took the form of a postcard from an American gal in Paris who, disregarding her father's likely objections, decided to stay in Europe for good.

"Prehistoric Man" is the thrilling song-and-dance number by Betty Comden, Adolph Green (lyric), and Roger Edens (music) that was written for the 1949 film version of the Broadway musical *On the Town*. In a Manhattan anthropology museum, New Yorkers Anne Miller and Betty Garrett joined sailors Gene Kelly, Jules Munshin, and Frank Sinatra in a tribute to the animal in us all and then performed a rousing dance among the anthropological exhibits. Sally Mayes made a distinctive recording of the song in 1994.

"Prince Ali" is the silly and tuneful production number in the animated musical *Aladdin* (1992) in which the "street rat" Aladdin, disguised as a prince, arrived in Agrabah with a massive singing and dancing entourage. The Genie (voice of Robin Williams) led the parade, and Howard Ashman (lyric) and Alan Menken (music) wrote the daffy song that sung the ridiculous praises of the young prince. Later in the film the evil wizard Jafar (voice of Jonathan Freeman) reprised the song with different lyrics, gloating over his revenge on Aladdin.

"Princesses on Parade" is a splashy spoof of old Hollywood production numbers that David Zippel (lyric) and Lex de Azevedo (music) wrote for the animated fairy tale *The Swan Princess* (1994). At a ball given for the eligible bachelor Prince Derek, the Chamberlain (voice of Davis Gaines) and the ensemble sang about the alluring princess want-to-be's that descended on the prince as if in a beauty pageant. It then became an extravagant Busby Berkeley–type number, complete with the requisite overhead shot as the girls formed colorful patterns with their bodies.

"Public Melody No. 1" is a delightful spoof of the G-Man list of criminals that took the form of a combustible dance number in *Artists and Models* (1937). E. Y. Harburg (lyric) and Harold Arlen (music) wrote the song, staged by Vincente Minnelli (in his first screen assignment) in a Harlem setting where Martha Raye (in blackface), Louis Armstrong, and a dancing chorus acted out several clichés about the neighborhood, from fancy loose women to crime in the streets.

"Puppet on a String" is the soft ballad by Sid Tepper and Roy Bennett that claims one's sweetheart holds the strings and so one will do whatever she wishes. Nightclub singer Elvis Presley sang the straightforward love song to millionaire's daughter Shelley Fabares as they walked beside a Florida motel pool in the spring break musical *Girl Happy* (1965). Later in the film he reprised the number as the two of them sailed through the harbor in Fort Lauderdale. Presley recorded the number with the Jordanaires.

"Pure Imagination" is the lyrical ballad by Anthony Newley and Leslie Bricusse inviting one to use creative thinking to open up a whole new world. Candy wizard Gene Wilder sang the number to his guests at the candy factory in the fantasy musical *Willy Wonka and the Chocolate Factory* (1971). Julie Budd made a memorable recording of the song.

"Put 'Em in a Box, Tie 'Em With a Ribbon, and Throw 'Em in the Deep Blue Sea" is the uptempo list song that band singer Doris Day sang with the Page Cavanaugh Trio in *Romance on the High Seas* (1948) in a bar aboard a ship in the Havana harbor. Jule Styne composed the jaunty melody, and Sammy Cahn wrote the the list of all the romantic things you can toss overboard, from kisses and flowers to songs sung by "Frankie Boy" and Mister C." Day's recording was a Number One bestseller, and there were also notable records by Eddy Howard and Nat "King" Cole.

"Put It There, Pal" is the buddy song by Johnny Burke (lyric) and James Van Heusen (music) that Bing Crosby and Bob Hope sang together in *Road to Utopia* (1946) as they dog–sledded through the snow–covered forests of Alaska. The title phrase asks for a handshake, and the lyric is a series of alternating compliments and insults with many references to the two stars' physical features, other films, and careers in general. The two performers recorded the duet, which would not make much sense sung by anyone else.

"Put Me to the Test" is the song of determination that nightclub hoofer Gene Kelly sang as he rehearsed dancing with a dummy in a dress shop in *Cover Girl* (1944), soon replacing it with Rita Hayworth. Later in the film Kelly reprised the number with Phil Silvers and a male chorus on the back of a military truck as they clowned around and did Hawaiian, jazz, and boogie-woogie versions of the song. "Put Me to the Test" began as a list song by the Gershwin brothers written for *Damsel in Distress* (1937), and George Gershwin's music was used for a dance routine by Fred Astaire, George Burns, and Gracie Allen but the lyric was dropped. Years later, when Ira Gershwin was slated to write the lyrics for Jerome Kern's music for *Cover Girl*, he resurrected the clever lyric that listed all the things a lover would do to prove his love, from going over Niagara Falls in a barrel to getting tickets to the latest Noel Coward play. Kern wrote an original melody (which, ironically, was very Gershwinesque in flavor), and by request the lyrics were toned down to less daunting exploits, such as swimming in the Radio City fountain and doing kitchen chores. Bobby Short made a memorable recording of the unusual ballad in the 1970s.

"Puttin' on the Ritz" is the dapper song of sophistication by Irving Berlin that is often wrongly attributed to Cole Porter because of its debonair quality. Berlin wrote the number for the 1930 film musical of the same name, where Harry Richman (in his screen debut) sang it with the chorus on stage of a Broadway theatre in front of a surreal backdrop with the Manhattan buildings taking on human characteristics and moving in time to the music. The original lyric was about Harlem and mocked the well-dressed black citizens who were stepping out for the evening. With a revised lyric about Park Avenue swells, the song was sung by Fred Astaire in *Blue Skies* (1946), where he performed a vivacious dance (choreographed by Hermes Pan) with eight miniature Astaires on a split screen. It is this version of the song that has become a standard and has been recorded hundreds of times. Early records were made by Richman, Leo Reisman, Astaire (made in 1930 with his fancy footwork on the track), and others. A 1983 recording by Dutch–Indonesian singer Taco was at the top of the charts, and recent recordings have been made by Mandy Patinkin, Michael Feinstein, Lee Roy Reams, and Andrea Marcovicci. James R. Morris describe's the music as "a superb example of Irving Berlin's rarely equaled talent for shifting rhythmic emphasis about in a way that brings vitality to a song and propels it forward." As for the lyric of "Puttin' on the Ritz," Philip Furia calls it "Berlin's greatest rhythm song of all" and notes that it "carries the principle of lyrical ragging to the furthest possible extreme." The song was used in two memorable sequences in nonmusical films: Clark Gable and "Les Blondes" performed it in *Idiot's Delight* (1939), and it became a satiric soft-shoe song-and-dance routine for Dr. Frankenstein (Gene Wilder) and his monster (Peter Boyle) in *Young Frankenstein* (1974).

Q

"Queen Bee" is the enthralling rock-and-roll song by Rupert Holmes that struggling singer Barbra Streisand and two African-Americans (Clydie King and Venetta Fields) sang as the group the Oreos in a small club in the remake of *A Star Is Born* (1976). The lyric uses a variety of animal images (wasp, black widow spider, male-killing praying mantis, and so on) to describe the dangerous woman of the title, and then goes on to compare her to such famous queens as Cleopatra, Isabella, Nefertiti, and others.

"Queen of the Hunt Am I" is a delicious comic number sung by Beatrice Lillie (in her first of few screen appearances) with her unique giddy delivery and silly high notes that made her a favorite on stage. Grace Henry (lyric) and Morris Hamilton (music) wrote the number that was used in a farcical sequence in *Are You There?* (1930). London private eye Lillie, disguised as "Diana" for a fox hunt, was thrown by a temperamental horse and landed under a tree, where the fox happily jumped into her lap. All the hunters joined Lillie in singing of her exploits in a scene not dissimilar from the title song number from the stage and film versions of the musical *Mame*.

R

"Rainbow Connection" is the Oscar-nominated ballad by Paul Williams and Kenny Ascher that served as the theme song for *The Muppet Movie* (1979). Kermit the Frog (voice of Jim Henson) sat on his favorite log in a swamp, strummed his banjo, and sang the wistful number that apologized for being yet another song about rainbows, explaining that he needed to express a yearning for a bright and colorful world. Henson's recording was quite popular and the song became Kermit's signature song.

"Rainbow on the River" is the optimistic title song by Paul Francis Webster (lyric) and Louis Alter (music) for the sentimental 1936 Bobby Breen vehicle. Orphaned Southern boy Breen sang the cheerful song that was later recorded by Guy Lombardo (vocal by Carmen Lombardo), Ted Weems (vocal by Perry Como), and Tony Martin. The number remained familiar for years because it was used as the theme song for the popular radio program *Dr. Christian.*

"A Rainy Night in Rio" is the appealing song by Leo Robin (lyric) and Arthur Schwartz (music) that served as a memorable production number in the backstager *The Time, the Place and the Girl* (1946). As the finale of a Broadway revue, Jack Carson, Martha Vickers, Dennis Morgan, and Janis Paige found themselves caught in a sudden shower in a Rio de Janeiro square, so they took refuge in a nearby nightclub, where they sang and danced the samba with Carmen Cavallaro on the piano. Others joined them, and the sequence ended with everyone back in the rainy square dancing with umbrellas.

"Rap Tap on Wood" is the vibrant Cole Porter dance song that was used to display the superior tap dancing talents of Eleanor Powell in *Born to Dance* (1936). Powell, as a new arrival to Manhattan, took a room at the Lonely Hearts

Club and entertained the residents there with her quicksilver tapping feet, proving once and for all that she was the finest female tap artist Hollywood ever had. Frances Langford made a disk of the incendiary song and, years later, Bobby Short did a distinctive version on record.

"Readin', Ritin', Rhythm" is the vivacious song about education that Helen Kane, dressed in professorial gown, cap, and spectacles, sang and danced to in *Heads Up* (1930). Don Hartman (lyric) and Victor Schertzinger (music) wrote the song, and the chorus joined Kane in singing it while Charles "Buddy" Rogers and Margaret Breen danced. *Heads Up* was Kane's last film, for Hollywood rarely knew how to use the unique "Boop-a-Doop" girl who came from the stage.

"Ready, Willing and Able" is the ballad of availability that New England lonelyheart Doris Day sang in the musical melodrama *Young at Heart* (1954). Al Rinker, Floyd Huddleston, and Dick Gleason collaborated on the deep-felt song of yearning.

"Red Robins, Bob Whites and Blue Birds" is the swinging help-the-war-effort song by Mack Gordon (lyric) and James Monaco (music) that Martha Raye sang in a patriotic production number in *Pin-Up Girl* (1944). In a New York nightclub, Raye urged one to take a lesson from the patriotic birds of the title and join in the singing and fighting, while a chorus on roller skates wearing red, white, and blue plumes created birdlike waves and geometric patterns.

"Reflection" is the knowing "I am" song that the young Chinese girl Mulan (singing voice of Lea Salonga) sang in the animated adventure *Mulan* (1998) as she wondered if anyone would ever understand what she is really like inside. David Zippel (lyric) and Matthew Wilder (music) wrote the slightly-pop ballad which Mulan sang as she prayed to her ancestors, her face reflected dozens of times on the shiny stone tablets in the family shrine.

"Remember Me?" is the Oscar-nominated ballad that takes a tongue-in-cheek look back to the courtship, wedding, honeymoon, and early married years of a married couple. Al Dubin (lyric) and Harry Warren (music) wrote the not-so-nostalgic number, which was sung by Kenny Baker in the radio backstager *Mr. Dodd Takes the Air* (1937). A successful recording by Hal Kemp (vocal by Skinnay Ennis) helped keep the song on *Your Hit Parade* for eleven weeks, and the number was used a decade later in *Never Say Goodbye* (1946).

"Remember Me to Carolina" is the Oscar-nominated hit song by Paul Francis Webster (lyric) and Harry Revel (music) that was introduced in the sentimental show biz musical *Minstrel Man* (1944). Entertainer Judy Clark, raised by strangers after the death of her mother, was reunited with her father Benny Fields on stage as the two of them performed the country-flavored song that soon became popular.

"Remember My Forgotten Man" is the passionate Depression-era plea by Al Dubin (lyric) and Harry Warren (music) that Ethan Mordden called "one of Hollywood's most bitter arraignments of economic injustice" as it climaxed the smart and cynical backstager *Gold Diggers of 1933* (1933). The eight-minute sequence about forgotten veterans of World War One and how they were faring in the Depression was staged by Busby Berkeley, and though it is a bit garish and preachy, it is appropriately haunting as well. Streetwalker Joan Blondell sang about the former heroes, commenting that "forgetting him, you see, means you're forgetting me." She was joined by Etta Moten singing in a window as a cop was about to arrest a vagrant, but Blondell shows the officer the bum's medal and he is released. An ironic flashback showed hundreds of soldiers marching off to war, but it soon dissolved to the same hundreds standing in soup lines. The sequence climaxed with silhouettes of soldiers forming a massive archway and Blondell reprising her plea. Dubin's lyric is tough and slangy while Warren's music is a slow blues that easily turns into a march. The whole number is the quintessential Depression musical sequence.

"Remind Me" is a vintage Dorothy Fields–Jerome Kern song that was, according to Roy Hemming, "virtually thrown away in an early scene" of the first Abbott and Costello film *One Night in the Tropics* (1940). The Latin-flavored number was introduced by Peggy Moran and Allan Jones in a nightclub scene as they reminded each other not to fall in love with each other again unless, of course, they should forget. Kern's music is insistent and rhythmic with the pulse of a rumba. (The music had been written years before and not used, so Kern reworked it with a Latin beat as the scene required.) Fields' lyric "is not only perfect, it couldn't have been written by anyone else," according to Deborah Grace Winer, who sees it as "probably the best argument for the case that Dorothy Fields' popular songs are essentially feminine in viewpoint." The song was ignored until Mabel Mercer rescued it from obscurity by recording it in the late 1940s and singing it in clubs, and today it is a standard. Scott Holmes and Elaine Delmar performed the number in the Broadway revue *Jerome Kern Goes to Hollywood* (1986), and it has more recently been recorded by Barbara Carroll and Andrea Marcovicci.

"Return to Sender" is the jumping torch song by Otis Blackwell and Winfield Scott about a lover whose love letters to a sweetheart keep coming back marked "no such person." Charter boat pilot Elvis Presley sang the high-pitched, moaning rock-and-roll number in a waterside nightclub in *Girls! Girls! Girls!* (1962), and his recording, released before the film opened, eventually sold over a million disks.

"Rhumboogie" is the swinging Latin number that the Andrews Sisters sang in their film debut in *Argentine Nights* (1940). Don Raye and Hughie Prince wrote the song that, as the title implied, mixed rumba with boogie–woogie. The sisters sang the number as three gals on the lam in South America. Their recording was a bestseller, and there were also disks by Ray McKinley with Will Bradley's Orchestra and by piano-playing bandleader Bob Zurke.

"Rhythm of the Rain" is the fancy-free ballad by Jack Meskill (lyric) and Jack Stern (music) that celebrates the pitter-patter of a rain shower. It was presented as a nightclub number in *Folies Bergère* (1935) with Maurice Chevalier, Ann Sothern, and a chorus singing and dancing down the street in a rain shower as their umbrellas twirled in pleasing patterns. The song was recorded by the bands of Abe Lyman, Vincent Rose, and the Dorsey Brothers (vocal by Kay Weber).

"Rhythm on the River" is the lyrical title song by Johnny Burke (lyric) and James Monaco (music) for the 1940 musical, where ghost songwriter Bing Crosby sang about his peaceful home in a dilapidated houseboat. Crosby recorded the number, as did Wingy Manone and his Orchestra.

"Ride, Cossack, Ride" is the grandiose song of encouragement that George Forrest, Robert Wright (lyric), and Herbert Stothart (music) wrote for the costume operetta *Balalaika* (1939). Russian prince Nelson Eddy, disguised as a Cossack to win the heart of a revolutionary peasant, sang the fervent number.

"Ride, Tenderfoot, Ride" is the cowboy standard by Johnny Mercer (lyric) and Richard Whiting (music) in the "pop western" tradition that used the steady canter of a horse for its musical rhythm. City boy Dick Powell turned into a singing cowpoke on the radio and crooned the song in *Cowboy From Brooklyn* (1938). The popular number was recorded by Powell, Dick Todd, and the bands of Eddy Duchin, Freddie Martin, Orrin Tucker, and Guy Lombardo.

"The Right Girl for Me" is a dreamy ballad that baseballer-vaudevillian Frank Sinatra sang in the period musical *Take Me Out to the Ball Game* (1949) as he listed the various ways he will be able to tell when the perfect girl for him comes along. Betty Comden, Adolph Green (lyric), and Roger Edens (music) wrote the song, which was later recorded by Sammy Kaye (vocal by Tony Alamo). The number is sometimes listed as "She's the Right Girl for Me."

"The Right Romance" is the touching "I am" song for the Philadelphia girl Jeanne Crain (dubbed by Louanne Hogan) in the period musical *Centennial Summer* (1946). Jerome Kern (in his last film assignment before his death) wrote the flowing music, and Leo Robin provided the piquant lyric that imagined an ideal romance that "will never go wrong."

"The Right Somebody for Me" is the optimistic song of affection by Jack Yellen (lyric) and Lew Pollack (music) that mawkishly taught that worldly riches will not cheer you up but putting your arms around that special someone will make the future seem bright. As sung by Shirley Temple to her guardian Guy Kibbee in *Captain January* (1936), the advice didn't seem trite at all. The song was followed by an absurd dream sequence in which Temple, dressed as a miniature nurse, tended to a baby-sized Kibbee in his high chair.

"The Ritz Roll and Rock" is Cole Porter's nod to the new rock-and-roll sound of the late 1950s, but this jazzy song, written for the 1957 film version of Porter's Broadway musical *Silk Stockings*, was more in the jitterbug mode with a bit of Russian angst thrown in. Fred Astaire sang the number with five top-hatted male singers in the Paris Ritz Hotel and then went into a nimble dance with Russian commissar Cyd Charisse. Porter's lyric describes the rock sound that all the rich folks have adopted, but it was the traditional Astaire footwork that seemed to rule the day.

"River Song" is the atmospheric theme song by Richard M. and Robert B. Sherman for the 1973 musical version of *Tom Sawyer*. Charlie Pride and the chorus sang the number on the soundtrack as various points in the period musical.

"Road to Morocco" is the waggish title song that Bing Crosby and Bob Hope sang while riding on a camel across the African desert at the start of their adventures in the 1942 "Road" picture. Johnny Burke (lyric) and James Van Heusen (music) wrote the prankish duet that made allusions to the previous "Road" comedies (including references to the studio and co-star Dorothy Lamour) and merrily commented that "like Webster's dictionary," they were "Morocco bound." A Crosby recording became popular, strangely enough, three years after the film was released. In the Broadway revue *Swinging on a Star* (1995), the number was sung by Lewis Cleale and Michael McGrath and reprised by McGrath and Kathy Fitzgerald.

"Rock and Roll," written in 1934 by Sidney Clare (lyric) and Richard Whiting (music), was not about the pop sound that would invade the airwaves twenty years later but a rhythm number that referred to the rocking and rolling of an ocean liner on the high seas. The song was introduced in the nautical musical mystery *Transatlantic Merry-Go-Round* (1934), where Mitzi Green sang it while the ship's passengers danced in the grand ballroom. Later in the film the number was reprised as a floor show by the Boswell Sisters in stageprop rowboats singing while chorines in sailor garb merrily danced about them.

"Rockin' and Reeling" is the Big Band number that Don Raye (lyric) and Gene De Paul (music) wrote for the Abbott and Costello vehicle *Ride 'Em Cowboy* (1942). Ella Fitzgerald sang the lively number with the Merry Macs as entertainment on a dude ranch.

"The Rogue Song" is the philosophical title number that Clifford Grey (lyric) and Herbert Stothart (music) wrote (based on Franz Lehar's "Gypsy Love") for the 1930 operetta set in Russia. Opera singer Lawrence Tibbitt made his film debut as a dashing bandit fighting against the Cossacks and sang the fighting number proclaiming no decent man "dies in bed." Recordings were made by Tibbitt, the Shilkert Orchestra, and the Columbia Photo Players.

"Roll Along, Prairie Moon" is the Western song that struggling songwriter Harry Stockwell wrote and sang in the show biz musical *Here Comes the Band* (1935). Ted Fio Rito, Cecil Mack, and Albert Von Tilzer collaborated on the ballad, which had successful recordings by Al Bowlly and the bands of Smith Ballew and Henry "Red" Allen. The song was featured in the Roy Rogers western *King of the Cowboys* (1943).

"Romance" is the lush ballad by Edgar Leslie (lyric) and Walter Donaldson (music) that riverboat gambler J. Harold Murray sang in the New Orleans period musical *Cameo Kirby* (1930). The song enjoyed momentary popularity and then fifteen years later was a hit all over again after it was featured in the Sonja Henie vehicle *It's a Pleasure* (1945). Subsequent recordings by Tony Martin, Mario Lanza, and Jimmy Dorsey and his Orchestra were hits, and there were also records by John Boles, the Casa Loma Orchestra, and Ray Herbeck's Orchestra, which adopted the number as their theme song.

"Romance and the Rhumba" is the dance song by Mack Gordon (lyric) and James Monaco (music) that proclaims "what a lovely combination" the two make. American tourist Alice Faye and local Romeo Cesar Romero sang and danced the catchy number in a Cuban nightclub in *Week-End in Havana* (1941).

"Rosalie" is the title ballad by Cole Porter that West Point cadet Nelson Eddy sang to serenade Vassar student Eleanor Powell beneath her dorm window in the 1937 costume musical. The song is reprised several times later by the ensemble and was familiar enough to audiences by the end of the film that it became a hit. Porter himself disliked the song, writing six drafts of the romantic tribute before studio head Louis B. Mayer was pleased. Porter filled the lyric with several Tin Pan Alley clichés and then dismissed the number, being all the more surprised when it was so popular. (Irving Berlin's advice to Porter: "Listen, kid, . . . never hate a song that's sold a half million copies.") "Rosalie" was sung by a trio of street singers in the Porter bio-musical *Night and Day* (1946).

"The Rose" is the fervent title song by Amanda McBroom for the 1979 film musical loosely based on the life of self-destructive rock star Janis Joplin. The tender ballad about death and the fragile nature of a rose was not used in the film proper, but Bette Midler sang it over the final credits and her recording was very popular.

"The Rose in Her Hair" is gushing ballad by Al Dubin (lyric) and Harry Warren (music) that was featured in the radio backstager *Broadway Gondolier* (1935). Taxicab-driver-turned-singer Dick Powell sang the number in English and Italian and recorded it, as did Ted Fio Rito and his Orchestra.

"A Rose Is Not a Rose" is the quiet ballad that Richard M. and Robert B. Sherman wrote for the musical animal film *The Magic of Lassie* (1978). The number was sung by Alice Faye (in her last film appearance) as she accompanied the singing voice of Pat Boone coming from a jukebox.

"Rose of the Rancho" is the Spanish-flavored title song by Leo Robin (lyric) and Ralph Rainger (music) for the exotic 1935 operetta. Government agent John Boles sang the waltzing tribute to Gladys Swarthout, proclaiming her both a flame and a flower.

"Roses in December" is the love ballad that wealthy heir Gene Raymond sang with working–class sweetheart Harriet Hilliard in *The Life of the Party* (1937), knowing he will lose his fortune if he marries her. George Jessel and Ben Oakland wrote the infatuated number, and Hilliard recorded it with Ozzie Nelson's Orchestra.

"Rosie the Riveter" is the wartime song of salute to the women working in factories by Redd Evans and John Jacob Loeb that the King Sisters and Alvino Rey introduced in a nightclub floor show in *Follow the Band* (1943). The song caught on and was used in the war effort musical *Rosie the Riveter* (1944) and served as the patriotic finale for the film. In the later film airplane factory worker Jane Frazee was given an award by a senator and all the gals in the plant celebrated by singing the lively tribute to the female work force as they joyfully flew model airplanes on sticks. The song was recorded by the Four Vagabonds.

"Rumble, Rumble, Rumble" is the vivacious comic number by Frank Loesser that Betty Hutton, as silent film star Pauline White, sang in *The Perils of Pauline* (1947) as she complained about the pianist in the next apartment who played boogie-woogie all the time. Hutton recorded the furious ditty.

"Run Little Raindrop Run" is the peppy song by Mack Gordon (lyric) and Harry Warren (music) that tells the rain and clouds to get gone because he has a "date with the sun." The sprightly song was written for *The Great American Broadcast* (1941) but was cut before filming began. A year later Broadway stars Betty Grable and John Payne sang and danced the number dressed in raincoats on a drizzly Central Park stage setting in *Springtime in the Rockies* (1942); they were joined by a whistling chorus who dashed back and forth through the raindrops. Later in the film Grable and Cesar Romero danced to the music at a fashionable resort on Lake Louise.

"A Russian Rhapsody" is the lush ballad by Paul Francis Webster (lyric) and Walter Jurmann (music) that combined romantic trills with Russian angst. Broadway star Marta Eggerth delivered the operatic air as a Russian princess in a Broadway show in the backstager *Presenting Lily Mars* (1943).

S

"Sailing for Adventure" is the rousing sea chant that Barry Mann and Cynthia Weil wrote for the musical adventure farce *Muppet Treasure Island* (1996?). Tim Curry (as Long John Silver), Kevin Bishop (as Jim Hawkins), and the sailors and passengers on the *Hispanola* sang the Gilbert and Sullivan–like chorus number as they set off from England to find treasure in the Caribbean.

"Sailor Beware" is the uptempo ballad that was written by Leo Robin (lyric) and Richard Whiting (music) for the first film version of the Broadway hit *Anything Goes* (1936). Stowaway Bing Crosby sang the congenial number (with help from the chorus) to British heiress Ida Lupino and later recorded it as well.

"A Sailor With an Eight Hour Pass" is the brash comic number by Ben Raleigh and Bernie Wayne from the Eddie Bracken vehicle *Out of This World* (1945). Cass Daley performed the number, according to Clive Hirschhorn, "in a fair imitation of a whirling dervish."

"Salome" is the sexy narrative ballad by Ralph Freed, E. Y. Harburg (lyric), and Burton Lane (music) that Virginia O'Brien delivered with comic aplomb in *DuBarry Was a Lady* (1943). The Freed-Harburg lyric told of the gal who predated all the "umph" girls and strippers of today, making her "the grandma of them all." The comic number is sometimes listed as "No Matter How You Slice It, It's Still Salome."

"Salud (Here's Cheers)" is the happy toast song by Johnny Mercer (lyric) and Saul Chaplin (music) that was featured in the Big Top musical *Merry Andrew* (1958). The sprightly number was sung by Danny Kaye, as a schoolteacher-turned-ringmaster, Salvatore Baccaloni, as the owner of the circus, beautiful Pier Angeli, and the chorus.

"Saludos Amigos" is the festive title number by Ned Washington (lyric) and Charles Wolcott (music) and the theme song for the 1943 part live-action, part animated musical travelogue about South America. The Oscar-nominated song was sung on the soundtrack by a chorus welcoming Americans to the colorful world of their neighbors to the south of them.

"San Francisco" is the marchlike title song by Gus Kahn (lyric) and Bronislau Kaper (music) for the 1936 classic that Stanley Green described as "that exceedingly limited film genre, the disaster musical." The tuneful tribute to the California city was sung four times in the film. At the Paradise cabaret, singer Jeanette MacDonald rehearsed the number as a slow and loving hymn until owner Clark Gable ordered her to pick up the tempo, which she did, the scene dissolving into the performance that night. A crowd of citizens reprised the song at an outdoor political rally later in the film, and MacDonald jazzed up the number for a reprise at the competition at the Chicken's Ball. The number was sung once more, as a solemn hymn, sung by the survivors of the earthquake as they overlooked their ravaged city. "San Francisco" was heard by chorus or orchestra in other films set in the city: *Hello, Frisco, Hello* (1943), *Nob Hill* (1945), and the Kahn bio-musical *I'll See You in My Dreams* (1952).

"Sand in My Shoes" is the gentle standard by Frank Loesser (lyric) and Victor Schertzinger (music) that Connie Boswell introduced in the Hollywood backstage musical *Kiss the Boys Goodbye* (1941). The song wistfully recalls a love affair in Havana, and Boswell's recording was a major hit. There were also disks by Helen Morgan, Sammy Kaye (vocal by Tommy Ryan), and Sonny Dunham and his Orchestra.

"Santa Fe" is the eager "I am" song for the orphaned newsboy Christian Bale in the period musical *Newsies* (1992). Jack Feldman (lyric) and Alan Menken (music) wrote the number about the longing to escape 1899 Manhattan and head out West, and Bale sang it as he wandered the streets late at night, breaking into a rousing cowboy dance step as he imagined a new life for himself in the great outdoors. Debbie Shapiro Gravitte made a lovely recording of the song.

"Satan's Holiday" is the spirited number that Irving Kahal (lyric) and Sammy Fain (music) wrote for Ruth Etting to sing in a nightclub in the Ed Wynn vehicle *Follow the Leader* (1930). But at the last minute Etting was replaced by Broadway singer Ethel Merman, who (in her feature film debut) belted out the irreverent number with her characteristic bravado.

"Saturday Afternoon Before the Game" is the jubilant march by Mack Gordon (lyric) and Josef Myrow (music) that the chorus sang with Debbie Reynolds in the show biz musical *I Love Melvin* (1953). After singing with anticipation for the weekend football game, the male members of the ensemble tossed Reynolds about like a football in a merry dance.

"Savages" is the potent chorus number by Stephen Schwartz (lyric) and Alan Menken (music) that was featured with great effect in the animated romance *Pocahontas* (1995). English governor Ratcliffe (voice of David Ogden Stiers) and the other European settlers sang about the heathen Native Americans in Virginia, who are "barely even human," and their hopes of driving them away from the colony. Then the number was reprised by the natives who, seeing the settlers destroy the natural resources, sang about the invading savages from Europe. Soon the two choruses are united in a warlike chant of destruction.

"Save Me, Sister" is the revival–like number that musical comedy star Al Jolson (in his last starring film role) sang with Cab Calloway and Wini Shaw in the show biz musical *The Singing Kid* (1936). E. Y. Harburg (lyric) and Harold Arlen (music) wrote the song, one of their earliest screen assignments together.

"Sawdust, Spangles and Dreams" is the hopeful song by Roger Edens that was interpolated into the Rodgers and Hart score for the 1962 film version of the Broadway circus musical *Jumbo*. After Jimmy Durante's circus is destroyed, Doris Day, Stephen Boyd (dubbed by James Joyce), Martha Raye, and Durante sang this teary-eyed tribute to the Big Top as they plan to rebuild the business at the end of the film.

"Say a Prayer for Me Tonight" is the wistful musical plea that the nervous Leslie Caron (dubbed by Betty Wand) sang to her cat the night before her first grown-up date in *Gigi* (1958). The song had been written by Alan Jay Lerner (lyric) and Frederick Loewe (music) two years earlier for Julie Andrews to sing the night before the embassy ball in the Broadway musical *My Fair Lady* (1956), but the number was cut in New Haven. Lerner disliked the song and was glad to let it die, but Loewe remembered it fondly and played it for producer Arthur Freed (when Lerner was not present) and it was put into *Gigi*. (Later Lerner admitted that he did like the number better in the context of the film.) The music is a gentle waltz, not at all hymnlike, and the lyric is engaging as the young girl anticipates a Waterloo and hopes "I'll be Wellington, not Bonaparte."

"Say It (Over and Over Again)" is the smooth harmonizing ballad by Frank Loesser (lyric) and Jimmy McHugh (music) that pleads for repetitive romantic affirmation. Ellen Drew, Virginia Dale, and Lillian Cornell, as a performing trio auditioning in a recording studio, introduced the number in the Jack Benny vehicle *Buck Benny Rides Again* (1940) and then reprised it later in a nightclub. The song was featured on *Your Hit Parade* for seven weeks, and the two most popular recordings of the ballad were by Glenn Miller (vocal by Ray Eberle) and Tommy Dorsey (vocal by Frank Sinatra).

"Say It With a Kiss" is a demonstrative ballad by Johnny Mercer (lyric) and Harry Warren (music) that Maxine Sullivan sang in the horseracing musical *Going Places* (1938). It was recorded by Sullivan, as well as by Teddy Wilson, Gene Krupa (vocal by Irene Daye), and Artie Shaw (vocal by Helen Forrest).

"Say It With Firecrackers" is a routine holiday song by Irving Berlin that provided Fred Astaire with one of his most famous numbers, "a snappy routine," according to Roy Hemmings, "that is reputedly the fastest precision dance that he or anyone else ever filmed." As part of the Fourth of July show in *Holiday Inn* (1942), a chorus in patriotic garb sang the number about celebrating the day with firecrackers (the title is a slant on Berlin's more famous song "Say It With Music"); then Astaire launched into a tap solo, tossing lit firecrackers down around him as his feet matched the rapid fire of the many small explosions.

"Say That We're Sweethearts Again" is the romantically sly plea written by Earl Brent for the backstager *Meet the People* (1944). Virginia O'Brien's knowing rendition of the number was the highlight of the film.

"Says My Heart" is the ballad of conflicting emotions that Frank Loesser (lyric) and Burton Lane (music) wrote for the nightclub backstager *Cocoanut Grove* (1938). Harriet Hilliard sang the number with Harry Owens Orchestra in the famous night spot, explaining how her heart tells her one thing but her head tells her differently. The number went to the top spot on *Your Hit Parade* and stayed on the show for twelve weeks. Hilliard recorded the song with Ozzie Nelson's Orchestra, and there were also records by Billie Holiday, Tommy Dorsey, Jimmie Grier, and George Hall (vocal by Holly Dawn).

"Says Who, Says You, Says I" is an agreeable love song by Johnny Mercer (lyric) and Harold Arlen (music), but it was never taken very seriously because of the way it was introduced in *Blues in the Night* (1941). Buck-toothed comedienne Mabel Todd, who was known for perking up many a Warners musical, sang the number with the Will Bradley Orchestra, delivering it in a shrill and very funny manner. Underneath lay what Alec Wilder described as "a very charming and eccentric little rhythm song."

"Scales and Arpeggios" is an inventive music lesson written by

Robert M. and Robert B. Sherman for the animated Gallic tale *The Aristocats* (1970). The feline Duchess (voice of Eva Gabor) and her three kittens practiced their piano in their wealthy Paris home by jumping back and forth on the keyboard, singing about how important it is to master the two techniques of the song title.

"Seal It With a Kiss" is the rhapsodic ballad that Edward Heyman (lyric) and Arthur Schwartz (music) wrote for the Lily Pons vehicle *That Girl from Paris* (1936). Pons, as an opera singer traveling with a swing band, sang the infatuated aria.

"The Second Time Around" is the engaging ballad by Sammy Cahn (lyric) and James Van Heusen (music) that proposes that a mature, second-chance love affair is much more comfortable and agreeable. Widower Bing Crosby decided to go to college in *High Time* (1960) to get the education he never had time for, and he sang this number when he fell in love with the French professor Nicole Maurey. Frank Sinatra's recording of the Oscar-nominated song was a bestseller.

"Secret Love" is the Oscar-winning ballad by Paul Francis Webster (lyric) and Sammy Fain (music) that Doris Day introduced in *Calamity Jane* (1953) and her recording sold over a million copies, the biggest hit record of her career. Sharpshooter Day sang the reflective ballad leaning against a tree, realizing that she loved Bill Hickock (Howard Keel) but that she had been hiding her feeling even from herself. The oft-recorded number was a bestseller for Slim Whitman, and it was revived successfully in 1966 by Billy Stewart and again in 1975 by Freddy Fender. International singer Caterina Valente and Carmen McRae each recorded it with success, and Judy Kaye made a distinctive recording in 1998.

"See You Later, Alligator" is the rock-and-roll hit by Robert Guidry that was introduced by Bill Haley and the Comets in the first rock-and-roll film *Rock Around the Clock* (1955). Haley's best-selling recording was in the Top Ten in all categories.

"Seeing's Believing" is the lighter-than-air song by Johnny Mercer (lyric) and Harry Warren (lyric) that got a lighter-than-air staging by choreographer Robert Alton in the period musical *The Belle of New York* (1952). Manhattan playboy Fred Astaire was smitten by Salvation Army lass Vera-Ellen and sang of her charms, proclaiming that they must be seen to be believed. Astaire then went into a high-flying dance in Washington Square, floating through the air and landing on top of the famous arch, where he performed a joyous tap routine.

"Seize the Day" is the hymnlike march sung by David Moscow and the other newsboys when they went on strike and danced through the streets of 1899 New York in *Newsies* (1992). Jack Feldman (lyric) and Alan Menken (music) wrote the stirring number that had an impelling Irish jig flavor to it. Debbie Shapiro Gravitte recorded the song in 1994.

"Send Me a Man, Amen" is the swinging novelty number by Ray Gilbert (lyric) and Sidney Miller (music) that was the highlight of the out-West musical *Moonlight and Cactus* (1944). The Andrews Sisters, as staff members at an all-girl ranch, introduced the slangy hymn.

"Sentimental and Melancholy" is the simple but affecting torch song by Johnny Mercer (lyric) and Richard Whiting (music) that West End singing star Wini Shaw sang in the Broadway backstager *Ready, Willing and Able* (1937). The plaintive number was recorded by Glen Gray and the Casa Loma Orchestra, Phil Harris, and Teddy Wilson.

"September in the Rain" is the enthralling standard by Johnny Mercer (lyric) and Harry Warren (music) that wistfully recalls a love affair in the fall but concludes that even though it is now spring, the disheartened one is still in September. The ballad was written for opera star James Melton to sing in *Stars Over Broadway* (1935), but by the final cut the music was heard only in the background. Melton finally got to sing it as a temperamental bandleader in *Melody for Two* (1937), and the song has remained popular ever since. Warren's music is gently swinging and Mercer's lyric work is expert, filled with flowing internal rhymes and atmospheric imagery. Melton's recording was popular, but the George Shearing Quintet had the biggest hit with the ballad in 1949. It was revived all over again in 1961 with a best-selling record by Dinah Washington.

"Serenade in Blue" is the perennial Big Band favorite by Mack Gordon (lyric) and Harry Warren (music) that remembers a past romance every time a certain serenade is heard. Glenn Miller and his Orchestra (vocal by Lynn Bari, who was dubbed by Pat Friday) introduced the entrancing number at an Iowa City concert in the Big Band musical *Orchestra Wives* (1942), and the Miller recording with vocalists Ray Eberle and the Modernaires was a bestseller. Warren's music is particularly haunting, Alec Wilder noting that the "release is a daring reiteration of notes . . . six measures start with the same four notes, but there is a very subtle variation in each of the second halves of these measures." Warren credited Miller as the inspiration for the song, saying, "I knew Glenn could play anything I put on paper and that he would arrange the music in a way that could only enhance it." The ballad was most recently recorded by Andrea Marcovicci.

"A Serenade to the Stars" is the "affectedly saccharine" (according to Roy Hemming) ballad by Harold Adamson (lyric) and Jimmy McHugh (music) that wished for happiness from celestial friends. Wealthy teenager Deanna Durbin, a student at a posh Swiss boarding school, sang the song in *Mad About Music* (1938) as she yearned for a father and a family.

"Shadow Waltz" is the insistent and memorable serenade by Al Dubin (lyric) and Harry Warren (music) that was featured in a famous Busby Berkeley–staged sequence in *Gold Diggers of 1933* (1933). Struggling songwriter Dick Powell sang the waltzing ballad to Ruby Keeler in his Manhattan apartment, and soon the scene dissolved to dozens of girls in white dresses and white wigs playing white violins as they waltzed across a dark floor. The scene then went to black and only the illuminated violins could be seen, making patterns in the darkness and even forming an outline of one giant violin. The six-minute sequence concluded with white-suited Powell reprising the song to Keeler. Warren's music for the verse is unusually melodic and could stand on its own quite well. As for the swirling refrain, Tony Thomas calls it "a superior piece of composition that takes it place among the handful of great American waltzes." Bing Crosby's recording of the song was a bestseller, and there were also popular records by Al Bowlly with Ray Noble and his Orchestra and by Rudy Vallee. "Shadow Waltz" was featured in the film *Cain and Mabel* (1936) and in the Broadway musical *42nd Street* (1980), where it was sung by Tammy Grimes, Carole Cook, and the chorus girls.

"Shall We Dance?" is the zippy title song by Ira Gershwin (lyric) and George Gershwin (music) for the 1937 Fred Astaire and Ginger Rogers vehicle. (The film title dropped the question mark.) In a revue at a Manhattan rooftop theatre, Astaire performed an artsy ballet routine with Harriet Hector and then broke into tap and modern dance as he sung the invitational number. As a stage full of chorus girls all wearing Ginger Rogers masks surrounded him; he danced among them until he discovered the genuine Rogers, and then the two performed a swinging pas de deux. The film was scheduled to be called *Stepping Toes*, but producer Pandro S. Berman requested a new song that could also serve as the film's title. After the song became popular, a woman in Montana sued the studio because she had written a waltz titled "Shall We Dance?" but the suit was dropped when the copyright office listed six other songs with the same title. (Thirteen years later Rodgers and Hammerstein would write a memorable number with the same title for *The King and I*) Astaire made a record of the song with Johnny Green's Orchestra, Bobby Short recorded it in 1990, and it was sung by Harry Groener and Jodi Benson in the Broadway musical *Crazy for You* (1992).

"Shanghai Lil" is the narrative song by Al Dubin (lyric) and Harry Warren (music) that became a Busby Berkeley extravaganza in the legendary backstager

FootlightParade (1933). As part of an onstage entertainment in a movie theatre, sailor Jimmy Cagney searched the Shanghai bars and opium dens for his lost sweetheart Lil. When he found her (Ruby Keeler in Chinese makeup and clothes), the two vigorously tap danced on the top of a bar until it was time for all the sailors to return to the ship. After performing military drills and a lot of flagwaving, the face of FDR was created by holding up hundreds of cards, and the patriotic number (and the film) came to its finale with Keeler in sailor garb stowing away on the troop ship.

"She Is Not Thinking of Me" is the vivacious waltz number from *Gigi* (1958) that uses film and music in a creative and enthralling manner. At Maxim's Restaurant in Paris, the bachelor Louis Jourdan sat at his table and his thoughts were heard in song on the soundtrack as he watched his lover Eva Gabor waltz with other men on the dance floor. As his suspicions of her unfaithfulness increased, the song and the dancing got more furious; and the sequence ended with Jourdan dumping a glass of champagne down her dress and leaving Maxim's. Frederick Loewe composed the vigorous music and Alan Jay Lerner wrote the just as furious lyric, rhyming "ooh-la-la-la-la" with "she's so untrue-la-la-la-la." When the scene was originally shot in Paris, two few closeups of Jourdan were filmed and the final product was confusing. At considerable expense, Maxim's was rebuilt in Hollywood and the whole scene was shot again to clarify the subjective point of view. The song, which is sometimes listed as "Waltz at Maxim's," was sung by Daniel Massey in the 1973 Broadway version of *Gigi*.

"She Reminds Me of You" is a touching ballad by Mack Gordon (lyric) and Harry Revel (music) that explains that the reason for the singer's new love is that she reminds him of his old flame. The song was introduced by sailor Bing Crosby, who sang it to his pet bear on a yacht in *We're Not Dressing* (1934), and Crosby recorded it. There was also a noteworthy record by Eddy Duchin (vocal by Lew Sherwood).

"She Was a China Teacup and He Was Just a Mug" is the daffy song by Leo Robin (lyric) and Ralph Rainger (music) that provided for an equally daffy production number in *International House* (1933). Sterling Holloway sang the oriental-flavored ditty as he danced with chorus girls costumed as teacups.

"The Shepherd's Serenade" is the melodic ballad by Clifford Grey (lyric) and Herbert Stothart (music) that French general Ramon Novarro sang in the early costume musical *Devil May Care* (1929). Recordings of the ardent love song were made by Smith Ballew, Frank Munn, and Leo Reisman and his Orchestra.

"She's a Latin from Manhattan" is the playful narrative ballad by Al Dubin (lyric) and Harry Warren (music) about an exotic dancing star named Dolores, who turns out to be Broadway chorine Susie from Tenth Avenue. Al Jolson sang the rumba–like number in a nightclub show in *Go Into Your Dance* (1935) and was joined by Señorita Ruby Keeler and chorus girls; the sequence climaxed with Jolson and Keeler atop a huge globe of planet earth. The song, filled with traces of a tango, spoofed the then-common Hollywood practice of fabricating exotic foreign origins for American stars. Jolson recorded the number, Jack Carson and Joan Leslie sang it in *The Hard Way* (1942), and Evelyn Keyes and the chorus performed it in *The Jolson Story* (1946). Bobby Short made a distinctive recording in 1995.

"Shoes With Wings On" is the fleet-of-foot number by Ira Gershwin (lyrics) and Harry Warren (music) that provided Fred Astaire with a singular opportunity for dance in *The Barkleys of Broadway* (1949). In a Broadway revue number, shoe repairman Astaire was left with a dancer's white shoes and sang about how his feet seem to have wings when dancing. The pair of shoes started to perform some steps, so Astaire put them on and was soon dancing all over the shop, other pairs of shoes joining in. The numbers got more and more chaotic and ended with Astaire shooting all the footwear dead. In an unusual twist, Astaire's singing was only on the soundtrack, so we hear his thoughts during the number. Gershwin's lyric is carefree and joyous ("the world's in rhyme"), and Warren's music has a brassy quality that eventually erupts into a military march.

"Shootin' the Works for Uncle Sam" is the patriotic call to arms written by Cole Porter for the wartime musical *You'll Never Get Rich* (1941). Fred Astaire and a chorus of comely girls sang and danced to the marchlike number that explained how the men in all professions are dropping their old jobs and enlisting in the U.S. Army.

"Should I (Reveal)?" is the reflective ballad by Arthur Freed (lyric) and Nacio Herb Brown (music) that debated whether or not to make known one's true feelings in a romance. Songwriter-performer Charles Kaley sang the number in the early backstager *Lord Byron of Broadway* (1930), where it was reprised by Ethelind Terry. Georgia Carroll sang it with Kay Kyser's Orchestra in *Thousands Cheer* (1943), and Wilson Wood performed it in *Singin' in the Rain* (1952). Two standout recordings of the ballad were those by Jack Fulton with Paul Whiteman's Orchestra and by the Arden and Ohman Orchestra.

"Shout It Out" is the celebratory rock-and-roll song by Bill Giant, Bernie Baum, and Florence Kaye that didn't fit at all into the period musical *Frankie and Johnny* (1966) but was enjoyable all the same. Riverboat singer Elvis Presley sang the number about dropping inhibitions at a Mardi Gras ball in New

Orleans, and the partying crowd happily joined in.

"Shuffle Off to Buffalo" is the wily song about honeymooners that Al Dubin (lyric) and Harry Warren (music) wrote for an amusing production number in a Broadway-bound show in *Forty-Second Street* (1933). Newlyweds Ruby Keeler and Clarence Nordstrom took the *Niagara Ltd.* to Niagara Falls and sang with anticipation with the other honeymooning couples. Also on the train are two gold diggers (Ginger Rogers and Una Merkel), who slyly sang about how short-lived such romances are and how many of the couples would be seeking divorces in the near future. The number climaxed with all the pajama-clad passengers performing up and the down the length of the train. Busby Berkeley's staging was atypical in that the scene looked as if it really could fit on a Broadway stage. The song immediately caught on, thanks to recordings by Hal Kemp, Don Bestor, and others. Jack Carson and Joan Leslie sang the number in *The Hard Way* (1942), and it was performed by Karen Prunscik, Joseph Bova, Carole Cook, and several bridal couples in the Broadway version of *42nd Street* (1980). In 1994 the complete film score was recorded, and the number was sung by Ann Morrison, Guy Stroman, Debbie Shapiro Gravitte, and Judy Blazer.

"The Siamese Cat Song" is the brief but memorable little ditty that Sonny Burke and Peggy Lee wrote for the animated canine romance *Lady and the Tramp* (1955). A pair of mischievous felines (both voiced by Lee) sang in harmony as they checked out their new home and merrily started to destroy it as the abashed cocker spaniel Lady tried to stop them. Bobby McFerrin made a delightful double-track recording of the song in 1995, and the group the Jazz Networks recorded it in 1996.

"Silhouetted in the Moonlight" is the enchanting romantic ballad by Johnny Mercer (lyric) and Richard Whiting (music) that was featured in the Tinsel Town backstager *Hollywood Hotel* (1938). At the deserted Hollywood Bowl, Rosemary Lane stepped onto the vast stage and sang the ballad while Dick Powell, silhouetted in the moonlight, sang back to her. Later in the film Frances Langford and Jerry Cooper reprised the song with Robert Paige's Orchestra as part of a broadcast from the Orchid Room of the Hollywood Hotel. Langford recorded the ballad, as did Benny Goodman and his Orchestra.

"Silver Bells" is the holiday standard by Jay Livingston and Ray Evans that was introduced in the Bob Hope vehicle *The Lemon Drop Kid* (1951) and has received hundreds of recordings over the years. Small-time hood Hope, dressed as a ragged Santa Claus, sang the number with Marilyn Maxwell while strolling down a New York City street and various passersby joined in the singing. The song is unusual for a Christmas carol on two accounts: It is written in a brisk 3/4 time and the lyric paints a picture of "Christmastime in the city" rather than the usual rural setting for holiday songs. The carol is so constructed that the verse and refrain can be sung simultaneously with extra words written for the refrain lyric. Of the many recordings, the biggest seller was a duet version by Bing Crosby and Carol Richards.

"The Simple Things in Life" is the mellow but optimistic Depression chaser that Rochelle Hudson sang in the Shirley Temple vehicle *Curly Top* (1935) as she strummed a ukelele in a benefit show for the orphanage. Ted Koehler (lyric) and Ray Henderson (music) wrote the uplifting number that promised that smiles would soon be in style again.

"Since I Kissed My Baby Goodbye" is the Oscar-nominated torch song by Cole Porter that has an unsentimental streak running through it. In a U.S. Army guard house, inmates played by the Delta Rhythm Boys sang the jazzy song of lost love in *You'll Never Get Rich* (1941) while Fred Astaire danced to the rhythmic number. The scene was filmed in such a way that Astaire and the African-American singers were never in the same shot together but appeared to be in the same room, a result of crosscutting. In this way the distributors could cut the Delta Rhythm Boys out of the scene for screenings in the South. Astaire recorded the song, and years later David Allen made a notable disk of it as well.

"Sing a Song of Sunbeams" is the rosy ballad by Johnny Burke (lyric) and James Monaco (music) that cab driver Bing Crosby sang in *East Side of Heaven* (1939). The lyric gleefully looks at life's sunny side, and the music, as described by Ethan Mordden, has a "melody with vocal bubbles so that it dances about the ear." Crosby recorded the number, as did Bob Crosby and the Bob Cats (vocal by Marion Mann) and Gray Gordon (vocal by Cliff Grass).

"Sing a Tropical Song" is the pseudo-calypso number by Frank Loesser (lyric) and Jimmy McHugh (music) that satirized all the exotic island songs written for the movies. Beachcomber Dick Powell sang the ridiculous ditty with Eddie Bracken, Sir Lancelot, and the Caribbean locals in the opening number of *Happy Go Lucky* (1943), describing the wonders of the island, where people accent the wrong syllables so that everything sounds exotic. The number became a novelty favorite, the first calypso song to become a commercial hit. The Andrews Sisters sang it in *Her Lucky Night* (1945), and their recording was a bestseller. Jack Smith also made a disk of the number, and Loesser himself recorded it.

"Sing, Baby, Sing" is the rhythmic title song by Jack Yellen (lyric) and Lew Pollock (music) for the 1936 musical about Hollywood. Nightclub singer Alice Faye sang the swinging torch song as she suggested singing as a cure for the blues.

"Sing Before Breakfast" is the joyous song of ambition that Broadway hopefuls Eleanor Powell and Vilma and Buddy Ebsen sang on their tenement roof in *Broadway Melody of 1936* (1935) as they waited for that one big break. Arthur Freed (lyric) and Nacio Herb Brown (music) wrote the vivacious number, and Powell was featured and became a star with this, her second film.

"Sing Me a Song of the Islands" is a peppy Hawaiian chant by Mack Gordon (lyric) and Harry Warren (music) that has more than a touch of Broadway in it. Betty Grable, on a small boat heading back home to Ami-Oni-Oni Isle, sang the number in *Song of the Islands* (1942) about returning to the land of high hearts and a low moon, and the welcoming natives joined her in singing it.

"Sing, You Sinners" is the rousing revival number by Sam Coslow (lyric) and W. Franke Harling (music) and one of the first hits to usher in the swing era of the 1930s. Spunky Southern heiress Lillian Roth and aristocrat Skeets Gallagher, posing as a butler in *Honey* (1930), came upon a revival meeting where black plantation workers were celebrating, and before long the two joined right in and were leading the crowd. Then the youth Mitzi Green encored the number with the African-American children and the sequence climaxed with joyous singing and dancing by all. Coslow got the idea for the number after attending a Sunday night revival meeting outside of San Diego, and the lyric he wrote is sassy without being irreverent. Roth popularized the song on records and in clubs, as did vaudeville star Belle Barker. Other recordings of note include those by Duke Ellington's Orchestra (billed then as the Charleston Chasers) with vocalist Irving Mills, the High Hatters, Smith Ballew, the Columbia Photo Players, the Revellers, and Margaret Whiting. Tony Bennett revived the number in the 1950s, and Sammy Davis, Jr., did the same in the 1960s. Billy Daniels performed "Sing, You Sinners" in *Cruisin' Down the River* (1953), Susan Hayward sang it in the Roth bio-musical *I'll Cry Tomorrow* (1955), and Pamela Myers was heard singing the song in *The Day of the Locust* (1975).

"Singin' in the Rain" is that rare case of a song that is remembered more for its later appearance on screen than in its initial film. The delectable standard by Arthur Freed (lyric) and Nacio Herb Brown (music) has been featured in a handful of movies but was originally written for *Hollywood Revue of 1929* (1929), where Cliff Edwards and a chorus (which included Buster Keaton, Marion Davies, Joan Crawford, the Brox Sisters, and songwriter Brown himself) all in wet slickers sang the number in an artificial downpour. Jimmy Durante sang the song in *Speak Easily* (1932), and Judy Garland gave it a soaring rendition in

Little Nellie Kelly (1940). But it was Gene Kelly's five-minute song-and-dance treatment of the standard in *Singin' in the Rain* (1952) that will always remain the definitive screen version. It was also sung in that film by Debbie Reynolds and Donald O'Connor with Kelly. The jubilant song had its oddest screen treatment in the dark science fiction film *A Clockwork Orange* (1971), where it became a lietmotif for violence when sung by Malcolm McDowell. (The Kelly recording was played over that film's final credits.) Early recordings were made by Edwards, Gus Arnheim and his Orchestra, and the Frohne Sisters Quartet, and there have been many others over the years.

"Singing a Vagabond Song" is the crooning serenade written by Val Burton, Harry Richman, and Sam Messenheimer that Richman jauntily sang and danced in a cheap vaudeville theatre in *Puttin' on the Ritz* (1930). Richman recorded the ballad about being carefree and singing like a wandering vagabond, and he used it as his theme song on radio and in nightclubs for years. The Ritz Brothers did a parody version of the number in *Sing, Baby, Sing* (1936) and Van Johnson sang it in *Kelly and Me* (1957).

"Sisters" is the simple but delightful Irving Berlin song about the mutual affection and mutual rivalry of female siblings, much in the style of an old vaudeville soft-shoe number. Sisters Rosemary Clooney and Vera-Ellen (dubbed by Trudy Ewen) sang the number with large feather fans in a Miami nightclub in *White Christmas* (1954), and it was later reprised by Bing Crosby and Danny Kaye comically mouthing the sisters' record of the song. Peggy Lee made a memorable disk of the number, and real-life sisters Rosemary and Betty Clooney recorded it with Paul Weston's Orchestra.

"Sittin' on a Backyard Fence" is a coy production number from *Footlight Parade* (1932) in which Ruby Keeler, Billy Taft, and the chorus, all dressed like cats, sang and cavorted in a back alley. The number was supposedly a rehearsal, but it looked pretty polished the way Busby Berkeley staged it. Irving Kahal (lyric) and Sammy Fain (music) wrote the ditty, which was recorded by Paul Whiteman and Freddy Martin (vocal by Terry Shand).

"Slap That Bass" is an ingenious rhythm song by Ira Gershwin (lyric) and George Gershwin (music) that, urging one to play an instrument and fight off the blues, uses a mechanical beat to set the tempo. Dudley Dickerson and the other crew members in the boiler room of an ocean liner in *Shall We Dance* (1937) first sang the number (one of them actually playing a bass) then Fred Astaire sang it before he tapped, rapped, and danced to the the cadence of the pulsating engine set the beat. The lyric effectively repeated the word "zoom" to link up with the driving rhythm, and the whole sequence seemed like impromptu fun. Astaire recorded the song with Johnny Green's Orchestra, and in the

Broadway musical *Crazy for You* (1992) the number was sung by Harry Groener, Beth Leavel, Stacey Logan, Brian M. Nalepka, and the company.

"Sleepy Valley" is an old-time minstrel ballad by Andrew B. Sterling (lyric) and James F. Hanley (music) that was used effectively in the early sentimental musical *The Rainbow Man* (1929). On stage the minstrel singer Eddie Dowling started to sing the warm tribute to his rural home when he spotted his old love Marian Nixon in the audience, so he used the song to plead with her to return to him.

"Sleigh Ride in July" is the Oscar-nominated ballad by Johnny Burke (lyric) and James Van Heusen (music) that rues a lost love and regrets that one "didn't know enough to come in out of the moonlight." Saloon singer Dinah Shore sang the lament in *Belle of the Yukon* (1944), and her recording of the number was a bestseller. There were also notable disks by Bing Crosby, Tommy Dorsey (vocal by Bonnie Lou Williams), Les Brown (vocal by Gordon Drake), and most recently Mary Clare Haran.

"The Slipper and the Rose Waltz" is the pleasant fairy tale waltz from the musical fable *The Slipper and the Rose: The Story of Cinderella* (1977). The captivating number by Richard M. and Robert B. Sherman was first heard as dance music at the ball and then was sung as a duet by prince Richard Chamberlain and Cinderella Gemma Craven when they were alone. The Oscar-nominated song is sometimes listed as "He Danced With Me/She Danced With Me."

"Sluefoot" is the swinging dance song by Johnny Mercer that urged one to "put your posterior up" and dance as the college kids do. The number was sung by a quintet with Ray Anthony's Orchestra at a college dance in *Daddy Long Legs* (1955); then millionaire Fred Astaire danced to it with his ward Leslie Caron while all the college students sang it.

"Slumming on Park Avenue" is Irving Berlin's musical antithesis of his "Puttin' on the Ritz" (Stanley Green titles it "puttin' down the swells") in that the lower classes spy on the upper and sing satirically about their posh ways. The song's honky-tonk music also contrasts nicely with the sophisticated airs of "Puttin' on the Ritz," and the lyric is slangy and fun. The song was introduced as part of a Broadway revue in *On the Avenue* (1937), where Alice Faye and her tenement neighbors dressed up in flashy clothes and headed for Park Avenue. The song was reprised later in the film by the Ritz Brothers with Harry Ritz in drag and his brothers Al and Jimmy in top hat and tails. In addition to Faye's recording were records by the orchestras of Ray Noble (vocal by the Merry Macs), Red Norvo (vocal by Mildred Bailey), and Jimmie Lunceford. Both

Michael Feinstein and Andrea Marcovicci recorded the song with its opposite counterpart "Puttin' on the Ritz."

"Small Fry" is the unlikely hit song by Frank Loesser (lyric) and Hoagy Carmichael (music) that takes the form of a lecture about the sins of youth. In a bizarre routine in *Sing, You Sinners* (1938), family patriarch Bing Crosby (with a white beard) and wife Fred MacMurray (in drag smoking a corncob pipe) sang to their thirteen-year-old youngun' Donald O'Connor (in his screen debut) that he must stop skipping school to hang around the pool hall, smoke cigarettes, bet on the ponies, and engage in other sinful activities. Crosby and Johnny Mercer recorded the song together and it was a surprise hit. There was also a recording by Mildred Bailey that enjoyed some success.

"Small Towns Are Smile Towns" is the rosy tribute to rural America that Jane Powell, as the daughter of a small-town judge, sang in *Small Town Girl* (1953). The homey but not corny number was written by Leo Robin (lyric) and Nicholas Brodszky (music). Nat "King" Cole made a distinctive record of the song.

"Smarty" is the quick-witted ballad by Ralph Freed (lyric) and Burton Lane (music) that pleads with a loved one to stop being so heartless and get smart about love. Bing Crosby introduced the number in *Double or Nothing* (1937) and recorded it, as did Count Basie's Band.

"Smokey Mountain Boy" is the country music march that Lenore Rosenblatt and Victor Millrose wrote for the hillbilly Elvis Presley vehicle *Kissin' Cousins* (1964). Military officer Presley sang the easygoing number about returning to the hills (and girls) of his Tennessee home as he drove a U.S. Army jeep and senior officer Jack Albertson whistled along with the soldiers in the convoy behind them.

"A Snake in the Grass" is the jazzy and tongue-in-cheek number that Bob Fosse, as a snake dressed in a black lounge lizard outfit, shades, derby, and trademark dangling cigarette, sang and danced in the allegorical musical *The Little Prince* (1974). Fosse appeared out of nowhere in the desert and offered the royal youth Steven Warner an escape from the pains of life by providing a deadly sting that would end all his troubles. Fosse choreographed the odd number, his slick Broadway style looking rather incongruous in the barren setting as he leapt over rocks and sand dunes and even sprinkled some sand from his pocket before he went into a soft-shoe routine. Frederick Loewe composed the tango-like music and Alan Jay Lerner wrote the high-style lyric that noted "how relaxed you can be posthumously."

"So Do I" is the heartfelt ballad by Johnny Burke (lyric) and Arthur Johnston (music) that street singer Bing Crosby sang in *Pennies From Heaven* (1936) while Edith Fellows danced. The anxious serenade was recorded by Crosby (with Georgie Stoll's Orchestra), Tony Martin, and Eddy Duchin and his Orchestra.

"So It's Love" is a pleasing romantic ballad of discovery that Alice Faye sang in the Broadway backstager *You're a Sweetheart* (1937). Mickey Bloom, Arthur Quenzer, and Lou Bing collaborated on the number, which was presented as part of a Broadway revue.

"So Near and Yet So Far" is the driving ballad of indecision that Cole Porter wrote for *You'll Never Get Rich* (1941), using much of the melody from a song of his called "Kate the Great" that was cut from the Broadway hit *Anything Goes* (1934). Fred Astaire sang the song to Rita Hayworth as part of a servicemen's show, and then the two performed an entrancing ballroom dance sequence. Porter's music is a very compelling beguine, and his lyric wavers as it tries to determine the true feelings of one who seems so distant at times. Bobby Short recorded it, and Mary Clare Haran made a distinctive record of the song in 1994.

"Sobbin' Women" is the merry (if politically incorrect) narrative song about how the ancient Romans, anxious for feminine companionship, took the Sabine women by force. Backwoodsman Howard Keel sang the number to his six love-starved brothers in *Seven Brides for Seven Brothers* (1954), and the song encouraged them to abduct their six sweethearts from the town. Johnny Mercer (lyric) and Gene De Paul (music) wrote the lighthearted, country-flavored song, the title of which came from the Stephen Vincent Benet story that inspired the film. David-James Carroll sang the number in the 1982 Broadway version of *Seven Brides for Seven Brothers,* and it was sung by Edmund Hockridge in a 1994 British recording of the full score.

"Sold My Soul to Rock and Roll" is the inflammatory rock song by Gene Pustilli about the destructive camaraderie of sex and music. Rock singer Bette Midler (in her screen debut) sang the desperate number on stage in *The Rose* (1979), and the audience broke out in a riot after she finished the song and abruptly left the stage.

"Some Day My Prince Will Come" is the plaintive song of yearning that Snow White (voice of Andriana Caselotti) sang as she dreamt of Prince Charming in the legendary animated fairy tale *Snow White and the Seven Dwarfs* (1937). Larry Morey wrote the simple but poignant lyric, and Frank Churchill composed the operetta-like aria. The group the Jazz Networks recorded the ballad in 1996.

"Some Other Time" is an infatuated love ballad that playwright Frank Sinatra and showgirl Gloria De Haven sang in *Step Lively* (1944), the musical version of *Room Service*. Sammy Cahn wrote the potent lyric that admitted resistance was possible some other time but not now, and Jule Styne composed the old-fashioned music that was expansive and lush. Michael Feinstein made a notable recording of the ballad in 1991.

"Somebody From Somewhere" is the delicate lullaby by Ira Gershwin (lyric) and George Gershwin (music) that Scottish immigrant Janet Gaynor sang herself to sleep with in *Delicious* (1930), longing for the right man to come along. Perhaps because of Gaynor's thin singing voice the number got little attention at the time, but it was revived twenty-five years later by Shannon Bolin and enjoyed some popularity. Other notable recordings were made by Bob Clauser (vocal by Kenny Sargent) and Ella Fitzgerald.

"Someone at Last" is a simple-minded ditty that Ira Gershwin (lyric) and Harold Arlen (music) wrote to spoof empty-headed movie ballads of anxious longing. The number was a springboard for Judy Garland's tour de force one-woman satire in *A Star Is Born* (1954) in which she acted out for husband James Mason the entire plot and score of her latest Hollywood extravaganza. Jumping around their living room and using furniture, lamp shades, and pillows, Garland sang and enacted the tale of a Miss Lonelyhearts who traveled to Africa, China, Brazil, and wherever searching for a someone "who's the someone for me."

"Someone to Care for Me" is a ballad of wistful yearning by Gus Kahn (lyric), Bronislau Kaper, and Walter Jurmann (music) that was used in contrasting ways in the domestic musical *Three Smart Girls* (1937). Calculating gold digger Binnie Barnes sang the ballad (off-key) at a dinner party to catch the eye of the divorced Charles Winninger. Later that night his daughter Deanna Durbin reprised the song in her bedroom to show Winninger how the number should be sung. Durbin's recording of the ballad was her very first disk.

"Someone's Waiting for You" is the Oscar-nominated song of assurance written by Carol Connors, Ayn Robbins (lyrics), and Sammy Fain (music) for the animated adventure *The Rescuers* (1977). While kidnapped orphan Penny put her teddy bear to bed and hoped of being rescued, Shelby Fleet sang the tender lullaby on the soundtrack, encouraging her to be brave and be patient.

"Something Better" is the hopeful ballad that Barry Mann and Cynthia Weil wrote for the farcical adventure *Muppet Treasure Island* (1996?). Orphaned Kevin Bishop sang the heartfelt "I am" song with Rizzo the Rat (voice of Steve Whitmire) and Gonzo (voice of Dave Goelz) as they cleaned up the tavern and imagined a life of adventure rather than drudgery.

"Something Good" is one of the two songs written for the 1965 film version of the Broadway musical *The Sound of Music*, replacing the stage song "An Ordinary Couple." Governess Julie Andrews and her employer Christopher Plummer (dubbed by Bill Lee) sang the quiet duet after he proposed marriage to her, both of them wondering what good deed in their past accounted for their good fortune in finding each other. Richard Rodgers wrote both music and lyrics, his lyricist-partner Oscar Hammerstein having died in 1960.

"Something There" is a charming character song by Howard Ashman (lyric) and Alan Menken (music) written for the animated fairy tale *Beauty and the Beast* (1991). As Belle (voice of Paige O'Hara) started to see the Beast in a new light and even began to fall in love with him, she sang this restless and contemplative number with musical comments from Mrs. Potts (voice of Angela Lansbury), both noticing something there that "wasn't there before."

"Something to Shout About" is the robust title song by Cole Porter for the 1943 Broadway backstager in which chorus girl Janet Blair went on for the leading lady at the last moment and became a star. Blair sang the exultant number as a solo (the something to shout about was "something's that's known as love") and reprised it at the end of the film with William Gaxton, Don Ameche, Jack Oakie, Veda Ann Borg, and the ensemble. The musical was titled *Wintergarden* until the studio heard the Porter song and changed the title.

"Something's Gotta Give" is the hypnotic Johnny Mercer standard (he wrote both music and lyric) that points out the laws of physics that lead to love. The gentle swing number has a propellant energy that builds into a dance all on its own, and Fred Astaire, who commissioned Mercer to write it and introduced it in *Daddy Long Legs* (1955), sang and danced to the number while riding the crest of this energy. (It was the last song that Astaire made into a hit.) Millionaire Astaire sang the number to French ward Leslie Caron on a penthouse balcony, the two slid into a smooth pas de deux, and then the song continued under a montage of the two of them visiting all the chic Manhattan night spots. The Oscar-nominated number was recorded by Astaire, the McGuire Sisters, Sammy Davis, Jr., and Ella Fitzgerald, and all four records were hits. Joanne Woodward sang it in *The Stripper* (1963), it was performed by Fay DeWitt and Denise Nolan in the Off-Broadway revue *Nightclub Confidential* (1984), and Jessica Molaskey sang it in the Broadway revue *Dream* (1997).

"Somewhere in the Night" is the atmospheric ballad by Mack Gordon (lyric) and Josef Myrow (music) that Atlantic City gold digger Vivian Blaine sang in *Three Little Girls in Blue* (1946). The dreamy number enjoyed some popularity through recordings by Betty Jane Rhodes, Ginny Simms, Martha Tilton, and Dick Haymes.

"The Son of a Gun Is Nothing But a Tailor" is a frolicsome Gilbert and Sullivan–like number from the legendary comic operetta *Love Me Tonight* (1932), in which French aristocrats C. Aubrey Smith, Jeanette MacDonald, and various servants at the chateau expressed their dismay when they found out that dashing Maurice Chevalier was only a tailor. Richard Rodgers wrote the fussy music and Lorenz Hart provided the crafty lyric.

"Song of Surrender" is a torchy ballad by Al Dubin (lyric) and Harry Warren (music) that the Boswell Sisters introduced in the musical farce *Moulin Rouge* (1934). The Boswells recorded the number, as did the orchestras of Eddy Duchin, Wayne King, Ted Weems, and Emil Coleman.

"Song of the Marines" is the patriotic finale number by Al Dubin (lyric) and Harry Warren (music) for the military musical *The Singing Marine* (1937). Dick Powell and his fellow Leathernecks sang the hearty salute to the corps before they shipped off to action. The song was a radio favorite and enjoyed newfound popularity during World War Two. Powell recorded the number, which is sometimes listed as "We're Shovin' Right Off."

"A Song Was Born" is an ambitious musical sequence written by Don Raye and Gene De Paul for *A Song Is Born* (1948), in which the various origins of popular music are identified and performed. At the stuffy Totten Institute in Manhattan, several musicians and singers gathered to help musicologist Danny Kaye record the roots of American music, from Negro spirituals to jazz to swing. Nightclub singer Virginia Mayo (dubbed by Jeri Sullivan) helped with the experiment, but the number was a rare treasure because of the musical contributions of the Golden Gate Quartet, Louis Armstrong, Mel Powell, Tommy Dorsey, Lionel Hampton, and Benny Goodman all playing themselves.

"The Song's Gotta Come from the Heart" is the razzamatazz duet that ex-GI Frank Sinatra and school janitor Jimmy Durante sang in *It Happened in Brooklyn* (1947), citing sincerity as the key to all good performing. Sammy Cahn (lyric) and Jule Styne (music) wrote the the no-holds-barred number, which received an antic duet recording by Durante and Helen Traubel.

"Sonny Boy" was the first giant hit song to come out of Hollywood; in fact, it was one of the best-selling popular songs of all time. The sentimental standard was written by B. G. DeSylva, Lew Brown (lyric), and Ray Henderson (music) for Al Jolson to sing at various points in the melodrama *The Singing Fool* (1929). Entertainer Jolson held his three-year-old son Davey Lee on his lap on Christmas Eve and introduced the heart-throbbing ballad. Jolson reprised it later in the film when the youth was dying, and he sang it again at the climax of the musical when he collapsed in grief as he tried to perform the number on stage. An Irving Berlin song was originally recorded and filmed, but test audiences were not moved by the number and so Jolson phoned the illustrious Broadway team of DeSylva, Brown, and Henderson in New York to come up with a new ballad. Legend has it that the team, not particularly excited about the assignment, crammed as many mawkish clichés as they could in the song and called Jolson back in four hours, delivering what they felt was a joke. But Jolson loved it and so did audiences. Over three million copies of sheet music were sold, and Jolson's recording sold over a million disks. (When he recorded the song again in 1946, that recording also sold over a million copies.) The Andrews Sisters' 1941 record was another bestseller. Jolson provided the singing voice for Larry Parks when he sang "Sonny Boy" in *The Jolson Story* (1946) and in *Jolson Sings Again* (1949). In the DeSylva, Brown, and Henderson bio-musical *The Best Things in Life Are Free* (1956) the song was sung once again by Jolson with Gordon MacRae, Ernest Borgnine, and Dan Dailey (as the songwriting trio) joining in. The most recent recording of note is that by Mandy Patinkin in 1989.

"Soon" is the anticipatory but not overly eager ballad that Lorenz Hart (lyric) and Richard Rodgers (music) wrote for Lanny Ross to sing in the period musical melodrama *Mississippi* (1935). But Ross was replaced by Bing Crosby, who ended up performing the song in the film as a riverboat singer in the South, and recorded it as well.

"Soon" is the hopeful "I am" song by Jack Feldman, Bruce Sussman (lyric), and Barry Manilow (music) for the tiny princess in the animated fairy tale *Thumbelina* (1994). In her miniature bedroom, Thumbelina (voice of Jodi Benson) dreamt of meeting someone her own size someday. Later in the film the ballad was reprised with altered lyrics by her mother (voice of Barbara Cook) as she waited for Thumbelina to return home from her journey, hoping that soon there would be a happy ending. The number is notable for being a very rare film record of the Broadway diva Cook's crystal clear soprano singing voice.

"Sooner or Later" is the warm song of affection that Southern sharecropper Hattie McDaniel sang to Uncle Remus (James Baskett) as she fed him some of her fresh apple pie in a live-action sequence in *Song of the South* (1946). Ray Gilbert (lyric) and Charles Wolcott (music) wrote the pleasant number about the inevitabilities in life, and it was recorded by Sammy Kaye (vocal by Betty Barclay) and Les Brown (vocal by Doris Day).

"Sooner or Later (I Always Get My Man)" is the Oscar-winning song of seduction written by Stephen Sondheim for the stylized musical *Dick Tracy* (1990). Madonna, as nightclub vamp Breathless Mahoney, introduced the sultry number on stage wearing a slinky black dress and warning "you're mine on a platter." She was later heard reprising the song on the soundtrack during a montage of detective Tracy's raids on illegal operations across town. Rachel York sang the bluesy number in the Off-Broadway revue *Putting It Together* (1993), and the ballad has been recorded by Madonna, Karen Akers, Bernadette Peters, Karen Ziemba, and Jane Krakowski.

"So-o-o-o-o in Love" is the demonstrative song of romantic joy that show girl Vera-Ellen (dubbed by June Hutton) sang on stage with Cecil Cunningham and the Goldwyn Girls in the Danny Kaye fantasy *Wonder Man* (1945). Leo Robin (lyric) and David Rose (music) wrote the Oscar-nominated song, and there was a popular recording by Ray Noble and his Orchestra.

"Speaking Confidentially" is the breezy ballad by Dorothy Fields (lyric) and Jimmy McHugh (music) about not-so-secret secrets that Alice Faye, Frances Langford, and Patsy Kelly, as three workers in a mint-julep factory who are aching to be singers, performed in *Every Night at Eight* (1935). Langford was the only one of the trio to record the number.

"Spice Up Your Life" is the soft rock anthem from the novelty piece *Spice World* (1998) that urges "people of the world" to shake, slam, and dance their way to a spicier existence. The number was written by Richard Stannard, Matt Rowe, and the five British fashion icons of the group the Spice Girls, who sang it at London's Albert Hall at the end of the film. Their recording of the enthusiastic song was a bestseller.

"A Spoonful of Sugar" is the tuneful march by Richard M. and Robert B. Sherman that taught how to help the distasteful "medicine go down." Nanny Julie Andrews sang the catchy ditty in *Mary Poppins* (1964) as she snapped her fingers and magically made her charges' room tidy and then added sugar to their bedtime medicine, making all of life's unpleasantries fun. At one point in the song Andrews trilled away in duet with a chirping bird sitting on her finger. The number's music was used throughout the film as a kind of theme song for Poppins and her unorthodox ways. Burl Ives made a notable recording of the song.

"Spreading Rhythm Around" is the sleek, jazzy number by Ted Koehler (lyric) and Jimmy McHugh (music) that Alice Faye and Thomas "Fats" Waller sang in the backstage musical *King of Burlesque* (1935). The "smooth as satin" song was recorded individually by Faye and Waller with great success, and the number (with some additional lyric work by Richard Maltby, Jr.) was performed by the company of the Broadway musical revue *Ain't Misbehavin'* (1978).

"Spring Again" is the gushing song about the season when robins sing and it is time to fall in love. Kenny Baker, as a gondolier on a Venice movie set, sang the demonstrative number to Vera Zorina as they floated along a studio-created canal in the Tinsel Town backstager *The Goldwyn Follies* (1938). The film was scored by the Gershwin brothers but George Gershwin died during production and so Vernon Duke composed the music for the Ira Gershwin lyric.

"Spring Fever" is the harmonizing rock-and-roll travel song that Bill Giant, Bernie Baum, and Florence Kaye wrote for the Elvis Presley vehicle *Girl Happy* (1965). Chicago singer Presley and his group (Gary Crosby, Joby Baker, and Jimmy Hawkins) sang the sportive number about the fun and romance awaiting them as they drove down to Fort Lauderdale. At the same time coed Shelley Fabares and her two college classmates sang the number as they drove south to Florida for their spring break.

"Spring Is Sprung" is the sweet duet by Dorothy Fields (lyric) and Arthur Schwartz (music) that merrily welcomed the season of young love. Auto inventor Red Skelton and and his sweetheart Sally Forrest sang the upbeat ballad in the period musical *Excuse My Dust* (1951).

"Spring Isn't Everything" is the reflective ballad about love being not only for the young that Ralph Blane (lyric) and Harry Warren (music) wrote for the period musical *Summer Holiday* (1948) based on Eugene O'Neill's domestic comedy *Ah, Wilderness*. A touching scene where the Connecticut family patriarch Walter Huston sang the tender number to his wife Selena Royle was recorded and filmed but cut from the final print. Warren always considered the number one of his finest achievements and later published it himself. The indelible ballad was included in the 1948 recording of the film's score.

"Spring, Spring, Spring" is the melodic number by Johnny Mercer (lyric) and Gene De Paul (music) that joyously celebrates the time when "each day is mother's day" and all new things come to life. The bucolic song was sung by the six courting couples in *Seven Brides for Seven Brothers* (1954), and Mercer's expert lyric is filled with many lyrical animal references and cunning rhymes, including an amoeba that sings "Ach du lieber."

"Stand Up and Cheer" is the perky title song that moppet Shirley Temple sang in her screen debut in the 1934 patriotic musical. Six-year-old Temple performed the number with James Dunn, singing and dancing around him in a high-waisted polka dot dress. Not only did she become a star but even the dress was a hit and became the favored style for little girls. Lew Brown (lyric) and Harry Akst (music) wrote the sunny number.

"The Stanley Steamer" is the catchy travel song by Ralph Blane (lyric) and Harry Warren (music) that recalls Warren's earlier motion numbers such as "Chattanooga Choo Choo" and "On the Atchinson, Topeka and the Santa Fe." This jovial song was sung by Gloria De Haven, Mickey Rooney, Selena Royle, and Walter Huston as they all took a family auto ride through the Connecticut countryside after graduation ceremonies in the period musical *Summer Holiday* (1947). Jo Stafford made a notable recording of the merry song.

"Star!" is the Oscar-nominated title song by Sammy Cahn (lyric) and James Van Heusen (music) that Julie Andrews sang over the credits for the 1968 bio-musical of British stage star Gertrude Lawrence. The sparkling number, one of two original songs in a score full of Lawrence hits, happily lists the ways you can tell if a person is a star, from being "chicer than chic" to the number of fans that love her from the second balcony. Frank Sinatra had a successful recording of the swinging song.

"Star Eyes" is the dreamy ballad that Don Raye (lyric) and Gene De Paul (music) wrote for the musical farce *I Dood It* (1943). Bob Eberle and Helen O'Connell sang the number with Jimmy Dorsey's Orchestra, and their recording of the number was popular.

"Stars in My Eyes" is the expansive waltz that dressmaker-in-disguise Grace Moore sang in the period operetta *The King Steps Out* (1936). The music was written by Fritz Kreisler for the song "Who Can Tell" (lyric by William Le Baron) in the Broadway musical *Apple Blossoms* (1919). But Dorothy Fields wrote a new lyric when the song was put into the film, creating an enchanting romantic aria.

"Stay as Sweet as You Are" is the romantic request not to change that college student tenor Lanny Ross crooned in the campus musical *College Rhythm* (1934). Mack Gordon (lyric) and Harry Revel (music) wrote the oft-recorded ballad, which gave Jimmie Grier and his Orchestra a Number One hit. Other contemporary disks were made by Ross, Guy Lombardo and the Royal Canadians, Art Kassel, Little Jack Little, Jolly Coburn, and Archie Blyer. Frankie Laine's 1947 recording revived the ballad and Nat "King" Cole had success with it in the 1950s.

"Stay Awake" is the reverse psychology lullaby by Richard M. and Robert B. Sherman that nanny Julie Andrews sang to her charges in *Mary Poppins* (1964) to get them asleep after an exciting day of fantasy and adventure. Poppins sang of lively and stimulating things to do, urging the children to keep awake; but the music was soothing and warm and soon the two kids were in slumber. Louis Prima and Gia Maione made recordings together in English and Italian.

"Stay With Me" is the slow but pulsating rock song by Jerry Ragavoy and George Weiss about being left by a lover. Drugged-out rock singer Bette Midler sang the desperate number in a concert in her home town in *The Rose* (1979); soon after she collapsed and died.

"Step in Time" is the vibrant polka number that provided chimney sweep Dick Van Dyke, nanny Julie Andrews, and a crew of sooty sweeps to sing and dance on the rooftops of London in *Mary Poppins* (1964). Richard M. and Robert B. Sherman wrote the vigorous song that randomly chose words or phrases as an excuse to dance in time with the music.

"Steppin' Out With My Baby" is the contagious Irving Berlin song about painting the town red that inspired a memorable production number in *Easter Parade* (1948). As part of a Broadway revue, Fred Astaire sang the toe-tapping song with the Mel-Tones and the Lyttle Sisters and then launched into a cane-twirling tap routine. As the dance progressed, Astaire performed in slow motion while the chorus behind him was in regular time, a feat that took four weeks to rehearse and synchronize so that the sound and movement of each matched. The song was a popular favorite by Joe Bushkin and his Orchestra, the Three Suns and Gordon MacRae each made a successful disk of the number, and recently it was recorded by Mandy Patinkin and by Andrea Marcovicci.

"Stetson" was a routine chorus song about hats from Texas, but as filmed by choreographer Busby Berkeley (in his film debut) it was an important step in the development of the film musical. Gus Kahn (lyric) and Walter Donaldson (music) wrote the peppy number for the 1930 film version of the Broadway smash *Whoopee*, where it was sung by comic sidekick Ethel Shutta and the Goldwyn Girls. Then the chorines ducked behind a ledge where a row of stetons were sitting, each girl popping up and putting her hat on in closeup and smiling directly into the camera. It was the first use of a closeup in a musical to highlight individual chorus girls, a practice Berkeley (and others) would use for decades. Berkeley also dispensed with the practice of shooting a dance number with three cameras and editing the sequence together afterward. By insisting on a sole camera, he was able to control the focus of the musical numbers and allow them to build theatrically.

"Stiff Upper Lip" is the droll song that Ira Gershwin (lyric) and George Gershwin (music) wrote for *Damsel in Distress* (1937), giving very British advice on maintaining poise while doing such British things as "muddling through" and attempting to "carry on." (Years after writing the song, Ira Gershwin found out that the title phrase was Bostonian in origin rather than English.) Gracie Allen sang the satiric number at an amusement park in England and then joined George Burns and Fred Astaire for an inventive dance through a fun house, the number ending with the trio dancing in front of huge concave and convex mirrors. The farcical number was sung by Harry Groener, Jodi Benson, Stephen Temperley, and the company in the Broadway musical *Crazy for You* (1992).

"Still the Bluebird Sings" is the hopeful ballad that Bing Crosby, as showman Gus Edwards, sang in the bio-musical *The Star Maker* (1939). Johnny Burke (lyric) and James Monaco (music) wrote the optimistic song and Crosby recorded it.

"Stolen Dreams" is a largely forgotten ballad by Otto Harbach (lyric) and Jerome Kern (music) from the completely forgotten musical melodrama *Men of the Sky* (1931). Irene Delroy, as a French woman in love with an American flyer, sang the beguiling number at several points, turning it into the theme song for the film.

"Stop, You're Breaking My Heart" is the seriocomic duet that Ted Koehler (lyric) and Burton Lane (music) wrote for the daffy musical comedy *Artists and Models* (1937). Ben Blue and Judy Canova sang and danced the number in the film, and there were popular recordings by Hal Kemp (vocal by Skinnay Ennis) and Claude Thornhill's Combo (vocal by Maxine Sullivan).

"Straight From the Shoulder (Right From the Heart)" is the no-nonsense love song by Mack Gordon (lyric) and Harry Revel (music) that gently and simply expresses affection without embellishment. Princeton student Bing Crosby sang the ballad to fiancee Kitty Carlisle in the musical farce *She Loves Me Not* (1934), and Crosby recorded it, as did Hal Kemp and his Orchestra.

"Straighten Up and Fly Right" is the swinging song of advice by Nat "King" Cole and Irving Mills that recommends that one mend one's ways and get back on track. The popular wartime number was introduced by the King Cole Trio in *Here Comes Elmer* (1944), and Cole's recording sold a half million copies. The Andrews Sister also had a major hit with the song and sang it in *Her Lucky Night* (1945). Linda Ronstadt revived the number with a recording in 1986, Natalie Cole recorded it in 1991, and Diana Krall gave it a memorable interpretation in 1996. According to the younger Cole, her father got the idea for the lyric from his father, who was a preacher, who once gave a sermon about a buzzard who took a monkey for a ride in the air.

"Strange Enchantment" is the starry-eyed ballad by Frank Loesser (lyric) and Frederick Hollander (music) that Dorothy Lamour sang in the Jack Benny vehicle *Man About Town* (1939). Lamour recorded the love song, as did

Skinnay Ennis, Bob Crosby (vocal by Marion Mann), and Ozzie Nelson and his Orchestra.

"Streets of Gold" is the throbbing rock song by Tom Snow and Dean Pitchford that explains how New York City can be a hotspot of opportunity for those with the savvy to do more than just survive it. The street-smart canine Rita (singing voice of Ruth Pointer) and some back-up singers sang the number to the orphan kitten Oliver in the animated contemporary version of *Oliver Twist* titled *Oliver and Co.* (1988).

"Strictly on the Corny Side" is the hyperactive duet that adolescents Jane Powell and Scotty Beckett sang and danced to in teenager Elizabeth Taylor's mansion in the youth-oriented musical *A Date With Judy* (1948). Stella Unger and Alec Templeton wrote the robust hoe-down number that celebrated the joy of being a hick in the country, and Stanley Donen choreographed the vivacious dance routine. The song is sometimes listed as "I'm Strictly on the Corny Side."

"Strictly U.S.A." is the patriotic list song by Betty Comden, Adolph Green (lyric), and Roger Edens (music) from the period musical *Take Me Out to the Ball Game* (1949), itemizing everything from candied yams to Bing Crosby that means America. Frank Sinatra, Gene Kelly, Esther Williams, and Betty Garrett led the ensemble in the flag-waving hoe-down number.

"The Stuff That Dreams Are Made Of" is the merry list song by Sammy Cahn (lyric) and Vernon Duke (music) that chronicles all the domestic little things that mean true love. The upbeat song was performed by college footballer Gene Nelson and burlesque-star-turned-student Virginia Mayo at a faculty party in *She's Working Her Way Through College* (1952) as they demonstrated for the guests a number from the upcoming student show. Later in the film the song was reprised (with a different lyric) by the same two students dressed as Marc Antony and Cleopatra in the campus revue.

"Style" is the easygoing soft-shoe song and dance that racketeers Frank Sinatra and Dean Martin sang to milquetoast Bing Crosby in *Robin and the Seven Hoods* (1964) as they tried to teach him how to dress and behave in high style. Sammy Cahn (lyric) and James Van Heusen (music) wrote the catchy number, and the trio performed it with traditional straw hats and canes.

"Suddenly It's Spring" is the bubbly song by Johnny Burke (lyric) and James Van Heusen (music) that was interpolated into the score for the 1944 film version of the Ira Gershwin–Kurt Weill Broadway musical *Lady in the Dark*. Magazine editor Ginger Rogers imagined herself a bride on her wedding day in one of the film's elaborate dream sequences, singing the merry number with the

Joseph J. Lilley Choir and then dancing with Don Loper. But by the final cut by the studio, Rogers' vocal was eliminated and only the chorus was heard. Glen Gray and his Casa Loma Orchestra (vocal by Eugenie Baird) popularized the song and Hildegarde made a distinctive recording of it.

"Summer Magic" is the appreciative title song about the gifts of nature that Richard M. and Robert B. Sherman wrote for the 1963 period musical set in a small Maine town. The song was sung by Boston widow Dorothy McGuire (dubbed by Marilyn Hooven) to her children Haley Mills, Eddie Hodges, and Jerry Mathers on the steps of their new home in the country. The lullaby number was accompanied by nature footage showing the evening activities of the local animals.

"Summer Night" is the lush song by Al Dubin (lyric) and Harry Warren (music) that playboy James Melton sang to the stars in *Sing Me a Love Song* (1936). Melton recorded the enraptured number, as did Enoch Light, Abe Lyman (vocal by Sonny Schuyler), and Dick Stabile. There were popular recordings later by Hal McIntyre, Ralph Marterie, and Clark Dennis.

"Sunday, Monday, or Always" is the romantic standard by Johnny Burke (lyric) and James Van Heusen (music) that Bing Crosby introduced as songwriter Daniel Decatur Emmett in the bio-musical *Dixie* (1943). Crosby's recording of the fervent plea for long-lasting affection was his biggest wartime hit, though Frank Sinatra's later recording was even more popular. The ballad remained on *Your Hit Parade* for eighteen weeks and was featured in the films *Make It Big* (1944) and *Road to Utopia* (1945), where Crosby was heard singing it off camera. The George Shearing Orchestra also recorded the song, which was sung by Alvaleta Guess in the Broadway revue *Swinging on a Star* (1995).

"Sunny Side Up" is the buoyant title song by B. G. DeSylva, Lew Brown (lyric), and Ray Henderson (music) that urged one to "be like two fried eggs" and keep smiling. Janet Gaynor, as a poor girl from Yorkville, sang the number with her neighbors at a block party to Long Island playboy Charles Farrell during a Fourth of July celebration in the 1929 musical romance.The optimistic rouser was reprised by Marjorie White and Frank Richardson later in the film. In *The Best Things in Life Are Free*, the 1956 bio-musical of DeSylva, Brown, and Henderson, the number was sung by Gordon MacRae, Ernest Borgnine, and Dan Dailey (as the songwriters) with Sheree North. Notable recordings of the song, sometimes listed as "Keep Your Sunny Side Up" or "Sunnyside Up," were made by Earl Burnett and his Orchestra and by Johnny Hamp's Kentucky Serenaders (vocal by Frank Luther), the latter used on the soundtrack of the film *Paper Moon* (1973).

"Sunshine Cake" is the slaphappy song by Johnny Burke (lyric) and James Van Heusen (music) that taught one how to find happiness without finding money. Horse trainer Bing Crosby sang the upbeat number with sweetheart Colleen Gray and stable hand Clarence Muse in *Riding High* (1950) as they beat out the rhythm on coffee pots, frying pans, and other found objects. Crosby recorded the exhilarating song.

"Super-cali-fragil-istic-expi-ali-docious" is the nonsense song by Richard M. and Robert B. Sherman that is so nicely patterned rhythmically that the ridiculous title is memorable and even easy to remember. Julie Andrews sang the fun number, using the invented word to express her feelings after winning a horse race in a fantasy sequence in *Mary Poppins* (1964). She was joined by Dick Van Dyke and the Pearlies (animated buskers) and soon kids all over America were singing the ditty. Louis Prima and Gia Maione made recordings together in English and Italian.

"Sure Thing" is a beguiling ballad by Ira Gershwin (lyric) and Jerome Kern (music) that insists that one found a sure thing when one found a certain sweetheart. In a flashback sequence in *Cover Girl* (1944), entertainer Rita Hayworth (dubbed by Nan Wynn) sang the song with the chorus at Tony Pastor's in what Gershwin described as a "pre–World War One music hall number with a racetrack background." The two songwriters had written the number back in 1939, but Gershwin penned a new lyric for the film. Kern could not locate the sheet music nor could he remember the melody until his daughter, who did recall it, hummed it for him. The music is unusual in its length (an atypical twenty-eight measures) and in the way the refrain moves out of its key of E flat for four measures, creating an effective diversion. Alec Wilder considers it "one of the most American-sounding of Kern's later ballads." Glen Gray and the Casa Loma Orchestra made a notable disk of the song, and more recently there have been recordings by Mary Clare Haran and Andrea Marcovicci.

"Surprise, Surprise" is the Oscar-nominated song about the wonder of sex that Edward Kleban (lyric) and Marvin Hamlisch (music) wrote for the 1984 film version of their long-running Broadway musical *A Chorus Line.* Auditioning dancer Greg Burge sang about his sexual initiation and was backed by the other auditionees in song and dance. The pounding jazz number replaced the stage musical's song about adolescence called "Hello Twelve, Hello Thirteen, Hello Love."

"A Sweater, a Sarong and a Peek-a-Boo Bang" is the in-joke novelty number that Paulette Goddard, Dorothy Lamour, and Veronica Lake (dubbed by Martha Mears) sang in *Star-Spangled Rhythm* (1942), spoofing their Hollywood image. Later in the film Arthur Treacher, Walter Catlett, and Sterling

Holloway reprised the song in drag, spoofing the spoof. Harold Arlen wrote the simple, narrow-range music (only Lamour was a real singer), and Johnny Mercer penned the farcical lyric.

"Sweepin' the Clouds Away" is the lighter-than-air song by Sam Coslow that served as the spectacular finale for the early film revue *Paramount on Parade* (1930). Chimney sweep Maurice Chevalier sang the number on a Paris rooftop and was then joined by a chorus of comely sweepettes who danced and formed kalidescopic designs. The number climaxed with Chevalier ascending a ladder up to a rainbow, literally sweeping the clouds aside as he climbed. Chevalier recorded the song, and there were also disks by Glen Gray and the Casa Loma Orchestra (vocal by Jack Richman), Charles "Buddy" Rogers and his Band, the Photo Players, and the Coon-Sanders Orchestra. Helen Mack sang the number in *You Belong to Me* (1934).

"Sweet as a Song" is the crooning ballad that Tony Martin sang in the show biz musical *Sally, Irene, and Mary* (1938). The Mack Gordon (lyric) and Harry Revel (music) number was recorded with success by Horace Heidt and his Orchestra.

"Sweet Dreams, Sweetheart" is the loving goodnight song by Ted Koehler (lyric) and M. K. Jerome (music) that Joan Leslie and Kitty Carlisle sang as part of an all-star revue in the popular wartime musical *Hollywood Canteen* (1944). The Oscar-nominated ballad was recorded by Carlisle as well as by Ray Noble and his Orchestra (vocal by Larry Stewart).

"Sweet Is the Word for You" is a love song in which the quality of sweetness is applied to both a girl and a fruit. Bing Crosby, as the PR man in Hawaii for a Miss Pineapple Contest, sang the sunny number in *Waikiki Wedding* (1937) and recorded it as well. Leo Robin (lyric) and Ralph Rainger (music) wrote the ballad, and there were also recordings by Hal Kemp (vocal by Bob Allen) and Tommy Dorsey (vocal by Jack Leonard).

"Sweet Leilani" is the Oscar-winning ballad by Harry Owens that conjured up visions of an idyllic Hawaii to people across the nation and became the leading standard of the tropical island genre. Bing Crosby introduced the song in *Waikiki Wedding* (1937), and his recording of the number sold over a million disks. Composer Ralph Rainger and lyricist Leo Robin wrote the score for the film, but Crosby asked as a favor if Hawaiian bandleader Owens' song could be interpolated. "Sweet Leilani" became the biggest hit of the musical, outselling such popular competition as "Sweet Is the Word for You" and "Blue Hawaii." Pan flutist Kim Kahuna and the Royal Palms Orchestra made a distinctive recording of the ballad.

"Sweet Love Child" is a disarmingly tender song of seduction that Anthony Newley sang to innocent-looking Connie Kreski on a carousel before crudely ravishing her in the erotic fantasy musical *Can Heironymus Merken Ever Forget Mercy Humppe and Find True Happiness?* (1969). Newley wrote the flowing music and Herbert Kretzmer provided the double entendre lyric.

"Sweet Music" is the lyrical title song by Al Dubin (lyric) and Harry Warren (music) for the 1935 Rudy Vallee vehicle, an expansive ballad that championed the power of music. Vallee recorded the number, as did the orchestras of Will Osborne, Archie Bleyer, Lud Gluskin (vocal by Buddy Clark), Freddy Martin, and Victor Young.

"Sweet Potato Piper" is the tangy specialty number that Bing Crosby sang while Bob Hope accompanied him on the pipes and Dorothy Lamour strummed a guitar in the first "Road" film *Road to Singapore* (1940) as they entertained the Polynesian locales in order to sell their phoney cleaning fluid. Johnny Burke (lyric) and James Monaco (music) wrote the song about a piper whose sweet music could calm the savage and soften one's heart.

"The Sweetest Music This Side of Heaven" is the dreamy ballad by Carmen Lombardo and Cliff Friend that was introduced by Lombardo and Guy Lombardo and the Royal Canadians in the George Burns–Gracie Allen vehicle *Many Happy Returns* (1934). The song's title was used as the slogan for the Lombardo Orchestra for decades.

"Sweethaven" is the driving folk song by Harry Nilsson that opened the somewhat surreal musical *Popeye* (1980). The odd citizens of the seaside town of Sweethaven sang the number as they went about their daily habits, noting that God must love the town in order for it to keep standing at all.

"Swing High, Swing Low" is the rhythmic title song by Ralph Freed (lyric) and Burton Lane (music) for the 1937 musical, an alluring song that encouraged swing music as a prelude for romance. The chorus sang the number over the credits, and the song was recorded by Dorothy Lamour, the Ink Spots, Phil Harris, and Ruby Newman (vocal by Ray Heatherton).

"Swing Low Sweet Rhythm" is the mellow swing number that Walter Bullock (lyric) and Jule Styne (music) wrote for the airways backstager *Hit Parade of 1941* (1940). Frances Langford, as the co-owner of a small radio station, sang the agreeable rhythm number.

"Swing Me an Old Fashioned Song" is a clever swing number by Walter Bullock (lyric) and Harold Spina (music) that orphan Shirley Temple sang in *Little Miss Broadway* (1938) as she and the chorus gave a lesson on how to enliven old songs with the new sound. "Down By the Old Mill Stream," "In the Evening By the Moonlight," and other old-time favorites were jazzed up in the playful musical sequence.

"Swing Your Partner Round and Round" has the title of a country hoedown or a square dance number, but it was, in fact, an intoxicating waltz that Johnny Mercer (lyric) and Harry Warren (music) wrote for *The Harvey Girls* (1946). Waitress Judy Garland, Marjorie Main, and the Harvey girls tried to introduce the waltz to their small pioneer town with the song, but the result was a comic dance number that was as contagious as Warren's flowing melody.

"Swingin' the Jinx Away" is the jazzy song of optimism that Cole Porter wrote for *Born to Dance* (1936) and inspired the spectacular finale of the film. On a sleek art deco battleship, Frances Langford sang the breezy number with a male quartet in white military uniforms. Then Buddy Ebsen joined her and did an agile dance routine with the chorus. Finally, Eleanor Powell was spotted in the crow's nest, descended onto the deck by way of a catwalk, and then launched into an energetic dance that involved rapid tapping and cartwheels. Musical director Roger Edens later admitted the number "haunts me as an embarrassment of bad taste . . . but the audience loved it." Porter worked diligently on the music, studying American folk songs in order to achieve a pure American melody. The studio was not impressed with the number and after filming the elaborate sequence cut it out of the film and asked Porter to write a different song. He refused, and so they had no option but to reinstate it. The finale remains a wonderfully silly cliché that would be satirized for years after. The entire sequence was lifted and edited into *I Dood It* (1943) with a few closeups of Red Skelton spliced in to fool unsuspecting audiences. Langford made a notable recording of the song.

"Swinging on a Star" is the Oscar-winning song by Johnny Burke (lyric) and James Van Heusen (music), a clever and amusing list song that uses different animals to illustrate some of the seven deadly sins and merrily teach a lesson. Roman Catholic priest Bing Crosby and the Robert Mitchell Boys Choir sang the song on stage at the Metropolitan Opera House as part of an audition for a music publisher in *Going My Way* (1944). Burke, who got the idea for the song after hearing Crosby scold one of his sons for "acting like a mule," developed the list song, which was childlike but also poetic with the memorable wish to bring "moonbeams home in a jar." Van Heusen's music gently swings in a flowing manner and then stops abruptly on "mule," "fish," and the other animal names that end each musical phrase. Crosby's recording of the song with the Williams Brothers and the John Scott Trotter Orchestra sold over a million disks, and Crosby joined Betty Hutton, Dorothy Lamour, Diana Lynn, and

Arturo Cordova in a parody of the number in *Duffy's Tavern* (1945). Frank Sinatra sang it (with some lyric revision by Harry Harris) in *The Joker Is Wild* (1957), and it was performed by the cast of the Broadway revue *Swinging on a Star* (1995). Folk singer Burl Ives also made an estimable disk of the song.

T

"Take a Number from One to Ten" is the swinging love song by Mack Gordon (lyric) and Harry Revel (music) that coed Lyda Roberti sang in *College Rhythm* (1934) as she asked footballer Jack Oakie to guess about the quantitative state of her affections. Recordings of the ballad were made by Roberti, Oakie, and the orchestras of Tom Coakley (vocal by Kay Thompson), Art Kassel, and Jimmie Grier.

"Take It Easy" is the song of musical advice written by Dorothy Fields (lyric) and Jimmy McHugh (music) for the show biz musical *Every Night at Eight* (1935). Alice Faye, Patsy Kelly, and Frances Langford, as factory workers who have their sights on Broadway, sang the soothing swing number.

"Take It Easy" is the Big Band number that Albert De Bru, Irving Taylor, and Vic Mizzy wrote for *Two Girls and a Sailor* (1944), the wartime musical about a soldiers' canteen. Virginia O'Brien sang the number with Lina Romay, the Wilde Twins, and Xavier Cugat and his Orchestra.

"Take It From There" is the old-time romantic ballad from the period musical *Coney Island* (1943), where singer Betty Grable sang it on a saloon stage in a nostalgic picture-frame setting wearing a black Lillian Russell-like gown and was serenaded by a chorus of men in formal wear. Grable reprised the song later in the film as her audition for impressario Oscar Hammerstein and sang it once again from a Broadway stage at the end of the musical. Leo Robin penned the pastiche lyric that offered one's heart for further development, and the flowing music was by Ralph Rainger, one of the last songs he wrote before his death in a plane crash the year before. The song is sometimes listed as "I Love You to Take It From There."

"Take Me to Broadway" is the rhythmic number by Leo Robin (lyric) and Nicholas Brodszky (music) that inspired a clever dance sequence in *Small Town Girl* (1953). Clerk Bobby Van sang the number about his show biz ambitions and then performed a merry dance all over town that consisted of a series of energetic hops and bounces.

"Take My Hand, Paree" is the French pastiche number that country cat Mewsette (voice of Judy Garland) sang in the animated romance *Gay Purr-ee* (1962) as she yearned to be part of the high life of the big city. E. Y. Harburg wrote the heartfelt lyric and Harold Arlen provided the quaint Gallic music.

"Take My Love" is the lush love song written by Helen Deutsch (lyric) and Bronislau Kaper (music) for the arty version of *Cinderella* called *The Glass Slipper* (1954). Prince Michael Wilding sang the gushing ballad, which was reprised by Leslie Caron as Cinderella. Eddie Fisher's recording of the song was very popular.

"Takes Two to Make a Bargain" is the uptempo proposal of marriage that Broadway songwriter Bing Crosby sang in the backstager *Two for Tonight* (1935). Mack Gordon (lyric) and Harry Revel (music) wrote the jaunty number and Crosby recorded it.

"Taking Care of You" is the sentimental ballad that Lew Brown (lyric) and Harry Akst (music) wrote for showman Harry Richman to sing in the show biz musical *The Music Goes Round* (1936). The song was revived a half dozen years later when it was featured in *Stars on Parade* (1944).

"Talk to the Animals" is the Oscar-winning ditty by Leslie Bricusse that served as the theme song for the musical fantasy *Doctor Dolittle* (1967). Prompted by his parrot Polynesia, British veterinarian Rex Harrison sang about mastering the languages of the animal kingdom; he was joined in the number by the squealing and squawking of the various animals in his surgery office. Louis Armstrong and Sammy Davis, Jr., each made a notable recording of the popular song, and Bricusse's usual songwriting partner Anthony Newley recorded it as well.

"Tallahassee" is the echoing duet written by Frank Loesser that merrily extolled the joy of Southern living and, in particular, the town that is "Dixie at its very best." Alan Ladd and Dorothy Lamour sang the spiffy number in *Variety Girl* (1947), and there were popular duet recordings by Bing Crosby and the Andrews Sisters and by Dinah Shore and Woody Herman, as well as a solo disk by Loesser himself.

"Tangerine" is the pop standard by Johnny Mercer (lyric) and Victor Schertzinger (music) about an exotic gal from the Argentine who bewitches all who encounter her but whose heart belongs only to herself. The beguiling number was introduced by band singers Helen O'Connell and Bob Eberle singing the number as a duet with Jimmy Dorsey's Orchestra at San Francisco's Swingland Dance Hall in *The Fleet's In* (1942). The Dorsey-O'Connell–Eberle recording was a giant bestseller and dozens of other records followed, from the cool jazz version by saxophonist Boots Randolph to the choral ode by the Norman Luboff Choir. The ballad was revived in 1976 with a disco instrumental version by the Salsoul Orchestra, and it was sung by Brooks Ashmanskas and the company of the Broadway Mercer revue *Dream* (1997).

"The Tapioca" is a silly pastiche number by Sammy Cahn (lyric) and James Van Heusen (music) that spoofed the 1920s dance craze when a new step could be named for anything. Flapper Julie Andrews and her beau James Fox invented the song and the new dance in *Thoroughly Modern Millie* (1967) because she had had tapioca pudding at lunch that day.

"Teddy Bear" is the Elvis Presley hit from *Loving You* (1957) pleading to be treated like a pet toy that is pampered and loved. The rock-and-roll number was written by Kal Mann and Bernie Lowe and gas-station-attendant-turned-singing-star Presley sang it with a back-up group in a concert to the pleasure of screaming fans. Presley's record of the song, sometimes listed as "Let Me Be Your Teddy Bear," sold over a million disks.

"Tee Dum—Tee Dee" is the contagious march that Oliver Wallace, Ted Sears, and Winston Hibler wrote for the animated fantasy *Peter Pan* (1953). John (voice of Tommy Luske), Michael (voice of Paul Collins), and the Lost Boys sang the bouncy number as they set out to explore the island of Neverland. The tuneful sing-along song is also known as "Following the Leader" and "March of the Lost Boys."

"Tell Me Lies" is the bluesy torch song written by Randy Newman for the animated spoof of Hollywood called *Cats Don't Dance* (1996). The hard-boiled feline secretary Sawyer (singing voice of Natalie Cole) sang the moody lament about a lost love and a dream destroyed.

"Temptation" is the fuming romantic standard by Arthur Freed (lyric) and Nacio Herb Brown (music) that laments the bondage of love in a self-pitying manner. The driving ballad was introduced by Bing Crosby as he sang it weepingly in a Tijuana bar in *Going Hollywood* (1933). As he sang it he saw the face of his true love in his glass of tequila, and the number climaxed as he threw the glass against the wall and left the bar. Crosby's rendition of the song in the film and on record made him a top box office star in Hollywood. The throbbing ballad was also featured in the films *A Date With Judy* (1948), *The Seven Hills of Rome* (1958), and *Viva Las Vegas* (1964). Recordings over the decades include those by Mario Lanza, the Percy Faith Orchestra, Xavier Cugat (a very distinctive rendition), Artie Shaw, Perry Como, Red Ingle, Dorothy Kirsten, and the Everly Brothers. The most unusual recording was a novelty disk titled "Timtayshun" by Cinderella G. Stump (AKA Jo Stafford) with Red Ingle and his Natural Seven. Melissa Gilb sang the song in the Broadway musical version of *Singin' in the Rain* (1985).

"Ten Pins in the Sky" is the dreamy ballad sung by teenager Judy Garland in the domestic musical drama *Listen, Darling* (1938). Joseph McCarthy (lyric) and Milton Ager (music) wrote the wistful number, recorded by Clyde McCoy and his Orchestra.

"Tess's Torch Song (I Had a Man)" is the swinging lament by Ted Koehler (lyric) and Harold Arlen (music) about a gal who lost her man and her best friend at the same time. WAC lieutenant Dinah Shore (in her film debut) sang the blues number with a chorus of soldiers in *Up in Arms* (1944) as she entertained the troops on a transport ship in the Pacific. Later in the film Shore and Danny Kaye reprised the song in an antic scat version with different lyrics. Ella May Morse's recording of the song was a bestseller.

"Thank Heaven for Little Girls" is the opening and closing number for the musical classic *Gigi* (1958) and the theme song for the film as well. Parisian boulevardier Maurice Chevalier eyed the young girls in the Bois de Boulogue and sang of their charms as he imagined what they would be like when they grew up. Frederick Loewe composed the pleasant music, and Alan Jay Lerner wrote the expert lyric that wryly concludes with the observation that without little girls "what would little boys do?" One of the lyric's most potent images, about how a girl's eyes can "flash and send you crashing through the ceiling," was cut by Lerner because he thought it ridiculously hyperbolic; but Loewe convinced him it was appropriate to the song and it was reinstated. Alfred Drake sang the delectable song in the 1973 Broadway version of *Gigi*.

"Thank Heaven for You" was a droll spoof by Leo Robin (lyric) and Ralph Rainger (music) that allowed Rudy Vallee to poke fun at his own image in *International House* (1933). In a guest star sequence Vallee self-mockingly sang the sentimental number into his megaphone while W. C. Fields made wisecracks at every musical rest.

"Thank You, Mr. Currier, Thank You, Mr. Ives" is a nostalgic pastiche number by Johnny Mercer (lyric) and Harry Warren (music) that celebrated the idealized views of American life as illustrated by the famous team of lithographers. Salvation Army gal Vera-Ellen sang about the team in front of a series of Currier and Ives backdrops as she imagined living and dancing through the four seasons with Manhattan playboy Fred Astaire. The song is also known as "The Bride's Wedding Song."

"Thank You Very Much" is the Oscar-nominated song of mock appreciation that Leslie Bricusse wrote for the musical version of *A Christmas Carol* called *Scrooge* (1970). Londoner Anton Rogers led the ensemble at Scrooge's funeral in the sarcastic song, thanking the old miser for dying and making the world a better place. Scrooge himself, played by Albert Finney, watched the festivities and, unaware that it was his future funeral he was seeing, joined in the singing and dancing.

"Thank Your Lucky Stars" is the cheery title song by Frank Loesser (lyric) and Arthur Schwartz (music) for the 1943 star-packed wartime musical. Dinah Shore and the chorus sang the optimistic number as part of the charity show presented in the film.

"A Thankful Heart" is the uptempo Christmas song by Paul Williams that promises to "hold you close" with gratitude for the season. Michael Caine, as the reformed Ebenezer Scrooge, sang the song with various human and cloth citizens of London at the end of *The Muppet Christmas Carol* (1992).

"Thanks" is a gentle torch song by Sam Coslow (music) and Arthur Johnston (music) that takes the form of a serenade thanking the departed lover for all the happy moments now past. Broadway crooner Bing Crosby sang the ballad in the backstager *Too Much Harmony* (1933) and also recorded the number with Jimmie Grier's Orchestra. Records were also made by Will Osborne, Carl Brisson, and the orchestras of Victor Young (vocal by Scrappy Lambert), Meyer Davis, and Irving Aaronson and his Commanders.

"Thanks a Lot But No Thanks" is the comic list song by Betty Comden, Adolph Green (lyric), and André Previn (music) that rejects all kinds of material wealth (yacht, solid gold sink, Ford factory, the State of Maine) while waiting for "a faithful lad." Dolores Gray gave the song a slinky interpretation on a television program in *It's Always Fair Weather* (1955). Recently Sally Mayes and Judy Kaye each recorded the sly number.

"Thanks a Million" is the heartfelt ballad by Gus Kahn (lyric) and Arthur Johnston (music) that conveys appreciation to the beloved who "made a million dreams come true." Gubernatorial candidate Dick Powell sang the song in the 1935 political musical comedy of the same name, and there were recordings of the number made by Powell, the Mound City Blowers, Louis Armstrong, and the orchestras of Paul Whiteman, Johnny Hamp, and Paul Pendarvis.

"Thanks for Ev'rything" is the enraptured title song by Mack Gordon (lyric) and Harry Revel (music) for the 1938 musical *Thanks for Everything* about the world of advertising. Tony Martin introduced the ballad, and a later recording by Artie Shaw's Orchestra was Number One on the charts. There were also disks by Connie Boswell with Woody Herman's Orchestra and by Tommy Dorsey and his Orchestra.

"Thanks for the Memory" is the Oscar-winning song by Leo Robin (lyric) and Ralph Rainger (music) that is mostly known as Bob Hope's theme song. But the number is a smart and revealing character song and a musical scene that stands dramatically on its own. At a bar on the ocean liner *S.S. Gigantic* in *The Big Broadcast of 1938* (1937), ex-spouses Shirley Ross and Bob Hope (in his film debut) met again after a long separation and wistfully thanked each other for the good times in the past. The tone of the lyric is somewhat mocking, but there is a great deal of pathos and aching between the lines and the number anticipates the subtle tension not seen in musicals for another decade. It is arguably Robin's finest lyric, a superb list of everyday activities (rainy afternoons, crap games, beef and kidney pie, burnt toast) that seem mundane but develop into a very romantic statement. The song made Hope a film star and he used it on his numerous radio, television, and concert appearances for six decades. A recording by Ross and Hope was a bestseller in 1938, and over the years the song was recorded by Mildred Bailey, Shep Fields and his Orchestra, Michael Feinstein, and by Spider Saloff and Ricky Ritzel in 1989. The song was featured in the film *Thanks for the Memory* (1938) and was sung by the company of the Broadway revue *A Day in Hollywood—A Night in the Ukraine* (1980).

"That Foolish Feeling" is the song of romantic discovery that Harold Adamson (lyric) and Jimmy McHugh (music) wrote for the nightclub backstager *Top of the Town* (1937). Ella Logan belted the ballad with the energy of a battalion in the film, and a quieter rendition was recorded by Edythe Wright with Tommy Dorsey's Orchestra. The song is sometimes listed as "I Feel That Foolish Feeling Coming On."

"That Little Dream Got Nowhere" is the comic lament that Betty Hutton, as a gal who confesses to a murder she didn't commit, sang in the whodunit musical *Cross My Heart* (1946). Johnny Burke (lyric) and James Van Heusen (music) wrote the specialty number.

"That Old Black Magic" is the torchy standard by Johnny Mercer (lyric) and Harold Arlen (music) that has shown up in more films than perhaps any other contemporary number. GI Johnny Johnston sang the lengthy, bewitching ballad in *Star-Spangled Rhythm* (1942) as part of an all-star show while a scantily clad Vera Zorina danced amid snowflakes to choreography by George Balanchine. Glenn Miller (vocal by Skip Nelson and the Modernaires) popularized the song with their best-selling disk, but the number is most associated with Billy Daniels, who sang it in nightclubs for years and whose recording sold over two million copies. Arlen always credited Mercer's lyric for the song's success. It is a passionate piece of writing with the metaphor of a flame to express the power of love, for only "your kiss can put out the fire." But Arlen's music is brilliantly inventive, dropping a full octave three times in the song (which corresponds effectively with the lyric's "down I go, 'round and 'round I go") and sustaining long musical phrases with almost unbearable results. Alec Wilder notes that the song "has the longest pedal point (identical base notes) of any song I know . . . it lasts for fifteen measures." Among the notable recordings over the years have been those by Frank Sinatra, Keely Smith, Louis Prima, Sammy Davis, Jr., Bobby Rydell, and Julie Wilson and a spoof version by Spike Jones. Some of the Oscar-nominated song's film appearances include Bing Crosby (satirizing Sinatra) in *Here Come the Waves* (1944), Frances Langford in *Radio Stars on Parade* (1945), Daniels in *When You're Smiling* (1950), Lizbeth Scott in *Dark City* (1950), Sinatra in *Meet Danny Wilson* (1952), Marilyn Monroe in *Bus Stop* (1956), Prima and Smith in *Senior Prom* (1958), Jerry Lewis in *The Nutty Professor* (1963), and Ann-Margaret in *The Swinger* (1966). The number was sung by the ensemble in the Off-Broadway revue *Nightclub Confidential* (1984) and by Lesley Ann Warren in the Broadway revue *Dream* (1997).

"That Old Feeling" is the Oscar-nominated torch ballad by Lew Brown (lyric) and Sammy Fain (music) that concerns an old love rekindled when one sights a former flame from yesteryear. Virginia Verrill introduced the song in the fashion show musical *Vogues of 1938* (1937) and it proved to be one of 1938's most popular ballads in nightclubs and on the radio. Recordings were made by the orchestras of Shep Fields and Jan Garber, and Jane Froman sang the number on the soundtrack for Susan Hayward in the Froman bio-musical *With a Song in My Heart* (1952).

"That's Amore" is the most popular song to emerge from the many Jerry Lewis–Dean Martin films, this one written by Jack Brooks (lyric) and Harry Warren (music) for *The Caddy* (1953). Golfer-turned-singing-idol Martin sang the song to his mother and other family members at an Italian restaurant; Lewis joined him with his nasal singing, and then all the family sang and danced to the uptempo number. The psuedo-Italian ballad about the omens of love and food imagery (e.g., the moon hits you in the face like a pizza) is more satirized today than taken seriously, but Martin's disk at the time was a bestseller. The Martin recording was used on the soundtrack of *Moonstruck* (1988).

"That's Entertainment" is the sprightly song about show business that, thanks to the 1974 documentary of the same title about the MGM musicals, has become the unofficial anthem for film musicals in general. Howard Dietz (lyric) and Arthur Schwartz (music) wrote the sparkling number for the backstager *The Band Wagon* (1953), which used stage songs by the team for the rest of its score. Broadway producer Jack Buchanan wanted to present an arty musical version of *Faust*, but hoofer Fred Astaire sang to him that what the public wanted was escapism because "the world is a stage, the stage is a world of entertainment." He was joined in his argument by Nanette Fabray, Oscar Levant, and Cyd Charisse (dubbed by India Adams) as they took over an empty stage and acted out the various kinds of entertainment audiences will and will not accept. Schwartz's music is contagiously upbeat, and Dietz's lyric is filled with funny examples and outrageous rhymes, such as his description of *Hamlet* as a "ghost and prince meet" and "everyone ends in mincemeat." The song became popular again after the 1974 documentary; and in new footage for the 1976 sequel *That's Entertainment II*, an aging Gene Kelly and Fred Astaire sang it with a revised lyric. Lee Roy Reams made a snappy recording of the number with the Cincinnati Pops Orchestra in 1995.

"That's for Me" is the romantic ballad that Johnny Burke (lyric) and James Monaco (music) wrote for *Rhythm on the River* (1940), the musical about the songwriting business. Ghost songwriters Bing Crosby and Mary Martin sang the number together and Crosby later recorded it.

"That's for Me" is a graceful love-at-first-sight ballad by Oscar Hammerstein (lyric) and Richard Rodgers (music) that retains its romantic nature as it moves along in a sprightly manner. Vivian Blaine sang the number from a bandstand at the Iowa State Fair in *State Fair* (1945) and then fairgoers Dana Andrews and Jeanne Crain (dubbed by Louanne Hogan) reprised it. Rodgers' music is unusually structured with a short verse and an economic refrain that builds beautifully with Hammerstein's "I saw . . . I knew . . . I liked . . . I said," reaching a high E where the crucial word "that's" sits. Pat Boone sang the number in the 1962 remake of *State Fair*, and the number was performed by Ben Wright in the 1996 Broadway version. Notable recordings include those by Dick Haymes, Jo Stafford, and Kay Kyser (vocal by Mike Douglas and the Campus Kids).

"That's How I Got My Start" is the mock-striptease number that Southern chorus girl Mary Martin sang in the satiric musical *Kiss the Boys Goodbye* (1941) when she came to Hollywood to try to land the part of Scarlett

O'Hara in *Gone With the Wind*. Frank Loesser wrote the wily lyric and Victor Schertzinger composed the vampy music.

"That's How It Went, All Right" is the pop number that Dory Langdon Previn (lyric) and André Previn (music) wrote for the Hollywood backstager *Pepe* (1960). Guest stars Bobby Darin and Shirley Jones sang the number with Matt Mattox and Michael Callan in one of the film's many specialty spots.

"That's Southern Hospitality" is the sassy number by Sam Coslow that Phil Harris and his Orchestra performed at a furniture store Silver Jubilee show in the astrology musical *Turn Off the Moon* (1937). Harris was long identified with the song, which he sang on his radio show for years. Rudy Vallee and his Orchestra recorded the number, which is sometimes listed as "Southern Hospitality."

"That's the Rhythm of the Day" is the pulsating finale for the Broadway backstager *Dancing Lady* (1933) in which an unknown Nelson Eddy sang about the frantic life of the big city. The busy production number featured Joan Crawford and the chorus dancing, crowds rushing by, aged matrons getting youthful makeovers in beauty parlors, and other urban activities. Richard Rodgers composed the driving music, and Lorenz Hart penned the aggressive lyric about a city where love is electric and has its own beat.

"That's the Song of Paree" is the melodic tribute to Paris written by Lorenz Hart (lyric) and Richard Rodgers (music) for the innovative musical *Love Me Tonight* (1932). Parisian tailor Maurice Chevalier, Marion Bryon, George "Gabby" Hayes, and other neighbors sang the number, which utilized the sounds of cars honking, people arguing, and other city noises in the music.

"That's What Friends Are For" is the harmonizing chorale number, reminiscent of a barbershop quartet number, that was written by Richard M. and Robert B. Sherman for the animated Kipling tale *The Jungle Book* (1967). The Indian youth Mowgli (voice of Bruce Reitherman) came upon a trio of vultures (J. Pat O'Malley, Chad Stuart, and Lord Tim Hudson) who blend their voices in song and offer to help the young man-cub. Oddly, the three birds sported Liverpool accents, perhaps a passing nod to the popularity of the Beatles at the time. The song is sometimes listed as "The Vulture Song."

"That's What I Like" is the affable ballad that Bob Hilliard (lyric) and Jule Styne (music) interpolated into their Broadway score of *Hazel Flagg* (1953) when it was turned into the film musical *Living It Up* (1954). Dean Martin, as a doctor with questionable ethics, sang the number in the film, and the group Don,

Dick 'n' Jimmy made a popular record of it.

"That's What I Want for Christmas" is the altruistic song of selflessness that Shirley Temple sang in *Stowaway* (1936), tugging mercilessly at the heartstrings of audiences everywhere. Standing before a Christmas tree, the orphaned moppet sang that she didn't want model trains or expensive toys for the holiday but would rather have love and warmth for her foster parents and shoes for poor children. Irving Caesar (lyric) and Gerald Marks (music) wrote the unabashed number.

"That's What Makes Paris Paree" is the cheery tribute to the City of Light by Sammy Cahn (lyric) and Vernon Duke (music) that also lists several of Paris' shortcomings, from antique plumbing to overpriced clothes. American showgirl Doris Day and European diplomat Claude Dauphin sang the merry list song in a French restaurant floor show in *April in Paris* (1952).

"That's What Makes the World Go Round" is the tuneful song about survival of the fittest that Richard M. and Robert B. Sherman wrote for the animated legend *The Sword in the Stone* (1963). The wizard Merlin (voice of Karl Swenson) turned himself and his pupil Wart (voice of Ricky Sorenson) into fish and they swam in the castle moat and explored the world underwater. The lesson Merlin sings of has to do not with love but with understanding all the ups and downs and ins and outs of life.

"Theme from *New York, New York*" is the rousing hit song by Fred Ebb (lyric) and John Kander (music) from the 1940s pastiche musical *New York, New York* (1977) that praises the city as challenging but superlative and was one of the biggest hits to come out of the movies in the 1970s. The song's melody is first heard in the film when musician Robert De Niro at the piano in his apartment plucked out the tune as a song he was working on. Later in the film his wife Liza Minnelli reads to him part of the lyric she had written for the melody. An instrumental version was later heard on the radio and also in a jazz club. Then finally, near the end of the film, movie star Minnelli sang the full number, music and lyric, at a high class Manhattan nightclub. Minnelli's recording was a bestseller but even more popular was Frank Sinatra's 1980 record which so endeared the number to the city that it was made the official song of New York City. The number was sung by the cast of the Off-Broadway revue *And the World Goes 'Round* (1991). The reason for the lengthy title: so that the song would not be confused with the standard "New York, New York" by Betty Comden, Adolph Green (lyric), and Leonard Bernstein (music).

"Then It Isn't Love" is the intriguing musical lesson by Leo Robin (lyric) and Ralph Rainger (music) that teaches that pain and torment are signs of true love. Carole Lombard half sang, half talked the number in *Swing High, Swing Low* (1937). The songwriters originally wrote the song for Marlene Dietrich to sing in *The Devil Is a Woman* (1935), but it was cut. The number is often listed as "If It Isn't Pain Then It Isn't Love."

"There Goes That Song Again" is the reflective ballad by Sammy Cahn (lyric) and Jule Styne (music) that recalls an old love when an old melody is heard. Kay Kyser and his Orchestra (vocal by Harry Babbitt) introduced the popular song in *Carolina Blues* (1944) and recorded it as well. Other disks were made by Russ Morgan and his Orchestra, Sammy Kaye (vocal by Nancy Norman), Billy Butterfield (vocal by Margaret Whiting), and Kate Smith. Dick Haymes sang the ballad in *Cruisin' Down the River* (1953).

"There Goes the Ball Game" is the swinging torch song that band singer Liza Minnelli performed in a recording studio in the 1940s pastiche musical *New York, New York* (1977). John Kander wrote the breezy music, and Fred Ebb supplied the clever lyric that uses baseball imagery to describe a love affair that struck out and batted zero. Only a short section of the number was heard in the film, but the song was sung in its entirely by Brenda Pressley, Karen Mason, and Karen Ziémba in the Off-Broadway revue *And the World Goes 'Round* (1991).

"There Will Never Be Another You" is the delectable ballad by Mack Gordon (lyric) and Harry Warren (music) that bids a lover farewell, reflecting that there will be other songs to sing and other seasons but there will never be a true love like this one. Joan Merrill introduced the number with Sammy Kaye's Orchestra in an elegant Reykjavik hotel dining room in the Sonja Henie vehicle *Iceland* (1942). Warren's music is exceptionally well structured, ascending and descending in a way that makes for what James R. Morris calls an "almost geometrically balanced" melody. Alec Wilder describes the music as "sinuous, graceful, gracious, sentimental, totally lacking in cliché . . . it just may be the loveliest of all Warren songs." Dennis Day sang the ballad in *I'll Get By* (1950), and among the many memorable recordings over the years are those by Day, Woody Herman (vocal by Herman), Kaye (vocal by Nancy Norman), the Four Freshmen, Nat "King" Cole, and Chris Montez, who revived the song with his 1966 record. Most recently it was recorded by Ann Hampton Callaway.

"There's a Breeze on Lake Louise" is the light-footed song that Mort Greene (lyric) and Harry Revel (music) wrote for the musical melodrama *The Mayor of 44th Street* (1942). Band singer Joan Merrill sang the Oscar-nominated number with Freddy Martin's Orchestra in the film, and Martin recorded the song with success. The number is sometimes listed as "When

There's a Breeze on Lake Louise."

"There's a Fellow Waiting in Poughkeepsie" is the delicious character song that WAVE Betty Hutton sang in a U.S. Navy show in *Here Come the Waves* (1944), boasting about all the sweethearts she had left pining for her in different cities spread across the nation. Johnny Mercer wrote the sly lyric and Harold Arlen composed the sunny music.

"There's a Lull in My Life" is the popular torch song by Mack Gordon (lyric) and Harry Revel (music) that describes the emptiness one feels when a lover is far away. Radio advice columnist Alice Faye sang the lament with Ben Bernie's Orchestra on a radio broadcast in *Wake Up and Live* (1937), and her recording of the number was the biggest-selling disk of her career. Alec Wilder describes the song as "a very unusual and experimental ballad" where whole notes are interspersed with an eighth-note scale line and the release uses repetition (twelve repeated notes) with great success. Other distinctive recordings were made by Teddy Wilson, George Hall (vocal by Dolly Dawn), and Duke Ellington (vocal by Ivie Anderson).

"There's a Rainbow 'Round My Shoulder" is the Al Jolson specialty number that Billy Rose, Jolson (lyric), and Dave Dreyer (music) wrote for *The Singing Fool* (1928). Entertainer Jolson sang the song about the expansive feeling that love gave him, then decades later he recorded it again for Larry Parks in the bio-musical *The Jolson Story* (1946). The song was featured in *There's a Rainbow 'Round My Shoulder* (1952) and was most recently recorded by Mandy Patinkin.

"There's a Tear for Every Smile in Hollywood" is the poignant, cautionary song about the fickle nature of the film business that washed-up movie star Blanche Sweet sang to newcomer Alice White in the early Tinsel Town backstager *Show Girl in Hollywood* (1930). Bud Green (lyric) and Sam Stept (music) wrote the touching number that spoke of "a million dreams" that are born daily but "keep fading away." The song was beautifully delivered by Sweet, a silent screen star going back to the days of D. W. Griffith, who was herself going out of vogue.

"There's Danger in a Dance" is the elaborate finale number from the period musical *Coney Island* (1943), a lush song that warns of the romantic complications that can come from dancing with that certain person. Leo Robin (lyric) and Ralph Rainger (music) wrote it for saloon singer Betty Grable's big Broadway debut and Hermes Pan choreographed the lengthy number that included debonair New Yorkers out on the town, Southern plantation couples at a ball, and a colorful Latin American festival, the dancers all disappearing into the stage floor on ramps as each part of the dance ended. For one section of the number Robin wrote new lyrics for some old Stephen Foster favorites, continuing his theme of the dance as something perilous.

"There's Danger in Your Eyes, Cherie" is the oft-recorded love song by Harry Richman, Jack Meskill, and Pete Wendling that speaks of the irresistible and fatalistic nature of a woman's charm. Song-and-dance-man Richman sang the number in his New York nightclub in *Puttin' on the Ritz* (1930) and was the first to record it. He was followed by Irving Kaufman, Guy Lombardo's Royal Canadians (vocal by Carmen Lombardo), Sid Gray, Fred Waring's Pennsylvanians, Smith Ballew with Ed Lloyd's Orchestra, Vincent Lopez, James Melton, and others. Danielle Darrieux sang the ballad in *Rich, Young and Pretty* (1951).

"There's No Two Ways Around Love" is the languid ballad that Lena Horne sang in a nightclub in *Stormy Weather* (1943), taking the fatalistic view that there is nothing between being in and out of love. Ted Koehler wrote the chilly lyric, and Irving Mills and James P. Johnson collaborated on the easygoing music. Horne recorded the number with Cab Calloway and his Orchestra.

"There's Nothing Too Good for My Baby" is the uptempo love song by Harry Akst, Benny Davis, and Eddie Cantor that slyly claims one's sweetheart deserves the best but is satisfied with a gift from the five-and-ten store. Cantor, as an inept spiritualist's assistant who sings when he's nervous, introduced the number in *Palmy Days* (1931) and recorded the song with Leo Reisman's Orchestra.

"There's Something in the Air" is the dreamy ballad by Harold Adamson (lyric) and Jimmy McHugh (music) that Tony Martin sang in *Banjo on My Knee* (1936). Recordings were made by Martin, Ruth Etting, and the orchestras of Ray Noble (vocal by Al Bowlly), Mal Hallett, and Shep Fields.

"They All Fall in Love" is the first song Cole Porter wrote for the screen and was given to Gertrude Lawrence to sing in her film debut in *The Battle of Paris* (1929). Paris songstress Lawrence sang the witty list song in a cabaret filled with Yankee soldiers, mugging delightfully as she recounted the many types of Parisians who fall in love, from cold-fish types to "red-hot mammas." Because the film was so unsuccessful at the box office, Lawrence rarely returned to the screen, but the song became a favorite of nightclub performers.

"They All Laughed" is a delectable love song by Ira Gershwin (lyric) and

George Gershwin (music) that never once uses the word "love" (something the lyricist was very proud of). Ginger Rogers sang the uptempo ballad in a nightclub atop a Manhattan hotel in *Shall We Dance* (1937), and then she and Fred Astaire performed a competitive dance routine. At the end of the film the two of them briefly reprise the number at the same club. The music is jaunty and almost self-mocking and the lyric is a masterpiece of construction and wit. The title comes from the popular ad for music lessons that stated "they all laughed when I sat down to play the piano," but Gershwin turns it into a list of famous men (Edison, Columbus, Fulton, and so on) who were laughed at, comparing the situation to a new romance and ending with "who's got the last laugh now?" The lyric inserts "ho ho ho" and "hee hee hee" between the lyric lines so that the song literally laughs. Astaire recorded the number with Johnny Green's Orchestra, and there were notable recordings by the orchestras of Tommy Dorsey (vocal by Edythe Wright), Jimmy Dorsey, Ozzie Nelson, a duet version by Ella Fitzgerald and Louis Armstrong, and a more recent record by Michael Feinstein.

"They Call Me Sister Honky Tonk" is the sassy number that Mae West sang in *I'm No Angel* (1933), a sexy song with a psuedo-Arabian beat but a honky–tonk melody. It was written by Gladys DuBois, Ben Ellison, and Harvey Brooks, and singing vamp West delivered the number with suggestive ad libs ("do I make myself clear, boys?") and nasal moaning that led into musical notes. West recorded the song complete with all her characteristic asides and moans.

"They Can't Take That Away from Me" is the captivating list song by the Gershwin brothers and arguably the finest song they ever wrote for the movies. Fred Astaire sang the beguiling number to Ginger Rogers on a ferryboat to Manhattan in *Shall We Dance* (1937) as they contemplated their impending divorce. Ira Gershwin's lyric chronicles the little everyday details (how you sip tea, wear your hat, sing off key, and so on) that can never be erased from memory. The flowing lyric is inseparable from George Gershwin's music, which is concise and compact with no extraneous notes. In fact, the complete melodic statement is not completed until the release. The verse is also unusual in that it has a recitative quality, postponing melody until the last possible moment. The lovely ballad was nominated for the Oscar (George Gershwin's only nomination in his career). Astaire recorded it with Johnny Green's Orchestra, and other early recordings were made by Tommy Dorsey, Ozzie Nelson, and Billie Holiday. The song became even more beloved with time, and a later Frank Sinatra recording was the biggest seller of them all, while Sarah Vaughan's was the most unusual. Astaire reprised the number in *The Barkleys of Broadway* (1949), where he sang it to Rogers as part of a benefit show. Harry Groener performed it in the Broadway musical *Crazy for You* (1992).

"They Met in Rio" is the entrancing serenade by Mack Gordon (lyric) and Harry Warren (music) that was featured in the south-of-the-border romance *That Night in Rio* (1941). Nightclub crooner Don Ameche (in his first musical role) sang the Latin number in Portuguese in a ritzy bar with a group of guitar-strumming men backing him up. Then wealthy patron Alice Faye picked up the song, singing in English about a romance in Rio de Janeiro.

"They're Either Too Old or Too Young" is the comic lament written by Frank Loesser (lyric) and Arthur Schwartz (music) about the shortage of men on the home front during World War Two and how difficult romance was for the women left behind. Betty Davis introduced the ingenious number in *Thank Your Lucky Stars* (1943) as part of a charity show and then demonstrated the problem by jitterbugging with the youth Conrad Wiedell and singing to the elderly Jack Norton. Loesser's lyric is suggestive and playful, noting that whatever is good is in the Army and what is left "cannot harm me." The Oscar-nominated song had a hit recording by Jimmy Dorsey (vocal by Kitty Kallen), Jane Froman sang it on the soundtrack for Susan Hayward in the bio-musical *With a Song in My Heart* (1952), and it was also recorded by Hildegarde, Pearl Bailey, and more recently Andrea Marcovicci.

"Things Are Looking Up" is the jovial song by the Gershwin brothers that describes the sensation of a newfound love. American hoofer Fred Astaire sang the jaunty number to British heiress Joan Fontaine in *Damsel in Distress* (1937) as they skipped through the estate of Totleigh Castle. The sequence then turned into a dance of sorts as Astaire pranced through the scenery while nondancer Fontaine's footwork was disguised by bushes, fences, and other convenient props. Ira Gershwin took a familiar expression and turned it into an entrancing lyric, and George Gershwin composed the fleet-footed music, the release being particularly notable, according to Alec Wilder, for being "strictly based on repeated notes and is a minor masterpiece of understated invention." Astaire recorded the song, which was later sung by Harry Groener in the Broadway musical *Crazy for You* (1992).

"The Things I Want" is the superb music hall number that riverboat chanteuse Dorothy Lamour sang to farmer Randolph Scott, Alan Hale, and other patrons in the pioneer musical *High, Wide and Handsome* (1937). Jerome Kern composed the blues music and Oscar Hammerstein wrote the caustic lyric about material possessions.

"Think Pink" is the sparkling song by Leonard Gershe (lyric) and Roger Edens (music) that was interpolated into the Gershwins' score for the 1957 film musical *Funny Face* (1957). Fashion magazine editor Kay Thompson sang the opening number about the latest trend for all things pink in clothing, and the melody was used throughout the film as a leitmotif for the fashion business.

"This Heart of Mine" is the enchanting ballad by Arthur Freed (lyric) and Harry Warren (music) that inspired a self-contained mini-musical in the revue *Ziegfeld Follies* (1946). At a formal embassy ball, top-hatted jewel thief Fred Astaire's intended victim was the lovely Lucille Bremer, but when he met her the smitten thief sang to her how she has stolen his heart and sent it dancing. The two went into an entrancing dance together, he subtly stole her bracelet, she guessed his intentions and gave him her bejeweled necklace, and the two continued dancing into the night. The twelve-minute sequence was choreographed by Robert Alton (at one point Astaire and Bremer were dancing on conveyor belts moving in opposite directions) and remains, as described by Rick Altman, "one of the [American film] musical's most elegant narrative dances." Judy Garland made a notable recording of the ballad, and the song was used effectively as background in *The Barkeleys of Broadway* (1949). Most recently it was recorded by Mary Clare Haran.

"This Is Always" is a ballad of long-lasting commitment that Mack Gordon (lyric) and Harry Warren (music) wrote for the period musical *Three Little Girls in Blue* (1946). Atlantic City gold digger June Haver introduced the song, and there were subsequent recordings made by Dick Haymes, Jo Stafford, Harry James (vocal by Buddy Di Vito), Ginny Simms, and Betty Rhodes.

"This Is Halloween" is the pulsating holiday song written by Danny Elfman for the stop-action musical fantasy *The Nightmare Before Christmas* (1993). In the opening number of the film, the ghoulish residents of Halloween Town celebrated another successfully ghastly October 31 with this insistent and stirring song that rarely departed from a series of repeated notes.

"This Is My Night to Dream" is the starry-eyed ballad by Johnny Burke (lyric) and James Monaco (music) that doctor Bing Crosby crooned in *Doctor Rhythm* (1938) and also recorded with success. The song is most associated with bandleader Abe Lyman, who recorded it and featured it on his radio show. Years later Nat "King" Cole made a distinctive recording of the ballad.

"This Is the Beginning of the End" is the torchy list song by Frank Loesser (lyric) and Alfred Newman (music) that warns of the unmistakable signs that a romance is waning. Dorothy Lamour sang the number for a group of patrons at the Club Paradise in the melodrama *Johnny Apollo* (1940). Lamour recorded the ballad, as did Tommy Dorsey (vocal by Frank Sinatra), Buddy Clark, and Al Donahue (vocal by Paula Kelly), and it was revived in 1952 with a Don Cornell record.

"This Is the Moment" is the expansive psuedo-aria written by Leo Robin (lyric) and Frederick Hollander (music) for the period operetta *That Lady in Ermine* (1948). The Oscar-nominated ballad was sung by European countess Betty Grable, a rare foray into the operetta genre for the leggy performer.

"This Is the Night" is the enchanting title ballad by Sam Coslow (lyric) and Ralph Rainger (music) for the 1932 musical comedy of manners. American Lily Damita stared down from her Venice balcony at gondolier Donald Novis, who sang the song in Italian; then the number was picked up by American playboy Roland Young walking below, who sang it in English to the lady above.

"This Is Where I Came In" is the wise, self-knowing ballad by Walter Bullock (lyric) and Harold Spina (music) that realizes the affair is over when one is dancing to the same music that one started with. Singing manicurist Alice Faye sang the engaging number in *Sally, Irene and Mary* (1938) as she grew tired of the love merry-go-round and concluded, "I'd rather be lonely."

"This Isn't Heaven" is the smooth ballad that reporter Bobby Darrin sang to farmgirl Pamela Tiffin in the 1962 remake of *State Fair* where he acknowledged she was not an angel but theirs was true love all the same. Richard Rodgers wrote both music and lyric for the number, his lyricist partner Oscar Hammerstein having died two years before.

"This Time the Dream's on Me" is the blues standard by Johnny Mercer (lyric) and Harold Arlen (music) that band singer Priscilla Lane introduced in the musical melodrama *Blues in the Night* (1941). The bittersweet ballad about the need for romantic fantasy in life has received many notable recordings over the years, among them disks by Woody Herman (vocal by Herman), Glenn Miller (vocal by Ray Eberle), Ella Fitzgerald, and Julie Wilson. The number has always been a favorite of jazz musicians, and alto saxophonist Charlie "Bird" Parker made a distinctive recording that was used on the soundtrack of the bio-musical *Bird* (1988). Margaret Whiting, Lesley Ann Warren, and John Pizzarelli sang the ballad in the Broadway revue *Dream* (1997).

"This Year's Kisses" is the languid but spirited ballad by Irving Berlin that dismisses new lovers because they do not compare favorably to a true love of the past. Broadway star Alice Faye sang the number at a rehearsal in *On the Avenue* (1937) as she leaned against the proscenium arch and sighed that she was "still wearing last year's love." Faye recorded the alluring ballad.

"Thoroughly Modern Millie" is the vivacious Oscar-nominated song by Sammy Cahn (lyric) and James Van Heusen (music) and the title number for the 1967 pastiche musical about flappers in the 1920s. Julie Andrews sang the razzamatazz ditty about a free-thinking gal who bobbed her hair and raised her skirts, during the opening and closing credits of the film. Louis Armstrong made a scintillating recording of the song.

"The Three Caballeros" is the hyperactive title song for the 1945 musical travelogue that used animation and live action to explore the exotic side of South America. Manuel Esperon wrote the rapid Latin music, and Ray Gilbert adapted Ernesto Cortazar's Spanish lyric in which Donald Duck (voice of Clarence Nash) and his feathered friends Joe Carioca (voice of José Olivera) and Panchito (voice of Joaquin) introduced themselves and professed their friendship. The animated sequence was filled with visual slapstick and furious comic bits that hilariously illustrated the lyric. Bing Crosby recorded the number with the Andrews Sisters, and the song was performed by Jack Weston, F. Murray Abraham, and Paul B. Price in a gay bathhouse in the farce *The Ritz* (1976).

"Three Little Sisters" is the harmonizing swing number that the Andrews Sisters sang in the war effort musical *Private Buckaroo* (1942). Irving Taylor and Vic Mizzy wrote the tailormade number about sisterhood. The Sisters recorded it, as did Vaughn Monroe and Horace Heidt and his Orchestra.

"Three Little Words" is the breezy standard by Bert Kalmar (lyric) and Harry Ruby (music) that celebrated the importance of the phrase "I love you." The song was introduced by the Rhythm Boys (Bing Crosby, Harry Barris, and Al Rinker) with Duke Ellington's Orchestra in the Amos and Andy vehicle *Check and Double Check* (1930). The producers thought so little of the song that they tried to cut it, but it ended up on the soundtrack only, heard in the background during a birthday party. But the Ellington–Rhythm Boys record went to the top of the charts, and best-selling recordings by Ethel Waters, Rudy Vallee, and Patti Page over the years kept the song popular. In the Kalmar-Ruby bio-musical *Three Little Words* (1950), the song was sung by Fred Astaire and Red Skelton as the two songwriters.

"Three Times a Day" is a comic song of seduction that Leo Robin (lyric) and Richard Whiting (music) wrote for the frothy comedy of manners *One Hour With You* (1932). Physician Maurice Chevalier musically recommends to his patient Genevieve Tobin that a certain tonic be taken thrice daily, and she responds by asking to see the doctor three times a day for romance

"Through a Thousand Dreams" is the gushing ballad that Leo Robin (lyric) and Arthur Schwartz (music) wrote for the backstager *The Time, the Place and the Girl* (1946). Dennis Morgan and Martha Vickers introduced the number with Carmen Cavallaro at the piano, and there were notable recordings by Jo Stafford and by the orchestras of Desi Arnez and George Olsen.

"Thumbelina" is the simple children's ditty that Frank Loesser wrote for the bio-musical *Hans Christian Andersen* (1952), a narrative song about the miniature princess, who learns if your "heart is full of love, you're nine feet tall." Danny Kaye, as the Danish storyteller, sang the number from a window in his jail cell to a little girl outside, turning his thumb into the princess and acting out the story. Kaye recorded the Oscar-nominated song with Gordon Jenkins' Orchestra.

"Thunder Over the Prairie" is the lyrical love duet sung by government agent John Boles and spy Gladys Swarthout (backed by a chorus of Spanish guitarists) in the operetta *Rose of the Rancho* (1935). Leo Robin (lyric) and Ralph Rainger (music) wrote the lush number, which was recorded by Isham Jones (vocal by Woody Herman).

"Ticket to Ride" is the lighthearted rock song by John Lennon about a gal who has the freedom to travel and see life but "she don't care." It was written and recorded for the Beatles' second film, *Help* (1965), but was released as a single before the film opened, the disk identifying the number as written for *Eight Arms to Hold You*, the title of the film until it was changed at the last minute. In the movie the foursome were heard singing the song on the soundtrack during a skiing escapade in the Austrian Alps, the Liverpool lads falling down a lot (which was spontaneous, since none of them could actually ski) and cavorting in the snow. Years later Lennon described the song as "one of the earliest heavy metal records made" because of, as Steve Turner describes, its "insistent, clanking riff underpinned by a heavy drum beat." In England many fans thought the title referred to a train ticket to the town of Ryde on the Isle of Wight. The Beatles' single went to the Number One spot on the charts, and in 1970 the Carpenters recorded it with success.

"Tico-Tico" is the contagious Latin number that arrived in the United States from Brazil in the early 1940s and found recognition when interpolated into the animated travelogue musical *Saludos Amigos* (1942). Zequinha Abreu composed the festive music, Ervin Drake adapted Aloysio de Oliveira's Portuguese lyric, and Oliviera sang it on the soundtrack while Donald Duck and Joe Carioca visited a carnival in Rio de Janeiro. The number appeared in a number of films in the 1940s, including *Thousands Cheer* (1943), where it was danced to by Maxine Barrett and Don Loper; *Bathing Beauty* (1944). where organist Ethel Smith played it with Xavier Cugat's Orchestra and the song was long associated with her; as background in *Kansas City Kitty* (1944); and *Copacabana* (1947), where Carmen Miranda sang it. Popular recording were made by Smith, Miranda, Charles Wolcott and his Orchestra, and the Andrews Sisters.

"Till the End of Time" is the popular serenade that was fashioned out of one of Chopin's works and used as a romantic song in the classical bio-musical *A Song to Remember* (1945). Buddy Kaye and Ted Mossman adapted Chopin's "Polonaise in A Flat Major" (Opus 53) and supplied the hyperbolic lyric, which was sung in the background in the film. The ballad immediately caught on and remained on *Your Hit Parade* for nineteen weeks (seven of them in the Number One spot) thanks to recordings by Perry Como (which sold over two million disks), Les Brown (vocal by Doris Day), and Dick Haymes. The number was used as the theme song for the melodrama *Till the End of Time* (1946).

"Time After Time" is the beguiling ballad by Sammy Cahn (lyric) and Jule Styne (music) that pledges to repeat over and over how fortunate it is to be in love. Frank Sinatra sang the number in Jimmy Durante's apartment in *It Happened in Brooklyn* (1947) as a lyric he has just written to go with Peter Lawford's music. The number was reprised by Kathryn Grayson later in the film. The music is hauntingly memorable, Alec Wilder proclaiming it Styne's best song, with "a strong, pure, dramatic, uncluttered, unselfconscious melody." Sinatra's recording was very popular, and the ballad was revived in the 1960s with records by Frankie Ford, Sarah Vaughan with Teddy Wilson, and Chris Montez. More recently it has been recorded by Valerie Carr, Johnny Mathis, Michael Feinstein, Carly Simon, and Judy Kuhn.

"Time and Time Again" is the enraptured ballad by Earl Brent and Fred Spielman from the ocean liner romance *Nancy Goes to Rio* (1950). Jane Powell, as an actress fighting with her mother over the same part and the same man (Barry Sullivan), sang the song about how consistent her love will always be.

"The Time for Parting" is the hymnlike farewell song that GIs Gene Kelly, Dan Dailey, and Michael Kidd (dubbed by Jud Conlin) sang (with some assist by David Burns) in *It's Always Fair Weather* (1955) as they pledged to meet again in ten years and rekindle their friendship. Betty Comden, Adolph Green (lyric), and André Previn (music) wrote the harmonic trio.

"Tip Toe Through the Tulips With Me" is the naive love song that sold millions of copies of sheet music and has remained one of the most recognized of all American popular songs. Al Dubin (lyric) and Joseph Burke (music) wrote the catchy ditty for *Gold Diggers of Broadway* (1929), where Nick Lucas sang it in a big production number, inviting a sleeping girl to tip toe out of her bed and into the garden, where they can kiss amidst the tulips in the moonlight. Lucas recorded the song, and the old disk was used on the soundtrack of *The Great Gatsby* (1974). Jean Goldkette's Orchestra (vocal by Frank Munn) was also popular in the 1930s. The song was featured in the film *Painting the Clouds With Sunshine* (1951), where it was sung by Lucille Norman, Virginia

Mayo, Virginia Gibson, and Gene Nelson and was revived in 1968 by a popular recording by Tiny Tim.

"Tired of It All" is the languid lament by Bert Kalmar (lyric) and Harry Ruby (music) that Ruth Etting sang in the musical farce *Hips, Hips, Hooray* (1934). Etting recorded the ballad, as did the Glen Gray and the Casa Lama Orchestra (vocal by Kenny Sargent) and George Hall and his Orchestra.

"Today I Love Ev'rybody" is the exuberant number that Dorothy Fields (lyric) and Harold Arlen (music) wrote for the period musical *The Farmer Takes a Wife* (1953). Betty Grable, as a cook on a boat on the Erie Canal, walked the streets of Rome, New York, and sang the joyous song that offered indiscriminate affection because "everybody loves me." She was joined by the children of the town in singing the song, and at the end of the film Grable and the kids reprised it on her wedding day.

"Tom Sawyer" is the robust title song by Richard M. and Robert B. Sherman for the 1973 film musical of the Mark Twain classic. Celeste Holm, as Aunt Polly, sang the number with Joshua Hill Lewis and Susan Joyce, about the mischievous nature of the youth Tom (Johnny Whitaker).

"Tom Thumb's Tune" is the merry "I am" song by Peggy Lee for the miniature hero of *Tom Thumb* (1958), a musicalization of the famous Grimm fairy tale. Russ Tamblyn, as the energetic Tom, and the chorus sang the number about the freewheeling little man.

"Tom, Tom the Piper's Son" is a bouncy little ditty by E. Y. Harburg (lyric) and Burton Lane (music) about a lad who stole a tune and how he turned it into a hit record. Struggling actress Judy Garland sang the swinging number at a highbrow party in an Indiana town in the backstager *Presenting Lily Mars* (1943).

"Tomorrow" is the superb blues song that Paul Williams wrote for the all-kids musical *Bugsy Malone* (1976). The hired hand Fizzy (played by Albin Jenkins and singing dubbed by Archie Hahn), who dreamt of being a dancer, swept the floor of the speakeasy and sang of his bleak future while the chorus girl Velma (Vivienne McKane) slowly danced in the background. The captivating number is alarmingly potent without being mawkish. Fizzy saw tomorrow as "a resting place for bums, a trap set in the slums" and pessimistically noted "tomorrow never comes." Ethan Modden describes the sequence as "one of the best four or five minutes of song and dance produced in the 1970s." The song is a startling antithesis to the popular ballad of the same name from *Annie* that was written the next year, both sung by poor children in the Depression looking to the future.

"Tomorrow Is Another Day" is the optimistic number by Bud Green (lyric) and Sam Stept (music) that Al Jolson sang in *Big Boy* (1930). The happy-go-lucky jockey Gus (Jolson in blackface), on the night before he has to fight a duel, recalled the song his Mammy sang to him when he was a child and burst into the cheery ballad. At the end of the film Jolson dropped character (and the blackface) and reprised the song.

"Tomorrow Is Another Day" is the upbeat ballad that used the by-then popular phrase from the novel *Gone With the Wind* to make its hopeful point. Gus Kahn (lyric), Walter Jurmann, and Bronislau Kaper (music) wrote the number, which was sung by Allan Jones in the Marx Brothers vehicle *A Day at the Races* (1937).

"Tonight and Every Night" is the appealing title song by Sammy Cahn (lyric) and Jule Styne (music) from the 1945 wartime musical about entertaining the troops in a London theatre that never closes. Janet Blair sang the zestful song in an entertaining production number in which personages from a newsreel enter from behind the screen and join in the Jack Cole and Val Raset choreography.

"Too Late Now" is an intoxicating ballad by Alan Jay Lerner (lyric) and Burton Lane (music), one of the finest ballads either of them ever wrote for the screen. American entertainer Jane Powell sang the song to Brit Peter Lawford in *Royal Wedding* (1951) as they strolled along a moonlit lake in England, telling her timid suitor that it is too late now to ever love anyone else. The fluid music has a perfectly symmetrical and balanced structure, and Lerner's lyric, which lists the things (your smile, your voice, and so on) that it is too late to forget, is disarmingly simple and effective. James R. Morris describes the song as "one of the most lyrical and lovely of American ballads." The Oscar-nominated number was recorded by Powell, Dick Haymes, Dinah Shore, Marilyn Maye, Toni Arden, Dorothy Loudon, and many others. Recently the ballad has come back into popularity with recordings by Michael Feinstein, Ann Hampton Callaway, and Andrea Marcovicci.

"Too Marvelous for Words" is the sterling Johnny Mercer (lyric) and Richard Whiting (music) song that lists all the words that are not good enough to describe one's sweetheart. The lighthearted love song was introduced in *Ready, Willing and Able* (1937) in a bizarre but effective production number. In a scene from a Broadway revue, Ross Alexander (dubbed by James Newill) dictated a letter to his secretary Wini Shaw, singing his verbal list to sweetheart Ruby Keeler. When Keeler received the letter, she phoned Alexander back and sang the same sentiments to him. Then Keeler and Lee Dixon performed a tap routine on a giant typewriter with chorus girls in black as the ribbon and the lyric printed on the huge paper in the background. The tingling song was on *Your Hit Parade* for six weeks and was later featured in *Young Man With a Horn* (1950), where Doris Day sang it with Harry James' Orchestra, and in *On the Sunny Side of the Street* (1951), where it was performed by Frankie Laine. Margaret Whiting began her singing career when she performed her father's song on the radio in 1940. Bobby Short featured it in his act for many years; of the many recordings over the years, Ella Fitzgerald's was one of the most memorable. On Broadway the song was sung by the cast of the revue *A Day in Hollywood—A Night in the Ukraine* (1980) and by Charles McGowan and company in the Mercer revue *Dream* (1997).

"Too Much in Love" is the Oscar-nominated ballad by Kim Gannon (lyric) and Walter Kent (music) about a romance too overwhelming to dismiss. Juvenile Hollywood star Jane Powell (in her screen debut) introduced the infatuated number in *Song of the Open Road* (1944).

"Too Romantic" is the warm ballad by Johnny Burke (lyric) and James Monaco (music) that fears the night, moonlight, and stars because their charms "can make such a fool of me." Millionaire's son Bing Crosby sang the number with Polynesian local Dorothy Lamour in *Road to Singapore* (1940), the first of the Crosby–Bob Hope "Road" films.

"Toot Sweets" is the merry song about a new candy that Richard M. and Robert B. Sherman wrote for the musical fantasy *Chitty Chitty Bang Bang* (1968). Crackpot inventor Dick Van Dyke sang the foot-stomping march with Sally Ann Howes and the children Adrian Hill and Heather Ripley about a candy whistle that you can both blow and eat. In a lavish production number in a candy factory, Van Dyke tried to sell the product to the sweets manufacturers and the whole place became a symphony of whistles with Van Dyke conducting all the employees. But all the dogs in the neighborhood went berserk with the whistling and destroyed the factory.

"Top Hat, White Tie and Tails" is the quintessential Fred Astaire number, a breezy, sophisticated song by Irving Berlin in which one responds to a formal invitation by getting dressed to the nines and ready to hit the town. Astaire sang it in the opening night performance of a London revue in *Top Hat* (1935); he then moved into an elegant tap routine that climaxed with his shooting down a row of chorus boys with his cane used as a gun (a dance bit he had performed on stage in the 1930 musical *Smiles*). While the song has always been identified with Astaire (it might argued that it was his theme song of sorts), it is also one of Berlin's finest works. The melody was written years before for a

Broadway revue that was never produced, but the music seemed composed with Astaire in mind. The verse about getting an invitation in the mail is justly famous for the way the words and phrases are "ragged" to sit on the tricky musical accents. The refrain is rhythmic with a honky–tonk flavor, yet the effect is smooth and sophisticated. William Hyland observes that the "verse glides into the chorus on three descending notes, landing squarely on a solid E natural in the key of C major. The middle release is unusually intricate for Berlin, a repetition of descending chromatic figures that magically find their way back to the main refrain." In addition to Astaire's recording, there have been notable disks by the Boswell Sisters, the orchestras of Archie Bleyer, the Dorsey brothers, and Joe Bushkin, as well as by Frankie Carle, Phil Ohman, Mandy Patinkin, and Andrea Marcovicci.

"Top of the Town" is the pleasant title song by Harold Adamson (lyric) and Jimmy McHugh (music) for the 1937 backstager about a Manhattan nightclub. The number was used in the clever opening credits, Ella Logan, Gertrude Niesen, George Murphy, and Doris Nolan each singing a line or two of the song as a way of introducing the cast. Niesen recorded the whole song, and there was a disk by Clarence Williams and his Washboard Band (vocal by Eva Taylor).

"Toscanini, Iturbi and Me" is the comic ditty by Walter Bullock (lyric) and Harold Spina (music) that Jimmy Durante sang in the otherwise sentimental melodrama *Music for Millions* (1944). As the manager for the classical maestro José Iturbi (who played himself in the film), Durante sang the sassy number about his dealings with the world of classical music.

"Treat Me Nice" is the rock-and-roll plea for affection and fidelity that was used throughout *Jailhouse Rock* (1957) to chart the rise of ex-con Elvis Presley to singing superstar. Mike Stoller and Jerry Leiber wrote the number, which Presley first sang in a recording studio trying for his breakthrough hit. The song was next heard on the radio as background while the D.J. did a dog food commercial. Finally the song caught on and was heard on the radio during a montage showing Presley's rise to fame. Victor Trent Cook performed the number in the Broadway revue *Smokey Joe's Cafe* (1995).

"The Trolley Song" is the Oscar-nominated song by Ralph Blane and Hugh Martin that captured the excitement of a trolley ride and the exuberance of young love in the period musical *Meet Me in St. Louis* (1944). The song, about how a boy and a girl met and fell in love during a short trolley ride, was sung by the passengers on a St. Louis trolley as an anxious Judy Garland watched out for Tom Drake. When he came running down the street and caught the moving car, Garland sang the joyous number as well. The lyric uses onomatopoeia, such as "clang clang clang" and "ding ding ding," to punctuate the musical accents, and the music has a driving rhythm that propels the song beautifully. Alec Wilder points out the "uncluttered melodic line that suggests everyone get out of the way . . . and it manages this inevitable motion within the confines of an octave." The song remained on *Your Hit Parade* for fourteen weeks thanks to best-selling recordings by Garland and the Pied Pipers. Other notable disks were made by Jo Stafford, Guy Lombardo (vocal by Stuart Foster), Vaughn Monroe's Orchestra (vocal by Monroe and Marilyn Duke), and the King Sisters. Donna Kane and the company performed the number in the 1989 Broadway version of *Meet Me in St. Louis.*

"Tropical Magic" is the dreamy ballad by Mack Gordon (lyric) and Harry Warren (music) that was used throughout the Latin-flavored musical *Week-End in Havana* (1941). The languid song, which describes the "black velvet sky" and other exotic images of the Caribbean, was first heard at the Casino Madrilena, where a male trio sang it in Spanish. Later in the film Alice Faye, as a Macy's clerk on vacation in Cuba, sang it in English as she leaned against a pillar on the casino's veranda. The number was reprised as a duet by Faye and John Payne as they rode together on the back of a donkey cart in the moonlight. The ballad was recorded by Gene Krupa (vocal by Johnny Desmond) and Dick Todd.

"True Blue Lou" is the torchy blues number by Sam Coslow, Leo Robin (lyric), and Richard Whiting (music) that tells the tale of a gal whose love for a worthless man breaks her heart. Comedian-singer Hal Skelly sang the jazzy lament in a third-rate vaudeville house in the early musical melodrama *Dance of Life* (1929), and the bittersweet lyric reflected Skelly's life with a selfless wife who put up with him. The "Frankie and Johnny"–type song was most associated with Ethel Waters, who recorded it and sang it in clubs throughout her career. There were also notable records by Russ Columbo, Larry Carr, Meyer Davis' Orchestra, Johnny Marvin, and Ben Pollock and his Orchestra. Frank Sinatra revived the ballad with a disk in the 1950s, and Tony Bennett did the same thing in the 1960s.

"True Love" is Cole Porter's most popular movie song, a straightforward sentimental ballad that he wrote for *High Society* (1956) that remained on *Your Hit Parade* for twenty-two weeks, outranking the new rock-and-roll hits. During a flashback sequence Newport millionaire Bing Crosby sang the love song to his wife Grace Kelly on their yacht as he played a concertina and she hummed along. Later in the film a drunk Kelly reprised the number to Frank Sinatra after they had a midnight swim. The Oscar-nominated ballad is one of Porter's simplest and least typical. Philip Furia is among those who find it lacking, noting that the lyric "fairly drips with feeling unrelieved by even the faintest flash of wit." Yet the music is undoubtedly alluring and in the flowing Jerome Kern style.

Crosby's recording sold over a million disks, and there were also popular ones by the McGuire Sisters and one Nero Young, as well as a duet version by Steve Lawrence and Eydie Gorme. In a 1994 British recording of the *High Society* score, the song was sung by Tracy Collier and Dennis Lotis, and it was performed by Daniel McDonald and Melissa Errico in the 1998 Broadway version of the film.

"Tumbling Tumbleweeds" is the bewitching title ballad by Bob Nolan from the 1934 Western musical and one of the few cowboy songs from the movies to become a mainstream hit. Gene Autry sang the atmospheric number about the open prairie and had a successful recording of it as well. Roy Rogers revived interest in the song when he sang it in *Silver Spurs* (1943); then the Sons of the Pioneers sang it in *Hollywood Canteen* (1944) and their disk was very popular, the number becoming their theme song. Autry reprised the ballad in *Don't Fence Me In* (1945). Other successful recordings include those by Bing Crosby, Glen Gray and the Casa Loma Orchestra (vocal by Kenny Sargent), by Larry Cotton and Fred Lowery in a duet version, Patti Page, Jo Stafford, Billy Vaughn, and the Norman Luboff Choir.

"Turn on the Heat" is the slaphappy song by B. G. DeSylva, Lew Brown (lyric), and Ray Henderson (music) from the early musical *Sunny Side Up* (1929) that inspired what many historians consider the first truly cinematic production number on film. Sammy Lee choreographed the tongue-in-cheek song in a way that defied the confines of the stage and opened up the possibilities for expansive musical fantasy. At a charity show on a Long Island estate, Sharon Lynn in Eskimo garb sang the song in a tundra setting about how her wild dancing is hot enough to melt the ice and snow. She was joined by a chorus of Eskimo gals who danced by the flashing of the Northern Lights. Then things warmed up, the girls dropped their furs to display revealing summer wear, palm trees rose out of the ground, and a hot tropical island was in full swing. Soon the island caught on fire, the girls dove into the cool water (a large glass tank that allowed the camera to shoot the swimmers at various angles), and the sequence ended with a wall of splashing water that took the place of a final curtain coming down. The melodic song served as dance music for Sheree North and Gordon MacRae in the DeSylva-Brown-Henderson bio-musical *The Best Things in Life Are Free* (1956), and there were recordings of the number by Lloyd Keating's Orchestra (vocal by Sammy Fain), Frankie Trumbauer's Orchestra (vocal by jazz violinist Joe Venuti), the Charleston Chasers with Eva Taylor, and Earl Burtnett's Orchestra.

"Two Blind Loves" is the pleasant little duet that Kenny Baker and Florence Rice sang sitting together at a lunch counter in the Marx Brothers' vehicle *At the Circus* (1939). E. Y. Harburg (lyric) and Harold Arlen (music) wrote the romantic number, which used the nursery rhyme "Three Blind Mice" both musically and lyrically as the starting point for the ballad. Baker recorded the song, as did Ted Weems (vocal by Perry Como) and Jack Teagarden (vocal by Kitty Kallen).

"Two Dreams Met" is the languishing ballad by Mack Gordon (lyric) and Harry Warren (music) about two lovers who must part but their hearts have met and will be together forever. The loving number was used effectively throughout *Down Argentine Way* (1940), first sung by the group Six Hits and a Miss in a Manhattan nightclub. The song was reprised in Spanish by the guitar-strumming Banda de Luna on an Argentine hacienda later in the film. Finally, American heiress Betty Grable sang it in English when she visited South America, and Argentine horse rancher Don Ameche (dubbed by Carlos Albert) joined her, singing it in Spanish. The ballad was recorded by the orchestras of Mitchell Ayres (vocal by Mary Ann Mercer), Tommy Dorsey (vocal by Connie Haines), and Eddy Duchin (vocal by Johnny Drake).

"200 Years" is the mock–patriotic song by Henry Gibson (lyric) and Richard Baskin (music) that opens the country-western satire *Nashville* (1975). During the extensive opening credits, Nashville singing star Gibson was seen in a recording studio trying to cut a record of the quasi-country song that patriotically boasted that America must be "doin' somethin' right" in order to "last two hundred years."

U

"The Ugly Bug Ball" is the narrative ballad that town postmaster Burl Ives sang to a young Jerry Mathers in the period musical *Summer Magic* (1963). Richard M. and Robert B. Sherman wrote the gentle ragtime song about an ugly caterpillar who found romance at an annual ball for unsightly crawling critters, and the number was accompanied by nature footage of insects and other bugs that seemed to keep time to the music.

"The Ugly Duckling" is the narrative song by Frank Loesser that Danny Kaye sang in the romanticized bio-musical *Hans Christian Andersen* (1952). Storyteller Kaye saw a young boy (Peter Votrian) whose head had been shaved because of illness, so the Danish writer sang to him the moralistic tale of the rejected ducking who grew into a lovely swan, punctuating his tale with animated expressions and comical duck sounds.

"Umbriago" is the comic number that Irving Caesar (lyric) and Jimmy Durante (music) wrote for *Music for Millions* (1944), the melodrama with a classical music background. Durante, as the manager for maestro José Iturbi, sang the specialty number, whose title is a corruption of the Italian word for "good-natured sot."

"The Unbirthday Song" is the silly but catchy song that Mack David, Al Hoffman, and Jerry Livingston wrote for the animated fantasy *Alice in Wonderland* (1951). Alice (voice of Kathryn Beaumont) stumbled upon a bizarre and endless tea party where the Mad Hatter (voice of Ed Wynn) and the March Hare (voice of Jerry Colonna) were celebrating their unbirthday. As the song merrily explains, everyone has only one birthday but 364 unbirthdays to enjoy.

"Under the Sea" is the Oscar-winning calypso number by Howard Ashman (lyric) and Alan Menken (music) that was the musical centerpiece of the animated fairy tale *The Little Mermaid* (1989). Sebastian the Crab (voice of Samuel E. Wright) tried to explain to the mermaid princess Ariel (voice of Jodi Benson) that life on land was terrible and that she would be much happier staying below the surface where she belongs. The scene started out as a clever list song about all the advantages of life under water, but soon it erupted into a Follies-like production number with various forms of sea life joining in the singing and dancing. Ashman's lyric is particularly artful in its use of the many marine animal names. *The Little Mermaid* and this number in particular was the start of the Disney studio's dominance of the musical film for the next decade. The group the Jazz Networks recorded a distinctive version of the song in 1996.

"United Nations on the March" is the patriotic production number that Kathryn Grayson and the ensemble sang (accompanied by José Iturbi) in a star-studded showcase in the wartime musical *Thousands Cheer* (1943). Herbert Stothart adapted the music from a melody by Dmitri Shostakovich, and E. Y. Harburg collaborated with Harold Rome on the stirring optimistic lyric.

"Up With the Lark" is the exhilarating waltz that Leo Robin (lyric) and Jerome Kern (music) wrote for the period musical *Centennial Summer* (1946). The chipper "good morning" song was sung at the beginning of the film by various members of a Philadelphia household: Kathleen Howard, Jeanne Crain (dubbed by Louanne Hogan), Constance Bennett, Dorothy Gish, Buddy Swan, Linda Darnell, and Walter Brennan. Later in the film the song was reprised by Cornel Wilde and Crain (Hogan). Cabaret singer Barbara Carroll made a distinctive recording of the song.

"Upholstery" is a delicious spoof of the Beach Boys and their kind of music, written by Paul Williams for the cult musical *Phantom of the Paradise* (1974), a disco spoof of *The Phantom of the Opera*. At the Paradise Discotheque, a group calling themselves "The Beach Bums" (Jeffrey Comanor as the lead singer) sang about the all-important "tuck-n-roll" upholstery in their car, noting that it's where "my baby sits up close to me."

"Used to You" is the crooning ballad that airwaves singer Al Jolson delivered in the early radio backstager *Say It with Songs* (1929). The number was written by the Broadway team of B. G. DeSylva, Lew Brown (lyric), and Ray Henderson (music) as a favor for Jolson.

V

"Valentine" is the Gallic ballad by Albert Willemetz (lyric) and Henri Christine (music) that Maurice Chevalier had sung in music halls in Paris. Herbert Reynolds wrote an English lyric, and Chevalier introduced the new version in *Innocents of Paris* (1929), the French star's feature film debut in America. Chevalier, as a Parisian junk dealer, sang the number with the title pronounced as a four-syllable word as in the original French; set amidst an English lyric, the contrast was enticing and comic. Chevalier recorded the ballad, reprised it in *Folies Bergère* (1935) and sang it throughout his career on radio, nightclubs, and television.

"Valentine Candy" is the reflective "I am" song that tomboy Leslie Ann Warren (in her screen debut) sang in the period musical *The Happiest Millionaire* (1967). Warren, as a Philadelphia heiress who likes to box for a hobby, looked at herself in her bedroom mirror and tried to find the woman between the society lady and the little girl with a sweet tooth. Richard M. and Robert B. Sherman wrote the warm and truthful song.

"Vamp of the Pampas" was a comic number by Leo Robin (lyric) and Richard Whiting (music) that spoofed a song that was introduced on the screen earlier the same year. In *Here Comes Cookie* (1935), Gracie Allen sang the narrative ditty about a provocative woman of renowned allure and danced as eight guitar-strumming choristers accompanied her. The Latin-flavored lyric, music, and production number were intentionally similar to the Busby Berkeley–staged "The Lady in Red" sequence in *In Caliente* (1935). Allen's clowning was superb, the parody being a comic tour de force that did not require knowledge of the original number being spoofed.

"A Veritable Smorgasbord" is the gleeful list song that Richard M. and Robert B. Sherman wrote for the animated children's musical *Charlotte's Web* (1973). A goose (voice of Agnes Moorehead) explained to the rat Templeton (voice of Paul Lynde) about the feast waiting for him if he travels with the human family to the county fair, and the two sang of all the goodies in store. Late at night at the fair Templeton reprised the eager number as he gorged on all the garbage he found.

"Viva Las Vegas" is the rocking country-western title song by Doc Pomus and Mort Shulman from the 1964 Elvis Presley vehicle set in the Nevada city. Presley sang the electric tribute to the city of twenty-four hours of excitement on the soundtrack during the opening credits and then reprised it later in a nightclub talent show, where he danced with some of the show girls. *Viva Las Vegas* was also the most popular of Presley's thirty-one films, and his recording of the song was a bestseller.

W

"Wait and See" is the hyperbolic love song by Johnny Mercer (lyric) and Harry Warren (music) that pledges eternal devotion and asks you to just wait and see for yourself if you don't believe it. In the western musical *The Harvey Girls* (1946), saloon proprietor Angela Lansbury sang part of the ballad as she rehearsed in her club. Then the whole song was heard later in the film when waitress Cyd Charisse (dubbed by Betty Russell) and her suitor Kenny Baker reprised it together. Judy Garland, who was in the film but didn't sing the number, recorded the ballad, as did Johnny Johnston.

"Wait 'Til You See Ma Cherie" is the grinning song of romantic boasting that Leo Robin (lyric) and Richard Whiting (music) wrote for Maurice Chevalier's first American film, *Innocents of Paris* (1929). Paris junk dealer Chevalier delivered the affectionate number in the film in his unique suggestive style and recorded it as well.

"Wait Till Paris Sees Us" is the tuneful opening number by Phil Moody and Pony Sherrell for *So This Is Paris* (1955), in which American sailors Tony Curtis, Gene Nelson and Paul Gilbert sang about how lucky the French capital is to have them as visitors. Nelson and Lee Scott provided the athletic and odd choreography which had the three tars climbing and dancing all over the rented car they are riding in to get from their ship to Paris.

"The Waiter and the Porter and the Upstairs Maid" is the delightful comic gem by Johnny Mercer from *Birth of the Blues* (1941), where it was performed by Bing Crosby, Mary Martin, and Jack Teagarden from the bandstand of a ritzy New Orleans restaurant. The narrative song tells of a guest at a stuffy party who sneaks down to the kitchen and has a great time singing and swinging with the hired help. Besides being funny and jazzy, the number also delivers a sociological point, making it, according to Ethan Mordden, "lyrically, musically and conceptually one of the supreme products of race-relating swing."

"Waitin' at the Gate for Katy" is the ingratiating ballad by Gus Kahn (lyric) and Richard Whiting (music) that John Boles and the chorus sang in the Hollywood backstager *Bottoms Up* (1934). The sprightly number was recorded by the orchestras of Don Bestor, Anson Weeks (vocal by Bob Crosby), Earl Burtnett, Adrian Rollini (vocal by Joey Nash), and Paul Small. An instrumental version of the song was featured in *The Fabulous Dorseys* (1947).

"Waiting at the End of the Road" is the stirring spiritual by Irving Berlin from the groundbreaking Negro folklore musical *Hallelujah* (1929). Southern farmer Daniel Haynes and plantation workers (singing voices by the Dixie Jubilee Singers) sat on their wagons and sang the choral number as they waited to have their harvested cotton weighed. The lyric is a heartfelt hope for peace and rest after traveling a long distance, the number serving as a metaphor for heaven's reward. Most of the score was comprised of actual Negro spirituals, yet Berlin's song is dignified, sincere, and free from cliché or stereotype. The number, sometimes listed as "At the End of the Road," was recorded by Paul Whiteman and his Orchestra, by the Revellers, and years later by Dorothy Loudon and Bobby Short.

"Wake Up and Live" is the spirited title song by Mack Gordon (lyric) and Harry Warren (music) from the 1937 radio backstager. Alice Faye, as the airways' "Wake Up and Live" girl, sang the uplifting number about pursuing your dreams, reprised later in the film by microphone-shy Jack Haley (vocal by Buddy Clark) singing with Ben Bernie's Orchestra into what he thought was a dead mike but was actually being broadcast nationwide. Faye recorded the song, as did the Andrews Sisters with Leon Belasco's Orchestra.

"Wake Up Jacob" is the incendiary number that Don Raye (lyric) and Gene De Paul (music) wrote for the Abbott and Costello vehicle *Ride 'Em Cowboy* (1942). The Merry Macs introduced the swinging revival number.

"Walk Through the World" is the lyrical love song by Leslie Bricusse from the 1969 film musicalization of the James Hilton sentimental classic *Goodbye, Mr. Chips*. Schoolteacher Peter O'Toole and his music hall singer wife Petulia Clark sang the ballad on their honeymoon, simply expressing the joys of spending their lives together.

"Waltzing in the Clouds" is the Oscar-nominated ballad that Gus Kahn (lyric) and Robert Stolz (music) wrote for the Viennese operetta *Spring Parade* (1940). Deanna Durbin, as a baker's daughter in the court of Emperor Franz Joseph, sang the melodic number.

"Warmer Than a Whisper" is the soothing ballad that Sammy Cahn (lyric) and James Van Heusen (music) wrote for the last Bob Hope–Bing Crosby "Road" movie, *The Road to Hong Kong* (1962). Although Joan Collins replaced Dorothy Lamour as the gal the two con men fight over, Lamour made a cameo appearance singing this endearing number in a nightclub sequence.

"Was It Rain?" is the tearful ballad by Walter Hirsch (lyric) and Lou Handman (music) from the radio backstager *The Hit Parade* (1937). Radio star Phil Regan and his new singing partner Frances Langford performed the number about two lovers recalling their past parting in the rain. Although some of the lyric work is suspect ("misty" is rhymed with "kiss me"), the song is rather appealing and was recorded by Langford and Regan separately.

"Watch Closely Now" is the rock song by Kenny Ascher and Paul Williams that was used throughout the 1976 remake of *A Star Is Born*. Burnt-out rock superstar Kris Kristofferson sang the number in various concerts, inviting one to partake of a dangerous love affair and warning "don't look down." At the end of the film Barbra Streisand reprised the song in a memorial concert after Kristofferson committed suicide in his Ferrari. Kristofferson's recording was on the charts.

"Watch the Birdie" is the comic nonsense song by Don Raye (lyric) and Gene De Paul (music) from the 1941 film version of the popular Broadway revue *Hellzapoppin'*. Martha Raye clowned her way through the zany number with her characteristic wide-mouthed expressions and gleefully belting voice.

"Watching My Dreams Go By" is the hit ballad that Al Dubin (lyric) and Joe Burke (music) wrote for the gangster musical melodrama *She Couldn't Say No* (1930). Nightclub blues singer Winnie Lightner performed the torch number on stage as she lamented her love for her racketeer-manager. A recording by Vincent Lopez and his Orchestra was very popular.

"The Way He Makes Me Feel" is the song of romantic realization that Alan and Marilyn Bergman (lyric) and Michel Legrand (music) wrote for the Eastern European tale *Yentl* (1983). Barbra Streisand, as a village girl disguised as a male Yeshiva student, sang the ballad about her fellow student Mandy Patinkin with whom she is falling in love. Streisand's recording of the Oscar-nominated song was a bestseller, and Johnny Mathis recorded it as "The Way She Makes Me Feel."

"The Way You Look Tonight" is the indelible Oscar-winning ballad and perhaps the finest collaboration of the team of Dorothy Fields (lyric) and Jerome Kern (music). In *Swing Time* (1936), Fred Astaire sat at the piano and accompanied himself as he sang the penetrating number about how in future and bleak times he will be comforted by the memory of her tonight. Ginger Rogers, shampooing her hair in the next room, was so moved by the song that she joined him, her head still in a lather. Later the ballad was reprised by bandleader Georges Metaxa as he sang it in a nightclub, and at the end of the film Astaire and Rogers reprised it contrapuntally with "A Fine Romance." The entrancing song, high on everybody's list of all-time favorites, has been described by Alex Wilder as "a lovely, warm song [that] flows with elegance and grace. It has none of the spastic, interrupted quality to be found in some ballads, but might be the opening statement of the slow movement of a cello concerto." Just as superb is Fields' effortless lyric that is romantically haunting with its picture of "when the world is cold" and how the memory of a laugh "touches my foolish heart." (With this song, Fields became the first woman to win a songwriting Oscar.) Of the hundreds of recordings over the years, those by Astaire, Skitch Henderson, the Lettermen, Eddy Duchin, Barbara Cook and Tommy Tune, and Andrea Marcovicci are among the notable ones. Scott Holmes performed the song in the Broadway revue *Jerome Kern Goes to Hollywood* (1986).

"We Mustn't Say Goodbye" is the Oscar-nominated ballad by Al Dubin (lyric) and James Monaco (music) that Lanny Ross sang in the wartime patriotic musical *Stage Door Canteen* (1943). Vaughn Monroe and his Orchestra popularized the number about a romantic parting.

"We Never Talk Much" is the delightful duet written by Sammy Cahn (lyric) and Nicholas Brodszky (music) that is both sly and romantic. French free-thinker Danielle Darrieux and her beau Fernando Lamas (in his screen debut) sang the number in *Rich, Young and Pretty* (1951), and it was reprised later in the film by Texas heiress Jane Powell and her beau Vic Damone (in his screen debut).

"We Saw the Sea" is the catchy sea ditty by Irving Berlin that is both rousing and deflating as it sings of the unromantic life of a sailor who joined the U.S. Navy to "see the world" but what he saw mostly was water. The sprightly number was used throughout the nautical musical *Follow the Fleet* (1936), most memorably at the beginning of the film where bandleader-sailor Fred Astaire sang it with his fellow seamen on deck. Astaire recorded the comically frustrated song.

"We Should Be Together" is the bright and sentimental duet that Walter Bullock (lyric) and Harold Spina (music) wrote for the Shirley Temple vehicle *Little Miss Broadway* (1938). Orphan Temple sang the bouncy number with vaudevillian George Murphy about how well they blend together; then they launched into an intricate dance routine to prove it. The music alternates back and forth between a waltz and a jazzy swing number, and the two move from a strutting walk to a full-fledged tap dance in the sequence.

"We Will Always Be Sweethearts" is the waltzing song by Leo Robin (lyric) and Oscar Straus (music) that Jeanette MacDonald sang to her old friend Genevieve Tobin in *One Hour With You* (1932) about how happily married she was. Later in the film the affectionate song was reprised by MacDonald and her husband Maurice Chevalier.

"We'd Make a Peach of a Pair" is the cheery love song by George Marion, Jr., (lyric) and Richard Whiting (music) that anticipates married bliss. It was interpolated into the 1930 film version of the popular Broadway musical *Follow Thru* and was used no less than four times in the movie, sung by golf pro Nancy Carroll and her coach-sweetheart Charles "Buddy" Rogers. Russ Columbo's best-selling disk popularized the ballad, which is sometimes listed as "A Peach of a Pair."

"The Wedding Cake Walk" is the boogie–woogie wedding song that Cole Porter wrote for the lavish finale of the military musical *You'll Never Get Rich* (1941). Martha Tilton sang the jumping song, and then Fred Astaire and Rita Hayworth danced to it. The sequence climaxed on a giant wedding cake with dozens of chorus boys and girls dancing on the different layers and Astaire and Hayworth getting married by a real preacher that Astaire substituted at the last minute to keep Hayworth from marrying the wrong man.

"The Wedding of the Painted Doll" is the jolly song by Arthur Freed (lyric) and Nacio Herb Brown (music) that inspired a groundbreaking musical sequence in *The Broadway Melody* (1929). While tenor James Burrows sang of a puppet wedding, a chorus of sixty doll–like dancers jumped about the stage in a frantic and carefree manner. Ethan Mordden comments that Brown's music "jitters back and forth from major to minor in a jumpy vocal line suggestive of dancing puppets." The scene, added to the film after the principal shooting was complete, is unique on two fronts: It was the first use of a primitive two-color Technicolor process, and it was the first prerecorded musical number on film. The later innovation, which would eventually become standard practice, came about because the first version of the scene was deemed unacceptable. So using the soundtrack already recorded on the studio set, the number was reshot with the actors dubbing their own voices. The result was sometimes awkward (several of the chorus members don't match the voices very well), but it was an important step for film musical production. Harold Lambert,

Leo Reisman, and Charles King recorded the song, which was sung by the chorus in the musical classic *Singin' in the Rain* (1952) and in the 1985 Broadway version of it.

"Week-End in Havana" is the Latin-flavored invitation to come and enjoy the charms of Cuba that Mack Gordon (lyric) and Harry Warren (music) wrote for the 1941 musical of the same name. At the opening of the movie, a cardboard display advertising Havana in a Manhattan travel agency's window came to life and Carmen Miranda and a mariachi band preformed the number. At the end of the film the song was reprised by Alice Faye, John Payne, Miranda, and Cesar Romero. Miranda recorded the song, as did Bob Crosby (vocal by Liz Tilton), and most recently Judy Kaye.

"A Weekend in the Country" is a droll little ditty by Ira Gershwin (lyric) and Harry Warren (music) that sings merrily about the joys of nature, small-town life, and the lure of the countryside. Fred Astaire and Ginger Rodgers sang the number as they strolled down a country road in *The Barkleys of Broadway* (1949) while Oscar Levant tagged along and made disparaging remarks, asking "What's the next train out?"

"Welcome to My Dream (and How Are You?)" is the warm ballad by Johnny Burke (lyric) and James Van Heusen (music) that invites a beautiful girl to share in a romantic fantasy. Bing Crosby sang it to saloon gal Dorothy Lamour in *Road to Utopia* (1945) as he accompanied himself on the piano in her boudoir. Recordings were made by Crosby, by Woody Herman (vocal by Frances Wayne), and many years later by Tiny Tim.

"We'll Make Hay While the Sun Shines" is the bucolic number by Arthur Freed (lyric) and Nacio Herb Brown (music) about the rewards of country life. In a dream sequence in *Going Hollywood* (1933), Marion Davies imagined herself riding along in a horse and buggy with Bing Crosby, who sang the ballad to her. They then got out of the carriage, danced with a scarecrow, ran from a rain shower, and ended up cuddling close together in front of a glowing fire. Crosby's recording was very popular, and there was also a notable record by Nye Mayhew and his Orchestra.

"We're in Business" is the chipper number by Dorothy Fields (lyric) and Harold Arlen (music) from the period musical set on the Erie Canal called *The Farmer Takes a Wife* (1953). Canal boat cook Betty Grable, driver Dale Robertson, and much of the rest of the cast sang the catchy number about business booming on the Erie waterway as they played and splashed in the water of the canal. Jack Cole choreographed the number, which featured Grable and an uncredited Gwen Verdon in an effervescent dance atop the canal boat roof.

"We're in the Money" is the perky standard that thumbed its nose at the Depression by playfully hyperbolizing the power of money when so few had any. Al Dubin (lyric) and Harry Warren (music) wrote the blindly optimistic song for *Gold Diggers of 1933* (1933), where it was sung at the top of the film by Ginger Rogers and the other chorus girls wearing oversized coins in a rehearsal for a Broadway show. Rogers sang part of the number in pig Latin, for no other reason than that it was funny. Warren's music is jaunty and tuneful, and Dubin's bold lyric is filled with 1930s expressions such as "bread lines," "new silver dollar," and "Old Man Depression." Rogers, Dick Powell, and Leo Reisman and his Orchestra each made early disks of the song favorite, which was featured in *We're in the Money* (1935); *The Jolson Story* (1946), where it was sung by Evelyn Keyes; and *Painting the Clouds With Sunshine* (1951), where it was performed by Dennis Morgan and the chorus. In the Broadway musical *42nd Street* (1980), the number was sung by Karen Prunczik, Wanda Richert, Ginny King, Jeri Kausas, Lee Roy Reams, and the ensemble.

"We're Off to See the Wizard" is the scampering theme song by E. Y. Harburg (lyric) and Harold Arlen (music) for the musical classic *The Wizard of Oz* (1939). Judy Garland sang the merry march with the ensemble of Munchkins as she set off for the Emerald City; she then reprised it with scarecrow Ray Bolger, tin man Jack Haley, and cowardly lion Bert Lahr as she encountered each of them along the yellow brick road. The song is among the most recognizable from the famous film score.

"We're Working Our Way Through College" is the pie-eyed song of joy about college life that Johnny Mercer (lyric) and Richard Whiting (music) wrote for *Varsity Show* (1937). Dick Powell and the other students sang the keyed-up number as they paraded across the campus of Winfield College. With a slightly altered lyric it became the title song for the film musical *She's Working Her Way Through College* (1952), where it was sung by Gene Nelson, Virginia Mayo, and fellow collegians.

"What a Little Thing Like a Wedding Ring Can Do" is the charming and suggestive duet written by Leo Robin (lyric) and Oscar Straus (music) for the musical comedy of manners *One Hour With You* (1932). Married couple Jeanette MacDonald and Maurice Chevalier sang about how a ring makes everything, even sin, official and proper.

"What a Perfect Combination" is the eager romantic number that Eddie Cantor introduced in a lavish Busby Berkeley–staged production number in *The Kid from Spain* (1932). At a nightclub floor show, Cantor (in blackface) and a chorus of girls sang the Latin-flavored song as their bodies formed a giant tortilla and then, when viewed from above, the head of a bull. Bert Kalmar and

Irving Caesar collaborated on the lyric and the music was by Harry Ruby and Harry Akst. The song was recorded by Cantor and also by Ozzie Nelson and his Orchestra.

"What Am I Gonna Do About You?" is the questioning love duet by Sammy Cahn (lyric) and Jule Styne (music) that country boy Eddie Bracken sang with city girl Virginia Welles in the radio backstager *Ladies' Man* (1946). Harry James (vocal by Art Lund) and Joan Edwards recorded the ballad that asked what one does when struck with love.

"What Can You Lose?" is the beguiling torch song of sorts that Stephen Sondheim wrote for the cartoonish musical *Dick Tracy* (1990). Nightclub pianist Mandy Patinkin and saloon singer Madonna briefly sang the ambivalent love song at a rehearsal in the club, noting that one can never tell the truth about love but "with so much to win, there's too much to lose." The intriguing number was cut down to just snippets heard in the film, but Guy Haines (AKA Bruce Kimmel) recorded the full song in 1997.

"What Goes on Here in My Heart?" is the swinging musical question that Betty Grable posed to Jack Whiting, John Hubbard, and the other U.S. Navy officers she flirted with at a dance in *Give Me a Sailor* (1938). The answer had to do with "all that bumpin' and thumpin' and jumpin' — that's what!" The lively number by Leo Robin (lyric) and Ralph Rainger (music) was recorded by the orchestras of Benny Goodman, Henry Busse, Frank Dailey, Dick Jurgens, and Gene Krupa.

"What Have You Got That Gets Me?" is the torchy but spirited lament by Leo Robin (lyric) and Ralph Rainger (music) that asks why one is so drawn to such an unromantic and unappealing person. The number was introduced in the fashion show musical *Artists and Models Abroad* (1938) by the Yacht Club Boys with Joyce Compton, Jack Benny, and Joan Bennett. Recordings were made by Bob Crosby (vocal by Marion Mann) and Kay Kyser (vocal by Ginny Simms).

"What Makes the Sunset?" is the gentle list song by Sammy Cahn (lyric) and Jule Styne (music) that asks eleven difficult questions about the ways of nature. Frank Sinatra, as a sailor on leave in Hollywood, sang the ballad in *Anchors Aweigh* (1945) and recorded it as well.

"What Would You Do?" is the comic gem by Leo Robin (lyric) and Richard Whiting (music) that Maurice Chevalier sang in the domestic comedy of manners *One Hour With You* (1932). Slightly unfaithful husband Chevalier explained to the camera how he fell to the charms of another woman, listing her alluring qualities and posing the title question. The clever lyric ended with his answer: "That's what I did too." Chevalier recorded the cunning number, which is sometimes listed as "Now I Ask You What Would You Do?"

"What Wouldn't I Do for That Man?" is the ballad of unflinching devotion that Helen Morgan introduced in the groundbreaking musical drama *Applause* (1929). E. Y. Harburg (lyric) and Jay Gorney (music) wrote the torch song that saloon singer Morgan sang a cappella on the floor of her apartment looking through old love letters and photographs. In one of the earliest uses of split screen, the film showed her unfaithful lover across the hall in another room kissing another woman. Morgan recorded the ballad, reprised it in *Glorifying the American Girl* (1929), and made it a specialty in her act for several years. Other recordings of note were made by Annette Hanshaw and the Charleston Chasers with Eva Taylor.

"What's Buzzin' Cousin?" is a farcical little ditty by Mack Gordon (lyric) and Harry Owens (music) that asks a series of vague questions filled with jive talk and rhyming slang. Jack Oakie sang the burlesque number to a pretty native girl as he strummed a ukelele in *Song of the Islands* (1942).

"What's Good About Goodbye?" is the heartfelt ballad that jewel thief Tony Martin sang on a balcony to his beloved Marta Toren in *Casbah* (1948), pleading with her not to depart. Leo Robin wrote the plaintive lyric, and Harold Arlen composed the bewitching music that climbs the scale in an intriguing manner and then reverses itself back to the original note. Martin recorded the song, but it was a disk by Margaret Whiting that became the bestseller. Years later Diahann Carroll made a distinctive recording of the number.

"What's Good About Goodnight?" is the parting ballad by Dorothy Fields (lyric) and Jerome Kern (music) that was used in an interesting manner in *Joy of Living* (1938). The song was performed by the chorus in a production number at the beginning of the film; it was then reprised by Broadway star Irene Dunne in a radio studio later in the film. Because she is anxious to retreat, Dunne hurried along the temperamental conductor Franklin Pangborn and the performance sped up to a comic climax. The number is sometimes listed as "Tell Me What's Good About Goodnight?"

"What's This?" is the fast and excited song of discovery that Danny Elfman wrote for the stop-action animated fantasy *The Nightmare Before Christmas* (1993). The discontented Pumpkin King Jack Skellington (voice of Elfman) landed in Christmas Town and eagerly asked himself the meaning of all the snow, colored lights, making of toys, and warmth of human spirit.

"When a Woman Loves a Man" is the fatalistic lament that Billy Rose (lyric) and Ralph Rainger (music) wrote for Fanny Brice to sing in her film debut in *Be Yourself* (1930). Smart-aleck nightclub singer Brice introduced the torch song with Marjorie Kane, Gertrude Astor, and the chorus on stage; she then reprised it later in the film by herself. Recordings were made by Libby Holman (with Roger Wolfe Kahn's Orchestra) and Annette Hanshaw, but the number was always associated with Brice, who recorded it and sang it in clubs for years. The ballad was also Rainger's first film hit and launched his prodigious composing career.

"When Did You Leave Heaven?" is the starry-eyed ballad that Tony Martin (in his screen debut) sang to his "angel" in *Sing, Baby, Sing* (1936). The Oscar-nominated serenade by Walter Bullock (lyric) and Richard Whiting (music) was on *Your Hit Parade* for thirteen weeks thanks to popular recordings by Martin and the orchestras of Ben Bernie and Charlie Barnet.

"When I Grow Too Old to Dream" is the warm and touching ballad that Oscar Hammerstein (lyric) and Sigmund Romberg (music) wrote for the sentimental operetta *The Night Is Young* (1935) and is Romberg's most recorded film song. Archduke Ramon Novarro and the common ballet dancer Evelyn Laye that he loves sang the beautiful parting song in which both pledge to carry the memory of each other forever. Hammerstein was not comfortable with the title line, questioning how someone could be too old to dream. He searched for an alternative phrase but was persuaded to keep the expression after hearing Romberg's dreamy melody. José Ferrer sang the waltzing favorite in the Romberg bio-musical *Deep in My Heart* (1954), and the dozens of recordings made at the time included those by Irene Dunne, Nelson Eddy and Jeanette MacDonald, Allan Jones, Rose Murphy, Robert Merrill and Dorothy Kirsten, Jane Pickens, and Dennis Day. Orchestra disks were released by Glen Gray and the Casa Loma Orchestra (vocal by Kenny Sargent), Benny Goodman, George Hall (vocal by Sonny Schuyler), Bob Crosby, Arnett Cobb, and others. The song was revived by a Nat "King" Cole record in 1951 and again by Ed Townsend in 1958. Della Reese made a memorable disk, and most recently the melodic ballad was recorded by Mandy Patinkin.

"When I Grow Up" is the cheerful ditty that Edward Heyman (lyric) and Ray Henderson (music) wrote for the Shirley Temple vehicle *Curly Top* (1935). At a benefit show for the orphanage, Temple sang of the happiness she felt was in her future and then fantasized about being a princess, a bride, and a contented old lady in a rocking chair, changing into costume for each role. Later in the film the butler Arthur Treacher and the cook Billy Gilbert reprised the number in the kitchen.

"When I Look at You (I Hear Music)" is a lush ballad by Paul Francis Webster (lyric) and Walter Jurmann (music) that is crooned and parodied in the Broadway backstager *Presenting Lily Mars* (1943). Operetta star Marta Eggerth sang the melodic number to producer Van Heflin at a rehearsal for a new Broadway musical and then reprised it briefly in his apartment. The number was heard later in the film at a posh Manhattan nightclub, where up-and-coming singer Judy Garland sang it with Bob Crosby and his Bob Cats, mimicking the old operetta style with exaggerated trills and vocal excess.

"When I Look in Your Eyes" is the enamored hit song that was more a curiosity when first presented in the musical fantasy *Doctor Dolittle* (1967). Veterinarian Rex Harrison bid farewell to his pet seal Sophie (who wore a dress and hat) and sang tenderly to her, commenting that the "wisdom of the world" can be found in her eyes. Leslie Bricusse wrote the ballad, which was very popular at the time.

"When I Love I Love" is the musical boast of an oversexed Carmen Miranda as she sang in a nightclub in *Week-End in Havana* (1941) and searched for the kind of love that feels like "Mickey Mouses" running up and down her spine. Mack Gordon wrote the comic lyric and Harry Warren composed the rapid Latin music. Judy Kaye made a delightful recording of the number in 1998.

"When I See an Elephant Fly" is the jaunty comic song by Ned Washington (lyric) and Oliver Wallace (music) that Jim Crow (voice of Cliff Edwards) and the other crows sang in *Dumbo* (1941) about the possibility of baby elephant Dumbo flying up into the tree where he has been found. The song was reprised by the chorus on the soundtrack at the end of the film when Dumbo became a star and rode off into the sunset on the circus train with his mother. The jazzy number is filled with puns ("a rubber band . . . a peanut stand") and musically is very ambitious. For a while the sequence was deemed offensive to African-Americans (the crow's name is the only overtly stereotypic aspect of the scene), and the film was not shown much. But later and more enlightened audiences have found it to be the most musically vibrant aspect of *Dumbo*. Jane Froman made a recording of the clever number.

"When I'm Looking at You" is the entrancing ballad by Clifford Grey (lyric) and Herbert Stothart (music) that opera singer Lawrence Tibbitt (in his screen debut) sang in the early film operetta *The Rogue Song* (1930), and for the first time audiences heard a full-blown classical voice on film and they loved it. The dashing Russian bandit rescued princess Catherine Dale Owen from the Cossacks and took her to his mountain hideout, where he sang this song of beguilement. Tibbett's recording was a bestseller.

"When I'm With You" is the sentimental song by Mack Gordon (lyric) and Harry Revel (music) that was used throughout the Shirley Temple vehicle *Poor Little Rich Girl* (1936). The popular song was first heard on the radio sung by an unbilled Tony Martin; then Temple sang it to her father Michael Whalen as she sat on his lap and offered such extreme sentiments as "marry me and let me be your wife." The song was heard a third time when vaudevillian Alice Faye reprised it on the radio. Temple reprised the song as part of a medley at the piano in *Rebecca of Sunnybrook Farm* (1938). The recording by Ray Noble and his Orchestra (vocal by Al Bowlly) was the biggest-selling of the many made in the 1930s.

"When Is Sometime?" is the gentle song of romantic yearning that medieval lady Rhonda Fleming sang for her uncle the king and members of his court in *A Connecticut Yankee in King Arthur's Court* (1949). Johnny Burke (lyric) and James Van Heusen (music) wrote the flowing ballad about waiting for that "sometime" when the special "someone" of your dreams will arrive on the scene.

"When Love Goes Wrong (Nothing Goes Right)" is the astute ballad that Harold Adamson (lyric) and Hoagy Carmichael (music) interpolated into the score for the 1953 film of the Broadway musical *Gentlemen Prefer Blondes*. Down-on-their-luck gold diggers Marilyn Monroe and Jane Russell sang the smooth number about the trouble with men as they were seated at a Paris sidewalk cafe; soon the two attracted a group of bystanders, and so the duo launched into a sizzling dance routine. At the end a taxi pulled up, and before they left Russell whispered under her breath to Monroe: "No bows, honey. Exit bars and off."

"When My Dreams Come True" is the operetta-like love duet that Oscar Shaw and Mary Eaton warbled together in the first Marx Brothers' film *The Cocoanuts* (1929). The song was reprised later in the film by Harpo on the harp and again by Eaton when she fretted over temporarily losing Shaw. Irving Berlin wrote the number and added it to his Broadway score, becoming the first of many songs he would write directly for the screen. Paul Whiteman and his Orchestra recorded the ballad, and it was sung by Alec Timerman and Becky Watson in the 1996 Off-Broadway revival of *Cocoanuts*.

"When My Ship Comes In" is the hopeful ballad by Gus Kahn (lyric) and Walter Donaldson (music) that nebbish Eddie Cantor sang in *Kid Millions* (1934) to his sweetheart on a Brooklyn barge while an orchestra of kids played in the background. The lyric painted a picture of all the philanthropic things he would do if he were rich, such as open an ice cream factory and give free samples to all the kids. In the film's color finale, Cantor reprises the number as he does indeed open such a factory and hundreds of children stuff themselves with ice cream sodas and sundaes. Cantor recorded the ballad, as did the orchestras of Mal Hallett, George Hall, and Emil Coleman.

"When the Boys Meet the Girls" is the snappy title song by Jack Keller and Howard Greenfield for the 1965 hip version of the Gershwins' *Girl Crazy*. Connie Francis, who ran a dude ranch for divorcees, sang the number with the chorus and it enjoyed some popularity for a time.

"When Winter Comes" is the romantic song tribute to the snowy season by Irving Berlin about the desire for the cold weather to come so one can cuddle up to one's sweetheart. Rudy Vallee introduced the ballad in the Hollywood backstager *Second Fiddle* (1939), where he sang it to Sonja Henie at a Tinsel Town pool party. There were disks of the slightly swinging number by Vallee and the bands of Artie Shaw, Hal Kemp (vocal by Nan Wynn), and Frankie Master.

"When You Hear the Time Signal" is an amorous song by Johnny Mercer (lyric) and Victor Schertzinger (music) that gets its title from radio announcers' standard phrase when delivering the time. Nightclub singer Dorothy Lamour turned the expression into a romantic call for love in the wartime musical *The Fleet's In* (1942).

"When You Pretend" is the pleasant song of optimism by Jack Brooks (lyric) and Harry Warren (music) that argues for a vivid imagination in order for wishes to come true. Jerry Lewis sang the upbeat number to unemployed artist Dean Martin in *Artists and Models* (1955) as he pantomimed all the creature comforts that they were lacking. Then Martin reprised the song to his image in his bedroom mirror, the two Martins harmonizing together in a crooning duet. The number was briefly reprised at the end of the film by Martin, Lewis, Shirley MacLaine, and Dorothy Malone as part of a production number.

"When You Wish Upon a Star" is one of the most beloved of all movie songs, a dreamy and optimistic number by Ned Washington (lyric) and Leigh Harline (music) that became the theme song for Walt Disney's entertainment empire. The plaintive ballad about wishes coming true if you firmly believe in yourself was first heard (minus the touching release) at the beginning of the animated fantasy *Pinocchio* (1940), where Jiminy Cricket (voice of Cliff Edwards) sang it as the camera moved into Gepetto's house and the story began. The ballad immediately became a favorite, won the Oscar, and was forever after associated with Disney, being used as the theme song for his weekly television show to ads plugging the various theme parks. In the 1980s and 1990s the song was recorded by Ringo Starr, Johnny Mathis, Linda

Ronstadt, and Billy Joel.

"When You're Dancing the Waltz" is the entrancing dance song that Boston dance instructor Charles Collins, shanghaied to a picturesque Mexican town, sang to the pretty local Steffi Duna as dozens of other couples circled around them in the swashbuckling musical *The Dancing Pirate* (1936). Lorenz Hart penned the glowing lyric and Richard Rodgers provided one of his ever-effective waltz melodies.

"When You're in Love" is the lilting ballad about the mystery of love written by Johnny Mercer (lyric) and Gene De Paul (music) that newlywed Jane Powell sang to her backwoodsman husband Howard Keel on their wedding night in *Seven Brides for Seven Brothers* (1954), with her at the bedroom window and him sitting outside on the limb of a tree. The expressive ballad was reprised by Keel later in the film as he sang it for his youngest brother Russ Tamblyn who was deep in confusion about love.

"When You're Loved" is a teary ballad by Richard M. and Robert B. Sherman that is unique only in that it was sung by a dog in a nonanimated film. Debbie Boone provided the singing voice for the famous collie in the canine musical *The Magic of Lassie* (1978).

"Whenever You're Away from Me" is a Big Band pastiche number by John Farrar that was used in a fantasy sequence in the disco musical *Xanadu* (1980). Millionaire Gene Kelly recalled a girl he once loved, a band singer in the 1940s, and then she appeared as Olivia Newton-John in military uniform. The elder Kelly in the present and the illusionary Newton-John from the past sang the romantic paean together and then danced a stylized routine that includes an agreeable tap dance.

"Where Am I? (Am I in Heaven?)" is the disbelieving ballad by Al Dubin (lyric) and Harry Warren (music) that questions one's own happiness in getting such a sweetheart. Radio singer James Melton introduced the gushing ballad in the airways backstager *Stars Over Broadway* (1935). The song, according to Tony Thomas, "has remained a favorite among musicians, who feel its melodic line lends itself to instrumental playing, particularly for woodwinds." There were records of the number by Melton and the bands of Ray Noble, Little Jack Little, and Hal Kemp.

"Where Are You?" is the torchy cry of a disillusioned woman that Harold Adamson (lyric) and Jimmy McHugh (music) wrote for Gertrude Niesen to sing in *Top of the Town* (1937), one of her rare film appearances. Niesen delivered the sentimental lament in a candle-lit club, singing in the sultry and heartwrenching style that made her so potent on the stage. The ballad was on *Your Hit Parade* for seven weeks thanks to popular recordings by Niesen, Connie Boswell with Ben Pollack's Band, Bunny Berigan, Tommy Dorsey (vocal by Jack Leonard), Barry Wood, and Will Osborne. The song was revived a decade later with a recording by Les Brown and his Band.

"Where Does Love Begin (and Where Does It End)?" is the swinging song by Sammy Cahn (lyric) and Jule Styne (music) about the fickle nature of love that asks how to find "that dividing line." Gloria De Haven, George Murphy, and the chorus of a Broadway show sang the number in *Step Lively* (1944), and the song was reprised later in the film by Frank Sinatra and Ann Jeffreys.

"Where Is It Written?" is the prayerlike song by Alan and Marilyn Bergman (lyric) and Michel Legrand (music) that served as the "I am" song for the eager village girl Barbra Streisand in *Yentl* (1983). The ambitious Streisand asked why women were not allowed an education in her Eastern European world and wished to know what law of God she would be breaking if she pursued her dream. Legrand's music is unusual in that it has the flavor of a hymn yet is busy with notes and races up and down the scale in an almost jazzy manner. Opera diva Jessye Norman made a notable recording of the ballad.

"Where Is My Love?" is the waltzing aria written by Leo Robin (lyric) and Ralph Rainger (music) that Spanish spy Gladys Swarthout sang in the operetta *Rose of the Rancho* (1935). While she wondered when "my love will come riding," the chorus echoed her sentiments and asked why he hesitates. Although the number was pure operetta, the song was accompanied by flamenco stompings to retain the required Spanish flavor.

"Where the Blue of the Night Meets the Gold of the Day" is the crooning ballad that Bing Crosby sang in his first starring role, as a radio singer in *The Big Broadcast* (1932), and it became his theme song. Crosby and Roy Turk wrote the evocative lyric and Fred A. Ahlert composed the gliding music. In addition to Crosby's popular recording, disks were made by Russ Columbo and Bob Crosby.

"Where the Boys Are" is the yearning title song by Howard Greenfield (lyric) and Neil Sedaka (music) that Connie Francis tearfully sang in the 1960 musical about vacationing youth in Ft. Lauderdale, vowing to go south to find love in the sun. Francis' recording went to the top of the charts, the most popular "beach movie" song of them all. The number was featured in four Off-Broadway revues about the music of the 1960s: Alison Fraser sang it in *Beehive* (1986), the company performed it in *Suds* (1988), Karen Curlee sang it in *The*

Taffetas (1988), and Wendy Edmead cried it in *A Brief History of White Music* (1996).

"Where the Lazy River Goes By" is the atmospheric ballad by Harold Adamson (lyric) and Jimmy McHugh (music) that Barbara Stanwyck (in a rare musical role and doing her own singing) and Tony Martin sang in the Mississippi River musical *Banjo on My Knee* (1936). The popular number was recorded by Martin, Phil Harris, Ray Noble (vocal by Al Bowlly), Teddy Wilson (vocal by Midge Williams), Mal Hallett, and Roy Eldridge.

"Where There's Music" is the gushing finale that Roger Edens wrote for the backstager *Presenting Lily Mars* (1943) when the studio was not pleased with the simple ending originally shot. Indiana-gal-turned-star Judy Garland sang the number about finding love wherever there is music, and she was joined by a chorus of gowned ladies, gentlemen in tails, and Tommy Dorsey and his Orchestra, all part of a scene from a Broadway show on opening night.

"Where You Are (That's Where I Want to Be)" is the wistful ballad by Mack Gordon (lyric) and Harry Warren (music) from *The Great American Broadcast* (1941), the musical about the early days of radio. Alice Faye and the chorus sang the gently swinging number promising to go anywhere her true love goes.

"While Hearts Are Singing (Live for Today)" is the piece of musical advice that hard-boiled Claudette Colbert and her band sang to officer Maurice Chevalier in the fairy tale romance *The Smiling Lieutenant* (1931). Clifford Grey wrote the upbeat lyric and Oscar Straus composed the waltzing music.

"Whispers in the Dark" is the Oscar-nominated ballad about nocturnal love that Connie Boswell sang with Andre Kostalanetz's Orchestra in the fashion industry musical *Artists and Models* (1937). Leo Robin (lyric) and Frederick Holander (music) wrote the number for Marlene Dietrich to sing in *Desire* (1936), but it was cut and only the music was heard in the background. Recordings of the number were made by Boswell with Ben Pollack's Band, Hal Kemp, Bob Crosby (vocal by Kay Weber), Claude Thornhill, and Clyde Lucas.

"Whistle While You Work" is the catchy ditty by Larry Morey (lyric) and Frank Churchill (music) that Snow White (voice of Adriana Caselotti) sang and whistled as she and her animal friends cleaned up the cottage of the dwarfs in the animated classic *Snow White and the Seven Dwarfs* (1937). The simple number is one of the most recognizable in American pop culture, mainly heard on children's records. Artie Shaw (vocal by Leo Watson) made a distinctive recording of the song.

"Whistling Away the Dark" is the Oscar-nominated ballad by lyricist Johnny Mercer (his last film score) and Henry Mancini (music) that provided the pathos in the farcical romantic comedy *Darling Lili* (1969). Music hall entertainer (and a German spy) Julie Andrews sang the tender song of hope on a World War I–era London stage near the beginning and end of the film. Mancini's music is disarming and haunting and the lyric, using the touching image of a child walking alone and afraid to describe the fearful world situation, is Mercer's last powerful creation. Johnny Mathis made a standout recording of the ballad several years later.

"The Whistling Boy" is the delicate ballad by Dorothy Fields (lyric) and Jerome Kern (music) that Australian diva Grace Moore sang to a group of children who have come to hear her rehearse in *When You're in Love* (1937). The charming waltz had a touching lyric that was pretty much indecipherable with Moore's operatics.

"White Christmas" is the Oscar-winning holiday song by Irving Berlin that holds an armful of all-time records: the most popular Christmas song written in the twentieth century, the highest-selling nonreligious song of all time, over fifty million records sold in over 400 different versions, and so on and on. It is ironic that such a blockbuster is so quiet and low-key a song, musically and lyrically restrained. The verse, about living in Southern California and wishing to be back East, where there is snow, is often omitted in performances and recordings, but it is quite expert (even if it makes the geographical mistake of putting Beverly Hills in Los Angeles) and sets up the famous refrain nicely. While the dreamy song is about Christmas yearnings, it has a nostalgic flavor that refers to any fervent wish to be back home. The song was particularly popular with troops overseas during World War Two and other conflicts. "White Christmas" was introduced in *Holiday Inn* (1942) in a manner as unobtrusive as the song itself. In his snow-covered Connecticut farmhouse, Bing Crosby played the song (which he has recently written for a holiday show at his inn) on the piano and taught it to singer Marjorie Reynolds (dubbed by Martha Mears) for her to audition with. She joined him in singing the ballad as he tapped out some of the notes with his pipe on the Christmas tree ornaments hanging nearby, and the number becomes a romantic duet. At the end of the film the same situation was re-created on a Hollywood stage set, where Crosby and Reynolds were reunited after a falling out. The ballad was reprised by Crosby in *Blue Skies* (1946) and by Crosby and the company at the end of *White Christmas* (1954). Crosby's record has sold over thirty million copies over the years, and 1942 recordings by Freddy Martin and Frank Sinatra sold over a million each. Other notable disks were made by Charlie Spivak, Jo Stafford, and Perry Como. For the thirtieth anniversary of the song, records by Pat Boone, Paul Anka, Steve Lawrence, Peggy Lee, and Ella Fitzgerald were all hits. In fact, it is easier to list the recognized artists that did *not* record "White Christmas" than to identify all that did.

"Who Am I?" is the Oscar-nominated ballad that gave composer Jule Styne his first Hollywood success. Walter Bullock wrote the reflective lyric, which was sung by small-time radio singers Frances Langford and Kenny Baker in the airwaves musical *Hit Parade of 1941* (1940). Langford recorded the number, as did Count Basie (vocal by Helen Humes) and Charlie Barnet (vocal by Dolores O'Neill).

"Who Are You?" is the melodic ballad that Lorenz Hart (lyric) and Richard Rodgers (music) wrote for the 1940 film version of their Broadway success *The Boys From Syracuse*. Allan Jones sang the ardent number to Rosemary Lane, asking who this woman is who has stolen his heart and changed his life.

"Who Did? I Did" is the sassy duet that Bob Hope and his health-nut fiancée Betty Hutton sang in the wartime farce *Let's Face It* (1943) based on a popular Broadway show. Sammy Cahn (lyric) and Jule Styne (music) wrote the comic number of self-accusation that was interpolated into Cole Porter's stage score.

"Who Knows?" is the affectionate ballad by Cole Porter that anticipates romantic fulfillment, a concise little love song made up of short lyric phrases punctuated by the repeated title question. Lois Clements (dubbed by Camille Sorey, who later changed her name to Julie Gibson) sang the number in a gleaming white nightclub in *Rosalie* (1937); the song was reprised later in the film by Clements and Nelson Eddy, followed by a dance by Eddy and Eleanor Powell. The ballad was recorded by Tommy Dorsey (vocal by Jack Leonard) and Leo Reisman and his Orchestra.

"Who Wants to Be a Millionaire?" is the sprightly duet by Cole Porter that magazine reporters Celeste Holm and Frank Sinatra sang while checking out a lavish Newport mansion in the musical comedy of manners *High Society* (1956). The clever lyric asks a series of questions about being wealthy, each one ending with "I don't" because "all I want is you." Carl Wayne and Tracy Collier sang the number in the 1994 British recording of the full score, and Randy Graff and Stephen Bogardus performed the duet in the 1998 Broadway version of *High Society*.

"A Whole New World" is the expansive Oscar-winning song by Tim Rice (lyric) and Alan Menken (music) that celebrates the exhilarating feeling of freedom and blossoming love. In the animated adventure *Aladdin* (1992), the Princess Jasmaine (singing voice of Lea Salonga) escaped from the confines of the palace and saw the world with Aladdin (voice of Brad Kane), the two of them singing the melodic ballad as they traveled across the globe on a flying carpet. Peabo Bryson and Regina Belle recorded a duet version of the song that was very popular.

"Whose Side Are You On?" is the grasping rock song by Kenny Hopkins and Charley Williams that opened *The Rose* (1979), the thinly disguised bio-musical based on the life of Janis Joplin. Bette Midler (in her screen debut) sang the self-destructive number, about not believing one is worthy of anything, during the opening credits and in the film's first concert sequence.

"Why Am I So Gone (About That Gal)?" is the questioning Cole Porter ballad that entertainer Gene Kelly asked in *Les Girls* (1957), listing all the things he does not like about the girl and yet admitting he was still crazy about her. The number was followed by a comic dance routine with Mitzi Gaynor that spoofed the leather-jacketed Marlon Brando look of the motorcycle drama *The Wild One* (1953).

"Why Do I Dream Those Dreams?" is the enthralling ballad that Al Dubin (lyric) and Harry Warren (music) wrote for the show biz musical *WonderBar* (1934). Bandleader and songwriter Dick Powell sang the love song to Dolores Del Rio, explaining how he kept seeing the two of them happily married in his dreams. The number was recorded with success by Eddy Duchin and his Orchestra.

"Why Dream?" is the flowing song by Leo Robin (lyric), Ralph Rainger, and Richard Whiting (music) that advises one to stop fantasizing about love and start in with the romancing. The number was used throughout the radio backstager *The Big Broadcast of 1936* (1935), most confusingly by Henry Wadsworth (dubbed by Kenny Baker), who is dubbing for radio star Jack Oakie on a broadcast. (Ironically, Oakie recorded the number himself later on.) Harold Nicholas reprised the song later in the film, and there were band recordings by Ray Noble (vocal by Al Bowlly) and Little Jack Little.

"Why Fight the Feeling?" is the comic song about a fateful romance by Frank Loesser that argues it is too late to escape because the "beguine has begun." Betty Hutton sang the persuasive love song in *Let's Dance* (1950), and the music was used later in the film for a dream pas de deux for Hutton and Fred Astaire.

"Why Should I Care?" is a charming character song that Cole Porter wrote for the gigantic operetta-college musical *Rosalie* (1937). Frank Morgan sang the number, explaining how all his worries about money fade away when he realizes "my sweetheart is still there."

"Why Should I Worry?" is the driving "I am" song by Dan Hartman and Charlie Midnight for the street-wise canine Dodger (voice of Billy Joel) in the animated updating of *Oliver Twist* called *Oliver and Company* (1988). The confident dog sang the pulsating rock song to the young feline Oliver as he showed him how to survive in New York City using "street savoir faire."

"The Wild, Wild West" is the caustic character song that waitress Virginia O'Brien sang in the western musical *The Harvey Girls* (1946), lamenting that she has not yet found anything out West that is wild, from outlaws to cowboys to kidnapped damsels. Johnny Mercer wrote the wry lyric and Harry Warren composed the honky–tonk music.

"Wilhelmina" is the Oscar-nominated song by Mack Gordon (lyric) and Josef Myrow (music) that Broadway star Betty Grable sang in a revue production number in the period musical *Wabash Avenue* (1950). On a Copenhagen setting, a male chorus sang and danced the number with Grable about the Danish girl who all the boys called "Willie." Perry Como's recording of the mellow but swinging number was a bestseller, and there were also records by Art Lund with Leroy Holmes' Orchestra and Kay Kyser (vocal by Mike Douglas).

"Wish I Had a Braver Heart" is the wry character lament by Ralph Blane (lyric) and Harry Warren (music) about wanting to be less fearful of love, hoping to be more like the famous femme fatales of history or a "lady Jekyll or Mrs. Hyde." The reflective ballad was sung by Connecticut teenager Gloria De Haven in the period musical *Summer Holiday* (1948).

"Wish I May, Wish I Might" is the contagious number that Hugh Martin and Ralph Blane interpolated into their Broadway score for the 1943 film version of *Best Foot Forward*. June Allyson, Kenny Bowers, Gloria De Haven, Jack Jordan, Sara Haden, Donald MacBride, and other cadets and guests sang the rousing song as they arrived at the prom at Winsocki Military Academy.

"With a Kiss" is the Continental soft-shoe number by Ralph Blane, Robert Wells (lyric), and Josef Myrow (music) that explains how a Frenchman cannot say hello, goodbye, or anything else without a peck on the hand or the cheek or the lips. Paris entertainer Gilbert Roland and a bevy of models sang the number to Texas heiress Jane Russell in a New York City fashion salon in *The French Line* (1954).

"With a Smile and a Song" is the buoyant "I am" song for Snow White (voice of Adriana Caselotti) that Larry Morey (lyric) and Frank Churchill (music) wrote for the groundbreaking animated musical *Snow White and the Seven Dwarfs* (1938). Near the beginning of the film, orphaned Snow White sang the song to her animal friends in the forest about her philosophy for happiness.

"With Every Breath I Take" is the elegant ballad by Leo Robin (lyric) and Ralph Rainger (music) that millionaire crooner Bing Crosby sang at the Cocoanut Grove in *Here Is My Heart* (1934), expressing an affection as constant as breathing. Over the years several top singers (Crosby, Frank Sinatra, and Perry Como among them) have fallen in love with the song and recorded it, yet the lovely ballad never caught on and became the standard it was hoped for. The song is sometimes listed as "I Dream of You With Every Breath I Take."

"With My Eyes Wide Open I'm Dreaming" is the romantic song of disbelief that Mack Gordon (lyric) and Harry Revel (music) wrote for the sideshow backstager *Shoot the Works* (1934). Dorothy Dell and Jack Oakie introduced the ballad with Ben Bernie's Orchestra, and it enjoyed modest popularity until 1950, when Patti Page (singing on four different tracks and calling herself the "Patti Page Quartet") recorded it and the disk sold over a million copies. Dean Martin sang the song in *The Stooge* (1953).

"With Plenty of Money and You (Oh, Baby, What I Couldn't Do)" is the catchy standard by Al Dubin (lyric) and Harry Warren (music) that insurance-salesman-turned-Broadway-producer Dick Powell sang in *Gold Diggers of 1937* (1936). The breezy number about spending money on the girl of one's dreams was often recorded, the best disks being those by Art Tatum and Turner Layton. Doris Day sang the optimistic song in *My Dream Is Yours* (1949), and Virginia Mayo and the Blackburn Twins performed it in *She's Working Her Way Through College* (1952).

"With the Sun Warm Upon Me" is the lazy and contented ballad by Dorothy Fields (lyric) and Harold Arlen (music) about the various sounds of spring and how they echo one's feelings. Canal boat driver Dale Robertson sang the bucolic number as he laid back in a field in the period musical *The Farmer Takes a Wife* (1953); he was joined by canal boat cook Betty Grable for the last line of the lyric.

"With You" is the Irving Berlin ballad that was used effectively throughout the show business musical *Puttin' on the Ritz* (1930). Songwriter Harry Richman sang it to his collaborator Joan Bennett, who joined him in the duet. The two were next seen performing the number in a lavish Broadway revue.

Many months later, at the end of the film, a distraught Bennett is on a stage and tries to sing the number but falters when she thinks of her lost love Richman. But Richman, sitting in the balcony, belted it out to her; they sang it together and were reunited for a happy ending. Richman's recording was very popular, as were disks by Fred Waring and Guy Lombardo and his Royal Canadians.

"With You on My Mind" is the torch song by Lew Brown (lyric) and Lew Pollack (music) about a love that cannot be shaken from one's memory. Ethel Merman sang the number in the horse-racing musical *Straight, Place and Show* (1938). The song contained an intriguing patter section about trying to dispel the blues in Harlem, but it was cut from the final print.

"Without a Word of Warning" is a ballad by Mack Gordon (lyric) and Harry Revel (music) about a romance that appears on the scene suddenly. Broadway songwriter Bing Crosby sang the number in the backstager *Two for Tonight* (1935) and had success with a recording of it as well.

"Wolf Call" is the playful rock-and-roll number about the romantic call of the wild that Bill Giant, Bernie Baum, and Florence Kaye wrote for the Florida-set musical *Girl Happy* (1965). Chicago singer Elvis Presley sang the howling song in a Ft. Lauderdale nightclub while his group (Gary Crosby, Joby Baker, and Jimmy Hawkins) accompanied and harmonized with him.

"A Woman in Love" is the Latin ballad that Frank Loesser interpolated into his Broadway score for the 1955 film version of the smash stage hit *Guys and Dolls*. The languid love song, which observes that "your eyes are the eyes of a woman in love," was first sung in Spanish by an uncredited male singer at a Havana restaurant; it was then reprised in English by Reneé Renor. Back in New York, gambler Marlon Brando and mission gal Jean Simmons sang the number together as they arrived from their Cuban escapade. The song replaced the popular stage number "I've Never Been in Love Before," but the new ballad enjoyed some popularity as well, thanks to recordings by Frankie Laine and the Four Aces.

"The Woman in the Moon" is the surging song by Kenny Ascher and Paul Williams about the power of women who are not afraid to push and dream. Fledgling singer Barbra Streisand sang the number with backup singers at a benefit concert in the 1976 remake of *A Star Is Born* when she was pushed out on stage by her lover Kris Kristofferson.

"The Woman in the Shoe" is the sprightly song by Arthur Freed (lyric) and Nacio Herb Brown (music) that inspired an early Technicolor sequence in *Lord Byron of Broadway* (1930). Ethelind Terry appeared as the nursery rhyme character in a dream sequence, complete with a shoe for a house and dozens of hungry children. She sang the song with an off-screen chorus in the fantasy in which a prince arrived and then turned her old shoe into a sleek modern high-rise high heel, famous Mother Goose characters entered and danced, and all ended happily with everyone ascending a gold staircase.

"Wonder Bar" is the snappy title song that nightclub owner Al Jolson sang about his Parisian watering hole in the 1934 musical. Al Dubin (lyric) and Harry Warren (music) wrote the number that extolled the qualities of the place.

"Wonder Why" is the Oscar-nominated ballad by Sammy Cahn (lyric) and Nicholas Brodszky (music) in which a romance is mysteriously revealed to the two in love. Texas girl Jane Powell sang the duet with Vic Damone, a man she has fallen for in Paris, in the youthful musical *Rich, Young and Pretty* (1951).

"Wonderful Copenhagen" is the sweeping waltz number that Frank Loesser wrote for the bio-musical *Hans Christian Andersen* (1952) and it became one of the most recognized of all postwar movie melodies. The vivacious tribute to the "salty old queen of the sea" was first sung by an uncredited fisherman on his boat; it was then picked up by storyteller Danny Kaye and his apprentice Joey Walsh as they viewed the Copenhagen harbor for the first time. The song takes the form of a sea chanty and Loesser, who had never been to Denmark, wrote the lyric less as a salute to the city and more as the sigh of a sailor who misses his home port. The Danes loved the song and invited Loesser to Copenhagen, where they made him a national hero.

"Wonderful, Wonderful Day" is the waltzing song of joy by Johnny Mercer (lyric) and Gene De Paul (music) that celebrates the wonders of nature and, indirectly, the wonders of love. Newlywed Jane Powell sang the exhilarating number to husband Howard Keel in *Seven Brides for Seven Brothers* (1954) as they stopped on their ride through the mountains to water the horse and admire a field of flowers. Debbie Boone and the brides sang the song in the 1982 Broadway version of the tale, and in the 1994 British recording of the complete score, the ballad was sung by Bonnie Langford. Judy Kaye made a notable recording of the number in 1998.

"The Words Are in My Heart" is the ballad by Al Dubin (lyric) and Harry Warren (music) of a timid lover who cannot express himself verbally, fearing rejection, so he keeps his emotions inside. The song provided choreographer Busby Berkeley the inspiration for one of his most memorable musical sequences. Dick Powell sang the ballad in the backstager *Gold Diggers of 1935* (1935) to Gloria Stuart in a small boat, but the scene soon dissolved into Powell serenading Stuart in nineteenth-century clothes in a period setting.

Then fifty-six ladies in white gowns were seen playing fifty-six white pianos that moved about into various patterns and ended up as a dance floor where Powell and Stuart performed a waltz. The effect was created by having a technician dressed in black under each piano manipulating it. Also, part of the sequence was filmed backwards, so the pianos seemed to come together magically. Powell recorded the flowing song.

"The World Is a Circle" is the childlike ditty that Hal David (lyric) and Burt Bacharach (music) wrote for the 1973 musical version of the fantasy favorite *Lost Horizon*. Liv Ullmann sang the insistent little song ("nobody knows where the circle ends") with a group of school children in the Tibetan kingdom of Shangri-La. Like it or not, the tune stuck in one's head.

"The Worry Song" is not the most memorable of movie songs but it did provide for one of the most cherished of all film musical scenes: the vivacious dance by sailor Gene Kelly and the animated Jerry the Mouse in *Anchors Aweigh* (1945). Ralph Freed (lyric) and Sammy Fain (music) wrote the bombastic song in which Kelly tried to cheer up the grumpy character from the *Tom and Jerry* cartoons, but the number really took off when he tried to teach the little fellow to dance.

"Would You?" is the amorous invitation that Jeanette MacDonald sang to Clark Gable as they waltzed together in the period musical *San Francisco* (1936). Arthur Freed (lyric) and Nacio Herb Brown (music) wrote the flowing number, reprised later in the film by MacDonald at a rehearsal for a nightclub floor show. Bing Crosby's recording with Victor Young's Orchestra was popular. Debbie Reynolds sang the number in *Singin' in the Rain* (1952), and it was performed by Mary D'Arcy in the 1985 Broadway version of that musical.

X

"Xanadu" is the lite-rock title song by Jeff Lynne for the 1980 musical fantasy that mixed old and new musical styles. In the film's finale, the glitzy Club Xanadu opened to great fanfare as the crowd sang (with the Electric Light Orchestra) about "a place where nobody dared to go" and the multilevel club was filled with roller skating dancers (led by Gene Kelly), tap dancing muses (including Olivia Newton-John), zoot suiters, disco and Big Band musicians, and even cowgirls. Newton-John's recording with the Electric Light Orchestra went to the Top Ten on the charts.

Y

"The Yam" is another of Irving Berlin's catchy dance songs, this one a lighthearted fox trot that asked the musical question "any yam today?" The song was sung by socialite Ginger Rogers at a country club dance in *Carefree* (1938); then she and her psychiatrist Fred Astaire led the country clubbers in a merry dance line that went in and out of the clubhouse. Rogers recorded the staccato number, but it was a disk by Jimmy Dorsey's Orchestra that became a bestseller. During World War Two Berlin rewrote the lyric into "any bonds today?" and it was used for fundraising. Years later the song was recorded as a duet by Bobby Short and Dorothy Loudon.

"The Yawning Song" is a novelty number by Kermit Goell and Fred Spielman that was used in a clever way in the musical fairy tale *Tom Thumb* (1958). The clownish sleep ditty was performed by a puppet, and Stan Freberg provided the singing voice.

"Yes, Indeedy" is the comic number by Betty Comden, Adolph Green (lyric), and Roger Edens (music) that moves from soft-shoe to western hoedown to mock blues as vaudevillians Gene Kelly, Frank Sinatra, and Jules Munchin in *Take Me Out to the Ball Game* (1949) recalled past experiences, all of them frightening, with various gals they have encountered in their travels.

"Yes to You" is the entrancing ballad by Sidney Clare (lyric) and Richard Whiting (music) that nineteen-year-old Alice Faye performed in *365 Nights in Hollywood* (1934) in her straightforward but warm manner that would characterize her work in later films. Movie star hopeful Faye sang the romantic song in a sequined gown in a glittering ballroom; the scene then turned into a dream sequence where she danced into various locales around the world, her dress magically changing for each new location. The ballad is sometimes listed as "How I'd Like to Say Yes to You."

"Yolanda" is the swinging serenade that Fred Astaire sang to Lucille Bremer in the surreal musical *Yolanda and the Thief* (1945) as he strummed on a harp and then tapped danced on it as well. Arthur Freed wrote the flowing lyric that found music and poetry in the woman's name, and Harry Warren composed the subtle Latin-flavored music that gently moved into jazz as Astaire's dance got more vigorous. Artie Shaw and his Orchestra recorded the number and featured it in Shaw's concerts for years.

"You (Gee, But You're Wonderful)" is the gushing song of adoration that Harold Adamson (lyric) and Walter Donaldson (music) wrote for the lavish bio-musical *The Great Ziegfeld* (1936). The song was presented as a typical Ziegfeld wedding production number, where it was sung by dozens of brides and bridegrooms in a show on the New Amsterdam rooftop theatre. Jimmy Dorsey (vocal by Bob Eberle) had a popular recording of the ballad.

"You and Me" is the breezy soft-shoe duet that male impersonator Julie Andrews and her mentor Robert Preston sang and danced in a (literally) gay Paris nightclub in the cross-dressing musical *Victor/Victoria* (1982), claiming to be "the kind of people other people want to be." Andrews reprised the number by Leslie Bricusse (lyric) and Henry Mancini (music) with Tony Roberts in the 1995 Broadway version of the musical.

"You and Your Kiss" is the adoring ballad that Dorothy Fields (lyric) and Jerome Kern (music) wrote for the premiere Abbott and Costello vehicle *One Night in the Tropics* (1940). Allan Jones serenaded Nancy Kelly with the pleasing number on board a cruise ship.

"You Are My Lucky Star" is the simple but beloved standard by Arthur Freed (lyric) and Nacio Herb Brown (music) that has provided a high spot for many a Hollywood musical. The dreamy serenade was introduced in *Broadway Melody of 1936* (1935), where Frances Langford sang it on a radio program. Later in the film it was reprised in a dream sequence as Eleanor Powell sang and danced it in a deserted theatre and imagined she was the star of a big Broadway hit. Other memorable performances of the ballad in films: Jean Harlow and the waiters in *Riff-Raff* (1935), Betty Jaynes in *Babes in Arms* (1939), in the background in *Born to Sing* (1942), Phil Regan in *Three Little Words* (1950), Gene Kelly and Debbie Reynolds in *Singin' in the Rain* (1952), Twiggy in *The Boy Friend* (1971), and Liza Minnelli in *New York, New York* (1977). Notable recordings over the years include those by the Dorsey brothers (vocal by Bob

Eberle), Eleanor Powell with Tommy Dorsey's Orchestra, and the bands of Don Bestor, Archie Bleyer, and Eddie Duchin. In the 1985 Broadway version of *Singin' in the Rain*, the wistful song was performed by Don Correia and Mary D'Arcy and reprised by the ensemble.

"You Are My Sunshine" is the country-western hit that crossed over and enjoyed many successful recordings by mainstream singers. Jimmie Davis and Charles Mitchell wrote the simple metaphorical ballad for Tex Ritter to sing in the cowboy musical *Take Me Back to Oklahoma* (1940), and soon the number was recorded by Bing Crosby, Gene Autry, Bob Atcher, and others. In 1944 Davis used the number as his campaign song for the governorship of Louisiana and won. In 1962 the ballad became popular all over again through a top-selling record by Ray Charles. Bette Midler, Barbara Hershey, and Catherine Johnston sang it in the film *Beaches* (1988).

"You Are Too Beautiful" is the entrancing song by Lorenz Hart (lyric) and Richard Rodgers (music) that turned out to be, in the opinion of Clive Hirschhorn and others, "one of the loveliest ballads (Al) Jolson ever sang." The number was written for the Depression musical *Hallelujah, I'm a Bum* (1933), where Central Park hobo Jolson sang it to Madge Evans as they danced in her room to the music coming from a nearby dance hall. Hart's lyric is fervent and warm, acknowledging that she is too wonderful for just one man but pleading for her eternal affection anyway. Rodgers' music seems casual, but because of what William Hyland describes as an "unusual melodic line and darting harmonies," the song lingers in one's memory. Jolson recorded the ballad, and a superb disk by Dick Haymes a decade later was popular.

"You Belong to My Heart" is the hit ballad that Mexican singing star Dora Luz sang to Donald Duck in the part animation, part live-action travel musical *The Three Caballeros* (1944). The alluring serenade was based on the Mexican song "Solamente Una Vez" by Augustin Lara and was given English lyrics by Ray Gilbert for the film. The ballad immediately caught on and was often recorded, the most popular disk being one by Bing Crosby with Xavier Cugat's Orchestra. Years later Englebert Humperdinck also had a top-selling version of the song. "You Belong to My Heart" was sung by Tito Guizar in the Roy Rogers musical *The Gay Ranchero* (1948), and Ezio Pinza sang it in his film debut in *Mr. Imperium* (1951).

"You Brought a New Kind of Love to Me" is the expansive love song by Irving Kahal (lyric), Pierre Norman, and Sammy Fain (music) that Maurice Chevalier sang in *The Big Pond* (1930) and recorded with great success. Venice tour guide Chevalier serenaded American tourist Claudette Colbert with the ballad as they went down the canal in a gondola. Later in the film Chevalier reprised the song as the singing commercial "I Brought a New Kind of Gum to You." Noteworthy recordings of the ballad include those by Ben Bernie, the High Hatters (vocal by Belle Barker), and Paul Whiteman's Orchestra. The Marx Brothers had fun lip-syncing to the popular Chevalier recording of the number in *Monkey Business* (1931), Frank Sinatra sang it over the titles to *A New Kind of Love* (1963), and Liza Minnelli performed it in *New York, New York* (1977).

"You Came to My Rescue" is the thankful ballad by Leo Robin (lyric) and Ralph Rainger (music) from the radio backstager *The Big Broadcast of 1937* (1936). Small-town radio singer Shirley Ross and network celebrity crooner Frank Forrest sang the number.

"You Can Bounce Right Back" is the frenzied number by Sammy Cahn (lyric) and James Van Heusen (music) from the second film version of *Anything Goes* (1956). Donald O'Connor, as a Broadway star on a cruise searching for a leading lady, sang and danced the number about resiliency in his unique animated manner.

"You Can Do No Wrong" is the wistful song of forgiveness by Cole Porter that Caribbean lass Judy Garland sang to actor Gene Kelly, praising him as the perfection of manhood, after knocking him down in a temper tantrum in *The Pirate* (1948). Garland recorded the hyperbolic number, as did Harry James (vocal by Marion Morgan).

"You Can Fly" is the exhilarating song by Sammy Cahn (lyric) and Sammy Fain (music) that was used so effectively in the animated fantasy *Peter Pan* (1953). After Peter (voice of Bobby Driscoll) sprinkled the fairy dust on them, Wendy (voice of Kathryn Beaumont), Michael (voice of Paul Collins), and John (voice of Tommy Luske) rhythmically repeated the lyric that Peter intoned; then the song was picked up by the offscreen chorus as the foursome flew out of the nursery and over Victorian London. Susan Egan made a standout recording of the song in 1996.

"You Can't Have Everything" is the spirited title song by Mack Gordon (lyric) and Harry Revel (music) that fledgling playwright Alice Faye sang in the 1937 Broadway backstager. The number, which urges one to find happiness with reasonable and practical expectations, was recorded by Louis Prima, Bob Crosby (vocal by Kay Weber), and Judy Garland.

"You Can't Run Away From Love Tonight" is the soft romantic ballad by Al Dubin (lyric) and Harry Warren (music) that Dick Powell introduced in the military musical *The Singing Marine* (1937). Bashful U.S. Marine Powell is pushed into singing the atmospheric number by his buddies at a moonlit weanie roast in order to put the lady guests into an amorous mood.

"You Can't Say No to a Soldier" is the wartime credo that Joan Merrill sang with Sammy Kaye and his Band at a nightclub in the Sonja Henie vehicle *Iceland* (1942); Merrill recorded the song as well. Mack Gordon (lyric) and Harry Warren (music) wrote the sly number about romantic patriotism and Spike Jones and the City Slickers did a wacky version on disk. Five decades later Andrea Marcovicci made a zesty recording of it.

"You Couldn't Be Cuter" is that rare thing: a swing number by lyrical composer Jerome Kern, who usually disdained the new sound. Alec Wilder points out, "The song not only swings but it builds in the last section of twelve measures . . . to perfection." Dorothy Fields wrote the slangy lyric ("the well-known goose is cooked"), first heard in *Joy of Living* (1938), where Broadway star Irene Dunne sang the song and played it on a toy piano in her two nieces' room to lull them to sleep. The ploy did not work, for Dunne fell asleep singing it and the two young girls had to finish the number.

"You Dear" is the romantic ballad that Ralph Freed (lyric) and Sammy Fain (music) wrote for the wartime musical *Two Girls and a Sailor* (1944). Harry James and his Orchestra (vocal by Buddy Moreno) performed the number at a servicemen's canteen.

"You Do" is the pliable song of affection by Mack Gordon (lyric) and Josef Myrow (music) that was used throughout the period musical *Mother Wore Tights* (1947). Vaudevillian Dan Dailey performed the number as a jazzy song-and-dance routine; then later it was reprised by his performer-wife Betty Grable as a slow tempo solo on stage. Near the end of the film, their young daughter Mona Freeman sang the warm ditty to her parents at her school graduation. The Oscar-nominated song was recorded by Vaughn Monroe and his Orchestra, Vic Damone, Margaret Whiting, and Bing Crosby with Carmen Cavallaro and his Orchestra, but the biggest seller of the ballad was a disk by Dinah Shore that went to the top of the charts.

"You Do the Darnd'st Things, Baby" is the merry serenade written by Sidney Mitchell (lyric) and Lew Pollack (music) for the campus musical *Pigskin Parade* (1936). Football coach Jack Haley sang the number to Arline Judge, and there were notable orchestra recordings by Charlie Barnet and Joe Sanders.

"You Don't Have to Know the Language" is the slick song by Johnny Burke (lyric) and James Van Heusen (music) that explains why foreign language proficiency is not necessary for romance with the right person and the moonlight above. Bing Crosby and the Andrews Sisters performed the song in *Road to Rio* (1947) as they entertained passengers on an ocean liner, mixing boogie–woogie with Latin themes. The Sisters' recording was very popular, and the number was heard on Broadway years later when performed by the cast of the revue *Swinging on a Star* (1995).

"You Don't Know What Love Is" is the haunting torch song by Don Raye (lyric) and Gene De Paul (music) that Carol Bruce sang in the Abbott and Costello vehicle *Keep 'Em Flying* (1941). The moody ballad has long been a favorite of jazz musicians, probably because, according to James R. Morris, the melody is made up "entirely of rising and falling scale passages supported by rich harmonic underpinning." Bruce reprised the lament in *Behind the Eight Ball* (1942) and recorded it, as did Dick Haymes, Ella Fitzgerald, Billy Eckstine and Earl Hines, Dinah Washington, Teddi King, with jazz versions in the 1950s by Miles Davis and Sonny Rollins.

"You Give a Little Love" is the joyous finale number by Paul Williams for the pint-sized gangster musical *Bugsy Malone* (1976). The entire cast of children sang the sing-along number at Fat Sam's Grand Slam Speakeasy after their whipped cream shootout, acknowledging that love offered to others "all comes back to you."

"You Go Your Way (and I'll Go Crazy)" is the funny specialty number that Mort Greene (lyric) and Harry Revel (music) wrote for struggling musician Ray Bolger to sing and dance in the wartime musical farce *Four Jacks and a Jill* (1941). The vivacious sequence was later used in the anthology film *Make Mine Laughs* (1949).

"You Gotta Eat Your Spinach, Baby" is the innocent little ditty that did more to promote the disdained vegetable than even Popeye was capable of. Mack Gordon (lyric) and Harry Revel (music) wrote the song that was used in a radio broadcast in the Shirley Temple vehicle *Poor Little Rich Girl* (1936). Vaudevillian Alice Faye sang the number to husband-performer Jack Haley and then the two delivered it to Temple, who responded in recitative that she had been sent "by the kids of the nation" to explain why they all hated spinach. The adults insisted, so Temple joined them in singing the praises of the vegetable.

"You Gotta S-M-I-L-E to Be H-A-Double P-Y" is the Depression-chaser by Mack Gordon (lyric) and Harry Revel (music) that moppet Shirley Temple sang in *Stowaway* (1936), at one point getting down on one knee and doing an animated Al Jolson imitation. The lyric argued that hard times is no excuse for pessimism and urged one to march through life swinging one's arms as if a soldier going past a reviewing stand. Temple's recording was used (incongruously) under the credits for the sex fantasy *Myra Breckinridge* (1970).

"You Hit the Spot" is the soothing song of romantic satisfaction that Frances Langford sang in the campus frolic *Collegiate* (1936). Mack Gordon (lyric) and Harry Revel (music) wrote the buoyant number, which was recorded by Langford, Kay Thompson, Richard Himbler (vocal by Allen Stuart), Bob Howard, and the Mound City Blue Blowers. The song was revived two decades later when featured in the Dean Martin and Jerry Lewis vehicle *Scared Stiff* (1953).

"You Keep Coming Back Like a Song" is the Oscar-nominated Irving Berlin ballad that was introduced among a flock of older Berlin standards in *Blue Skies* (1946). The mournful song about a love that cannot be forgotten was sung in the film by entertainer Bing Crosby and a male quartet in a small nightclub, and Crosby recorded it as well. Other notable disks were made by Jo Stafford, Dinah Shore, and most recently Andrea Marcovicci.

"You Leave Me Breathless" is the amorous ballad by Ralph Freed (lyric) and Frederick Hollander (music) that bandleader Fred MacMurray and band singer Harriet Hilliard sang in the nightclub backstager *Cocoanut Grove* (1938). Hilliard recorded the song with Ozzie Nelson's Orchestra, and there were records by the bands of Tommy Dorsey (vocal by Jack Leonard), George Hall (vocal by Dolly Dawn), and Jimmie Grier.

"You Let Me Down" is the song of disillusionment that Jane Froman sang in the radio backstager *Stars Over Broadway* (1935), the first film of her disappointing screen career. Al Dubin (lyric) and Harry Warren (music) wrote the torchy number, recorded by the bands of Jimmie Lunceford (vocal by Dan Grissom) and Wingy Manone.

"You Make Me Feel So Young" is the vibrant love song by Mack Gordon (lyric) and Josef Myrow (music) in which love makes the lovers feel like kids again. The popular ballad was introduced in *Three Little Girls in Blue* (1946), where it was sung and danced by gold digger Vera-Ellen (dubbed by Carol Stewart) and Atlantic City waiter Charles Smith (dubbed by Del Porter). Dennis Day sang a comic rendition of the song in *I'll Get By* (1950), and it was featured in *As Young As You Feel* (1951) and *But Not for Me* (1958). Long a favorite of jazz musicians, the number was often recorded, the most popular disk being that by Frank Sinatra.

"You Must Have Been a Beautiful Baby" is the sly and romantic number by Johnny Mercer (lyric) and Harry Warren (music) that makes love to a woman by praising the child she once was. Dick Powell sang the nimble song to Olivia De Havilland as they rode in a rowboat in Central Park lake in *Hard to Get* (1938). Doris Day sang the number in *My Dream Is Yours* (1949), and Eddie Cantor dubbed it for Keefe Brasselle in *The Eddie Cantor Story* (1953). Sam Costa and Dorothy Carless recorded a duet version of the popular ditty, there were many records throughout the 1940s, and then the number enjoyed a revival in the 1960s with hit recordings by Bobby Darrin and the Dave Clark Five. Toni Tennille recorded the song with Matt Catingub's Big Band in 1994, and Charles McGowan and Darcie Roberts sang it in the Broadway revue *Dream* (1997).

"You Must Love Me" is the Oscar-winning song that Tim Rice (lyric) and Andrew Lloyd-Webber (music) interpolated into their Broadway score for the 1997 film version of *Evita*. During her final days, the ailing Eva Peron was heard on the soundtrack, through the voice of Madonna, pleading to be remembered by her husband and her people. Madonna's recording was popular.

"You, My Love" is the loving ballad that Mack Gordon (lyric) and James Van Heusen (music) wrote for the musical melodrama *Young at Heart* (1955). Bitter songwriter Frank Sinatra and New Englander Doris Day sang the heartfelt number as a duet in the film.

"You Never Looked So Beautiful (Before)" is the pastiche number by Harold Adamson (lyric) and Walter Donaldson (music) that echoed the musical tributes of the *Ziegfeld Follies*. The song served as a production number in the bio-musical *The Great Ziegfeld* (1936), where a chorus of top-hatted men sang the praises of Virginia Bruce in a revue at the New Amsterdam rooftop theatre. Judy Garland sang the number in another Ziegfeld-era musical, *Ziegfeld Girl* (1941).

"You Say the Sweetest Things, Baby" is the uptempo ballad by Mack Gordon (lyric) and Harry Warren (music) that claims you can say anything (even lies), but not goodbye. It was the only new song in the period musical *Tin Pan Alley* (1940) that used standards from 1915 to 1919 for its score. In a quiet nightclub, songwriters John Payne and Jack Oakie sang their new effort with singer Alice Faye, and it became the young publishing company's first hit. The song was then heard during a montage, where it was performed by various vaudeville acts across the country. Finally, the number was reprised as a romantic duet by Payne and Faye as they rode the Staten Island Ferry together. Notable recordings of the ballad were made by Glen Gray and the Casa Loma Orchestra (vocal by Pee Wee Hunt) and Tommy Dorsey (vocal by Connie Haines). For many years Faye held that "You Say the Sweetest Things, Baby" was her favorite of all the songs she introduced.

"You Started Something" is the high-spirited ballad that Leo Robin (lyric) and Ralph Rainger (music) wrote for the Florida musical *Moon Over Miami* (1941), playfully admitting that one started believing in Santa Claus and in all of one's dreams since meeting that certain someone. Millionaire Bob Cummings sang the cheery number to gold digger Betty Grable as he played the piano on a Miami hotel veranda. After singing it with him, she joined the Condos Brothers in a rapid-fire tap routine devised by Hermes Pan in which the trio remained seated throughout the dance. Soon after, Don Ameche reprised the song to Grable on the hotel dance floor. Successful recordings of the ballad were made by Grable, Jan Savitt (vocal by Bon Bon), Art Jarrett (vocal by the Smoothies), Larry Clinton (vocal by Peggy Mann), Bea Wain, and Tommy Tucker and his Orchestra.

"You Stepped Out of a Dream" is the gushing paean to beauty that Gus Kahn (lyric) and Nacio Herb Brown (music) wrote for a production number in the period musical *Ziegfeld Girl* (1941). Tony Martin sang the lyrical tribute on stage as Hedy Lamarr, Lana Turner, and Judy Garland emerged out of a cloud in dazzling sequin dresses. Martin recorded the song, as did Kay Kyser (vocal by Harry Babbitt), Glenn Miller (vocal by the Modernaires), Guy Lombardo (vocal by Carmen Lombardo), Bobby Hackett, the George Shearing Orchestra, the Four Freshmen, and years later Johnny Mathis and Liza Minnelli. In the Broadway version of *Singin' in the Rain* (1985), the ballad was sung by Mary D'Arcy.

"You Took the Words Right Out of My Mouth" is the sprightly song of affection that Parisian entertainer Maurice Chevalier sang in the musical farce *Folies Bergère* (1935). Harold Adamson wrote the ingratiating lyric, and a very young Burton Lane provided the music.

"You Took the Words Right Out of My Mouth" is the amorous duet that Dorothy Lamour and Lief Ericson sang a few times in the shipboard musical *The Big Broadcast of 1938* (1938). At one point Lamour sang it to Ericson and a hidden microphone picked up her voice and broadcast it into the ballroom, where her boyfriend Bob Hope heard it with chagrin. Leo Robin (lyric) and Ralph Rainger (music) wrote the quiet ballad, which Lamour recorded with success.

"You Turned the Tables on Me" is the wry ballad by Sidney Mitchell (lyric) and Louis Alter (music) about a calculating woman who gets her comupance when she falls for the guy that she drove away. Nightclub singer Alice Faye sang the cool yet jazzy number in *Sing, Baby, Sing* (1936), and the song soon became popular, especially with jazz musicians. Memorable recordings were made by Louis Armstrong, Benny Goodman (vocal by Helen Ward), the Merry Macs, Ella Fitzgerald, and Gene Krupa (vocal by Dolores

Hawkins). The song was featured in *The Benny Goodman Story* (1955).

"You Were Meant for Me" is the unforgettable standard by Arthur Freed (lyric) and Nacio Herb Brown (music) and one of the first song hits to come from the talkies. The straightforward ballad was introduced in the groundbreaking musical *The Broadway Melody* (1929,) where hoofer Charles King sang it to Anita Page in her hotel room, declaring his love in the (rare for its time) nontheatrical setting. Edwin Bradley points out that it is "the first song in a movie musical to advance a plot." The music is simple and spare (only sixty-two notes), but its use of repetition and economy of musical phrases makes the song work. The ballad immediately caught on and was heard in two other musical films that same year: Conrad Nagle (dubbed by King) sang it to Page in *Hollywood Revue of 1929* (1929), and it was performed by Bull Montana and Winnie Lightner in *Show of Shows* (1929). Years later Frank Morgan performed it in *Hullabaloo* (1940), a group of schoolgirls chanted it in *Forty Little Mothers* (1940), Dan Dailey sang it to Jeanne Crain in *You Were Meant for Me* (1948), and Gene Kelly serenaded Debbie Reynolds with the number in *Singin' in the Rain* (1952). Early recordings were made by the Ben Selvin Orchestra and Nat Shilkret and the Victor Orchestra, followed by many others over the decades.

"You Were Never Lovelier" is the scintillating title song by Johnny Mercer (lyric) and Jerome Kern (music) from the 1942 romantic musical where nightclub hoofer Fred Astaire sang it to Rita Hayworth and then the two of them danced to the tingling number. Kern's music is slightly swinging, and Mercer's lyric asks pardon for staring but her beauty was never as dazzling as it is tonight. Astaire recorded the song, as did Vaughn Monroe, Paul Whiteman and his Orchestra, and most recently Andrea Marcovicci. John Pizzarelli sang the number in the Broadway revue of Mercer songs called *Dream* (1997).

"You Will Remember Vienna" is a sparkling number that Broadway operetta creators Oscar Hammerstein (lyric) and Sigmund Romberg (music) wrote for the original film operetta *Viennese Nights* (1930). Lieutenant Walter Pidgeon, Viennese music student Alexander Gray, and their sidekick Bert Roach sang the number about past love affairs in the romantic city. Later in the film the song was reprised by Vivienne Segal and the chorus in a more teary, torchy rendition. Hildegarde made a memorable recording of the ballad in 1939 and Helen Traubel sang it in the Romberg bio-musical *Deep in My Heart* (1954).

"You Wonderful You" is the flexible song about love and show business that was used in various ways throughout the backstager *Summer Stock* (1950). Stage director Gene Kelly sang the number to farmgirl Judy Garland, trying to explain to her how a musical comedy song can reveal deep emotions about a subject and about oneself. The song's music was next heard behind Kelly's ingenious solo dance on an empty stage covered with newspapers, Kelly tapping and cutting up the papers with his feet. The number was reprised as a vaudeville act in the show, Kelly and Garland wearing stripped blazers and beanies and performing the song as an affectionate duet. Harry Warren wrote the pastiche music, and Jack Brooks and Saul Chaplin rewrote a Mack Gordon lyric for the number. Kelly and Alan Dale each recorded it.

"You'd Be Hard to Replace" is the plaintive ballad by Ira Gershwin (lyric) and Harry Warren (music) that struck audiences deeply when performed in the final Fred Astaire–Ginger Rogers vehicle *The Barkleys of Broadway* (1950). After working with various partners in other films, the two stars were reunited as a battling married couple in this film. When Astaire tried to patch up a recent quarrel by singing the adoring number to Rogers, audiences were once again convinced that the team was irreplaceable.

"You'd Be So Nice to Come Home To" is the very warm and very atypical Cole Porter ballad that Janet Blair and Don Ameche sang in the Broadway backstager *Something to Shout About* (1943). The music is simple and flowing while the lyric is one of Porter's rare songs about home and domestic bliss. The Oscar-nominated number was on *Your Hit Parade* for eighteen weeks and became a popular favorite with wartime audiences missing home and loved ones. Dinah Shore's recording with Paul Weston's Orchestra was a bestseller, but there were also successful records by Dick Jurgens (vocal by Harry Cool), Six Hits and a Miss, Jane Froman, Barbara Carroll, and the Percy Faith Orchestra. Diane Keaton sang the ballad in the nostalgic film *Radio Days* (1987).

"You'll Have to Swing It (Mr. Paganini)" is the jazzy ditty that introduced and launched Martha Raye's film career and became her theme song, with Raye singing it in concerts and USO tours around the world. Sam Coslow wrote the number, about a boisterous gang of hepcats performing at Carnegie Hall, for Raye and she sang it for her first screen test. She and the song were featured in *Rhythm on the Range* (1936), where she played a cowboy's loud-mouthed sister and performed the number with jazz licks ad libbed throughout. Raye recorded the song, which she reprised in *Four Jills and a Jeep* (1944). A favorite with jazz musicians and singers, the number was also recorded by Sophie Tucker, harpist Caspar Reardon, and Ella Fitzgerald, whose seven-minute recording with Chick Webb's Orchestra took two sides of the record to include all the jazz improvisation of the performers. The song is also listed as "Mr. Paganini" and "If You Can't Sing It You'll Have to Swing It."

"You'll Never Know" is the romantic standard about hidden affection that became a symbol of the loneliness people felt for loved ones far away during World War II. The ballad had a direct and knowing lyric ("you'll never know — if you don't know now") by Mack Gordon, Harry Warren wrote the warm music, and it was introduced in the period musical *Hello, Frisco, Hello* (1943). In a beer hall with painted scenery depicting San Francisco and New York, vaudevillian Alice Faye in California sang the number on the telephone to John Payne in Manhattan; then separated lovers Jack Oakie and June Havoc followed suit. At the end of the film the positions were reversed as Faye in New York sang it to Payne in San Francisco. The song won the Oscar and sold more sheet music than any other in Warren's long career. Dick Haymes' recording with the Song Spinners sold over a million copies, and Frank Sinatra's record with the Bobby Tucker Singers was also very popular. Other records of note over the years were those by Rosemary Clooney (with Harry James' Orchestra), the Platters, Skitch Henderson, Englebert Humperdinck, Johnny Mathis, Willie Nelson, and Judy Kaye. Faye reprised the song in *Four Jills in a Jeep* (1944), Ginger Rogers sang it in *Dreamboat* (1952), and the Faye recording was used in *Alice Doesn't Live Here Anymore* (1975).

"Young and Healthy" is the ardent tribute to youthful love that Al Dubin (lyric) and Harry Warren (music) wrote for the classic backstager *Forty-Second Street* (1933). Dick Powell sang the number to Toby Wing as part of a Broadway revue; then Wing and a chorus of brides reprised it as they formed kaleidoscopic patterns with their flowing dresses. The Busby Berkeley–staged sequence ended with one of his much-copied trademarks: The camera moved through a tunnel of chorine legs and the scene ended with a closeup of Powell and Wing smiling through the final pair of gams. Bing Crosby, Fred Waring (vocal by Tom Waring), and Ben Selvin recorded the number, as did Brent Barrett in 1994, when the complete score of the film was recorded. The song, sometimes listed as "I'm Young and Healthy," was sung by Lee Roy Reams and Wanda Richert in the 1980 Broadway version spelled *42nd Street*.

"Young Man With a Horn" is the narrative ballad by Ralph Freed (lyric) and George Stoll (music) about a musician and his romancing ways. Canteen worker June Allyson sang the number with Harry James and his Orchestra in the wartime musical *Two Girls and a Sailor* (1944), and both performed it again a decade later in *The Opposite Sex* (1956).

"Your Broadway and My Broadway" is the splashy tribute to the entertainment street by Arthur Freed (lyric) and Nacio Herb Brown (music) that served as the opulent finale for *Broadway Melody of 1938* (1937). Sophie Tucker led the film's principals (including Judy Garland, George Murphy, Eleanor Powell, and Buddy Ebsen) and the large chorus in tux and gowns in the paean to the Great White Way as they sang and danced in front of a glittering art deco version of Broadway.

"Your Dream (Is the Same as My Dream)" is the enticing romantic ballad by Oscar Hammerstein, Otto Harbach (lyric), and Jerome Kern (music) that was presented in a rather awkward way in the Abbott and Costello vehicle *One Night in the Tropics* (1940) and never caught on as it should have. The song came from a 1938 Broadway musical, *Gentlemen Unafraid*, that never opened and it was refitted for the film. On a tropical veranda Nancy Kelly (dubbed by an uncredited singer) sang the ballad to a bullfighter in order to make Allan Jones jealous; later in the film he sang it to Peggy Moran to make Kelly jealous.

"Your Head on My Shoulder" is the homey ballad by Harold Adamson (lyric) and Burton Lane (lyric) that paints a picture of domestic bliss filled with simple joys. Ann Sothern and George Murphy sang the popular love song as a pair of quarreling lovers in the Eddie Cantor vehicle *Kid Millions* (1934), the pair rehearsing the song at the piano on an ocean liner heading to Egypt. Later in the musical farce the lovers reprised the ballad as Southern plantation owners in a musical number as part of a shipboard entertainment. There were successful recordings by the orchestras of the Dorsey brothers (vocal by Kay Weber), Anson Weeks (vocal by Kay St. Germaine), George Hall, Tom Coakley (vocal by Carl Ravazza), and Mal Hallett. It was most recently recorded by Michael Feinstein in 1991.

"Your Mother and Mine" is the comic number by Joe Goodwin (lyric) and Gus Edwards (music) that Charles King sang with instrument-playing comics Jack Benny, Karl Dane, and George K. Arthur in the first plotless film revue, *The Hollywood Revue of 1929* (1929). Later that same year Frank Fay, Beatrice Lillie, Louise Fazenda, and Lloyd Hamilton sang it in *Show of Shows* (1929).

"You're a Lucky Fellow, Mr. Smith" is the swinging patriotic number by Sonny Burke, Don Raye (lyric), and Hughie Prince (music) that praised the average American soldier and claimed he was lucky to be in such a great army. The Andrews Sisters sang the bouncy song to departing draftees at Grand Central Station in the wartime rouser *Buck Privates* (1941).

"You're a Sweet Little Headache" is the backhanded love song by Leo Robin (lyric) and Ralph Rainger (music) that Texas tourist Bing Crosby sang to European peasant Franciska Gaal in *Paris Honeymoon* (1938). Recordings of the ballad by Artie Shaw (vocal by Helen Forrest) and Nan Wynn were both popular.

"You're a Sweetheart" is the uplifting title song by Harold Adamson (lyric) and Jimmy McHugh (music) that Alice Faye sang to George Murphy in the 1937 backstager when they both realized they were meant for each other. The two then broke into an intricate dance routine that was the highlight of the film. The popular ballad stayed on *Your Hit Parade* for eleven weeks, and Frank Sinatra revived the number when he sang it in *Meet Danny Wilson* (1952).

"You're All the World to Me" is a marvelous list song by Alan Jay Lerner (lyric) and Burton Lane (music) that compares one's love to various places around the globe, from Paris to New York to Loch Lomond, in a zesty and romantic manner. The song itself is not so well known because it was upstaged by Fred Astaire's subsequent dance routine on the walls and ceiling of his London hotel room in *Royal Wedding* (1951). The song's melody actually began as "I Want to Be a Minstrel Man" with a lyric by Harold Adamson that was used for the film *Kid Millions* (1934). Lane composed the music with Astaire's jaunty style in mind and then rewrote it when the song was given to the Nicholas Brothers to perform in the earlier movie. When asked to write a number for Astaire to sing and dance to in *Royal Wedding*, Lane remembered the old tune and re-created it with Lerner's new lyric. The music has an urgency to it rare in a romantic ballad, and Lerner's tongue-in-cheek lyric makes it a true original. Astaire sang the number to a framed picture of his beloved Sarah Churchill and then launched into the justly famous dance that defied gravity. The idea for the sequence was Lerner's: At a production meeting he said that he had a dream where Astaire danced on the walls and ceiling; director-choreographer Stanley Donen picked up the idea and pushed for the technical staff to devise a way to do it. (The room was rotated and a stationary camera attached to it kept filming so that Astaire seemed to climb the walls.) Blossom Dearie, Tony Bennett, and Michael Feinstein are among the too few who have recorded the song.

"You're Always in My Arms (But Only in My Dreams)" is the waltzing ballad that Joseph McCarthy (lyric) and Harry Tierney (music) wrote for the 1929 film version of the Broadway hit *Rio Rita*, one of the first successful film operettas. Texas Ranger John Boles sang the number to Bebe Daniels, who later reprised it herself. The song (and the film) were very big hits, and Daniels made a record of it.

"You're an Angel" is the demonstrative ballad by Dorothy Fields (lyric) and Jimmy McHugh (music) that producer Gene Raymond and actress Ann Sothern sang in the Broadway backstager *Hooray for Love* (1935). Morton Downey's recording of the song was quite popular.

"You're as Pretty as a Picture" is an innocent song of affection that teenager Deanna Durbin sang with her friends in an amateur show in the youthful musical *That Certain Age* (1938). Harold Adamson (lyric) and Jimmy McHugh (music) wrote the number, which was recorded by the orchestras of Tommy Dorsey (vocal by Edythe Wright), George Hall (vocal by Dolly Dawn), and Henry King.

"You're Dancing Into My Heart" is the wistful ballad that Ralph Freed (lyric) and Burton Lane (music) wrote for the bittersweet musical *Hideaway Girl* (1937). Shirley Ross, as a woman unhappily married to a phony count, sang the infectious song when a new love shows up in her life.

"You're Dangerous" is the ironic love song that alluring Dorothy Lamour sang to milquetoast Bob Hope as they sat on a log together in the jungle in the safari "Road" film *Road to Zanzibar* (1941). Johnny Burke (lyric) and James Van Heusen (music) wrote the ballad that was quite romantic when removed from its original setting. Bing Crosby recorded it, as did Benny Goodman, Tommy Dorsey (vocal by Connie Haines), and Tommy Tucker (vocal by Ann Arnell).

"You're Easy to Dance With" is the light-footed musical compliment that Fred Astaire sang to Virginia Dale in *Holiday Inn* (1942) before the two of them glided across the dance floor in a New York nightclub. The number was written by Irving Berlin (who seemed never to run out of memorable dance songs) and recorded by Dick Stabile (vocal by Gracie Barrie) and Shep Fields (vocal by Ken Curtis).

"You're Getting to Be a Habit With Me" is the snappy song of affection that Al Dubin (lyric) and Harry Warren (music) wrote for the legendary backstage musical *Forty-Second Street* (1933). Broadway star Bebe Daniels sang the song atop a piano at a rehearsal and then danced with a quartet of men, the number ending bizarrely with her dancing off with a man dressed like Mahatma Gandhi. Bing Crosby had the most successful of the many recordings of the song. Although the lyric is filled with double entendres, Dubin, who had a morphine addiction, denied that the song was about the underground world of drugs among musicians at the time. Regardless, the song was popular in the 1960s and 1970s with groups who saw the number as clearly about drugs. Doris Day sang it (and danced with Gene Nelson) in *Lullaby of Broadway* (1951), and in the 1980 Broadway version of *42nd Street*, the number was sung by Tammy Grimes, Wanda Richert, Lee Roy Reams, and the ensemble. Maureen McGovern made a disk of the song in 1987, and Judy Blazer sang it in the 1994 recording of the complete score of the film classic.

"You're Gonna Lose That Girl" is the cautionary song by John

Lennon to a guy who doesn't appreciate his girlfriend; the singer states that he himself will pursue her if the guy doesn't start treating her right. The number was sung by the Beatles in a recording studio scene in *Help!* (1965), and while they taped the song some overanxious fans chasing Ringo Starr cut a hole around him and his drums from the ceiling of the room beneath him. The group's recording of the song was very popular.

"You're Just Too, Too" is the Cole Porter list song that runs out of adjectives to describe one's beloved, so each refrain ends with the all-inclusive title phrase. In what Stanley Green describes as a "seemingly spontaneous" routine, Gene Kelly and Kay Kendall (partially dubbed by Betty Wand) performed the number in the Paris nightclub musical *Les Girls* (1957).

"You're Laughing at Me" is a lesser-known but splendid Irving Berlin ballad in which the singer feels his romantic sincerity is not being taken seriously. Broadway producer Dick Powell sang the number to society dame Madeleine Carroll in *On the Avenue* (1937) as they sat on a bench in Central Park. Berlin's music is unusual and ambitious, having a wide range (an octave and a half) and shifting keys from section to section in an appealing way. Best-selling records of the ballad were made in the 1930s by Thomas "Fats" Waller, Mildred Bailey, and Wayne King.

"You're My Thrill" is a gushing ballad by Sidney Clare (lyric) and Jay Gorney (music) that took over twenty years to become popular. Slogan writer James Dunn sang the song in the romantic comedy *Jimmy and Sally* (1933), and it gained little attention until best-selling records were made by Doris Day and Harry James and his Orchestra in the 1950s.

"You're My Thrill" is the early swing number that Burton Lane (lyric) and Ned Washington (music) wrote for *Here Comes the Band* (1935), the film about the music business. Clarinetist and bandleader Ted Lewis performed the uptempo love song in the film.

"You're Nearer" is the elegant and tender love song that Lorenz Hart (lyric) and Richard Rodgers (music) interpolated into their Broadway score for the 1940 film version of the campus musical *Too Many Girls*. Heiress Lucille Ball (dubbed by Trudi Erwin) sang the sensitive ballad to an absent love, and the song was reprised later in the film by Frances Langford with Ann Miller, Libby Bennett, and Ball/Erwin.

"You're on Your Own" is the pliable song by Harold Adamson (lyric) and Jimmy McHugh (music) that took on different meanings when sung by various characters in *Higher and Higher* (1943). Mel Tormé, Marcy McGuire,

Frank Sinatra, Barbara Hale, and Michele Morgan each took a turn singing parts of the song, some wanting to be left alone, others taking care of themselves, still others realizing "when it comes to love you're on your own."

"You're Sensational" is the cool song of affection by Cole Porter that journalist Frank Sinatra sang to heiress Grace Kelly at the bar of her wealthy Newport mansion in *High Society* (1956), calling her "Miss Frigid Air" because of her aloofness but claiming that he was "the proper squire" to melt her down. Sinatra recorded the song, and years later Carl Wayne sang it on a 1994 British recording of the complete film score. Stephen Bogardus sang the number to Melissa Errico in the 1998 Broadway version of the musical.

"You're Slightly Terrific" is the unabashed ballad by Sidney Mitchell (lyric) and Lew Pollack (music) that uses Hollywood promotional terms like "gigantic," "stupendous," and "super-colossal" to describe one's sweetheart. Collegian Tony Martin sang the complimentary number to an indifferent Dixie Dunbar at a football rally in the campus musical *Pigskins Parade* (1936). Martin recorded the song, as did Joe Sanders' Band.

"You're Such a Comfort to Me" is a playful and self-mocking song by Mack Gordon (lyric) and Harry Revel (music) that uses timeworn similes ("like a port in a storm" and "like honey to a bee") to praise in a silly manner. Songwriters Jack Oakie and Jack Haley sang the number with Hollywood starlets Ginger Rogers and Thelma Todd in *Sitting Pretty* (1933). Records were made by the Pickens Sisters, George Hall (vocal by Loretta Lee), and Leo Reisman and his Orchestra.

"You're the Cause of It All" is the elegant number that Virginia Mayo (dubbed by Dorothy Ellers) sang in a nightclub in the Danny Kaye vehicle *The Kid From Brooklyn* (1946), citing her loved one as the reason for her sleeplessness and trembling heart. Sammy Cahn (lyric) and Jule Styne (music) wrote the ballad, which was recorded by Fred Martin (vocal by Clyde Rogers) and Kay Kyser (vocal by Lucy Ann Polk).

"You're the Cure for What Ails Me" is the sunny ballad by E. Y. Harburg (lyric) and Harold Arlen (music) that entertainer Al Jolson sang to moppet Sybil Jason, thanking her for helping to restore his voice in the show business musical *The Singing Kid* (1936). The cheerful number was reprised comically later in the film by Edward Everett Horton and Allen Jenkins.

"You're the One That I Want" is the pastiche love song written by John Farrar and interpolated into the pseudo-1950s score for the 1978 film version of the Broadway blockbuster *Grease*. Greaser John Travolta and his girl

Olivia Newton-John led the students of Rydell High School in singing the propulsive rock-and-roll song at the school carnival near the end of the film. The Travolta–Newton-John recording went to the top of the charts.

"Yours and Mine" is the mutual song of endearment by Arthur Freed (lyric) and Nacio Herb Brown (music) that lists all the things, from the stars above to the dreams in their hearts, that the two lovers share. Eleanor Powell, accidentally entering songwriter Robert Taylor's train compartment, helped him come up with the words to a song he was trying to compose in *Broadway Melody of 1938* (1937), and then she sang the number to him. Later in the film the ballad was sung by a young Judy Garland and the Robert Mitchell Boys Choir.

"You've Got Me Out on a Limb" is the pleasant ballad that Joseph McCarthy (lyric) and Harry Tierney (music) wrote for the 1940 film version of their 1919 musical hit *Irene*. Sales clerk Anna Neagle sang and danced to the sentimental number, which was recorded by Harry James (vocal by Dick Haymes) and Charlie Barnet (vocal by Mary Ann McCall). It was the last song written by either of the two Broadway songwriters.

"You've Got Me This Way (Whatta Ya Gonna Do About It?)" is the jaunty ballad by Johnny Mercer (lyric) and Jimmy McHugh (music) that band singer Harry Babbitt sang with Kay Kyser's Orchestra in the musical thriller *You'll Find Out* (1940) while entertaining a ritzy crowd at a party. Babbitt and Kyser recorded the number, as did Glenn Miller (vocal by Marion Hutton), Jimmy Dorsey (vocal by Helen O'Connell), and Tommy Dorsey (vocal by Jo Stafford and the Pied Pipers).

"You've Got Something There" is the diverting duet by Johnny Mercer (lyric) and Richard Whiting (music) that admits to the stirrings of romance in each other. Broadway producer Dick Powell and student Rosemary Lane (in her screen debut) sang the number together on the campus of Winfield College in the collegiate musical *Varsity Show* (1937). Later in the film the team of Buck and Bubbles reprised the number as a dance routine. Powell recorded the ballad as a solo.

"You've Got to Hide Your Love Away" is the Bob Dylan–like folk song that John Lennon wrote for the Beatles' second film *Help!* (1965), a ballad about a secret love and (Lennon later said) a paean to Dylan and his style of songwriting. The famous foursome performed the song on the soundtrack during a scene where religious cultist Eleanor Bron visits the Beatles' terraced house to steal a mystical ring. Some have pointed out that "You've Got to Hide Your Love Away" was the first gay rock song, written to and about homosexual producer Brian Epstein. In addition to the Beatles' popular recording, the folk quartet Silkie had a Top Ten record of it as well.

"You've Got What Gets Me" is a slaphappy duet that the Gershwin brothers wrote for the 1931 film version of their Broadway success *Girl Crazy*. Manhattan taxicab-driver-turned-Wild-West-sheriff Bert Wheeler sang the raucous number with Dorothy Lee, and then it was danced to by young Mitzi Green. Ira Gershwin (lyric) and George Gershwin (music) wrote the song as "Your Eyes, Your Smile" for the Broadway musical *Funny Face* (1927), but it was dropped before opening. They wrote a new verse and added a middle section for the song and interpolated it into their *Girl Crazy* score, providing one of the highlights of the film.

Z

"Zero to Hero" is the pulsating mock-rhythm-and-blues song by David Zippel (lyric) and Alan Menken (music) that was used to chronicle the young athlete's rise to fame in the animated musical *Hercules* (1997). The six Greek muses (voices of Lilias White, Tawatha Agee, Cheryl Freeman, La Chanze, Roz Ryan, and Vanessa Thomas) sang the comic tribute filled with anachronistic slang, outrageous puns, and a slick Motown sound.

"Zing a Little Zong" is the Oscar-nominated song by Leo Robin (lyric) and Harry Warren (music) that uses a Dutch accent ("zing some zentimental melody") to create a picture of lovers gazing out over the Zuyder-Zee. Theatre producer Bing Crosby and his fiancée Jane Wyman sang the delectable duet in *Just for You* (1952) at the opening-night party of a Broadway show where the song was supposedly featured. Crosby's recording of the lighthearted number was very popular.

"Zip-A-Dee-Doo-Dah" is the Oscar-winning song of joy by Ray Gilbert (lyric) and Allie Wrubel (music) that was featured in the early and groundbreaking mixture of animation and live action *Song of the South* (1946). James Baskett, as Negro storyteller Uncle Remus, began to relate the first story to the youth Bobby Driscoll and the film moved into animation for the first time with a live action Remus walking along a road singing and being joined by cartoon animals. At the end of the film Driscoll, Baskett, and Luana Patten reprised the happy song with an offscreen chorus as they walked into the sunset. While the song has a lazy Southern flavor to it, the number moves along both musically and lyrically. Johnny Mercer's recording with the Pied Pipers was a bestseller, and there were also successful records by Sammy Kaye and his

Orchestra and the Modernaires with Paula Kelly. The song remained popular because it was used by Disney on his television show, but it was on the charts again in 1962 with a best-selling record by Bob B. Sox and the Blue Jeans. A hip version by Rick Ocasek in the 1990s was also a hit.

Alternate Song Titles

Titles of film songs have varied from the screen credits to the published sheet music to record labels. Listed below are some of the most common alternate titles for songs discussed. The alternate title is followed by the title used in this book.

All of a Sudden My Heart Sings	My Heart Sings
And the World Goes 'Round	But the World Goes 'Round
Aren't We All?	I'm a Dreamer
At the End of the Road	Waiting at the End of the Road
Boston	The Back Bay Polka
The Bride's Wedding Song	Thank You, Mr. Currier, Thank You, Mr. Ives
Bring on Those Wonderful Men	Bring on the Beautiful Girls
Bury Me Not on the Lone Prairie	Carry Me Back to the Lone Prairie
But Not in Boston	The Back Bay Polka
Caldonia Boogie	Caldonia
Dig You Later	A Hubba Hubba Hubba
The Dying Cowboy	Carry Me Back to the Lone Prairie
Easy to Remember	It's Easy to Remember
Following the Leader	Tee Dum — Tee Dee
The Glamorous Life	The Letter Song
The Gold Diggers' Song	We're in the Money
Good News	I've Got News for You
Hand Me Down My Walking Stick	My Walking Stick
He/She Danced With Me	The Slipper and the Rose Waltz
How I'd Love to Say Yes to You	Yes to You

How Would You Like to Be the Love of My Life?	The Love of My Life
I Can't Help Falling in Love With You	Can't Help Falling in Love
I Don't Understand the Parisians	The Parisians
I Dream of You With Every Breath I Take	With Every Breath I Take
I Feel That Foolish Feeling Coming On	That Foolish Feeling
I Hear Music	When I Look at You
I Like New York in June	How About You?
I Love a Military Man	Military Man
I Love You, Take It From There	Take It From There
I Still Suits Me	Ah Still Suits Me
I'd Love to Spend One Hour With You	One Hour With You
If It Isn't Pain Then It Isn't Love	Then It Isn't Love
If You Can't Sing It You'll Have to Swing It	You'll Have to Swing It
I'm a Mountie Who Never Got His Man	The Mountie Who Never Got His Man
I'm Strictly on the Corny Side	Strictly on the Corny Side
I'm Young and Healthy	Young and Healthy
Isn't This a Silly Song?	The Dwarf's Yodel Song
It Seems I Heard That Song Before	I've Heard That Song Before
It's Getting Fair and Warmer	Fair and Warmer
It's Our Home Town	Our Home Town
I've Got a Lot in Common With You	A Lot in Common
I've Got Beginner's Luck	Beginner's Luck
Java Junction	Coffee Time
Keep Your Sunny Side Up	Sunny Side Up
Let Me Be Your Teddy Bear	Teddy Bear
The Liar Song	How Could You Believe Me When I Said I Loved You . . . ?
Lookie, Lookie, Lookie, Here Comes Cookie	Here Comes Cookie
Looking at You	Across the Breakfast Table
Love Theme from *A Star Is Born*	Evergreen
March of the Lost Boys	Tee Dum—Tee Dee
The Mother of Three	The Jolly Tar and the Milkmaid
Mr. Paganini	You'll Have to Swing It
My Lucky Star	You Are My Lucky Star
Nasty Man	Oh, You Nasty Man
Now I Ask You What Would You Do?	What Would You Do?
Our Love Is Here to Stay	Love Is Here to Stay
Pavement Artist	Chim Chim Cheree
A Peach of a Pair	We'd Make a Peach of a Pair

Pretty Little Poppy	Amapola
Read All About It	I've Got News for You
Running Around in Circles Getting Nowhere	Getting Nowhere
She's Working Her Way Through College	We're Working Our Way Through College
The Silly Song	The Dwarf's Yodel Song
Southern Hospitality	That's Southern Hospitality
Tell Me What's Good About Goodnight	What's Good About Goodnight
That Girl on the Cover	Cover Girl
There Must Be Happiness Ahead	Happiness Ahead
This Is a Lovely Way to Spend an Evening	A Lovely Way to Spend an Evening
Timtayshun	Temptation
Waltz at Maxim's	She Is Not Thinking of Me
The Way They Do It in Paree	Paree
We're Shovin' Right Off	Song of the Marines
Whatever It Is, I'm Against It	I'm Against It
When There's a Breeze on Lake Louise	There's a Breeze on Lake Louise
Where Are You Now That I Need You?	Now That I Need You
The World Goes 'Round	But the World Goes 'Round
The Worry Bird	Let the Worry Bird Worry for You
The Vulture Song	That's What Friends Are For
You Are the Melody	I Am the Words
You're So Square, Baby, But I Don't Care	Baby, I Don't Care

Famous Movie Songs from Other Sources

There are hundreds of movie musical moments using songs from Broadway or Tin Pan Alley. Here is a selective list of some of the most memorable, indicating one of the films the song was featured in and the origin of the song. Titles and dates refer to the Broadway (or Off-Broadway) production where the song was first presented; all these songs are discussed in *The American Musical Theatre Song Encyclopedia*. If only a date is indicated in the origin column, the song is from Tin Pan Alley and published in the year indicated.

Song	Film	Origin
The Aba Daba Honeymoon	*The King of Jazz*	1914
After the Ball	*Show Boat*	*A Trip to Chinatown* (1892)
Ah! Sweet Mystery of Life	*Naughty Marietta*	*Naughty Marietta* (1910)
Ain't Misbehavin'	*Stormy Weather*	*Hot Chocolates* (1929)
Ain't She Sweet?	*You Were Meant for Me*	1927
Ain't We Got Fun	*I'll See You in My Dreams*	1921
Alexander's Ragtime Band	*Alexander's Ragtime Band*	1911
All of You	*Silk Stockings*	*Silk Stockings* (1955)
All the Things You Are	*Till the Clouds Roll By*	*Very Warm for May* (1939)
All Through the Night	*Anything Goes*	*Anything Goes* (1934)
Almost Like Being in Love	*Brigadoon*	*Brigadoon* (1947)
Always	*Christmas Holiday*	1925
Always True to You in My Fashion	*Kiss Me, Kate*	*Kiss Me, Kate* (1948)
America the Beautiful	*With a Song in My Heart*	1895
Anything Goes	*Anything Goes*	*Anything Goes* (1934)
April in Paris	*April in Paris*	*Walk a Little Faster* (1932)
April Showers	*The Jolson Story*	*Bombo* (1921)

Aquarius	*Hair*	*Hair* (1968)
Arrividerci Roma	*The Seven Hills of Rome*	1956
As Long as He Needs Me	*Oliver!*	*Oliver!* (1963)
A-Tisket A-Tasket	*Two Girls and a Sailor*	1938
At the Hop	*Let the Good Times Roll*	1958
Babes in Arms	*Babes in Arms*	*Babes in Arms* (1937)
Baby Face	*Jolson Sings Again*	1926
Bali Ha'i	*South Pacific*	*South Pacific* (1949)
The Band Played On	*Strawberry Blonde*	1895
Baubles, Bangles and Beads	*Kismet*	*Kismet* (1953)
Beautiful Dreamer	*Swanee River*	1864
Before the Parade Passes By	*Hello, Dolly!*	*Hello, Dolly!* (1964)
Begin the Beguine	*Broadway Melody of 1940*	*Jubilee* (1935)
The Best Things in Life Are Free	*Good News*	*Good News* (1927)
Bewitched	*Pal Joey*	*Pal Joey* (1940)
Big Spender	*Sweet Charity*	*Sweet Charity* (1966)
Bill	*Show Boat*	*Show Boat* (1927)
Birth of the Blues	*Birth of the Blues*	*George White's Scandals* (1926)
Black Bottom	*The Best Things in Life Are Free*	*George White's Scandals* (1926)
Blow, Gabriel, Blow	*Anything Goes*	*Anything Goes* (1934)
Blue Moon	*Words and Music*	1934
Blue Skies	*The Jazz Singer*	*Betsy* (1926)
Blue Suede Shoes	*G.I. Blues*	1956
Body and Soul	*The Man I Love*	*Three's a Crowd* (1930)
Brush Up Your Shakespeare	*Kiss Me, Kate*	*Kiss Me, Kate* (1948)
Buckle Down, Winsocki	*Best Foot Forward*	*Best Foot Forward* (1941)
But Not for Me	*Girl Crazy*	*Girl Crazy* (1930)
Button Up Your Overcoat	*Follow Through*	*Follow Thru* (1929)
By Myself	*The Band Wagon*	*Between the Devil* (1937)
By the Beautiful Sea	*The Story of Vernon and Irene Castle*	1914
By the Light of the Silvery Moon	*Birth of the Blues*	*Follies of 1909* (1909)
Bye Bye Blackbird	*Pete Kelly's Blues*	1926
Bye Bye Love	*All That Jazz*	1957
Cabaret	*Cabaret*	*Cabaret* (1966)
California, Here I Come	*The Jolson Story*	*Bombo* (1923)
Camelot	*Camelot*	*Camelot* (1960)
Camptown Races	*I Dream of Jeanie*	1850
Can't Help Lovin' Dat Man	*Show Boat*	*Show Boat* (1927)
Carolina in the Morning	*The Dolly Sisters*	*The Passing Show of 1922*
Carry Me Back to Old Virginny	*With a Song in My Heart*	1878
C'est Magnifique	*Can-Can*	*Can-Can* (1953)

Chantilly Lace	*The Buddy Holly Story*	1958
Charleston	*Tea for Two*	*Runnin' Wild* (1923)
Clap Yo' Hands	*Funny Face*	*Oh, Kay!* (1926)
Climb Ev'ry Mountain	*The Sound of Music*	*The Sound of Music* (1959)
Coal Miner's Daughter	*Coal Miner's Daughter*	1971
Come Down, Ma Evenin' Star	*Lillian Russell*	*Twirly Whirly* (1902)
Comedy Tonight	*A Funny Thing Happened on the Way to the Forum*	*A Funny Thing Happened on the Way to the Forum* (1962)
Consider Yourself	*Oliver!*	*Oliver!* (1963)
Cuddle Up a Little Closer	*Birth of the Blues*	*The Three Twins* (1908)
Dancing in the Dark	*The Band Wagon*	*The Band Wagon* (1931)
Day By Day	*Godspell*	*Godspell* (1971)
Deep in My Heart, Dear	*The Student Prince*	*The Student Prince* (1924)
Deep in the Heart of Texas	*With a Song in My Heart*	1941
The Desert Song	*The Desert Song*	*The Desert Song* (1926)
Diamonds Are a Girl's Best Friend	*Gentlemen Prefer Blondes*	*Gentlemen Prefer Blondes* (1949)
Dinah	*The Big Broadcast*	*Kid Boots* (1923)
Dixie	*With a Song in My Heart*	1860
Do Do Do	*Star!*	*Oh, Kay!* (1926)
Do Re Mi	*The Sound of Music*	*The Sound of Music* (1959)
Don't Cry for Me, Argentina	*Evita*	*Evita* (1979)
Don't Sit Under the Apple Tree	*Private Buckaroo*	*Yokel Boy* (1939)
Easter Parade	*Easter Parade*	*As Thousands Cheer* (1933)
Edelweiss	*The Sound of Music*	*The Sound of Music* (1959)
Embraceable You	*Girl Crazy*	*Girl Crazy* (1930)
Every Little Movement	*On Moonlight Bay*	*Madame Sherry* (1910)
Everything's Coming Up Roses	*Gypsy*	*Gypsy* (1959)
Falling in Love With Love	*The Boys From Syracuse*	*The Boys From Syracuse* (1938)
Fascinating Rhythm	*Girl Crazy*	*Lady, Be Good* (1924)
For Me and My Gal	*For Me and My Gal*	1917
Friendship	*DuBarry Was a Lady*	*DuBarry Was a Lady* (1939)
Funny Face	*Funny Face*	*Funny Face* (1927)
Get Happy	*Summer Stock*	*9:15 Revue* (1930)
Get Me to the Church on Time	*My Fair Lady*	*My Fair Lady* (1956)
Getting to Know You	*The King and I*	*The King and I* (1951)
The Girl That I Marry	*Annie Get Your Gun*	*Annie Get Your Gun* (1946)
Give My Regards to Broadway	*Yankee Doodle Dandy*	*Little Johnny Jones* (1904)
The Glow Worm	*Walkin' My Baby Back Home*	1902
God Bless America	*This Is the Army*	1939

God Bless the Child	*Lady Sings the Blues*	1941
Golden Days	*The Student Prince*	*The Student Prince* (1924)
A Good Man Is Hard to Find	*Meet Danny Wilson*	1918
Good Morning Heartache	*Lady Sings the Blues*	1946
Good Morning, Starshine	*Hair*	*Hair* (1968)
Good News	*Good News*	*Good News* (1927)
Good Night, My Someone	*The Music Man*	*The Music Man* (1957)
Goodnight, Sweetheart	*You Were Meant for Me*	*Earl Carroll Vanities of 1931*
Great Balls of Fire	*American Hot Wax*	1957
Great Day	*Funny Lady*	*Great Day* (1929)
Hallelujah	*Hit the Deck*	*Hit the Deck* (1927)
Happy Talk	*South Pacific*	*South Pacific* (1949)
Harrigan	*Yankee Doodle Dandy*	*Fifty Miles From Boston* (1908)
Heart	*Damn Yankees*	*Damn Yankees* (1955)
Heat Wave	*There's No Business Like Show Business*	*As Thousands Cheer* (1933)
Heather on the Hill	*Brigadoon*	*Brigadoon* (1947)
Hello, Dolly!	*Hello, Dolly!*	*Hello, Dolly!* (1964)
Hello, Frisco	*Hello, Frisco, Hello*	*Ziegfeld Follies* (1915)
Hello, Ma Baby	*Hello, Frisco, Hello*	1899
Hello, Young Lovers	*The King and I*	*The King and I* (1951)
Hernando's Hideaway	*The Pajama Game*	*The Pajama Game* (1954)
Hey, There	*The Pajama Game*	*The Pajama Game* (1954)
Honeysuckle Rose	*Tin Pan Alley*	1929
Honky Tonk Girl	*Coal Miner's Daughter*	1954
Hooray for Captain Spaulding	*Animal Crackers*	*Animal Crackers* (1928)
Hound Dog	*Grease*	1953
How Are Things in Glocca Morra?	*Finian's Rainbow*	*Finian's Rainbow* (1947)
How Deep Is the Ocean?	*Blue Skies*	1932
How Long Has This Been Going On?	*Funny Face*	*Funny Face* (1927)
I Believe in You	*How to Succeed in Business . . .*	*How to Succeed in Business . . .* (1961)
I Cain't Say No	*Oklahoma!*	*Oklahoma!* (1943)
I Can't Give You Anything But Love	*Stormy Weather*	*Blackbirds of 1928*
I Could Have Danced All Night	*My Fair Lady*	*My Fair Lady* (1956)
I Could Write a Book	*Pal Joey*	*Pal Joey* (1940)
I Didn't Know What Time It Was	*Too Many Girls*	*Too Many Girls* (1939)
I Don't Care	*In the Good Old Summertime*	*The Blonde in Black* (1903)

I Don't Know How to Love Him	*Jesus Christ Superstar*	*Jesus Christ Superstar* (1971)
I Enjoy Being a Girl	*Flower Drum Song*	*Flower Drum Song* (1958)
I Found a Million Dollar Baby	*Funny Lady*	*Crazy Quilt* (1931)
I Get a Kick Out of You	*Anything Goes*	*Anything Goes* (1934)
I Got Plenty o' Nuttin'	*Porgy and Bess*	*Porgy and Bess* (1935)
I Got Rhythm	*Girl Crazy*	*Girl Crazy* (1930)
I Got the Sun in the Morning	*Annie Get Your Gun*	*Annie Get Your Gun* (1946)
I Guess I'll Have to Change My Plan	*The Band Wagon*	*The Little Show* (1929)
I Hate Men	*Kiss Me, Kate*	*Kiss Me, Kate* (1948)
I Love a Piano	*Easter Parade*	*Stop! Look! Listen!* (1915)
I Love Paris	*Can-Can*	*Can-Can* (1953)
I Talk to the Trees	*Paint Your Wagon*	*Paint Your Wagon* (1951)
I Wanna Be Loved By You	*Three Little Words*	*Good Boy* (1928)
I Want to Be Happy	*Tea for Two*	*No No Nanette* (1925)
I Wonder Who's Kissing Her Now	*The Time, the Place and the Girl*	*The Prince of Tonight* (1909)
If Ever I Would Leave You	*Camelot*	*Camelot* (1960)
If He Walked Into My Life	*Mame*	*Mame* (1966)
If I Loved You	*Carousel*	*Carousel* (1945)
If My Friends Could See Me Now	*Sweet Charity*	*Sweet Charity* (1966)
If You Knew Susie	*The Great Ziegfeld*	*Big Boy* (1925)
I'll Build a Stairway to Paradise	*An American in Paris*	*George White's Scandals* (1922)
I'll See You Again	*Bitter Sweet*	*Bitter Sweet* (1929)
I'll See You in My Dreams	*I'll See You in My Dreams*	1924
I'm Always Chasing Rainbows	*Ziegfeld Girl*	*Oh, Look!* (1918)
I'm Falling in Love With Someone	*The Great Victor Herbert*	*Naughty Marietta* (1910)
I'm Gonna Wash That Man Right Outa My Hair	*South Pacific*	*South Pacific* (1949)
I'm Just Wild About Harry	*Jolson Sings Again*	*Shuffle Along* (1921)
I'm Looking Over a Four Leaf Clover	*Jolson Sings Again*	1927
The Impossible Dream	*Man of La Mancha*	*Man of La Mancha* (1965)
In My Merry Oldsmobile	*The Merry Monihans*	1905
In the Good Old Summertime	*In the Good Old Summertime*	*The Defender* (1902)
Indian Love Call	*Rose-Marie*	*Rose-Marie* (1924)
It Ain't Necessarily So	*Porgy and Bess*	*Porgy and Bess* (1935)
It Had to Be You	*I'll See You in My Dreams*	1924
Italian Street Song	*Naughty Marietta*	*Naughty Marietta* (1910)

It's a Wonderful World	*Roustabout*	1954
It's All Right With Me	*Can-Can*	*Can-Can* (1953)
It's Been a Long, Long Time	*I'll Get By*	1945
It's De-Lovely	*Anything Goes*	*Red, Hot and Blue* (1936)
I've Got a Crush on You	*Three for the Show*	*Treasure Girl* (1928)
I've Grown Accustomed to Her Face	*My Fair Lady*	*My Fair Lady* (1956)
I've Told Ev'ry Little Star	*Music in the Air*	*Music in the Air* (1932)
The Japanese Sandman	*Rose of Washington Square*	1920
June Is Bustin' Out All Over	*Carousel*	*Carousel* (1945)
Just in Time	*Bells Are Ringing*	*Bells Are Ringing* (1956)
Just One of Those Things	*Night and Day*	*Jubilee* (1935)
La Bamba	*La Bamba*	1959
The Lady Is a Tramp	*Words and Music*	*Babes in Arms* (1937)
The Last Time I Saw Paris	*Till the Clouds Roll By*	1941
Lazy	*Alexander's Ragtime Band*	1924
Let Me Entertain You	*Gypsy*	*Gypsy* (1959)
Let the Sunshine In	*Hair*	*Hair* (1968)
Let's Do It	*Can-Can*	*Paris* (1928)
Let's Misbehave	*Pennies From Heaven*	1927
Let's Twist Again	*Let the Good Times Roll*	1961
Life Is Just a Bowl of Cherries	*Pennies From Heaven*	*George White's Scandals* (1931)
Little Darlin'	*La Bamba*	1957
Little Girl Blue	*Jumbo*	*Jumbo* (1935)
A Little Girl from Little Rock	*Gentlemen Prefer Blondes*	*Gentlemen Prefer Blondes* (1949)
Liza	*The Jolson Story*	*Show Girl* (1929)
Look for the Silver Lining	*Till the Clouds Roll By*	*Sally* (1920)
Look to the Rainbow	*Finian's Rainbow*	*Finian's Rainbow* (1947)
Love Is Like a Firefly	*The Firefly*	*The Firefly* (1912)
Love Me or Leave Me	*Love Me or Leave Me*	*Whoopee* (1928)
The Love Nest	*The Helen Morgan Story*	*Mary* (1920)
Lover, Come Back to Me	*Deep in My Heart*	*The New Moon* (1928)
Luck Be a Lady	*Guys and Dolls*	*Guys and Dolls* (1950)
Make Believe	*Show Boat*	*Show Boat* (1927)
Makin' Whoopee	*Whoopee*	*Whoopee* (1928)
Mame	*Mame*	*Mame* (1966)
The Man I Love	*Rhapsody in Blue*	1928
Mandy	*Kid Millions*	*Yip Yip Yaphank* (1918)
Manhattan	*Words and Music*	*Garrick Gaieties* (1925)
March of the Toys	*The Great Victor Herbert*	*Babes in Toyland* (1903)
Maria	*West Side Story*	*West Side Story* (1957)
Mary's a Grand Old Name	*Yankee Doodle Dandy*	*Forty-Five Minutes From Broadway* (1906)
Matchmaker, Matchmaker	*Fiddler on the Roof*	*Fiddler on the Roof* (1964)

Me and My Shadow	*Feudin', Fussin', and A-Fightin'*	*Harry Delmar's Revels* (1927)
Meet Me in St. Louis	*Meet Me in St. Louis*	1904
Minnie the Moocher	*The Cotton Club*	1931
Missouri Waltz	*The Story of Vernon and Irene Castle*	1916
Momma Look Sharp	*1776*	*1776* (1969)
More Than You Know	*Hit the Deck*	*Great Day* (1929)
The Most Beautiful Girl in the World	*Jumbo*	*Jumbo* (1935)
Mother Machree	*My Wild Irish Rose*	*Barry of Ballymore* (1910)
Mountain Greenery	*Words and Music*	*Garrick Gaieties* (1926)
The Music Goes 'Round and 'Round	*The Five Pennies*	1935
My Buddy	*I'll See You in My Dreams*	1922
My Favorite Things	*The Sound of Music*	*The Sound of Music* (1959)
My Funny Valentine	*Pal Joey*	*Babes in Arms* (1937)
My Gal Sal	*My Gal Sal*	1905
My Heart Belongs to Daddy	*Night and Day*	*Leave It to Me!* (1938)
My Heart Stood Still	*A Connecticut Yankee*	*A Connecticut Yankee* (1927)
My Mammy	*The Jazz Singer*	*Sinbad* (1918)
My Man	*The Great Ziegfeld*	*Ziegfeld Follies* (1921)
My Melancholy Baby	*Birth of the Blues*	1912
My Old Kentucky Home	*I Dream of Jeanie*	1853
My Romance	*Jumbo*	*Jumbo* (1935)
My Wild Irish Rose	*My Wild Irish Rose*	*A Romance of Athlone* (1899)
New Sun in the Sky	*Dancing in the Dark*	*The Band Wagon* (1931)
New York, New York	*On the Town*	*On the Town* (1944)
Night and Day	*The Gay Divorcee*	*The Gay Divorce* (1932)
The Night Was Made for Love	*The Cat and the Fiddle*	*The Cat and the Fiddle* (1931)
Oh, How I Hate to Get Up in the Morning	*Alexander's Ragtime Band*	*Yip Yip Yaphank* (1918)
Oh, Suzanna	*I Dream of Jeanie*	1848
Oh, What a Beautiful Mornin'	*Oklahoma!*	*Oklahoma!* (1943)
Oh, You Beautiful Doll	*For Me and My Gal*	1911
Oklahoma	*Oklahoma!*	*Oklahoma!* (1943)
Ol' Man River	*Show Boat*	*Show Boat* (1927)
Old Devil Moon	*Finian's Rainbow*	*Finian's Rainbow* (1947)
Old Folks at Home	*I Dream of Jeanie*	1851
On a Clear Day You Can See Forever	*On a Clear Day You Can See Forever*	*On a Clear Day You Can See Forever* (1965)
On Broadway	*All That Jazz*	1963
On Moonlight Bay	*On Moonlight Bay*	1912

On the Banks of the Wabash	*My Gal Sal*	1897
On the Street Where You Live	*My Fair Lady*	*My Fair Lady* (1956)
On the Sunny Side of the Street	*On the Sunny Side of the Street*	*The International Revue* (1930)
Once in Love With Amy	*Where's Charley?*	*Where's Charley?* (1948)
One Kiss	*The New Moon*	*The New Moon* (1928)
Over There	*Yankee Doodle Dandy*	1917
Pack Up Your Troubles in Your Old Kit Bag	*On Moonlight Bay*	*Her Soldier Boy* (1916)
Paris Loves Lovers	*Silk Stockings*	*Silk Stockings* (1955)
The Party's Over	*Bells Are Ringing*	*Bells Are Ringing* (1956)
Peg o' My Heart	*Oh, You Beautiful Doll*	1913
Peggy Sue	*The Buddy Holly Story*	1957
People	*Funny Girl*	*Funny Girl* (1964)
People Will Say We're in Love	*Oklahoma!*	*Oklahoma!* (1943)
The Peppermint Twist	*American Graffiti*	1961
Play a Simple Melody	*There's No Business Like Show Business*	*Watch Your Step* (1914)
Pretty Baby	*Is Everybody Happy?*	*A World of Pleasure* (1915)
A Pretty Girl Is Like a Melody	*The Great Ziegfeld*	*Ziegfeld Follies* (1919)
Put on a Happy Face	*Bye Bye Birdie*	*Bye Bye Birdie* (1960)
Put Your Arms Around Me, Honey	*In the Good Old Summertime*	*Madame Sherry* (1910)
The Rain in Spain	*My Fair Lady*	*My Fair Lady* (1956)
Rock-a-Bye Your Baby to a Dixie Melody	*The Jolson Story*	*Sinbad* (1918)
Rock Around the Clock	*Rock Around the Clock*	1953
Roll Over Beethoven	*American Hot Wax*	1956
Rose-Marie	*Rose-Marie*	*Rose-Marie* (1924)
Row, Row, Row	*The Seven Little Foys*	*Ziegfeld Follies of 1912*
'S Wonderful	*An American in Paris*	*Funny Face* (1927)
Say It With Music	*Alexander's Ragtime Band*	*Music Box Revue* (1921)
Second Hand Rose	*My Man*	*Ziegfeld Follies* (1921)
See You in September	*American Graffiti*	1959
Send in the Clowns	*A Little Night Music*	*A Little Night Music* (1973)
September Song	*Knickerbocker Holiday*	*Knickerbocker Holiday* (1938)
Seventy-Six Trombones	*The Music Man*	*The Music Man* (1957)
Shall We Dance?	*The King and I*	*The King and I* (1951)
Shine On, Harvest Moon	*The Great Ziegfeld*	*Follies of 1908*
A Shine on Your Shoes	*The Band Wagon*	*Flying Colors* (1932)
Short'ning Bread	*Louisiana Hayride*	1928
The Sidewalks of New York	*The Dolly Sisters*	1894

Sing for Your Supper	*The Boys From Syracuse*	*The Boys From Syracuse* (1938)
Sit Down, You're Rockin' the Boat	*Guys and Dolls*	*Guys and Dolls* (1950)
Sixteen Candles	*American Graffiti*	1959
Small World	*Gypsy*	*Gypsy* (1959)
Smiles	*Applause*	*Passing Show of 1918*
Smoke Gets in Your Eyes	*Roberta*	*Roberta* (1933)
Softly, as in a Morning Sunrise	*Deep in My Heart*	*The New Moon* (1928)
Some Enchanted Evening	*South Pacific*	*South Pacific* (1949)
Some of These Days	*All That Jazz*	1910
Somebody Loves Me	*Rhapsody in Blue*	*George White's Scandals* (1924)
Someone to Watch Over Me	*Star!*	*Oh, Kay!* (1926)
Something to Remember You By	*Dancing in the Dark*	*Three's a Crowd* (1930)
Something Wonderful	*The King and I*	*The King and I* (1951)
Sometimes I'm Happy	*Hit the Deck*	*Hit the Deck* (1927)
Somewhere	*West Side Story*	*West Side Story* (1957)
Somewhere That's Green	*Little Shop of Horrors*	*Little Shop of Horrors* (1982)
The Sound of Music	*The Sound of Music*	*The Sound of Music* (1959)
South American Way	*Down Argentine Way*	*The Streets of Paris* (1939)
Speak Low	*One Touch of Venus*	*One Touch of Venus* (1943)
St. Louis Blues	*Birth of the Blues*	1914
Star Dust	*Star Dust*	1929
Steam Heat	*The Pajama Game*	*The Pajama Game* (1954)
Stormy Weather	*Stormy Weather*	1933
Stouthearted Men	*Deep in My Heart*	*The New Moon* (1928)
Stranger in Paradise	*Kismet*	*Kismet* (1953)
Strike Up the Band	*Strike Up the Band*	*Strike Up the Band* (1930)
Summertime	*Porgy and Bess*	*Porgy and Bess* (1935)
Sunrise, Sunset	*Fiddler on the Roof*	*Fiddler on the Roof* (1964)
Surrey With the Fringe on Top	*Oklahoma!*	*Oklahoma!* (1943)
Swanee	*A Star Is Born*	*Demi-Tasse Revue* (1919)
Sweet Georgia Brown	*The Helen Morgan Story*	1925
Sweet Rosie O'Grady	*Sweet Rosie O'Grady*	1896
Sweethearts	*Sweethearts*	*Sweethearts* (1913)
Sympathy	*The Firefly*	*The Firefly* (1912)
Take Me Out to the Ball Game	*Take Me Out to the Ball Game*	1908
Take the "A" Train	*Reveille With Beverly*	1941
Taking a Chance on Love	*Cabin in the Sky*	*Cabin in the Sky* (1940)
Tea for Two	*Tea for Two*	*No No Nanette* (1925)
Ten Cents a Dance	*Love Me or Leave Me*	*Simple Simon* (1930)

That'll Be the Day	*The Buddy Holly Story*	1957
There Is Nuthin' Like a Dame	*South Pacific*	*South Pacific* (1949)
There's a Small Hotel	*Words and Music*	*On Your Toes* (1936)
There's No Business Like Show Business	*Annie Get Your Gun*	*Annie Get Your Gun* (1946)
These Foolish Things	*Ghost Catchers*	1936
They Call the Wind Maria	*Paint Your Wagon*	*Paint Your Wagon* (1951)
They Didn't Believe Me	*Till the Clouds Roll By*	*The Girl From Utah* (1914)
They Say It's Wonderful	*Annie Get Your Gun*	*Annie Get Your Gun* (1946)
This Can't Be Love	*The Boys From Syracuse*	*The Boys From Syracuse* (1938)
Thou Swell	*Words and Music*	*A Connecticut Yankee* (1927)
Till the Clouds Roll By	*Till the Clouds Roll By*	*Oh, Boy!* (1917)
Till There Was You	*The Music Man*	*The Music Man* (1957)
Till We Meet Again	*On Moonlight Bay*	1918
Together	*Gypsy*	*Gypsy* (1959)
Tomorrow	*Annie*	*Annie* (1977)
Tonight	*West Side Story*	*West Side Story* (1957)
Too Darn Hot	*Kiss Me, Kate*	*Kiss Me, Kate* (1948)
Too-Ra-Loo-Ra-Loo-Rah	*Going My Way*	1914
Toot, Toot, Tootsie	*The Jazz Singer*	*Bombo* (1921)
Toyland	*Babes in Toyland*	*Babes in Toyland* (1903)
Triplets	*The Band Wagon*	*Between the Devil* (1937)
The Twist	*Let the Good Times Roll*	1958
Two Lost Souls	*Damn Yankees*	*Damn Yankees* (1955)
Under the Bamboo Tree	*Meet Me in St. Louis*	*Sally in Our Alley* (1902)
The Varsity Drag	*Good News*	*Good News* (1927)
Wait Till the Sun Shines, Nellie	*Rhythm Parade*	1905
Waiting for the Robert E. Lee	*Babes on Broadway*	1912
What I Did for Love	*A Chorus Line*	*A Chorus Line* (1975)
What'll I Do?	*Alexander's Ragtime Band*	*Music Box Revue* (1923)
What's the Use of Wond'rin'?	*Carousel*	*Carousel* (1945)
When I'm Not Near the Girl I Love	*Finian's Rainbow*	*Finian's Rainbow* (1947)
When Irish Eyes Are Smiling	*Coney Island*	*The Isle o' Dreams* (1913)
When the Moon Comes Over the Mountain	*The Big Broadcast*	1931
When You Were Sweet Sixteen	*Little Miss Broadway*	1898
Where or When	*Babes in Arms*	*Babes in Arms* (1937)
Who?	*Till the Clouds Roll By*	*Sunny* (1925)

Why Can't You Behave?	*Kiss Me, Kate*	*Kiss Me, Kate* (1948)
Why Do I Love You?	*Show Boat*	*Show Boat* (1927)
Why Was I Born?	*Sweet Adeline*	*Sweet Adeline* (1929)
Wild Rose	*Sally*	*Sally* (1920)
Will You Remember?	*Maytime*	*Maytime* (1917)
With a Little Bit of Luck	*My Fair Lady*	*My Fair Lady* (1957)
With a Song in My Heart	*Words and Music*	*Spring Is Here* (1929)
A Wonderful Guy	*South Pacific*	*South Pacific* (1949)
Wouldn't It Be Loverly?	*My Fair Lady*	*My Fair Lady* (1956)
Wunderbar	*Kiss Me, Kate*	*Kiss Me, Kate* (1948)
Y.M.C.A.	*Can't Stop the Music*	1979
Yakety Yak	*Stand By Me*	1958
The Yankee Doodle Boy	*Yankee Doodle Dandy*	*Little Johnny Jones* (1904)
Yes Sir, That's My Baby	*I'll See You in My Dreams*	1925
Yes, We Have No Bananas	*The Eddie Cantor Story*	1923
You Are Love	*Show Boat*	*Show Boat* (1927)
You Do Something to Me	*Night and Day*	*Fifty Million Frenchmen* (1929)
You Made Me Love You	*Broadway Melody of 1938*	*The Honeymoon Express* (1913)
You Took Advantage of Me	*A Star Is Born*	*Present Arms* (1928)
You'll Never Walk Alone	*Carousel*	*Carousel* (1945)
Younger Than Springtime	*South Pacific*	*South Pacific* (1949)
Your Cheatin' Heart	*Your Cheatin' Heart*	1952
You're a Grand Old Flag	*Yankee Doodle Dandy*	*George Washington, Jr.* (1906)
You're Just in Love	*Call Me Madam*	*Call Me Madam* (1950)
You're the Cream in My Coffee	*The Best Things in Life Are Free*	*Hold Everything* (1928)
You're the Top	*Anything Goes*	*Anything Goes* (1934)
Zing! Went the Strings of My Heart	*Lullaby of Broadway*	*Thumbs Up!* (1934)

Best Song Oscars

The Academy of Motion Picture Arts and Sciences has given an "Oscar" for Best Song since the 1934 presentation. Listed below are all the winning songs and the films in which they first appeared. Those songs marked * are from film musicals and are included in this book.

1934	"The Continental"*	*The Gay Divorcee*
1935	"Lullaby of Broadway"*	*Gold Diggers of 1935*
1936	"The Way You Look Tonight"*	*Swing Time*
1937	"Sweet Leilani"*	*Waikiki Wedding*
1938	"Thanks for the Memory"*	*The Big Broadcast of 1938*
1939	"Over the Rainbow"*	*The Wizard of Oz*
1940	"When You Wish Upon a Star"*	*Pinocchio*
1941	"The Last Time I Saw Paris"**	*Lady, Be Good*
1942	"White Christmas"*	*Holiday Inn*
1943	"You'll Never Know"*	*Hello, Frisco, Hello*
1944	"Swinging on a Star"*	*Going My Way*
1945	"It Might as Well Be Spring"*	*State Fair*
1946	"On the Atchison, Topeka and the Santa Fe"*	*The Harvey Girls*
1947	"Zip-A-Dee-Doo-Dah"*	*Song of the South*

** "The Last Time I Saw Paris" by Oscar Hammerstein (lyrics) and Jerome Kern (music) was not written for any film but was interpolated into *Lady Be Good* because of its popularity. When it won the Oscar, there were protests by many, including Hammerstein and Kern, and the Academy's rules regarding Best Songs were subsequently changed to include only songs written directly for the screen.

1948	"Buttons and Bows"*	*The Paleface*
1949	"Baby, It's Cold Outside"*	*Neptune's Daughter*
1950	"Mona Lisa"	*Captain Carey, USA*
1951	"In the Cool, Cool, Cool of the Evening"*	*Here Comes the Groom*
1952	"High Noon"	*High Noon*
1953	"Secret Love"*	*Calamity Jane*
1954	"Three Coins in the Fountain"	*Three Coins in the Fountain*
1955	"Love Is a Many-Splendored Thing"	*Love Is a Many-Splendored Thing*
1956	"Whatever Will Be, Will Be"	*The Man Who Knew Too Much*
1957	"All the Way"*	*The Joker Is Wild*
1958	"Gigi"*	*Gigi*
1959	"High Hopes"	*A Hole in the Head*
1960	"Never on Sunday"	*Never on Sunday*
1961	"Moon River"	*Breakfast at Tiffany's*
1962	"Days of Wine and Roses"	*Days of Wine and Roses*
1963	"Call Me Irresponsible"	*Papa's Delicate Condition*
1964	"Chim-Chim-Cheree"*	*Mary Poppins*
1965	"The Shadow of Your Smile"	*The Sandpiper*
1966	"Born Free"	*Born Free*
1967	"Talk to the Animals"*	*Doctor Dolittle*
1968	"The Windmills of Your Mind"	*The Thomas Crown Affair*
1969	"Raindrops Keep Fallin' on My Head"	*Butch Cassidy and the Sundance Kid*
1970	"For All We Know"	*Lovers and Other Strangers*
1971	"Theme from *Shaft*"	*Shaft*
1972	"The Morning After"	*The Poseidon Adventure*
1973	"The Way We Were"	*The Way We Were*
1974	"We May Never Love Like This Again"	*The Towering Inferno*
1975	"I'm Easy"*	*Nashville*
1976	"Evergreen"*	*A Star Is Born*
1977	"You Light Up My Life"	*You Light Up My Life*
1978	"Last Dance"	*Thank God It's Friday*
1979	"It Goes Like It Goes"	*Norma Rae*
1980	"Fame"*	*Fame*
1981	"Arthur's Theme"	*Arthur*
1982	"Up Where We Belong"	*An Officer and a Gentleman*
1983	"Flashdance . . . What a Feeling"	*Flashdance*
1984	"I Just Called to Say I Love You"	*The Woman in Red*
1985	"Say You, Say Me"	*White Nights*
1986	"Take My Breath Away"	*Top Gun*

1987	"(I've Had) The Time of My Life"	*Dirty Dancing*
1988	"Let the River Run"	*Working Girl*
1989	"Under the Sea"*	*The Little Mermaid*
1990	"Sooner or Later"*	*Dick Tracy*
1991	"Beauty and the Beast"*	*Beauty and the Beast*
1992	"A Whole New World"*	*Aladdin*
1993	"Streets of Philadelphia"	*Philadelphia*
1994	"Can You Feel the Love Tonight?"*	*The Lion King*
1995	"Colors of the Wind"*	*Pocahontas*
1996	"You Must Love Me"*	*Evita*
1997	"My Heart Will Go On"	*Titanic*

Oscar-Nominated Film Musicals

Despite their popularity, film musicals have not often been winners of the Oscar for Best Picture. In fact, since sound films were developed, only forty-five movie musicals have been nominated for the award. Listed below are the film musicals that were nominated for Best Picture (the nine actual winners are in **bold** type) and the year in which they were cited.

1929	***Broadway Melody***
	The Hollywood Revue
1930	*The Love Parade*
1931	*One Hour With You*
	The Smiling Lieutenant
1933	*Forty-Second Street*
	She Done Him Wrong
1934	*Flirtation Walk*
	The Gay Divorcée
	One Night of Love
1935	*Broadway Melody of 1936*
	Naughty Marietta
	Top Hat
1936	***The Great Ziegfeld***
	San Francisco
	Three Smart Girls
1937	*In Old Chicago*
	One Hundred Men and a Girl
1938	*Alexander's Ragtime Band*
1939	*The Wizard of Oz*
1942	*Yankee Doodle Dandy*

1944	*Going My Way*
1945	*Anchors Aweigh*
	The Bells of St. Mary's
1948	*The Red Shoes*
1951	*An American in Paris*
1954	*Seven Brides for Seven Brothers*
1956	*The King and I*
1958	*Gigi*
1961	*West Side Story*
1962	*The Music Man*
1964	*Mary Poppins*
	My Fair Lady
1965	*The Sound of Music*
1967	*Doctor Dolittle*
1968	*Oliver!*
	Funny Girl
1969	*Hello, Dolly!*
1971	*Fiddler on the Roof*
1972	*Cabaret*
1975	*Nashville*
1979	*All That Jazz*
1980	*Coal Miner's Daughter*
1991	*Beauty and the Beast*
1997	*Evita*

Film Musicals

All the songs discussed in the *Encyclopedia* are included in this alphabetical list of film musicals. Films based on Broadway or Off-Broadway musical plays are indicated and the year of the stage production's New York City premiere is given. Many other songs from these stage musicals can be found in *The American Musical Theatre Song Encyclopedia*.

Adorable   (Fox 1933)
Adorable

Aladdin   (Disney 1992)
Arabian Nights
Friend Like Me
One Jump Ahead
Prince Ali
A Whole New World

Alexander's Ragtime Band   (Fox 1938)
My Walking Stick
Now It Can Be Told

Alice in Wonderland   (Disney/RKO 1951)
Alice in Wonderland
All in a Golden Afternoon
I'm Late
The Un-Birthday Song

All the King's Horses   (Paramount 1935)

A Little White Gardenia

Anastasia (Fox 1997)
In the Dark of the Night
Journey to the Past
Once Upon a December
Paris Holds the Key

Anchors Aweigh (MGM 1945)
The Charm of You
I Begged Her
I Fall in Love Too Easily
My Heart Sings
What Makes the Sunset?
The Worry Song

And the Angels Sing (Paramount 1944)
Bluebirds in My Belfry
His Rocking Horse Ran Away
It Could Happen to You

Annie (Columbia 1982) [Broadway 1977]
Let's Go to the Movies

Anything Goes (Paramount 1936) [Broadway 1934]
Moonburn
My Heart and I
Sailor Beware

Anything Goes (Paramount 1956)
You Can Bounce Right Back

Applause (Paramount 1929)
Give Your Baby Lots of Lovin'
I've Got a Feeling I'm Falling
What Wouldn't I Do for That Man?

April in Paris (Warner 1952)
I'm Gonna Ring the Bell Tonight
That's What Makes Paris Paree

April Love (Fox 1957)
April Love

Are You There? (Fox 1930)
Queen of the Hunt Am I

Are You With It? (Universal 1048) [Broadway 1945]
Down at Baba's Alley

Argentine Nights (Universal 1940)
Rhumboogie

The Aristocats (Disney 1970)
The Aristocats
Ev'rybody Wants to Be a Cat
Scales and Arpeggios

Artists and Models (Paramount 1937)
I Have Eyes
Public Melody No. 1
Stop, You're Breaking My Heart
Whispers in the Dark

Artists and Models (Paramount 1955)
Artists and Models
Innamorata
When You Pretend

Artists and Models Abroad (Paramount 1938)
What Have You Got That Gets Me?

At the Circus (MGM 1939)
Lydia, the Tattooed Lady
Two Blind Loves

Athena (MGM 1954)
I Never Felt Better
Imagine

Babes in Arms (MGM 1939) [Broadway 1937]
Good Morning

Babes on Broadway (MGM 1941)
Anything Can Happen in New York
Babes on Broadway
Chin Up, Cheerio, Carry On

How About You?

Balalaika (MGM 1939)
Ride, Cossack, Ride

The Band Wagon (MGM 1953) [Broadway 1931]
That's Entertainment

Banjo on My Knee (Fox 1936)
There's Something in the Air
Where the Lazy River Goes By

The Barkleys of Broadway (MGM 1949)
My One and Only Highland Fling
Shoes With Wings On
A Weekend in the Country
You'd Be Hard to Replace

The Battle of Paris (Paramount 1929)
They All Fall in Love

Be Yourself (United Artists 1930)
Cooking Breakfast for the One I Love
When a Woman Loves a Man

Beauty and the Beast (Disney 1991)
Be Our Guest
Beauty and the Beast
Belle
Gaston
Something There

Because You're Mine (MGM 1952)
Because You're Mine

Bedknobs and Broomsticks (Disney 1971)
Age of Not Believing
The Beautiful Briny

A Bedtime Story (Paramount 1933)
In the Park in Paree
Look What I've Got

Behind the Eight Ball (Universal 1942)
Mister Five By Five

The Belle of New York (MGM 1952)
Baby Doll
I Wanna Be a Dancin' Man
Oops!
Seeing's Believing
Thank You, Mr. Currier, Thank You, Mr. Ives

Belle of the Nineties (Paramount 1934)
My Old Flame

Belle of the Yukon (International/RKO 1944)
Like Someone in Love
Sleigh Ride in July

The Bells of St. Mary's (Rainbow/RKO 1945)
Aren't You Glad You're You?

Best Foot Forward (MGM 1943) [Broadway 1941]
Wish I May, Wish I Might

Big Boy (Warner 1930) [Broadway 1925]
Tomorrow Is Another Day

The Big Broadcast (Paramount 1932)
Crazy People
Here Lies Love
It Was So Beautiful
Please
Where the Blue of the Night Meets the Gold of the Day

The Big Broadcast of 1936 (Paramount 1935)
Double Trouble
I Wished on the Moon
It's the Animal in Me
Miss Brown to You
Why Dream?

The Big Broadcast of 1937 (Paramount 1936)
Here's Love in Your Eye
I'm Talking Through My Heart

You Came to My Rescue

The Big Broadcast of 1938 (Paramount 1938)
Mama, That Moon Is Here Again
Thanks for the Memory
You Took the Words Right Out of My Mouth

The Big Pond (Paramount 1930)
Living in the Sunlight — Loving in the Moonlight
You Brought a New Kind of Love to Me

Birth of the Blues (Paramount 1941)
The Waiter and the Porter and the Upstairs Maid

Blonde From Brooklyn (Columbia 1945)
My Baby Says Yes

Bloodhounds of Broadway (Fox 1952)
Bye Low

Blossoms on Broadway (Paramount 1937)
Blossoms on Broadway

Blue Hawaii (Paramount 1961)
Can't Help Falling in Love

Blue Skies (Paramount 1946)
A Couple of Song and Dance Men
Getting Nowhere
You Keep Coming Back Like a Song

Blues in the Night (Warner/1st National 1941)
Blues in the Night
Hang on to Your Lids, Kids
Says Who, Says You, Says I
This Time the Dream's On Me

Born to Dance (MGM 1936)
Easy to Love
Hey, Babe, Hey!
I've Got You Under My Skin
Love Me, Love My Pekinese
Rap Tap on Wood

Swingin' the Jinx Away

Bottoms Up (Fox 1934)
Waitin' at the Gate for Katy

The Boys From Syracuse (Universal 1940) [Broadway 1938]
Who Are You?

Bright Eyes (Fox 1934)
On the Good Ship Lollipop

Broadway Gondolier (Warner 1935)
Lulu's Back in Town
Outside of You
The Rose in Her Hair

The Broadway Melody (MGM 1929)
Broadway Melody
The Wedding of the Painted Doll
You Were Meant for Me

Broadway Melody of 1936 (MGM 1935)
Broadway Rhythm
I've Got a Feelin' You're Foolin'
On a Sunday Afternoon
Sing Before Breakfast
You Are My Lucky Star

Broadway Melody of 1938 (MGM 1937)
Everybody Sing
I'm Feelin' Like a Million
Your Broadway and My Broadway
Yours and Mine

Broadway Melody of 1940 (MGM 1940)
Between You and Me
I Concentrate on You
I've Got My Eyes on You
Please Don't Monkey With Broadway

Broadway Rhythm (MGM 1944) [on Broadway as *Very Warm for May* 1939]
Amor

Irresistible
Milkman, Keep Those Bottles Quiet

Broadway Through a Keyhole (20th Century/United Artists 1933)
Doin' the Uptown Lowdown

Buck Benny Rides Again (Paramount 1940)
My! My!
Say It

Buck Privates (Universal 1941)
Boogie Woogie Bugle Boy
Bounce Me Brother With a Solid Four
You're a Lucky Fellow, Mr. Smith

Bugsy Malone (Rank/Paramount 1976)
Bugsy Malone
Ordinary Fool
Tomorrow
You Give a Little Love

Bye Bye Birdie (Columbia 1963) [Broadway 1960]
Bye Bye Birdie

Cabaret (ABC/Allied Artists 1972) [Broadway 1966]
Maybe This Time
Mein Herr
Money, Money

Cabin in the Sky (MGM 1943) [Broadway 1940]
Happiness Is (Just) a Thing Called Joe
Life's Full of Consequence

The Caddy (Paramount 1953)
That's Amore

Cain and Mabel (Warner 1936)
I'll Sing You a Thousand Love Songs

Cairo (MGM 1942)
Buds Won't Bud

Calamity Jane (Warner 1953)

The Black Hills of Dakota
The Deadwood Stage
Just Blew in From the Windy City
Secret Love

Call Me Mister (Fox 1951) [Broadway 1946]
I Just Can't Do Enough for You
Love Is Back in Business

Cameo Kirby (Fox 1930)
Romance

Can Heironymus Merkin Ever Forget Mercy Humppe and Find True Happiness? (Universal 1969)
On the Boards
Piccadilly Lily
Sweet Love Child

Can't Help Singing (Universal 1944)
Any Moment Now
Californ-i-ay
Can't Help Singing
More and More

Captain January (Fox 1936)
At the Codfish Ball
Early Bird
The Right Somebody to Love

Carefree (RKO 1938)
Change Partners
I Used to Be Color Blind
The Yam

Carnegie Hall (Federal/United Artists 1947)
Beware My Heart

Carnival in Costa Rica (Fox 1947)
Another Night Like This

Carolina Blues (Columbia 1944)
There Goes That Song Again

Casbah (Marston/Universal 1948)
For Every Man There's a Woman
Hooray for Love
It Was Written in the Stars
What's Good About Goodbye?

Cats Don't Dance (Warner 1996)
Nothing's Gonna Stop Us Now
Tell Me Lies

Centennial Summer (Fox 1946)
All Through the Day
Cinderella Sue
In Love in Vain
The Right Romance
Up With the Lark

Charlotte's Web (Paramount 1973)
Charlotte's Web
Mother Earth and Father Time
A Veritable Smorgasbord

Chasing Rainbows (MGM 1930)
Happy Days Are Here Again

Check and Double Check (RKO 1930)
Three Little Words

Chitty Chitty Bang Bang (Warfield/United Artists 1968)
Chitty Chitty Bang Bang
Hushabye Mountain
Toot Sweets

A Chorus Line (Universal 1984) [Broadway 1975]
Let Me Dance for You
Surprise, Surprise

Cinderella (Disney 1950)
Bibbidi, Bobbidi, Boo
A Dream Is a Wish Your Heart Makes
Sing, Sweet Nightingale

Clambake (United Artists 1967)

The Girl I Never Loved

Close Harmony (Paramount 1929)
I Want to Go Places and Do Things

C'mon Let's Live a Little (Paramount 1967)
Over and Over

Cocoanut Grove (Paramount 1938)
Says My Heart
You Leave Me Breathless

The Cocoanuts (Paramount 1929) [Broadway 1925]
When My Dreams Come True

Colleen (Warner-Vitaphone 1936)
A Boulevardier From the Bronx

College Humor (Paramount 1933)
Down Old Ox Road
Learn to Croon
Moonstruck

College Rhythm (Paramount 1934)
College Rhythm
Let's Give Three Cheers for Love
Stay As Sweet As You Are
Take a Number From One to Ten

College Swing (Paramount 1938)
College Swing
How 'dya Like to Love Me?
I Fall in Love With You Every Day
Moments Like This

Collegiate (Paramount 1936)
I Feel Like a Feather in a Breeze
You Hit the Spot

Coney Island (Fox 1943)
Beautiful Coney Island
Lulu From Louisville
Take It From There

There's Danger in a Dance

A Connecticut Yankee in King Arthur's Court (Paramount 1949)
Busy Doing Nothing
If You Stub Your Toe on the Moon
Once and Far Away
When Is Sometime?

Copacabana (United Artists 1947)
Go West, Young Man
Let's Do the Copacabana

Coronado (Paramount 1935)
How Do I Rate With You?
Keep Your Fingers Crossed

The Court Jester (Paramount 1956)
I'll Take You Dreaming
The Maladjusted Jester

Cover Girl (Columbia 1944)
Cover Girl
Long Ago and Far Away
Make Way for Tomorrow
Put Me to the Test
Sure Thing

Cowboy From Brooklyn (Warner 1938)
Cowboy From Brooklyn
I'll Dream Tonight
Ride, Tenderfoot, Ride

Cross My Heart (Paramount 1946)
That Little Dream Got Nowhere

Cuban Love Song (MGM 1931)
Cuban Love Song
The Peanut Vendor

The Cuckoos (RKO 1930) [on Broadway as *The Ramblers* 1926]
I Love You So Much
I'm a Gypsy

Curly Top (Fox 1935)
Animal Crackers in My Soup
Curly Top
The Simple Things in Life
When I Grow Up

Daddy Long Legs (Fox 1955)
Something's Gotta Give
Sluefoot

Dames (Warner-Vitaphone 1934)
Dames
The Girl at the Ironing Board
I Only Have Eyes for You

Damsel in Distress (RKO 1937)
A Foggy Day
I Can't Be Bothered Now
The Jolly Tar and the Milkmaid
Nice Work If You Can Get It
Stiff Upper Lip
Things Are Looking Up

Dance Girl Dance (RKO 1940)
Oh Mother, What Do I Do Now?

Dance of Life (Paramount 1929)
True Blue Lou

Dancing Lady (MGM 1933)
Everything I Have Is Yours
Heigh-Ho, the Gang's All Here
Let's Go Bavarian
My Dancing Lady
That's the Rhythm of the Day

Dancing on a Dime (Paramount 1941)
Dancing on a Dime
I Hear Music

The Dancing Pirate (RKO 1936)
When You're Dancing the Waltz

Dangerous When Wet (MGM 1953)
Ain't Nature Grand
I Got Out of Bed on the Right Side

Darling Lili (Paramount 1970)
I'll Give You Three Guesses
Whistling Away the Dark

A Date With Judy (MGM 1948)
Cuanto Le Gusta
I'm Cookin' With Gas
It's a Most Unusual Day
Judaline
Strictly on the Corny Side

A Day at the Races (MGM 1937)
All God's Chillun Got Rhythm
Tomorrow Is Another Day

Delicious (Fox 1931)
Blah, Blah, Blah
Delishious
Somebody From Somewhere

Devil May Care (MGM 1929)
Charming
If He Cared
The Shepherd's Serenade

Diamond Horseshoe (Fox 1945)
I Wish I Knew
In Acapulco
The More I See You
A Nickel's Worth of Jive
Play Me an Old-Fashioned Melody

Dick Tracy (Touchstone/Disney 1990)
Back in Business
More
Sooner or Later
What Can You Lose

Dimples (Fox 1936)

Picture Me Without You

Dixie (Paramount 1943)
Sunday, Monday, or Always

Doctor Dolittle (APJAC/Fox 1967)
Talk to the Animals
When I Look in Your Eyes

Doctor Rhythm (Major/Paramount 1938)
My Heart Is Taking Lessons
On the Sentimental Side
This Is My Night to Dream

Doll Face (Fox 1945)
Here Comes Heaven Again
A Hubba Hubba Hubba

The Dolly Sisters (Fox 1945)
I Can't Begin to Tell You

Double or Nothing (Paramount 1937)
All You Want to Do Is Dance
It's On, It's Off
It's the Natural Thing to Do
Listen My Children and You Will Hear
The Moon Got in My Eyes
Smarty

Double Trouble (MGM 1967)
Could I Fall in Love?

Down Among the Sheltering Palms (Fox 1953)
I'm a Ruler of a South Sea Island

Down Argentine Way (Fox 1940)
Down Argentina Way
Two Dreams Met

DuBarry Was a Lady (MGM 1943) [Broadway 1939]
I Love an Esquire Girl
Madam, I Love Your Crepes Suzettes
Salome

Duck Soup (Paramount 1933)
The Country's Going to War
Freedonia Hymn

Duffy's Tavern (Paramount 1945)
Doin' It the Hard Way

Dumbo (Disney/RKO 1941)
Baby Mine
Pink Elephants on Parade
When I See an Elephant Fly

Earl Carroll Vanities (Republic 1945)
Endlessly

East Side of Heaven (Universal 1939)
East Side of Heaven
Hang Your Heart on a Hickory Limb
Sing a Song of Sunbeams

Easter Parade (MGM 1948)
Better Luck Next Time
A Couple of Swells
A Fella With an Umbrella
It Only Happens When I Dance With You
Steppin' Out With My Baby

The Emperor Waltz (Paramount 1948)
The Kiss in Your Eyes

Every Day's a Holiday (Paramount 1937)
Every Day's a Holiday
Fifi
Jubilee

Every Night at Eight (Paramount 1935)
I Feel a Song Comin' On
I'm in the Mood for Love
Speaking Confidentially
Take it Easy

Everybody Sing (MGM 1938)
The One I Love

Everything I Have Is Yours (MGM 1952)
Derry Down Dilly

Evita (Hollywood Pictures 1997) [Broadway 1979]
You Must Love Me

Excuse My Dust (MGM 1951)
Spring Is Sprung

Fame (MGM 1980)
Fame
Hot Lunch Jam
I Sing the Body Electric
Out Here on My Own

The Farmer Takes a Wife (Fox 1953)
Today I Love Ev'rybody
We're in Business
With the Sun Warm Upon Me

The Firefly (MGM 1937) [Broadway 1912]
The Donkey Serenade

First Love (Universal 1939)
Amapola

The Five Pennies (Dena/Paramount 1959)
The Five Pennies
Lullaby in Ragtime

The 5,000 Fingers of Dr. T (Columbia 1953)
Dream Stuff
The Dressing Song
The Kid's Song

The Fleet's In (Paramount 1942)
Arthur Murray Taught Me Dancing in a Hurry
Build a Better Mousetrap
I Remember You
Not Mine
Tangerine

Flirtation Walk (1st National 1934)

Flirtation Walk
I See Two Lovers
Mr. and Mrs. Is the Name

Flying Down to Rio (RKO 1933)
The Carioca
Flying Down to Rio
Music Makes Me
Orchids in the Moonlight

Folies Bergère (20th Century/United Artists 1935)
I Was Lucky
Rhythm of the Rain
You Took the Words Right Out of My Mouth

Follow That Bird (Warner 1985)
Ain't No Road Too Long
Grouch Anthem
One Little Star

Follow the Band (Universal 1943)
Rosie the Riveter

Follow the Boys (Universal 1944)
I'll Walk Alone
Is You Is or Is You Ain't My Baby?

Follow the Boys (MGM 1962)
Follow the Boys

Follow the Fleet (RKO 1936)
But Where Are You?
Get Thee Behind Me, Satan
I'd Rather Lead a Band
I'm Putting All My Eggs in One Basket
Let Yourself Go
Let's Face the Music and Dance
We Saw the Sea

Follow the Leader (Paramount 1930) [on Broadway as *Manhattan Mary* 1927]
Satan's Holiday

Follow Through (Paramount 1930) [on Broadway as *Follow Thru* 1929]
It Must Be You
We'd Make a Peach of a Pair

Footlight Parade (Warner 1933)
By a Waterfall
Honeymoon Hotel
Shanghai Lil
Sittin' on a Backyard Fence

Footlight Serenade (Fox 1942)
I Heard the Birdies Sing
I'm Still Crazy for You

A Foreign Affair (Paramount 1948)
Illusions

Forty-Second Street (Warner-Vitaphone 1933)
Forty-Second Street
Shuffle Off to Buffalo
Young and Healthy
You're Getting to Be a Habit With Me

Four Jacks and a Jill (RKO 1941)
You Go Your Way

Four Jills in a Jeep (Fox 1944)
How Blue the Night
How Many Times Do I Have to Tell You?

Fox Movietone Follies of 1929 (Fox 1929)
Big City Blues

Frankie and Johnny (RKO 1936)
Give Me a Heart to Sing

Frankie and Johnny (United Artists 1966)
Look Out Broadway
Please Don't Stop Loving Me

The French Line (RKO 1954)
Any Gal From Texas
Lookin' for Trouble

With a Kiss

Fun and Fancy Free (RKO 1947)
I'm a Happy-Go-Lucky Fellow

Funny Face (Paramount 1957) [Broadway 1927]
Bonjour, Paris!
Think Pink

Funny Girl (Rastar/Columbia 1968) [Broadway 1964]
Funny Girl

Funny Lady (Rastar/Columbia 1975)
How Lucky Can You Get?
I Like Him
Isn't This Better?
Let's Hear It for Me

The Gang's All Here (Fox 1943)
The Lady in the Tutti-Frutti Hat
A Journey to a Star
The Polka Dot Polka
No Love, No Nothin'

Garden of the Moon (1st National 1938)
Confidentially
The Girl Friend of the Whirling Dervish
Love Is Where You Find It

The Gay Divorcee (RKO 1934) [on Broadway as *The Gay Divorce* 1932]
The Continental
Don't Let It Bother You
Let's K-nock K-nees

Gay Purr-ee (UPA/Warner 1962)
Little Drops of Rain
Paris Is a Lonely Town
Take My Hand, Paree

Gentlemen Prefer Blondes (Fox 1953) [Broadway 1949]
Ain't There Anyone Here for Love
When Love Goes Wrong

George White's Scandals (Fox 1934)
Hold My Hand
Oh, You Nasty Man

George White's Scandals (Fox 1935)
According to the Moonlight

Gigi (MGM 1958)
Gigi
I Remember It Well
I'm Glad I'm Not Young Anymore
It's a Bore
The Night They Invented Champagne
The Parisians
Say a Prayer for Me Tonight
She's Not Thinking of Me
Thank Heavens for Little Girls

The Girl Can't Help It (Fox 1956)
Blue Monday
The Girl Can't Help It

Girl Crazy (RKO 1932) [Broadway 1930]
You've Got What Gets Me

Girl Happy (1965)
I've Got News for You
Puppet on a String
Spring Fever
Wolf Call

The Girl Most Likely (RKO 1958)
I Don't Know What I Want

The Girl Next Door (Fox 1953)
Nowhere Guy

The Girl Rush (Paramount 1955)
Birmin'ham
An Occasional Man

Girls, Girls, Girls (Paramount 1962)
Return to Sender

Give a Girl a Break (MGM 1953)
Applause, Applause
In Our United State
It Happens Every Time

Give Me a Sailor (Paramount 1938)
Just a Kiss at Twilight
What Goes on Here in My Heart?

Give Out, Sisters (Universal 1942)
Pennsylvania Polka

Give Us This Night (Paramount 1936)
Music in the Night

The Glass Slipper (MGM 1954)
Take My Love

Go Into Your Dance (Warner 1935)
About a Quarter to Nine
Go Into Your Dance
The Little Things You Used to Do
She's a Latin from Manhattan

Go West Young Man (Paramount 1937)
I Was Saying to the Moon

Godspell (Columbia 1973) [Off Broadway 1971]
Beautiful City

Goin' to Town (Paramount 1935)
Now I'm a Lady

Going Hollywood (Cosmopolitan/MGM 1933)
After Sundown
Beautiful Girl
Cinderella's Fella
Going Hollywood
Our Big Love Scene
Temptation
We'll Make Hay While the Sun Shines

Going My Way (Paramount 1944)

The Day After Forever
Going My Way
Swinging on a Star

Going Places (Warner 1938)
Jeepers Creepers
Mutiny in the Nursery
Say It With a Kiss

Gold Diggers in Paris (Warner 1938)
Day Dreaming
The Latin Quarter
I Wanna Go Back to Bali

Gold Diggers of Broadway (Warner 1929)
Painting the Clouds With Sunshine
Tip Toe Through the Tulips With Me

Gold Diggers of 1933 (1st National-Vitaphone 1933)
I've Got to Sing a Torch Song
Pettin' in the Park
Remember My Forgotten Man
Shadow Waltz
We're in the Money

Gold Diggers of 1935 (1st National-Vitaphone 1935)
Lullaby of Broadway
I'm Going Shoppin' With You
The Words Are in My Heart

Gold Diggers of 1937 (1st National 1937)
All's Fair in Love and War
Let's Put Our Heads Together
With Plenty of Money and You

Golden Girl (Fox 1951)
Never

The Goldwyn Follies (Goldwyn/United Artists 1938)
I Love to Rhyme
I Was Doing All Right
Love Is Here to Stay
Love Walked In

Spring Again

Good News (MGM 1947) [Broadway 1927]
The French Lesson
Pass That Peace Pipe

Goodbye, Mr. Chips (APJAC/MGM 1969)
Fill the World With Love
Walk Through the World

Grease (Paramount 1978) [Broadway 1972]
Grease
Hopelessly Devoted to You
You're the One That I Want

Grease 2 (Paramount 1982)
Back to School Again
Girl for All Seasons

The Great American Broadcast (Fox 1941)
It's All in a Lifetime
Where You Are

The Great Caruso (MGM 1951)
The Loveliest Night of the Year

The Great Muppet Caper (ITC 1981)
Couldn't We Ride?

The Great Waltz (MGM 1938)
One Day When We Were Young

The Great Ziegfeld (MGM 1936)
You
You Never Looked So Beautiful

Gulliver's Travels (Paramount 1939)
Bluebirds in the Moonlight
Faithful Forever
It's a Hap-Hap-Happy Day

Guys and Dolls (Goldwyn/MGM 1955) [Broadway 1950]
Adelaide

Pet Me Poppa
A Woman in Love

Hallelujah (MGM 1929)
Waiting At the End of the Road

Hallelujah, I'm a Bum (United Artists 1933)
Hallelujah, I'm a Bum
You Are Too Beautiful

Hans Christian Andersen (Goldwyn/RKO 1952)
Anywhere I Wander
I'm Hans Christian Andersen
The Inch Worm
No Two People
Thumbelina
The Ugly Duckling
Wonderful Copenhagen

The Happiest Millionaire (Disney, 1967)
Fortuosity
Valentine Candy

Happiness Ahead (Warner-Vitaphone 1934)
Happiness Ahead
Pop! Goes Your Heart

Happy Days (Fox 1930)
Crazy Feet

Happy Go Lucky (Republic 1943)
The Fuddy Duddy Watchmaker
Happy Go Lucky
Let's Get Lost
Murder, He Says
Sing a Tropical Song

A Hard Day's Night (United Artists 1964)
And I Love Her
Can't Buy Me Love
A Hard Day's Night
I Should Have Known Better

Hard to Get (Warner 1938)
You Must Have Been a Beautiful Baby

The Harvey Girls (MGM 1946)
In the Valley
It's a Great Big World
On the Atchison, Topeka and the Santa Fe
Swing Your Partner Round and Round
Wait and See
The Wild, Wild West

Hawaii Calls (RKO 1938)
Down Where the Trade Winds Blow

Heads Up (Paramount 1930) [Broadway 1929]
Readin', Ritin', Rhythm

Hearts in Dixie (Fox 1929)
Mammy's Gone

Hello, Dolly! (Fox 1969) [Broadway 1964]
Just Leave Everything to Me
Love Is Only Love

Hello, Everybody! (Paramount 1933)
Moon Song

Hello, Frisco, Hello (Fox 1943)
You'll Never Know

Hellzapoppin' (Universal 1941) [Broadway 1938]
Watch the Birdie

Help! (United Artists 1965)
Help!
Ticket to Ride
You're Gonna Lose That Girl
You've Got to Hide Your Love Away

Hercules (Disney 1997)
Go the Distance
The Gospel Truth
I Won't Say I'm in Love

Zero to Hero

Here Come the Waves (Paramount 1944)
Ac-cent-chu-ate the Positive
I Promise You
Let's Take the Long Way Home
There's a Fellow Waiting in Poughkeepsie

Here Comes Cookie (Paramount 1935)
Vamp of the Pampas

Here Comes Elmer (Republic 1944)
Straighten Up and Fly Right

Here Comes the Band (MGM 1935)
Roll Along, Prairie Moon
You're My Thrill

Here Comes the Groom (Paramount 1951)
Bonne Nuit — Goodnight
In the Cool, Cool, Cool of the Evening
Misto Cristo Colombo

Here Is My Heart (Paramount 1934)
June in January
Love Is Just Around the Corner
With Every Breath I Take

Here's to Romance (Paramount 1935)
Midnight in Paris

Hideaway Girl (Paramount 1937)
You're Dancing Into My Heart

High Society (Siegle/MGM 1956)
I Love You, Samantha
Mind If I Make Love to You?
Now You Has Jazz
True Love
You're Sensational
Who Wants to Be a Millionaire?

High Society Blues (Fox 1930)

I'm in the Market for You

High Time (Fox 1960)
The Second Time Around

High, Wide and Handsome (Paramount 1937)
Allegheny Al
Can I Forget You?
The Folks Who Live on the Hill
High, Wide and Handsome
The Things I Want

Higher and Higher (RKO 1943) [Broadway 1940]
I Couldn't Sleep a Wink Last Night
I Saw You First
A Lovely Way to Spend an Evening
The Music Stopped
You're on Your Own

Hips Hips Hooray (RKO 1934)
Keep on Doin' What You're Doin'
Tired of It All

His Butler's Sister (Universal 1943)
In the Spirit of the Moment

Hit Parade of 1937 (Republic 1937)
Was It Rain?

Hit Parade of 1941 (Republic 1941)
In the Cool of the Evening
Swing Low Sweet Rhythm
Who Am I?

Hit Parade of 1943 (Republic 1943)
Change of Heart

Hit the Deck (Radio 1930) [Broadway 1927]
Keepin' Myself for You

Hold That Ghost (Universal 1941)
Aurora

Holiday Inn (Paramount 1942)
Abraham
Be Careful, It's My Heart
Happy Holiday
I'll Capture Your Heart Singing
Let's Start the New Year Right
Say It With Firecrackers
White Christmas
You're Easy to Dance With

Hollywood Canteen (Warner 1944)
Corns for My Country
Don't Fence Me In
Sweet Dreams, Sweetheart

Hollywood Hotel (1st National 1937)
Hooray for Hollywood
I'm Like a Fish Out of Water
I've Hitched My Wagon to a Star
Let That Be a Lesson to You
Silhouetted in the Moonlight

Hollywood Party (MGM 1934)
Feelin' High

The Hollywood Revue of 1929 (1929)
Gotta Feelin' for You
Nobody But You
Orange Blossom Time
Singin' in the Rain
Your Mother and Mine

Honey (Paramount 1930)
Let's Be Domestic
Sing, You Sinners

Honky Tonk (Warner 1929)
He's a Good Man to Have Around
I'm the Last of the Red Hot Mammas

Honolulu (MGM 1939)
Honolulu
The Leader Doesn't Like Music

Hooray for Love (RKO 1935)
Hooray for Love
You're an Angel

Horse Feathers (Paramount 1932)
Everybody Says I Love You
I'm Against It

The Hot Heiress (First National 1931)
Nobody Loves a Riveter

The Hunchback of Notre Dame (Disney 1996)
The Bells of Notre Dame
God Help the Outcasts
A Guy Like You
Heaven's Light/ Hellfire
Out There

I Could Go on Singing (Barbican/United Artists 1963)
I Could Go on Singing

I Dream Too Much (RKO 1935)
I Dream Too Much
I Got Love
The Jockey on the Carousel

I Dood It (MGM 1943)
Star Eyes

I Love Melvin (MGM 1953)
I Wanna Wander
A Lady Loves
Saturday Afternoon Before the Game

Iceland (Fox 1942)
It's a Lovers' Knot
There Will Never Be Another You
You Can't Say No to a Soldier

If I Had My Way (Universal 1940)
April Played the Fiddle
I Haven't Time to Be a Millionaire
Meet the Sun Half Way

I'll Take Romance (Columbia 1937)
I'll Take Romance

I'll Take Sweden (United Artists 1965)
I'll Take Sweden
Nothing Can Compare With You

I'm No Angel (Paramount 1933)
I Found a New Way to Go to Town
I'm No Angel
They Call Me Sister Honky Tonk

In Caliente (1st National 1933)
The Lady in Red
Muchacha

In Old Chicago (Fox 1938)
In Old Chicago
I've Taken a Fancy to You

In Person (RKO 1935)
Don't Mention Love to Me
I Got a New Lease on Life
Out of Sight, Out of Mind

In Society (Universal 1944)
My Dreams Are Getting Better All the Time

Innocents of Paris (Paramount 1929)
Louise
On Top of the World, Alone
Valentine
Wait 'Til You See Ma Cherie

International House (Paramount 1933)
My Bluebird's Singing the Blues
She Was a China Teacup and He Was Just a Mug
Thank Heaven for You

Irene (RKO 1940) [Broadway 1919]
You've Got Me Out on a Limb

It Happened in Brooklyn (MGM 1947)

Brooklyn Bridge
I Believe
It's the Same Old Dream
The Song's Gotta Come From the Heart
Time After Time

It's a Great Feeling (Warner 1949)
At the Cafe Rendezvous
Blame My Absent Minded Heart
Fiddle Dee Dee
It's a Great Feeling

It's Always Fair Weather (MGM 1955)
Baby, You Knock Me Out
I Like Myself
Music Is Better Than Words
Thanks a Lot But No Thanks
Time for Parting

Jailhouse Rock (MGM 1957)
Baby, I Don't Care
Jailhouse Rock
Treat Me Nice

James and the Giant Peach (Disney 1996)
Family

The Jazz Singer (Warner-Vitaphone 1927)
Mother of Mine, I Still Have You

The Jazz Singer (EMI 1980)
America
Love on the Rocks

Jimmy and Sally (Fox 1933)
You're My Thrill

Johnny Apollo (Fox 1940)
This Is the Beginning of the End

The Joker Is Wild (AMBL/Paramount 1957)
All the Way

The Jolson Story (Columbia 1946)
Anniversary Song

Joy of Living (RKO 1938)
Just Let Me Look at You
What's Good About Goodnight
You Couldn't Be Cuter

Jumbo (MGM 1962) [Broadway 1935]
Sawdust, Spangles and Dreams

The Jungle Book (Disney 1967)
The Bare Necessities
I Wan'na Be Like You
That's What Friends Are For

Jupiter's Darling (MGM 1955)
I Have a Dream
If This Be Slav'ry

Just Around the Corner (Fox 1938)
I Love to Walk in the Rain

Just for You (Paramount 1952)
I'll Si-Si Ya in Bahia
Zing a Little Zong

Just Imagine (Fox 1930)
I Am the Words

Keep 'Em Flying (Universal 1941)
Pig Foot Pete
You Don't Know What Love Is

The Kid From Brooklyn (Goldwyn/RKO 1946)
You're the Cause of It All

The Kid From Spain (United Artists 1932)
Look What You've Done
What a Perfect Combination

Kid Galahad (Mirisch/United Artists 1962)
King of the Whole Wide World

Kid Millions (Goldwyn/United Artists 1934)
An Earful of Music
I Want to Be a Minstrel Man
Okay Toots
When My Ship Comes In
Your Head on My Shoulder

King Creole (Paramount 1958)
Crawfish
Don't Ask Me Why
Hard Headed Woman

King of Burlesque (Fox 1935)
I'm Shooting High
I've Got My Fingers Crossed
Lovely Lady
Spreading Rhythm Around

King of Jazz (Universal 1930)
A Bench in the Park
Happy Feet
I Like to Do Things for You
It Happened in Monterey

The King Steps Out (Columbia 1936)
Stars in My Eyes

Kiss Me, Kate (MGM 1953) [Broadway 1948]
From This Moment On

Kiss the Boys Goodbye (Paramount 1941)
I'll Never Let a Day Pass By
Kiss the Boys Goodbye
Sand in My Shoes
That's How I Got My Start

Kissin' Cousins (Four Leaf/MGM 1964)
Kissin' Cousins
Smokey Mountain Boy

The Kissing Bandit (MGM 1948)
If I Steal a Kiss
Love Is Where You Find It

Klondike Annie (Paramount 1936)
Occidental Woman in an Oriental Mood for Love

Labyrinth (Tri-Star 1986)
Magic Dance

Ladies' Man (Paramount 1947)
I Gotta Gal I Love
What Am I Gonna Do About You?

Lady and the Tramp (Disney 1955)
Bella Notte
He's a Tramp
The Siamese Cat Song

Lady in the Dark (Paramount 1944) [Broadway 1941]
Suddenly It's Spring

The Lady Objects (Columbia 1938)
A Mist Is Over the Moon

Las Vegas Nights (Paramount 1941)
Dolores

The Las Vegas Story (RKO 1952)
My Resistance Is Low

Laughing Irish Eyes (Republic 1936)
All My Life

The Lemon Drop Kid (Paramount 1951)
It Doesn't Cost a Dime to Dream
Silver Bells

Les Girls (MGM 1957)
Ça, C'est L'Amour
Ladies-in-Waiting
Les Girls
Why Am I So Gone?
You're Just Too, Too

Let's Dance (1950)
Why Fight the Feeling?

Let's Face It (Paramount 1943) [Broadway 1941]
Who Did? I Did

Let's Fall in Love (Columbia 1934)
Let's Fall in Love

Let's Sing Again (Principal/RKO 1936)
Let's Sing Again

Life of the Party (Warner 1937)
Roses in December

Lillian Russell (Fox 1940)
Blue Lovebird

The Lion King (Disney 1994)
Be Prepared
Can You Feel the Love Tonight
Circle of Life
Hakuna Matata
I Just Can't Wait to Be King

Listen Darling (MGM 1938)
On the Bumpy Road to Love
Ten Pins in the Sky

The Little Mermaid (Disney 1989)
Kiss the Girl
Part of Your World
Poor Unfortunate Souls
Under the Sea

Little Miss Broadway (Fox 1938)
Swing Me an Old Fashioned Song
We Should Be Together

Little Miss Marker (Paramount 1934)
Laugh, You Son-of-a-Gun
Lowdown Lullaby

Little Nelly Kelly (MGM 1940)
It's a Great Day for the Irish

A Little Night Music (Sascha-Wein-New World 1978) [Broadway 1973]
The Letter Song

The Little Prince (Paramount 1974)
I Never Met a Rose
The Little Prince
A Snake in the Grass

Little Shop of Horrors (Geffen/Warner 1986) [Off-Broadway 1982]
Mean Green Mother From Outer Space

Living It Up (Paramount 1954) [on Broadway as *Hazel Flagg* 1953]
Money Burns a Hole in My Pocket
That's What I Like

Looking for Love (MGM 1964)
Looking for Love

Lord Byron of Broadway (MGM 1930)
A Bundle of Old Love Letters
Should I?
The Woman in the Shoe

Lost Horizon (Columbia 1973)
Lost Horizon
The World Is a Circle

Love Finds Andy Hardy (MGM 1938)
In-Between
Meet the Beat of My Heart

Love in Bloom (Paramount 1935)
Here Comes Cookie
My Heart Is an Open Book

Love in the Rough (MGM 1930)
Go Home and Tell Your Mother
I'm Learning a Lot From You

Love Me Forever (Columbia 1935)
Love Me Forever

Love Me or Leave Me (MGM 1955)

I'll Never Stop Loving You
Never Look Back

Love Me Tender (Fox 1956)
Love Me Tender
Poor Boy

Love Me Tonight (Paramount 1932)
Isn't It Romantic?
Love Me Tonight
Lover
Mimi
The Son of a Gun Is Nothing But a Tailor
That's the Song of Paree

The Love Parade (Paramount 1929)
Anything to Please the Queen
Dream Lover
Let's Be Common
March of the Grenadiers
My Love Parade
Nobody's Using It Now
Paris, Stay the Same

Love Thy Neighbor (Paramount 1940)
Dearest, Darest I?
Do You Know Why?
Isn't That Just Like Love

Lovely to Look At (MGM 1952) [on Broadway as *Roberta* 1933]
Lafayette

Loving You (Paramount 1957)
Loving You
Teddy Bear

Lucky Boy (Tiffany-Stahl 1929)
My Mother's Eyes

Lucky Me (Warner 1954)
I Speak to the Stars

Lullaby of Broadway (Warner 1951)

I Love the Way You Say Goodnight

Mad About Music (Universal 1938)
I Love to Whistle
A Serenade to the Stars

The Magic of Lassie (MGM 1978)
A Rose Is Not a Rose
When You're Loved

Make a Wish (RKO 1937)
Make a Wish
Music in My Heart
My Campfire Dreams

Make Mine Music (RKO 1946)
Blue Bayou
Johnny Fedora and Alive Blue Bonnet

Mammy (Warner-Vitaphone 1930)
Across the Breakfast Table
Let Me Sing and I'm Happy

Man About Town (Paramount 1939)
Fidgety Joe
Strange Enchantment

Many Happy Returns (Paramount 1934)
The Boogie Man
The Sweetest Music This Side of Heaven

Marianne (MGM 1929)
Just You, Just Me

Mary Poppins (Disney 1964)
Chim Chim Cheree
Feed the Birds
I Love to Laugh
Jolly Holiday
Let's Go Fly a Kite
A Spoonful of Sugar
Stay Awake
Step in Time

Super-cali-fragil-istic-expi-ali-docious

Mayor of 44th Street (RKO 1942)
There's a Breeze on Lake Louise

Meet Me in St. Louis (MGM 1944)
The Boy Next Door
Have Yourself a Merry Little Christmas
The Trolley Song

Meet the People (MGM 1944)
Say That We're Sweethearts Again

Melody Time (Disney 1948)
Blame It on the Samba
Blue Shadows on the Trail
Pecos Bill

Men of the Sky (First National 1931)
Every Little While
Stolen Dreams

Merry Andrew (MGM 1958)
Salud

Minstrel Man (PRC 1944)
Remember Me to Carolina

Mississippi (Paramount 1935)
Down By the River
It's Easy to Remember
Soon

Monte Carlo (Paramount 1930)
Always in All Ways
Beyond the Blue Horizon
Give Me a Moment, Please

Moon Over Miami (Fox 1941)
Is That Good?
The Kindergarten Conga
Oh Me, Oh Mi-ami
You Started Something

Moonlight and Cactus (Universal 1944)
Send Me a Man, Amen

Moonlight and Pretzels (Universal 1933)
Ah, But Is It Love?
Are You Makin' Any Money, Baby?

Mother Wore Tights (Fox 1947)
Kokomo, Indiana
On a Little Two-Seat Tandem
You Do

Moulin Rouge (20th Century/United Artists 1934)
The Boulevard of Broken Dreams
Coffee in the Morning
Song of Surrender

Mountain Music (Paramount 1937)
Good Mornin'

Movie Movie (Warner 1978)
Just Shows to Go Ya

Mr. Dodd Takes the Air (Warner 1937)
Am I in Love?
Remember Me?

Mr. Music (Paramount 1950)
Accidents Will Happen
And Then You'll Be Home
Life Is So Peculiar

Mulan (Disney 1998)
A Girl Worth Fighting For
Honor to Us All
Reflection

The Muppet Christmas Carol (Disney 1992)
A Thankful Heart

The Muppet Movie (ITC 1979)
I'm Going to Go Back There Some Day
Movin' Right Along

The Rainbow Connection

Muppet Treasure Island (Disney 1996)
Sailing for Adventure
Something Better

Murder at the Vanities (Paramount 1934)
Cocktails for Two
Ebony Rhapsody
Live and Love Tonight

Music for Millions (MGM 1944)
Toscanini, Iturbi and Me
Umbriago

The Music Goes 'Round (Columbia 1936)
Life Begins When You're in Love
Taking Care of You

Music in My Heart (Columbia 1940)
It's a Blue World

The Music Man (Warner 1962) [Broadway 1957]
Being in Love

My Blue Heaven (Fox 1950)
Don't Rock the Boat, Dear
Hallowe'en
I Love a New Yorker
Live Hard, Work Hard, Love Hard

My Dream Is Yours (Warner 1949)
My Dream Is Yours

My Gal Sal (Fox 1942)
Here You Are

My Lucky Star (Fox 1938)
I've Got a Date With a Dream

My Man (Warner-Vitaphone 1928)
I'd Rather Be Blue Over You
If You Want the Rainbow

My Sister Eileen (Columbia 1955)
Give Me a Band and My Baby
It's Bigger Than You and Me

Nancy Goes to Rio (Universal 1950)
Time and Time Again

Nashville (Paramount/ABC 1975)
Dues
I'm Easy
It Don't Bother Me
My Idaho Home
200 Years

Neptune's Daughter (MGM 1949)
Baby, It's Cold Outside

Never Steal Anything Small (Universal 1959)
I'm Sorry, I Want a Ferrari

New Faces of 1937 (RKO 1937)
Love Is Never Out of Season

New Moon (MGM 1940) [on Broadway as *The New Moon*, 1928]
Paree

New Orleans (United Artists 1947)
Do You Know What It Means to Miss New Orleans?

New York, New York (United Artists 1977)
But the World Goes 'Round
Happy Endings
Theme From *New York, New York*
There Goes the Ball Game

Newsies (Disney 1992)
Santa Fe
Seize the Day

A Night at the Opera (MGM 1935)
Alone
Cosi Cosa

The Night Is Young (MGM 1935)
When I Grow Too Old to Dream

The Night They Raided Minsky's (United Artists 1968)
The Night They Raided Minsky's
Perfect Gentlemen

The Nightmare Before Christmas (Touchstone/Disney 1993)
Jack's Lament
This Is Halloween
What's This?

No Leave, No Love (MGM 1946)
All the Time

Nob Hill (Fox 1945)
I Don't Care Who Knows It

Oliver and Company (Disney 1988)
Once Upon a Time in New York City
Perfect Isn't Easy
Streets of Gold
Why Should I Worry?

On a Clear Day You Can See Forever (Paramount 1970) [Broadway 1965]
Go to Sleep
Love With All the Trimmings

On an Island With You (MGM 1948)
I Can Do Without Broadway

On the Avenue (Fox 1937)
The Girl on the Police Gazette
He Ain't Got Rhythm
I've Got My Love to Keep Me Warm
Slumming on Park Avenue
This Year's Kisses

On the Riviera (Fox 1951)
On the Riviera
Popo the Puppet

On the Town (MGM 1949) [Broadway 1944]
Count on Me
Main Street
Prehistoric Man

On With the Show (Warner 1929)
Am I Blue?
Birmingham Bertha

The One and Only, Genuine, Original Family Band (Disney 1968)
Let's Put It Over With Grover
The One and Only, Genuine, Original Family Band

One Hour With You (Paramount 1932)
Oh, That Mitzi!
One Hour With You
Three Times a Day
We Will Always Be Sweethearts
What a Little Thing Like a Wedding Ring Can Do
What Would You Do?

One in a Million (Fox 1936)
One in a Million

One Night in the Tropics (Universal 1940)
Remind Me
You and Your Kiss
Your Dream

One Night of Love (Columbia 1934)
One Night of Love

One Sunday Afternoon (Warner 1948)
Girls Were Made to Take Care of Boys

Orchestra Wives (Fox 1942)
At Last
I've Got a Gal in Kalamazoo
People Like You and Me
Serenade in Blue

Out of This World (Paramount 1945)
I'd Rather Be Me

June Comes Around Every Year
Out of This World
A Sailor With an Eight-Hour Pass

Paint Your Wagon (Paramount 1969) [Broadway 1951]
The First Thing You Know
A Million Miles Away Behind the Door

The Paleface (Paramount 1948)
Buttons and Bows
Meetcha 'Round the Corner

Palm Springs (Paramount 1936)
The Hills of Old Wyomin'
I Don't Want to Make History

Palmy Days (Goldwyn/United Artists 1931)
Bend Down, Sister
There's Nothing Too Good for My Baby

Paradise, Hawaiian Style (Paramount 1966)
Datin'

Paramount on Parade (Paramount 1929)
All I Want Is Just One Girl
Any Time's the Time to Fall in Love
I'm True to the Navy Now
Sweepin' the Clouds Away

Paris Honeymoon (Paramount 1938)
The Funny Old Hills
Joobalai
You're a Sweet Little Headache

Paris in the Spring (Paramount 1935)
Paris in the Spring

Pennies From Heaven (Columbia 1936)
Let's Call a Heart a Heart
One, Two, Button Your Shoe
Pennies From Heaven
So Do I

Pepe (Posa/Columbia 1960)
Faraway Part of Town
Pepe
That's How It Went, All Right

The Perils of Pauline (Paramount 1947)
I Wish I Didn't Love You So
Poppa, Don't Preach to Me
Rumble, Rumble, Rumble

Pete Kelly's Blues (Mark VII/Warner 1955)
He Needs Me
Pete Kelly's Blues

Peter Pan (Disney 1953)
Tee Dum — Tee Dee
You Can Fly

Pete's Dragon (Disney 1977)
Candle on the Water

Phantom of the Paradise (Fox 1974)
Old Souls
Phantom's Theme
Upholstery

The Phantom President (Paramount 1932)
Give Her a Kiss

Pigskin Parade (Fox 1936)
Balboa
It's Love I'm After
You Do the Darnd'st Things, Baby
You're Slightly Terrific

Pin-Up Girl (Fox 1944)
Don't Carry Tales Out of School
Once Too Often
Red Robins, Bob Whites and Blue Birds

Pinocchio (Disney/RKO 1940)
Give a Little Whistle
Hi-Diddle-Dee-Dee

I've Got No Strings
When You Wish Upon a Star

The Pirate (MGM 1948)
Be a Clown
Love of My Life
Mack the Black
Niña
You Can Do No Wrong

Playboy of Paris (Paramount 1930)
My Ideal

Playmates (RKO 1942)
How Long Did I Dream?
Humpty Dumpty Heart

Pocahontas (Disney 1995)
Colors of the Wind
Just Around the Riverbend
Savages

Poor Little Rich Girl (Fox 1936)
But Definitely
Military Man
Oh, My Goodness
When I'm With You
You Gotta Eat Your Spinach, Baby

Popeye (Paramount/Disney 1980)
He Needs Me
Sweethaven

Presenting Lily Mars (MGM 1943)
A Russian Rhapsody
Tom, Tom the Piper's Son
When I Look at You
Where There's Music

Priorities on Parade (Paramount 1942)
Conchita, Marquita, Lolita, Pepita, Rosita, Juanita Lopez

Private Buckaroo (Universal 1942)

Three Little Sisters

Puttin' On the Ritz (United Artists 1930)
Puttin' On the Ritz
Singing a Vagabond Song
There's Danger in Your Eyes, Cherie
With You

Quest for Camelot (Warner 1998)
If I Didn't Have You
Looking Through Your Eyes

The Rainbow Man (Paramount 1929)
Sleepy Valley

Rainbow on the River (Principal/RKO 1936)
Rainbow on the River

Rainbow 'Round My Shoulder (Columbia 1952)
Girl in the Wood

Ready, Willing and Able (Warner 1937)
Sentimental and Melancholy
Too Marvelous for Words

Rebecca of Sunnybrook Farm (Fox 1938)
Come Get Your Happiness
An Old Straw Hat
Parade of the Wooden Soldiers

Reckless (MGM 1935)
Everything's Been Done Before

Red Garters (Paramount 1954)
Brave Man
Love Is Greater Than I Thought

Red, Hot and Blue (Paramount 1949) [Broadway 1936]
Now That I Need You

The Rescuers (Disney 1977)
Someone's Waiting for You

Reveille With Beverly (Columbia 1943)
Cow-Cow Boogie

Rhythm on the Range (Paramount 1936)
Empty Saddles
I Can't Escape From You
I'm an Old Cowhand
You'll Have to Swing It

Rhythm on the River (Paramount 1940)
Ain't It a Shame About Mame?
I Don't Want to Cry Anymore
Only Forever
Rhythm on the River
That's for Me

Rich, Young and Pretty (MGM 1951)
Dark Is the Night
How Do You Like Your Eggs in the Morning?
We Never Talk Much
Wonder Why

Ride 'Em Cowboy (Universal 1942)
I'll Remember April
Rockin' and Reelin'
Wake Up Jacob

Ridin' on a Rainbow (Republic 1941)
Be Honest With Me

Riding High (Paramount 1950)
Sunshine Cake

Rio Rita (MGM 1929) [Broadway 1927]
You're Always in My Arms

Road to Bali (Paramount 1953)
Chicago Style
The Merry-Go-Runaround

The Road to Hong Kong (Melnor/United Artists 1962)
Let's Not Be Sensible
Warmer Than a Whisper

Road to Morocco (Paramount 1942)
Ain't Got a Dime to My Name
Constantly
Moonlight Becomes You
Road to Morocco

Road to Rio (Paramount 1947)
But Beautiful
You Don't Have to Know the Language

Road to Singapore (Paramount 1940)
The Moon and the Willow Tree
Sweet Potato Piper
Too Romantic

Road to Utopia (Paramount 1945)
Good-Time Charley
It's Anybody's Spring
Personality
Put It There, Pal
Welcome to My Dreams

Road to Zanzibar (Paramount 1941)
It's Always You
You're Dangerous

Roadhouse Nights (Paramount 1930)
Everything Is on the Up and Up
It Can't Go on Like This

Roberta (RKO 1935) [Broadway 1933]
I Won't Dance
Lovely to Look At

Robin and the Seven Hoods (PC/Warner 1964)
Don't Be a Do-Badder
Mister Booze
My Kind of Town
Style

Robin Hood (Disney 1973)
Love
Oo-De-Lally

Rock-a-Bye Baby (Paramount 1958)
Dormi Dormi Dormi

Rock Around the Clock (Columbia 1955)
See You Later, Alligator

The Rogue Song (MGM 1930)
The Rogue Song
When I'm Looking At You

Roman Scandals (Goldwyn/United Artists 1933)
Build a Little Home
Keep Young and Beautiful
No More Love

Romance in the Dark (Paramount 1938)
The Nearness of You

Romance on the High Seas (Warner 1948)
I'm in Love
It's Magic
Put 'Em in a Box . . .

Rosalie (MGM 1937)
In the Still of the Night
I've a Strange New Rhythm in My Heart
Rosalie
Who Knows?
Why Should I Care?

The Rose (TCF 1979)
Midnight in Memphis
The Rose
Sold My Soul to Rock and Roll
Stay With Me
Whose Side Are You On?

Rose-Marie (MGM 1954)
The Mountie Who Never Got His Man

Rose of the Rancho (Paramount 1936)
If I Should Lose You
Rose of the Rancho

Thunder Over the Prairie
Where Is My Love?

Rose of Washington Square (Fox 1939)
I Never Knew Heaven Could Speak

Royal Wedding (MGM 1951)
Every Night at Seven
How Could You Believe Me When I Said I Loved You?
Open Your Eyes
Too Late Now
You're All the World to Me

Sadie McKee (MGM 1934)
All I Do Is Dream of You

Safety in Numbers (Paramount 1930)
Do You Play, Madame?
My Future Just Passed

Sally (1st National 1929) [Broadway 1920]
If I'm Dreaming, Don't Wake Me Too Soon

Sally, Irene and Mary (Fox 1938)
Got My Mind on Music
Half Moon on the Hudson
I Could Use a Dream
Sweet As a Song
This Is Where I Came In

Saludos Amigos (Disney/RKO 1942)
Brazil
Saludos Amigos
Tico-Tico

San Francisco (MGM 1936)
San Francisco
Would You?

Say It With Songs (Warner 1929)
Little Pal
Used to You

Scrooge (Cinema Center/Waterbury 1970)
Thank You Very Much

Second Chorus (Paramount 1940)
The Love of My Life

Second Fiddle (Fox 1939)
Back to Back
I Poured My Heart Into a Song
I'm Sorry for Myself
An Old-Fashioned Tune Is Always New
When Winter Comes

Seven Brides for Seven Brothers (MGM 1954)
Bless Your Beautiful Hide
Lonesome Polecat
Sobbin' Women
Spring, Spring, Spring
When You're in Love
Wonderful, Wonderful Day

Seven Days Leave (RKO 1942)
Can't Get Out of This Mood
I Get the Neck of the Chicken

Shall We Dance (RKO 1937)
Beginner's Luck
Let's Call the Whole Thing Off
Shall We Dance?
Slap That Bass
They All Laughed
They Can't Take That Away From Me

She Couldn't Say No (Warner 1930)
Watching My Dreams Go By

She Done Him Wrong (Paramount 1933)
A Guy What Takes His Time
I Wonder Where My Easy Rider's Gone

She Learned About Sailors (Fox 1934)
Here's the Key to My Heart

She Loves Me Not (Paramount 1934)
Love in Bloom
Straight From the Shoulder

She's Working Her Way Through College (Warner 1952)
Am I in Love?
I'll Be Loving You
The Stuff That Dreams Are Made Of

Ship Ahoy (MGM 1942)
I'll Take Tallulah
Last Call for Love
Poor You

Shipmates Forever (Cosmopolitan/Warner 1935)
Don't Give Up the Ship
I'd Love to Take Orders From You
I'd Rather Listen to Your Eyes

The Shocking Miss Pilgrim (Fox 1947)
Aren't You Kind of Glad We Did?
The Back Bay Polka
Changing My Tune
For You, For Me, For Evermore

Shoot the Works (Paramount 1934)
With My Eyes Wide Open I'm Dreaming

Show Boat (Universal 1936) [Broadway 1927]
Ah Still Suits Me
I Have the Room Above Her

Show Girl in Hollywood (First National 1930)
There's a Tear for Every Smile in Hollywood

Silk Stockings (MGM 1957) [Broadway 1955]
Fated to Be Mated
The Ritz Roll and Rock

Sing, Baby, Sing (Fox 1936)
When Did You Leave Heaven?
You Turned the Tables on Me

Sing Me a Love Song (1st National 1936)
Summer Night

Sing You Sinners (Paramount 1938)
Don't Let That Moon Get Away
I've Got a Pocketful of Dreams
Small Fry

Sing Your Way Home (RKO 1945)
I'll Buy That Dream

Singin' in the Rain (MGM 1952)
Make 'Em Laugh

The Singing Fool (Warner 1928)
Sonny Boy
There's a Rainbow 'Round My Shoulder

The Singing Hills (Republic 1941)
Blueberry Hill

The Singing Kid (1st National 1936)
I Love to Sing-A
Save Me, Sister
You're the Cure for What Ails Me

The Singing Marine (Warner 1937)
Cause My Baby Says It's So
I Know Now
Night Over Shanghai
Song of the Marines
You Can't Run Away From Love Tonight

Sis Hopkins (Republic 1941)
Look at You, Look at Me

Sitting Pretty (Paramount 1933)
Did You Ever See a Dream Walking?
Good Morning Glory
You're Such a Comfort to Me

The Sky's the Limit (RKO 1943)
A Lot in Common

My Shining Hour
One for My Baby

Sleeping Beauty (Disney 1959)
Once Upon a Dream

Slightly French (Columbia 1949)
Fifi From the Folies Bergère

The Slipper and the Rose: The Story of Cinderella (Paradine 1977)
The Slipper and the Rose Waltz

Small Town Girl (MGM 1953)
I've Got to Hear That Beat
Small Towns Are Smiling Towns
Take Me to Broadway

The Smiling Lieutenant (Paramount 1931)
While Hearts Are Singing

Snow White and the Seven Dwarfs (Disney/RKO 1937)
The Dwarf's Yodel Song
Heigh-Ho
I'm Wishing
One Song
Someday My Prince Will Come
Whistle While You Work
With a Smile and a Song

So Dear to My Heart (Disney/RKO 1949)
County Fair
Lavender Blue

So This Is College (MGM 1929)
I Don't Want Your Kisses

So This Is Paris (Universal 1955)
If You Were There
Looking for Someone to Love
Wait Till Paris Sees Us

Some Like It Hot (Paramount 1939)
The Lady's in Love With You

Somebody Loves Me (Paramount 1952)
Love Him

Something for the Boys (Fox 1944)
I Wish We Didn't Have to Say Goodbye
In the Middle of Nowhere

Something to Shout About (Columbia 1943)
Something to Shout About
You'd Be So Nice to Come Home To

Son of Paleface (Paramount 1952)
Am I in Love?
California Rose

A Song Is Born (Goldwyn/RKO 1948)
Daddy-O
A Song Was Born

Song of the Islands (Fox 1942)
Down on Ami-Oni-Oni Isle
O'Brien Has Gone Hawaiian
Sing Me a Song of the Islands
What's Buzzin', Cousin?

Song of the Open Road (United Artists 1944)
Too Much in Love

Song of the South (Disney/RKO 1946)
Everybody Has a Laughing Place
How Do You Do?
Sooner or Later
Zip-A-Dee-Doo-Dah

A Song to Remember (Columbia 1945)
Till the End of Time

The Sound of Music (Argyle/Fox 1965) [Broadway 1959]
I Have Confidence in Me
Something Good

South Pacific (Fox 1958) [Broadway 1949]
My Girl Back Home

Spice World (Columbia 1998)
Spice Up Your Life

Spinout (Euterpe/MGM 1966)
Adam and Evil
All I Want

Spring Is Here (1st National 1930)
Cryin' for the Carolinas

Spring Parade (Universal 1940)
Waltzing in the Clouds

Springtime in the Rockies (Fox 1942)
I Had the Craziest Dream
Pan American Jubilee
Run Little Raindrop Run

St. Louis Blues (Paramount 1938)
I Go for That
Kinda Lonesome

Stage Door Canteen (Lesser/United Artists 1943)
The Girl I Love to Leave Behind
We Mustn't Say Goodbye

Stage Struck (1st National 1936)
Fancy Meeting You
In Your Own Quiet Way

Stand Up and Cheer (Fox 1934)
Baby, Take a Bow
Broadway's Gone Hillbilly
Stand Up and Cheer

Star! (Fox 1968)
Star!

A Star Is Born (Transcona/Warner 1954)
Born in a Trunk
Gotta Have Me Go With You
Here's What I'm Here For
It's a New World

Lose That Long Face
The Man That Got Away
Someone at Last

A Star Is Born (Warner/Barwood/First Artists 1976)
Evergreen
I Believe in Love
Queen Bee
Watch Closely Now
Woman in the Moon

The Star Maker (Paramount 1939)
An Apple for the Teacher
Go Fly a Kite
A Man and His Dream
Still the Bluebird Sings

Star-Spangled Rhythm (Paramount 1942)
He Loved Me Till the All-Clear
Hit the Road to Dreamland
I'm Doing It for Defense
A Sweater, a Sarong and a Peek-a-Boo Bang
That Old Black Magic

Stars Over Broadway (Warner 1935)
Carry Me Back to the Lone Prairie
September in the Rain
Where Am I?
You Let Me Down

State Fair (Fox 1945)
All I Owe Ioway
Isn't It Kinda Fun?
It Might As Well Be Spring
It's a Grand Night for Singing
Our State Fair
That's for Me

State Fair (Fox 1962)
More Than Just a Friend
Never Say No to a Man
This Isn't Heaven

Step Lively (RKO 1944)
And Then You Kissed Me
As Long As There's Music
Come Out, Come Out, Wherever You Are
Some Other Time
Where Does Love Begin?

Stork Club (Paramount 1945)
Doctor, Lawyer, Indian Chief
If I Had a Dozen Hearts
I'm a Square in a Social Circle

Stormy Weather (Fox 1942)
I Lost My Sugar in Salt Lake City
There's No Two Ways About Love

The Story of Vernon and Irene Castle (RKO 1939)
Only When You're in My Arms

Stowaway (Fox 1936)
Goodnight, My Love
I Wanna Go to the Zoo
One Never Knows, Does One?
That's What I Want for Christmas
You Gotta S-M-I-L-E to Be H-A-Double P-Y

Straight, Place and Show (Fox 1938)
With You on My Mind

Strike Me Pink (Goldwyn/United Artists 1936)
First You Have Me High, Then You Have Me Low
The Lady Dances

Strike Up the Band (MGM 1940) [Broadway 1930]
Nobody
Our Love Affair

The Strip (MGM 1951)
A Kiss to Build a Dream On

The Student Prince (MGM 1954) [Broadway 1924]
Beloved
I'll Walk With God

Student Tour (MGM 1934)
A New Moon Is Over My Shoulder

Summer Holiday (MGM 1947)
Afraid to Fall in Love
Our Home Town
Spring Isn't Everything
The Stanley Steamer
Wish I Had a Braver Heart

Summer Magic (Disney 1963)
Summer Magic
The Ugly Bug Ball

Summer Stock (MGM 1950)
Friendly Star
If You Feel Like Singing, Sing
You Wonderful You

Sun Valley Serenade (Fox 1941)
Chattanooga Choo-Choo
I Know Why
It Happened in Sun Valley
The Kiss Polka

Sunny (First National 1930) [Broadway 1925]
I Was Alone

Sunny Side Up (Fox 1929)
If I Had a Talking Picture of You
I'm a Dreamer (Aren't We All?)
Sunny Side Up
Turn On the Heat

The Swan Princess (Nest 1994)
Far Longer Than Forever
Princesses on Parade

Sweater Girl (Paramount 1942)
I Don't Want to Walk Without You, Baby
I Said No

Sweet and Low-Down (Fox 1944)

I'm Making Believe

Sweet Charity (Universal 1969) [Broadway 1966]
My Personal Property

Sweet Music (Warner-Vitaphone 1935)
Ev'ry Day
Fare Thee Well Annabelle
Sweet Music

Sweet Rosie O'Grady (Fox 1943)
My Heart Tells Me

Sweetheart of Sigma Chi (Monogram 1946)
Five Minutes More

Sweetie (Paramount 1929)
Alma Mammy
He's So Unusual
My Sweeter Than Sweet

Swing High, Swing Low (Paramount 1937)
Panamania
Swing High, Swing Low
Then It Isn't Love

Swing It, Soldier (Universal 1941)
I'm Gonna Swing My Way to Heaven

Swing Parade of 1946 (Monogram 1945)
Caldonia

Swing Time (RKO 1936)
Bojangles of Harlem
A Fine Romance
Never Gonna Dance
Pick Yourself Up
The Way You Look Tonight

The Sword in the Stone (Disney 1963)
That's What Makes the World Go Round

Syncopation (Radio 1929)

I'll Always Be in Love With You
Jericho

Take a Chance (Paramount 1933) [Broadway 1932]
Come Up and See Me Sometime

Take Me Back to Oklahoma (Monogram 1940)
You Are My Sunshine

Take Me Out to the Ball Game (MGM 1949)
It's Fate, Baby, It's Fate
The Right Girl for Me
Strictly U.S.A.
Yes, Indeedy

Tars and Spars (Columbia 1946)
I'm Glad I Waited for You

Texas Carnival (MGM 1951)
It's Dymamite

Thank Your Lucky Stars (Warner 1943)
The Dreamer
How Sweet You Are
Ice Cold Katie
I'm Ridin' for a Fall
Love Isn't Born, It's Made
Thank Your Lucky Stars
They're Either Too Young or Too Old

Thanks a Million (Fox 1935)
I'm Sitting High on a Hilltop
Thanks a Million

Thanks for Everything (Fox 1938)
Thanks for Ev'rything

That Certain Age (Universal 1938)
My Own
You're as Pretty As a Picture

That Girl From Paris (RKO 1936)
Love and Learn

Seal It With a Kiss

That Lady in Ermine (Fox 1948)
This Is the Moment

That Night in Rio (Fox 1941)
Boa Noite
Cae Cae
Chica Chica Boom Chic
I, Yi Yi Yi Yi
They Met in Rio

There's No Business Like Show Business (Fox 1954)
A Man Chases a Girl

Thin Ice (Fox 1937)
I'm Olga From the Volga

This Is Spinal Tap (Embassy 1984)
Big Bottom
Hell Hole

This Is the Night (Paramount 1932)
This Is the Night

Thoroughly Modern Millie (Universal 1967)
The Tapioca
Thoroughly Modern Millie

Those Redheads From Seattle (Paramount 1953)
Baby, Baby, Baby

Thousands Cheer (MGM 1943)
I Duga Ditch
The Joint Is Really Jumpin' in Carnegie Hall
United Nations on the March

The Three Caballeros (Disney/RKO 1945)
The Three Caballeros
You Belong to My Heart

Three Darling Daughters (MGM 1948)
The Dickey Bird Song

365 Nights in Hollywood (Fox 1934)
Yes to You

Three Little Girls in Blue (Fox 1946)
On a Boardwalk in Atlantic City
Somewhere in the Night
This Is Always
You Make Me Feel So Young

Three Sailors and a Girl (Warner 1954)
Face to Face
The Lately Song

Three Smart Girls (Universal 1937)
My Heart Is Singing
Someone to Care for Me

Thrill of a Romance (MGM 1945)
I Should Care
Please Don't Say No, Say Maybe

Thumbelina (Warner 1994)
Follow Your Heart
Marry the Mole
On the Road
Soon

The Time, the Place and the Girl (Warner 1946)
A Gal in Calico
Oh, But I Do
Rainy Night in Rio
Through a Thousand Dreams

Tin Pan Alley (Fox 1940)
You Say the Sweetest Things, Baby

To Beat the Band (RKO 1935)
Eeny, Meeny, Miney, Mo
If You Were Mine

The Toast of New Orleans (MGM 1950)
Be My Love

Tom Sawyer (United Artists/Readers Digest 1973)
Freebootin'
River Song
Tom Sawyer

Tom Thumb (Pal/MGM 1958)
Tom Thumb's Tune
The Yawning Song

Tommy (Hemdale 1975)
Champagne

Tonight and Every Night (Columbia 1945)
Anywhere
Tonight and Every Night

Too Many Girls (RKO 1940) [Broadway 1939]
You're Nearer

Too Much Harmony (Paramount 1933)
Black Moonlight
The Day You Came Along
Thanks

Top Hat (RKO 1935)
Cheek to Cheek
Isn't This a Lovely Day?
No Strings
The Piccolino
Top Hat, White Tie and Tails

Top of the Town (Universal 1937)
That Foolish Feeling
Top of the Town
Where Are You?

Torch Singer (Paramount 1933)
Give Me Liberty or Give Me Love
It's a Long, Dark Night

Transatlantic Merry-Go-Round (Small/United Artists 1934)
If I Had a Million Dollars
Rock and Roll

A Troll in Central Park (Warner 1994)
Absolutely Green

Tropic Holiday (Paramount 1938)
Havin' Myself a Time

True to Life (Paramount 1943)
The Old Music Master

Tumbling Tumbleweeds (Republic 1934)
Tumbling Tumbleweeds

Turn Off the Moon (Paramount 1937)
Jammin'
That's Southern Hospitality

Twenty Million Sweethearts (Warner 1934)
Fair and Warmer
I'll String Along With You
Out for No Good

Two for Tonight (Paramount 1935)
From the Top of Your Head
Takes Two to Make a Bargain
Without a Word of Warning

Two Girls and a Sailor (MGM 1944)
Take It Easy
You Dear
Young Man With a Horn

Two Girls on Broadway (MGM 1940)
My Wonderful One, Let's Dance

Two Guys From Texas (Warner 1948)
Ev'ry Day I Love You

Two Sisters From Boston (MGM 1946)
G'wan, Your Mudder's Callin'

Two Tickets to Broadway (RKO 1951)
The Closer You Are
Let the Worry Bird Worry for You

Up in Arms (Avalon/RKO 1944)
Now I Know
Tess's Torch Song

The Vagabond King (Paramount 1930) [Broadway 1925]
If I Were King

The Vagabond Lover (Radio 1929)
Heigh-Ho, Everybody, Heigh-Ho
If You Were the Only Girl in the World
A Little Kiss Each Morning

Variety Girl (Paramount 1947)
Tallahassee

Varsity Show (Warner 37)
Have You Got Any Castles, Baby?
Love Is on the Air Tonight
We're Working Our Way Through College
You've Got Something There

Victor/Victoria (MGM 1982)
Chicago, Illinois
Crazy World
Le Jazz Hot
You and Me

Viennese Nights (Warner 1930)
You Will Remember Vienna

Viva Las Vegas (MGM 1964)
The Lady Loves Me
Viva Las Vegas

Vogues of 1938 (Wanger/United Artists 1937)
That Old Feeling

Wabash Avenue (Fox 1950)
Baby, Won't You Say You Love Me?
Wilhelmina

Waikiki Wedding (Paramount 1937)
Blue Hawaii

Sweet Is the Word for You
Sweet Leilani

Wake Up and Dream (Fox 1946)
Give Me the Simple Life
I Wish I Could Tell You

Wake Up and Live (Fox 1937)
I'm Bubbling Over
It's Swell of You
Never in a Million Years
There's a Lull in My Life
Wake Up and Live

Week-End in Havana (Fox 1941)
The Nango
Romance and the Rhumba
Tropical Magic
A Week-End in Havana
When I Love I Love

Welcome Stranger (Paramount 1947)
As Long As I'm Dreaming
My Heart Is a Hobo

We're Not Dressing (Paramount 1934)
Goodnight, Lovely Little Lady
Love Thy Neighbor
May I?
Once in a Blue Moon
She Reminds Me of You

When the Boys Meet the Girls (MGM 1965)
When the Boys Meet the Girls

When You're in Love (Columbia 1937)
Our Song
The Whistling Boy

Where Do We Go From Here? (Fox 1945)
All at Once
The Nina, the Pinta and the Santa Maria

Where the Boys Are (MGM 1960)
Where the Boys Are

White Christmas (Paramount 1954)
The Best Things Happen When You're Dancing
Count Your Blessings
Love, You Didn't Do Right By Me
Sisters

Whoopee (Goldwyn/United Artists 1930) [Broadway 1928]
My Baby Just Cares for Me
Stetson

Willy Wonka and the Chocolate Factory (Wolper/Paramount 1971)
The Candy Man
Pure Imagination

The Wizard of Oz (MGM 1939)
Ding-Dong! The Witch Is Dead!
Follow the Yellow Brick Road
If I Only Had a Brain
If I Were King of the Forest
The Merry Old Land of Oz
Over the Rainbow
We're Off to See the Wizard

Wonder Bar (1st National 1934)
Don't Say Goodnight
Goin' to Heaven on a Mule
Why Do I Dream Those Dreams?
Wonder Bar

Wonder Man (Beverley/RKO 1945)
Bali Boogie
So-o-o-o-o in Love

Xanadu (Universal 1980)
Magic
Whenever You're Away From Me
Xanadu

Yellow Submarine (King/Apple 1968)
All Together Now

Yentl (United Artists/Barwood 1983)
No Wonder
Papa, Can You Hear Me?
A Piece of Sky
The Way He Makes Me Feel
Where Is It Written?

Yes, Giorgio (MGM 1982)
If I Were in Love

Yolanda and the Thief (MGM 1945)
Angel
Coffee Time
Yolanda

You Can't Have Everything (Fox 1937)
Afraid to Dream
Danger — Love at Work
Please Pardon Us, We're in Love
You Can't Have Everything

You Were Never Lovelier (Columbia 1942)
Dearly Beloved
I'm Old Fashioned
You Were Never Lovelier

You'll Find Out (RKO 1940)
The Bad Humor Man
I'd Know You Anywhere
You've Got Me This Way

You'll Never Get Rich (Columbia 1941)
Dream Dancing
So Near and Yet So Far
Shootin' the Works for Uncle Sam
Since I Kissed My Baby Goodbye
The Wedding Cake Walk

Young at Heart (Armin/Warner 1954)
Hold Me in Your Arms
Ready, Willing and Able
You My Love

Young People (Fox 1940)
I Wouldn't Take a Million

You're a Sweetheart (Universal 1937)
Oh, Oh, Oklahoma
So It's Love
You're a Sweetheart

Youth on Parade (Paramount 1942)
I've Heard That Song Before

The Ziegfeld Follies (MGM 1946)
Bring on the Beautiful Girls
Love
This Heart of Mine

Ziegfeld Girl (MGM 1940)
Minnie From Trinidad
You Stepped Out of a Dream

Bibliography

General Works on Film Musicals

Altman, Rick. *The American Film Musical.* Bloomington: Indiana University Press, 1987

_____ (ed.). *Genre: The Musical.* London: Routledge and Kegan Paul, 1981.

Aylesworth, Thomas G. *Broadway to Hollywood.* New York: Gallery Books-W.H. Smith Publishers, 1985.

Barrios, Richard. *A Song in the Dark: The Birth of the Musical Film.* New York: Oxford University Press, 1995.

Bergman, Andrew. *We're in the Money: Depression America and Its Films.* New York: Harper & Row, 1971.

Bradley, Edwin M. *The First Hollywood Musicals.* Jefferson, NC: McFarland, 1996.

Burton, Jack. *The Blue Book of Hollywood Musicals.* Watkins Glen, NY: Century House, 1975.

Croce, Arlene. *The Fred Astaire and Ginger Rogers Book.* New York: Dutton, 1987.

Crowther, Bosley. *The Lion's Share: The Story of an Entertainment Empire.* New York, E.P. Dutton & Co., 1957.

Druxman, Michael B. *The Musical from Broadway to Hollywood.* New York: Barnes, 1980.

Eames, John Douglas. *The MGM Story.* New York: Crown Publishers, 1975.

_____. *The Paramount Story.* New York: Crown Publishers, 1985.

Fehr, Richard, and Frederick G. Vogel. *Lullabies of Hollywood: Movie Music and the Movie Musical, 1915–1992.* Jefferson, NC: McFarland, 1993.

Feuer, Jane. *The Hollywood Musical.* Bloomington, Indiana: Indiana University Press, 1982.

Fitzgerald, Michael G. *Universal Pictures: A Panoramic History.* Westport, CT: Arlington House, 1977.

Fordin, Hugh. *The World of Entertainment: Hollywood's Greatest Musicals.* New York: Avon Books, 1975.

Geduld, Harry M. *The Birth of the Talkies.* Bloomington: Indiana University Press, 1975.

Gottfried, Martin. *All His Jazz: The Life and Death of Bob Fosse.* New York: Bantam

Books, 1990.

Green, Stanley. *Encyclopedia of Musical Film*. New York: Oxford University Press, 1981.

____. *Hollywood Musicals, Year by Year*. Milwaukee, WI: Hal Leonard Publishing Corp., 1990.

Halliwell, Leslie. *Halliwell's Film Guide*. New York: Harper & Row, Publishers, 1989.

Harvey, Stephen. *Directed by Vincente Minnelli*. New York: Museum of Modern Art/Harper and Row, 1989.

Hirschhorn, Clive. *The Hollywood Musical*. New York: Crown Publishers, 1981.

____. *The Universal Story*. New York: Crown Publishers, 1983.

____. *The Warner Bros. Story*. New York: Crown Publishers, 1979.

Jewell, Richard B., and Vernon Harbin. *The RKO Story*. New York: Arlington House, 1982.

Katz, Ephraim. *The Film Encyclopedia*. 3rd Ed. New York: HarperCollins Publishers, 1998.

Kobal, John. *Gotta Sing, Gotta Dance: A Pictorial History of Film Musicals*. London/New York: Hamlyn, 1971.

Kreuger, Miles (ed.). *The Movie Musical: From Vitaphone to 42nd Street*. New York: Dover, 1975.

Lasky, Betty. *RKO: The Biggest Little Major of Them All*. Englewood Cliffs, NJ: Prentice-Hall, 1984.

Lynch, Richard Chigley. *Movie Musicals on Record*. Westport, CT: Greenwood Press, 1989.

Maltin, Leonard. *The Disney Films*. New York: Hyperion, 1995.

Mast, Gerald. *Can't Help Singin': The American Musical on Stage and Screen*. Woodstock, NY: Overlook Press, 1987.

McVay, Douglas. *The Musical Film*. London: A. Zwemmer/New York: A.S. Barnes, 1967.

Mielke, Randall G. *The Road to Box Office: The Seven Comedies of Bing Crosby, Bob Hope and Dorothy Lamour, 1940–1962*. Jefferson, NC: McFarland, 1996.

Mordden, Ethan. *The Hollywood Musical*. New York: St. Martin's Press, 1981.

Parish, J. R., and Ronald L. Bowers. *The MGM Stock Company: The Golden Era*. New York: Bonanza Books, 1972.

Parish, J. R., and Michael R. Pitts. *The Great Hollywood Musicals*. Metuchen, NJ: Scarecrow Press, 1992.

Reed, William. *Rock on Film*. New York: Delilah/Putnam, 1982.

Rubin, Martin. *Showstoppers: Busby Berkeley and the Tradition of Spectacle*. New York: Columbia University Press, 1993.

Sennett, Ted. *Hollywood Musicals*. New York: Harry Abrams, 1982.

____. *Warner Brothers Presents*. Secaucus, NJ: Castle Books, 1971.

Silverman, Stephen W. *Dancing on the Ceiling: Stanley Donen and His Movies*. New York: Alfred A. Knopf, 1996.

Springer, John. *All Talking! All Singing! All Dancing!* New York: Citadel Press, 1966. Reissued as *They Sang, They Danced, They Romanced*, 1991.

Stern, Lee Edward. *The Movie Musical*. New York: Pyramid Books, 1974.

Taylor, John Russell, and Arthur Jackson. *The Hollywood Musical*. New

York: McGraw-Hill, 1971.

Thomas, Lawrence B. *The MGM Years*. New York: Columbia House/Arlington House, 1971.

Thomas, Tony. *Music for the Movies*. New York: A.S. Barnes and Co., 1973.

Thomas, Tony, and Aubrey Solomon. *The Films of 20th Century Fox*. Secaucus, NJ: Citadel Press, 1979.

Vallance, Thomas. *The American Musical*. New York: A.S. Barnes & Co., 1970.

Walker, John (ed.). *Halliwell's Filmgoer's Companion*. 12th Ed. New York: HarperCollins, 1997.

Wiley, Mason, and Damien Bona. *Inside Oscar: The Unofficial History of the Academy Awards*. New York: Ballantine Books, 1996.

Wlaschin, Ken. *Opera on Screen*. Los Angeles: Beachwood Press, 1997.

Woll, Allen L. *The Hollywood Musical Goes to War*. Chicago: Nelson-Hall, 1983.

Works on Film Songs and Songwriters

Armitage, Merle. *George Gershwin: Man and Legend*. New York: Duell, Sloane and Pearce, 1958.

Arbold, Elliot. *Deep in My Heart: Sigmund Romberg*. New York: Duell, Sloane and Pearce, 1949.

Bach, Bob, and Ginger Mercer (eds.). *Our Huckleberry Friend: The Life, Times and Lyrics of Johnny Mercer*. Secaucus, NJ: Lyle Stuart, 1982.

Barrett, Mary Ellin. *Irving Berlin: A Daughter's Memoir*. New York: Simon & Schuster, 1994.

Benjamin, Ruth, and Arthur Roseblatt. *Movie Song Catalog*. Jefferson, NC: McFarland, 1993.

Bergreen, Laurence. *As Thousands Cheer: The Life of Irving Berlin*. New York: Viking Press, 1990.

Bookspan, Martin, and Ross Yockey. *André Previn: A Biography*. Garden City, NY: Doubleday, 1981.

Bordman, Gerald. *Days to Be Happy, Years to Be Sad: The Life and Music of Vincent Youmans*. New York: Oxford University Press, 1982.

____. *Jerome Kern: His Life and Music*. New York: Oxford University Press, 1980.

Burton, Humphrey. *Leonard Bernstein*. New York: Doubleday, 1994.

Cahn, Sammy. *I Should Care: The Sammy Cahn Story*. New York, Arbor House, 1974.

Carmichael, Hoagy. *Sometimes I Wonder*. New York: DaCapo Press, 1976.

____. *The Stardust Road*. Bloomington: Indiana University Press, 1946-1983.

Citron, Stephen. *Noel and Cole: The Sophisticates*. New York: Oxford University Press, 1993.

____. *The Wordsmiths: Oscar Hammerstein II and Alan Jay Lerner*. New York: Oxford University Press, 1995.

Collier, James Lincoln. *Duke Ellington*. New York: Oxford University Press, 1987.

Comden, Betty. *Off Stage: My Non–Show Business Life*. New York: Limelight Editions, 1996.

Coslow, Sam. *Cocktails for Two: The Many Lives of Giant Songwriter Sam Coslow*. New Rochelle, NY: Arlington House, 1977.

Craig, Warren. *Great Songwriters of Hollywood*. New York: A.S. Barnes, 1980.

___. *Sweet and Low Down: America's Popular Song Writers*. Metuchen, NJ: Scarecrow Press, 1978.

David, Lee. *Bolton and Wodehouse and Kern*. New York: James H. Heineman, 1993.

Davis, Sheila. *The Craft of Lyric Writing*. Cincinnati, Ohio: Writers Digest Books, 1985.

Deutsch, Didier C. *VideoHound's Soundtracks: Music from the Movies, Broadway and Television*. Detroit: Visible Ink Press, 1998.

Dietz, Howard. *Dancing in the Dark*. New York: Quadrangle Books/New York Times Book Co., 1979.

Dowling, William J. *Beatlesongs*. New York: Fireside/Simon & Schuster, 1989.

Duke, Vernon. *Passport to Paris*. Boston: Little, Brown, 1955.

Eells, George. *The Life That Late He Led: A Biography of Cole Porter*. New York: G.P. Putnam's Sons, 1967.

Ewen, David. *American Songwriters*. New York: H.W. Wilson Co., 1987.

___. *George Gershwin: His Journey to Greatness*. Westport, CT: Greenwood Press, 1977.

___. *Great Men of American Popular Song*. Englewood Cliffs, NJ: Prentice-Hall, 1972.

___. *Richard Rodgers*. New York: Holt, 1957.

___. *The World of Jerome Kern*. New York: Holt, 1960.

Fehr, Richard, and Frederick G. Vogel. *Lullabies of Hollywood: Movie Music and the Movie Musical, 1915–1992*. Jefferson, NC: McFarland & Co., 1993.

Fordin, Hugh. *Getting to Know Him: A Biography of Oscar Hammerstein II*. New York: Random House, 1977.

Freedland, Michael. *Irving Berlin*. New York: Stein and Day, 1974.

___. *Jerome Kern*. New York: Stein and Day, 1981.

Furia, Philip. *Ira Gershwin: The Art of the Lyricist*. New York: Oxford University Press, 1996.

___. *The Poets of Tin Pan Alley: A History of America's Great Lyricists*. New York: Oxford University Press, 1990.

Grafton, David. *Red, Hot and Rich: An Oral History of Cole Porter*. New York: Stein and Day, 1987.

Grattan, Virginia L. *American Women Songwriters: A Biographical Dictionary*. Westport, CT: Greenwood Press, 1993.

Green, Stanley. *Rodgers and Hammerstein Fact Book*. Milwaukee: Lynn Farnol Group/Hal Leonard Publishers, 1986.

___. *The Rodgers and Hammerstein Story*. New York: John Day Co., 1963.

Hamm, Charles. *Irving Berlin*. New York: Oxford University Press, 1997.

Hammerstein, Oscar, II. *Lyrics*. Rev. ed. Milwaukee: Hal Leonard Books, 1985.

Harris, Charles K. *After the Ball: Forty Years of Melody*. New York: Frank Maurice, 1926.

Hart, Dorothy. *Thou Swell, Thou Witty: The Life and Lyrics of Lorenz Hart*. New York: Harper & Row, 1976.

Hart, Dorothy, and Robert Kimball (eds.). *The Complete Lyrics of Lorenz Hart*. New York: Alfred A. Knopf, 1986.

Hemming, Roy. *The Melody Lingers On: The Great Songwriters and Their Movie*

Musicals. New York: Newmarket Press, 1986.

Herman, Jerry, with Marilyn Stasio. *Showtune.* New York: Donald I. Fine Books, 1996.

Hischak, Thomas S. *Word Crazy: Broadway Lyricists From Cohan to Sondheim.* New York: Praeger Press, 1991.

Hyland, William G. *Richard Rodgers.* New Haven, CT: Yale University Press, 1998.

____.*The Song Is Ended: Songwriters and American Music, 1900–1950.* New York: Oxford University Press, 1995.

Jablonski, Edward. *Gershwin.* Garden City, NY: Doubleday & Co., 1987.

_____. *Gershwin Remembered.* London: Farber and Farber, 1992.

_____. *Harold Arlen: Happy With the Blues.* Garden City, NY: Doubleday & Co., 1961; De Capo Press, 1986.

Jablonski, Edward, and Lawrence D. Stewart. *The Gershwin Years.* Garden City, NY: Doubleday & Co., 1958/1973.

Jacobs, Dick, and Harriet Jacobs. *Who Wrote That Song?* Cincinnati: Writer's Digest Books, 1994.

Jay, David. *The Irving Berlin Songography.* New Rochelle, NY: Arlington House, 1969.

Kendall, Alan. *George Gershwin: A Biography.* New York: Universe Books, 1987.

Kimball, Robert (ed.). *Cole.* New York: Holt, Rinehart and Winston, 1971.

____. *The Complete Lyrics of Cole Porter.* New York: Alfred A. Knopf, 1983.

____. *The Complete Lyrics of Ira Gershwin.* New York: Alfred A. Knopf, 1993.

____. *The Complete Lyrics of Lorenz Hart.* New York: Alfred A. Knopf, 1986.

Kimball, Robert, and Alfred Simon. *The Gershwins.* New York: Athenaeum, 1973.

Lees, Gene. *Inventing Champagne: The Worlds of Lerner and Loewe.* New York: St. Martin's Press, 1990.

Lerner, Alan Jay. *The Street Where I Live.* New York: W.W. Norton & Co., 1978.

Lerner, Alan Jay, and Benny Green (ed.). *A Hymn to Him: The Lyrics of Alan Jay Lerner.* New York: Limelight Editions, 1987.

Loesser, Susan. *A Most Remarkable Fella: Frank Loesser and the Guys and Dolls in His Life.* New York: Donald I. Fine Books, 1993.

Mancini, Henry, with Gene Lees. *Did They Mention the Music?* Chicago: Contemporary Books, 1990.

Marx, Samuel, and Jan Clayton. *Rodgers and Hart: Bewitched, Bothered and Bewildered.* New York: G.P. Putnam's Sons, 1976.

McGuire, Patricia Dubin. *Lullaby of Broadway: The Life of Al Dubin.* Secaucus, NJ: Citadel Press, 1983.

Meyerson, Harold, and Ernie Harburg. *Who Put the Rainbow in* The Wizard of Oz? *Yip Harburg, Lyricist.* Ann Arbor: University of Michigan Press, 1993.

Mordden, Ethan. *Rodgers and Hammerstein.* New York: Harry N. Abrams, 1992.

Nolan, Frederick. *Lorenz Hart: A Poet on Broadway.* New York: Oxford University Press, 1994.

____ . *The Memory of All That: The Life of George Gershwin.* New York: Simon & Schuster, 1993.

____. *The Sound of Their Music: The Story of Rodgers and Hammerstein.* New York: Walker & Co., 1978.

Peyser, Joan. *The Memory of All That: The Life of George Gershwin.* New York:

Simon & Schuster, 1993.

Previn, André. *No Minor Chords: My Days in Hollywood*. New York, Doubleday, 1991.

Rodgers, Richard. *Musical Stages: An Autobiography*. New York: Random House, 1975.

Rosenberg, Deena. *Fascinating Rhythm: The Collaboration of George and Ira Gershwin*. New York: Dutton, 1991.

Schwartz, Charles. *Cole Porter: A Biography*. New York: Dial Press, 1977.

_____. *Gershwin, His Life and Music*. Indianapolis: Bobbs-Merrill Co., 1973.

Secrest, Meryle. *Leonard Bernstein*. New York: Alfred A. Knopf, 1994.

_____. *Stephen Sondheim: A Life*. New York: Alfred A. Knopf, 1998.

Suskin, Steven. *Berlin, Ken, Rodgers, Hart and Hammerstein: A Complete Song Catalogue*. Jefferson, NC: McFarland and Company, 1990.

_____. *Richard Rodgers: A Checklist of His Published Songs*. New York: New York Public Library, 1984.

Taylor, Deems. *Some Enchanted Evenings: The Story of Rodgers and Hammerstein*. New York: Harper and Brothers, 1953.

Taylor, Theodore. *Jule: The Story of Composer Jule Styne*. New York: Random House, 1979.

Thomas, Tony. *Harry Warren and the Hollywood Musical*. Secaucus, NJ: Citadel Press, 1975.

Turner, Steve. *A Hard Day's Write: The Stories Behind Every Beatles' Song*. New York: HarperCollins Publishers, 1994.

Waller, Maurice, and Anthony Calabrese. *Fats Waller*. New York: Schirmer Books, 1977.

Whitcomb, Ian. *Irving Berlin and Ragtime America*. New York: Limelight Editions, 1988.

White, Mark. *"You Must Remember This . . . " ; Popular Songwriters, 1900–1980*. New York: Charles Scribner's Sons, 1985.

Wilder, Alec. *American Popular Song: The Great Innovators, 1900–1950*. New York: Oxford University Press, 1972.

Wilk, Max. *They're Playing Our Song*. New York: Athenaeum, 1973.

Winer, Deborah Grace. *On the Sunny Side of the Street: The Life and Lyrics of Dorothy Fields*. New York: Schirmer Books, 1997.

Woll, Allen L. *Songs from Hollywood Musical Comedies, 1927 to the Present: A Dictionary*. New York: Garland Press, 1976.

Works on American Popular Music

Burton, Jack. *The Blue Book of Tin Pan Alley*. Watkins Glen, NY: Century House, 1951.

Cooke, Deryck. *The Language of Music*. New York: Oxford University Press, 1959.

Dachs, David. *Anything Goes: The World of Popular Music*. Indianapolis: Bobbs-Merrill, 1964.

Ewen, David. *All the Years of American Popular Music*. Englewood Cliffs, NJ: Prentice-Hall, 1977.

_____. *American Popular Songs*. New York: Random House, 1966.

_____. *History of Popular Music*. New York: Barnes and Noble, 1961.

_____. *The Life and Death of Tin Pan Alley: The Golden Age of American Popular Music*. New York: Funk & Wagnalls, 1964.

Ferrara, Lawrence. *Philosophy and Analysis of Music: Bridges to Musical Sound, Form and Reference*. Westport, CT: Greenwood Press, 1991.

Freeman, Graydon Laverne. *The Melodies Linger On*. Watkins Glen, NY: Century House, 1951.

Gammond, Peter. *The Oxford Companion to Popular Music*. New York: Oxford University Press, 1991.

Goldberg, Isaac. *Tin Pan Alley*. New York: John Day Co., 1930.

Hamm, Charles. *Yesterdays: Popular Song in America*. New York: W.W. Norton, 1979.

Jacobs, Dick, and Harriet Jacobs. *Who Wrote That Song?* Cincinnati: Writer's Digest Books, 1994.

Jasen, David A. *Tin Pan Alley: The Composers, the Songs, the Performers, and Their Times*. New York: Donald I. Fine, 1988.

Lax, Roger, and Frederick Smith. *The Great Song Thesaurus*. 2nd ed. New York: Oxford University Press, 1989.

Lissauer, Robert. *Lissauer's Encyclopedia of Popular Music, 1888 to the Present*. New York: Paragon House, 1991.

Morris, James R., J.R. Taylor and Dwight Blocker Bowers. *American Popular Song: Six Decades of Songwriters and Singers*. Washington, DC: Smithsonian Institution Press, 1984.

Murrells, Joseph. *Million Selling Records From the 1900s to the 1980s*. New York: Arco Publishing, 1984.

Palmer, Tony. *All You Need Is Love: The Story of Popular Music*. New York: Grossman, 1976.

Parish, James Robert, and Michael R. Pitts. *Hollywood Songsters: A Biographical Dictionary*. New York: Garland, 1991.

Paymer, Marvin E. (Gen. ed.). *Facts Behind the Songs: A Handbook of American Popular Music From the Nineties to the 90s*. New York: Garland Publishing, 1993.

Popular Music: An Annotated Index of American Popular Songs, 18 volumes. Editors: Nat Shapiro (1964–1973); Bruce Pollock (1984–1994). New York: Adrien Press, 1964–1973; Detroit: Gale Research, 1984–1994.

Robinette, Richard. *Historical Perspectives in Popular Music: A Historical Outline*. Dubuque, IA: Kendall-Hunt, 1980.

Smith, F. Joseph. *The Experiencing of Musical Sound: Prelude to a Phenomenology of Music*. New York: Gordon and Breach, 1979.

Spaeth, Sigmund. *A History of Popular Music in America*. New York: Random House, 1948.

Stambler, Irwin. *Encyclopedia of Popular Music*. New York: St. Martin's Press, 1965.

Whitcomb, Ian. *After the Ball: Pop Music From Rag to Rock*. New York: Simon & Schuster, 1973.

Index

About the Author

THOMAS S. HISCHAK is Professor of Theatre at the State University of New York, College at Cortland and a playwright who is a member of the Dramatists Guild, Inc. His previous publications include *The Theatregoer's Almanac* (Greenwood, 1997), *The American Musical Theatre Song Encyclopedia* (Greenwood, 1995), which received the 1995 *Choice* Outstanding Academic Book award, *Stage It With Music* (Greenwood, 1993), and *Word Crazy* (Praeger, 1991). He is also the author of eighteen published plays.